FOUR CENTURIES OF ITALIAN-AMERICAN HISTORY

FOUR CENTURIES
OF
ITALIAN-AMERICAN HISTORY

by
Giovanni Schiavo

2000
Center for Migration Studies
New York

The Center for Migration Studies is an educational, nonprofit institute founded in New York in 1964 to encourage and facilitate the study of sociological, demographic, historical, legislative and pastoral aspects of human migration movements and ethnic group relations. The opinions expressed in this work are those of the author. This book is a reprint from the Fourth American Edition (1957) with the kind permission of Giovanni Schiavo's daughters, Giovanna S. Masterson and Eleanor S. Leonard, to whom this book is dedicated. A partial grant toward the publication of this book from The National Italian American Foundation is greatly acknowledged.

Reprint 2000 by
Center for Migration Studies of New York, Inc.
209 Flagg Place
Staten Island, New York 10304

ISBN 0-934733-70-8

Printed in the United States of America

TABLE OF CONTENTS

Part I

Part II

FROM THE AMERICAN REVOLUTION TO WORLD WAR II

PREFACE

I consider Giovanni Schiavo the most important writer of Italian contributions to the creation of America. He was not a historian in the academic sense of the word. He was really an investigative reporter, with a knack of digging up important facts. He was an indefatigable worker. But above all, he saw the overall picture: the Italians, when we consider the discoveries, the explorations, the contributions in music, art, law, philosophy of government, architecture, agriculture, and military service were undoubtedly an important ethnic group in the coalescing of a new nation from the fifteenth century to the Civil War.

At a time when publishers were not interested in writing about Italian influence, he had the energy to raise money for the publication of his books. And in doing so, he discerned the Italian leaders in the United States during the twentieth century.

Schiavo was simply a fantastic researcher and writer. No one has approached him in the breadth of his writings, then or since. He has provided material for research for a hundred years to come. He has inspired a whole school of writing on Italian contributions and has given a new aspect to history, an aspect that is still neglected in many school textbooks.

Peter Sammartino
Fairleigh Dickinson University

Giovanni E. Schiavo is now acknowledged as "the pioneer historian and encyclopedist of Italians in America" (*Il Progresso,* March 13, 1983). He left us a rich inheritance in his many books reflecting his sixty years of research and publication. "He blazed the trail and pointed the way for us all (Ernest Falbo, S.U.N.Y. at Buffalo).

Schiavo's sixty years of dedicated research in America and many European countries, investigating the role of Italians in the discovery, exploration and development of America from the fifteenth through the twentieth centuries yielded ten historical volumes packed with many reproductions of rare records, journals, manuscripts, drawings, maps, photographs, title pages of books and newspaper articles and other documents previously unknown or not easily available... There is no question that the really impressive magnitude and wealth of historical information that crowd the pages of his books constitute a veritable saga of the Italians in America.

Remigio U. Pane
Rutgers University

FOREWORD

> "Citizens by birth or choice, of a common country, that country has a right to concentrate your affections. The name of American which belongs to you in your national capacity, must always exact the just pride of patriotism, more than any appellation derived from local discriminations. . . ."
>
> (*From Washington's Farewell Address*)

The present volume is intended primarily as a tribute to America, as a glorification of America's insuperable power of assimilation. A tribute not so much to America as a land of economic opportunities, but as the land of freedom, in the truest and widest sense of the word.

This volume aims to show once more that America's influence on her children, regardless of nationality or year of arrival, has been greater than the influence exerted by those children on America. At any time. But it also aims to remind our fellow-Americans that without the contributions of the immigrants from all parts of the world, America would not be what she is today.

Over and above everything else, this volume intends to prove, as it proves in an unquestionable manner that the Italians do not belong to the so-called "new immigration." As a matter of fact, the Italians have been coming to, and settled in, the territory that is today the United States of America, before any other national group, with the exception of the Spanish. An Italian discovered America; another Italian gave her his name; still another Italian first planted the English flag on American soil and gave England her claim to North America and the American people their first claim to independence; other Italians explored, or helped to explore, her coasts, from the Atlantic to the Gulf of Mexico and the Pacific, as well as her interior, from Florida to the Mississippi, from Arizona to Kansas, from Minnesota to Louisiana. Later, Italian fur traders and missionaries spread Christianity, civilization and good will among the Indians of the Northwest, thus making American settlements easier and more secure.

In art and music, probably no other ethnical group has contributed to American musical and artistic appreciation as the Italian, from the days of Thomas Jefferson to our own. In agriculture, Italian truck gardeners have made our meals more varied and more pleasant, and have added to our health.

Of course, the Italians have brought also some problems, but which national group has not? Problems, large or small, are inevitable in the life of any individual as in the life of any nation, especially when millions of heterogeneous immigrants are involved. But let the crucible cool off, take out the dross, and you will find among the Italians as fine a group of citizens as any in our nation. The thousands of professional men of Italian extraction today, the hundreds of outstanding business executives, the scores upon scores of distinguished artists, musicians, scientists, public officials, judges, and even baseball and football players, prove conclusively that our immigrants from Italy have been and are an asset to our country, economically, culturally, spiritually, and morally.

Finally, it is on the battlefield that the Americans of Italian extraction have proved their right to citizenship. For it is easy to wave a flag or to profess allegiance; it is not so easy to make the supreme sacrifice. The thousands of Italian-Americans who have died for Old Glory, the dozens of Congressional Medals of Honor and Navy Crosses, the hundreds of Distinguished Service Crosses, the tens of thousands of Purple Hearts, are the most eloquent proof of their loyalty to their country. Not one Italian-American has ever been found guilty of, or has been indicted for, treason to America.

The present volume, I should add, does not aim to discuss, no matter how briefly, the social implications of Italian immigration, a subject that belongs properly to sociology and not to history. This is primarily a source book, or an outline of the history of the Italians in America, to serve as a guide to writers of American history in general, and as an incentive to other investigators; for much remains to be done. Attention should be turned primarily to a study of the Italians in agriculture, in maritime trade, in engineering and inventions, and other fields which we have not been able to study as thoroughly as we wished.

Obviously, in a work like the present one, which was begun more than a quarter of a century ago, I have received the assistance of a large number of people, mostly librarians, from New York and Washington to San Diego and Spokane. The names of the libraries which helped me to obtain the necessary photographs and photostats are indicated under the reproductions in the present volume. But then there are the individual librarians, some of whom have gone out of their way to facilitate my work: men like Mr. F. Ivor Avellino, Mr. Sylvester Vigilante and Mr. J. A. Gault of the New York Public Library, for instance. To all of them, including those whose names never reached me, I owe a debt of gratitude

To my good friend, Ario Flamma, wha has helped me in the preparation of the biographical section of this work, my special thanks.

Above all, I wish to express my appreciation to all those fellow-citizens of Italian origin whose encouragement and support made this work possible. Particularly, I wish to single out my good friends: the Hon. Charles J. Margiotti of Pittsburgh, Judge Felix Forte of the Superior Court of Massachusetts, Mr. Vincent Ferrara of Chicago, Mr. John Riccardi of Detroit, and Mr. James V. Funaro of Cleveland.

GIOVANNI SCHIAVO

New York, February 20, 1952.

THE DISCOVERY OF AMERICA BY CHRISTOPHER COLUMBUS AND AMERICUS VESPUCIUS

Allegory by Joannes Stradanus, engraving by A. Callaert. From the title page of the book *Americae retectio* (*Pars Quarta*) . . . *expressa a Theodoro de Bry*, Frankfort, Germany, 1594.

INTRODUCTION TO PART ONE

Names and Nationality

At the outbreak of the Revolution there were in the Thirteen Colonies thousands of people whose ancestry could be traced, directly or indirectly, to Italy. Even more important than their number, however, was their quality.

Our conclusions, we are perfectly aware of it, are at variance with those of the experts whose data were accepted by the Congress of the United States as a basis for computing immigration quotas from the various European countries. The result, we know, was the Johnson Bill of 1927. Nor do our conclusions agree with those of more recent experts, including a professor of Italian extraction at one of America's leading universities, according to whom there were no Italians to speak of in America at the end of the 18th century. He even took the trouble to count all the "Italian" names in the New York and Philadelphia city directories for the period, and was good enough to inform us that in all there were only twenty names in the former and eight in the latter. Unfortunately, most of the names listed by him were not even Italian, as any linguist could easily tell, or as one could ascertain by looking them up in the various available dictionaries of biography. Thus, according to our "Italian" source, the Italian population in America in 1790, when the first census of the United States was taken, was practically non-existent.

A much more important and more reliable study is that by the American Council of Learned Societies started in 1927 and completed on February 8, 1932. It consists of various reports by Mr. Howard F. Barker and Dr. Marcus L. Hansen, and was published in Vol. I of the Annual Report of the American Historical Association for 1931.

Those reports are most impressive but, in our opinion, they are not as scientific as they are claimed to be. To mention one major shortcoming, the authors failed to take into consideration the thousands of foreigners in London (French, Dutch, Italian, etc.) whose names were Anglicized in England, long before they, or their descendants, came to America. Many of them came over, but since they came from English ports, in English ships, there is no way anyone can tell whether the immigrants with names similar to those of the London aliens were English or continental Europeans. Nor would it be correct to include them among the English contingent even if they were natives of England, for nationality in those days extended beyond the second and third generations. Mr. Barker, to be sure, assigns seven per cent of the total American population in 1790 to miscellaneous groups (about 220,000 people out of a total of more than 3,172,000), thereby allowing some margin for names hard to classify, but we are inclined to believe that the percentage was much higher. The general report, however, ends by stating that "the results are far from final. They indicate that continued study of surnames both in Europe and in the United States is likely to throw more light upon the origin and composition of the American population." It is in this spirit that the following notes of ours are presented.

As indicated and documented in the present volume, we know that a certain number of Italians settled in the present territory of the United States between 1565 and 1776. The largest group was composed of Piedmontese Protestants, generally known as Waldenses, 300 of whom arrived in 1657. Many others came in later years, but, for the sake of argument, we shall limit ourselves to the first group. Now, if we were to double their number every twenty-five years, as it is computed by some population experts, by 1790 there would have been more than 10,000 descendants of the original Piedmontese immigrants. Of course, it does not always work out that way. Sometimes family groups double in twenty-five years, sometimes they fall below the mark, at other times they jump far above the expected ratio. For instance, if the descendants of the Venetian Alberti, who settled in Amsterdam in 1635, had simply doubled every fourth of a century, by 1785 they would have been 64. But we know that Alberti had seven children, all born before 1654. If we start then with the 8 members of the family having Italian blood in 1654, they would have reached the figure of 256 by 1779. Italians, as we know, have always had large families, as the increase in the population of Italy during the last few centuries amply shows. By the same method of computation, the 16 Venetian glassworkers who settled in Virginia in 1622 would have had 1024 descendants in 1772 and 2050 in 1797. Even if our figures are wide of the mark, taking into consideration the return to Europe of some immigrants, death before marriage, and so forth, it is unquestionable that the Italian strain in America's population was not negligible, even as early as 1790.

So far we have dealt with persons who, we are positive, came from Italy. But how many more immigrants of Italian birth or origin settled in the Colonies about whom we know nothing at all? How many names that seem strictly English or French were not actually Italian? We shall mention some of them in Chapters Five and Six. Here let us call attention to the fact that the American custom of changing names is not of very recent date, as it is generally supposed. By that we do not mean to assert that immigrants changed their names themselves, by applying to a local court or otherwise, as it has been done often during the last half century. Names were changed by clerks or recorders who did not know how to spell them, and wrote them phonetically. Hence, names like Paca at times are found spelled as Pecker, Taliaferro as Tolliver or Tailfer, Bressani as Bressany. Some good Irish Catholics a century ago used to call Father Mazzuchelli as Father Kelly. Poor handwriting added to the confusion. For instance, in one document we have found Father Bressani listed as a native of Rouen, evidently the result of poor writing or hasty reading, for we know that he was born in Rome. Mazzei's name often is spelled as Mazzie. De Lieto appears as Desliettes, and possibly also as Du Lhut.

The strange thing is that the Anglicization of Italian names took place even in England, where clerks were supposed to have been a little better educated. In the *Return of Aliens in London in* 1567, we find, for instance, such names of Italian residents as Fox, Pickering, Gillam, Moore, Fortune, Kennythe, Rise, Pitcher, Benson, and so on. That they were Italians there is no doubt (see facsimiles on page 13). We do not know, of course, if any of those Italians with English names, or their children, ever came to America. But if they did, is there an expert in the world who could single out their descendants in the 1790 census?

As for family trees or histories, unless they are of recent date, or in exceptional cases, they are unreliable, as explained in Chapters Five and Six. The same thing may be said for the religious affiliations of early Italian immigrants. The Italian-Americans of those days were anything but Catholic, at least nominally. Was not Mazzei a member of the Calvinistical Reformed Church of Virginia?

That there were numerous Americans of Italian extraction as early as 1776 is demonstrated by the names of those who rose to prominent positions before and after the Revolution. To deny such a fact would be to ascribe to the Italians a superiority out of proportion to that of other national groups, not excluding the English. But, of course, we do not advance any such theory. We believe, instead, that for each family that distinguished itself there must have been many others that sank into oblivion.

A wood engraving of a caravel, after a drawing which is said to have been made by Columbus. (From *the letter by Columbus to Sanchez printed in Rome in* 1493.)

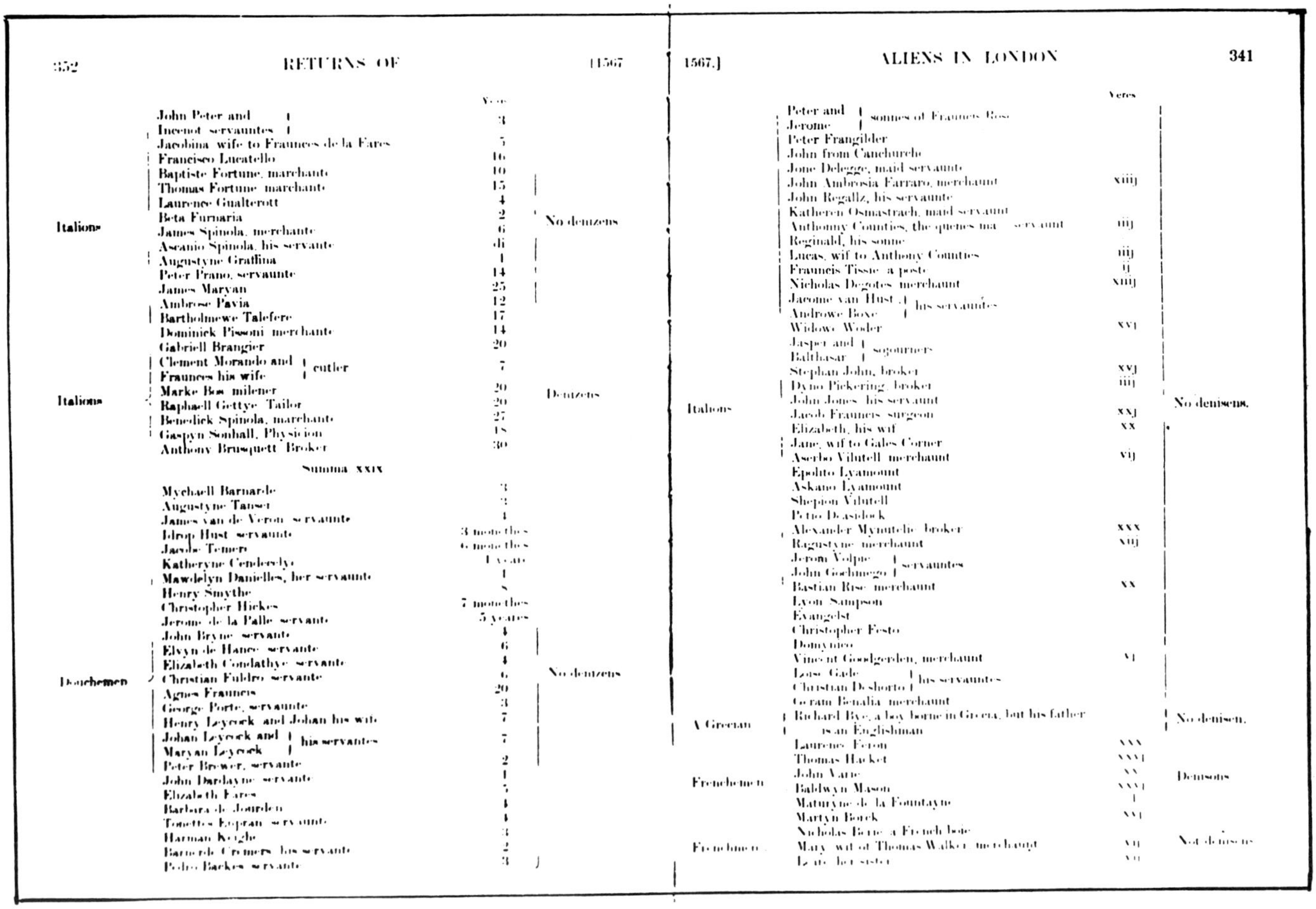

352 RETURNS OF [1567

		Yeres	
Italions	John Peter and Incenot servauntes	3	No denzens
	Jacobina wife to Fraunces de la Fares	5	
	Francisco Lucatello	16	
	Baptiste Fortune, marchante	10	
	Thomas Fortune marchante	15	
	Laurence Gualterott	4	
	Beta Furnaria	2	
	James Spinola, merchante	6	
	Ascanio Spinola, his servante	di	
	Augustyne Gratlina	1	
	Peter Prano, servaunte	14	
	James Maryan	25	
	Ambrose Pavia	12	
	Bartholmewe Talefere	17	
	Dominick Pissoni merchante	14	
	Gabriell Brangier	20	
Italions	Clement Morando and Fraunces his wife, cutler	7	Denzens
	Marke Bos milener	20	
	Raphaell Gettye Tailor	20	
	Benedick Spinola, marchante	27	
	Gaspyn Sonhall, Physicion	18	
	Anthony Brusquett Broker	30	

Summa xxix

Douchemen	Mychaell Barnarde	3	No denzens
	Augustyne Tanser	2	
	James van de Veron servaunte	4	
	Idrop Hust servaunte	3 monethes	
	Jacobe Temers	6 monethes	
	Katheryne Cenderedye	1 yeare	
	Mawdelyn Danielles, her servaunte	1	
	Henry Smythe	8	
	Christopher Hickes	7 monethes	
	Jerome de la Palle servante	5 yeares	
	John Bryne servante	4	
	Elvyn de Hance servante	6	
	Elizabeth Condathye servante	4	
	Christian Fuldro servante	6	
	Agnes Fraunces	20	
	George Porte, servaunte	3	
	Henry Leycock and Johan his wife	7	
	Johan Leycock and Maryan Leycock, his servantes	7	
	Peter Brewer, servante	2	
	John Dardayne servante	1	
	Elizabeth Fares	5	
	Barbara de Jourden	4	
	Tonettes Expran servaunte	4	
	Harman Keighe	3	
	Barnerde Cremers his servante	2	
	Pedro Backes servante	3	

1567.] ALIENS IN LONDON 341

		Yeres	
Italions	Peter and Jerome, sonnes of Fraunces Bose		No denisens.
	Peter Frangilder		
	John from Canchurche		
	Jone Delegge, maid servaunte		
	John Ambrosia Farraro, merchaunt	xiiij	
	John Regallz, his servaunte		
	Katheren Osmastrach, maid servaunt		
	Anthonny Counties, the quenes ma[ ] servaunt	iiij	
	Reginald, his sonne		
	Lucas, wif to Anthony Counties	iiij	
	Fraunceis Tissie a poste	ij	
	Nicholas Degotes merchaunt	xiiij	
	Jacome van Hust and Androwe Boxe, his servauntes		
	Widowe Woder	xvj	
	Jasper and Balthasar, sojourners		
	Stephan John, broker	xvj	
	Dyno Pickering, broker	iiij	
	John Jones his servaunt		
	Jacob Fraunceis surgeon	xxj	
	Elizabeth, his wif	xx	
	Jane, wif to Gales Corner		
	Aserbo Vilutell merchaunt	vij	
	Epolito Lyamount		
	Askano Lyamount		
	Shepion Vilutell		
	Petro Deasidock		
	Alexander Myntelie broker	xxx	
	Ragustyne merchaunt	xiij	
	Jerom Volpe and John Gochmego, servauntes		
	Bastian Rise merchaunt	xx	
	Lyon Sampson		
	Evangelst		
	Christopher Festo		
	Domynico		
	Vincent Goodgerden, merchaunt	vj	
	Lose Gade and Christian Deshorto, his servauntes		
	Goram Benalia merchaunt		
A Grecian	Richard Bye, a boy borne in Grecia, but his father is an Englishman		No denisen.
Frenchemen	Laurence Feron	xxx	Denisons
	Thomas Hacket	xxxj	
	John Varne	xx	
	Baldwyn Mason	xxxj	
	Maturyne de la Fountayne	l	
	Martyn Borck	xvj	
Frenchmen	Nicholas Berne a French boie		Not denisens
	Mary wif of Thomas Walker merchaunt	vij	
	Lewis her sister	vij	

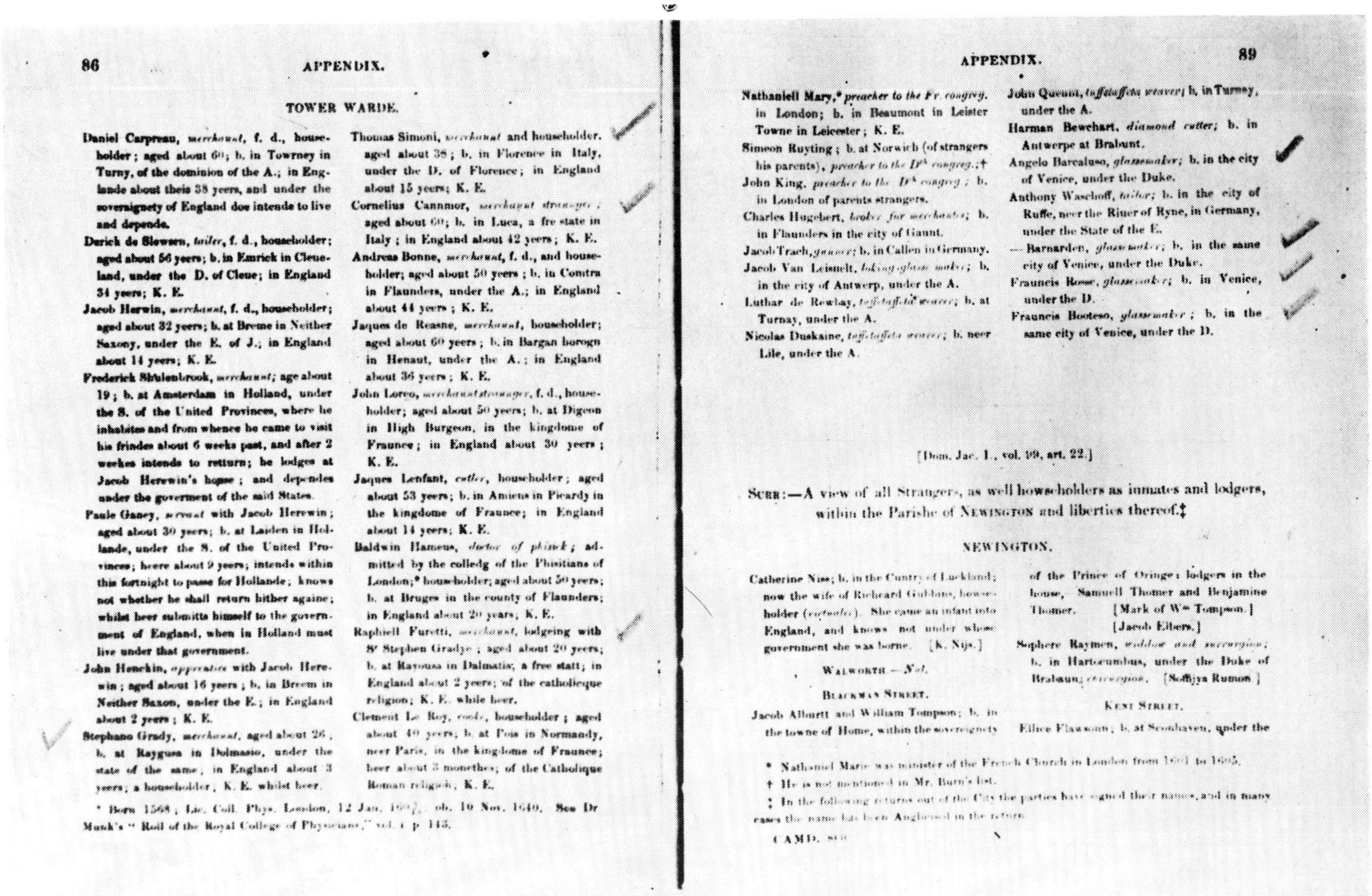

86 APPENDIX.

TOWER WARDE.

Daniel Carpreau, *merchaunt*, f. d., householder; aged about 60; b. in Towrney in Turny, of the dominion of the A.; in Englande about theis 38 yeers, and under the soveraignety of England doe intende to live and depende.

Derick de Slewsen, *tailer*, f. d., householder; aged about 56 yeers; b. in Emrick in Cleueland, under the D. of Cleue; in England 34 yeers; K. E.

Jacob Herwin, *merchaunt*, f. d., householder; aged about 32 yeers; b. at Breme in Neither Saxony, under the E. of J.; in England about 14 yeers; K. E.

Frederick Shulenbrook, *merchaunt*; age about 19; b. at Amsterdam in Holland, under the S. of the United Provinces, where he inhabites and from whence he came to visit his frindes about 6 weeks past, and after 2 weekes intends to returne; he lodges at Jacob Herewin's house; and dependes under the goverment of the said States.

Paule Ganey, *servant* with Jacob Herewin; aged about 30 yeers; b. at Laiden in Hollande, under the S. of the United Provinces; heere about 9 yeers; intends within this fortnight to passe for Hollande; knows not whether he shall return hither againe; whilst heer submitts himself to the government of England, when in Holland must live under that government.

John Henchin, *apprentice* with Jacob Herewin; aged about 16 yeers; b. in Breem in Neither Saxon, under the E.; in England about 2 yeers; K. E.

Stephano Grady, *merchaunt*, aged about 26; b. at Rayguse in Dolmasio, under the state of the same; in England about 3 yeers; a householder; K. E. whilst heer.

Thomas Simoni, *merchaunt* and householder. aged about 38; b. in Florence in Italy, under the D. of Florence; in England about 15 yeers; K. E.

Cornelius Cannmor, *merchaunt straunger*; aged about 60; b. in Luca, a fre state in Italy; in England about 42 yeers; K. E.

Andreas Bonne, *merchaunt*, f. d., and householder; aged about 50 yeers; b. in Contra in Flaunders, under the A.; in England about 44 yeers; K. E.

Jaques de Reasne, *merchaunt*, householder; aged about 60 yeers; b. in Bargan borogn in Henaut, under the A.; in England about 36 yeers; K. E.

John Loreo, *merchaunt straunger*, f. d., householder; aged about 50 yeers; b. at Digeon in High Burgeon, in the kingdome of Fraunce; in England about 30 yeers; K. E.

Jaques Lenfant, *cutler*, householder; aged about 53 yeers; b. in Amiens in Picardy in the kingdome of Fraunce; in England about 14 yeers; K. E.

Baldwin Hameus, *doctor of phisick*; admitted by the colledg of the Phisitians of London;* householder; aged about 50 yeers; b. at Bruges in the county of Flaunders; in England about 20 years; K. E.

Raphiell Furetti, *merchaunt*, lodgeing with Sr Stephen Gradye; aged about 20 yeers; b. at Rayousa in Dalmatia, a free statt; in England about 2 yeers; of the catholicque religion; K. E. while heer.

Clement Le Roy, *cook*, householder; aged about 40 yeers; b. at Fois in Normandy, neer Paris, in the kingdome of Fraunce; heer about 3 monethes; of the Catholique Roman religion; K. E.

* Born 1568; Lic. Coll. Phys. London, 12 Jan. 1609/10, ob. 10 Nov. 1640. See Dr Munk's "Roll of the Royal College of Physicians," vol. i. p. 143.

APPENDIX. 89

Nathaniell Mary,* *preacher to the Fr. congreg.* in London; b. in Beaumont in Leister Towne in Leicester; K. E.

Simeon Ruyting; b. at Norwich (of strangers his parents), *preacher to the Dch congreg.*;†

John King, *preacher to the Dch congreg.*; b. in London of parents strangers.

Charles Hugebert, *broker for merchantes*; b. in Flaunders in the city of Gaunt.

Jacob Trach, *gunner*; b. in Callen in Germany.

Jacob Van Leisnelt, *looking-glass maker*; b. in the city of Antwerp, under the A.

Luthar de Rewlay, *tuff-taffeta weaver*; b. at Turnay, under the A.

Nicolas Duskaine, *tuff-taffeta weaver*; b. neer Lile, under the A.

John Queunt, *tuffetaffeta weaver*; b. in Turnay, under the A.

Harman Bewchart, *diamond cutter*; b. in Antwerpe at Brabunt.

Angelo Barcaluso, *glassmaker*; b. in the city of Venice, under the Duke.

Anthony Waschoff, *tailor*; b. in the city of Ruffe, neer the Riuer of Ryne, in Germany, under the State of the E.

— Barnarden, *glassmaker*; b. in the same city of Venice, under the Duke.

Fraunceis Bosse, *glassmaker*; b. in Venice, under the D.

Fraunceis Booteso, *glassmaker*; b. in the same city of Venice, under the D.

[Dom. Jac. I., vol. 99, art. 22.]

SURR:—A view of all Strangers, as well howseholders as inmates and lodgers, within the Parishe of NEWINGTON and liberties thereof.‡

NEWINGTON.

Catherine Nise; b. in the Cuntry of Luckland; now the wife of Richeard Gibbons, howseholder (*victualer*). She came an infant into England, and knows not under whose government she was borne. [K. Nijs.]

WALWORTH.—*Nil.*

BLACKMAN STREET.

Jacob Albertt and William Tompson; b. in the towne of Home, within the soveraignety of the Prince of Oringe: lodgers in the house, Samuell Thomer and Benjamine Thomer. [Mark of Wm Tompson.] [Jacob Elbers.]

Sophere Raymen, *widdow and surgeon*; b. in Hartocumbus, under the Duke of Brabaun; *chirurgion*. [Soffiya Rumon.]

KENT STREET.

Elline Flawsonn; b. at Scoahaven, under the

* Nathaniel Marie was minister of the French Church in London from 1601 to 1605.

† He is not mentioned in Mr. Burn's list.

‡ In the following returns out of the City the parties have signed their names, and in many cases the name has been Anglicised in the return.

CAMD. SOC.

(*Top*) Partial list of Italian residents in London in 1618. Notice the names of Cornelius Cannmor and Francis Bosse. Other Anglicized Italian names appear in the same volume. (From *Publications of the Camden Society,* Vol. 82) (*Bottom*) Two pages from the Return of Aliens in London in 1567. Notice the Anglicization of Italian, Dutch and French names and, on page 352, the name of Bartholmewe Talefere (Bartholomew Taliaferro). Other Italians with Anglicized names, as listed in the same volume, were Lambert Garrett, Arnold Giles, Godfrey Sokes, Peter Fox, James Flotrye, John Gillam, Giles Corner, etc. (From *Huguenot Society Publications,* Vol. X) See also Vol. XXVII.

The earliest illustration of the landing of Columbus in America. It first appeared in the title page of Dati's poem published at Florence in 1493, and later in the frontispiece of Vespucci's Letters published also at Florence in 1504.

CHAPTER ONE

CHRISTOPHER COLUMBUS

The history of America begins with its discovery by Columbus in 1492. What went on before him belongs to archaeology, ethnology, geology, paleontology, anthropology, but not to history.

It is said, with a devotion worthy of a better cause, that white men—the Vikings—reached North America before Columbus. Most likely they did. But what of it? Of their voyages only an obscure saga or legend had remained by the time Columbus planned his great adventure—a legend of absolutely no scientific or historical significance and most certainly of no practical value. To assert otherwise is to display one's ignorance of the facts connected with Columbus's first voyage, its preparation, and its course.

It has been said also that had Columbus not discovered America, someone else would have done so, sooner or later. There is no doubt about that. But, by the same token, the same thing may be said of most, if not all, other inventions or discoveries in the history of mankind. The argument is too childish to deserve further consideration. As for the Portuguese Cabral, who landed in Brazil in the year 1500, more than one historian is of the opinion that he went off his course to ascertain whether there was land beyond the line of demarcation set by the Papal Bull as a consequence of Columbus's voyage.

In the history of humanity there is nothing that surpasses or even equals Columbus's achievement, with the exception of the coming of Christ—but Christ was the son of God. It is not, indeed, because of the vagaries of some historians that Modern Age begins with the landing of the Genoese Navigator in the New World.

THE BOY COLUMBUS
by Giulio Monteverde. (Courtesy, *Boston Museum of Fine Arts*)

The house in which Columbus spent his childhood in his native Genoa. (Courtesy, *City of Genoa, Italy*)

Christopher Columbus was born in Genoa, Italy, between the months of August and October, 1451. His father, Domenico Colombo, belonged to an Italian Catholic family that has been traced to the 12th century; his mother, Susanna Fontanarossa, hailed from the Bisagno Valley, also in the Genoa district. Columbus did not have a speck of blood in his veins that was not purely Italian.

We know little with certainty regarding Columbus's life previous to his arrival in Spain; about 1476 he moved to Portugal; later he traveled to England and to Madeira; about 1479 or 1480 he married Filippa Moniz Perestrello, who bore him one son, Diego, who was born about 1480 or 1481. In 1485 he presented his plan for a voyage across the ocean to the king of Portugal, who turned him down. From the end of 1485, or the beginning of 1486, he lived in Spain, almost uninterruptedly, pleading his case until he reached an agreement with the Spanish sovereigns. It was signed on April 17, 1492.

Volumes upon volumes have been written on what Columbus did or did not do before 1492; little of it is based on historical evidence; much of it is the product of the imagination of historians and would-be historians, who have tried to reconstruct the life of the navigator on the biased evidence presented by Columbus's enemies as well as friends during the inheritance lawsuits which were protracted for years through the civil courts of Spain. For, one must remember, a large fortune was at stake, a fortune involving the rights of Columbus's descendants to inherit the privileges and income guaranteed by the sovereigns of Spain before Columbus left Palos on his first voyage. On the one side the Court was trying to prove that Columbus's discovery was of little importance; on the other, his descendants were bound to exaggerate their claims, at times distorting the truth, even if unwittingly, in order to score a point.

There are, however, a few facts concerning Columbus about which there is not the least doubt; facts based on evidence which no one can deny. Most of them deal with Columbus's consummate skill as a mariner and the most thorough manner with which he organized his voyage. Those are the only facts that count; the rest we may relegate among academic discussions, petty squabbles, wild hypotheses, conjectures, suppositions, ifs and buts. We shall refer to them as we go along in this concise illustration of the main events in the Navigator's life.

THE DEPARTURE OF THE CARAVELS FROM PALOS

A fresco of the late 19th century in the D'Albertis Castle in Genoa, Italy. (Courtesy, *City of Genoa, Italy*)

CHRISTOPHER COLUMBUS

A portrait atributed to Rodolfo del Ghirlandaio in the Naval Museum of Genoa, Italy. (Courtesy, *City of Genoa.*) There are no portraits of Columbus painted from life. The above is one of the best known.

SINCE I WAS BORN IN GENOA ....

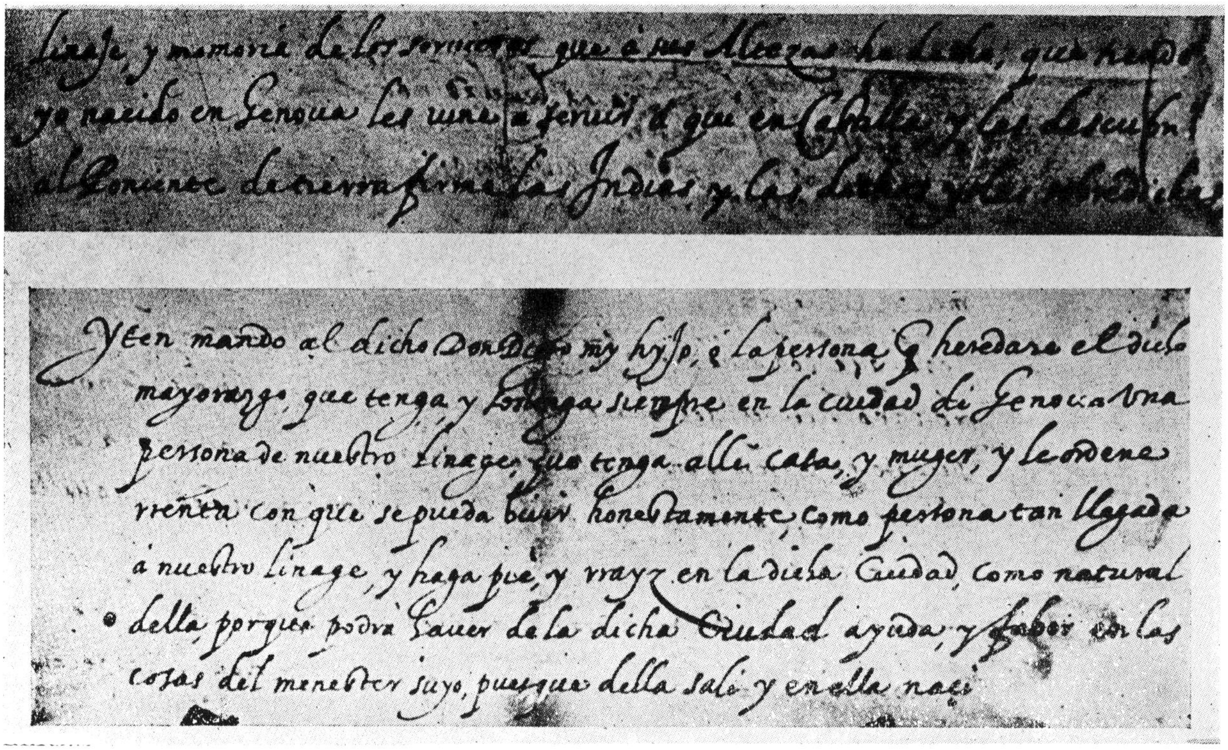
linaje, y memoria de los servicios que a sus Altezas he hecho, que siendo
yo nacido en Genoua les vine a servir aqui en Castilla y les descubri
al Poniente de tierra firme las Indias y las dichas yslas sobredichas

Yten mando al dicho Don Diego my hijo, o a la persona que heredare el dicho
mayorazgo, que tenga y sostenga siempre en la ciudad de Genova una
persona de nuestro linage, que tenga alli casa, y muger, y le ordene
renta con que se pueda bivir honestamente, como persona tan llegada
a nuestro linage, y haga pie, y rayz en la dicha Ciudad, como natural
della, porque podra haver de la dicha Ciudad ayuda, y favor en las
cosas del menester suyo, puesque della sali y en ella naci

There are many documents that prove beyond the shadow of a doubt that Columbus was born in Genoa. One of them is the Majorat, or will, which Columbus instituted on February 22, 1498, in favor of his son Diego.

In this will, the authenticity of which has been proved by two scholars, one a Spaniard and the other an American, Columbus refers more than once with endearing terms to the city of Genoa. Two passages, reproduced in facsimile on this page, may be sufficient. In the one above, first and second lines, he says unequivocally that he was born in Genoa: *siendo yo nacido en Genova* (since I was born in Genoa). In the other (from the fourth line on, *above*) he orders his son and heirs to keep a person of their lineage in the city of Genoa, to have there house and wife "since from it I came and in it I was born" (*puesque della sali y en ella naci.*)

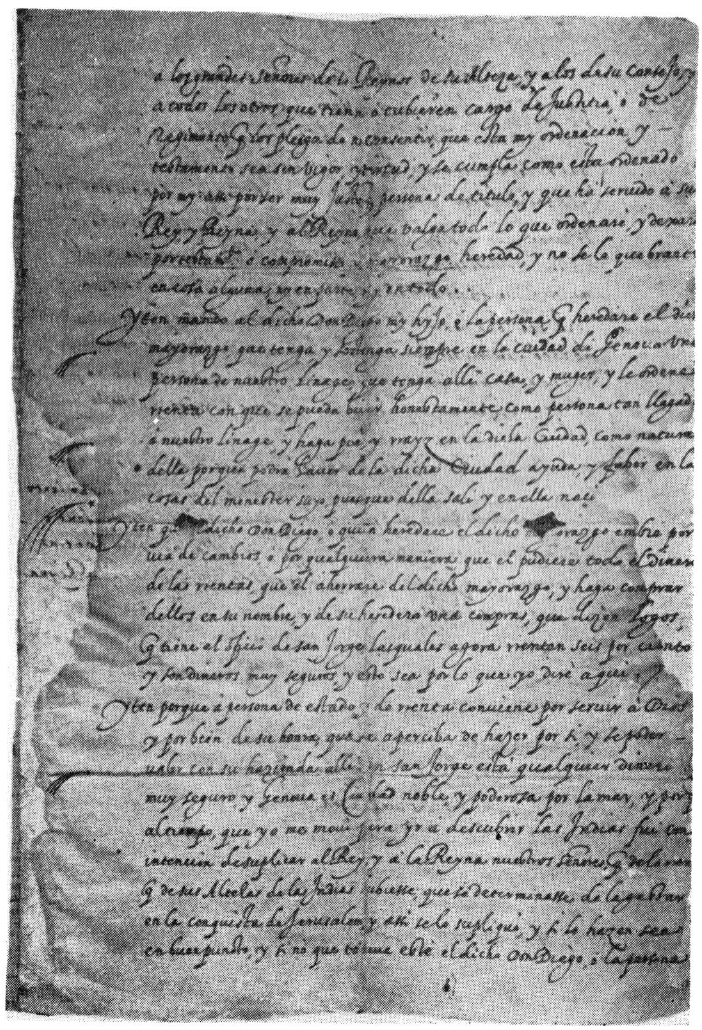

For the full text in facsimile and for other supporting material see the large volume "*Christopher Columbus, Documents and Proofs of his Genoese Origin* (English and German edition) put out by the City of Genoa in 1932. See esp. pp. 238-241. See also Almagia', R.—*I Primi Esploratori dell'America* in the series *L'Opera del Genio Italiano al l'Estero,* Rome, 1937, pp. 3-10, 160, and 439, note 97, and Revelli P.A., *Cristoforo Colombo e la scuola cartografica genovese,* Genoa, 1937, Chapter IV.

On this page are reproduced in facsimiles a page from the majorat (*right*) and two enlarged passages from it (*above*).

A

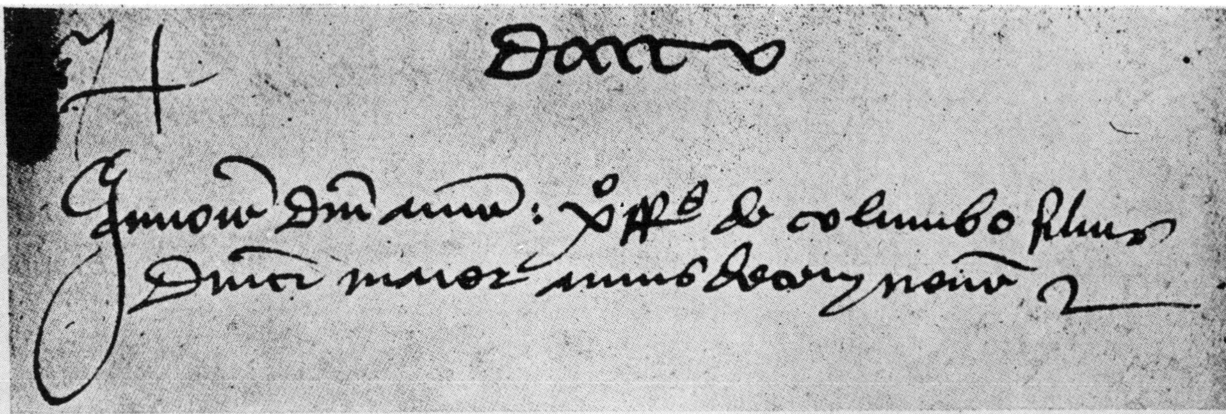

B

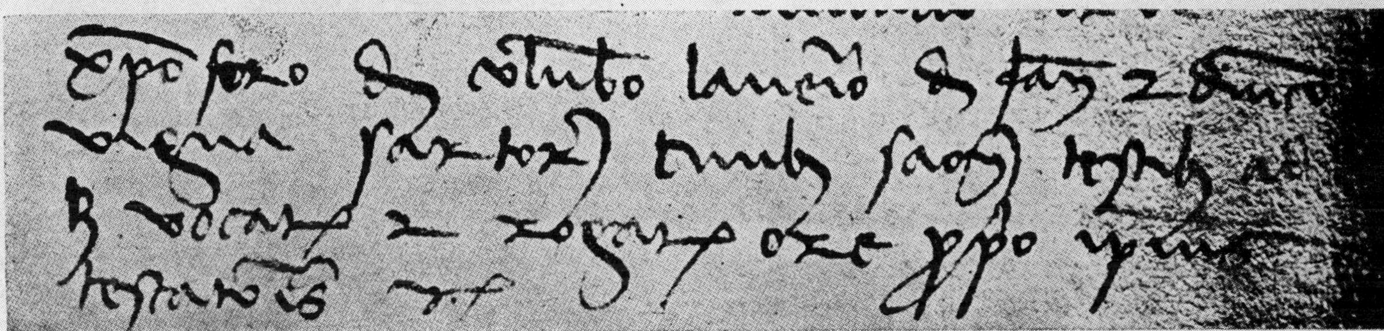

C

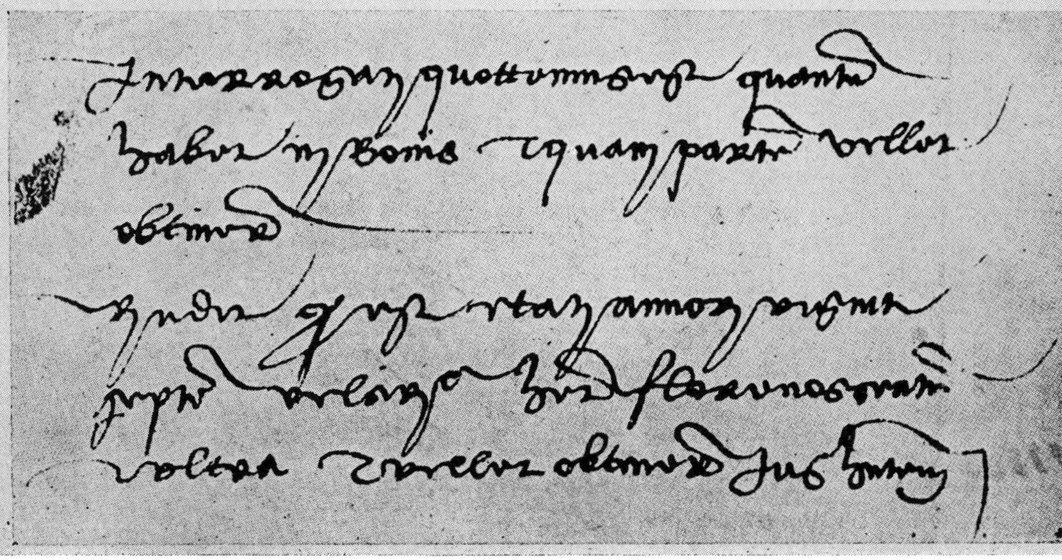

Enlarged passages from notarial deeds proving that Columbus was born in Genoa, Italy. (A) In a deed drawn in Genoa on Oct. 31, 1470, Columbus is said to be over 19 years old. (B) In a deed drawn at Savona on March 20, 1472, Columbus is called "wool worker of Genoa." (C) In a deed drawn at Genoa on August 25, 1479, Columbus states that he is about 27 years old. (From Revelli, P., *Cristoforo Colombo e la Scuola Cartografica Genovese,* Genoa, 1937) See also City of Genoa, Christopher Columbus, *op. cit. pp.* 132, 146 and 136.

COLUMBUS' OFFER TO THE BANK OF ST. GEORGE

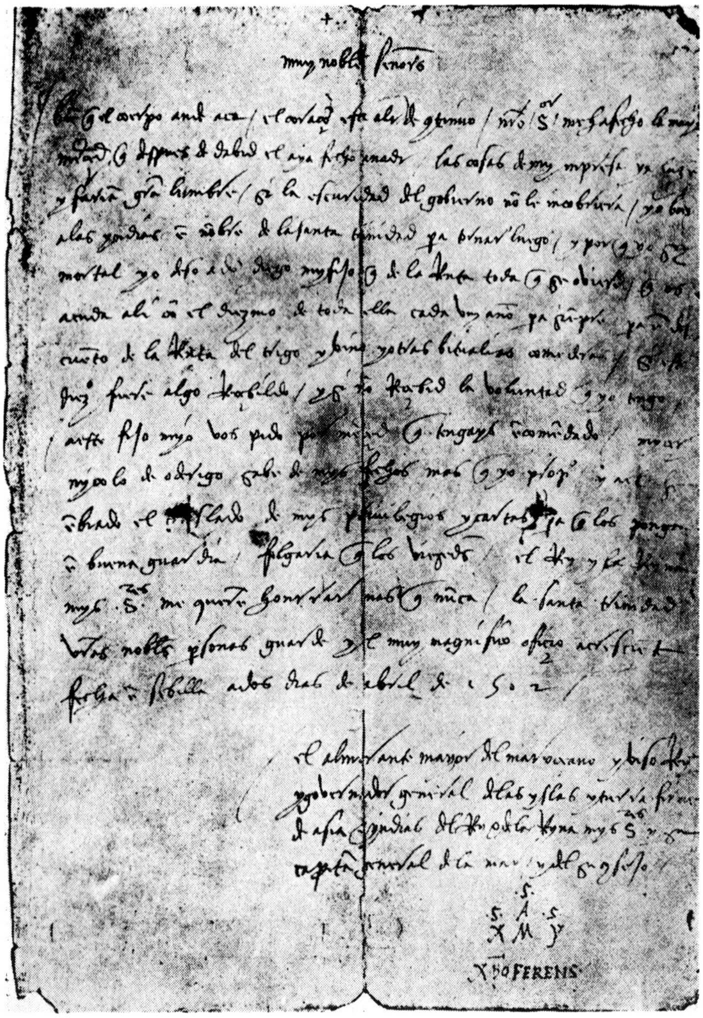

On April 2, 1502, just before he left on his fourth voyage, Columbus drew up a temporary will in which he left one tenth of all income to be derived from his discoveries, to the Bank of St. George in the city of Genoa. He wrote about it to the directors of the Bank in a letter which is reproduced in facsimile on this page. (*Left*) The letter begins with the words *Bien que el coerpo ande aca, el coracon esta ali de continuo* (Though my body walks here, my heart is always with you)—one more proof that Columbus in his hour of triumph had not forgotten his native city.

On his return from his fourth voyage Columbus found no reply from the Bank to his generous offer and resenting what he thought was a discourtesy or lack of appreciation he cancelled his donation to the Bank. He wrote about it, in complaining terms, to Niccolo Oderisio, the Genoese representative in Spain, in a letter dated Seville, December 27, 1504. As a matter of fact, the Bank had replied to Columbus's letter and thanked him, in a letter dated December 8, 1502, but unfortunately the missive never reached the Admiral. In that letter the Bank refers three times to Columbus as a native of Genoa. That is why the donation to the Bank is not repeated in the Navigator's final will.

(For further data on this point see Almagia, *op. cit.* pp. 187 and 209).

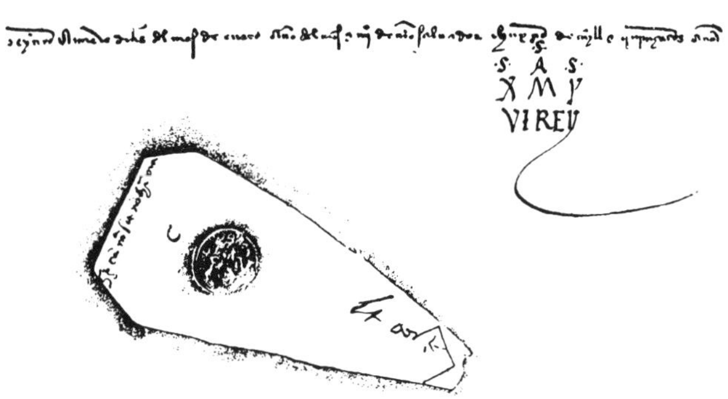

COLUMBUS' SIGNATURE AS VICEROY

and his seal with the words "Jesus cum Maria sit nobis in via." (From *Autografos de Cristobal Colon,* edited by the Duchess of Berwick and Alba)

THE BANK OF ST. GEORGE PALACE

in Genoa, Italy. (Courtesy, *City of Genoa*)

COLUMBUS AND THE ITALIAN LANGUAGE

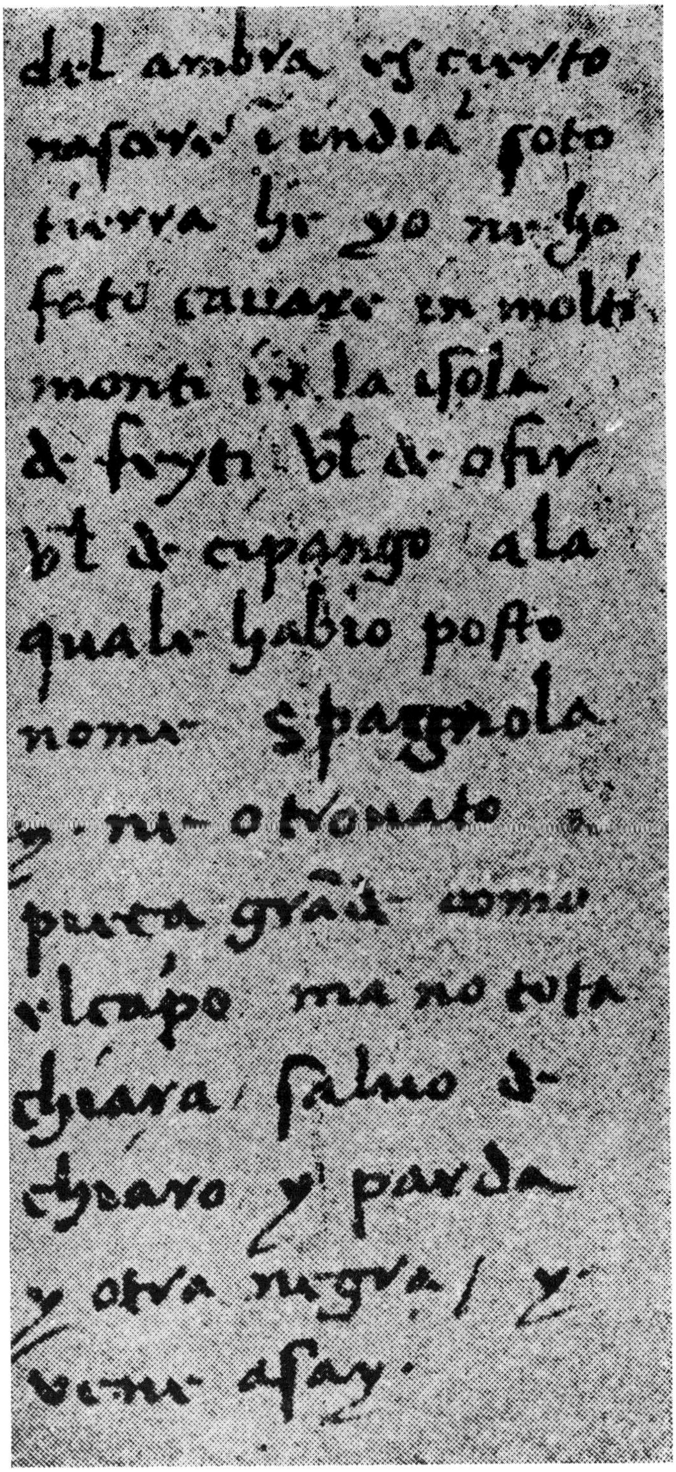
del ambra et cristo
nasarsi i' india soto
tierra lo yo ne ho
fato cavare en molti
monti in la isola
de feyti ut de ofir
ut de cipango ala
quale habio posto
nome spagnola
y ne o trovato
piezza grãde como
el capo ma no tuta
chiara salvo de
chiaro y parda
y otra negra / y
vene asay.

(*Above*) (enlarged) Notes by Columbus to Pliny's History. Notice the Italian words "isola," "quale," "nome Spagnola." (From Revelli, *op. cit.*) (Right) First page of "Libretto de Tutta La Nauigatione De Re De Spagna" translated and published by Angelo Trevisan in Venice on April 10, 1504. Notice the first three words "Christophoro Colobo Zenouese" (Christopher Columbus Genoese). Trevisan was a personal friend of the Navigator. A well-known biographer of Columbus, in his determination to prove that the original name was not Columbus, pointed out that even the Italians called him Colobo, thus revealing his ignorance of paleography. In early printed books the sign ~ over a letter stood in place of the letters *m* or *n*. Thus Colobo was to be read Colombo. (From the photostat of the only copy in existence, Marciana Library, Venice)

One of the most stupid charges advanced by those critics who are determined to prove that Columbus was not an Italian, is the fact that all of the Columbus letters which have reached us are in Spanish, including those to other Italians, like the directors of the Bank of St. George, Father Gorricio and Niccolo Oderisio.

Columbus, one must remember, spoke the Genoese dialect, which is quite different from literary Italian. It was therefore only natural for him to write in Spanish, a language which he knew much better. Literary Italian has always been like another language for all natives of Italy, with the exception of the Tuscans, for it required special study. As late as 1870 many of the Piedmontese noblemen whom Victor Emmanuel II took with him to Rome as members of his Court, could hardly speak Italian, for they were used to speaking the Piedmontese dialect or French. In the United States, as well as in Latin America, most Italians whose education has been primarily English or Spanish do not use the Italian language when corresponding with each other. Even when they know literary Italian they prefer to use English or Spanish by force of habit, if nothing else. (See Ramon Menendez Pidal, *La Lengua de Cristobal Colon*, Buenos Aires, 1942).

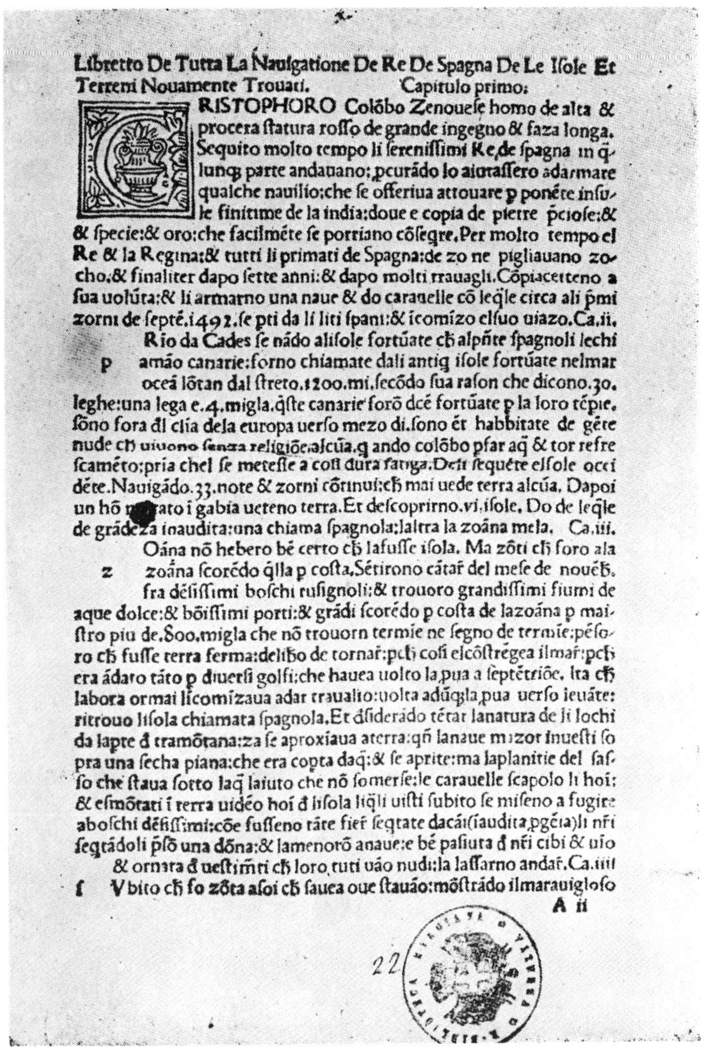
Libretto De Tutta La Nauigatione De Re De Spagna De Le Isole Et
Terreni Nouamente Trouati. Capitulo primo:
CRISTOPHORO Colõbo Zenouese homo de alta &
procera statura rosso de grande ingegno & faza longa.
Sequito molto tempo li serenissimi Re de spagna in q̃
lunq; parte andauano; pcurãdo lo aiutassero adarmare
qualche nauilio; che se offeriua attouare p ponẽte insu
le finitime de la india; doue e copia de pietre pciose: &
& specie: & oro: che facilmẽte se porriano cõsegre. Per molto tempo el
Re & la Regina: & tutti li primati de Spagna: de zo ne pigliauano zo
cho. & finaliter dapo sette anni: & dapo molti trauagli. Cõpiacetteno a
sua uolũta: & li armarno una naue & do carauelle cõ leq̃le circa ali pmi
zorni de septẽ. 1492. se pti da li liti spani: & icomizo elsuo uiazo. Ca. ii.
PRio da Cades se nãdo alisole fortũate ch alpñte spagnoli lechi
amão canarie: forno chiamate dali antiq isole fortũate nelmar
oceã lõtan dal streto. 1200. mi. secõdo sua rason che dicono. 30.
leghe: una lega e. 4. migla. q̃ste canarie forõ dcẽ fortũate p la loro tẽpie.
sõno fora dl clia dela europa uerso mezo di. sono ẽt habbitate de gẽte
nude ch uiuono senza religiõe alcũa. q ando colõbo psar aq̃ & tor refre
scamẽto; pria chel se metesse a cosi dura fatiga. Deli sequẽte elsole occi
dẽte. Nauigãdo. 33. note & zorni cõtinui: ch mai uede terra alcũa. Dapoi
un hõ [illegible]ato i gabia ueteno terra. Et descoprirno. vi. isole. Do de leq̃le
de grãdeza inaudita: una chiama spagnola; laltra la zoãna mela. Ca. iii.
ZOãna nõ hebero bẽ certo ch lafusse isola. Ma zõti ch foro ala
zoãna scorẽdo q̃lla p costa. Sẽtirono cãtar del mese de nouẽb.
fra dẽsissimi boschi rusignoli: & trouoro grandissimi fiumi de
aque dolce: & bõissimi porti: & grãdi scorẽdo p costa de lazoãna p mai
stro piu de. 800. migla che nõ trouorn termie ne segno de termie; pẽso
ro ch fusse terra ferma: delibo de tornar: pch cosi elcõstrẽgea ilmar: pch
era ãdato tãto p diuersi golfi; che hauea uolto la pua a septẽtriõe. Ita ch
labora ormai licomizaua adar trauaglio: uolta adũq̃la pua uerso leuãte:
ritrouo lisola chiamata spagnola. Et dsiderãdo tẽtar lanatura de li lochi
da lapte d tramõtana: za se aproxiaua aterra: qñ lanaue mazor inuesti so
pra una secha piana: che era copta daq̃: & se aprite: ma laplanitie del sas
so che staua sotto laq̃ laiuto che nõ somerse: le carauelle scapolo li hoi:
& esmõtati i terra uidẽo hoi d lisola liq̃li uisti subito se miseno a fugire
aboschi dẽsissimi: cõe fusseno tãte fier seqtate dacãi (iaudita pgẽia) li nri
seqtãdoli psõ una dõna: & lamenorõ anaue: e bẽ pasiuta d nri cibi & uio
& ornata d uestimẽti ch loro tuti uão nudi: la lassarno andar. Ca. iiii
SVbito ch fo zõta asoi ch sauea oue stauão: mõstrãdo ilmarauiglioso
A ii

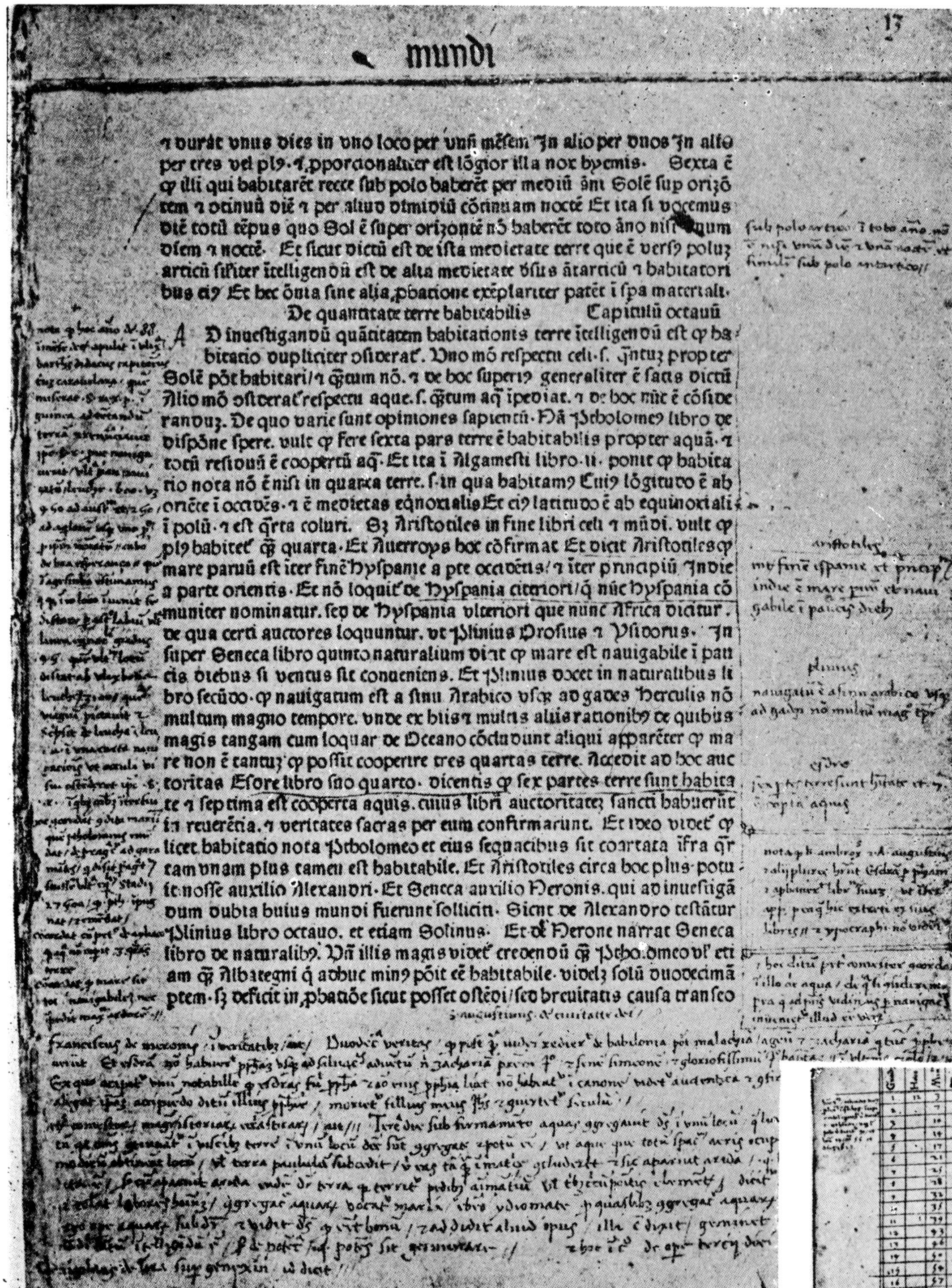

mundi 17

& durat vnus dies in vno loco per vnū mēsem In alio per duos In alio per tres vel pl9 & pporcionaliter est lōgior illa nox hyemis. Sexta ē q illi qui habitarēt recte sub polo haberēt per mediū ānū Solē sup orizōtem & dimidiū diē & per aliud dimidiū cōtinuam noctē Et ita si vocemus diē totū tēpus quo Sol ē super orizontē nō haberēt toto āno nisi vnum diem & noctē. Et sicut dictū est de ista medietate terre que ē vers9 poluz articū sīliter itelligendū est de alia medietate vsus ātarticū & habitatoribus ei9 Et hec ōnia sine alia pbatione exēplariter patēt ī spa materiali.

De quantitate terre habitabilis Capitulū octauū

Ad inuestigandū quātitatem habitationis terre itelligendū est q habitatio dupliciter osiderat'. Vno mō respectu celi. s. q̄ntuz propter Solē pōt habitari & q̄tum nō. & de hoc superi9 generaliter ē satis dictū Alio mō osiderat' respectu aque. s. q̄tum aq̄ ipediat. & de hoc nūc ē cōsiderandus. De quo varie sunt opiniones sapientū. Nā Ptholome9 libro de dispōne spere. vult q fere sexta pars terre ē habitabilis propter aquā. & totū residuū ē coopertū aq̄. Et ita ī Almagesti libro. ii. ponit q habitatio nota nō ē nisi in quarta terre. s. in qua habitam9 Cui9 lōgitudo ē ab oriēte ī occidēs. & ē medietas eq̄noxialis Et ei9 latitudo ē ab equinoxiali ī polū. & est q̄rta coluri. Sz Aristotiles in fine libri celi & mūdi. vult q pl9 habitet' q̄ quarta. Et Auerroys hoc cōfirmat Et dicit Aristotiles q mare paruū est iter finē Hyspanie a pte occidēts & iter principiū Indie a parte orientis. Et nō loquit' de Hyspania citteriori q̄ nūc Hyspania cōmuniter nominatur. sed de Hyspania vlteriori que nunc Africa dicitur. de qua certi auctores loquuntur. vt Plinius Orosius & Ysidorus. Insuper Seneca libro quinto naturalium dicit q mare est nauigabile ī paucis diebus si ventus sit conueniens. Et Plinius docet in naturalibus libro secūdo. q nauigatum est a sinu Arabico vsq ad gades Herculis nō multum magno tempore. vnde ex hiis & multis alijs rationib9 de quibus magis tangam cum loquar de Occeano cōcludunt aliqui apparēter q mare non ē tantuz q possit cooperire tres quartas terre. Accedit ad hoc auctoritas Esdre libro suo quarto. dicentis q sex partes terre sunt habitate & septima est cooperta aquis. cuius libri auctoritatē sancti habuerūt in reuerētia. & veritates sacras per eum confirmarunt. Et ideo videt' q licet habitatio nota Ptholomeo et eius sequacibus sit coartata īfra q̄rtam vnam plus tamen est habitabile. Et Aristotiles circa hoc plus potuit nosse auxilio Alexandri. Et Seneca auxilio Neronis. qui ad inuestigādum dubia huius mundi fuerunt solliciti. Sicut de Alexandro testātur Plinius libro octauo. et etiam Solinus. Et de Nerone narrat Seneca libro de naturalib9. Vn̄ illis magis videt' credendū q̄ Ptholomeo vl' etiam q̄ Albategni q̄ adhuc min9 pōit eē habitabile. videlz solū duodecimā ptem. sz deficit in pbatiōe sicut possēt ostēdi sed breuitatis causa transeo

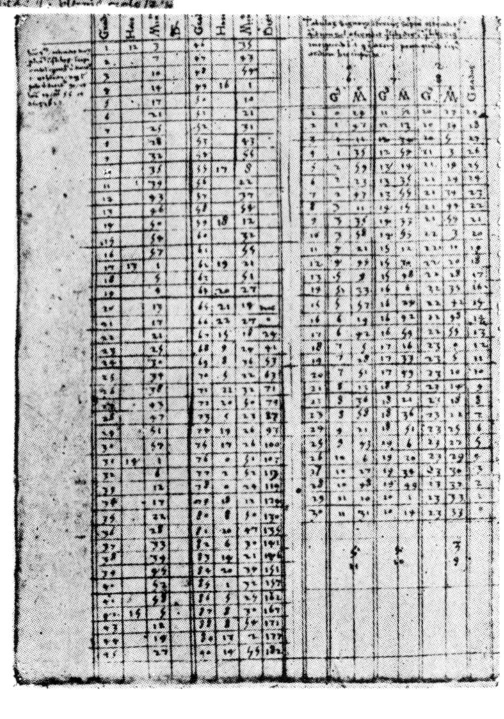

(*Above*) A page from "Imago Mundi" by Pierre D'Ailly, with notes by Columbus in his own handwriting. (*Right*) Columbus' calculations, also in his own handwriting, of the length of the days of the month at various latitudes, and of the declination of the sun. (*Columbian Library, Seville, Spain*)

SIX YEARS OF PLEADING, WAITING AND DREAMING

COLUMBUS BEFORE THE COUNCIL OF SALAMANCA

From an old print. (Courtesy, *New York Public Library*)

While waiting for his plan to be approved or rejected, Columbus did not remain idle or day-dreaming. Instead, he studied all scientific treatises he could get hold of, noting down whatever conflicted with his personal views, observations, or practical experience. (See the opposite page).

As the American scholar, G. E. Nunn, stated in his book *The Geographical Conceptions of Columbus* (New York, 1924), "Christopher Columbus in the art of navigation exceeded without doubt all others who lived in his day."

Armored with his scientific convictions, Columbus never wavered and struggled for almost eight years to secure royal support. To quote another leading American scholar, Prof. Samuel E. Morison, author of the admirable book *Admiral of the Ocean Sea* (Boston, 1942) Columbus's voyage to America and back "was no blind chance, but the creation of his own brain and soul, long studied, carefully planned, repeatedly urged on indifferent princes, and carried through by virtue of his courage, sea-knowledge, and indomitable will."

(*Right*) Statuary group carved out of a single block of Carrara marble by Larkin Goldsmith Meade, an American sculptor living in Florence, between 1868 and 1874. It was purchased for $30,000 by D. O. Mills and presented to the State of California on December 22, 1883. It now stands in the Rotunda of the California State Capitol at Sacramento. (Courtesy, *California State Library, Sacramento, Cal.*)

COLUMBUS EXPLAINING TO QUEEN ISABELLA HIS THEORY OF A WESTERN VOYAGE

ITALIAN MERCHANTS OFFER FINANCIAL ASSISTANCE

It has been stated over and over again that it was Luis de Santangel, the Jewish treasurer of the Court of Aragon (not of Castile) who finally induced Queen Isabel to approve Columbus's plan and who advanced the money for the expedition. According to recent research, however, it would seem that Santangel actually did not put out any or much money out of his own coffers, and that most of the funds, if not all of them, were advanced by Italian merchants in Spain.

Columbus, it is obvious, went to Spain with letters of introduction to some of his influential countrymen there. The very fact, as Rinaldo Caddeo points out, that he was able to be presented at Court in a relatively brief period of time, shows that he had influential connections. As for the merchants who came to his assistance, it is also obvious that they helped him over such a long period of time (more than six years) not because he was one of their countrymen, but because his plan, if successful, offered them not only a profit but also a new outlet to their activities.

According to Sig. Caddeo, Santangel had no personal reason whatever to help Columbus; not even profit, for he received only a few thousand *maravedis* (the equivalent of a few dollars today) for his trouble in advancing the money he is alleged to have advanced. Why should he have risked any money, as well as his position at court, in the event of failure? Columbus himself stated more than once, and corroborating documents show, that he advanced one half of the total cost of the expedition, and that the other half was put up by the Spanish sovereigns. The voyage cost about two million maravedis, something like $6,000 according to pre-World War I values, or about $20,000 according to the purchasing power of the dollar in 1950.

There is no doubt that Santangel advanced 1,400,000 maravedis, or more than half of the total, but Santangel was not alone in providing the money, for he was associated with Francisco Pinelo, also a treasurer, like Santangel, of the Sancta Hermandad. Pinelo was a member of the old Genoese family of Pinelli, and a wealthy merchant of Seville. At one time he guaranteed a loan of five million maravedis made to the King of Spain and at another time he advanced to Santangel other sums to be loaned also to the King.

Without going into further details, all of which can be found in Signor Caddeo's book mentioned below, it would seem that Pinelo put out the greater share of, if not all, the money which Santangel loaned to the Spanish Sovereigns for the Columbus expedition. Whether or not such was the case, and whether or not Pinelo furnished the full amount of the Santangel loan, it is well established that Columbus raised the other half—or about half—of the total amount required to finance his first voyage. Columbus, as we know, had no money of his own. Where, then, did he get the money? As it appears from unimpeachable documents, he got it from friends of his, all of them Italian. Three of them, we know, were Genoese. One was a Tuscan, Zuanoto Berardi, the representative in Seville of the powerful banking house of Medici.

For documentary material on this point see Caddeo, R., *Le Historie della Vita e dei Fatti di Cristoforo Colombo,* 2 vols. Milan, 1930, Vol. II, Appendix F, pp. 346-360 and Almagia', *op. cit.* pp. 79-80.

THE RECALL OF COLUMBUS
By A. G. Heaton, (Courtesy, *Library of Congress*)

TOWARDS THE UNKNOWN

THE DEPARTURE OF COLUMBUS
FOR AMERICA
(From a rare print)

Columbus left Palos on Friday, August 3, 1492. The three caravels, it would seem, consisted of 120 men, of whom from 42 to 45 were on the *Santa Maria,* 25 on the *Pinta* and about 20 on the *Nina.*

At least three Italians were with Columbus on his first voyage. They were: Giacomo del Rio, of Genoa, who died in America; Antonio of Calabria, a servant of Martin Alonso Pinzon; and Giovanni of Venice. Many other Italians came over in the following voyages. (See Gould, A. Nueva lista documentada de los tripulantes de Colon en 1492. *Boletin de la Academia de Historia,* Vol. 88, pp. 721-784.)

COLUMBUS LEAVING PALOS
(A painting by Ricardo Balaca in the Provincial Museum at Cadiz, Spain)

SAIL ON, AND ON, AND ON

COLUMBUS LEAVING SPAIN

A mural by Ezra Winter in the center of the Great Hall in the Cunard White Star Building in New York City. (*Cunard White Star Photo by W. A. Probst*)

No voyage in the history of the world ever surpassed in drama Columbus's plunge into the uncharted ocean. Danger lurking from every side, not only from the elements or from the mystery of the unknown, but also from the crew itself, superstitious and quick to mutiny, only a man with an almost superhuman character like Columbus could persist in what practically all his men soon came to consider a foolhardy adventure. But, had not Columbus possessed such an indomitable will, he would have not discovered America. The story, however, is an old one and we may dispense with repeating it here.

Let us remind some people, however, that the voyage of the Vikings was like sailing on a lake compared to that of Columbus, for they sailed in view of, or not far from, the coast, whereas the Genoese Navigator had only the sun and the stars to go by.

As God willed, Columbus weathered the storms of both nature and men, amid sudden hopes and even more sudden disappointments, but always supremely confident of God's help and his own calculations. How well-founded his confidence was, events soon proved.

THE SANTA MARIA

as reconstructed by Capt. E. A. D'Albertis. Naval Museum, Genoa, Italy. (Courtesy, *City of Genoa*)

LAND, AT LAST!

THE DISCOVERY GROUP
by Luigi Persico, at the entrance to the Rotunda of the United States Capitol in Washingon, D. C. It was carved in Italy at a cost of $24,000. (Courtesy, *The Architect of the Capitol*)

THE DISCOVERY OF LAND
by Luigi Gregori, a mural in the University of Notre Dame. (Courtesy, *University of Notre Dame*)

THE DEBARKATION OF COLUMBUS
By Edward Moran. (Courtesy, *Philadelphia Museum of Art*)

INDIANS BRINGING GIFTS TO COLUMBUS AT HISPANIOLA
(From an old engraving by De Bry)

OCTOBER 12, 1492

At 2 o'clock, in the morning of October 12, 1492, San Salvador, or Watlings Island, in the Bahamas, was at last sighted. There, at daylight, Columbus, followed by some of his men, landed, knelt down, thanked the Lord, and planted the royal standard of Spain. On that fateful Friday morning, Modern History was born.

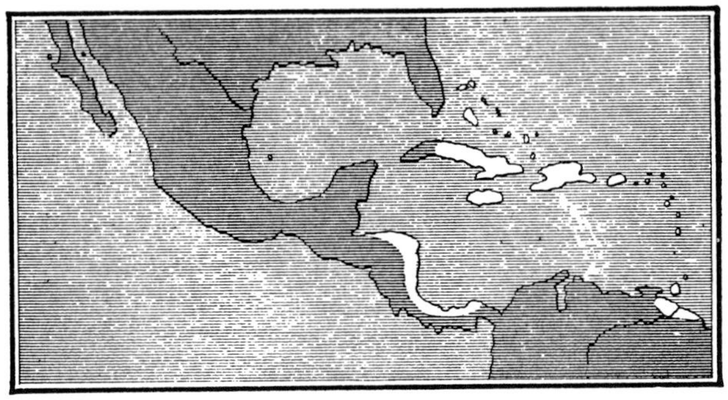

Map showing (in white space) the lands discovered by Columbus during his four voyages. If John Cabot did not go beyond Newfoundland, and if Vespucius did not land on the shores of South America before 1499, the honor of the discovery of the Continent belongs to Columbus (Aug. 5, 1498).

THE LANDING OF COLUMBUS
at one of the smaller Bahama Islands called Guanahani by the natives. A painting by John Vanderlyn in the Rotunda of the United States Capitol. (Courtesy, *Library of Congress*)

THE HOUR OF TRIUMPH — THE RECEPTION AT COURT

THE RETURN OF COLUMBUS AND HIS RECEPTION AT COURT
A mural by Luigi Gregori in the University of Notre Dame. (Courtesy, *University of Notre Dame*)

On March 15, 1493, Columbus was back at Palos. The Spanish sovereigns were then holding court at Barcelona, and there a month later Columbus was received by the King and Queen with great pomp and exceptional solemnity. His titles, privileges and rights were confirmed as "Admiral of the Ocean Sea, Viceroy and Governor of the Islands now discovered in the Indies."

Unfortunately, soon they were to forget their solemn promises.

THE RETURN OF CHRISTOPHER COLUMBUS
A painting by Eugene Delacroix. (Courtesy, *Toledo Museum of Art*, Toledo, Ohio)

THE RETURN OF COLUMBUS
A fresco by Lazzaro Tavarone in the ceiling of the Belimbay Palace, Genoa, Italy. (Courtesy, City of Genoa)

COLUMBUS RECEIVED BY FERDINAND AND ISABELLA AT BARCELONA
A painting by Ricardo Balaca in the Seville Library, Seville, Spain.

A PAGE THAT NEEDS NO WORDS

COLUMBUS IN CHAINS
(*Left*) From a painting by J. Tower. (*Below*) From an old print. (Courtesy, *New York Public Library*)

Columbus's days of triumph were not to last long. His influence at Court having been undermined by his enemies who did not find it hard to arouse the jealousies of other Spaniards (Columbus was a foreigner, we must remember), he was not able to enforce his authority in the New World. As a governor Columbus was rather a failure; one must bear in mind, however, that he had to deal with turbulent people who had come over to find gold, not to work. At any rate, in 1500 the Spanish Sovereigns sent one of their trusted men, the infamous Bobadilla, with unlimited powers, to take charge of the situation at Hispaniola. Bobadilla put Columbus and his two brothers in chains and sent them, still in chains, to Spain. The captain of the ship carrying the Admiral offered to remove the chains, but he refused. He was still in chains when he reached Seville. Only in December 1500, more than two months later, were the chains removed by order of the Sovereigns, who restored his income and some of his rights.

As discoveries followed upon discoveries and the magnitude of the New World became apparent, the Spanish Sovereigns repented having granted such rights and privileges to the Discoverer. As Prof. Morison well points out, the only favor King Ferdinand granted Columbus was the permission to ride a mule.

The great navigator made still another voyage, his fourth and last, also of great scientific value, but of no immediate financial importance. Neglected, except by a few friends and relatives, Columbus died at Valladolid on May 20, 1506.

DEATH AND IMMORTALITY

THE DEATH OF COLUMBUS
A fresco by Luigi Gregori in the University of Notre Dame. (Courtesy, *University of Notre Dame*)

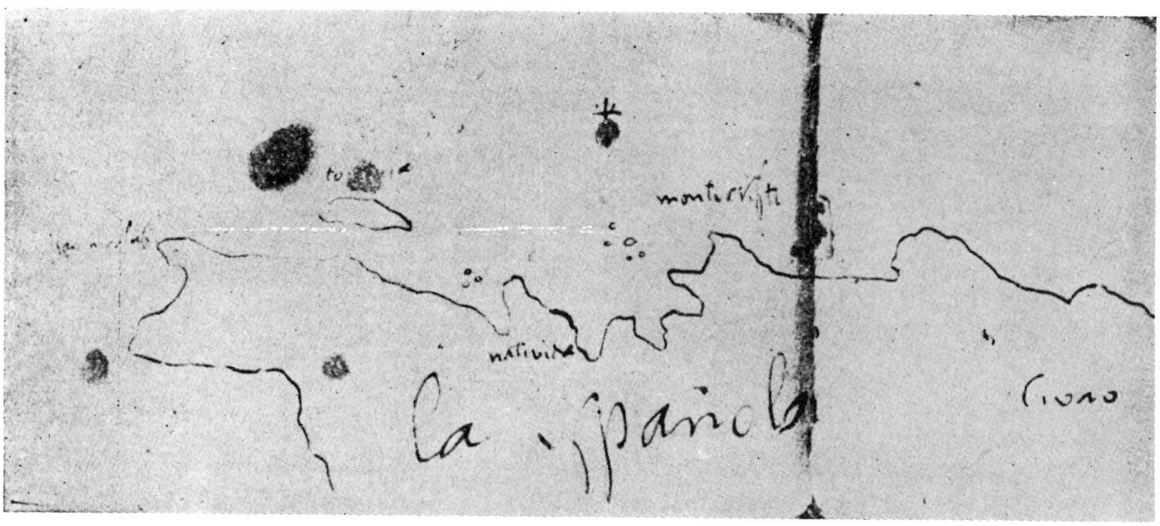

SKETCH OF HISPANIOLA (HAITI) AS DRAWN BY COLUMBUS
(Madrid, Archives of the Dukes of Alba)

WHERE IS COLUMBUS BURIED?

COLUMBUS' COAT OF ARMS

Nobody knows exactly where Columbus's remains are buried today.

Between 1541 and 1547 they were transferred to Santo Domingo, in compliance with the written request of Diego Columbus for a permanent family tomb in that city. In 1796 they were exhumed and transferred to the Cathedral of Havana, Cuba. A century later, in 1899, following the Spanish-American War, they were exhumed once more and transferred to Seville, where they are said to rest.

However, according to some authorities, the remains taken to Spain were not those of Columbus, but of his son, Diego. Those of the Admiral, it is claimed, are still in Santo Domingo. The Government of Haiti is now erecting a most grandiose monument in honor of the Navigator.

THE TOMB OF COLUMBUS

In the Cathedral of Santo Domingo (Courtesy, *Pan American Union,* Washington, D.C.)

THE TOMB OF COLUMBUS

In the Cathedral of Seville, Spain.

Les autorités attendant l'arrivée de la Giralda »

Premier sépulcre de Colomb à la Havane

THE REMOVAL OF WHAT ARE BELIEVED TO BE COLUMBUS'S REMAINS, TO SPAIN

(*Above, left*) The Spanish authorities awaiting the arrival of the warship "Giralda" with Columbus's remains on board. (*Above, right*) The first tomb of Columbus at Havana, Cuba. (*Below*) The artillery cortege. (From *L'Illustration,* Paris, February 4, 1899)

THE FIRST COLUMBUS CELEBRATION IN 1792

Some of our fellow-citizens do not seem to appreciate the fact that had it not been for Columbus, God only knows where we Americans would be today, granting that our parents would have met as they did. For no intelligent person with a smattering of education can deny that Columbus changed the course of history.

In Oregon, for instance, the enlightened Legislature of that progressive State recently (1950) abolished Columbus Day as a State holiday, following a campaign based on ignorance and sheer stupidity.

Our forefathers, however, were the first in the world to express their gratitude to the discoverer of our Land. Long before either Spain or Italy thought of it, American cities from Baltimore to Philadelphia to New York to Boston, and most likely other cities, suitably observed the third centenary of the discovery of America by publicly honoring Columbus. Actually they had honored him years before, when, at the very beginning of the Revolution, they named one of our first warships after him. (Two of the other three ships, incidentally, were named after Italians, one after Cabot, and the other after Andrea Doria, the Genoese liberator of his country.)

The first man to honor Columbus with a monument was a Frenchman, Chevalier Charles D'Annemour, Consul General of France in Baltimore, who erected at his own expense a shaft in honor of the Navigator on the grounds of his own villa. That monument is still standing, and is still in good condition, at the corner of what are now North Avenue and Harford Road. The cornerstone was laid on August 3, 1792, the 300th anniversary of Columbus's departure from Palos. (See *Maryland Historical Society Magazine,* Vol. I, p. 246). A few days later, on August 17, a writer in the Philadelphia *Mail* suggested that steps be taken to observe in a fitting manner the anniversary of the fateful landing of Columbus on our shores.

Boston, among other cities, also celebrated the third centenary of the discovery of America with special ceremonies sponsored by the Massachusetts Historical Society, as one can read in the facsimile reproduced on the next page.

The most impressive ceremony, however, took place in New York City, where the Tammany Society erected a 14-foot obelisk and organized a celebration that would put our contemporaries to shame. As the facsimile on the next page is legible, we dispense from repeating here the details of that solemn observance. For the benefit of some benighted individuals, however, we shall only call attention to the words *Columbus was born at Genoa.*

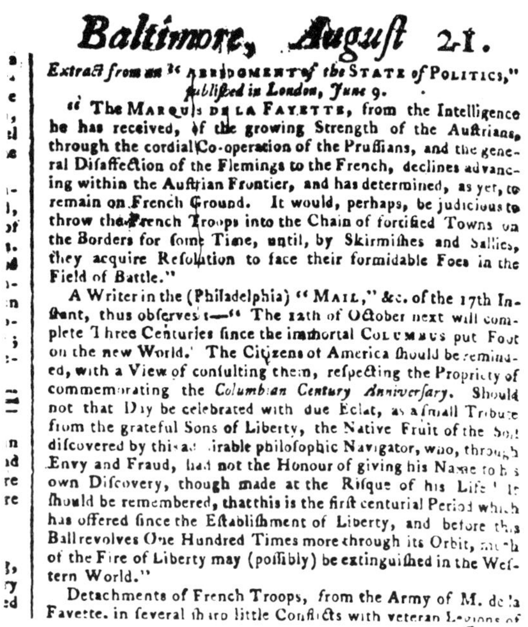

Baltimore, August 21.

*Extract from an "*ABRIDGEMENT *of the* STATE *of* POLITICS,*" published in London, June 9.*

"The MARQUIS DE LA FAYETTE, from the Intelligence he has received, of the growing Strength of the Austrians, through the cordial Co-operation of the Prussians, and the general Disaffection of the Flemings to the French, declines advancing within the Austrian Frontier, and has determined, as yet, to remain on French Ground. It would, perhaps, be judicious to throw the French Troops into the Chain of fortified Towns on the Borders for some Time, until, by Skirmishes and Sallies, they acquire Resolution to face their formidable Foes in the Field of Battle."

A Writer in the (Philadelphia) "MAIL," &c. of the 17th Instant, thus observes:—"The 12th of October next will complete Three Centuries since the immortal COLUMBUS put Foot on the new World.' The Citizens of America should be reminded, with a View of consulting them, respecting the Propriety of commemorating the *Columbian Century Anniversary.* Should not that Day be celebrated with due Eclat, as a small Tribute from the grateful Sons of Liberty, the Native Fruit of the Soil discovered by this admirable philosophic Navigator, who, through Envy and Fraud, had not the Honour of giving his Name to his own Discovery, though made at the Risque of his Life! It should be remembered, that this is the first centurial Period which has offered since the Establishment of Liberty, and before this Ball revolves One Hundred Times more through its Orbit, much of the Fire of Liberty may (possibly) be extinguished in the Western World."

Detachments of French Troops, from the Army of M. de la Fayette, in several sharp little Conflicts with veteran Legions of

Item regarding the third centenary of the Discovery of America in the "Maryland Journal and Baltimore Advertiser" for August 21, 1792. (Courtesy, *Library of Congress*)

THE FIRST MONUMENT TO COLUMBUS IN THE UNITED STATES, AT BALTIMORE, MD. (From an old photograph in the possession of the *Maryland Historical Society*)

Celebration of the diſcovery of A[illegible]

Tueſday laſt, the 23d inſt. being the 12th of the month, *old ſtile*, and the day on which the *Third Century* after the diſcovery of America by *Chryſtopher Columbus*, was compleated, that event was celebrated by the *Hiſtorical Society* of this Commonwealth, in the following manner :

The Members of the Society having aſſembled at a quarterly meeting, held at the houſe of the Rev. Dr. *Thacher*, they proceeded from thence to the Meeting Houſe in Brattle-Square.— Dr. *Thacher* opened the ſervice with a prayer peculiarly adapted to the occaſion. A diſcourſe was then delivered by the Rev. Dr. *Belknap*, who had been appointed by the Society for that purpoſe. This diſcourſe was diſtinguiſhed by a deep reſearch into the ſubject of the diſcovery of America, both as to the reaſons which led to it, and its conſequences ; by an entertaining account of the character and fortunes of the great Diſcoverer ; and, above all, by a liberality of ſentiment in politics and religion, which do honor to the age. After the diſcourſe, a prayer pertinent to the ſubject of the day, was made by the Rev. Mr. *Eliot*—and the whole was concluded with an Ode, by Mr. *Rea*, and others, in concert with the Organ.

His Excellency the Governor, His Honor the Lt. Governor, and ſuch of the Hon. Council, as were in town, favored the Society with their attendance on this occaſion ; and accompanied the Members to dine with the Hon. *James Sullivan*, Eſq. the Preſident, at his houſe, where the memory of *Columbus* was toaſted in convivial enjoyment—and the warmeſt wiſhes were expreſſed, that the bleſſings now diſtinguiſhing the United States, might be extended to every part of the world he has diſcovered.

On the 12th inſt. was celebrated in New-York, the completion of the third century ſince the diſcovery of America by *Columbus*. On this occaſion a monumental obeliſk was exhibited by the Tammany Society at their Great Wigwam ; where an animated oration on the great nautical hero was delivered by *J. B. Johnſon*, Eſquire.

The mode of chooſing Federal Re-

Two newspaper accounts of the 300th anniversary of the Discovery of America as reported (*above*) in the "Boston Independent Chronicle" for October 25, 1792, and (*right*) in the "New York Diary; or, Lowdon's Register" for October 19, 1792. (Courtesy, *New York Historical Society*)

THE DIARY; OR, LOUDON's REGISTER.

NEW-YORK: Printed by *SAMUEL LOUDON*, No. 5, WATER STREET;—where Eſſays, Advertiſements, *&c.* are gratefully received.

FRIDAY, OCTOBER 19, 1792. [No. 213.

NEW-YORK, *Oct.* 19.

It is reported, that John Stakes, Major of horſe in the weſtern army, is now on his way to this city, having reſigned his commiſſion.

Thomas Sprig, Eſq. is elected a Repreſentative in Congreſs from the ſtate of Maryland, for the 4th diſtrict of that ſtate.

The 12th inſt. being the commencement of the IVth COLUMBIAN CENTURY, was obſerved as a Century Feſtival by the Tammany Society, and celebrated in that ſtile of ſentiment which diſtinguiſhes this ſocial and patriotic inſtitution.

In the evening a monument was erected to the memory of Columbus, ornamented by *tranſparency*, with a variety of ſuitable devices.

This beautiful exhibition was expoſed for the gratification of public curioſity ſome time previous to the meeting of the ſociety.

An elegant oration was delivered by Mr. J. B. Johnſton, in which ſeveral of the principal events in the life of this remarkable man were pathetically deſcribed, and the intereſting conſequences to which his great atchievements had already, and muſt ſtill conduct the affairs of mankind, were pointed out in a manner extremely ſatiſfactory.

During the evening's entertainment, a variety of rational amuſement was enjoyed.—The following toaſts were drank :

1. The memory of Chriſtopher Columbus, the diſcoverer of this new world.
2. May the new world never experience the vices and miſeries of the old ; and be a happy aſylum for the oppreſſed of all nations and of all religions.
3. May peace and liberty ever pervade the United Columbian States.
4. May this be the laſt century feſtival of the Columbian Order that finds a ſlave on this globe.
5. Thomas Paine.
6. The Rights of Man.
7. May the 4th century be as remarkable for the improvement and knowledge of the rights of man as the firſt was for diſcovery, and the improvement of nautic ſcience.
8. La Fayette and the French nation.
9. May the liberty of the French riſe ſuperior to all the efforts of Auſtrian deſpotiſm.
10. A Burgoyning to the Duke of Brunſwick.
11. May the deliverers of America never experience that ingratitude from their country, which Columbus experienced from his King.
12. May the genius of liberty, as ſhe has conducted the ſons of Columbia with glory to the commencement of the fourth century, guard their fame to the end of time.
13. The DAY.
14. *Waſhington*, the deliverer of the new world.

Several moral and patriotic ſongs, inculcating the Love of Country and of Freedom, were gratifying in the higheſt degree. Among others an Ode was compoſed and ſung on the occaſion.

Deſcription of the Monument.

The monument is upwards of 14 feet in height, being well illuminated, and reſembling black marble ; it blended, in an agreeable manner, a grave and ſolemn, with a brilliant appearance.

At the baſe a globe appears, emerging out of the clouds and chaos ; preſenting a rude ſketch of the once uncultivated coaſt of America. On its pyramidal part, Hiſtory is ſeen drawing up the curtain of oblivion, which diſcovers the four following repreſentations :

Firſt, and on the right ſide of the obeliſk, is preſented a commercial port, and an expanding ocean ; here Columbus, while muſing over the inſignia of geometry and navigation, the favorite ſtudies of his youth, is inſtructed by ſcience to croſs the great Atlantic. She appears in luminous clouds, hovering over its ſkirts ; with one hand ſhe preſents Columbus with a compaſs, and with the other ſhe points to the ſetting ſun. Under her feet is ſeen a ſphere, the eaſtern half of which is made to repreſent the then known terraqueous globe ; the weſtern is left a blank. On the pedeſtal is the following inſcription :

THIS MONUMENT
WAS ERECTED BY THE
TAMMANY SOCIETY,
or,
COLUMBIAN ORDER,
OCTOBER 12, M,DCC,XCII,
TO COMMEMORATE
THE IVth COLUMBIAN CENTURY :
AN
INTERESTING AND ILLUSTRIOUS
ÆRA.

On the upper part of the obeliſk is ſeen the arms of Genoa, ſupported by the beak of a prone eagle.

The ſecond ſide or front of the monument ſhews the firſt landing of Columbus. He is repreſented in a ſtate of adoration ; his followers proſtrate as ſupplicants around him, and a group of American natives at a diſtance. Hiſtorical truth is attended to, and the inſcription on the pedeſtal is as follows.

SACRED
TO THE
MEMORY
OF
CHRISTOPHER COLUMBUS,
THE DISCOVERER
OF
A NEW WORLD,
October 12, 1492.

Above, the arms of Europe and America are blended, and ſupported as on the right ſide of the monument.

The third, or left ſide, exhibits the ſplendid reception of Columbus by the Court of Spain, on his firſt return from America. He is ſeated at the right hand of Ferdinand, and his illuſtrious patroneſs, Iſſabella. A map of the newly diſcovered countries, with ſome of their peculiar productions, laying at his feet, diſtinguiſh the intereſting ſcene. Above, the prone eagle ſupports the arms of Iſſabella, and on the pedeſtal is the following inſcription :

COLUMBUS
WAS BORN AT GENOA,
1447 ;
WAS RECEIVED BY THE COURT OF SPAIN
IN TRIUMPH,
1493 ;
WAS PUT IN CHAINS BY ITS ORDER,
September, 1500 ;
DIED AT VILLADOLID,
May 20, 1506.

The laſt ſcene exhibited on the rear or fourth ſide of the obeliſk ſtrongly contraſts with the one juſt deſcribed ; Columbus is ſeen in his chamber penſive and neglected. The chains with which he had been cruelly loaded hang againſt its bare walls, on which is ſeen written, '*The Ingratitude of Kings*.' To chear his declining moments, the *Genius of Liberty* appears before him : The glory which ſurrounds him ſeems to illuminate his ſolitary habitation. The emblems of deſpotiſm and ſuperſtition are cruſhed beneath her feet ; and to intimate the gratitude and reſpect of poſterity, ſhe points to a monument, ſacred to his memory, reared by the *Columbian Order*. On the pedeſtal, *Nature* is ſeen careſſing her various progeny ; her tawny offspring ſeem to mourn over the Urn of Columbus.

The upper part of the obeliſk is embelliſhed as on the other ſides. But the eagle, as an emblem of civil government, is ſeen no longer prone, or loaded with the decorations of heraldry : She ſoars in an open ſky, graſping in her talons a ſcrole, inſcribed,

THE RIGHTS OF MAN.

Murder ſtrangely Diſcovered.

THE FIRST MONUMENT TO COLUMBUS IN THE UNITED STATES

The first statue in honor of Columbus in the United States was erected in Louisburg Square in Boston late in 1849 or soon after. (The Baltimore monument was a shaft, without any sculpture).

The Boston statue is said to have arrived late in 1849 and to have been imported by a Greek merchant named Iasigi. According to another source, it was erected by Marquis Niccolò Reggio, a merchant of Italian extraction, who served as consul in Boston for the Papal States, the Kingdom of Sardinia, the Kingdom of the Two Sicilies, and the Kingdom of Spain. It is said that Reggio was prompted to erect the Columbus statue not to be outdone by his business competitor, Iasigi, who had erected one of Aristides in the same square. Regarding the first version see the booklet *Some Statues of Boston* by Allan Forbes and Ralph M. Eastman, published by the State Street Trust Co. of Boston in 1946. The photograph reproduced above is from said booklet.

BOSTON, 1849

PHILADELPHIA, 1876

Donated by the Italians of the city.

ST. LOUIS, MO., 1884

Donated by Henry Shaw, of St. Louis, the statue, in gilt bronze, was modeled and cast in Munich, Germany. (Courtesy, *Missouri Historical Society*, St. Louis, Mo.)

1869 - 1934

In New York City, as well as in New York State, there are several statues of Columbus. One, of no particular importance, is in Buffalo. Another is in front of Public School 69 in the Bronx. On this page and in the next, we reproduce four of the best-known.

(*Above*) The statue by Emma Stebbins, executed in 1869. Rediscovered in the Central Park Arsenal, it was erected in 1934 in Columbus Park, behind the New York County Court House. (Photograph by the author) (*Right*) Close-up of the column in Columbus Circle. See opposite page. (Courtesy, *New York City Park Department*)

1894

Sunol's statue in the Mall, Central Park, offered by a group of prominent New Yorkers at the behest of General Grant Wilson. The statue is a replica of the one surmounting the Columbus monument in Madrid, Spain.

1941

The Queens Borough monument at 31st Street and Astoria Boulevard. Angelo Rociuppi, Sculptor. (all photographs on this page by courtesy of the *New York City Park Department*)

THE COLUMBUS CIRCLE MONUMENT IN NEW YORK CITY

The most majestic monument to Columbus in the United States was dedicated on October 12, 1892, with the participation of outstanding representatives of the United States and other governments. For the occasion, Italy and Spain sent over a warship each. The work of the Sicilian sculptor, Gaetano Russo, the monument is located in Columbus Circle, at the entrance to Central Park, and reaches a height of 75 feet, including the statue, which is 14 feet high. It was donated by the Italians in the United States through subscriptions raised by the daily newspaper, "Il Progresso Italo-Americano," Carlo Barsotti, publisher.

IN CHICAGO

In the City of Chicago, Ill., there are at least seven statues of Columbus, three of which are shown on this page. The two at the left were exhibited at the World's Columbian Exposition in 1892. The one above is by Howard Kretchmar and is said to be now on the Lake Front. The one below, by Miss Mary Trimble Lawrence of New York, a pupil of Augustus St. Gaudens, stood at the east entrance to the Administration Building. The monument on the right, by Carlo Brioschi, was unveiled on August 3, 1933. It was donated by citizens of Italian origin and is located in Grant Park, Columbus Park at Roosevelt Road.

Another statue of Columbus, sculptor unknown, is in front of Englewood Engine Co. 51 station, 6345 Wentworth Ave. It was exhibited at the Columbian Exposition and was donated in 1893 by W. H. Mullins in honor of the firemen who lost their lives in the cold storage building fire at the exposition. Two more statues of Columbus may be seen in Chicago, one on the Columbus Memorial Building, State Street near Washington, Moses Ezekial sculptor, and the other at the Drake Fountain, 92nd and Exchange. The latter was presented to the City of Chicago on December 26, 1892, and was dedicated on October 11, 1908, after being removed from its site on Washington Street in front of the courthouse. Still another statue, by R. M. Park, is said to have been exhibited at the Columbian Exposition in 1892.

BALTIMORE, 1892

Donated by the local Italians. Achille Canessa, sculptor. (Photograph by the author)

NEW HAVEN, 1892

Donated by the local Italians. Sculptor unknown.

SCRANTON, 1892

Donated by the local Italians. Alberto Cottini, sculptor. Located in the city's main square. (Courtesy, *Mr. & Mrs. Angelo Fiorani,* Scranton)

PROVIDENCE, 1893

A replica of the statue by August Bertholdi, originally cast in silver for the Columbian Exposition, Chicago. Photo by Roger Williams. (Courtesy, *Judge Luigi De Pasquale,* Providence)

PUEBLO, COLO., 1905

Pietro Piai, sculptor. Donated by the Columbian Federation of Italian Societies in the United States.

DETROIT, MICH., 1912

A. Rivalta, sculptor. Donated by the local Italians, under the sponsorship of *La Tribuna Italiana d'America,* Detroit, Vincenzo Giuliano, publisher and editor.

WASHINGTON, 1912

The impressive monument by Loredo Taft which greets every visitor to the Capital of the United States on leaving Union Station.

NEWARK, N. J., 1927

Giuseppe Ciocchetti, sculptor. Donated by the local Italians under the auspices of the Giuseppe Verdi Society. Photo by George Van. (Courtesy, *F. Villani, Mayor,* Newark, N. J.)

HOBOKEN, N. J., 1931

(Courtesy, *Department of Parks and Public Property,* **Hoboken**)

RICHMOND, VA., 1927

Ferruccio Legnaioli, sculptor. Donated by the local Italians. (Courtesy, *Frank Realmuto,* Richmond)

ST. PAUL, MINN., 1931

Carlo Brioschi, Sculptor. The only monument to Columbus erected on any State Capitol grounds. Donated by the Minnesota State Federation of Italian-American Clubs.

MAMARONECK, N. Y., 1938

AKRON, O., 1938

WESTERLY, R. I., 1949

(*Left*) Henri Grenier, Sculptor. Donated by all the citizens of the village, regardless of race, color or creed. (Courtesy, *Wm. H. Johnson,* Village Manager, Mamaroneck, N. Y.) (*Center*) Donated by the Italians of the city under the sponsorship of the local Sicilian Society. (Courtesy, *S. Silecchia,* Akron) (*Right*) Chas. F. Pazzano, Sculptor. Donated by the local Italians. (Courtesy, *Atanasio Grasso,* Westerly)

THE COLUMBUS MURAL IN THE UNITED STATES CAPITOL
A fresco in the rotunda of the Capitol by Costantino Brumidi. (Courtesy, *Library of Congress*)

THE ROGERS BRONZE DOOR IN THE MAIN ENTRANCE TO THE UNITED STATES CAPITOL

The door, of solid bronze, is 19 feet high, 9 feet wide and weighs 20,000 pounds. It was modeled by Randolph Rogers in Rome in 1858 and cast in Munich in 1860 by F. von Muller. Its cost was $30,000. On it are nine panels, in high relief, representing the main events in Columbus's life from his appearance before the Council of Salamanca to his death. On the sides and between the panels are sixteen small statues of well-known contemporaries of Columbus, together with ten projecting heads of the historians of his voyages. On the transom arch is a bust of the Admiral. (Courtesy, *Library of Congress*)

CHAPTER TWO

IN THE WAKE OF COLUMBUS

VESPUCIUS, THE CABOTS, VERRAZZANO

AMERICUS VESPUCIUS

No man, next to Columbus, did so much to enlarge the world's horizon as Vespucius. No discoverer, next to the Genoese Admiral, has been so calumnied as the Florentine who was destined to give his name to the western hemisphere. It would seem that the greater one's achievements, the more abundant the calumnies and attempts to besmirch his glory. Washington, Jefferson, Lincoln, all had to endure vilifications, especially while they were living. But, like the giants of American history, Vespucius, too, is gaining stature as more light is thrown on his accomplishments.

Americus Vespucius was born in Florence in March, 1454. He spent his youth in his native city, where he devoted considerable time to the study of mathematics until, at the age of 25, he was sent to France as secretary to an uncle of his who was the Medicean envoy in Paris. Two years later he returned to Florence as an executive in the Medici banking house. In 1491 he was still with the same organization, at their branch office in Seville, then entrusted to Giannetto Berardi, the friend of Columbus. Berardi was active in fitting out ships for America from 1493 to the time of his death in 1495, when Vespucius became his testamentary executor and head of the Seville branch. It was there that the young Florentine became acquainted with the Genoese Admiral and developed a keen interest in the new discoveries.

Vespucius is said to have made his first transatlantic voyage in 1497-98, but there is no certainty on this point. At any rate, it is established that he took part as a pilot in the Ojeda expedition of 1499-1500. From Central America he undertook with two ships a voyage of his own during which he discovered Brazil (August, 1499). That was eight months before Cabral, the man who is generally credited with the discovery of that country.

Two years later, in May, 1501, Vespucius sailed across the ocean with a Portuguese expedition, apparently as a scientific observer. In August of that year, it would seem, he landed once more on the Brazilian coast, not far from the present city of Pernambuco. On December 13 he discovered the Bay of Rio de Janeiro. Later he is said to have reached Patagonia, but there is no consensus of opinion on this point, just as there is no agreement among historians regarding another voyage which he is said to have made later on.

At any rate, by 1505 Vespucius was back in Spain, as we know from the famous letter which Columbus wrote to his son, Diego, in which he refers to Vespucius in endearing terms and notes how he too, like many others, had not been very lucky.

Once in Spain, Vespucius became naturalized and was appointed "piloto mayor" of the *Casa de Contratacion de las Indias,* the first man to fill that office. As "piloto mayor" it was Vespucius's duty to examine and appoint all pilots and sea captains who planned to cross the ocean, no ship being allowed to go overseas without his permission. He was also in charge of the compilation of all maps and charts, no ship being permitted to follow a different route than the one marked by him. His most important trust was the study of all new discoveries which were to be reported to him. For a man who was born abroad that was a position of paramount significance, especially in those days when all routes and discoveries were kept with utmost secrecy.

Nor was Vespucius an impostor who, still according to Emerson, "managed in this lying world to supplant Columbus and baptize half the earth with his dishonest name." Vespucius was a man of the highest integrity and a scientist of superior skill. He was the first man to become convinced, as the result of his own voyages along the coast of South America, that the lands discovered by Columbus and his followers were not a part of Asia, as it had been believed until then, but a new continent, veritably a New World. As Prof. Pohl shows abundantly in his biography of the great Florentine, he was the greatest cosmographer of his age. Suffice it to mention that he was able to estimate the circumference of the earth within fifty miles of the correct figure.

Vespucius remained as "piloto mayor" of Spain until his death at Seville on February 22, 1512. That, too, should be an indication of the value the rulers of Spain attached to his ability and services.

Columbus was still insisting that he had found Asia when two pamphlets appeared, in both Paris and Florence, one bearing the title *Quatuor Americi Navigationes,* and the other with the most significant title of *Mundus Novus.* The former was a translation or adaptation of a letter which Vespucius is said to have written in 1504 to the House of Medici in Florence, from Lisbon; the second was an account of his voyage to Brazil. Both were published without Vespucius's knowledge.

In 1507 the German geographer Martin Waldseemuller (in Latin Hylacomylus) reprinted the *Quatuor navigationes,* preceded by a pamphlet entitled *Cosmographiae introductio cum quibusdam geometriae ac astronomiae*

AMERICA GETS HER NAME

Nūc vō & hę partes ſunt latius luſtratæ/& alia quarta pars per Americū Veſputiū(vt in ſequenti bus audietur)inuenta eſt/quā non video cur quis iure vetet ab Americo inuentore ſagacis ingenn vi ro Amerigen quaſi Americi terrā / ſiue Americam dicendā:cū & Europa & Aſia a mulieribus ſua ſor tita ſint nomina. Eius ſitū & gentis mores ex bis bi nis Americi nauigationibus quæ ſequunt liquide intelligi datur.

Ameri ca

The passage from Waldseemuller's *Cosmographiae* in which he suggested that the new world be called America. As translated by John Fiske, (*The Discovery of America,* Boston, 1892, Vol. II, p. 136), it reads: "But now these parts have been more extensively explored and another fourth part has been discovered by Americus Vespucius (as it will appear in what follows) wherefore I do not see what is rightly to hinder us from calling it Amerige or America, i.e. the land of Americus, a man of sagacious mind, since both Europe and Asia have got their names from women. Its situation and the manners and customs of its people will be clearly understood from the twice two voyages of Americus which follow."

AMERICUS VESPUCIUS AS A BOY
A fresco in the Church of All Saints, Florence. (School of Domenico Ghirlandaio)

principis ad eam rem necessariis, together with a map. (See page 50). In that pamphlet Waldseemuller suggested that since it had been Vespucius to advance the belief that the new lands discovered after Columbus's first voyage were not Asia but a new world, it should be called "ab Americo inventore, sagacis ingenii viro, Amerigen quasi Americi terram sive Americam," or "after its discoverer Americus, a man of sagacious mind, Amerige or America, the land of Americus." The suggestion was accepted by the other leading geographers of the time, but, as already stated, Vespucius had nothing to do with it. Nor was Columbus completely ignored by Waldseemuller for, as we can see in the map on page 50, the name America was applied only to the present South America, whereas the islands and the part of the Central American continent discovered by Columbus were credited to him. It was only in later years that the name America was applied to the entire western hemisphere.

VESPUCIUS OBSERVING THE SOUTHERN CROSS
(Drawing by Stradanus, engraved by Collaert)

AMERICUS VESPUCIUS

A fresco by Brumidi in the ceiling of the United States Capitol. (Courtesy, *Library of Congress*)

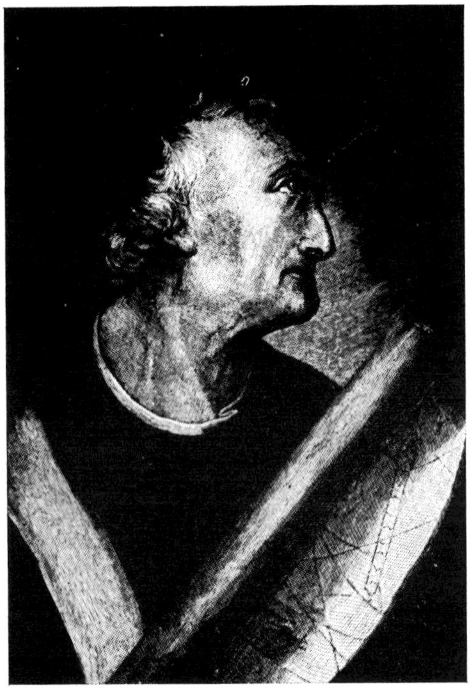

AMERICUS VESPUCIUS
A portrait by unknown author in the Galleria degli Uffizi, Florence.

PORTION OF WALDSEEMULLER'S GLOBE
(See page 48)

As stated on page 48, Waldseemuller first applied the name America to the southern part of the western hemisphere. (See the reproduction on this page of portion of his globe as it was first published together with his *Universalis Cosmografia.*)

Waldseemuller, however, did not ignore Columbus, for in a little box, about the middle of the map reproduced on this page, below the island of Hispaniola, near the coast of Paria (Central America) he inserted the words: "Iste insule per Columbum genuensem almirantem ex mandato regis Castellae invente sunt" or "these islands have been discovered by the Genoese admiral Columbus by order of the king of Castile." Notice the word, Genoese, one more early proof of Columbus's nationality, one year after his death.

The complete map is surmounted by two portraits, one of Ptolemy and the other of Vespucius, a clear indication that in the eyes of Waldseemuller and the other geographers of his day Vespucius was as important for the knowledge of the New World as Ptolemy was for that of the Old. As Prof. Almagià points out, one could hardly ask for a higher recognition of the achievements of the Florentine Navigator.

On Vespucius see Almagià, *op. cit.,* and the fundamental work by Alberto Magnaghi *Amerigo Vespucci,* 2nd edition, Milan, 1926. The best volume in English on the subject is Prof. Frederick J. Pohl's *Amerigo Vespucci: Pilot Major,* New York, 1944. It follows, largely, Magnaghi's theories.

JOHN CABOT GIVES ENGLAND HER CLAIM TO NORTH AMERICA

The fundamental thing about John Cabot an American should remember is the fact that it was because of his voyage of 1497 that the English took possession of North America. When Sir Humphrey Gilbert and Sir Walter Raleigh conceived the plan of establishing an English colony in the New World, their only legal claim was based on Cabot's voyage of discovery. (See facsimile in next column). Our founding fathers also based their claim for American independence on that first voyage by the Italian navigator. We quote from Benjamin Franklin's famous address on *Vindication for the Colonies* which he issued to the public on June 15, 1775:

> Forasmuch as the enemies of America in the Parliament of Great Britain, to render us odious to the nation, and give an ill impression of us in the minds of other European powers, having represented us as unjust and ungrateful in the highest degree; asserting on every occasion, that the colonies were settled at the expense of the same, proteced in their infancy ....
> And as by frequent repetitions these groundless assertions and malicious calumnies may, if not contradicted and refuted, obtain further credit.
> ....
> With regard to the first, *that the colonies were settled at he expense of Britain,* it is a known fact that none of the twelve united colonies were settled or even discovered at the expense of England. Henry VII, indeed, granted a commission to Sebastian Cabot, a Venetian, and his sons to sail into western seas for the discovery of new countries; but it was to be "suis corum propriis sumptibus et expensis," at their own cost and charges. They discovered, but soon slighted and neglected these northern territories; which were, after more than a hundred years dereliction, purchased of the natives ....

Franklin, of course, got his data a little mixed up, starting from Cabot's first name, but that matters little. What matters is the historical fact that Cabot financed his voyage at his own expense and that it was because of that voyage that the English eventually settled in Virginia.

The English flag was first planted on American soil by John Cabot on June 24, 1497. Little is known of Cabot, or Caboto, except that he became a citizen of Venice in the year 1476, after a residence of 15 years in that city. Nobody knows exactly where he was born. Some people say that he was a native of Genoa. Others trace his birth to Gaeta, the same city near Naples Henri Tonti came from. He had three sons, Louis, Sebastian and Sante (or Sancius, as we find his name in English documents). Only Sebastian became famous.

About the year 1491 or 1492 John Cabot took up residence in Bristol, England. It seems that between those years and 1496 he tried to sail out of that port in search of some mythical islands, but there is no evidence on this point. What we know for sure is that after Columbus made his first voyage, Cabot tried to come over, but he chose a northern route in order to avoid a possible conflict by England with Spain or Portugal.

At any rate, on March 5, 1496, Henry VII granted John Cabot and his three sons permission to fit out an expedition at their own expense. Most likely local merchants advanced most of the money, if not all of it. Not much, however, was required, because, although Cabot had permission to leave with five ships, he left with only one, the 50-ton *Matthew*. The crew consisted of 18 men. Thus Cabot's voyage was in a way even bolder than that by Columbus, except that the Genoese Admiral was sailing towards the unknown, whereas Cabot knew of the existence of land across the sea.

The *Matthew* remained out of Bristol only three months. It left on May 2 and returned on August 6, 1497. Land, as we have already noted, was first sighted on June 24, when the English flag was first planted in America. Cabot, however, did not forget Venice, for at the same time he planted the standard of St. Mark, or the Venetian flag. Nobody knows exactly where Cabot first landed, but most historians seem to agree that it was near the present town of Louisbourg, near Cape Breton. At least one Italian, a Genoese barber, or surgeon, named Castiglione, took part in that expedition, for Raimondo da Soncino, in his report to the Duke of Milan written in 1497, stated that he was one of the two men to whom Cabot had donated an island. The other was a Frenchman.

1622 **543**

The Countrey called VIRGINIA (so named by the late Virgin-Queene *Elizabeth* of blessed memory) being the rightfull inheritance of his Maiesty, as being first discouered at the costs and charges of that most prudent Prince of famous memory, *King Henry the Seauenth*, his Maiesties great Grandfather; The Patent whereof still extant to be seene, was granted to *Iohn Cabot* and diuers other of his subiects, who went thither with sixe Saile of Ships, and discouered as farre as from *Cape Florida* to *Neu-found-land*, all along the Coast, and tooke possession thereof to the Kings vse, about that time when *Ferdinando* and *Isabella* discouered the *Westerne Indies:* (by which title of first discouery the King of *Portugal* and *Spaine* hold and enioy their ample and rich Kingdomes in their *Indies East & West:*) A coast where *King Edward the Sixt* after planted his fishing to the *Neufound-land* by publike Act in Parliament, and of which *Philip Amadas* and *Arthur Barlow* tooke againe possession to the vse of the late *Queene Elizabeth:* and after them, [3] *Sir Richard Greenfield, Sir Ralph Lane,* and *Sir Walter Rawleigh;* at what time seuerall Colonies were there placed. And since his Maiesties most happy comming to the Crowne, being an

(*Right*) An early reference (1622) to England's title to North America based on Cabot's discovery. From *The Records of the Virginia Company of London* by S. M. Kingsbury. (Courtesy, *New York Public Library*) A still earlier reference is in Hakluyt's preface to his *Divers Voyages,* London, 1582.

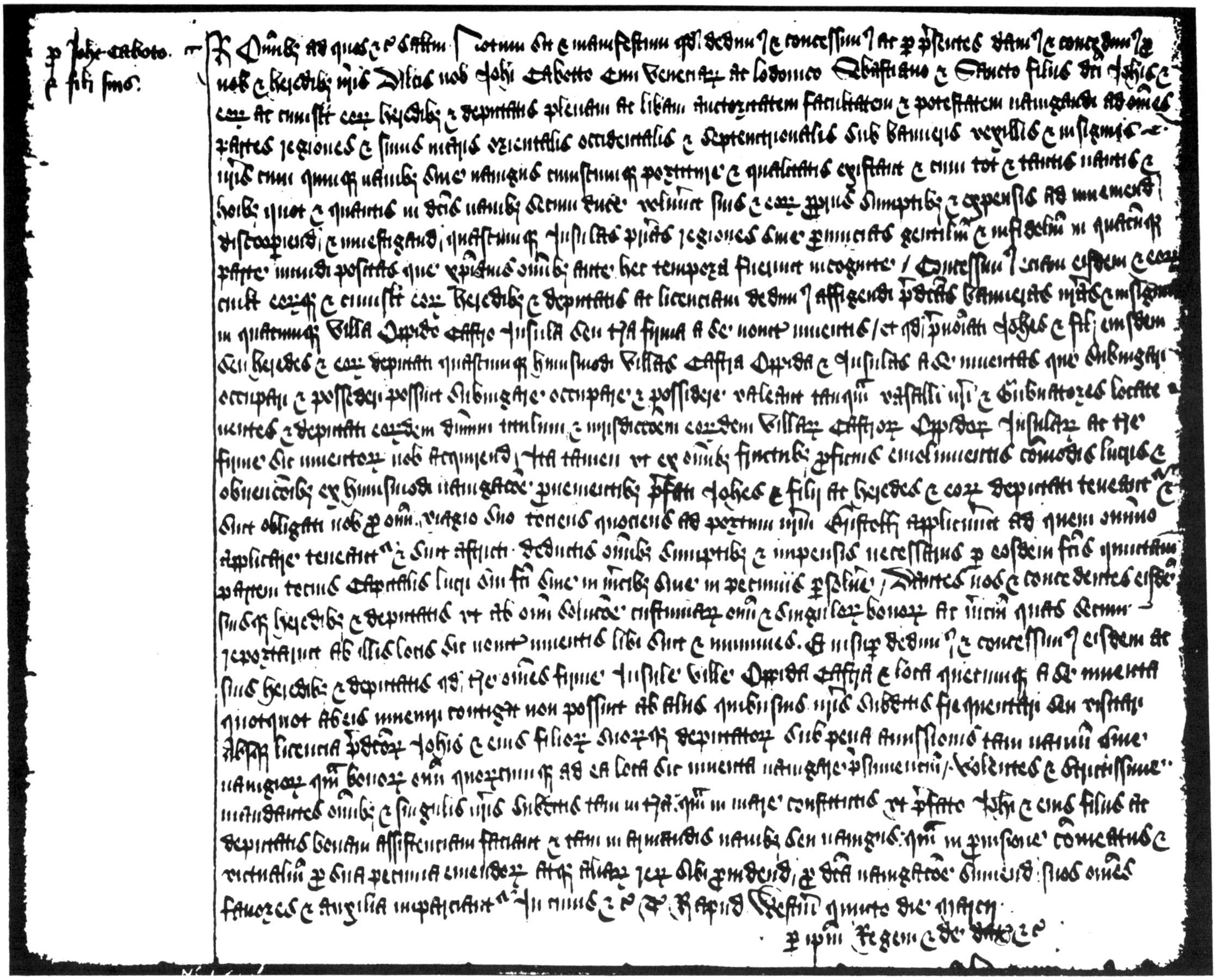

THE FIRST LETTER PATENT GRANTED BY HENRY VII TO JOHN CABOT AND HIS SONS. From *The Public Record Office, London, Chancery Treaty Roll* (C-76) No. 178 M8. (Courtesy, *British Museum, London*)

Translation from the Latin text as it appears above:

The King, to all to whom, etc. . . Greetings: Be it known and made manifest that we have given and granted as by these presents we give and grant, for us and our heirs, to our well-beloved John Cabot, citizen of Venice, and to Lewis, Sebastian and Sancio, sons of the said John, and to the heirs and deputies of them, and of any one of them, full and free authority, faculty and power to sail to all parts, regions and coasts of the eastern western and northern sea, under our banners, flags and ensigns, with five ships or vessels of whatsoever burden and quality they may be, and with so many and such mariners and men as they may wish to take with them in the said ships, at their own proper costs and charges, to find, discover and investigate whatsoever islands, countries, regions or provinces of heathens and infidels, in whatsoever part of the world placed, which before this time were unknown to all Christians.

We have also granted to them and to any of them, and have given licence to set up our aforesaid banners and ensigns in any town, city, castle, island or mainland whatsoever, newly found by them. And that the before-mentioned John and his sons or their heirs and deputies may conquer, occupy and possess whatsoever such towns, castles, cities, and islands by them thus discovered that they may be able to conquer, occupy and possess, as our vassals and governors, lieutenants and deputies therein, acquiring for us the dominion, title and jurisdiction of the same towns, castles, cities, islands and mainlands so discovered; in such way, nevertheless that of all the fruits, profits, emoluments, commodities, gains and revenues accruing from this voyage, the said John and sons and their heirs and deputies shall be bounden and under obligation for every voyage, as often as they shall arrive at our port of Bristol, at which they are bound and holden only to arrive, all necessary charges and expenses incurred by them having been deducted, to pay to us, either in goods or money, the fifth part of the whole capital gained, we giving and granting to them and to their heirs and deputies that they shall be free and exempt from all payments of customs on all and singular the goods and merchandise that they may bring back with them from those places thus newly discovered. And further we have given and granted to them and to their heirs and deputies, that all mainlands, islands, towns, cities, castles and other places whatsoever discovered by them, however numerous they may happen to be, may not be frequented or visited by any other subjects of ours whatsoever without the licence of the aforesaid John and his sons and their deputies, on pain of the loss as well as of the ships or vessels daring to sail to these places discovered, as of all goods whatsoever. Willing and strictly commanding all and singular our subjects as well by land as by sea, that they shall render good assistance to the aforesaid John and his sons and their deputies, and that they shall give them all their favour and help as well in fitting out the ships or vessels, as in bringing stores and provisions with their money and in providing the other things which they must take with them on the said voyage. In witness whereof. . . .

Translation from the Latin, as per facsimile above, from Williamson, J. A. *The Voyages of the Cabots and the English Discovery of North America under Henry VIII and Henry VIII,* London, 1929, pp. 25-27.

THE CABOT TOWER

at the entrance to the Port of Bristol from which John Cabot and his sons sailed on their voyage of discovery to North America in 1497. (British Official Photograph)

A 16th Century painting (restored in the 18th) representing the Navigation of John and Sebastian Cabot. The Central figure is that of Sebastian Cabot. (Venice, Ducal Palace, Sala dello Scudo)

Back in England, Cabot, like Columbus, was received with great honors by the King who granted him an annual pension of 20 pounds sterling, a sum equal to $100, but possibly having the purchasing value in those days of $2,000 in America today. On December 13, 1497, Henry VII renewed John Cabot's letters patent authorizing him to fit out another expedition of six ships. The new voyage took place with five ships in 1498. At least one Italian, one Giovanni Antonio de Carbonariis, went along, besides Cabot's son, Sebastian, and possibly his brothers. Nothing is known of that second voyage either, except that John Cabot continued to collect his annual pension as late as September, 1499. He may have died soon after, for he was no longer living in 1505. During that second voyage, according to modern historians, John Cabot sighted, or landed along, the Atlantic coast from the 38th parallel north, or from New York to Canada.

CABOT PLANTS THE VENETIAN FLAG ON AMERICAN SOIL

THE LION OF ST. MARK

Symbol of the Republic of Venice, whose flag John Cabot planted on American soil on June 24, 1497, side by side with that of England.

(*Above*) THE DISCOVERY OF NORTH AMERICA BY JOHN AND SEBASTIAN CABOT

(From Ballou's *Pictorial Drawing Room Companion,* 1855. Wood Engraving. *Library of Congress.*)

Oct. 11.
Sanuto Diaries, v. i. p. 573.

752. LORENZO PASQUALIGO to his Brothers ALVISE and FRANCESCO.

The Venetian, our countryman, who went with a ship from Bristol in quest of new islands, is returned, and says that 700 leagues hence he discovered land, the territory of the Grand Cham (*Gram Cam*). He coasted for 300 leagues and landed; saw no human beings, but he has brought hither to the King certain snares which had been set to catch game, and a needle for making nets; he also found some felled trees, wherefore he supposed there were inhabitants, and returned to his ship in alarm.

He was three months on the voyage, and on his return he saw two islands to starboard, but would not land, time being precious, as he was short of provisions. He says that the tides are slack and do not flow as they do here. The King of England is much pleased with this intelligence.

The King has promised that in the spring our countryman shall have ten ships, armed to his order, and at his request has conceded him all the prisoners, except such as are confined for high treason, to man his fleet. The King has also given him money wherewith to amuse himself till then, and he is now at Bristol with his wife, who is also Venetian, and with his sons; his name is Zuan Cabot, and he is styled the great admiral. Vast honour is paid him; he dresses in silk, and these English run after him like mad people, so that he can enlist as many of them as he pleases, and a number of our own rogues besides.

The discoverer of these places planted on his new-found land a large cross, with one flag of England and another of S. Mark, by reason of his being a Venetian so that our banner has floated very far afield.

London, 23 August 1497.

[*Italian. Entered in the Diaries on* 11 *September* 1497. *Translated and printed for the Philobiblon Society.*]

(*Right*) English translation of portion of a letter Lorenzo Pasqualigo, a Venetian living in London, wrote to his brothers in Venice soon after John Cabot's return from his voyage of discovery. (From Calendar of State Papers, London, edited by H. Brown. Courtesy, *New York Public Library*)

JOHN CABOT'S DEPARTURE FROM BRISTOL
(From the painting by Ernest Board, 1877, in the Bristol (England) Museum and Art Gallery)

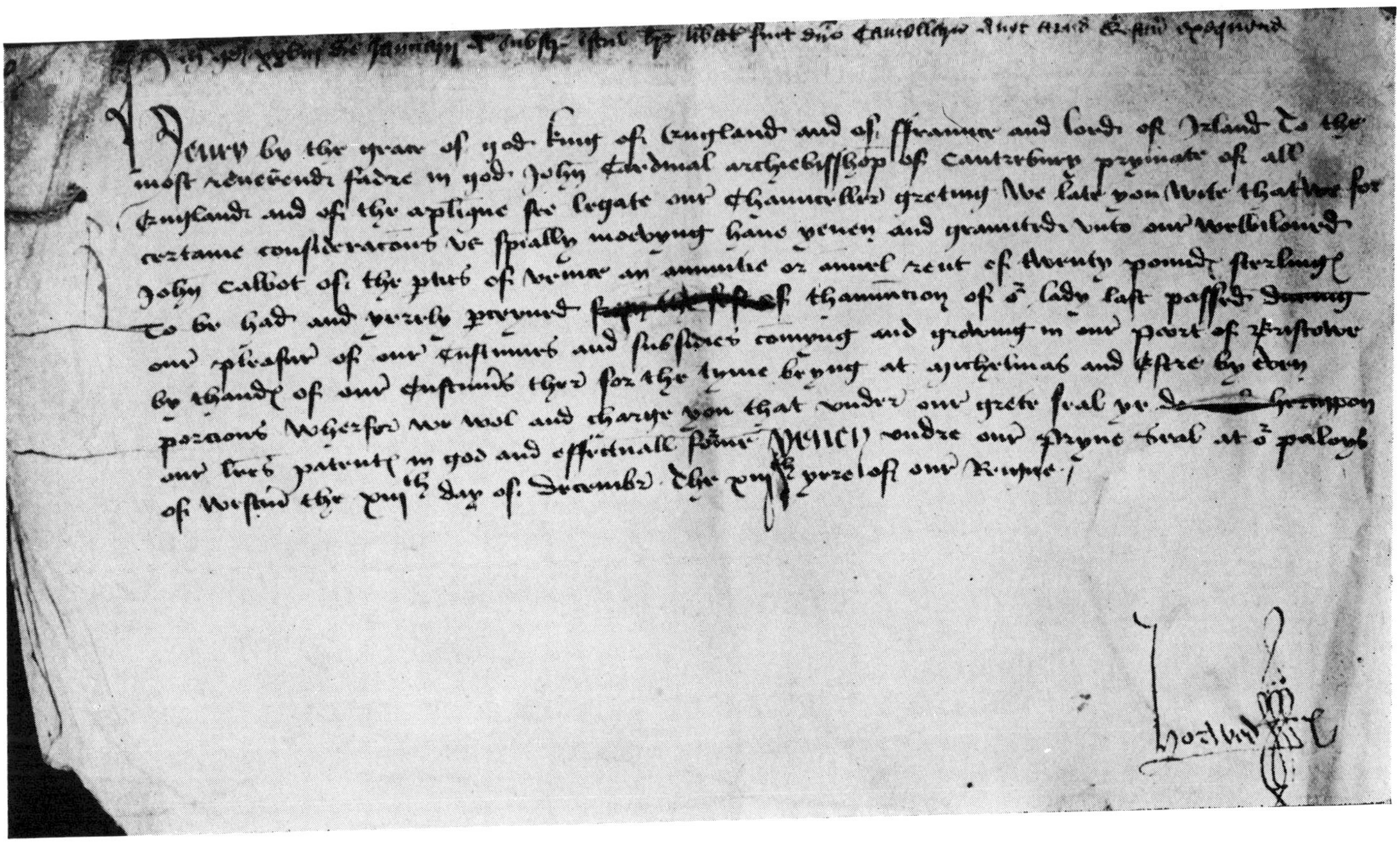

Henry by the grace of god king of England and of ffraunce and lord of Irland To the
most reverend fadre in god John Cardinal archebisshop of Canterbury primate of all
England and of the apostolique see legate our Chaunceller greting We late you wite that we for
certaine consideracions us specially moevyng have yeven and graunted unto our welbiloved
John Calbot of the parts of Venice an annuitie or annuel rent of twenty pounds sterling
to be had and yerely perceyved [illegible] fro thanunciacion of our lady last passed during
our pleasur of our custumes and subsidies comyng and growing in our poort of Bristowe
by thands of our custumers there for the tyme beyng at Michelmas and Estre by even
porcions Wherfor we wol and charge you that under our grete seal ye do [illegible]
our lettres patentes in good and effectuall forme Yeven under our pryve seal at our paloys
of Westminster the xiij day of Decembre the xiij yere of our Reigne

GRANT OF PENSION TO JOHN CABOT, DECEMBER 13, 1497
Notice in the fifth line the words "John Cabbot of the state of Venice an annuitie or annual rent of twenty pounds sterling. From the Public Record Office, London, Privy Seals, 13 Henry VII, December. (Courtesy, *British Museum,* London)

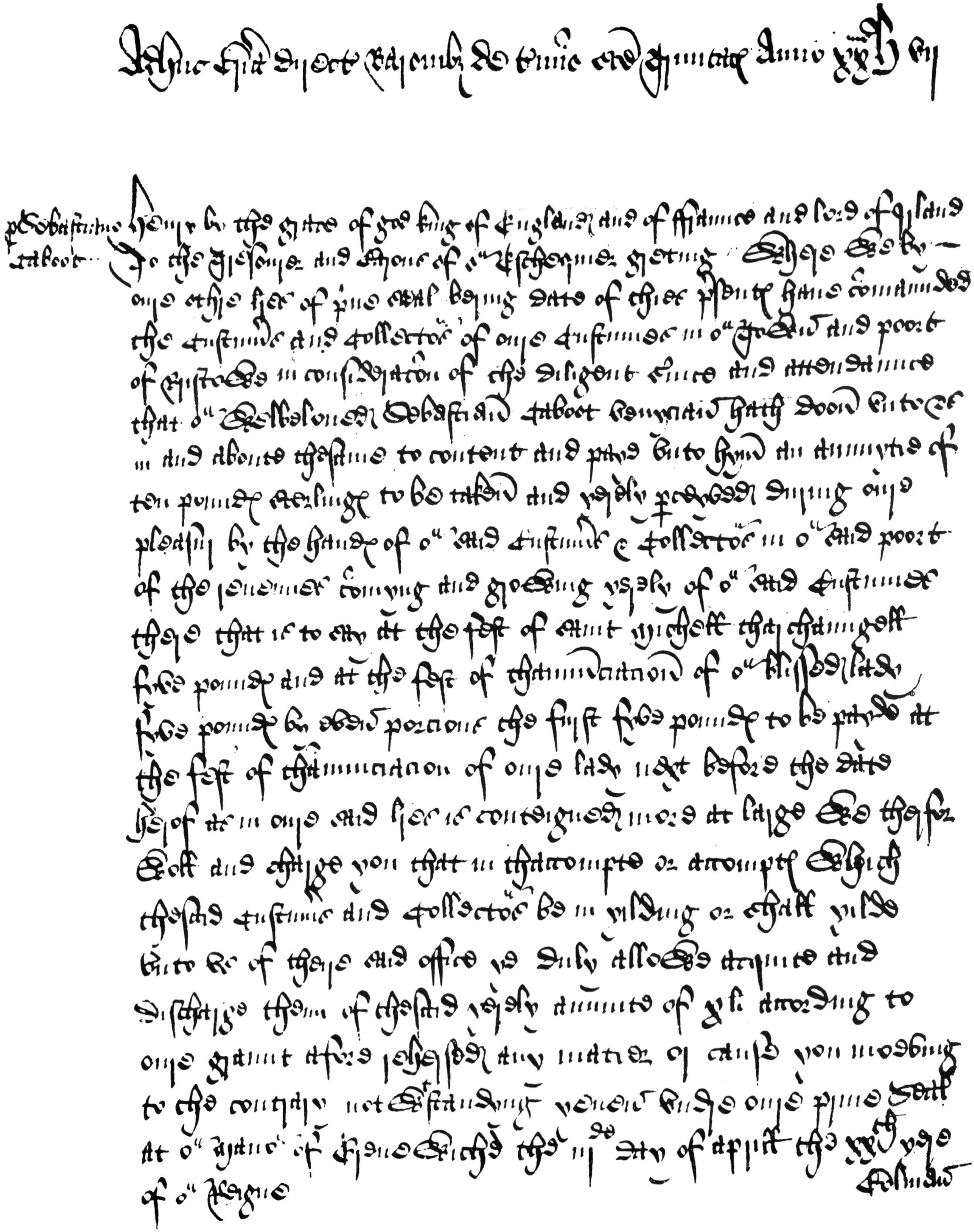

Adhuc Brevia direct' Baronibus de termino Sancti Hillarii Anno xxj R H vij

pro Sebastiano Caboot

Henry by the grace of god king of England and of Fraunce and lord of Irland To the Tresourer and Barons of our Eschequier greting Where as by our other lettres of prive seal beryng date of these presentes have commaunded the custumers and collectours of our custumes in our towne and poort of Bristowe in consideracion of the diligent service and attendaunce that our welbeloved Sebastian Caboot Venycian hath doon unto us in and aboute thesame to content and paye unto hym an annuytie of ten poundes sterlinge to be taken and yerely perceyved during our pleasur by the handes of our said custumers & collectours in our said poort of the revenues comyng and growing yerely of our said custumes there that is to say at the fest of Saint Michell tharchaungell five poundes and at the fest of thannunciacion of our blessed lady five poundes by even porcions the first five poundes to be payde at the fest of thannunciacion of our lady next before the date herof as in our said lettres is conteigned more at large We therfor woll and charge you that in thaccomptes or accomptes which thesaid custumers and collectours be in yelding or shall yelde unto you of their said office ye duly allowe theym and discharge theym of thesaid yerely annuitie of xli according to our graunt afore rehersed any matier or cause you movyng to the contrary notwithstanding yeven under our prive seal at our manoir of Grenewiche the iii[de] day of April the xx[th] yere of our Reigne

[illegible]

GRANT OF PENSION TO SEBASTIAN CABOT, APRIL 3, 1505

From the Public Record Office, London, Exchequer, (K.R. Memoranda Roll (E. 159) No. 283. (extract). (Courtesy, *British Museum, London*)

MONUMENT TO JOHN CABOT IN MONTREAL, CANADA

Guido Casini, Sculptor. Presented by the local Italians. Unveiled May 24, 1935. So far as we know, there is no monument in honor of John Cabot in the United States. It is interesting to recall, however, that one of the first four warships commissioned by the United States during the Revolution was named after John Cabot.

SEBASTIAN CABOT, CHIEF PILOT OF ENGLAND

SEBASTIAN CABOT

Portrait attributed to Holbein, destroyed by fire in 1845. From an engraving in Seyer's *Memoirs of Bristol,* 1824, Vol. II. A copy of the original portrait is said to be in the Historical Society of Massachusetts in Boston.

We have more information about Sebastian Cabot, who was born in Venice, of Venetian mother, about the year 1482. As we have seen, he accompanied his father in the 1498 voyage and possibly also in that of 1497. He was still in Bristol in 1505, when Henry VII granted him a pension of £10, "for services rendered to the city and port of Bristol." What those services were we do not know.

In 1508 (or 1509, according to the modern calendar, for in those times the English year began in March) Sebastian Cabot made a voyage under the English flag, also towards America, but in search of the North-West Passage, or the way to China. He left with two ships, also fitted out at his expense. Once more, we do not know much about that voyage, but it is believed that he reached Labrador and possibly entered Hudson Bay, which he thought to be the Pacific Ocean.

From 1512 to 1548 Sebastian was in the service of Spain, most of the time with the rank of "piloto mayor," a most important position. That alone should be sufficient to make one realize Cabot's skill and ability, for numerous and influential Spaniards were anxious to take his place. In 1526, while in the service of Spain, Sebastian Cabot undertook a most famous voyage which was not altogether successful. Nevertheless Cabot was able to reach and explore the entire basin of the Plata River, venturing inland through the Parana and Paraguay rivers. He even sent an overland expedition to the Andes. It was because of that voyage that South America became a possession of Spain rather than of Portugal. Here, again, let us recall that Italian merchants advanced two-thirds of the cost of the expedition, and that at least 30 Italians took part in it. Most of the Italians were either Venetians or Genoese, but there were also a Neapolitan, one of the officers, and a Sicilian.

From 1548 to the time of his death in 1557, Sebastian Cabot was once more in the service of England. The most important of his activities during this period was his organization in 1553 of the famous Company of Merchant Adventures of England, of which he was chosen governor for life. Students of English history need not be reminded that it was this company that started the British Empire on its march around the world. The first expedition sent out by Cabot was headed by Willoughby and Chancellor and marks the beginning of direct trade relations between Britain and Russia. Moreover, as George L. Baer states in his *The Origin of the British Colonial Empire* (New York, 1908, p. 6) "it was in searching for a northwestern route to the East, that Sir Humphrey Gilbert's interest was deflected to the colonization of America."

SEBASTIAN CABOT LEAVING LABRADOR
From a print in the *New York Public Library*

An interesting incident in Cabot's life is the offer he made to Venice, on two different occasions, in 1522 and in 1553, for an oversea voyage under the Venetian flag, but Venice turned him down, possibly because it was impossible for Venetian ships to get out of the Mediterranean without the consent of Spain and Portugal, who dominated the exit.

Sebastian Cabot, like Vespucius and Columbus, also has been the subject of attacks by people not well acquainted with the facts concerning his activities. Modern historians, however, are unanimous in praising him as one of the most skillful navigators and one of the most able scientists of his day. He certainly was one of the founders of the British Empire.

On the Cabots see: the article by Alberto Magnaghi in *Enciclopedia Italiana Treccani,* Vol. VIII, 199-202; Almagia,' *op cit.;* Williamson, *op. cit.;* Sercia, G., *Giovanni Caboto e la navigazione italiana del suo tempo,* Bologna, 1937. (Prof. Sercia's little book deals largely with the Gaeta origins of the Caboto family).

SEBASTIAN CABOT LEAVING FOR AMERICA

A mural by Ezra Winter (1921) in the ceiling of the Cunard White Star Building in New York City. *Cunard White Star photo by W. A. Probst.* (As we know, it was not Sebastian Cabot but his father, John, who first planted the English flag in North America. Sebastian was not born in Bristol, England, as stated by some misinformed persons, but in Venice)

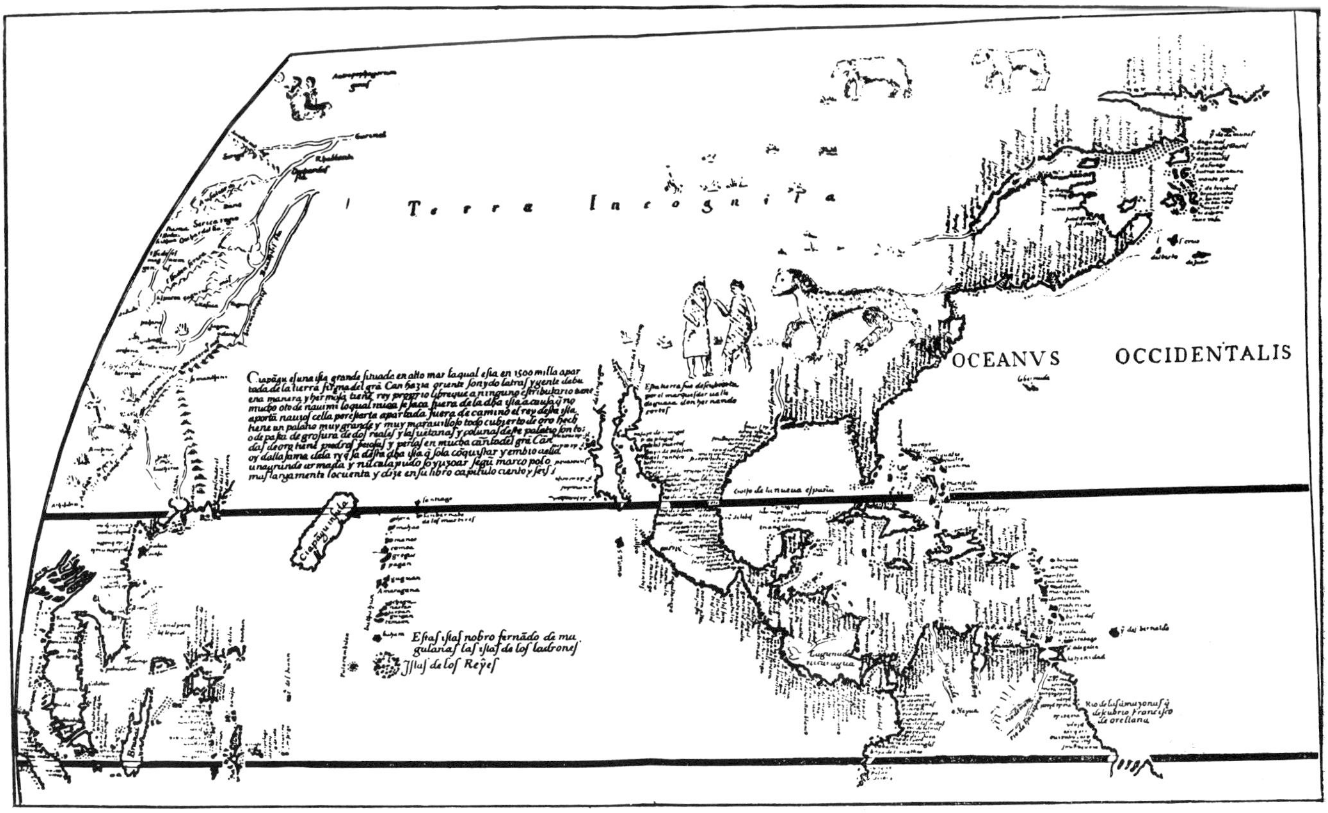

Portion of Sebastian Cabot's planisphere published probably at Norimberg in 1544. The only copy known to exist is in the Biblioteque Nationale in Paris. According to the late Prof. Magnaghi and other historians, Cabot had nothing to do with it. According to Prof. Almagià, it was based on a map which Cabot drew in 1541. At any rate, it seems that the cartographers drew largely on data furnished by Sebastian Cabot. One of the most remarkable notes on the margin of the map, note 8, in Spanish and Latin, reads: "This land was discovered by John Cabot, Venetian, and his son, Sebastian, in the year 1494" (Obviously an error). Also worthy of notice are the words, in Italian, "prima terra vista" (land first seen) near the location of Cape Breton.

VERRAZZANO IN NEW YORK HARBOR 85 YEARS BEFORE HUDSON

One of the most precious objects in the possession of the New York Historical Society is a copper globe made in Florence by Eufrosino Della Volpaia in 1542. Geographically it is not of paramount importance, except as a confirmation of the knowledge that existed at that time about the New World. Historically it is at least interesting, for it shows the Eastern Central Part of the United States under the name of Verrazana. The name was first suggested by Girolamo da Verrazzano, a brother of Giovanni da Verrazzano. Girolamo, a navigator and cartographer, had made a map in 1529 in which he had called all the land discovered by his brother "Verrazana or New France or Jucatanet." Apparently Della Volpaia consulted that map, and probably another globe which Giovanni da Verrazzano is said to have made but which has never been found. Be that as it may, it is to Giovanni da Verrazzano that we owe the first description of North America's coastline from South Carolina to Canada.

Not much is known of Verrazzano. He was born at Florence between 1481 and 1485. In his youth he sailed in the Mediterranean, and probably elsewhere, until 1522, when he settled in France. In 1524 he was entrusted by King Francis I of France with a voyage of discovery. Here again, as in the case of Columbus, the Cabots, and Vespucius, we must remind our readers that the Italians excelled all the other navigators of their day (with the possible exception of the Portuguese, who, however, did not surpass the Italians). Foreign kings, most certainly, would have chosen navigators of their nationality if they could find them. Several Florentines, incidentally, accompanied Verrazzano.

The voyage lasted from January to July, 1524, when Verrazzano was back in France. In 1528 he was entrusted with another expedition to North America. On this second voyage he had stopped at the Bahamas and was proceeding towards the Gulf of Darien (Panama) when he decided to explore an island which appeared to be uninhabited. Instead, he was met by some cannibals who set upon him, killed him and devoured him. His brother Girolamo saw it all from the deck of the ship but was unable to come to the assistance of Giovanni and the other six men who had gone ashore.

As to the legend that Verrazzano was a corsair in the service of France there is no evidence to prove it or disprove it.

Verrazzano deserves a prominent place in the history of American discovery, side by side with that of his fellow-Tuscan, Vespucius. For if the latter explored practically all the coast of South America, Verazzano reconnoitered all that of North America, from Florida to the Gulf of St. Lawrence, in a way that had never been done before.

The practical result of Verrazzano's voyage was the continued interest that the French took in North America, culminating in the voyage of Jacques Cartier in 1534. Now, however, it seems established that Cartier had accompanied Verrazzano during his first voyage. (See Lanctot, B., Cartier's first voyage to Canada in 1524, *Canadian Historical Review*, September, 1944, pp. 233-245.)

The other result of Verrazzano's voyage was the confirmation that the New World was not a part of Asia, or of Africa, as he clearly stated in the last page of his report to King Francis I.

Verrazzano's description of North America is one of the most interesting accounts we have of the United States

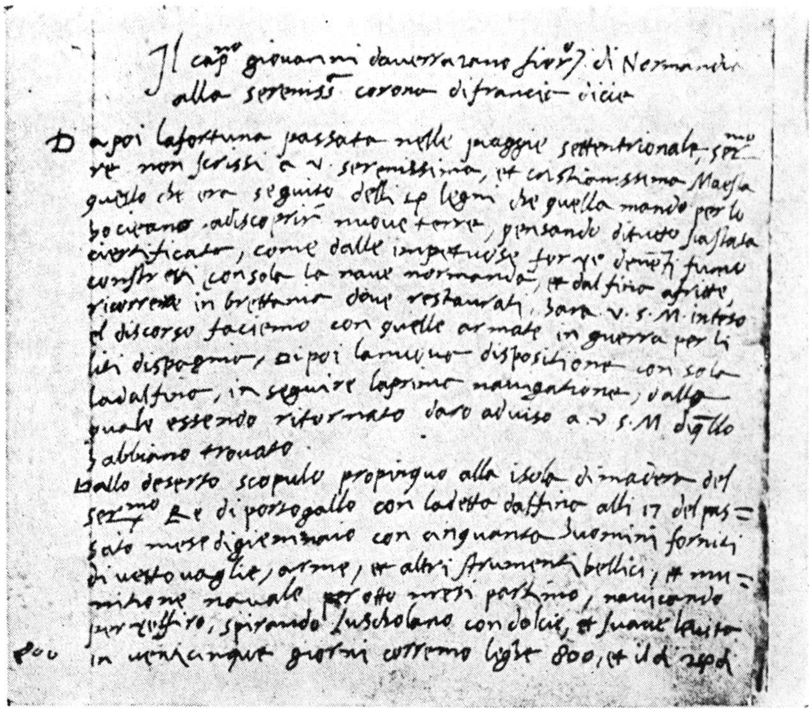
Il capno giovanni daverrazano fior.no di Normandia
alla serenissa corona di francia dicie
Dapoi la fortuna passata nelle plaggie settentrionali, Ser.mo
Re non scrissi a v. serenissima, et christianissima Maesta
quello che era seguito delli 4 legni che quella mando per lo
ociano a discoprir nuove terre, pensando di tutto sia stata
certificata, come dalle impetuose forze de venti fumo
constretti con sola la nave normanda, et dalfina afflicte,
ricorrere in brettania dove restaurati, harà v. S. M. inteso
il discorso faciemo con quelle armate in guerra per li
liti dispagnia, dipoi la nuova dispositione con sola
la dalfina, in seguire la prima navigatione, dalla
quale essendo ritornato darò adviso a v. S. M. di quello
habbiamo trovato.
Dallo deserto scopulo propinquo alla isola di madera del
ser.mo Re di portogallo con la detta dalfina alli 17 del pas=
sato mese di gienaio con cinquanta huomini forniti
di vettovaglie, arme, et altri strumenti bellici, et mu=
nitione navale per otto mesi partimo, navicando
per zefiro, spirando Eusbolano con dolcie, et suave levita
800 in venticinque giorni corremo leghe 800, et il di [illegible]

(*Left*) Beginning of the report Verrazzano sent to King Francis I of France upon his return from North America in 1525. Verrazzano made two copies, one of which he sent to Buonaccorso Ruccellai in Rome and another to a friend in Florence. Three copies of that report exist, but the most authoritative one, in manuscript form, was discovered by A. Bacchiani in the private library of the Cellere family in Rome in 1909. It is now in the Morgan Library in New York City. Notice the words "Il capno Giovanni da Verrazzano (Captain Giovanni da Verrazzano) a clear proof that Verrazzano was the captain and not a pilot, as someone has stated. Verrazzano would not have assumed a title which did not belong to him especially in his official report to the King who sent him out on his voyage of discovery.

MONUMENT TO VERRAZZANO IN NEW YORK CITY

The work of the Sicilian sculptor, Ettore Ximenes, it was donated by the Italians in the United States and dedicated on October 6, 1909. According to one source, the cost of the monument is said to have been borne by Mr. Carlo Barsotti, publisher of Il Progresso Italo-Americano.

The unveiling of the monument was a great day for the Italians of the city. The ceremony began with a parade in which some 40,000 people, representing 170 societies, took part with 42 bands and 400 flags. Three hundred thousand people are said to have watched the parade. One of the main features was the participation of 500 Italian cyclists and the crews of the Italian warships "Etna" and "Etruria" which had been sent to New York to take part in the 300th anniversary of the arrival of Henry Hudson in New York Bay.

The monument to Verrazzano is the only remembrance one finds in New York in honor of the great Florentine navigator, with the exception of a ferryboat which was named after him in 1950.

before it was settled by Europeans. His description of New York Harbor is of particular interest, for it preceded by 85 years the coming of Henry Hudson. He wrote:

> At the end of a hundred leagues we found a very agreeable situation located within two small prominent hills, in the midst of which flowed to the sea a very great river, which was deep within the mouth; which we found eight feet, any laden ship might have passed. . . . We were with the small boat, entering the said river to the land, which we found much populated. The people, almost like the others, clothed with the feathers of birds of various colors, came towards us joyfully, uttering very great exclamations of admiration, showing us where we could land with the boat more safely.

New Yorkers, apparently, have always excelled in hospitality, whether Indian or white!

Later Verrazzano stopped at Block Island, which he compared to the Island of Rhodes and called Louisa in honor of the King's mother, and entered the present Newport, R.I., inhabited by "the most beautiful people and the most civilized in customs that we have found in this navigation. . . . We formed a great friendship with them." After a sojourn of 15 days he proceeded north, until he reached the Gulf of St. Lawrence. Then he turned back. He had discovered "six hundred leagues and more of new land."

On Verrazzano see Almagia, *op. cit.* (valuable bibliography and notes) and Magnaghi's article in *Enciclopedia Italiana Treccani*. The English translation of Verrazzano's report, by E. H. Hall, is in the 1910 report of the *American Scenic and Historic Preservation Society*.

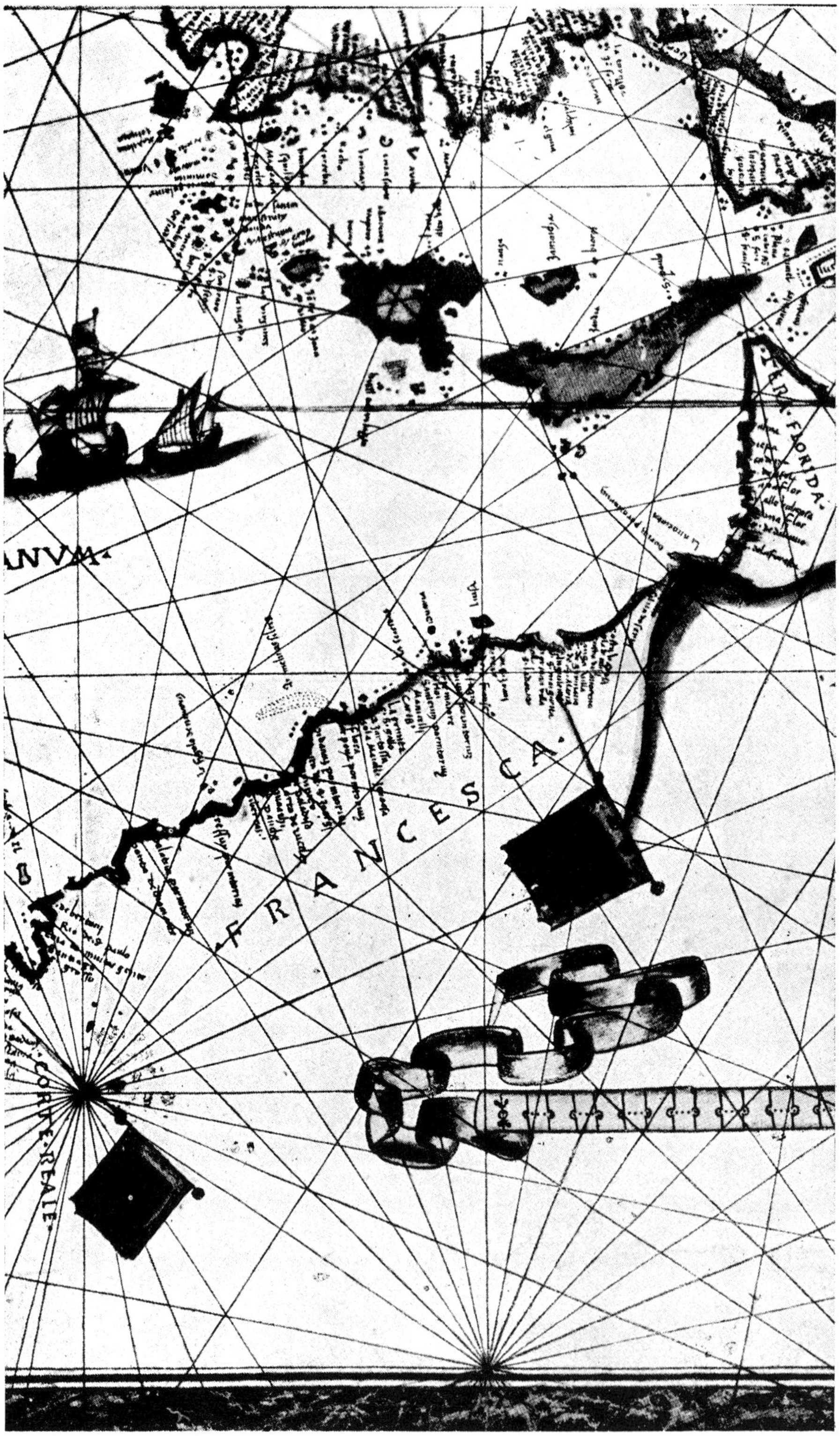

Portion of the planisphere made by Vesconte Maggiolo in Genoa in 1527. Only one copy, now in the Ambrosiana Library in Milan, is known to exist. All the land discovered by Verrazzano is called Francesca in honor of King Francis I of France. The map includes several Tuscan names like Valle Ombrosa, San Miniato, Orto de Rucelay, etc. In the facsimile reproduced above are omitted the words found at the extreme top in the original map, which read, translated from the Spanish, "Land now discovered by Christopher Columbus, Genoese, for account of the King of Spain." Once more, notice Columbus's nationality.

CHAPTER THREE

UNDER THE SPANISH FLAG

What is left of the house built by Diego Columbus, the son of the Admiral, at Santo Domingo, during his residence there as governor and viceroy of Hispaniola. (Courtesy, *Pan American Union, Washington, D.C.*)

In all probability there was not a single expedition sent by the Spaniards to the New World soon after the discovery of America, in which some Italians did not take part. That is easy to explain.

From the end of the 15th century to the end of the 18th, Italy was directly, or indirectly, under the dominion or influence of Spain. Aside from that, thousands upon thousands of Italians were settled in Spain, where they occupied positions of importance, from that of prime minister down. Especially numerous were the bankers or merchants and the seamen and soldiers in the Spanish service. Among the latter the engineers or artillery-men occupied leading places. Suffice it to mention that over a long period of years most of the fortifications erected throughout the Spanish Empire, from Flanders to the New World, were entrusted to Italians. One of them, Tiburcio Spanoqui (Tiburzio Spannocchi), was chief engineer while Spain was at the peak of her power and glory. No less notable was the Antonelli family, as we shall presently see.

Italian seamen or sailors took part in the early voyages of discovery and exploration. Columbus had Italians with him in everyone of his four voyages.

As soon as colonization began Italian business men were among the first, and probably the leading, merchants to fit out expeditions, to finance shipments of provisions and military material and to undertake colonization projects, from the West Indies, Mexico and Florida all the way to Argentina.

The conquistadores, we are certain, had Italian officers and men with them. Balboa, De Soto, Coronado, Menendez, Pizarro, Cortes, Magellan, all had their share of natives of Italy.

Italian missionaries, as we have shown in Volume Two of *Italian-American History,* played an important role in the Christianization of Central and North America. One of them, as related in the next page, became the first bishop of the New World.

Officials and civilians of Italian birth and extraction also came over, from viceroys to plain adventurers. It was not by mere chance that the first printing presses in the Western Hemisphere, namely, in Mexico and Peru, were established by Italians.

Nor should one forget the travellers, men in search of knowledge or adventure, like Benzoni or the globe-trotter from Calabria, Gemelli Careri.

Finally, we come to the Italians who settled in Louisiana and Missouri during its Spanish rule, but since the activities of most of them extend well-over the post-Revolutionary period, we shall deal with them in the second part of the present work.

How many Italians came over to Spanish North America we do not know. The names given in the following pages are only a few—out of the many—for historical truth compels us to limit ourselves only to those about whom we have found evidence of their Italian origins. On this account we have discarded names like Serra, Crespi and Costanso, to mention three well-known figures in early California history, as we have no positive proofs of their Italian birth or ancestry. Often, very often, as students of Romance languages know, it is hard to distinguish an Italian from a Spanish name. Not seldom Italian names assumed Spanish forms; names like Garcia, Pablo, Espindola, Spanoqui.

Above all, one must bear in mind that names recorded in histories and in legal documents are, obviously, only a few, compared to the thousands which remained either undistinguished or unrecorded.

(For a summary view of the Italians in Spain see Schiavo, *Italian-American History,* Vol. II Chap. I and notes, pp. 406-408.)

DIEGO COLUMBUS, VICEROY

At least three of Christopher Columbus's relatives held commanding roles in the New World. Bartholomew Co-
tivities of most of them extend well over the post-Revolu-

governor of Hispaniola in 1495; he was named adelantado and went back to Spain in chains with his brother, on Bobadilla's orders, in 1500. Later he was set free and accompanied his brother in his fourth voyage.

Diego Columbus, another brother, was for a time at the head of the government at Hispaniola. He also went back to Spain in chains in 1500. Later he became a priest and a naturalized Spanish citizen. He returned to America with his nephew, Diego.

Diego Columbus, the Admiral's eldest son, inherited his father's title of Admiral, but not that of Viceroy. In 1509 he was named governor of Hispaniola and in 1511, following his marriage with Maria de Toledo, the member of one of the most powerful families in Spain, he was finally given the title of viceroy, which rightfully belonged to him as solemnly promised to his father before he set out on his voyage of 1492. Diego Columbus lived in Santo Domingo with brief interruptions until 1523 and died in Spain in 1526. He is remembered primarily because in 1521 he set free some 150 Indians from the South Carolina coast whom a Spanish slave hunter had lured to Hispaniola with a view to sell them to plantation owners.

OTHER PIONEERS

In the *Diccionario autobiografico de conquistadores y pobladores de Nueva España* (Autobiographical dictionary of conquistadores and settlers of New Spain) published by Francisco A. D. Icaza at Madrid in 1923, one finds a list of some 1385 persons who addressed petitions to the King of Spain asking for relief. Among them one finds one Xristobal Despindola, (Spinola) well-known "hidalgo," and Bernardo Peloso of Genoa, both of whom accompanied De Soto to Florida. More is said about Espindola in this chapter. As for Peloso, according to his petition, he married the daughter of a Genoese conquistador and was responsible for the safe escape to Mexico of the survivors of the De Soto expedition. Another man who was in Florida and married the daughter of a conquistador was Jacomo Rolando of San Remo. Three Sicilian pioneers were Juan Siciliano, who came over in 1502, took part in the conquest of Mexico City and had at one time "arms and horses"; Francisco Rojo, who came to the land of Cibola (Arizona) with his own "arms and horses," but received no compensation with the exception of a few Indians; and Francisco de Mecina (Messina), who was one of the few men who were with Balboa when he discovered the Pacific Ocean. He is also referred to as Francisco de Lentin, Siciliano. (See J. T. Medina, *El Descubrimiento del Oceano Pacifico,* Vol. I, p. 90). Icaza lists other Italians, including John Paul (Pablo) of Brescia, the man who established the first printing press in the New World, but later was compelled to live on charity, and Benito del Nero, of Bologna, who also owned "arms and horses" before he became poor.

Everything considered, only a few Italians are listed in the *Diccionario,* but that does not militate against the coming to the New World of a notable group of men of Italian birth and ancestry. The Spaniards who came over were either conquistadores, on the one hand, or people without a future at home, on the other. No man with a position or occupation at home would have been tempted to leave the certain for the uncertain. On the other hand, most of the Italians who came over, aside from the usual percentage of adventurers, were either military technicians or merchants. Hence their low percentage among those who found themselves stranded in the New World. Other pioneer settlers are listed in Almagia's *I Primi Esploratori dell'America,* pages 459-467.

(*Above*) BALBOA TAKING POSSESSION OF THE PACIFIC OCEAN. At least one Italian, a native of Sicily, was with him when he first sighted the Pacific Ocean. (From the title page of the second decade of Herrera's *Historia General, Madrid,* 1726) (*Left*) Title page of Geraldini's "Itinerarium" published at Rome in 1631. (Courtesy, *New York Public Library*) Alessandro Geraldini, the first Catholic Bishop of the New World, was born at Amelia, near Perugia, Italy, in 1455, and died at Haiti in 1525.

MARCOS DE NIZA DISCOVERS ARIZONA

Fray Marcos de Niza, as his name in Spanish clearly indicates, was a native of Nizza (Nice, a French city since 1859), the same city in which Garibaldi was born. That he was an Italian is admitted by the Spanish Encyclopedia (Espasa), which refers to him as "Franciscano y descubridor italiano," by the French "La Grande Encyclopedie" which calls him "franciscain italien," and by the United States Library of Congress which has adopted the Italian form, Marco da Nizza, instead of the Spanish "Marcos de Nizza," for its catalog heading. It is interesting to recall also that John Gilmary Shea in his "History of the Catholic Missions among the Indian Tribes of the United States" published in 1854, also referred to Mark of Nice as "the Italian friar."

Little is known of the life of Fray Mark. He was born in the latter part of the 15th century and went to New Spain in 1531, laboring at Panama, Nicaragua and Guatemala. In 1532 he accompanied Valalcazar to Peru where he (not Valverde) is said to have been the first missionary to labor among the Indians. However, Pizarro's cruel treatment of the natives so aroused him that in 1535 he left Mexico.

On March 7, 1539, Fray Mark, accompanied by a Negro named Estevanico (Stephen) and another Italian friar, named Onorato, set out to explore the land north of present Mexico, where the rich Seven Cities of Cibola were rumored to exist. Not long after their departure, however, Onorato became ill and only the monk and the Negro proceeded on their mission.

Their trek through the desert has already become legendary. For days they travelled through Northern Mexico, until Estevanico, who was going ahead, was killed by the Indians because, it is said, he was getting bolder and bolder

FRAY MARCOS DE NIZA
An artist's conception based on available evidence, but not actually a portrait. It forms part of an exhibit in the National Park Service museum at Tumacacori National Monument, Arizona. (Courtesy, *U. S. National Park Service, Region Three, Santa Fe, New Mexico*)

The rock with Fray Mark's inscription in what is today Phoenix Mountain Park, or Pima Canyon, near Phoenix, Arizona. There are no proofs as to the authenticity of the carving, but the Italian spelling of the word Coronado (Corona to) adds to the belief that it was made by the monk or by some other Italian with him. On that spot, about May 1, 1539, the friar took possession of the desert by planting the Cross of Christ. Today the rock is protected by a grill (*right*). The author was standing by when the above photograph was taken by his friend, Mr. Harry Frothingham of Chandler, Arizona, in August, 1950.

in demanding women and what he thought were turquoise stones. Then the friar continued alone until he came within sight of what he thought was the famed city of Cibola. What he saw we do not know, but the writer will never forget the mirages of which he was the victim when he crossed the same desert (in an automobile) in the summer of 1950. At any rate, satisfied with his discovery, the monk returned to Mexico with such a tale of splendors and wealth that the cupidity of the Spaniards was quickly aroused and a magnificent expedition was made ready.

It was thus on February 23, 1540, that Coronado set out from Compostela at the head of one of the most brilliant expeditions ever to venture inland into the present United States. Coronado, as we know, found no wealth, but only poor Indians living in mud-built pueblos. His disappointment was great, but his pride and hopes were greater. He determined to go as far as he could, until he reached the present State of Kansas. Then he returned to Mexico.

No benefits came to Spain from Coronado's expedition, but his discoveries added a famous chapter to the history of exploration in America, for it made known for the first time the interior of the United States, from the border of Mexico to Nebraska. How many Italians took part in that expedition, besides Fray Mark, we do not know. But, as we have seen, one Sicilian, Francisco Rojo, joined it with his own "arms and horses."

Fray Marcos returned to Mexico in 1541 to serve as Provincial of the Franciscan Fathers—the third in the history of the Order in America. He died at Mexico City on March 25, 1558.

FRAY MARK ENTERING ARIZONA
(From a drawing in "The Fray Marcos de Niza 400th Anniversary Edition," published by the *Arizona Republic* of Phoenix on November 20, 1938)

WITH DE SOTO FROM FLORIDA TO THE MISSISSIPPI

While Coronado was trudging from Arizona to Nebraska, another Spanish conquistador, Hernando de Soto, was writing one more glorious page in the history of North American exploration. Aroused by the reports of Cabeza de Vaca regarding the alleged wealth of Florida and the southern part of the present United States, he fitted out four ships, and followed by 620 foot soldiers and 123 horsemen, in May, 1939, he started out on the famous expedition that was to end with his death and almost disaster for his men. De Soto spent three years crossing from the Atlantic to the Mississippi. Like Coronado, he found no gold, but like his famous contemporary, he opened the entire Southern United States to civilization. After his death on the banks of the Mississippi in May, or June, 1542, his lieutenant, Alvarado, took charge and descended the river to the Gulf of Mexico. Finally, thanks to the work of a Genoese engineer, the survivors were able to reach Mexico, four years after they had landed in Florida.

HERNANDO DE SOTO

At least three Italians played important roles in that ill-fated venture. One was a Genoese engineer; the other two were calkers, one from Genoa and the other from Sardinia. According to the *Final Report of the U.S. De Soto Expedition Commission,* published by the U.S. Government Printing Office in 1939, "The Genoese and the Sardinian, especially a Genoese engineer called Maestre Francisco, turned out to be among the most essential members of the expedition since they were relied upon in building bridges during the march and constructed the boats in which the survivors finally escaped to Mexico." The other Genoese, a calker, may have been Bernardo Peloso, already noted.

Still another Genoese with De Soto was Christobal de Espindola, the same Xristobal we met among those who had been reduced to poverty and had asked the King of Spain for relief. In 1439, however, we learn from Garcilasso de la Vega, (see facsimile), he was a Captain of the Guard in charge of sixty halberdiers. According to the Gentleman of Elvas, he was a kinsman of Cabeza de Vaca.

Of them the most notable seems to have been Francisco the Engineer "a man from Genoa whom it was God's will to preserve (for without him they could not have left the land, as there was no other who knew how to build ships)." So we read in the *Relacion Verdadeira* by the Gen-

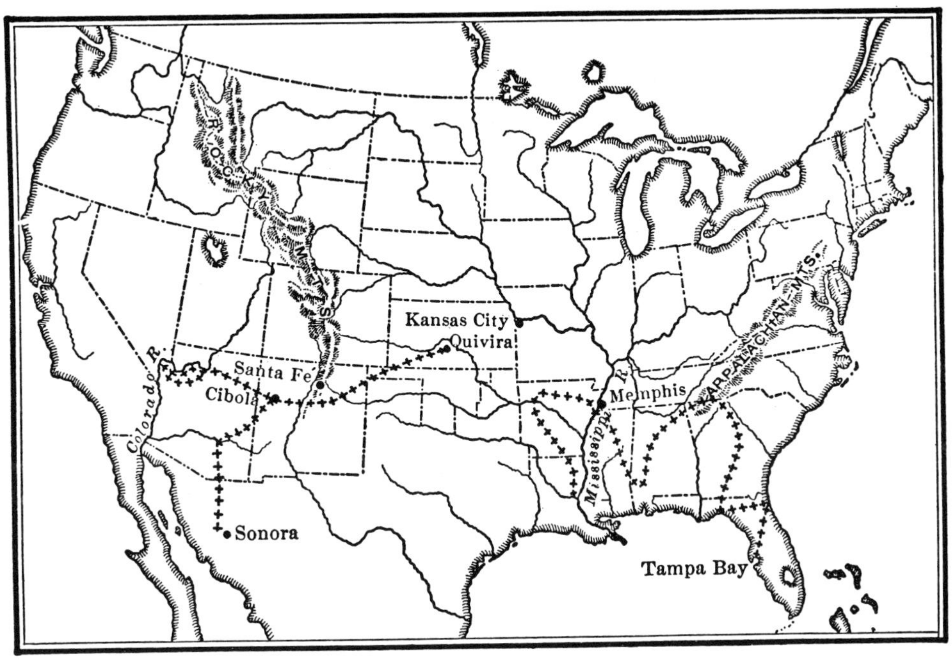

Map of the two most famous Spanish expeditions within the present territory of the United States, both started in 1539-1540. De Soto's, from Florida to the Mississippi; Coronado's, from Mexico to Kansas. (From D. H. Montgomery, *The leading facts of American History,* Boston, 1890)

tleman of Elvas. (See facsimile). According to Garcilasso de la Vega, he felled the biggest tree he could find and made a cross which he erected on an Indian mound, while De Soto and all the soldiers knelt down to thank God. The place, near New Madrid, Missouri. The year, 1541.

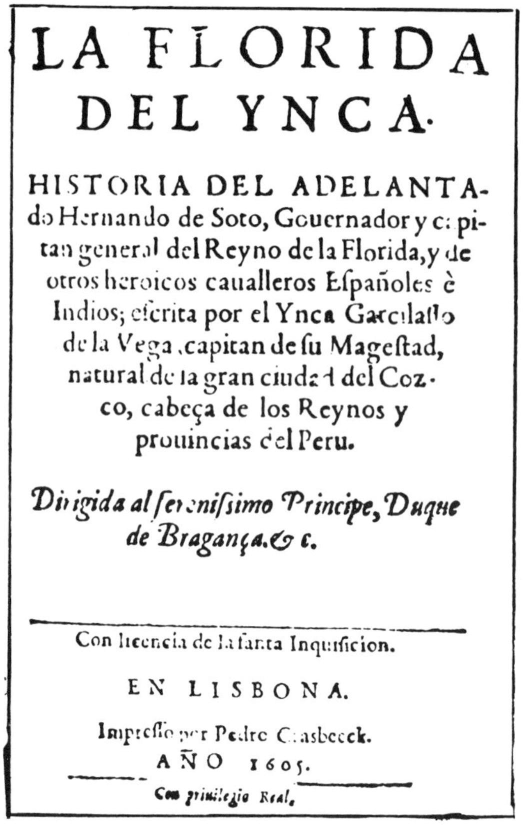

LA FLORIDA DEL YNCA.

HISTORIA DEL ADELANTADO Hernando de Soto, Gouernador y capitan general del Reyno de la Florida, y de otros heroicos caualleros Españoles è Indios; eſcrita por el Ynca Garcilaſſo de la Vega, capitan de ſu Mageſtad, natural de la gran ciudad del Cozco, cabeça de los Reynos y prouincias del Peru.

Dirigida al sereniſsimo Principe, Duque de Bragança. &c.

Con licencia de la ſanta Inquiſicion.

EN LISBONA.

Impreſſo por Pedro Craſbeeck.

AÑO 1605.

Con priuilegio Real.

(*Above*) DE SOTO ON THE BANKS OF THE MISSISSIPPI RIVER. (From an old print) (*Right*) Title page of Garcilasso de la Vega's account of the De Soto expedition. (Courtesy, *New York Public Library*)

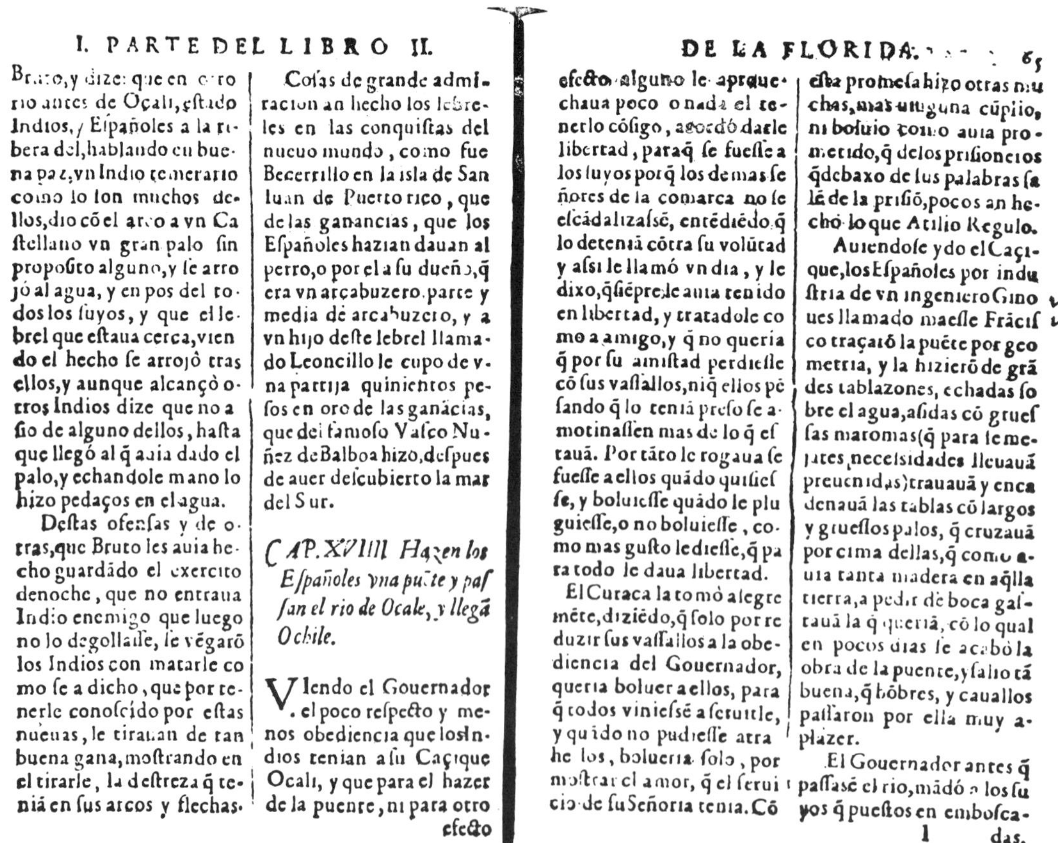

I. PARTE DEL LIBRO II.

Bruto, y dize: que en otro rio antes de Oçali, eſtado Indios, y Eſpañoles a la ribera del, hablando en buena paz, vn Indio temerario como lo ſon muchos dellos, dio cõ el arco a vn Caſtellano vn gran palo ſin propoſito alguno, y ſe arrojó al agua, y en pos del todos los ſuyos, y que el lebrel que eſtaua cerca, viendo el hecho ſe arrojô tras ellos, y aunque alcançò otros Indios dize que no aſio de alguno dellos, haſta que llegó al q̃ auia dado el palo, y echandole mano lo hizo pedaços en el agua.

Deſtas ofenſas y de otras, que Bruto les auia hecho guardādo el exercito denoche, que no entraua Indio enemigo que luego no lo degollaſſe, ſe vēgarō los Indios con matarle como ſe a dicho, que por tenerle conoſcido por eſtas nueuas, le tirauan de tan buena gana, moſtrando en el tirarle, la deſtreza q̃ tenian en ſus arcos y flechas.

Coſas de grande admiracion an hecho los lebreles en las conquiſtas del nueuo mundo, como fue Becerrillo en la isla de San Iuan de Puerto rico, que de las ganancias, que los Eſpañoles hazian dauan al perro, o por el a ſu dueño, q̃ era vn arcabuzero parte y media de arcabuzero, y a vn hijo deſte lebrel llamado Leoncillo le cupo de vna partija quinientos peſos en oro de las ganācias, que del famoſo Vaſco Nuñez de Balboa hizo, deſpues de auer deſcubierto la mar del Sur.

CAP. XVIIII Hazen los Eſpañoles vna puēte y paſſan el rio de Ocale, y llegā Ochile.

VIendo el Gouernador el poco reſpecto y menos obediencia que los Indios tenian a ſu Caçique Ocali, y que para el hazer de la puente, ni para otro

DE LA FLORIDA. 65

efecto alguno le aprouechaua poco o nada el tenerlo cõſigo, acordó darle libertad, para q̃ ſe fueſſe a los ſuyos porq̃ los demas ſeñores de la comarca no ſe eſcādalizaſsē, entēdiēdo q̃ lo detenia cõtra ſu volūtad y aſsi le llamó vn dia, y le dixo, q̃ ſiēpre le auia tenido en libertad, y tratadole como a amigo, y q̃ no queria q̃ por ſu amiſtad perdieſſe cõ ſus vaſſallos, ni q̃ ellos pēſando q̃ lo tenia preſo ſe amotinaſſen mas de lo q̃ eſtauā. Por tāto le rogaua ſe fueſſe a ellos quādo quiſieſſe, y boluieſſe quādo le pluguieſſe, o no boluieſſe, como mas guſto le dieſſe, q̃ para todo le daua libertad.

El Curaca la tomò alegremēte, diziēdo, q̃ ſolo por reduzir ſus vaſſallos a la obediencia del Gouernador, queria boluer a ellos, para q̃ todos vinieſsē a ſeruirle, y quādo no pudieſſe atraher los, bolueria ſolo, por moſtrar el amor, q̃ el ſeruicio de ſu Señoria tenia. Cõ eſta promeſa hizo otras muchas, mas ninguna cūplio, ni boluio como auia prometido, q̃ de los priſioneros q̃ debaxo de ſus palabras ſalē de la priſiō, pocos an hecho lo que Atilio Regulo.

Auiendoſe ydo el Caçique, los Eſpañoles por induſtria de vn ingeniero Ginoues llamado maeſſe Frācisco traçarō la puēte por geometria, y la hizierō de grādes tablazones, echadas ſobre el agua, aſidas cō grueſſas maromas (q̃ para ſemejantes neceſsidades lleuauā preuenidas) trauauā y encadenauā las tablas cō largos y grueſſos palos, q̃ cruzauā por cima dellas, q̃ como auia tanta madera en aq̃lla tierra, a pedir de boca gaſtauā la q̃ querian, cō lo qual en pocos dias ſe acabò la obra de la puente, y ſalio tā buena, q̃ hōbres, y cauallos paſſaron por ella muy aplazer.

El Gouernador antes q̃ paſſasē el rio, mādó a los ſuyos q̃ pueſtos en emboſcadas,

(*Above*) Two pages from Garcilasso de la Vega's *La Florida del Ynca* with the reference to the bridge-builder, "a Genoese engineer named Master Francisco." (*On the opposite page*) Four pages from the *Relacam Verdadeira* by the Gentleman of Elvas, published at Elvora in 1557. As translated in the J. A. Robertson edition for the Florida Historical Society (1933) the lower end of the top page on the right and the lower page on the left, read: ". . . and a man from Genoa whom it was God's will to preserve (for without him they could not have left that land, as there was no other who knew how to build ships), together with four or five other Basque carpenters who hewed the planks and knees for him, built the brigantines. . . . Two calkers, one a Genoese, and the other from Sardinia, calked them with tow from a plant like daffodils. . . ." (Courtesy, *New York Public Library*)

rã doētes de grandes τ perigosas
infirmidades, q̃ ó modorra tocauã.
Alli faleceo Andre de Vascõcelos
τ dous portugueses Deluas que a
elle hiã chegados: os quaes erã hir
mãos τ dalcunha se chamauam os
Sotis. Apousentaram se os xp̃aos
em hũ dos pouos, ho q̃ milhor lhes
pareceo: ho qual estaua cercado, τ
hũ quarto de legoa do rio grande.
Ho mayz quē ho outro pouo auia
se recolheo pera alli: τ todo se esti
mou em seys mil fanegas. E pera
fazer nauios auia alli milhor ma
deyra quē toda a terra da Frolida
auiam visto, com que todos deram
muitas graças a deos por tam assi
nada merce, τ cobraram esperança
de auer efeito ho que desejauam, q̃
era verem se em terra de xp̃aos.

¶ Cap. xxxvj. Como se fezerã se
te bragantins, τ partiram de
Aminoya.

[T]Anto q̃ Aminoya che
garam, ho gouernador
mãdou tomar as cade
as q̃ pera os indios ca
da hũ trazia: τ ajuntar
todo ho ferro ó moniçam τ todo ho
q̃ no real auia: τ mandou assentar
fragoa τ fazer crauaçã τ cortar ma
deyra pera os bragãtins. E hũ por
tugues de Ceita quē fez sendo cati
uo se auia ensinado a serrar cõ ser
ras q̃ pa esse efeito traziã, ēsinou a
outros q̃ o ajudauã a serrar madei
ra: τ hũ ginoues q̃ ds q̃s guardar (q̃
sem elle nã puderã sair daq̃lla tr̃ra
porq̃ nã auia outro q̃ soubesse fazer
nauios) este com outros quatro ou
cinco Bizcaynhos Carpinteyros,

que lhe falq̃jauam as tauoas τ cer
natões fazia os bragantins: τ dous
calafates, hũ ginoues τ outro ó cer
denha os calafeteauam cõ hũa esto
pa de hũa erua como abroteas, ó q̃
atras tenho dito que la se chama
Enequē: τ porq̃ nam auia auõdo cõ
linhas da terra τ de mantas, q̃ pa
isso desfiauã os calefetauam: adoe
ceo τ esteue a morte hũ Tenoeiro q̃
auia: τ nam auia outro q̃ daquelle
oficio soubesse: quis ds dar lhe sau
de: τ ainda q̃ muy fraco estaua τ nã
pode trabalhar, quinze dias antes
quepartissem fez pera cada bragan
tim dous piparotes q̃ os marinhei
ros chamam quartos: porq̃ quatro
fazē hũa pipa dagoa: os indios de
hũa prouincia que duas jornadas
ho rio arriba estaua q̃ Tagoanate
auia por nome: τ assi os de Anilco

τ Guachoya τ outros comarcãos
vendo q̃ os bragantins se faziã, pa
recendo lhe q̃ porq̃ suas colheitas
sam em agoa, q̃ era pera os hir bus
car: τ porq̃ ho gouernador lhes pe
dia mãtas por serē necessarias pa
velas, vinhã muitas vezes τ traziã
muitas τ muito pescado: τ certo se
parecia q̃rellos deos fauorecer em
tã grã necessidade, põdo ē vontade
aos indios q̃ as trouxessē, porq̃ pa
lhas yr tomar nam auia remedeo:
porq̃ no pouo dõde estauã, tanto q̃
entrou ho inuerno q̃darã aislhados
rodeados dagoa, q̃ se nã podia por
t̃rra andar mais q̃ hũa legoa ou le
goa τ mea: τ pera sahir dalli nã se
podiã leuar cauallos τ sem elles nã
erã parte pera os acometer por se
rē muitos: τ tantos por tantos a pe
por agoa τ por terra lhe faziãventa

LIBRO IIII. DE LA FLORIDA. 254

toda su familia de mugeres
y criados q̃ eran muchos.
El Gouernador dixo q̃ acep
taua su amistad, mas no su
casa, por no desacomodar-
le: y holgó de aposentarse
en vna huerta q̃ el mismo
Caçique señaló quãdo vio
q̃ no queria sus casas, dõde
los Indios, sin vna buena ca
sa que en ella auia hizierõ
cõ mucha presteza grãdes
y frescas ramadas, q̃ erã assi
menester: por ser ya Mayo,
y hazer calor. El exercito, se
alojó parte en el pueblo, y
parte ẽ las huertas dõde to
dos estuuierõ muy a plazer

*CAP. VI Hazese vna sole
ne processiõ de Indios y Es
pañoles para adorar la Cruz.*

TRes dias auia q̃ el exer
cito estaua alojado en
el pueblo llamado Casquin
cõ mucho cõtẽto del ndios
y Españoles, quãdo al quar
to dia el Curaca acõpaña-
do de toda la nobleza de su
tierra, q̃ la auia hecho cõuo
car para aq̃lla solẽnidad, se
puso ante el Gouernador, y
auiẽdo el y todos los suyos
hecho vna grandissima re
uerẽcia, le dixo: Señor, como nos hazes ventaja en el
esfuerço y en las armas, assi
creemos q̃ nos la hazes en
tener mejor Dios, q̃ nosotros. Estos q̃ ves aqui, q̃ son
los nobles de mi tierra (q̃
por la baxeza de su estado,
y poco merecimiẽto no o-
sarõ parecer delãte de ti) y
yo cõ todos ellos te suplica
mos, tengas por bien de pe
dir a tu Dios, que nos llue
ua, que nuestros sembra-
dos tienẽ mucha necessi-
dad de agua. El General res
põdio, que aunq̃ pecadores
todos los de su exercito, y
el suplicaria a Dios nuestro
Señor les hiziesse merced,
como padre de misericor-
dias. Luego en presencia
del Caçique mãdò a mae-
stre Francisco Ginoues grã
oficial de carpinteria, y de
fabrica de nauios, q̃ de vn
pino el más alto y gruesso,
que en toda la comarca se
hallasse hiziesse vna Cruz.
Tal

Tal fue el q̃ por auiso de
los mismos Indios se cortó
q̃ despues de labrado, quiero
dezir, quitada la corteza, y
redõdeado a mas ganar, co
mo dizen los carpinteros,
no lo podiã leuãtar del sue
lo ciẽ hõbres. El maestro hi
zo la Cruz en toda perfec-
cion en cuenta de cinco y
tres, sin quitar nada al ar-
bol de su altor: salio hermo
sissima por ser tan alta. Pu
sierõla sobre vn cerro alto
hecho a mano, q̃ estaua so
bre la barrãca del rio, y ser
uia a los Indios de atalaya,
y sobrepujaua en altura a o-
tros cerrillos q̃ por alli a-
uia. Acabada la obra q̃ ga-
starõ en ella dos dias, y pue
sta la Cruz, se ordenó el dia
siguiẽte vna solẽne processiõ, en q̃ fue el General, y los
capitanes, y la gẽte de mas
cuẽta, y quedó a la mira vn
esquadrõ armado de los in
fantes y cauallos que para
guarda y seguridad del e-
xercito era menester.
El Caçique fue al lado del
Gouernador, y muchos de
sus Indios nobles fuerõ en
tremetidos entre los Espa
ñoles. Delãte del General
de por si aparte en vn coro
yuã los Sacerdotes Cleri-
gos y frayles cãtãdo las Le
tanias, y los soldados respõ
diã. desta manera fuerõ vn
buẽ trecho mas de mil hõ-
bres entre fieles è infieles,
hasta q̃ llegarõ dõde la cruz
estaua: y delãte della hinca
rõ todos las rodillas y auiẽ
dose dicho dos o tres oracio
nes se leuãtarõ, y de dos en
dos fuerõ primero los Sacer
dotes, y cõ los ynojos en tie
rra adorarõ la Cruz, y la be
sarõ. Empos de los ecclesia
sticos fue el Gouernador, y
el Caçique con el, sin q̃ na-
die se lo dixesse, y hizo todo
lo q̃ vio hazer al General y
besò la Cruz: tras ellos fue
rõ los demas Españoles è In
dios, los quales hizirõ lo mis
mo q̃ los christianos haziã.
De la otra parte del rio
auia quinze o veynte mil
animas de ambos sexos,
y de todas las edades, los
quales estauan con los bra-
gg 2 ços

Two more pages from Garcilasso de la Vega's *La Florida del Ynca*. (*Above, second column*) De Soto orders Francisco the Genoese to fell the tallest tree he could find and make a cross out of it. (*Below, first column*) "Captain Mister Espindola, Genoese gentleman, who was captain of 60 halbardiers of the Governor's guard." (Courtesy, *New York Public Library*)

LIBRO I. DE LA FLORIDA. 11

capitan de infanteria yua
por capitan de otra nao
grande llamada sancta Bar
bara.
Alõso Romo de Cardeño
sa hermano de Arias Tino-
co, que tambien era nom
brado capitan de infante-
ria, yua por capitan de vn
galeoncillo, llamado san
Anton: con este capitan
yua otro hermano suyo lla
mado Diego Arias Tino-
co, nombrado para Alfe
rez general del exercito.
Estos tres hermanos eran
deudos del General. Por
capitan de vna carauela
muy hermosa yua Pedro
Calderon cauallero natu
ral de Badajoz, y en su com
pañia yua el Capitan Mi
cer Espindola, cauallero
Ginoues, el qual era Ca
pitan de sesenta alauar-
deros de la guardia del
Gouernador. Sin estos o-
cho nauios lleuauan dos
vergantines para serui-
cio de la armada, que por
ser mas ligeros, y mas fa
ciles de gouernar que las
naos gruessas, siruiessen co
mo espias de descubrir por
todas partes lo que huuies
se por la mar.
En estos siete nauios,
carauela, y vergantines,
se embarcaron los noue-
cientos y cinquenta hom
bres de guerra, sin los ma
rineros, y gente necessa-
ria para el gouierno y ser
uicio de cada nao. Sin
la gente que hemos di-
cho, yuan en la armada
doze Sacerdotes, ocho Cle
rigos, y quatro frayles: los
nombres de los Clerigos
que la memoria ha rete-
nido son, Rodrigo de Ga
llegos natural de Seuilla,
deudo de Balthasar de Ga
llegos, y Diego de Vañue
los, y Francisco del pozo
naturales de Cordoua. Dio
nisio de Paris natural de
Frãcia de la misma ciudad
de Paris. Los nombres de
los otros quatro clerigos se
hã oluidado. Los frayles se
llamauã F. Luis de Soto, na
tural de Villa nueua de Bar
carrota, deudo del gouerna
dor Hernãdo de Soto. Fray
Iuan de Gallegos natural
de Seuilla, hermano del ca
pitan Baltasar de Gallegos
ambos frayles de la orden
de sancto Domingo. Fray
Iuan de Torres natural de
Seuilla de la religion de
san Francisco, y fray Francisco de la Rocha natural
de Badajoz de la aduoca-
cion, è insignia de la san-
ctissima Trinidad: todos
ellos hombres de mucho
exemplo y doctrina.
Con esta armada de la
Florida yua la de Mexico,
q̃ era de veynte naos grues
sas, de laqual yua tambien
por general Hernando de
Soto hasta el paraje de la
isla de Sanctiago de Cuba,
de dõde se auia de apartar
para la Veracruz, y para de
alli adelante yua nombra
do por General della, vn ca
uallero principal llamado
Gonçalo de Salazar, el pri-
mer Christiano que nascio
en Granada despues que la
quitaron a los moros: por
lo qual aunque el era caua
llero hijo dalgo, los Reyes
catholicos de gloriosa me
moria que ganaron aque-
lla ciudad, le dieron grandes preuilegios, y hizieron
mercedes de que se fundo
vn mayorazgo para sus de
cendientes. El qual auia si-
do conquistador de Mexi
co, este cauallero boluio
por fator de la hazienda
imperial de la ciudad de
Mexico.
Con esta orden salieron
por la barra de san Lucar
las treynta naos de las dos
armadas, y se hizieron à la
vela a los seys de Abril del
año de mil y quinientos y
treinta ocho, y nauegaron
aq̃l dia y otros muchos con
toda la prosperidad, y bonã
ça de tiempo que se podia
dessear. La armada de la
Florida yua tan abasteci-
da de todo matalotage, q̃
a quantos yuan en ella se
daua racion doblada, cosa
bien impertinente, porque
se desperdiciaua todo lo q̃
sobraua, que era mucho:
mas la magnificencia del
B 3 Gene.

IN FLORIDA — 1564-1575

Although the Spaniards had actually explored a large section of the southern part of the present United States, the French paid little attention to their claims and rights and planned to establish French Huguenot settlements on the southern Atlantic coast. A first attempt by Jean Ribaut in Florida in 1562 failed, but two years later another expedition headed by René de Laudonnière met with more success and a fort, called Fort Caroline, was erected on the St. John's River a few miles north of the present St. Augustine.

The Spaniards met this threat to their American possessions by sending a powerful expedition under Don Pedro Menendez de Aviles. He landed in Florida near the location of the present St. Augustine on August 28, 1565, on the same day that another French expedition, headed also by Ribaut, arrived to reinforce de Laudonnière. Menendez soon surprised and annihilated the French garrison at Fort Caroline, which he renamed San Mateo. A few days later, on September 29, 1565, he put to death about 150 of the Frenchmen who had arrived with Ribaut, who met the same fate together with his remaining followers, shortly after. The place where that so-called massacre took place is known as "Matanzas," the Spanish word for "Slaughter" and forms today a part of Fort Matanzas National Monument, now entrusted to the United States National Park Service. The French, however, continued to harass the Spaniards along the Atlantic Coast line, as well as in the West Indies, with alternating fortunes. Menendez' nephew, Pedro Menendez Marques, continued for a time, up to 1580, to explore the entire coast from the Florida Keys to Chesapeake Bay, but soon after that the Spaniards entrenched themselves around St. Augustine and practically abandoned all claims to the northern part. A few years later the English tried their first colonization settlement in Virginia.

A number of Italians were active on both sides during the Franco-Spanish conflict in Florida between 1564 and 1575. Once more we must remind our reader that the only names that have reached us are those of men whose actions caused them to be mentioned in narratives or official reports. With the first French expedition, for instance, we find a Genoese named Stephen who became one of the ringleaders in a plot against Laudonniere, but eventually he was seized and put to death with the other conspirators.

Another Italian, Nicholas Ornano, a member of the famous Corsican family that gave so many military leaders by that name to France, was with Ribaut when they came over in 1565. Ornano, who is referred to in French and Spanish documents as Corsette and Corceto, was vice-admiral of the Ribaut fleet in charge of the ship Emerillon. Like Ribaut he also was killed at Matanzas by the Spaniards. Ten years later Nicola Strozzi, captain of the French ship "Prince" which had been wrecked at the bar of Santa Elena (Port Royal), was captured by Pedro Menendez Marques, the nephew of the first Menendez Aviles, and also put to death. He offered the Spanish Captain three thousand ducats if he would spare his life, but the Spaniard scorned the offer. What happened to Strozzi's money, if he had any with him, we do not know. In all probability

Fort Caroline, built in 1564 by the Huguenots headed by de Laudonnière near the mouth of the St. Johns River, Florida. The fort was captured by Pedro Menendez de Aviles on September 20, 1565. Most of the Frenchmen were killed and the name of the fort was changed to San Mateo. The river has long since washed out the land on which it stood. (From the drawing by Jacques Le Moyne)

he was the son of Simone Strozzi and Albiera di Iacopo Bindi, mentioned by Litta in his "Famiglie Celebri Italiane." Litta says that he served in France and in the Indies and was killed in 1576 while fighting against the Turks in the waters of Syracuse. However, he cautiously adds "I am not very sure about the data regarding this man."

As for the Italians who came over with the Spaniards, we are inclined to believe that a few must have come over, if we consider that a good many of the 2,646 men (in 34 vessels) who joined Menendez de Aviles, had been recruited among the Spaniards stationed in Italy. It is logical to infer that Italian sailors and soldiers may have enlisted. It is interesting to recall in connection with Menendez' expedition, that Tolomeo Espindola (Spinola) and other merchants of Saint-Jean-de-Luz, in France, not far from the Spanish frontier, offered him a premium of two thousand ducats a day if he would delay the departure of his fleet by three or four days. He refused. Another Espinola, or Spinola, whose first name was Augustin, also was connected for years with Menendez. Still another Italian we find in the records, one Genoese by name Francisco, was in charge of a patache, or tender, in the service of Menendez while in Florida.

An Italian servant of Francisco Lopez Mendoza Grajales, the chaplain of the expedition, however, was one of the very first men to set foot where now rises the city of St. Augustine. He had gone ashore with a few others to get some water, when in the moonlight he discovered underneath a tree a tortoise "the biggest and fiercest that up to that time had ever been seen." That was on August 28, 1565.

On the Italians who came over with the Spaniards and the French in 1564-1575 see, besides the works reproduced in facsimile in this chapter, Ruidiaz y Caravia, *La Florida, Su Conquista y Colonizacion,* Vols. I and II; *Coleccion de documentos ineditos,* Madrid, 1865, Vol. III, p. 444; G. Garcia—*Dos Antiguas Relaciones de la Florida,* Mexico City, 1902.

ENSAYO
CRONOLOGICO,
PARA LA
HISTORIA GENERAL
DE LA
FLORIDA.

CONTIENE LOS DESCUBRIMIENTOS, y principales ſuceſos, acaecidos en eſte Gran Reino, à los Eſpañoles, Franceſes, Suecos, Dinamarqueſes, Ingleſes, y otras Naciones, entre sì, y con los Indios: cuias Coſtumbres, Genios, Idolatria, Govierno, Batallas, y Aſtucias, ſe refieren: y los Viages de algunos Capitanes, y Pilotos, por el Mar de el Norte, à buſcar Paſo à Oriente, ò vnion de aquella Tierra, con Aſia.

DESDE EL AÑO DE 1512. QUE DESCUBRIÒ la Florida, Juan Ponce de Leon, haſta el de 1722.

ESCRITO

POR DON GABRIEL DE CARDENAS Z CANO

DEDICADO

AL PRINCIPE NUESTRO SEÑOR.

CON PRIVILEGIO: En MADRID.

En la OFICINA REAL, y à Coſta de NICOLAS RODRIGUEZ FRANCO, Impreſor de Libros. Año de CIↃ IↃCCXXII J.

Se hallaràn en ſu Caſa, en la Calle de el Poço, y en Palacio.

(*Above*) Title page of the "Chronological Essay for the General History of Florida from 1512 to 1722" by Gabriel de Cardenas y Cano, Madrid, 1722. (*Right*) A page from the "Ensayo," or Essay. Notice in the second column the words "un Genoves que se llamaba Estevan," one of the captains, "a Genoese, named Stephen," and the reference to him in the last line. The Genoese was one of the men who had plotted against Rene de Laudonnière. Later he was executed. (Courtesy, *New York Public Library*)

à la Hiſtoria de la Florida. 55

infinita en lo que debia hacer; de modo, que no ſe malogaſe lo trabajado. Renato agradeciò ſus buenos Servicios: tomò el Oro, y Plata, que traia, y no quiſo recibir Oro; antes le mandò bolver luego à Otina; y que, eſtando los Negocios mas adelantados, tomaria Reſolucion, ſobre darle Suceſor, ſi convenia.

Tambien ſe ſupo, en el Fuerte, por Relacion de los Indios, la Muerte de Pedro Ambie, que avia ſido Page, de Coligni; al qual avia dado Licencia Renato, de ir a reſcatar, donde le pareciese. El ſaliò, cargado de Mercaderias, con ſu Arcabuz: anduvo contratando con los Indios algunos Dias, con tanta maña, y habilidad, que le cobraron tanto cariño, que traian al Fuerte, con gran cuidado, las Cartas, que les daba, en que aviſaba à Renato, y Otros Amigos, la Fortuna, que tenia en ſu Comercio: que cauſaba baſtante embidia à los que eſtaban en èl.

Llegò à vna Isla, que forma el Rio, y los Indios le llevaron al Cacique, que ſe llamaba Adelano, y à breve tiempo le cobrò tanto cariño, que le diò vna Hija ſuia, por Muger; Autoriçandoſe con eſte Caſamiento entre los Isleños, de ſuerte, que quando el Cacique ſe auſentaba, quedaba por Dueño abſoluto de todo, y ſi eſtaba preſente, no ſe hacia nada, ſin tratarlo antes con èl.

Pedro, ſolo tenia cuidado de enriquecer, haciendo à los Indios, que le trageſen Oro, y Plata; y como no hallavan la que queria, los maltrataba de Obra, y de Palabra; con que poco à poco vinieron à perder el afecto, que le tenian, y eſtuvieron reſueltos algunos Principales à matarle, para librarſe de tan peſada carga; mas nunca ſe atrevieron à egecutarlo, por el Amor, que el Cacique le tenia, eſperando ocaſion, en que vengar las injurias padecidas, y diſimulandolas, con otras, que cada Dia aumentaban el aborrecimiento.

Aviendo recogido quanta Riqueça pudo Pedro de Ambie, y viendo, que yà los Indios no le traian coſa de importancia, determinò bolverſe al Fuerte, con ella; para lo qual pidiò Licencia al Cacique, perſuadiendole à que ſe la dieſe, las Ofertas, de las grandes Riqueças, con que bolveria preſto; de modo, que no ſe atreviò à negarla. Previno vna Canoa mui buena, Pedro, en la qual puſo todo el Oro, y Plata, y Piedras, que avia recogido; y mandò à dos Indios, le trageſen por el Rio, al Fuerte: metioſe en la Canoa, y aſi como perdieron de viſta al Cacique, y ſu Hija, y Otros, que ſalieron con èl, haſta la Ribera, ſe acordò vno de los Indios de vnos Palos, que le avia dado Pedro, el qual le dejò deſcuidar, y le partiò la Cabeça con vn Hacha, y huiò con el Otro Indio, contentos ambos de aver ſalido con tan buena ocaſion vengados, y ricos.

Los Amotinados iban eſtrechando ſus diſcurſos, traçando el modo de levantarſe con el Fuerte, y quanto avia en èl. Uno de ellos era Fornùx, Gran Hipocrita, y Embuſtero, y mas Avariento, que ninguno, aunque con diſimulacion; eſte dijo à los 30. que eſtaban de Acuerdo, que ſi eſperaban mas, era ſu muerte evidente; porque ò Renato avia de deſcubrir la trama, y juſticiarlos, ò avian de morir de hambre, pues en nada ſe ponia remedio; y aſi, que ſe adelantaſen, por lo menos, à conſervar la Vida: Reſpondieronle los Conjurados, que penſaſe lo que ſe avia de hacer, porque le elegian por ſu Capitan, y egecutarian quanto pudieſen, por ſalvar las Vidas. Fornùx ſe eſcusò del Cargo, pero no pudo reſiſtir à las inſtancias, que le hicieron, ſolo conſiguiò, que eligieſen por Capitanes tambien, à vn Genovès, que ſe llamaba Eſtevan, vn Gaſcon, llamado Le Seiñur, y à Otro Francès, llamado La Cruz, y trataron el modo de apoderarſe del Fuerte. Salieron à reducir Oficiales à ſu Partido, aſegurandoles, que todos eſtaban de vn Acuerdo, y que ſe perderia el que quiſieſe ſer ſingular, y oponerſe al Bien Comun, de que trataban. Eſtas Raçones, y el deſcontento de Algunos, motivaron à firmar vn Papel, que les enſeñaban; pero no ſe atrevieron à llegar à Ottigni, Le Caille, y Arlac; porque ſiendo tan Amigos de Renato, temieron ſu reſiſtencia, y que declaraſen la Conjuracion.

Pareciendoles, que yà tenian quanto neceſitaban para ſus diſignios, pocos dias deſpues, à la media Noche, Fornùx tomo la Caſa de Renato, con 20 Arcabuceros, y llegando à ſu Cama, en que eſtaba enfermo, le puſo vna Carabina à la Cara, diciendolo muchos oprobrios, y por fuerça le hiço mal veſtir, y echandole Cadenas, llevar preſo à la Nave, que eſtaba en el Puerto: Apoderoſe de quanto tenia en Caſa, y de las Llaves de los Almacenes, que era lo que èl mas deſeaba: La Cruz tomò la Caſa de ſu Teniente Ottigni, pero le tratò con mas piedad, porque ſolo le quitò las Armas, y le dejo ſobre palabra de no ſalir de ella, antes de amanecer: y lo miſmo hiço Eſtevan, el Genovès, con Arlac.

Le

PEDRO MENENDEZ DE AVILES
founder of St. Augustine, Fla., 1565.

Amigos aquellos Indios.

Hallabase el Adelantado con gran cuidado del Galeon San Pelayo, cuio paradero no sabia; y no pudiendo persuadirse à que se huviese perdido, segun el Rumbo llevaba, encargò à Francisco Ginovès (que en su Patache Espiritu Santo llevò à la Española, las Francesas, y Moços, que se avian salvado en el Fuerte de San Mateo) que si le hallase en algun Puerto, cargase su Patache del Bastimento, que en èl avia; pero aunque, aviendo dejado à los Franceses en la Española, le buscò en sus Puertos, y Baracoa, y despues en Cuba, donde separò su Patache, y fue à Puerto de Plata à cargar de Bastimento para los Fuertes de la Florida, en ninguna parte hallò noticia del Navio.

Causò gran pesar en el Adelantado este sucesso, y despachò à Gonçalo Gayon, en el Patache San Andrès, de 100 Toneladas, à vèr si avia llegado à aquellos Puertos; pero se bolviò de la misma suerte, que Francisco Ginovès, cargado de Bastimento à la Florida. Embiò el Vergantin San Mateo con Juan Rodriguez de Iela, su Maestre, à hacer la misma diligencia, en todos los Puertos;

Another page, with part of it enlarged, from the "Ensayo," with a reference to Francisco Ginoves, who in his boat, the "Espiritu Santo," had carried over to Santo Domingo the French women and children who had been spared when the Fort of San Mateo (the former Fort Caroline) was captured.

RUINS OF FORT MATANZAS IN 1872

XXXIX. PEDRO MENÉNDEZ MÁRQUES AL REY.

[54-5-9, 11.*
San Agustin, 3 Enero de 1580.]

[f. 1] †

C. R. M.

[ ] despues q̃ di qu^{ta} a Vra. mãg. con El cap^{an} R^{o} de Junco de lo q̃ hauia suçedido en estas proui^{as}. suçedieron çiertas cosas q̃ todo bendito nr̃o señor çuçedio bien. yo fui ha hazer la paga a s^{ta} helena a la gente de guerra q̃ alla rreside. y como los yndios no quisieron benir ablarme. ynbie Vna barca con doze honbres a tomar lengua dellos. y ablaronles desde la barca y rrespondieron los yndios que no querian amistad. y comencaron a flecharlos. la barca se boluio. y bisto esto enbie Vn batel segunda bez con beinte honbres rrequeriendoles con la paz. y estubieron tan rrebeldes q̃ estubo La gente fatigada E hirieron a cinco honbres bisto esto fui alla con sesenta honbres y salte en tierra y esperaron con buen animo. y tanto q̃ yo quede espantado. E hirieronme catorze honbres. pero ninguno murio. hizeles Vna burla lo mejor q̃ yo supe. de manera que q̃daron muertos muchos yndios y huieron todos. y dexaron la tierra. y buelto al fuerte por q̃ hera de alli a quinze leguas. antes q̃ pudiesen dar la nueba a otros pueblos rrebolui sobre vn pueblo Grande q̃ se dize coçapoy q̃ estaba muy fuerte y metido en Vn pantano. y a la media noche doy en el a donde hize mucho daño. y prendi Vn hijo del caçique. y a su muger y Vna hermana y a su madre. y murieron quemados mas de quarenta yndios y prendi dos françeses. y con esto me bolui al fuerte. de los françeses supe que quedauan en aquel pueblo otros doze françeses y que no se querian benir pã nosotros entre los q̃les estaba el piloto q̃ ya otra bez abra siete años se huyo de aqui ynbieles a dezir a los yndios me diesen los françeses y les daria las mugeres y aVnque tarde lo hizieron.y quedeme con el hijo del caçique en rrehenes. ellos estan de manera q̃ tengo dellos rruin esperança Vine a la lengua de guale. y andubieron buenos por q̃ luego me entregaron el cap^{an} q̃ se deçia nicolao estroçi y los demas q̃ tenian. Eçeto dos muchachos y vn soldado. q̃ estaban lexos. y los caçiques todos me binieron a ber. y

* 1 pliego. Original.—Lowery, III.- Smith.

XXXIX. PEDRO MENÉNDEZ MÁRQUES TO THE KING.

[54 5 9, 11.
St. Augustine, January 3, 1580.]

[f. 1] †

R. C. M.

After I gave your Majesty an account, through Captain Rodrigo de Junco, of what had occurred in these provinces, certain things happened which all turned out well, our Lord be thanked. I went to Santa Helena to distribute the pay to the soldiers who live there, and, as the Indians would not come to talk with me, I sent a boat with twelve men to seek information from them. The men spoke to them from the boat, and the Indians answered that they did not desire friendship, and began to shoot arrows at them. The boat returned, and when I heard this, I sent a boat a second time, with twenty men, notifying them to make peace; and they were so rebellious that the soldiers grew angry, and [the Indians] wounded five men. When I heard this, I went there with sixty men, and landed; and they waited with great courage, so much so that I marvelled, and they wounded fourteen of my men, but no one was killed. I worked a trick on them as well as I knew how, in such wise that many Indians were slain, and they all fled, and quit the country. I returned to the fort, which was fifteen leagues from there, and before they could spread the news to other villages, I went back and attacked a large village called Coçapoy, which was very well fortified and in the midst of a swamp. I fell upon it at midnight, and did much damage, and I captured a son of the cacique, his wife, a sister, and his mother. More than forty Indians were burned to death, and I seized two Frenchmen, and thereupon I returned to the fort. I learned from the Frenchmen that there were twelve other Frenchmen in that village, and that they did not wish to come to us. Among them was the pilot who, on another occasion, about seven years ago, escaped from here. I sent word to the Indians to give me the Frenchmen and I would give them the women, and they did so although they took their time. I kept the cacique's son as a hostage. They are in such a mood that I have little hope concerning them. I went to the province of Guale and they behaved well, for they delivered to me at once the captain who called himself Nicolao Estroçi, and the others they had, except two boys and one soldier who were far away; and all the

dieron la obidiençia de nuebo a Vr̃a mãg. al pareçer estan buenos aVnq̃ no se puede fiar mucho dellos y de alli me bine a este fuerte y lo estoi acabando. q̃ es muy buena pieça aunque hase hecho con mucho trabajo/no hize luego Justiçia de los françeses hasta agora enbie vn barco a s^{ta} hel^{a} por algunos dellos. y los demas se hizo alli Justiçia dellos y los q̃ binieron junte los con los que aqui auia q̃ por todos los de que hize Justiçia. fueron veinte y tres aqui y en santa hel^{a} y quedan tres muchachos y vn barbero y vn lonbardero q̃ son neçesarios en estas proui^{as} pã lenguas. solo quedã agora entre ellos a lo q̃ se entiende dos honbres y Vn moço/an quedado los yndios de entregarlos/bien mereçieron la muerte conforme a su confesion. porque confesaron auer saqueado y quemado la margarita y a cumana y a guadinilla y otros pueblos y tomar muchos nabios/El Cap^{an} hera rrico porque me ofreçio tres mill d^{o}s de rrescate. y le diese la uida. no me pareçio conbenia al seruiçio de Vr̃a mãg. q̃ vn honbre como este boluiese a françia. El hera de naçion florentin de buena casta.

[ ] de los mismos françeses y de los yndios supe q̃ los françeses trataron con los yndios q̃ ellos procurarian darles el fuerte. y conforme al conçierto q̃ tenian hecho. acudieron [f. 1v] los yndios pero binieron tarde. y [illegible] tiempano. poco les aprov[illegible] comun esto [illegible]

caciques came to see me, and renewed their allegiance to your Majesty. To all appearance they are friendly, although one cannot much rely on them. Thence I came to this fort, which I am finishing; it is a good piece, although it has been built with much difficulty. I did not at once work justice upon the Frenchmen; not until now. I sent a boat to Santa Helena for some of them, and then justice was worked upon the rest there. I added those who were brought to those who were here, so that those on whom I worked justice, here and at Santa Helena, numbered twenty-three altogether. There remain three boys, one barber and one gunner, who are needed in these provinces as interpreters. From what has been heard, only two men and one boy are now left among the Indians. They have agreed to surrender them. According to their confession, they well deserved death, for they admitted having sacked and burned Margarita Island, Cumana, Guadinilla and other villages, and captured many ships. The captain was rich, because he offered me three thousand ducats as ransom, if I would grant him his life. It did not appear to me expedient for your Majesty's service that a man like him should get back to France. He was of the Florentine nation, and of good lineage.[48]

I learned from those same Frenchmen and from the Indians, that the French had told the Indians that they would try to give them the fort; and in accordance with the agreement they had made, the Indians cam[illegible] But th[illegible] late, and even if

Spanish text and English translation of the letter in which Pedro Menendez Marques (nephew of Menendez de Aviles) tells his king how he refused 3,000 ducats to save the life of the Florentine Nicola Strozzi. (From *Publications of the Florida State Historical Society, No. 5. Vol. 2, translated and edited by Jeannette T. Connor*)

AN ITALIAN MARTYR IN VIRGINIA IN 1571

Christianity was first introduced into the eastern part of the present United States by Spanish priests as early as 1568, when the first Jesuit mission was established in Florida. They met with little success and after a few years they withdrew leaving, however, a few martyrs behind.

Among the latter there was an Italian friar, Brother Pedro Linares, whose real name is said to have been Mingoci or Mengozzi. He was among the Spaniards who went to Virginia with Father Segura and one of the eight religious men who were killed by the Indians on the banks of the River Rappahannock, not far from the present city of Washington, on February 4 and 9, 1571.

The Jesuits returned to Florida two centuries later when two Italian priests, Father Jose Maria Monaco and Father Jose Saverio Alagna, tried to convert the Miami, Santaluces and other tribes. The two landed at the mouth of the Rio de Ratones, probably the Miami River, on July 13, 1743, after tarrying for a while at Key West, where Father Alagna took scientific notes and mapped the Keys and nearby islets. They were not very successful. Nevertheless, they established a community of Catholic Indians who "retained their faith till the period of the Seminole Wars, when they were transported to Indian territory."

Father Monaco was born in Naples in 1704 and taught at the Jesuit College of Belen, Havana. He died in 1744, or a year after he landed in Florida. Father Alagna was born either at Palermo, or in Sardinia, in 1707 and taught also at Belen. He was the teacher of the noted historian, Father Alegre. He died at Havana in 1767. His portrait is said to be still hanging in the dining hall of the Jesuit College at Havana. Father Alegre used Father Alagna's diary in his "History of the Company of Jesus in New Spain."

Massacre of Father Baptista Segura, S.J. and Brother Linares, Zeballos, Gomez and Redondo at the Log Chapel in Ajacan, Virginia, February 9, 1571. (From M. Kenny, S.J., *The Romance of the Floridas, Milwaukee,* 1934, *by courtesy of the Burgess Publishing Co.*)

ITALIAN MILITARY ARCHITECTS IN THE AMERICAS

A notable group of Italians who were active in Spanish America, from Florida to the Strait of Magellan, during the 16th and 17th centuries consisted of military engineers sent over by Spain to fortify her possessions against the raiding pirates of England, France, Holland, and other nations.

In those days, it should be remembered, Spain had no technical experts, nor could she create them all of a sudden. As Prof. Diego Angulo Iñiguez of the Spanish Academy of History says in his study on "Bautista Antonelli," "that need was filled, above all, by Italian engineers, and Italians were several of the great engineers who in Europe, as well as in the Indies, worked at this time in the service of Philip II; its very chief engineer, Tiburcio Spanoqui, was also an Italian. Among them, one of the foremost places, both for number and for the skill of some of its members, was occupied by the Antonelli family."

Among the Antonellis we shall recall Giovanni Battista, who as early as 1529 proposed digging a canal through the present territory of Nicaragua, and his nephew, Battista, who was most active in the Western Hemisphere over a long period of years. In 1589 he laid the first stone of the Morro Castle in Havana. In 1596 he visited Florida,

1587. 329

1587.

and sick the number will be far less than they thought, to such an extent that his Majesty will be forced to raise new levies. The flagship of the New Spanish squadron in clearing the river at Saccaben went on the rocks.

The Earl of Morton, seeing how many delays in the way of the succours promised to his King are arising, and being convinced that the Armada cannot sail at present, has taken leave of the Cardinal, and is waiting to embark on board a carvel, they say, for Brittany, whence he will go to Paris before returning to Scotland. They say here that all the difficulties raised by the Marquis will be quite as serious in spring as now. For the King of Scotland, seeing that he is merely entertained with promises, may change his policy for fear of exposing himself and his kingdom to greater dangers; and especially now in view of the offers which are being made him by the Queen of England to name him heir to the English throne. Moreover, in this interval the Queen will have opportunity to fortify her coasts and to call in aid from other Princes. But the worst is that his Majesty must look to his own defences, for all the English corsairs, to the number of, perhaps, forty sail, are off Cape St. Vincent with the design of harrying Spanish shipping. They have captured various small vessels on their way from Seville to Cadiz, among them a very rich prize which had come from the Brazils; and if they do not send out some part of the Spanish fleet the English will grow so bold that they will attempt something of moment, while, even if it does go out, the Spanish ships are quite unable to pursue the English, whose ships are swifter, and themselves far better seamen. The Portuguese, at their wit's end, are going to send an Ambassador to the King to lay their condition before him, and to implore him to apply a remedy to so many ills by deigning to go in person to console those unhappy people who are groaning under this heavy calamity. But for many reasons, and chiefly that he may not be an eye witness of such ruin, it is thought that the King will not go to Portugal, and perhaps they will not even allow the Ambassador to come here.

The King is thinking of building three or four forts in Florida, and he has the plans in his rooms. Battista Antonelli is the engineer.

Madrid, 12th December 1587.

[*Italian; the part in italics deciphered.*]

English translation of the report by Girolamo Lippomano, Venetian Ambassador to Spain, to the Doge and Senate on Dec. 12, 1587. Notice in the last paragraph the reference to Antonelli. (From *Calendar of State Papers . . .* ed. by H. Brown, Vol. VIII) (Courtesy. *New York Public Library*) On Italian engineers in America see D. A. Iniguez, *Bautista Antonelli,* Madrid, 1942; Maggiorotti, L. A., *Gli Architetti Militari,* 3 vols., Rome, Laguno-Bermudez, *Noticias de los arquitectos y arquitectura de Espana,* 3 Vols. Madrid, 1829 (available in the Library of Congress); *Appleton's Cyclopaedia,* under Antonelli.

where apparently he ordered the erection of a new fort. He did much more in America, but space prevents us from getting into details. Battista's cousin, Cristobal Roda Antonelli, who arrived in 1591, was also active in Porto Rico, Cuba, and other parts of Central America. Many other Italian engineers worked in the New World. An Italian, in all probability, was also Miguel Costanso, who fortified San Diego and Monterey in 1769.

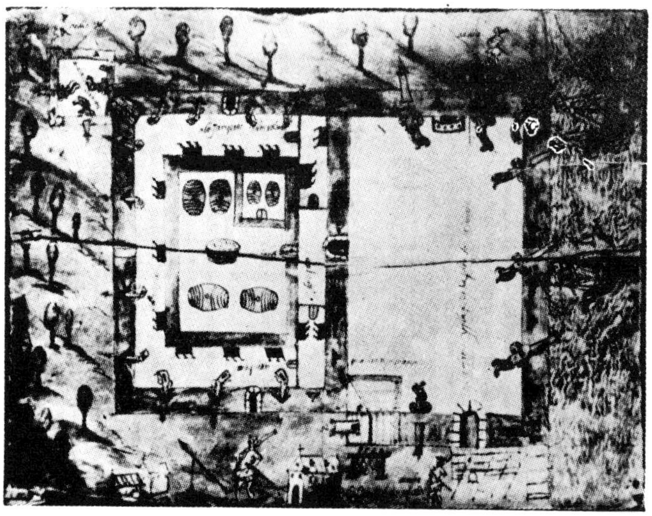

MAP OF ST. AUGUSTINE, FLA.
taken to Spain about 1549 by Hernando de Cestas, (*Archives of the Indies,* Seville) (*Below*) A modern view of Morro Castle, Havana, designed by G. B. Antonelli. (Courtesy, *Cuban Tourist Commission*)

FATHER CHINO, THE GIANT OF THE OLD SOUTHWEST

The Spanish missionaries failed along the Atlantic Coast, but they were more successful in Mexico. The reader, of course, will remember that as late as 1835-1849 Mexico extended so far North as to include the present states of California, Utah, New Mexico and the whole of Texas. Therefore, it was from what is now known as Old Mexico that the missionaries spread out to the outer borders of the Spanish possessions in North America. Most of them were either Franciscans or Jesuits.

The "Spanish" missionaries were not all natives of Spain. Quite a few of them were natives of Germany, the Flanders, France, Portugal and other countries. Those from Italy were probably more numerous than the others—with the exception, of course, of those born in Spain or Mexico. As related in detail in Vol. II of *Italian-American History,* their number may be judged by the fact that six or seven of the 73 provincials and at least eight of the 52 priests of the Society of Jesus who labored in Lower California from 1687 to 1767 were natives of Italy. At least four Italian missionaries were killed by the Indians in Mexico between 1632 and 1690.

The greatest Jesuit, and most likely the greatest missionary, to labor in the New World was the famous Father Eusebio Chino, a native of Segno, in the Val di Non, province of Trento, Italy. The family is still in existence there, but the name is Chini and not Chino. In Spanish it was spelled Kino, for phonetic reasons.

Father Chino was great as explorer, scientist, farmer, chronicler, and missionary. Out of the missions founded by him (he built more than 30 churches and chapels) from 1681 to the year of his death, 1711, were born in no small measure the cattle industry of the Southwest of the present United States and the fine orchards of modern California. Missions were in those days complete units by themselves, with gardens, orchards, ranches, workshops, water mills, and houses. Cattle, horses, sheep, goats, trees and plants of all kinds, from grapes to pomegranates, were introduced by the missionaries.

FATHER CHINO'S BIRTHPLACE AT SEGNO, ITALY

As Prof. Bolton has said, Father Chino was "easily the cattle king of his day and region." Prof. Bolton's map on the next page will give an idea of the immense territory covered by the tireless Father. Among the churches founded by him, two can still be seen in Arizona, not many miles south of Tucson. One is that of San Xavier del Bac (Bac means "where the water oozes from the sand"); the other, at Tumacacori, is a national monument, entrusted to the National Park Service, United States Department of the Interior.

THE MISSION OF SAN XAVIER DEL BAC

Still used by the Indians, the mission was founded by Father Chino in 1692, but the foundations of the Church were not laid until 1701. The Church as we see it today, however, was built by the Franciscan Fathers, mostly between 1772 and 1783. It has been improved since then. (Courtesy, *Franciscan Fathers of San Xavier Mission,* Tucson, Ariz.)

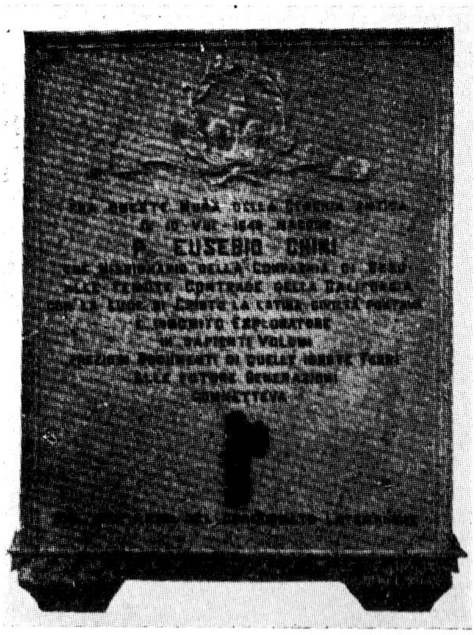

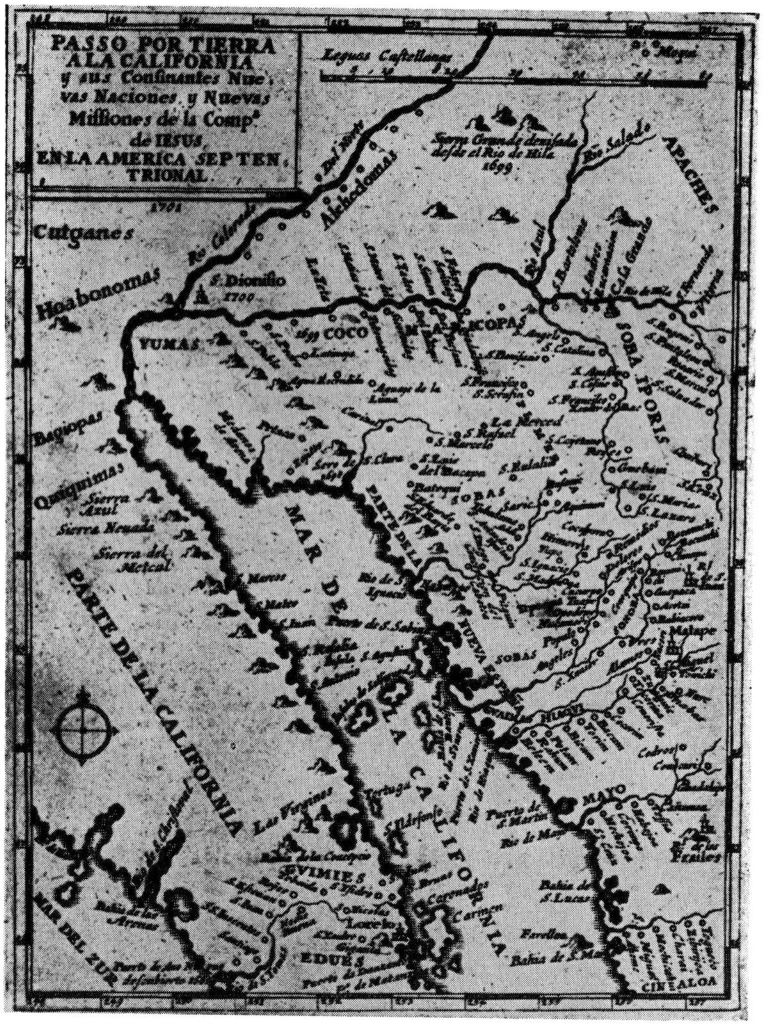

(*Above*) Tablet on the house in which Father Chino was born in 1645. (*Right*) Father Chino's Map showing California as a Peninsula, 1701. (From the original manuscript, as reproduced in H. E. Bolton's *Rim of Christendom,* Macmillan Co., New York, 1936) (*Below*) Map of Chino's Travels. (Courtesy, *Prof. H. E. Bolton*)

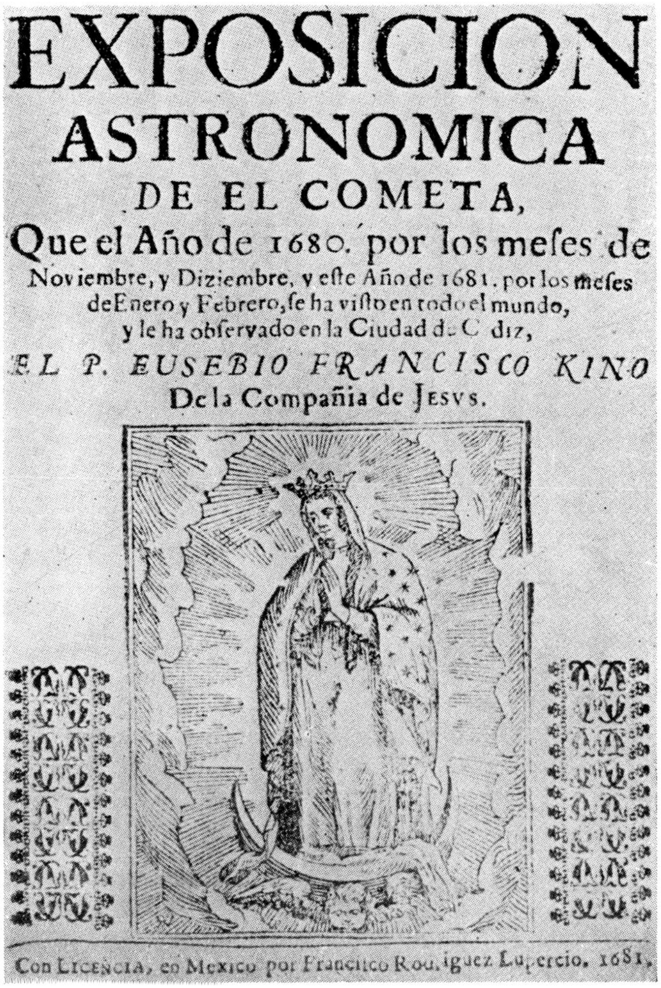

EXPOSICION
ASTRONOMICA
DE EL COMETA,
Que el Año de 1680. por los meses de
Noviembre, y Diziembre, y este Año de 1681. por los meses
de Enero y Febrero, se ha visto en todo el mundo,
y le ha observado en la Ciudad de Cadiz,
EL P. EUSEBIO FRANCISCO KINO
De la Compañia de JESUS.

Con Licencia, en Mexico por Francisco Rodriguez Lupercio. 1681.

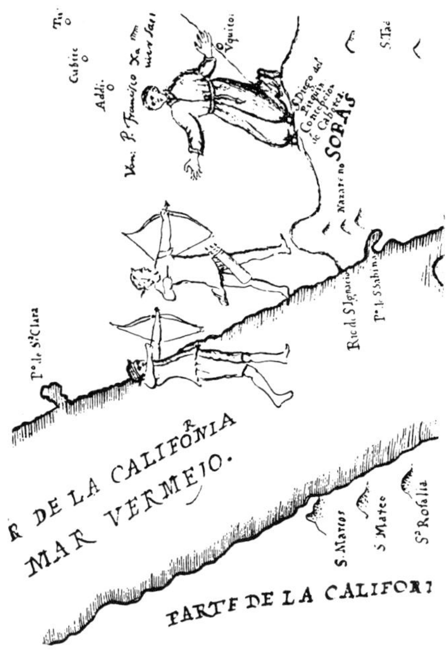

(*Left*) Title page of Father Chino's book on the comet, published in Mexico City in 1681. (*Above*) The martyrdom of the Sicilian Father Francesco Saverio Saetta in Pimeria, Mexico, in 1695, as drawn on Father Chino's Map of Pimeria Alta. (Both illustrations are from Prof. Bolton's *Rim of Christendom*)

MISSION CHURCH OF SAN JOSE' DE TUMACACORI

Established by Father Chino in 1691, it is a part of the Tumacacori National Monument, established by proclamation of President Theodore Roosevelt in 1908. It is 48 miles south of Tucson and 18 miles north of Nogales, on U. S. Highway No. 89. (Courtesy, *National Park Service*)

FATHER SALVATERRA, FOUNDER OF THE CALIFORNIA MISSIONS

The first of the historic California Missions was not established by Father Serra at San Diego in 1769; it was founded by Father Salvaterra at Loreto, in Lower California, in 1697.

Geographically, Upper California (the present State of California) and Lower California (Mexico) are a unit. They were united under the Spanish and Mexican flags up to 1849, when the upper part was joined to the United States. That explains, in part, why the history of the California Missions—which some historians date from the coming of Father Serra—actually starts with the founding of the first mission at Loreto. More important yet, without the Lower California Missions, in all probability Father Serra would not have been able to start his work in the present Golden State.

The first attempt to colonize and evangelize Lower California was made by Father Chino and Father Gogni in 1683, but they failed. The land was simply too sterile to support a mission. In 1697 Father Chino and Father Salvaterra were allowed to enter the Peninsula again, on condition that they ask for not a penny from the government. Father Chino at first felt that he could support the new mission with the produce and income from the Pimeria missions, but that was not enough. Besides, he was unable to remain. It was then that Father Salvaterra conceived the plan to establish a fund with an annual income sufficient to take care of the missions. Without getting into details, that is how the famous *Pious Fund* was started. All moneys collected were invested in lands and only the interest was used. By 1902 that Fund had increased to $1,420,682.67.

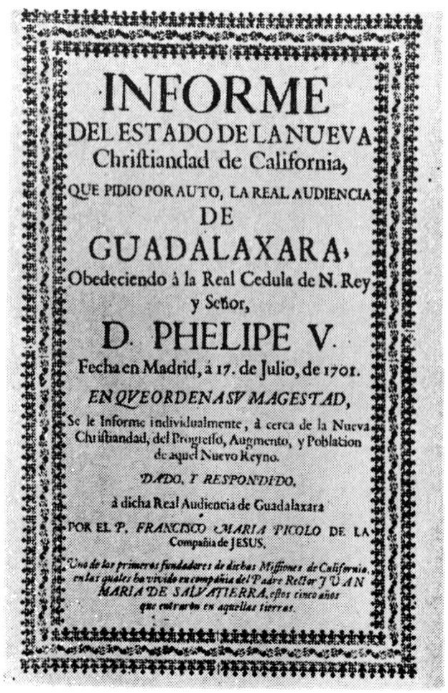

INFORME
DEL ESTADO DE LA NUEVA
Chriſtiandad de California,
QUE PIDIO POR AUTO, LA REAL AUDIENCIA
DE
GUADALAXARA,
Obedeciendo à la Real Cedula de N. Rey
y Señor,
D. PHELIPE V.
Fecha en Madrid, à 17. de Julio, de 1701.
EN QUE ORDENA SU MAGESTAD,
Se le Informe individualmente, à cerca de la Nueva
Chriſtiandad, del Progreſſo, Augmento, y Poblacion
de aquel Nuevo Reyno.
DADO, Y RESPONDIDO,
à dicha Real Audiencia de Guadalaxara
POR EL *P. FRANCISCO MARIA PICOLO* DE LA
Compañia de JESUS,
*Uno de los primeros fundadores de dichas Miſſiones de California,
en las quales ha vivido en compañia del Padre Rector JUAN
MARIA DE SALVATIERRA, estos cinco años
que entraron en aquellas tierras.*

Title page of Father Piccolo's *Informe.* (Courtesy, *New York Public Library*) In the National Library of Mexico City there is a life of Father Piccolo by Father Juan Antonio Balthasar (88 pages, no title page)

VERY REV. JUAN MARIA SALVATERRA
(Courtesy, *National Museum of History, Mexico City*)

When, after the expulsion of the Jesuits in 1767, the Franciscans were asked to take over the California missions, Father Serra was reluctant to accept. What made up his mind was the existence of the Pious Fund, which enabled him to carry on the work without the preoccupations which had beset the Italian pioneers.

Father Gianmaria Salvaterra (his name in Spanish was spelled Salvatierra) was born of a well-to-do family in Milan, Italy, on November 15, 1648. He labored in Mexico from 1675 to the end of his days, at Guadalajara, on July 17, 1717. In 1704 he was made Provincial of the Society of Jesus in New Spain. Together with his associates he founded seven missions in Lower California, starting with that of Loreto in 1697.

Several Italians were associated with Father Salvaterra in Lower California. The most notable of them, Father Francesco Piccolo, was born at Palermo on March 24, 1654, and came to America in 1683. He served in Lower California from 1697 to the time of his death on February 22, 1729. He founded three missions.

Other Italians who worked in Lower California between 1697 and 1767 were Fathers Geronimo Minutili of Sardinia, Benito Guisi, Ignazio Maria Napoli, Sigismondo Taraval of Lodi, Giacomo Druet of Turin, and Pietro Nascimbene of Venice.

TWO VICEROYS: BUCARELI AND BRANCIFORTE

ANTONIO MARIA DE BUCARELI
(Courtesy, *National Museum of History, Mexico City*)

Probably the most outstanding Spanish viceroy in New Spain, he was of Florentine extraction. In the National Library of Mexico there is a eulogy of him by Joseph Uribe, which was read in the Mexico City Cathedral on June 26, 1779 and the "Compendio Historico Genealogico de la Casa de Bucareli" by G. A. de Villar y Pinto.

The MARQUIS OF BRANCIFORTE
(Courtesy, *National Museum of History, Mexico City*)

A native of Sicily, he was a grandee of Spain, a captain general of the Spanish Army, and the brother-in-law of the famous Godoy. He founded the city of Santa Cruz, Cal., which was called Branciforte from 1797 until about 1845. Only an avenue in that city is now named after him. (See Bancroft, *History of Mexico*, Vol. III, and Berger, G. A., *The Franciscan Missions of California*)

EARLY ITALIAN TRAVELERS IN NEW SPAIN

The discovery of America aroused an unbounded curiosity in Italy, where the Renaissance was then in full bloom. Many Italians were prompted to come over by the spirit of adventure and by the desire to see and describe the marvels of the New World.

Three travellers who visited America before the Revolution deserve special attention. They were Benzoni, Boturini and Gemelli-Careri.

Girolamo Benzoni was probably the earliest wanderer in New Spain, which he visited between 1541 and 1556. A native of Milan, he was only 22 years old when he arrived. He wrote a book, *Historia del Mondo Nuovo,* which appeared in Venice in 1565 and was soon translated into French and Latin. Lorenzo Boturini Beneduci arrived in Mexico in 1736 and gathered a valuable collection of manuscripts regarding the Aztecs, most of which were lost. He also wrote a book.

GIROLAMO BENZONI
A portrait from the title page of his book "La Historia del Mondo Nuovo," Venice, 1565.

Giovanni Francesco Gemelli-Careri was born in Radicena, Calabria, in 1651 and died in Naples in 1725. In 1693 he undertook a trip around the world by way of Asia Minor and India. He visited the California Coast in 1698. He wrote a book entitled *Giro del Mondo* in 6 volumes, published at Naples in 1699-1700. A copy of the third edition is in the New York Public Library.

MALASPINA'S VOYAGE AROUND THE WORLD

Alessandro Malaspina was probably the first Italian to stop at San Francisco, where he landed on September 10, 1791. It is possible, however, that other sons of Italy may have preceded him.

Malaspina arrived in California at the head of one of the foremost scientific voyages in history, during which he surveyed the entire Pacific Coast from Alaska to Mexico.

He was born in Italy in 1754, the son of a marquis. His mother was the niece of Giovanni Fogliani, Prime Minister of Charles III of Spain. As a boy he entered the Spanish Naval Service, for Italy in those days offered no opportunity to ambitious young men. In 1786-88 he made his first voyage around the world. A year later he was put in charge of the greatest voyage, next to those of Columbus and Magellan, ever to sail under the Spanish flag.

During his voyage, besides surveying the Pacific Coast, he and his men made scientific observations and took measurements of great value. At Monterey, California, where he remained ten days, he and the members of his expedition made botanical and geological studies, took soundings in the bay, drew maps and charts, and interviewed local Indians.

On his return to Spain, Malaspina was received in triumph and was promoted to the rank of Brigadier of the Royal Navy. Not long after that, however, court intrigues (he was a foreigner) caused his arrest for reasons which are not clearly known to our own days. Only when Napoleon intervened in his behalf in 1802 was he set free and allowed to return to Italy. He died in his ancestral home on April 20, 1810.

ALESSANDRO MALASPINA
From the portrait in the Naval Museum, Madrid.

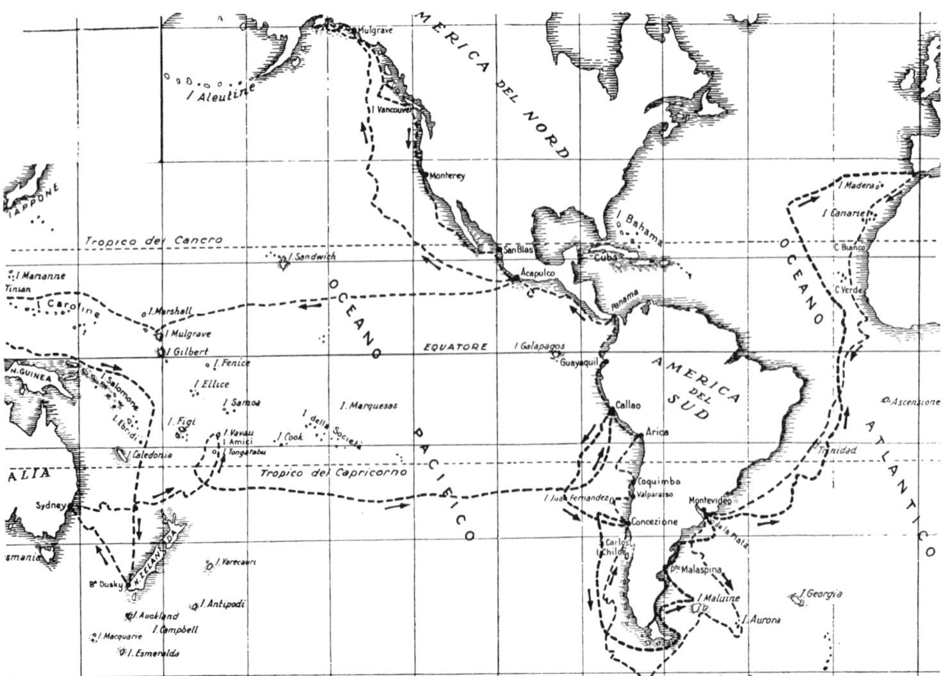

The routes followed by Malaspina in his voyage around the world from 1789 to 1794.
(From a rare map reproduced in E. Bona's, *Malaspina,* Rome, 1935)

CHAPTER FOUR

UNDER THE FRENCH FLAG

From Canada to Louisiana

Relations between Italy and France have always been very close from the days of Brennus and Caesar to our own. That is probably why the Italians and the French admire and detest each other so cordially.

Italians have been going to France in large numbers ever since St. Denis, the first Bishop of Paris, and other Italian missionaries crossed the Alps to evangelize Gaul. Later came the galaxy of Italian "students" at the University of Paris, like St. Thomas Aquinas, Archbishop Lanfranc and St. Anselm of Canterbury. From the 12th to the 15th century, Italian bankers and merchants went over or settled in considerable numbers in such centers as Marseilles, Lyons and Paris. Following the descent into Italy of Charles VIII, the movement to the North continued unabated. Merchants and bankers; soldiers and sailors, including a score of men who became marshals of France; artisans and technicians who were lured over to reveal some of the manufacturing secrets which had made Italy wealthy, especially weaving, glass and silk manufactures; politicians and princesses who acquired influential positions at court (two queens, a celebrated prime minister, ambassadors and what not); painters, sculptors and craftsmen, including Leonardo da Vinci (Michelangelo at one time was on the point of joining the other emigrants); religious refugees who became Huguenots; numberless musicians and dancers; scores of archbishops and bishops; physicians (like Guidi, founder of the medical school of the University of Paris), inventors and scientists (like the astronomers Cassini); adventurers and men without a profession or trade; even poets and writers found their way over.

In most instances the names of those Italians were so Gallicized that one would not be able to tell their national origin except for the fact that they acquired fame: names like Mazarin, Lully, Trivulce, Prioleau, Scaliger, Verrazan, and so on and on. Wars and revolutions added an even greater share of emigrants.

Not a few of the Italians who settled in France eventually found their way to America, from Canada to old Louisiana. Once more their names acquired a French spelling, like Tonty, Desliettes, Bressany, Du L'Hut, De L'Halle, Vigue (Vigo), Sarpy, Sanguinette, and similar cases. Who can tell, for instance, the original Italian spelling of names like Bouis and Yost, two of the first settlers in St. Louis, except for the fact that we know that they were born in Italy? The problem becomes unsurmountable when dealing with Piedmontese emigrants, especially the Waldenses, whose names were more French than anything else.

Under the circumstances it is hard to trace all the Italians who settled in New France. In the following pages, therefore, we have limited ourselves only to those few about whom we have positive proofs of their Italian birth or origin.

NIAGARA FALLS AS FIRST SEEN BY WHITE MEN
(From L. Hennepin's *A New Discovery of a Vast Country in America,* London, 1698)

FATHER BRESSANI TORTURED BY THE IROQUOIS IN 1644

One of the first Italians to live and labor within the present State of New York was the Roman, Father Francesco Giuseppe Bressani, S.J. (1612-1672). Coming over in 1642, he soon was ministering to the French at Quebec, but during the following year he was already laboring among the Algonquin Indians at Three Rivers, in Canada. In 1644 he was transferred for missionary work among the Hurons and was on his way to take up his new duties, when he was captured by the ferocious Iroquois who inhabited the central and western parts of New York State and who subjected him to indescribable tortures.

For two months Father Bressani bore all torments with a fortitude becoming a true soldier of the Catholic Faith. Finally, when he seemed about to die, he was sold as a slave for a few beads to an old Indian woman who, in turn, sold him for 300 francs to some Dutch sailors at Fort Orange (Albany). Through their kindness he was eventually sent to Governor Kieft at New Amsterdam (New York City), who treated him with utmost kindness and made possible his return to Europe.

A year later, however, Father Bressani was back in Canada, where he spent four more years, until he was called back to Italy in 1650.

Father Bressani was the first man to describe Niagara Falls, thirty years before Hennepin, and the second Catholic priest to visit the present site of the City of Albany. Jogues was the first. Of the early Jesuits in New France, he certainly was the most distinguished mathematician, astronomer, geographer and historian.

An artist's conception of Father Francesco Bressani. Drawing by Onorio Ruotolo.

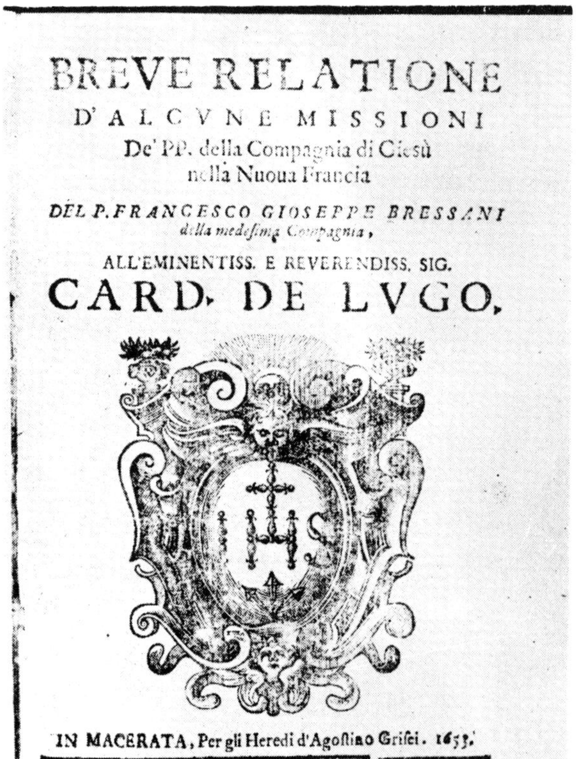

BREVE RELATIONE
D'ALCVNE MISSIONI
De' PP. della Compagnia di Giesù
nella Nuoua Francia
DEL P. FRANCESCO GIOSEPPE BRESSANI
della medesima Compagnia,
ALL'EMINENTISS. E REVERENDISS. SIG.
CARD. DE LVGO.

IN MACERATA, Per gli Heredi d'Agostino Grisei. 1653.
Con Licenza de' Signori Superiori.

(*Left*) An early map of the Huron Country, where Father Bressani was tortured by the Indians. (From Winsor's *Narrative and Critical History of America*) (*Above*) Title page of Father Bressani's *Relatione*, an account of his experiences in North America. (Courtesy, *New York Public Library*) He also wrote, in French, *Observations sur une Eclipse de Lune Faites à Quebec le* 18 *Novembre* 1649, which was inserted in the proceedings of the French Academy of Science.

ENRICO TONTI, TRAIL BLAZER IN THE MIDWEST

HENRY TONTI
A bas-relief by Edward Kemeys (Courtesy, *Chicago Historical Society,* owners of the original)

It so happens that the achievements of a lieutenant are often obscured by the fame of his captain, even if the latter has accomplished little more than promoting an undertaking and starting it on its way. Such was the relation between Henry Tonty and his superior, La Salle. As an American writer stated not long ago, "Despite the volumes that have been written about the great explorer (La Salle) and the acclaim which has accompanied his name down through the generations, I am convinced La Salle played a less important part in our immediate afffairs than did the unostentatious but most efficient lieutenant, Tonty." (*Illinois Catholic Historical Review,* Vol. III, p. 197).

Henri Tonty, as he signed his name, or Enrico Tonti, as it was originally in Italian, was born at Gaeta, not far from Rome, about 1650. That he was born in Italy we must assume from a letter dated July 17, 1651, which states that the Tonti family (with the exception of the father, Lorenzo) was still there at that time. (Ravaisson, F. *Archives de la Bastille,* Paris, 1874, Vol. VII, p. 294).

Henry was the son of Lorenzo and Isabella (De Lieto) Tonti. His father is still known today for the Tontine system of insurance which he introduced into France through Mazarin, and which later spread to the rest of the world. Its name is perpetuated in the United States by the Tontine Coffee House at Wall and Water streets in New York City. He is said to have been of humble origins. (Schipa, M., *Masaniello,* French edition, p. 112; *Les Mémoires d'Henri II de Lorraine, Duc de Guise,* New Edition, Paris, 1881, p. 35; Capecelatro, *Rivoluzione di Masaniello,* 3 vols. Naples, 1850-1854, Vol. II, p. 225). The name of Tonti, however, was an old one in Italy, as it appears from various manuscripts in the National Library of Naples and from other records in various parts of Italy (Spreti, V., *Enciclopedia Storico-Nobiliare Italiana,* 1932 ed., Vol. VI and Appendix, Part II.). One Count Antonio Tonti was also in the service of the Duke of Guise at the same time as Lorenzo, but we do not know whether the two were related. It is doubtful. (Innocenzo Fuidoro, or Vincenzo D'Onofrio, *Successi Storici Raccolti della Sollevatione di Napoli dalli 7 di luglio* 1647 *sino a' 6 d'Aprile* 1648. MS., Naples National Library, folios 206 and 220). Apparently Lorenzo was made a nobleman by Mazarin (See facsimile, next page), for his son Alphonse, Cadillac's companion, as we shall presently see, was often referred to as Baron of Paludy. (Paludi is a town near Naples).

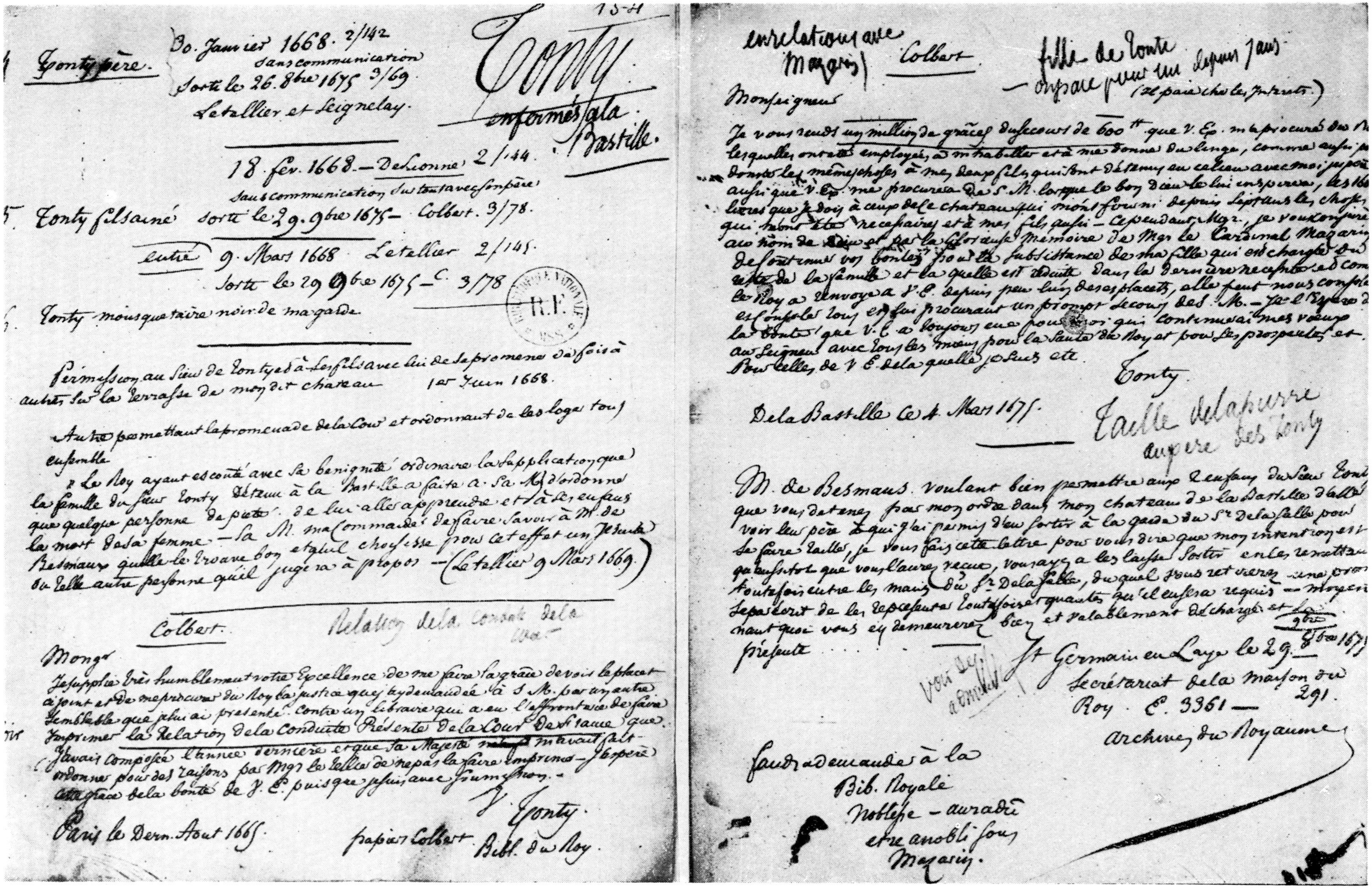

Facsimiles of two pages of manuscript notes in the Bibliotèque Nationale, Paris. (*Left*) *March* 9, 1669, a Jesuit priest is chosen to inform Lorenzo Tonti of the death of his wife. August 30, 1665, Lorenzo Tonti complains about a "relation" written by him and printed by a bookseller without his knowledge. (*Right*) March 4, 1675. Lorenzo Tonti thanks Colbert for the sum of 600 livres which the King had granted him. "In the name of God and of the glorious memory of Msgr. Cardinal Mazarin, I implore you to continue your assistance to my daughter who has charge of my family and who is in dire need." October 29, 1665. Tonti's two sons are allowed to visit their father, who had been released from prison in order to be operated. La Salle was held responsible for the two sons. Note at the bottom, left corner—Apparently Tonti had been made a nobleman by Mazarin. (Courtesy, *Dr. G. P. Ravera, Turin,* Italy)

At any rate, during the Masaniello revolution of 1647 in Naples, Lorenzo Tonti and his brother-in-law, Agostino De Lieto, served the Duke of Guise, Lorenzo as political representative in Rome, and Agostino as captain of the guard. When the revolution failed, both of them repaired to Paris, where Tonti gained the favor of Mazarin, a Sicilian, to whom he offered his system of insurance. We do not know what became of De Lieto, except that his sons later came to America (New France) where they served under the name of Desliette, DesLiettes, and possibly DuL'Hut, or Duluth. There Lorenzo became a prosperous banker until he became involved in a Spanish plot against the King of France, his mail was intercepted and he was imprisoned in the Bastille together with two of his sons. (Laloy, E., *La Révolte de Messine—L'Expédition de Sicile et la Politique Française en Italie*—3 vols. Paris, 1929-1931, Vol. I, 406-408.) All three of them remained in jail from 1668 until 1675, when they were set free. The father was released on October 26, so that he could be operated for gall bladder. On November 29 the two sons also were freed and entrusted to La Salle, on condition that he produce them whenever required.

Who those two sons were we do not know for certainty. Lorenzo's family was a large one, with several sons and daughters, nineteen in all. His wife died before March 9, 1669, whereupon his daughter took charge of the family (See facsimiles, March 9, 1669, and March 4, 1675, on next page).

From the above-mentioned documents it appears that Henry could not have been one of the two sons who shared their father's imprisonment in the Bastille from 1668 to 1675, for Henry in his petition to Count of Pontchartrain wrote that he served as a cadet in the army in the years 1668 and 1669 and later as *garde marine* (midshipman) for four years at Marseilles and Toulon. According to Ravaisson (*op cit.*), La Salle took the two Tontis entrusted to him to New France, where the older one died while serving with the rank of captain and the younger one distinguished himself in the wars against the Indians. The latter, a black musketeer of the royal guard, had an iron hand. Obviously there is a mistake somewhere, for Henry, the man with the iron hand, is never referred to as a royal musketeer in any of the records which have reached us about him.

La Salle, as we know, first went to Canada as an adventurer in 1666, and returned to France in 1674 with a letter of recommendation to Colbert. It was at that time, or a year later, to be exact, that the two sons of Lorenzo Tonti were entrusted to him. Soon after that La Salle returned to Canada and was made governor of Fort Frontenac. He was back in France in 1677 in order to secure financial assistance for his grand scheme of exploration and trade in the interior of America. Only July 14, 1678, La Salle and Henry Tonty sailed from la Rochelle for Quebec, where they landed on the following September 15. Now, if Henry Tonty was serving with the French in Sicily in 1677, as he states in his petition to Pontchartrain, he could not have been one of the two Tontis entrusted to La Salle, for between 1675 and 1678 La Salle was in America. It is possible, however, that they could have joined the army, whereas La Salle returned to Canada. On the other hand, how could La Salle pledge himself to produce the two Tontis if they were not with him? That certainly adds to the confusion regarding the various officers named Tonty one finds in New France during the last quarter of the 17th century.

Leaving the riddle for the time being, we know that Henry Tonty after serving as a cadet in the army from 1668 to 1669 and midshipman from about 1670 to 1673 or 1674, made seven campaigns, four on board ships of

The building in 1679 of the *Griffon*, the first ship to navigate the Great Lakes, by Tonti near Tonawanda, not far from Buffalo. (*From an old print*)

(*Above*) One of the Reliefs on the approach to the Michigan Boulevard Link Bridge in Chicago, erected in 1928. The inscription on the tablet reads: "The Discoverers." "Joliet, Father Marquette, LaSalle and Tonti will live in American history as fearless explorers who made their way through the Great Lakes and across this water-shed to the Mississippi in the late seventeenth century, and typify the spirit of brave adventure which had always been firmly planted in the character of the Middle West." (*Below*) A tablet on the Michigan Boulevard Bridge, in Chicago, in honor of La Salle and Tonti "who passed through this River on their way to the Mississippi in December 1681," placed by the Illinois Society of Colonial Dames of America, under the auspices of the Chicago Historical Society, in 1925. (Courtesy, *Chicago Historical Society*)

war and three in the galleys. In 1677 he took part in the French expedition which was sent against the Spaniards in Sicily in answer to an appeal from the Sicilians, and while at Messina "his right hand was shot away by a grenade, and he was taken prisoner, and conducted to Metasse, where he was detained six months, and then exchanged for the son of the governor of that place. He then went to France to obtain some favor from his Majesty, and the King granted him three hundred livres." After more service in Sicily as a volunteer in the galleys he returned to France, but being out of employment he decided to accompany La Salle to Canada.

Tonty's work in America is rather well-known. One of the first tasks assigned to him by La Salle was the construction of a boat to be used for fur-trading purposes in the upper lakes. He built it with a motley crew of 30 men, French, Flemings and Italians, at Niagara, all jealous of each other, and always threatening to mutiny. It was completed in record time and on August 7, 1679, it set sail for Lake Michigan, the first ship ever to navigate the Great Lakes. On its return trip, however, it foundered and nothing has ever been heard about it.

Tonty continued as a lieutenant of La Salle until 1682, when the Frenchman sailed for France to secure more

STARVED ROCK

Near the town of La Salle, 100 miles south of Chicago, it is 125 feet high and was so called because there a group of Indians defended themselves until they starved to death. There, in December 1682, La Salle and Tonti began the erection of Fort St. Louis, the first permanent fort built by the French in the Mississippi Valley. (Photo by the author)

Two tablets on Starved Rock. The one above was placed in 1918 by the Illinois Society of the Colonial Dames of America in memory of Joliet, Marquette, La Salle and Tonti. The other was erected by the State of Illinois to mark the sites of Fort St. Louis and of the Indian villages, possibly numbering 20,000 souls, which rose below the fort, "symbol of French protection to the Indian tribes of the Illinois." (Photos by the author.)

financial assistance for his grandiose scheme. During the time they were together the two worked to get a firm foothold for France in the interior of the present United States, travelling, exploring, erecting forts, and reaching amicable agreements with the various Indian tribes. Most of the work and of the responsibility fell on Tonty's shoulders.

Notwithstanding the disloyalty and desertion of a number of men, amid the ever-increasing opposition of the English who tried to arouse the Indians against him, (a Seneca warrior once stabbed him close to his heart), Tonty carried on his work in such a manner as to arouse the admiration of his contemporaries and of posterity. In 1680 he built Fort Crevecoeur on Lake Peoria. Two years later he accompanied La Salle down the Mississippi and was the second man to sign, next to La Salle, the proces-verbal on taking possession of Louisiana for France.

In March, 1683, he and La Salle completed Fort St. Louis on Starved Rock near the present city of La Salle, Ill. Then the Frenchman sailed back to France.

From then on, until the time of his death 20 years later, Tonty was the absolute ruler of the entire Mississippi Valley, which he dominated literally and figuratively with an iron hand. A statesman, he first created a great Indian confederation of about 20,000 men whom he made his friends and allies. A strategist, he saw to it that the ways of commerce were kept open. A businessman, he kept the goods flowing so that they could be bartered for Indian furs. A trail blazer, he explored most of the southern part of the Central United States, from Peoria to New Orleans and from Arkansas to Alabama (The people of Arkansas call him the Father of their State). Finally he made possible the establishment of the new colony of Louisiana and greatly facilitated the work of Iberville and Bienville.

As a fur trader, above all, Tonty was the pathfinder of the entire Mississippi Valley, which he knew as no other man did in his day. Thus he made possible the consolidation, however temporary, of French power in the Middle West, and the expansion of the United States one century, almost to the day, after his death at Mobile.

To conclude with the words of one of his recent biographers (E. R. Murphy, *Henry De Tonty*, Baltimore, 1941), "It is true that he seconded La Salle in all things, but while the latter conceived, Tonty achieved. . . . For seventeen years after La Salle's work ended, Tonty carried on. He possessed qualities of patience, endurance, and leadership which La Salle manifestly lacked. . . . How long is he destined to remain only the faithful lieutenant of La Salle, only the shadow of the explorer's greatness in the pages of history?"

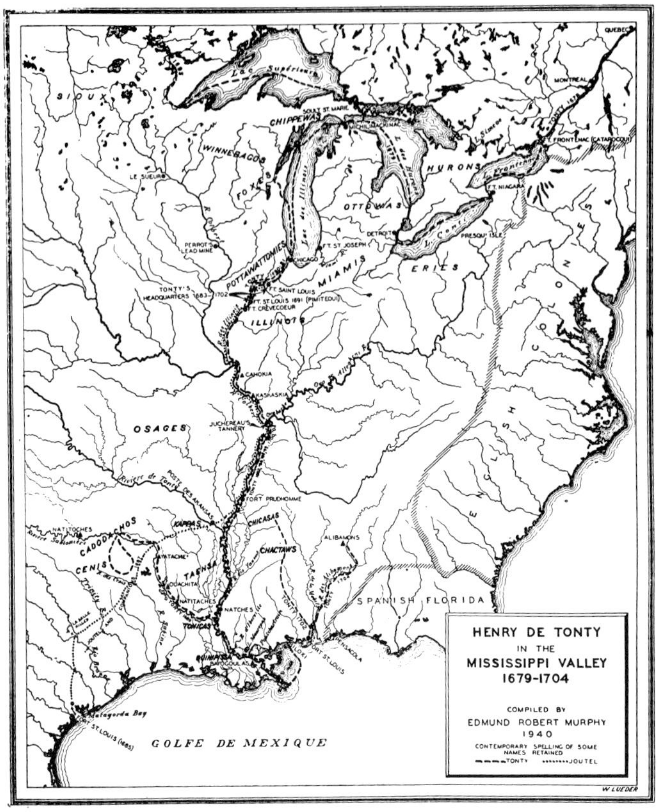

MAP OF TONTI'S VOYAGES
From E. R. Murphy's Henry de Tonty. (Courtesy, *The Johns Hopkins Press*)

LA SALLE AND TONTI TAKING POSSESSION OF THE MISSISSIPPI VALLEY FOR FRANCE
From the original drawing by W. H. Lippincott.

DULUTH EXPLORES THE NORTHWEST — DE LIETO GOVERNOR AT CHICAGO
TOMASO AND ANTONIO CRISAFI GOVERNORS AT THREE RIVERS AND ONONDAGA

Henry Tonty had been preceded to America by his cousin, Daniel Greysolon Du Lhut, as La Salle and Hennepin spelled the name, or Duluth, as he is best known. The city of that name in Minnesota was named after him.

How the two happened to be cousins nobody has been able to explain so far. It is possible that the name originally was De Lieto, although it would seem more likely that it was Greysolon or Grezollon, to judge by the name of Duluth's own brother, Claude Greysolon de la Tourette. A merchant named Grezollon was living between 1667 and 1670 in Lyons, a city long famous for its large colony of Italian merchants and bankers. According to Margry (*Découvertes et établissements. . . .* Vol. VI, p. 11) the Lyons Grezollon had a coat of arms with a rampant lion against a tree, more or less similar to a coat of arms of the Tonti family which can be seen in the National Library collection of Naples, Italy. (*18th century, folios* 61 *and* 88). We mention it as a mere curiosity, although the matter may deserve further study. At any rate, it seems established that Duluth had Italian blood in his veins and that he and Tonty were cousins. Moreover, the fact that in all probability Duluth was born about 1650 adds to the belief that he belonged to the De Lieto family that settled in Paris about that time.

Daniel Greysolon Duluth needs no introduction, for he was one of the boldest French explorers in what is now Minnesota. An American historian actually called him King of the Voyageurs. His brother, Claude Greysolon de la Tourette, also distinguished himself as a soldier and an explorer. He established a post to the north of Lake Superior.

Two or three cousins, not nephews, of Henry Tonty about whom we are positive were the brothers Desliettes. One of them, apparently Pierre, usually referred to as Sieur Desliette, was in charge at Chicago from 1698 to 1702, as he himself informs us in his memoir, known as *De Gannes Memoir*. Thus he seems to have been the first white man to reside for a considerable length of time where now rises the present city of Chicago. He served as commandant at Fort Illinois, on two different occasions, in 1704 and 1715, and was of great assistance to Bienville in Louisiana. Another Desliettes was commandant at Fort Chartres, near the present city of St. Louis, from 1726 to 1730. Still another brother, or nephew, Joseph Tonti Desliettes, was second in command at Green Bay, Wis. They were members of the De Lieto family mentioned in connection with Lorenzo Tonti in the preceding pages.

Among the other Italians in New France we might mention Antonio and Tomaso Crisafi, two political exiles from Messina, Sicily, who sought refuge in France after their city was abandoned by the French to the Spaniards.

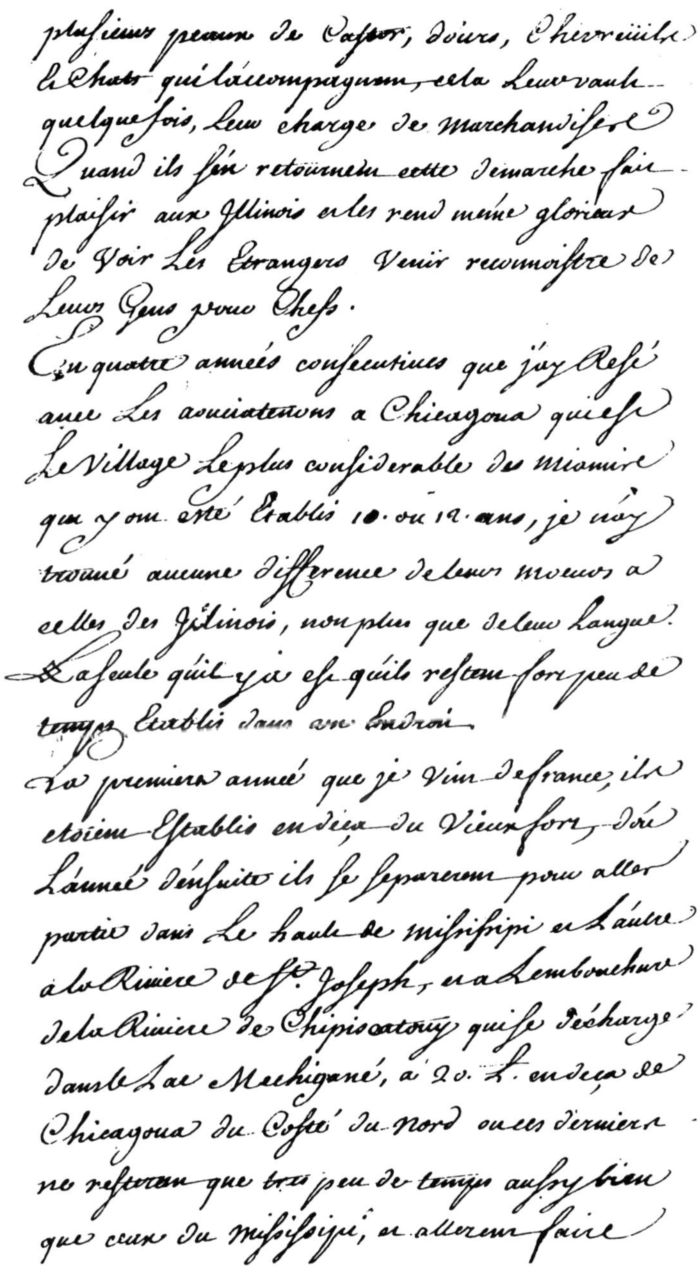
plusieurs peaux de Castor, d'ours, Chevreuils
le Chat qui l'accompagnent, cela leur vaut
quelquefois, leur charge de marchandises
Quand ils s'en retournent cette démarche fait
plaisir aux Illinois et les rend même glorieux
de Voir Les Etrangers Venir reconnoistre de
Leurs Gens pour Chefs.
En quatre années consecutives que j'ay Resté
avec Les ouiatanons a Chicagoua qui est
Le Village Le plus considerable des miamis
qui y ont esté Establis 10. ou 12. ans, je n'ay
trouvé aucune difference de leurs moeurs a
celles des Illinois, non plus que de leur Langue.
La seule qu'il y a est qu'ils restent fort peu de
temps Establis dans un Endroit.
La premiere année que je Vins de france, ils
etoient Establis en deça du Vieux fort, dés
L'année d'ensuite ils se separerent pour aller
partie dans Le haut de missisipi et L'autre
a la Riviere de St. Joseph, et a Lembouchure
de la Riviere de Chipiscatouy qui se décharge
dans le Lac Michigané, a 20. L. endeça de
Chicagoua du Costé du Nord ou ces derniers
ne resterent que tres peu de temps aussy bien
que ceux du missisipi, et allerent faire

A page from the *DeGannes Memoir,* in which Desliettes refers to the four years he spent at Chicago. (Courtesy, *Newberry Library,* Chicago, Ill.)

Both of them were captains. Antonio was governor at Three Rivers from 1703 to the time of his death in 1709. Previously, in 1696, he had been in charge of the new fort at Onondaga, near the present city of Syracuse.

(On the Crisafi brothers see Guardione, S., *La Rivoluzione di Messina contro la Spagna*, Palermo, 1906, and Laloy, *op. cit.*)

ALPHONSE TONTI CO-FOUNDER OF DETROIT

Alphonse Tonty, the younger brother of Henry Tonty, was one of the two founders of the City of Detroit, and its governor for twelve years. Some writers conveniently forget the *indispensable* role played by him in the very beginning of the new settlement, for without him Cadillac would have not been able to remain in the new post, surrounded by enemy Indians and by disloyal Frenchmen ready to desert him or to turn any situation to their own account at the least possible opportunity.

Tonty has been pictured as dishonest and unfit to command a post, by some local historians who apparently are not aware of the fact that Detroit's early history cannot be studied without taking into due account the conditions that prevailed there, as throughout New France, in colonial days. Not only in New France, but in all colonial possessions, at all times and under all flags, not excluding Virginia under English governors. We need not mention India under the famous Clive. It is possible that Tonty plied the Indians with liquor, but how many American Indian agents did not? As for the charges advanced against him, one must remember that, with a few exceptions, all prominent men in New France were exposed to similar attacks at one time or another. La Salle was surrounded by enemies. Frontenac was recalled. Cadillac himself had plenty of trouble, not only with the civilians and soldiers at the fort, but especially with the Jesuits, against whom he advanced even more serious charges than he did against Tonty. Aside from that, none of the charges against Tonty was ever proved, as a careful study of the Cadillac Papers reveals. It is possible, on the other hand, that he had very influential friends at Montreal and in Paris who whitewashed them, but had they been very serious he would have not been reinstated and left in charge for a period of seventeen years. Tonty, moreover, was a foreigner (a Neapolitan, as Cadillac called him) and the easy target of other Frenchmen who wanted to replace him. Other Italians in other countries had to go through similar charges. Columbus, Vespucius, Sebastian Cabot, for instance. It is simply ridiculous to judge a man in the wilderness of 17th century America by the moral standards of our own days.

THE LANDING OF CADILLAC AND TONTY AT DETROIT. From a drawing by Howard Pyle. (Courtesy, *New York Public Library*)

Alphonse Tonty was born in Paris in 1659 and came to America sometime before 1688. After serving in various capacities, including that of commandant at Mackinac, in 1700 he was chosen to accompany Cadillac as a captain, not as a lieutenant, as stated by some writers, to build a fort and start a new settlement at Detroit. In 1704 he was put in charge of Fort Frontenac, but in 1717 he returned to Detroit, where he ruled as governor for eleven more years. His daughter, Theresa, was the first white child born in what is now the great City of Detroit. He certainly had more to do with the early consolidation and development of the rising village than Cadillac himself, if residence alone is considered. (See Schiavo, *Italians in America Before the Civil War*, pp. 117-125.)

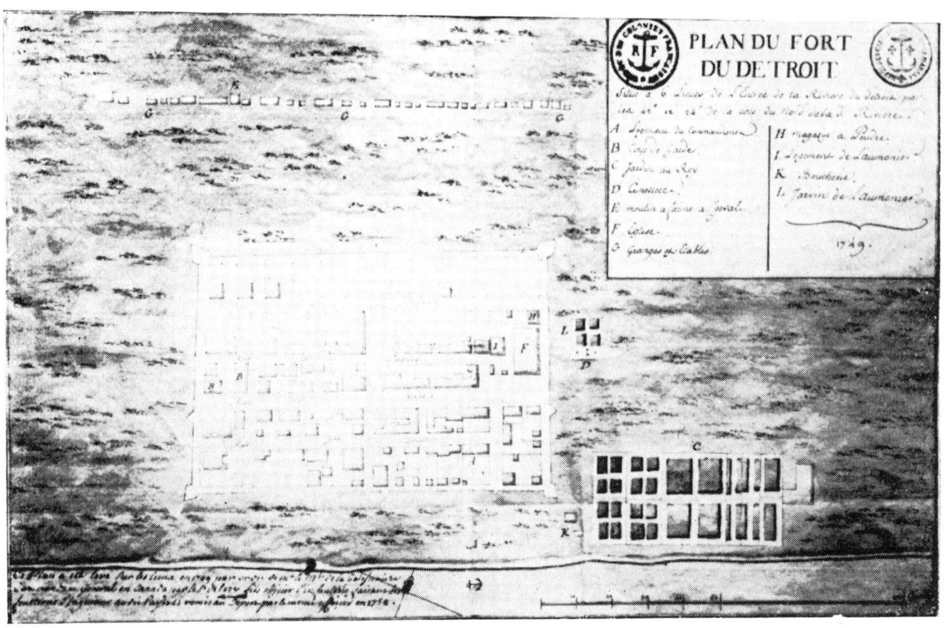

A MAP OF FORT DETROIT IN 1749. (Courtesy, *New York Public Library*)

400 ITALIAN FAMILIES IN LOUISIANA IN 1720?

The largest groups of Italian immigrants under the French Flag must have been either soldiers or political exiles, especially the former, many of whom served in such regiments as the *Royal Italien* (See *Historique des Corps de Troupe de l'Armée Française*, 1569-1900, Paris, 1900) and in the Carignan Regiment (See Benjamin Sulte, *Le Régiment de Carignan*, Montreal, 1922, and Regis Roy et Gerard Malchelosse, *Le Régiment de Carignan*, Montreal, 1925). To distinguish the nationality of the members of the Carignan Regiment is next to impossible. Take the name, for instance, of Pierre Salvage, equerry, Sieur de Fromont. How could one ever tell that he was an Italian, except for a note in the records according to which he was born in the parish of "Saint-Donnat, Ville de Peginerolle, Diocese de Gênes, Italie"? (Sulte, *op. cit.* p. 126.) He was granted one of the large islands of St. Ignace and is remembered by "La Riviere Salvaye." He died in 1689. Or again, take the case of Ensign Jean Nicalis de Brandis, a native of Turin, who served in Canada between 1665 and 1667. (Malcheloss, *op. cit.*, p. 113). The Regiment was raised by the Prince of Carignan in 1644 and was the first body of regular troops sent to Canada. It was made up of 20 companies. Most of the soldiers remained in America and settled in various parts of the present territory of the United States, primarily Indiana, Ohio and Missouri. Lest one should be misled by the "French" name of Carignan, let us remind the reader that Carignano is a city near Turin, in Italy, and that the name denotes the House of Savoy.

A notable, and possibly large, group of Italians settled in Louisiana in the 18th century, but when and how we do not know. Certainly there must have been quite a few of them at the beginning of the last century, if Col. Nichols of the British Artillery in the appeal that he issued to the population of New Orleans on August 29, 1814, addressed himself to the local "Spaniards, Frenchmen, Italians and Britons."

A prominent Italian to settle in that city was one Giovanni Gradenigo, a member of the famous Venetian family by that name, who settled there before the Revolution. For a time he lived in Mobile, Ala., but later he moved to Louisiana. Another prominent, but earlier family, was that of François Reggio, who was a member of the first Cabildo, or Council, in 1796. His granddaughter was the mother of the famous Civil War General, Pierre Gustave Toutant Beauregard. (See Hamilton Basso's Life of Beauregard). We do not know whether the Louisiana Reggio was related to the Admiral Reggio who was commander of the Spanish Squadron which fought Admiral Knowles in the West Indies in 1748. (See Stone, W. L., *Life and Times of Sir W. J. Johnson*, 2 vols., Albany, 1865, Vol. I, p. 369). Two other pioneer Italians in Louisiana were the Rev. Lupiano, who settled there in 1773, and one Mr. Istaffi, who was first in command. (*Georgia Gazette*, February 28, 1765.)

Our most intriguing and mysterious find regarding the emigration of Italians to New France is in connection with the proposed transportation of 400 Italian families to Louisiana in 1720.

As we know, John Law sought immigrants for his Mississippi Company in France, Switzerland, Germany and Italy. (Lavisse, E., *Histoire de France*, Vol. 8, pp. 35-36). In Italy a small group of men headed by one Chevalier de Fontana advanced and risked large sums of money for the transportation. Actually some 250 persons left Genoa on May, 1720, on the 300-ton ship "Our Lady of the Conception," Captain Vincent Blanc, master, directed to Agden, France. Whether the ship proceeded to Louisiana we have not been able to ascertain. (Extrait des Registres de la Chancellerie du Consulat de France à Gennes, (sic) Fol. 242. MS, *Bibliotèque Nationale*, Paris.) On this planned emigration to Louisiana there are in the National Library of Paris two other documents of which we have been able to obtain photographic copies. They are a six-page complaint by Fontana and a letter from Cardinal Gualterio, reproduced, in part, on the following page. Whether or not the Italians came over in large numbers at that time we have not been able to find out. The matter certainly deserves further investigation. (See also Chapter Twenty-One regarding the craftsmen who settled in Louisiana after 1751.)

MAIN ENTRANCE TO FORT CHAMBLY, QUEBEC, CANADA
Notice the name Carignan on the upper left corner. (Courtesy, *The Custodian, Fort Chambly*)

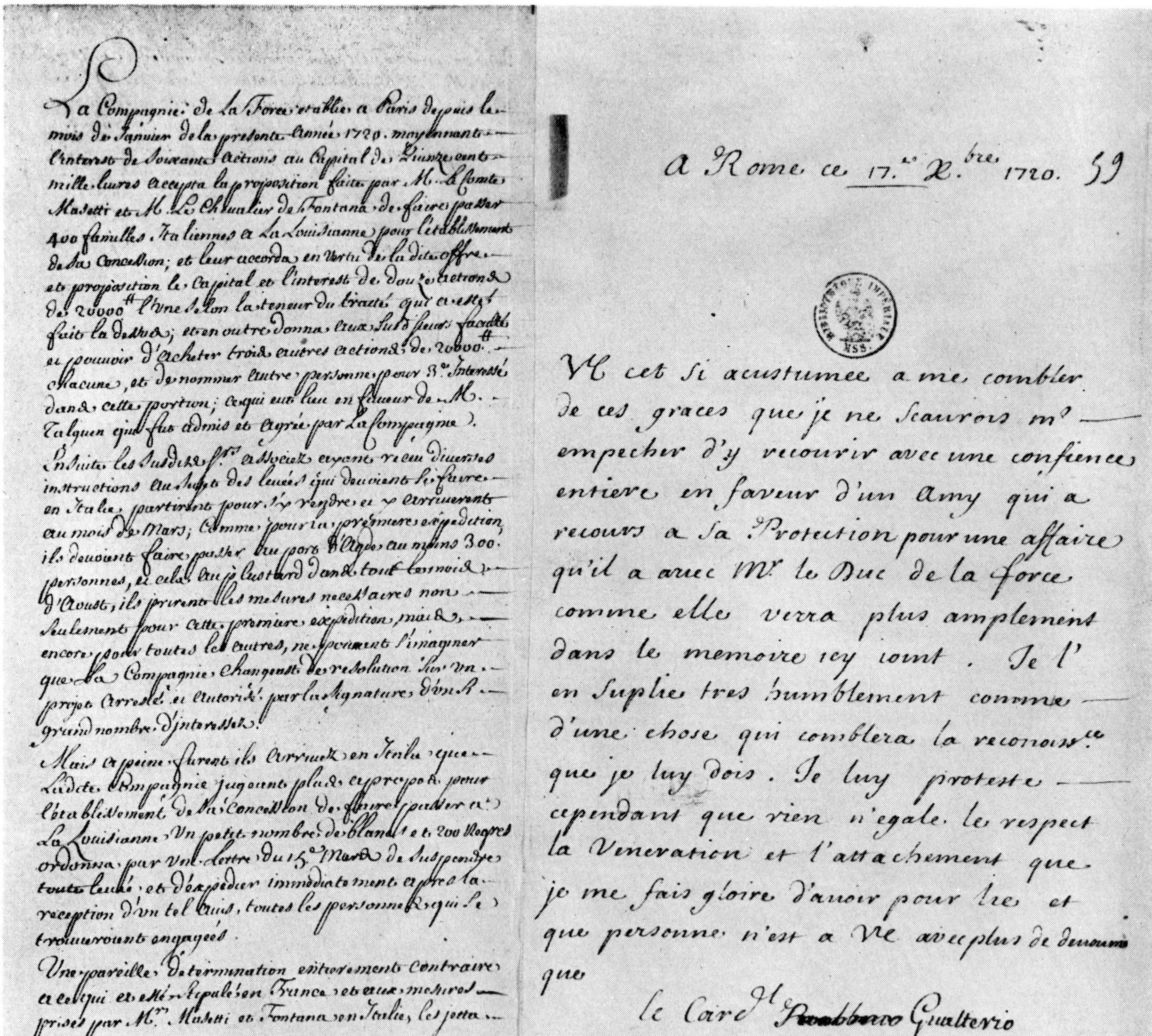

La Compagnie de la Force establie a Paris depuis le mois de Janvier de la presente Année 1720. moyennant l'interest de Soixante Actions au Capital de Quinze cent mille livres accepta la proposition faite par M. le Comte Masetti et M. le Chevalier de Fontana de faire passer 400 familles Italiennes a La Louisianne pour l'etablissement de sa Concession; et leur accorda en vertu de la dite offre et proposition le Capital et l'interest de douze actions de 20000# l'une selon la teneur du traité qui a esté fait la dessus; et en outre donna aux susd. sieurs faculté et pouvoir d'acheter trois autres actions de 20000# chacune, et de nommer autre personne pour S[r]. Interessé dans cette portion; cequi eut lieu en faveur de M. Talguen qui fut admis et agrée par La Compagnie.

Ensuite les susdits S[rs]. associez ayant receu diverses instructions au sujet des levées qui devoient se faire en Italie, partirent pour s'y rendre, et y arriverent au mois de Mars; Comme pour la premiere expedition ils devoient faire passer au port [illegible] au moins 300. personnes, et cela au plus tard dans tout le mois d'Aoust, ils prirent les mesures necessaires non seulement pour cette premiere expedition, mais encore pour toutes les autres, ne pouvant s'imaginer que La Compagnie changeroit de resolution sur un projet arresté et autorisé par la signature d'un grand nombre d'interessez.

Mais a peine furent ils arrivez en Italie que Ladite Compagnie jugeant plus a propos pour l'etablissement de sa Concession de faire passer a La Louisianne un petit nombre de blancs et 200 Negres ordonna par une lettre du 15.e Mars de suspendre toute levée, et d'expedier immediatement apres la reception d'un tel avis, toutes les personnes qui se trouveroient engagées.

Une pareille determination entierement contraire a celle qui estoit stipulée en France et aux mesures prises par M[rs]. Masetti et Fontana en Italie, les jetta

A Rome ce 17.e X.[bre] 1720. 59

V.E. est si acustumee a me combler de ses graces que je ne scaurois m'empecher d'y recourir avec une confience entiere en faveur d'un Amy qui a recours a sa Protection pour une affaire qu'il a avec M[r]. le Duc de la force comme elle verra plus amplement dans le memoire cy ioint. Je l'en Suplie tres humblement comme d'une chose qui comblera la reconoiss[ce] que je luy dois. Je luy proteste cependant que rien n'egale le respect la Veneration et l'attachement que je me fais gloire d'auoir pour V.E. et que personne n'est a V.E. aveeplus de deuouem[t] que

le Card.[l] ~~Scabbarco~~ Gualterio

Two pages from the Manuscript Collection of the Bibliotèque Nationale, Paris, regarding the proposed transportation of 400 Italian families to Louisiana in 1720. (*Left*) The first page of a six-page complaint by Chevalier de Fontana. Notice the 5th and 6th lines reading "de faire passer 400 familles Italiennes à La Louisianne pur l'etablissement de sa concession." (*Right*) A letter from Cardinal Gualterio supporting Fontana's claims. (Courtesy, *Dr. G. P. Ravera*, Turin, Italy)

CHAPTER FIVE

IN THE ENGLISH-SPEAKING COLONIES IN THE XVII CENTURY

In the Introduction, on page eleven, we stated: "In the *Return of Aliens in London in* 1567 we find, for instance, such names of Italian residents as Fox, Pickering, Gillam, Moore, Fortune, Kennythe, Rise, Pitcher, Benson, and so on. That they were Italians there is no doubt. We do not know, of course, if any of those Italians with strictly English names, or their children, ever came to America. But, if they did, is there an expert in the world who could single out their descendants in the 1790 census?" Who, for instance, would have been able to identify one Symn, who died at Warwick River, near Jamestown, in 1623, as an Italian, if we did not find his nationality next to his name? (Hotten, J. C., *The Original List of Persons of Quality,* London, 1874, p. 235.)

By the same token, who can tell us whether the Symn who died in 1623 was related to one Benjamin Symnes, who before 1648 endowed a free school in Virginia "With two hundred acres of land, a good house, forty milch cows and other appurtenances"? (Winsor, *Narrative and Critical History of America,* Vol. III, p. 147.) Another Symnes, incidentally, was a member of the Continental Congress and Chief Justice of New Jersey a century later; his daughter was the wife of President W. H. Harrison. Of course, we are not claiming any relationship between Chief Justice Symnes and the Italian Symn, but, on the other hand, who can deny that there was one? We happen to mention it only as a further proof of how hard it is to tell one's nationality by one's name.

One thing, however, we know; namely, that before and after the Reformation numerous Italians had settled or lived temporarily in England, where some of them married into English families. Some of them were connected with the Catholic Church (before the Reformation); others were artists, musicians, merchants, writers, educators. Men like Cornelio Vitelli, the earliest teacher of Greek at Oxford, or Polydore Virgil, the author of *Historia Anglica,* which he wrote at Henry VII's behest. Others were religious refugees, like Michael Angelo Florio, the father of Montaigne's translator, who was minister of the Italian church in London in 1550. Other outstanding Italians in England shortly before or during Elizabeth's reign were Acontius, Alberico Gentili, Petruccio Ubaldini, Sir Horatio Pallavicino, Cesare Adelmare (the father of Sir Julius Caesar), Thomas Lupo, all men of renown, whose biographical sketches can be found in the *Dictionary of National Biography* of London. Another immigrant was one Ciampanti, the great-grandfather of John Champante, who was appointed Agent of the Province of New York in 1699.

SIR HORATIO PALLAVICINO
A painting in the House of Lords, London, England, burned in part in 1834. From Litta's *Famiglie Celebri Italiane,* Vol. IV. (Courtesy, *New York Public Library*)

Both the Pallavicino and Caesar families were connected, directly or indirectly, with the establishment of the Virginia Company of London. As shown in the facsimiles reproduced on page 98, Edward Palavicine and Toby Palavicine were shareholders, or "adventurers," in the company. (Toby, in 1606, incidentally, married the daughter of Oliver Cromwell, the Protector's uncle). Edward Palavicine was one of the commissioners appointed by James I to create a new form of government for Virginia in 1624. Sir Julius Caesar also was appointed a commissioner at the same time. He was a member of the Privy Council, chancellor of the exchequer in 1606, and master of the rolls from 1614 to 1636. He "married Dorcas Martin, sister of Captain John Martin, one of the first councillors at Jamestown and the owner of 'Brandon' on James River. A John Caesar obtained a grant of land in King and Queen County in Virginia in 1690." (*Tyler's Quarterly,* Vol. 8, p. 273.)

Albino, or Albiano, Lupo, another shareholder of Italian birth or extraction, owned two and a half shares in 1620. At one time he and his wife owned 400 acres of land in Virginia. Lieutenant Lupo, one of the earliest English officers in the Colonies, arrived on the *Swan* in 1610. He was then 40 years old. His wife, Elizabeth, aged 28, came in the *George* in 1616. Their daughter, Temperance Lupo, was born in Virginia in 1620/21. The records show two more Lupos, Philip, aged 42, who arrived in the *George* in 1621 and William, who died in Virginia in 1623. (Hotten, *op. cit.*, p. 185 ff.)

It should not be necessary here to dwell at length on the Taliaferro family, the Italian origins of which seem to be well established. As early, or as late, as 1786, members of that family knew little about their ancestors, for in that year, George Wythe, the signer of the Declaration of Independence, who had married Elizabeth Taliaferro, asked Thomas Jefferson to trace her ancestors in Italy. Jefferson was at that time in Europe and did all he could to find the right information, but, in our opinion, he failed. According to Mr. William B. McGroarty (*William and Mary Quarterly,* April 1924, pp. 191, ff.) the family goes back to one Bartolomeo Taliaferro, a native of Venice who settled in London in the reign of Elizabeth, whom he served as a musician. He died in London in 1602. Most likely he was the same Bartholmewe Talefere whose name we have found in the *Return of Aliens in London in* 1567. (See facsimile on page 12, *ante.*) His grandson, or great-grandson, Robert, was born in 1635 and came to Virginia in 1655.

Also well known is the Fonda family which is said to have hailed originally from Genoa by way of Holland, coming to America in 1642. They settled near Albany. (W. A. Williams, *Early American Families,* Philadelphia, 1916, p. 24.) The family soon became so numerous that during the Revolution at least 49 persons named Fonda, Fondas, Fondey, and exclusive of Fonna and Funday, were listed. (*New York in the Revolution,* Office of the State Comptroller, Albany, 1941, Vol. I.)

Another famous pioneer family of Italian extraction was that of the Danas. Francis Dana, a member of the Continental Congress from 1776 to 1778, America's first minister to Russia, and Chief Justice of Massachusetts, did not know much about his Italian origin. Philip Mazzei called his attention to it, as we learn from a letter from Mazzei to Thomas Adams, dated June 10, 1780, now in the archives of the Virginia Historical Society. But Dana, as he noted in a postscript in his own handwriting to Mazzei's letter, did not care. All he was proud of was to be an American. As for his alleged French ancestry (See Spooner, W. F., *Historic Families of America,* Vol. III, p. 47), the name clearly is not of French origin. D'Anna, however, is common in Italy.

The same thing may be said of the name Rossi, which in America occasionally became Ross. Mr. Howard F. Barker, however, is mistaken in considering Rossi a French name, possibly because he found it in some list of French soldiers during the last century. (*Annual Report of the American Historical Association,* 1931, p. 149.) Rossi is nothing but Italian. (Pellegrino Rossi, the dean of the law school of the College de France, was born at Carrara, Italy.)

Were one to look for names that seem of Italian origin, and probably they were, one will find plenty of them in the early records of America. Names like Basse (Jeremiah

JAMESTOWN, VA., IN 1622
(From an old Dutch print)

Basse was governor of New Jersey in the 17th century); Amory; Benzio, a resident of New Haven in 1654; Carrico, in Maryland; Polentine, a burgess at Jamestown in 1624; Claude Ghiselin, who petitioned the King of England in 1621 for a concession in the Virginia Company; other persons also named Ghiselin who distinguished themselves in the colonies during the 17th and 18th century, hailing from Rouen, France; John Donne, the poet and divine, who was a shareholder in the Virginia Company; and many others whom we prefer not to add as their inclusion would be simply a matter of speculation. The same thing may be said about the antecedents of Paul Revere, or Sidney Lanier.

Limiting our inquiry to positive evidence, we know that a group of Venetian glassworkers arrived in 1622 to establish a glass factory; that another Venetian, named Cesare Alberti, landed in New Amsterdam (New York) in 1635 and became a landowner in Manhattan and in Long Island; that Italian immigrants were allowed to own land in Maryland in 1649; that 300 Piedmontese Protestants (Waldenses) landed in New Amsterdam in 1657; finally, that at least one prominent Huguenot minister of Italian origin, Prioleau, landed at Charleston in 1680. In the following chapter we shall deal with those who came in the 18th century.

SIR JULIUS CAESAR, KNT

Judge of the High Court of Admiralty, Master of the Rolls, Chancellor of the Exchequer and a Privy Councillor to Kings James and Charles the First. From the *Life of Sir Julius Caesar* by Edmund Lodge. (Courtesy, *New York Public Library*)

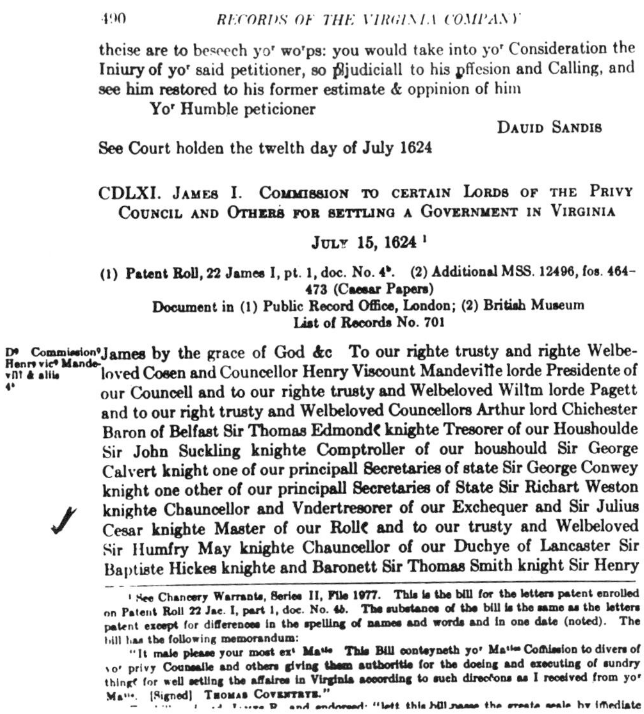

490 RECORDS OF THE VIRGINIA COMPANY

theise are to beseech yor wo'ps: you would take into yor Consideration the Iniury of yor said petitioner, so pjudiciall to his pffesion and Calling, and see him restored to his former estimate & oppinion of him

Yor Humble peticioner

DAUID SANDIS

See Court holden the twelth day of July 1624

CDLXI. JAMES I. COMMISSION TO CERTAIN LORDS OF THE PRIVY COUNCIL AND OTHERS FOR SETTLING A GOVERNMENT IN VIRGINIA

JULY 15, 1624 [1]

(1) Patent Roll, 22 James I, pt. 1, doc. No. 4b. (2) Additional MSS. 12496, fos. 464–473 (Caesar Papers)

Document in (1) Public Record Office, London; (2) British Museum

List of Records No. 701

D9 Commission9 Henr9 vic9 Mandevill & aliis 4b

James by the grace of God &c To our righte trusty and righte Welbeloved Cosen and Councellor Henry Viscount Mandevitte lorde Presidente of our Councell and to our righte trusty and Welbeloved Willm lorde Pagett and to our right trusty and Welbeloved Councellors Arthur lord Chichester Baron of Belfast Sir Thomas Edmondꝭ knighte Tresorer of our Houshoulde Sir John Suckling knighte Comptroller of our houshould Sir George Calvert knight one of our principall Secretaries of state Sir George Conwey knight one other of our principall Secretaries of State Sir Richart Weston knighte Chauncellor and Vndertresorer of our Exchequer and Sir Julius Cesar knighte Master of our Rollꝭ and to our trusty and Welbeloved Sir Humfry May knighte Chauncellor of our Duchye of Lancaster Sir Baptiste Hickes knighte and Baronett Sir Thomas Smith knight Sir Henry

[1] See Chancery Warrants, Series II, File 1977. This is the bill for the letters patent enrolled on Patent Roll 22 Jac. I, part 1, doc. No. 4b. The substance of the bill is the same as the letters patent except for differences in the spelling of names and words and in one date (noted). The bill has the following memorandum:

"It maie please your most ext Matie This Bill conteyneth yor Maties Comission to divers of yor privy Counsaile and others giving them authoritie for the doeing and executing of sundry thingꝭ for well setling the affaires in Virginia according to such direcĉons as I received from yor Matie. [Signed] THOMAS COVENTRYE."

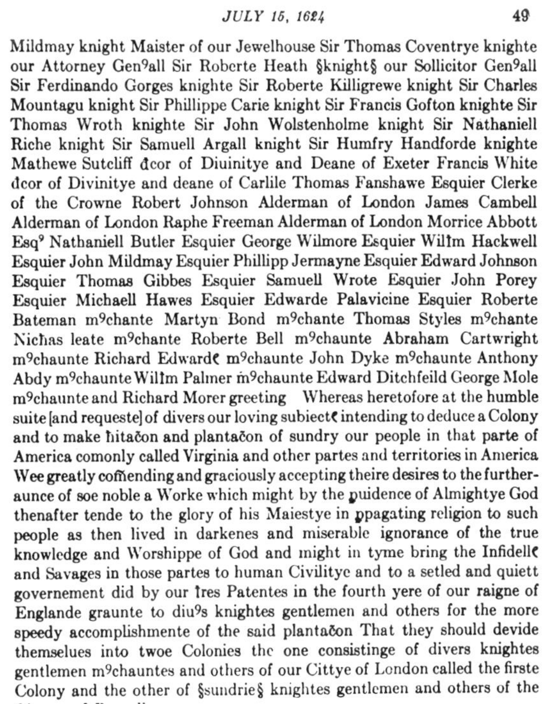

JULY 15, 1624 49

Mildmay knight Maister of our Jewelhouse Sir Thomas Coventrye knighte our Attorney Gen9all Sir Roberte Heath §knight§ our Sollicitor Gen9all Sir Ferdinando Gorges knighte Sir Roberte Killigrewe knight Sir Charles Mountagu knight Sir Phillippe Carie knight Sir Francis Gofton knighte Sir Thomas Wroth knighte Sir John Wolstenholme knight Sir Nathaniell Riche knight Sir Samuell Argall knight Sir Humfry Handforde knighte Mathewe Sutcliff dcor of Diuinitye and Deane of Exeter Francis White dcor of Divinitye and deane of Carlile Thomas Fanshawe Esquier Clerke of the Crowne Robert Johnson Alderman of London James Cambell Alderman of London Raphe Freeman Alderman of London Morrice Abbott Esq9 Nathaniell Butler Esquier George Wilmore Esquier Willm Hackwell Esquier John Mildmay Esquier Phillipp Jermayne Esquier Edward Johnson Esquier Thomas Gibbes Esquier Samuell Wrote Esquier John Porey Esquier Michaell Hawes Esquier Edwarde Palavicine Esquier Roberte Bateman m9chante Martyn Bond m9chante Thomas Styles m9chante Nichas leate m9chante Roberte Bell m9chaunte Abraham Cartwright m9chaunte Richard Edwardꝭ m9chaunte John Dyke m9chaunte Anthony Abdy m9chaunte Willm Palmer m9chaunte Edward Ditchfeild George Mole m9chaunte and Richard Morer greeting Whereas heretofore at the humble suite [and requeste] of divers our loving subiectꝭ intending to deduce a Colony and to make hitaĉon and plantaĉon of sundry our people in that parte of America comonly called Virginia and other partes and territories in America Wee greatly comending and graciously accepting theire desires to the furtheraunce of soe noble a Worke which might by the puidence of Almightye God thenafter tende to the glory of his Maiestye in ppagating religion to such people as then lived in darkenes and miserable ignorance of the true knowledge and Worshippe of God and might in tyme bring the Infidellꝭ and Savages in those partes to human Civilitye and to a setled and quiett governement did by our lres Patentes in the fourth yere of our raigne of Englande graunte to diu9s knightes gentlemen and others for the more speedy accomplishmente of the said plantaĉon That they should devide themselues into twoe Colonies the one consistinge of divers knightes gentlemen m9chauntes and others of our Cittye of London called the firste Colony and the other of §sundrie§ knightes gentlemen and others of the

Two pages from *The Records of the Virginia Company of London* edited by S. M. Kingsbury. The names of Sir Julius Cesar and Edwarde Palavicine, two of the founders of the Virginia Company, are checked on the margins. (Courtesy, *New York Public Library*)

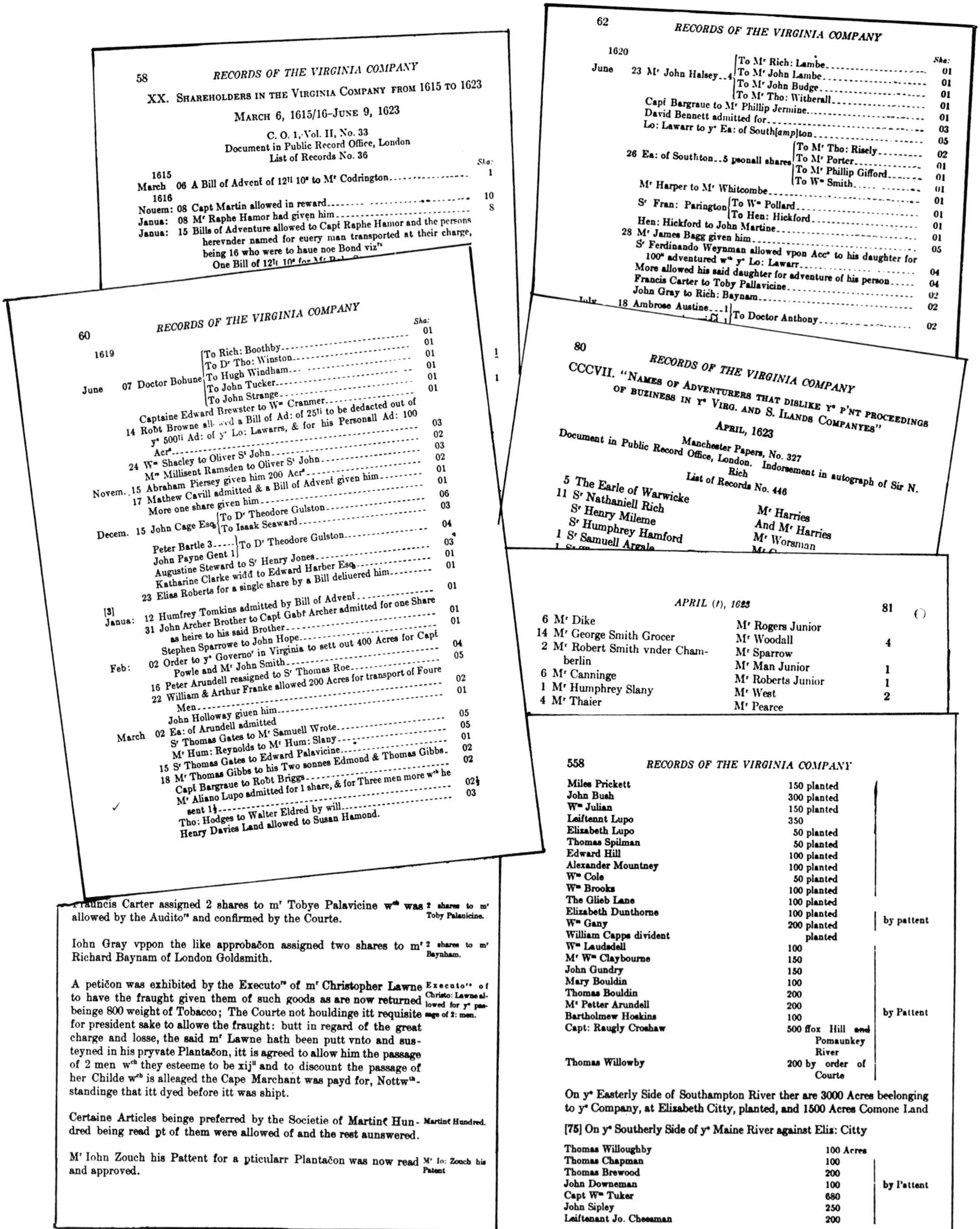

58 RECORDS OF THE VIRGINIA COMPANY

XX. SHAREHOLDERS IN THE VIRGINIA COMPANY FROM 1615 TO 1623

MARCH 6, 1615/16–JUNE 9, 1623

C. O. 1, Vol. II, No. 33
Document in Public Record Office, London
List of Records No. 36

		Sha:
1615 March 06	A Bill of Advent of 12li 10s to Mr Codrington	1
1616 Nouem: 08	Capt Martin allowed in reward	10
Janua: 08	Mr Raphe Hamor had given him	8
Janua: 15	Bills of Adventure allowed to Capt Raphe Hamor and the persons herevnder named for euery man transported at their charge, being 16 who were to haue noe Bond vizt	
	One Bill of 12li 10s for Mr R...	

60 RECORDS OF THE VIRGINIA COMPANY

		Sha:
1619 June 07	Doctor Bohune — To Rich: Boothby	01
	To Dr Tho: Winston	01
	To Hugh Windham	01
	To John Tucker	01
	To John Strange	01
	Captaine Edward Brewster to Wm Cranmer	01
14	Robt Browne all...d a Bill of Ad: of 25li to be dedacted out of ye 500li Ad: of ye Lo: Lawarrs, & for his Personall Ad: 100 Acrs	03
24	Wm Shacley to Oliver St John	02
	Mrs Millisent Ramsden to Oliver St John	03
Novem. 15	Abraham Piersey given him 200 Acrs	02
17	Mathew Cavill admitted & a Bill of Advent given him	01
	More one share given him	01
Decem. 15	John Cage Esq — To Dr Theodore Gulston	06
	To Isaak Seaward	03
	Peter Bartle 3 / John Payne Gent 1 — To Dr Theodore Gulston	04
	Augustine Steward to Sr Henry Jones	03
	Katharine Clarke widd to Edward Harber Esq	01
23	Elias Roberts for a single share by a Bill deliuered him	01
[3] Janua: 12	Humfrey Tomkins admitted by Bill of Advent	01
31	John Archer Brother to Capt Gabr Archer admitted for one Share as heire to his said Brother	01
	Stephen Sparrowe to John Hope	01
Feb: 02	Order to ye Governor in Virginia to sett out 400 Acres for Capt Powle and Mr John Smith	04
16	Peter Arundell resigned to Sr Thomas Roe	05
22	William & Arthur Franke allowed 200 Acres for transport of Foure Men	02
	John Holloway giuen him	01
March 02	Ea: of Arundell admitted	05
	Sr Thomas Gates to Mr Samuell Wrote	05
	Mr Hum: Reynolds to Mr Hum: Slany	01
15	Sr Thomas Gates to Edward Palavicine	02
18	Mr Thomas Gibbs to his Two sonnes Edmond & Thomas Gibbs	02
	Capt Bargraue to Robt Briggs	
	Mr Aliano Lupo admitted for 1 share, & for Three men more wch he sent 1½	02½
	Tho: Hodges to Walter Eldred by will	03
	Henry Davies Land allowed to Susan Hamond.	

62 RECORDS OF THE VIRGINIA COMPANY

		Sha:
1620 June 23	Mr John Halsey 4 — To Mr Rich: Lambe	01
	To Mr John Lambe	01
	To Mr John Budge	01
	To Mr Tho: Witherall	01
	Capt Bargraue to Mr Phillip Jermine	01
	David Bennett admitted for	01
	Lo: Lawarr to ye Ea: of South[amp]ton	03
26	Ea: of Southton 5 psonall shares — To Mr Tho: Risely	05
	To Mr Porter	02
	To Mr Phillip Gifford	01
	To Wm Smith	01
	Mr Harper to Mr Whitcombe	01
	Sr Fran: Parington — To Wm Pollard	01
	To Hen: Hickford	01
	Hen: Hickford to John Martine	01
28	Mr James Bagg given him	01
	Sr Ferdinando Weynman allowed vpon Acct to his daughter for 100li adventured wth ye Lo: Lawarr	05
	More allowed his said daughter for adventure of his person	04
	Francis Carter to Toby Pallavicine	04
	John Gray to Rich: Baynam	02
July 18	Ambrose Austine 1 — To Doctor Anthony	02

80 RECORDS OF THE VIRGINIA COMPANY

CCCVII. "NAMES OF ADVENTURERS THAT DISLIKE Ye P'NT PROCEEDINGS OF BUZINESS IN Ye VIRG. AND S. ILANDS COMPANYES"

APRIL, 1623

Document in Public Record Office, London. Manchester Papers, No. 327
Indorsement in autograph of Sir N. Rich
List of Records No. 446

5 The Earle of Warwicke	
11 Sr Nathaniell Rich	Mr Harries
Sr Henry Mileme	And Mr Harries
Sr Humphrey Hamford	Mr Worsman
1 Sr Samuell Argale	

APRIL (?), 1623 81

6 Mr Dike	Mr Rogers Junior	
14 Mr George Smith Grocer	Mr Woodall	4
2 Mr Robert Smith vnder Cham-berlin	Mr Sparrow	
	Mr Man Junior	1
6 Mr Canninge	Mr Roberts Junior	1
1 Mr Humphrey Slany	Mr West	2
4 Mr Thaier	Mr Pearce	

Francis Carter assigned 2 shares to mr Tobye Palavicine wch was allowed by the Auditors and confirmed by the Courte. — *2 shares to mr Toby Palauicine.*

Iohn Gray vppon the like approbacon assigned two shares to mr Richard Baynam of London Goldsmith. — *2 shares to mr Baynham.*

A peticon was exhibited by the Executors of mr Christopher Lawne to have the fraught given them of such goods as are now returned beinge 800 weight of Tobacco; The Courte not houldinge itt requisite for president sake to allowe the fraught: butt in regard of the great charge and losse, the said mr Lawne hath been putt vnto and susteyned in his pryvate Plantacon, itt is agreed to allow him the passage of 2 men wch they esteeme to be xijli and to discount the passage of her Childe wch is alleaged the Cape Marchant was payd for, Nottwth-standinge that itt dyed before itt was shipt. — *Executors of Christo: Lawne allowed for ye passage of 2: men.*

Certaine Articles beinge preferred by the Societie of Martins Hundred being read pt of them were allowed of and the rest aunswered. — *Martins Hundred.*

Mr Iohn Zouch his Pattent for a pticularr Plantacon was now read and approved. — *Mr Io: Zouch his Patent*

558 RECORDS OF THE VIRGINIA COMPANY

Miles Prickett	150 planted	
John Bush	300 planted	
Wm Julian	150 planted	
Leiftennt Lupo	350	
Elizabeth Lupo	50 planted	
Thomas Spilman	50 planted	
Edward Hill	100 planted	
Alexander Mountney	100 planted	
Wm Cole	50 planted	
Wm Brooks	100 planted	
The Glieb Lane	100 planted	
Elizabeth Dunthorne	100 planted	by pattent
Wm Gany	200 planted	
William Capps divident	planted	
Wm Laudsdell	100	
Mr Wm Claybourne	150	
John Gundry	150	
Mary Bouldin	100	
Thomas Bouldin	200	
Mr Petter Arundell	200	by Pattent
Bartholmew Hoskins	100	
Capt: Raugly Croshaw	500 ffox Hill and Pomaunkey River	
Thomas Willowby	200 by order of Courte	

On ye Easterly Side of Southampton River ther are 3000 Acres beelonging to ye Company, at Elizabeth Citty, planted, and 1500 Acres Comone Land

[75] On ye Southerly Side of ye Maine River against Eliz: Citty

Thomas Willoughby	100 Acres	
Thomas Chapman	100	
Thomas Brewood	200	
John Downeman	100	by Pattent
Capt Wm Tuker	680	
John Sipley	250	
Leiftenant Jo. Cheesman	200	

Several pages from *The Records of the Virginia Company of London,* edited by S. M. Kingsbury, showing the names of Toby Palavicine, Edward Palavicine, Aliano (Leiftenant) Lupo, and Elizabeth Lupo, as shareholders in the Virginia Company and landowners in Virginia in 1619 and 1620. That is, before the Pilgrim Fathers landed at Plymouth Rock. (Courtesy, *New York Public Library*)

VENETIAN GLASSWORKERS IN VIRGINIA IN 1622

Before the Pilgrim Fathers landed at Plymouth Rock, Italian artisans were already at work in Virginia.

Most likely, the first Italians to settle in the Old Dominion came over together with the French and Swiss skilled workers who arrived to produce silk and grapes, for we know that in those days both the Swiss and the French depended on Italian immigrants for the cultivation of mulberry trees and silk worms. (See, Savorgnan di Brazzà, *Tecnici ed Artigiani Italiani in Francia,* Rome, 1942, pp. 47-48.) It is hard to understand, therefore, how Switzerland and France could afford to provide a type of experts which they did not have for themselves; unless of course they were immigrants from Italy.

At any rate, we have definite proof of the arrival at Jamestown about 1621, or 1622, of another type of experts which England lacked in those days, namely, glassworkers.

According to John Strype's *Annals of the Reformation,* the first man to set up a glasshouse in London about 1580 was a Venetian named James Verselyn. Forty years later the English had not made much progress, if any at all, in that field, and were compelled to lure Venetian glassworkers to establish factories in England. Some of those workers went as far north as Scotland, and a few of them even came to Virginia. That much we learn from the reports of the Venetian Ambassador in London, Girolamo Lando, to his Government in Venice. Lando tried to convince the Venetians to return home, but he succeeded only in part. "The Republic," he sadly commented, referring to his own country, "has no more bitter enemies here than some of her own subjects." (*Calendar of State Papers,* Vol. 17, pp. 100 and 309.)

By 1622 some 16 glassworkers, "Italians, and others," had already arrived in Virginia, where they soon erected and operated a glasshouse, but some of them did not get along with the English colonists. According to George Sandys, the colonial treasurer (writing in 1624), the Italians were disorderly and one of them, Vincenzio, "had cracked the furnace with an iron bar."

What became of those Venetians we do not know exactly, with the exception that in February 1625, five of them were still working at the glasshouse. (*Virginia Magazine of History,* Vol. 23, p. 17.) One of them, Bernardo, had wife and child at Jamestown. (Hotten, *op. cit.,* p. 235.) Some of them may have returned to Europe, others remained, married and died in the country.

To us their coming is of importance, for it shows that in proportion to their number they contributed more than the English colonists to the founding and development of new industries in America.

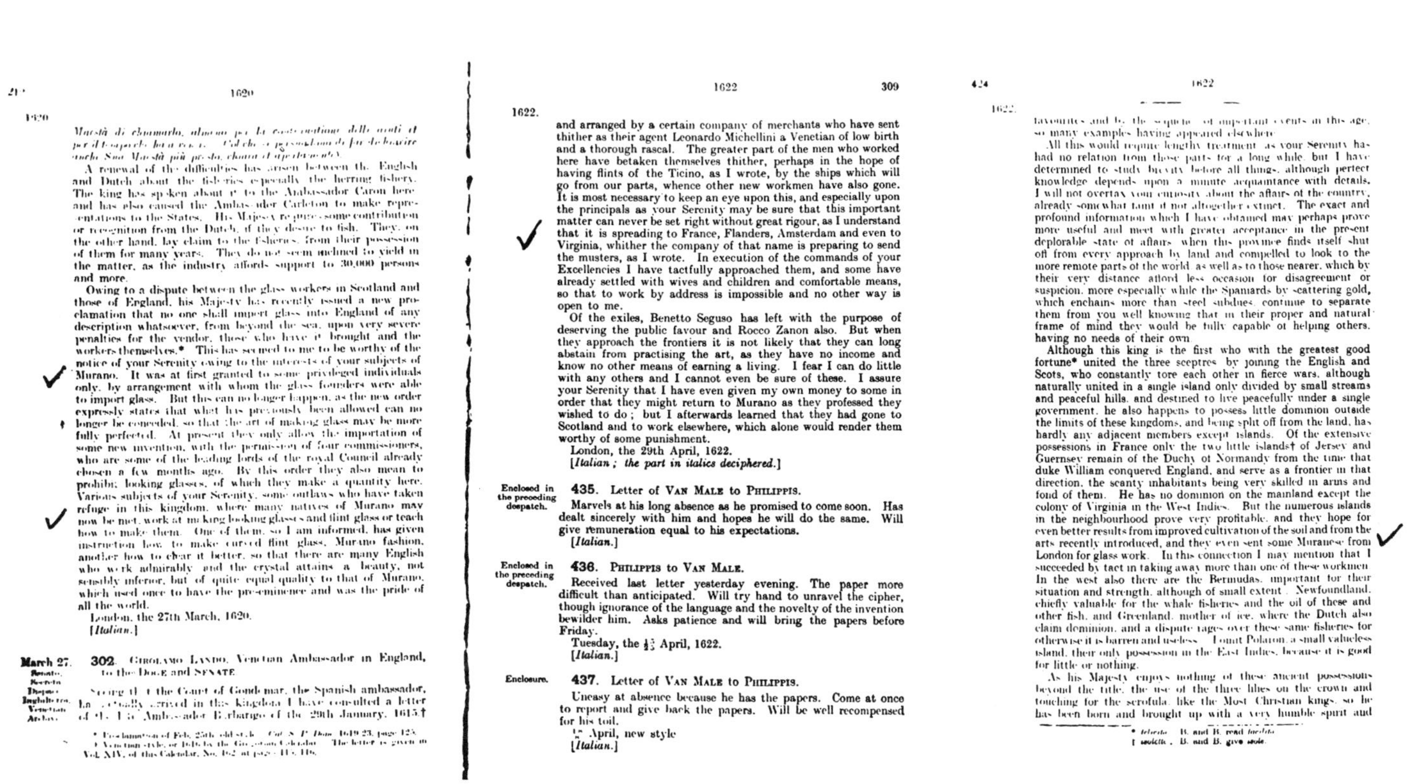
21[illegible] 1620

1620.

Maestà di chiamarlo, almeno per la [illegible] delle [illegible] et per il [illegible] Sua Maestà più presto, [illegible]

A renewal of the difficulties has arisen between the English and Dutch about the fisheries especially the herring fishery. The king has spoken about it to the Ambassador Caron here and has also caused the Ambassador Carleton to make representations to the States. His Majesty requires some contribution or recognition from the Dutch, if they desire to fish. They, on the other hand, lay claim to the fisheries, from their possession of them for many years. They do not seem inclined to yield in the matter, as the industry affords support to 30,000 persons and more.

Owing to a dispute between the glass workers in Scotland and those of England, his Majesty has recently issued a new proclamation that no one shall import glass into England of any description whatsoever, from beyond the sea, upon very severe penalties for the vendor, those who have it brought and the workers themselves.* This has seemed to me to be worthy of the notice of your Serenity owing to the interests of your subjects of Murano. It was at first granted to some privileged individuals only, by arrangement with whom the glass founders were able to import glass. But this can no longer happen, as the new order expressly states that what has previously been allowed can no longer be conceded, so that the art of making glass may be more fully perfected. At present they only allow the importation of some new invention, with the permission of four commissioners, who are some of the leading lords of the royal Council already chosen a few months ago. By this order they also mean to prohibit looking glasses, of which they make a quantity here. Various subjects of your Serenity, some outlaws who have taken refuge in this kingdom, where many natives of Murano may now be met, work at making looking glasses and flint glass or teach how to make them. One of them, so I am informed, has given instruction how to make curved flint glass, Murano fashion, another how to clear it better, so that there are many English who work admirably and the crystal attains a beauty, not sensibly inferior, but of quite equal quality to that of Murano, which used once to have the pre-eminence and was the pride of all the world.

London, the 27th March, 1620.

[*Italian.*]

March 27. Senato, Secreta, Dispacci, Inghilterra, Venetian Archives. **302**. GIROLAMO LANDO, Venetian Ambassador in England, to the DOGE and SENATE.

Seeing that the Court of Gondomar, the Spanish ambassador, [illegible] actually arrived in this kingdom I have consulted a letter of [illegible] Ambassador Barbarigo of the 29th January, 1615.†

* Proclamation of Feb. 25th, old style. *Cal. S. P. Dom.* 1619-23, page 125.
† Venetian style, or 1616 by the Gregorian Calendar. The letter is given in Vol. XIV. of this Calendar, No. 162 at pages 115, 116.

1622 309

1622.

and arranged by a certain company of merchants who have sent thither as their agent Leonardo Michellini a Venetian of low birth and a thorough rascal. The greater part of the men who worked here have betaken themselves thither, perhaps in the hope of having flints of the Ticino, as I wrote, by the ships which will go from our parts, whence other new workmen have also gone. It is most necessary to keep an eye upon this, and especially upon the principals as your Serenity may be sure that this important matter can never be set right without great rigour, as I understand that it is spreading to France, Flanders, Amsterdam and even to Virginia, whither the company of that name is preparing to send the musters, as I wrote. In execution of the commands of your Excellencies I have tactfully approached them, and some have already settled with wives and children and comfortable means, so that to work by address is impossible and no other way is open to me.

Of the exiles, Benetto Seguso has left with the purpose of deserving the public favour and Rocco Zanon also. But when they approach the frontiers it is not likely that they can long abstain from practising the art, as they have no income and know no other means of earning a living. I fear I can do little with any others and I cannot even be sure of these. I assure your Serenity that I have even given my own money to some in order that they might return to Murano as they professed they wished to do; but I afterwards learned that they had gone to Scotland and to work elsewhere, which alone would render them worthy of some punishment.

London, the 29th April, 1622.

[*Italian; the part in italics deciphered.*]

Enclosed in the preceding despatch. **435**. Letter of VAN MALE to PHILIPPIS.

Marvels at his long absence as he promised to come soon. Has dealt sincerely with him and hopes he will do the same. Will give remuneration equal to his expectations.

[*Italian.*]

Enclosed in the preceding despatch. **436**. PHILIPPIS to VAN MALE.

Received last letter yesterday evening. The paper more difficult than anticipated. Will try hand to unravel the cipher, though ignorance of the language and the novelty of the invention bewilder him. Asks patience and will bring the papers before Friday.

Tuesday, the $\frac{19}{29}$ April, 1622.

[*Italian.*]

Enclosure. **437**. Letter of VAN MALE to PHILIPPIS.

Uneasy at absence because he has the papers. Come at once to report and give back the papers. Will be well recompensed for his toil.

[illegible] April, new style

[*Italian.*]

424 1622

1622.

favourites and by the sequence of important events in this age, so many examples having appeared elsewhere.

All this would require lengthy treatment as your Serenity has had no relation from those parts for a long while, but I have determined to study brevity before all things, although perfect knowledge depends upon a minute acquaintance with details. I will not overtax your curiosity about the affairs of the country, already somewhat faint if not altogether extinct. The exact and profound information which I have obtained may perhaps prove more useful and meet with greater acceptance in the present deplorable state of affairs when this province finds itself shut off from every approach by land and compelled to look to the more remote parts of the world as well as to those nearer, which by their very distance afford less occasion for disagreement or suspicion, more especially while the Spaniards by scattering gold, which enchains more than steel subdues, continue to separate them from you well knowing that in their proper and natural frame of mind they would be fully capable of helping others, having no needs of their own.

Although this king is the first who with the greatest good fortune* united the three sceptres by joining the English and Scots, who constantly tore each other in fierce wars, although naturally united in a single island only divided by small streams and peaceful hills, and destined to live peacefully under a single government, he also happens to possess little dominion outside the limits of these kingdoms, and being split off from the land, has hardly any adjacent members except islands. Of the extensive possessions in France only the two little islands† of Jersey and Guernsey remain of the Duchy of Normandy from the time that duke William conquered England, and serve as a frontier in that direction, the scanty inhabitants being very skilled in arms and fond of them. He has no dominion on the mainland except the colony of Virginia in the West Indies. But the numerous islands in the neighbourhood prove very profitable, and they hope for even better results from improved cultivation of the soil and from the arts recently introduced, and they even sent some Muranese from London for glass work. In this connection I may mention that I succeeded by tact in taking away more than one of these workmen. In the west also there are the Bermudas, important for their situation and strength, although of small extent. Newfoundland, chiefly valuable for the whale fisheries and the oil of these and other fish, and Greenland, mother of ice, where the Dutch also claim dominion, and a dispute rages over these same fisheries for otherwise it is barren and useless. I omit Polaron, a small valueless island, their only possession in the East Indies, because it is good for little or nothing.

As his Majesty enjoys nothing of these ancient possessions beyond the title, the use of the three lilies on the crown and touching for the scrofula, like the Most Christian kings, so he has been born and brought up with a very humble spirit and

* *felicità*. B. and B. read *facilità*.
† *isolette*. B. and B. give *isole*.

Three pages from the *Calendar of State Papers, Venetian,* with references to Venetian glass workers in England and Scotland (Vol. 16, p. 212, and Vol. 17, pp. 309 and 424). (Courtesy, *New York Public Library*)

640 *RECORDS OF THE VIRGINIA COMPANY*

So there is 24. saile of Ships, with 500. Mariners in them imployed to these Plantations in this yeere.

Besides, there are now prouiding seuerall Ships in diuers parts of this Kingdome to transport to the Plantations aboue } 500. persons.

And for the greater benefit of the Plantations, these things following haue been here done this yeere.

16 Persons Italians, and others, haue been prouided and sent for the making of Beads for trade in the Countrey with the Natiues, and for making Glasse of all sorts.

57 Young maids haue bin sent to make wiues for the Planters, diuers of which were well married before the comming away of the Ships.

A Magazine hath bin sent of all necessaries for the Colony, to the value of 2000. pound, besides al priuate mens sending goods, which was very ample, Trade being set open for all his Maiesties Subiects.

A Ship called the *Discouery*, hath bin set out for the rich trade of Furres, which both the French, and Hollanders haue yeerely within our precincts, and within 50. leagues of vs.

25. Persons for the building of Boats, Pinnaces and Ships, for the necessary vse of the Colony for fishing, trade, and Discouery, &c.

7. Persons sent for planting the 1000. acres of land giuen to the *East-India Schoole.*

Other occurrents of note.

566 *RECORDS OF THE VIRGINIA COMPANY*

trade wthall, to wch end certen Italians and others to the number of 16 ꝑsons were already sent wch worke is hoped by this to be in a good forwardnes sett vp in aduancement whereof diuers Aduenturers had vnderwritten x^{li} a peece beinge the Some proposed to be paid by each Aduenturo^{r} wch is to be imployed in a Iointe Stocke: So that that perticuler Roll was already come to the Some of 500^{li}.

A second Roll was a Magazine for prouisions of Apparrell and other necessaries whereof the Colony stood in great need ...

DECEMBER 13, 1620 431

Mr Deputy signified that hee had receaved good store of Silkworme seed both out of Fraunce, Italy, and Spaine, and doubted not of much more verie shortlie, soe that their greatest want was of men skillfull in the orderinge of them, wherof they hadd some hope err longe to procure some out of Fraunce by the help of m^{r} Chamberline a man very carefull in y^{t} buisines In the meane time hee acquainted the Courte wth one y^{t} m^{r} Darnelly had ꝓcured for them beinge the servant of m^{r} — Silkwormes brought out of Fraunce C

16455—VOL 1—06——28

(*Above*) Title page of a foreign edition (Amsterdam, 1668) of Neri's "*Ars Vetraria*," the first practical handbook on the art of making glass.

(*Left*) A page from *The Records of the Virginia Company of London*, edited by S. M. Kingsbury, with the reference to the Italians who were sent to America to make beads and "Glasse of all sorts." (Courtesy, *New York Public Library*)

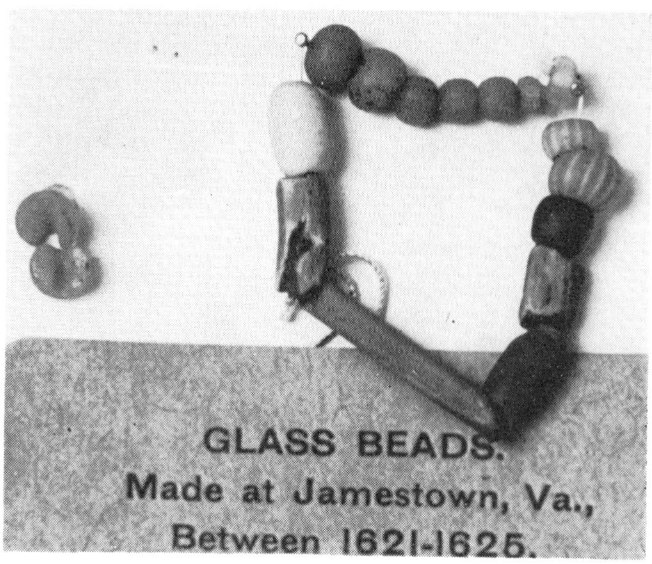

Some of the beads made by the Venetians at Jamestown. (Courtesy, *Philadelphia Museum of Art*)

A VENETIAN LANDOWNER IN MANHATTAN AND BROOKLYN IN 1635

Not even ten years had elapsed from the day the Dutch purchased Manhattan Island from the Indians, when a Venetian sailor, named Cesare Alberti, or Alberto, deserted his ship and settled in the rising New Amsterdam.

Where and when Alberti joined the Dutch crew we do not know, nor is it important. For centuries past, commercial relations between Italy and Holland had been close, both by land and by sea. Just before Alberti's arrival in 1635, Alvise Contarini, the Venetian Ambassador in England, reporting to the Doge and Senate in 1628, wrote that "good treatment and pay are given all along the coast of Flanders to mariners of any race whatever, and at Lubeck they reckon that more than 400 builders of ships and galleys from Provence and Italy have passed through that place." (*Calendar of State Papers, Venetian*, Vol. 20, p. 575.) At that time, we might add, the Dutch fleet that used to visit Leghorn regularly every year, included two ships for Venice (*op. cit.* Vol. 21, pp. 36-39.) Possibly it was on one of those voyages that Alberti joined the Dutch vessel.

Northeast and Southeast corners of Broad Street and Exchange Place, Manhattan, at the close of the 17th century. It was near this site that Alberti owned a house and garden before 1646 when he sold them. (From Valentine's *History of the City of New York*)

A partial view of New Amsterdam, now New York City, about 1667. (From an old print)

Alberti's life in America is of no historical importance, except for its implications regarding other Italian immigrants who may have come over the same way he did. One has indeed but to go through the *Records of the Reformed Dutch Church in New Amsterdam and New York*, to find numerous names which may have been of Italian origin.

Alberti married a Dutch woman in 1642 and became the father of seven children, six of whom were still living at the time of his death in 1655, apparently the victim of an Indian onslaught. His children moved to the interior of Long Island and, later, to the other colonies. One of them, William Alburtus, the son of Pietro (d. 1652) moved to Lawrenceville, near Princeton, N. J., served in the Hunterdon County, N. J., Grand Jury in 1714, and as a constable from 1722 to 1726. Thus he was, in all probability, the first Italian-American to fill a public office. In 1729 he owned 175 acres of land in New Jersey. (*Genealogical Magazine of New Jersey*, October 1938). The other sons also scattered through the colony. At any rate, it has been estimated that at the normal rates of prolification there should be in the United States today upwards of 3,000 descendants, directly or indirectly, of the Venetian pioneer.

Alberti was probably the first producer of tobacco at Wallabout, within the present city limits of Brooklyn, where his name is perpetuated by Alburtis Avenue. He also owned large tracts of land in various parts of Long Island and a house and garden along the canal, or graft, which used to run through what is now Broad Street, in Manhattan's financial district.

As related in Chapter Twenty, a physician by the name of Alberti was active in New York and Philadelphia between 1791 and 1837, but we have not been able to ascertain whether he was a descendant of the Venetian immigrant of 1635.

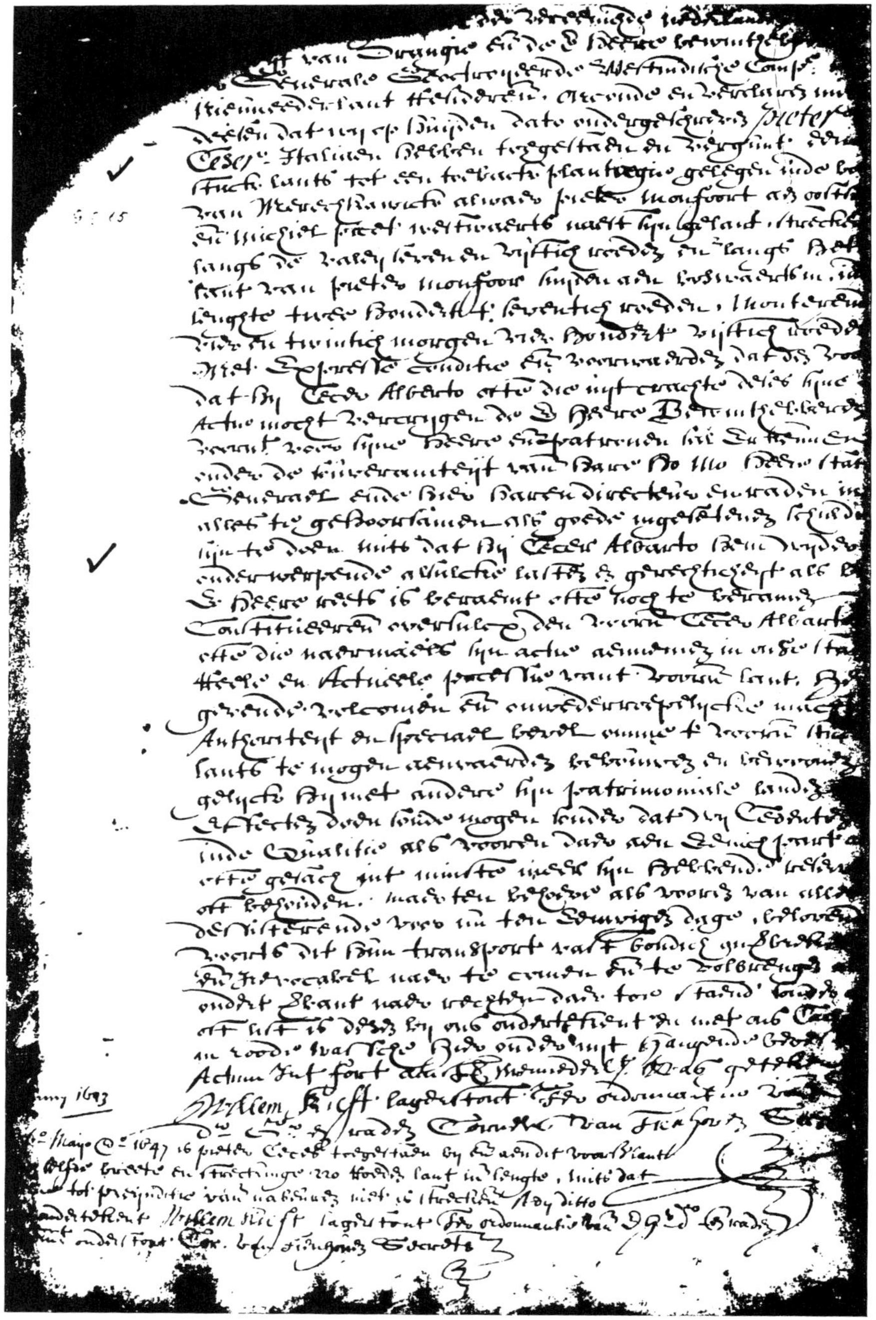

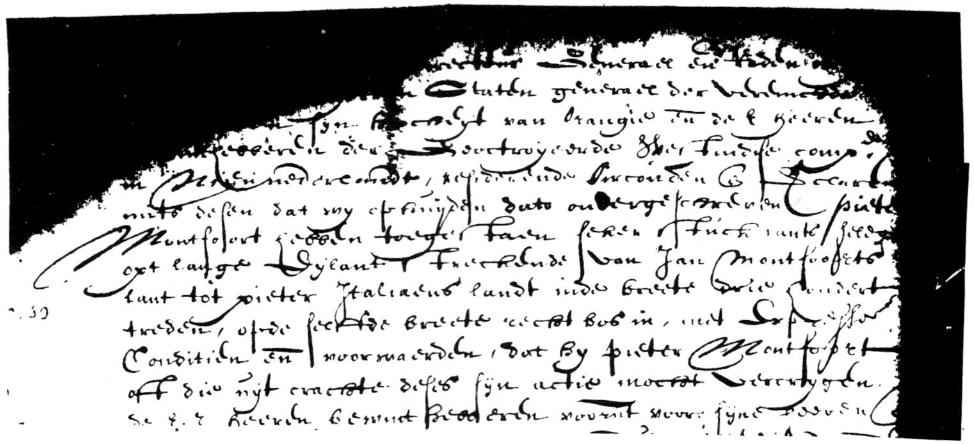

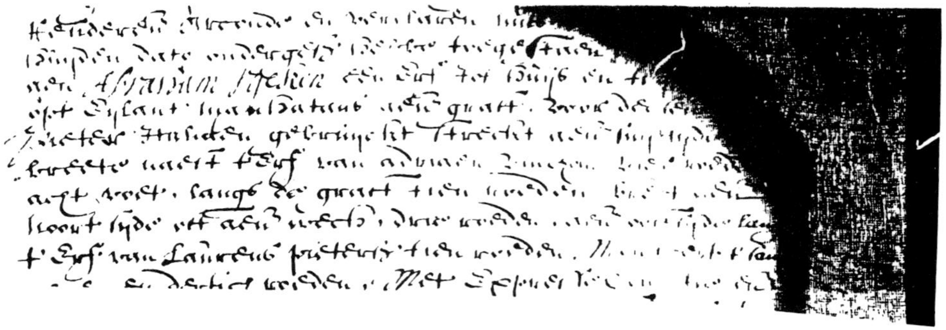

(*Above*) Patent dated May 29, 1641, to Peter Montfoort, on Long Island (Brooklyn), adjoining the property of Peter the Italian. Notice checks near Peter's name on each facsimile. (*Below*) Patent dated Feb. 14, 1646, to Abraham Rycken for a lot at the Graft on Manhattan Island (now Broad Street), heretofore occupied by Caesar Alberti. (*Left*) Patent dated June 17, 1643, by which Alberti was granted a piece of land 57 rods by 270 rods (a rod was equal to 16½ feet) in the bight of Merechkavick on Long Island (12th Ward, Brooklyn). A footnote adds that on May 1, 1647, 220 rods of land adjoining the above width, were granted also to Cesare Alberti. (For an English translation of the deeds see *Documents Relating to the Colonial History of New York,* Vol. XIV, old series, pp. 34 and 47.) (Courtesy, *New York State Library,* Albany.)
On Alberti, see De Forest, L. E. in *Atlantica,* March, 1936; Pyrke, B. A., *Long Island Forum,* August 1943; *N. Y. Genealogical and Biographical Record,* 1869-48: 114-15, besides the two works mentioned in the preceding page.

ITALIANS ALLOWED TO OWN LAND IN MARYLAND IN 1649

In the archives of the *Propaganda Fide* in the Vatican, there is a letter—never published, so far as we know—dated June 1, 1631, in which an English Jesuit, Father Stock, advanced the idea that it would have been a great honor for the Roman Catholic Church to establish in America an Italian colony with its own bishop. The suggestion did not materialize, for reasons best known to the Catholic authorities. (*Scritture antiche*. 100, f. 150.)

It would seem, however, that some Italians may have come to Maryland, the only place on the Atlantic seaboard, north of Florida, in which Catholics were allowed to settle as early as 1632. In 1649, religious toleration was formally established in Maryland, but it was to last only five years. It was put in force once more in 1661, continuing for thirty-one more years, until the Anglican Church was established in all the Colonies, including Maryland. During those years, whether religious toleration was in existence or not, some ships from Venice had come to the Maryland plantations, but when and how often we have not ascertained. (*Maryland Archives*, Vol. 3. p. 484.)

The fact that there were Italians in Maryland as early as 1649 is inferred from one of the twelve bills voted into law by the Maryland General Assembly (see facsimile below), according to which persons of "French, Dutch or Italian descent" who "either are already planted or shall hereafter come and plant in our said province" were allowed to own land and enjoy the same privileges of the English colonists.

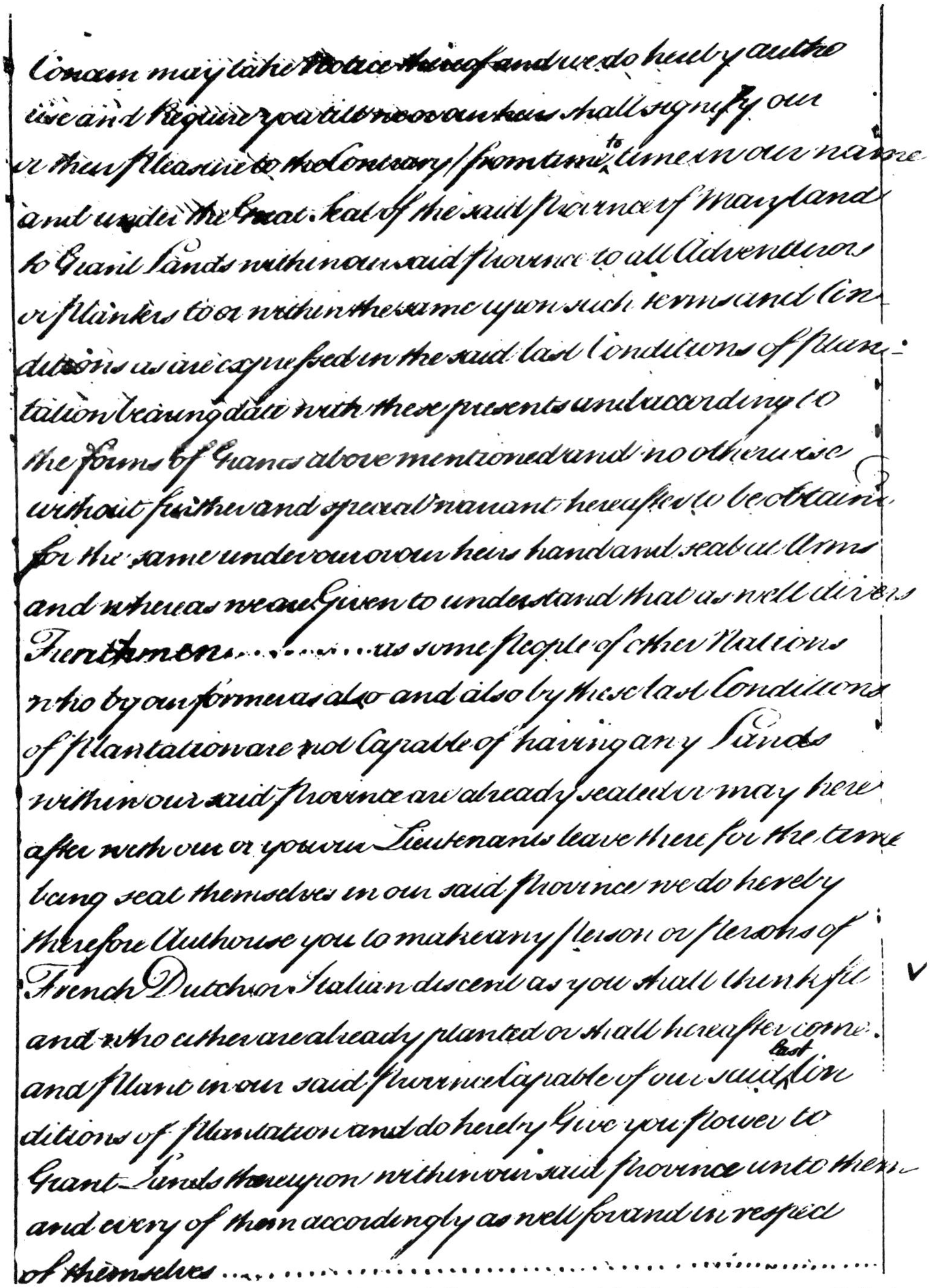
Concern may take Notice thereof and we do hereby autho-
rise and Require you until we or our heirs shall signify our
or their Pleasure to the Contrary) from time to time in our name
and under the Great Seal of the said Province of Maryland
to Grant Lands within our said Province to all Adventurers
or Planters to or within the same upon such terms and Conditions as are expressed in the said last Conditions of Plantation bearing date with these presents and according to
the forms of Grants above mentioned and no otherwise
without further and special warrant hereafter to be obtain-
for the same under our or our heirs hand and seal at Arms
and whereas we are Given to understand that as well divers
Frenchmen........ as some People of other Nations
who by our former as also and also by these last Conditions
of Plantation are not Capable of having any Lands
within our said Province are already seated or may hereafter with our or your or Lieutenants leave there for the time
being seat themselves in our said Province we do hereby
therefore Authorise you to make any Person or Persons of
French Dutch or Italian descent as you shall think fit
and who either are already planted or shall hereafter come
and Plant in our said Province Capable of our said last Conditions of Plantation and do hereby Give you Power to
Grant Lands thereupon within our said Province unto them
and every of them accordingly as well for and in respect
of themselves ....

Part of a page from the 1649 law allowing Italians to own land in Maryland. (Courtesy, *Hall of Records*, Annapolis, Md.)

AN EARLY ITALIAN MAP OF NEW YORK STATE AND NEW ENGLAND—1647

An early Italian map of New York State, and part of New England, engraved by Antonio Francesco Lucini, which appeared in Dudley's *Dell'Arcano del Mare,* Florence, 1647. (From E. B. O'Callaghan's *Documentary History of the State of New York,* Vol. I.)

300 PIEDMONTESE PROTESTANTS IN NEW YORK IN 1657

The first Italian mass immigration into the present territory of the United States took place in the Spring of 1657, when some 300 Protestants from the Valleys of Piedmont (according to Montanus, or 167 according to others) landed in New York. A few weeks later they were put on another ship and sent to Delaware, where on April 21, 1657, they organized the first government of the colony of New Amstel, now New Castle, Del.

From those days to our own, numerous groups of Protestants from Piedmont, or Waldenses, as they are known (after Waldo, the founder of their religious sect), have landed in North America, settling in the Atlantic Seaboard States, especially in New York, New Jersey, Pennsylvania and the Carolinas.

American historians have often included those Italian Protestants among the French immigrants, or among the Swiss, in part because the word Vaudois in French means both "Waldense" and "a native of the country of Vaud, Switzerland," but largely because the Waldenses had French names. There was, however, nothing French about them, except their names and their language. (Chinard, G. *Les Réfugiés Huguenots en Amérique*, Paris, 1925, p. 186.)

(*Right*) Title page of Montanus's Description of New Netherland, published at Amsterdam in 1671. (*Below*) The passage referring to the Waldenses (fourth line from the bottom, left column, to fourth line from the top, right column) reads: "In the year 1656, they shipped accordingly over to New Netherland seventy families, to which they added three hundred Waldenses who had been driven out of Piedmont. These embarked on the fifteenth of December by beat of drum." Translation in O'Callaghan, *Documentary History of the State of New York*, Vol. IV, p. 83. (Courtesy *New York Public Library*)

De NIEUWE en ONBEKENDE

WEERELD:

OF

BESCHRYVING

VAN

AMERICA

EN

'tZUID-LAND,

Vervaetende

d'Oorſprong der Americaenen en Zuid-landers, gedenkwaerdige togten derwaerds,

Gelegendheid

Der vaſte Kuſten, Eilanden, Steden, Sterkten, Dorpen, Tempels, Bergen, Fonteinen, Stroomen, Huiſen, de natuur van Beeſten, Boomen, Planten en vreemde Gewaſſchen, Gods-dienſt en Zeden, Wonderlijke Voorvallen, Vereeuwde en Nieuwe Oorloogen:

Verciert met Af-beeldſels na 't leven in America gemaekt, en beſchreeven

Door

ARNOLDUS MONTANUS.

t'AMSTERDAM,

By JACOB MEURS Boek-verkooper en Plaet-ſnyder, op de Kaiſars-gra ſchuin over de Weſter-markt, in de ſtad Meurs. *Anno* 1671. *Met Privilegie.*

134 TWEEDE BOEK:

'tNaer gehuil, welk 'twild gediert by nacht maekt, oordeelenze te zijn de klagten der geeſten uit goddelooſe lichaemen verhuiſt. De goede grond en gelegendheid van *Nieuw-Nederland* maekte d'Amſterdamſche Burgermeeſteren gaende, om derwaerds een volkplanting af te vaerdigen. Weshalven verdraegen met de Weſt-Indiſche Maetſchappy, onder goedvinden der Algemeine Staeten in *'s Graeven-Hage*. Op 't jaer ſeſtien honderd ſes en vijftig ſcheepten dieſhalven ſeventig huiſgeſinnen, waer by ſich voegden drie honderd verdreevene *Waldenſen* uit *Piemond*, na *Nieuw-Nederland* over. Den vijftienden van Wintermaend ſtaptenze by trommelſlag binnen ſcheeps-boord. De volkplanting ſette gelukkig voort: als ondertuſſchen d'oorlog tuſſchen d'Engelſche kroon en *'t Vereenigde Nederland* opſtond: ſulx na een tien-jaerig beſit, onmagtig tegen d'Engelſche, haer aen die landaerd over gaf. Zedert kreeg *Nieuw Amſterdam* de benaming *Nieuw-Jork*. De verheerde ingezetenen vervielen tot groote ongelegendheid, alſoo de koophandel t'eenemael ſtil ſtond.

Volk-planting na Nieuw-Nederland.

Vierde Hoofd-ſtuk:

VIRGINIA.

TEn tijde des koninginne *Elizabeth* waeren d'Engelſche ſterk in 't vaerwater, welk *'t Weſterſch Indien* beſpoelt. *Frans Draek*, geboortig in *Deven-ſhire* uit ſlechte ouders, voor een ieder wegende twintig pond: en voor *Lima* twaelf ſchepen, voerende veel zijde en een kiſt vol gemunt ſilver: de ſchippers jongen was alleenlijk binnen boort. Zedert verovert hy een

Verrichting van Draek, leer eedenk-

ITALIAN HUGUENOTS IN XVII CENTURY AMERICA

The Waldenses were not, of course, the only Italian Protestants who came to America in the 17th century.

During the Reformation and for more than a century after it, thousands of Italians left Italy for religious reasons and settled in Switzerland, France, the Netherlands, England, Germany, and even as far as Hungary and Poland.

It is only logical to suppose that some of those men who had left their own country to find religious freedom beyond the Alps may have longed to find even more freedom in a new country like America, but it is impossible for us to say at the present moment how many came over and what were their names. As we have already pointed out, Italian names often were spelled according to the way they sounded in French or in English. Thus Burlamacchi became Burlamaqui, Baldi was spelled Baldy, Priuli was transformed into Prioleau, D'Anna was shortened into Dana, and so on. (The same thing happened to French and German names in England and America.) The difficulty of ascertaining the original spelling, and therefore the nationality, of such names cannot be overemphasized.

The problem becomes even more difficult when dealing with Piedmontese immigrants, whose names were either French or were spelled according to French phonetics. One way, of course, would be to make a detailed study of French names in the baptismal and marriage records of Piedmontese towns, and then compare those names with similar ones found among the Huguenots who came to America. No such study at present exists, with the exception of a brief comparison made by the Rev. A. Stapleton in his *Memorials of the Huguenots in America,* (Carlisle Pa., 1904.) According to him, there is a connection between the names of Italian Protestants who were persecuted in Piedmont in 1655 and other families by that name in the United States, "with traditions of persecuted and martyred ancestors." (p. 39) Referring to the early immigrants in Pennsylvania (particularly in what used to be Delaware) he found that "the names of many have been irrevocably lost, while many who were unquestionably Huguenots are erroneously clased as Dutch and Swedish." (p. 42) Other "French" names, he found, have been credited to German and Scotch-Irish stocks.

Without getting deeper into the subject, we shall recall here only one prominent Huguenot family of Italian origin, the Prioleaus of South Carolina. The first distinguished member of that family to come to America seems to have been Elias Prioleau, founder and first pastor of the Huguenot Church at Charleston in 1687. He was followed by his brother Elisha. Both were the sons of the Rev. Samuel Prioleau of Pons, Saintonge, France, who was the son of Antonio Priuli, Doge of Venice in 1618. The American Prioleaus since then have been connected with some of the most noted families in America.

(Cf. in Chap. XII the names of the Waldenses who became Mormons about 1856.)

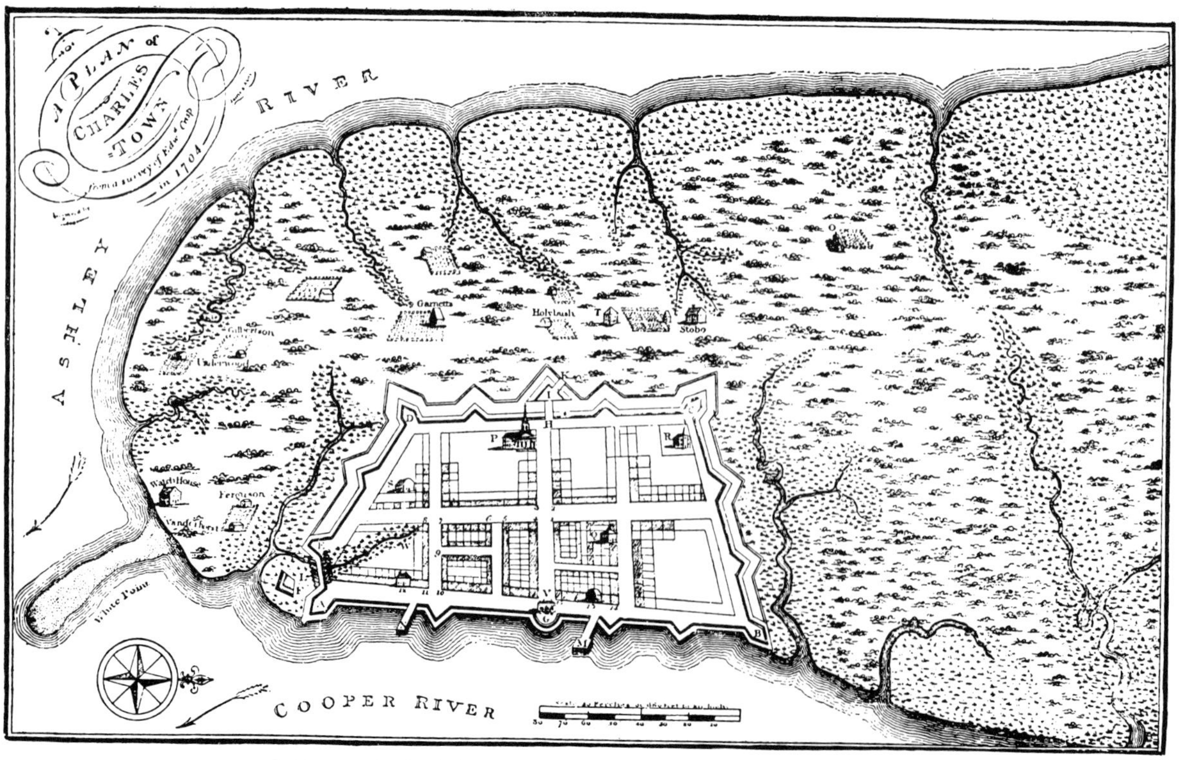

PLAN OF CHARLESTON. FROM A SURVEY OF EDWARD CRISP IN 1704.

In the foreground, on the spot marked by the letter Q, rose the French Church, founded by Elias Prioleau in 1687.

CHAPTER SIX

FROM FLORIDA TO NEW ENGLAND

in the XVIII Century

With the exception of the few groups indicated in the following pages, and notwithstanding the restrictions imposed by English navigation laws, the source of Italian immigration in the American Colonies is to be sought primarily in maritime trade.

A summary perusal of colonial newspapers clearly reveals the existence of direct trade between Italy and the Colonies. For instance, between June and August, 1774, to single out a brief period we happened to investigate during our work, the *Pennsylvania Journal and Weekly Advertiser* listed the arrival in Philadelphia of two ships from Trapani, two from Genoa and one from Leghorn. (June 15, June 22, July 20 and August 22.) But then there were other ships that were seized by the British while plying between Europe and the West Indies, like the vessel flying the Papal flag which was taken into the port of New York as a prize in 1757. The captain was a Genoese named Lorenzo Ghiglino.

During the Revolution Italian ships continued to come, risking capture by the English. One of them, the Neapolitan polacca S.S. *Nunziata e Giuseppe*, was seized in 1779 while on her way back from North Carolina with a cargo of tobacco and other American products. We do not know whether its crew included that lone "good Genoese sailor" who had tried to sail on the ship which was to take Mazzei to Europe, only to be captured by the English the day it set out from Virginia. Such traffic, at any rate, does not seem to have been rare. (See Andrews, G., *Guide to Materials for American History in the Public Record Office of Great Britain.*)

That quite a few Italians had settled in the Colonies appears evident from the records of St. Joseph's Catholic Church in Philadelphia. Limiting ourselves to colonial days, among the children baptized there we find Joseph, Francis, Dorothy, and Sarah Mignati, who were baptized, respectively, in 1763, 1765, 1768, and 1773; Peter Firmian Cancemi, who was baptized in 1767; Peter Gaspar Cangemy, who was baptized in 1769; Mary Mignio, who was born in 1776; Frances Louisa Orlandy, who was born in 1783; Anna Maria Orlandino, of Paul Orlandino, Genoese, who was born in 1780; Jacob Amico, who was baptized in 1782. In the same records, also before 1783, one finds the names of one Gaspar Polumbo, or Palumbo, who married one Susan Ogle in 1769, and of one Francis Morelli, who married one Elizabeth Miller in 1781. Many more names can

WILLIAM DIODATI'S COAT OF ARMS
(Courtesy, *Yale University*)

be found in the following years. One must bear in mind, however, that few colonial Italians had the opportunity or the desire to observe Catholic practices and that distance and poor means of communication prevented their attending church, except on very special occasions.

One of the most distinguished Italian names in 18th century America was that of William Diodati, the grandson of the famous Italian translator of the Bible. Like his ancestor, he was a Protestant. William lived in New Haven from 1717 to 1751. He was a banker and broker and "a trader in the various articles of gold and silver which were in use at the time". His daughter, Sarah, became the wife of John Griswold, son of the first Governor Griswold of Connecticut. (Salisbury, Edw. E., *Mr. William Diodate of New Haven from* 1717 *to* 1751 *and His Italian Ancestry*, New Haven, 1876.)

No less distinguished was the Castello family which settled in the English-speaking Colonies in 1712. Giovanni Battista Castello, painter, architect and sculptor, better known as "Il Bergamasco," from Bergamo, the province of his birth, settled in Spain in 1567, together with his

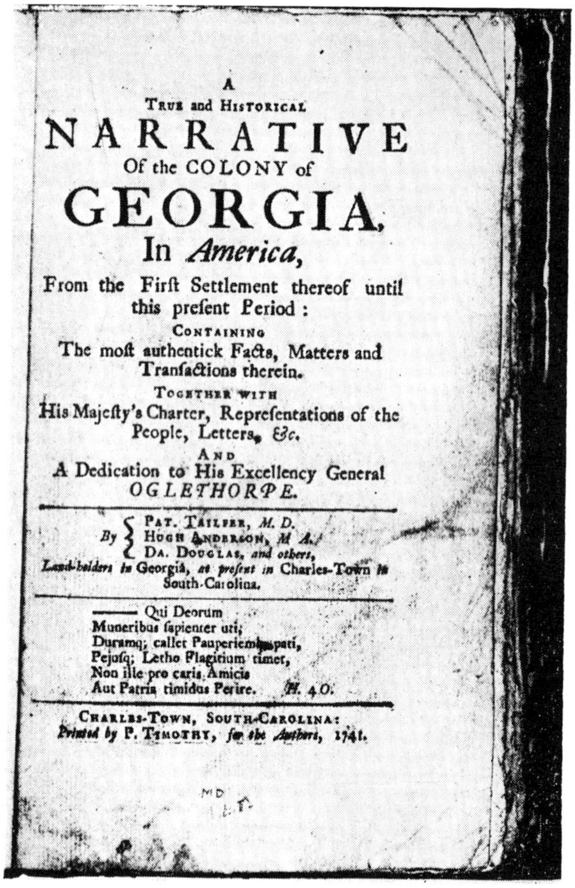

A
TRUE and HISTORICAL
NARRATIVE
Of the COLONY of
GEORGIA,
In *America*,
From the Firſt Settlement thereof until
this preſent Period:
CONTAINING
The moſt authentick Facts, Matters and
Tranſactions therein.
TOGETHER WITH
His Majeſty's Charter, Repreſentations of the
People, Letters, &c.
AND
A Dedication to His Excellency General
OGLETHORPE.

By { PAT. TAILFER, *M. D.*
HUGH ANDERSON, *M. A.*
DA. DOUGLAS, *and others*,
Land-holders in Georgia, *at preſent in* Charles-Town *in*
South-Carolina.

——— Qui Deorum
Muneribus ſapienter uti;
Duramq; callet Pauperiem pati,
Pejuſq; Letho Flagitium timet,
Non ille pro caris Amicis
Aut Patria timidus Perire. *H.* 40.

CHARLES-TOWN, SOUTH-CAROLINA:
Printed by P. TIMOTHY, *for the Authors*, 1741.

Title-page of a book written by Dr. Pat Tailfer (Taliaferro) and others and published at Charleston in 1741. It has been called "one of the few pieces of urbane literature produced in colonial Georgia." (Wright, L. B., *The Atlantic Frontier,* N. Y., 1947, pp. 300-301.) The authors were malcontents who had fled to South Carolina. (Courtesy, *New York Public Library.*)

sons, Gianello and Fabricio, who decorated some of the rooms of the Escurial palace in Madrid. From Spain the family later moved to the New World, settling in Pennsylvania, where Eugenio Castello, a noted American painter and sculptor, was born in 1851. (Thieme and Becker, *Allgemeines Lexikon der Bildenden Kunstler,* under Castello.) He died in Philadelphia in 1926.

Apparently also of Italian origin was James Latta, a teacher of ancient languages in Philadelphia in 1775. It has been said that Latta came from Ireland (see *American Descendants of James Latta* in the New York Public Library), but a summary search in Dublin and in books dealing with Irish and Scotch names failed to reveal any such antecedents. One Latta, a carrier, is mentioned in the *Boswell Journals* as a resident of London. James Latta was one of the seven men who graduated from the College, Academy and Charitable School of Philadelphia (now University of Pennsylvania) at its first commencement in 1757. Also in Philadelphia we find one John Philip Alberti, a pewterer, who advertised in a local German-language newspaper in 1764 (Coxe, P. A., *The Arts and Crafts in Philadelphia,* p. 107), and a surgeon, Dr. Joseph Batacchi, who arrived in the city in 1765. (See facsimile on this page.) Batacchi apparently was a Tuscan, probably related to the Giuseppe Batacchi whom Mazzei met in Leghorn in 1751.

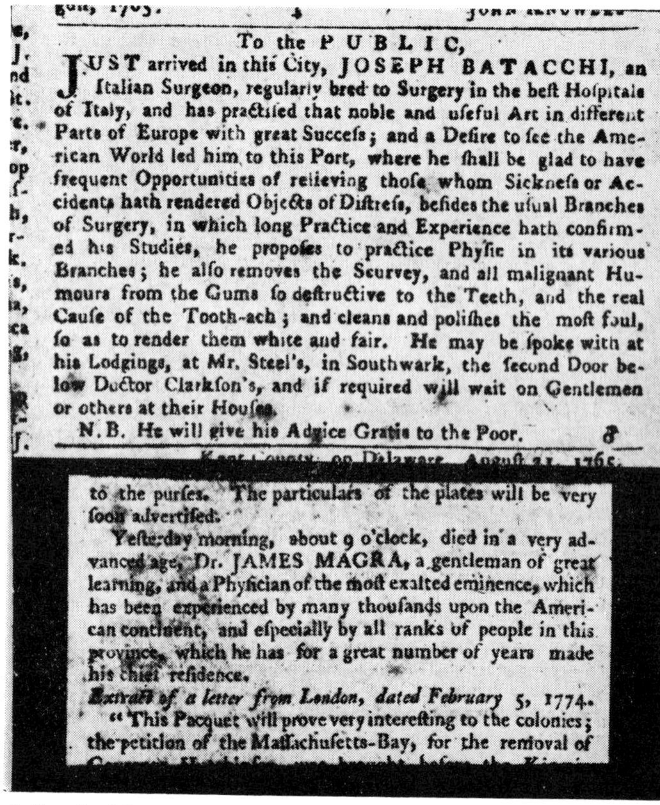

To the PUBLIC,
JUST arrived in this City, JOSEPH BATACCHI, an Italian Surgeon, regularly bred to Surgery in the beſt Hoſpitals of Italy, and has practiſed that noble and uſeful Art in different Parts of Europe with great Succeſs; and a Deſire to ſee the American World led him to this Port, where he ſhall be glad to have frequent Opportunities of relieving thoſe whom Sickneſs or Accidents hath rendered Objects of Diſtreſs, beſides the uſual Branches of Surgery, in which long Practice and Experience hath confirmed his Studies, he propoſes to practice Phyſic in its various Branches; he alſo removes the Scurvey, and all malignant Humours from the Gums ſo deſtructive to the Teeth, and the real Cauſe of the Tooth-ach; and cleans and poliſhes the moſt foul, ſo as to render them white and fair. He may be ſpoke with at his Lodgings, at Mr. Steel's, in Southwark, the ſecond Door below Doctor Clarkſon's, and if required will wait on Gentlemen or others at their Houſes.
N. B. He will give his Advice Gratis to the Poor.

to the purſes. The particulars of the plates will be very soon advertiſed.
Yeſterday morning, about 9 o'clock, died in a very advanced age, Dr. JAMES MAGRA, a gentleman of great learning, and a Phyſician of the moſt exalted eminence, which has been experienced by many thouſands upon the American continent, and eſpecially by all ranks of people in this province, which he has for a great number of years made his chief reſidence.
Extract of a letter from London, dated February 5, 1774.
"This Pacquet will prove very intereſting to the colonies; the petition of the Maſſachuſetts-Bay, for the removal of

(*Above*) Advertisement announcing Dr. Batacchi's arrival in Philadelphia in the *Pennsylvania Gazette* for August 29, 1765. (*Below*) Dr. Magra's obituary in *Rivington's New York Gazetteer* for April 21, 1774. (Courtesy, *New York Public Library.*)

In New York, one Dr. Bartholinus Gaspardo had his office at 12 Nassau Street and one Chis. Lewis Lente resided at 205 Water Street. (Barck, O. T., *New York City During the War of Independence,* New York, 1931, p. 180.) Another pioneer physician with an Italian name died in New York in 1774, but we are inclined to believe that he was of Irish birth or descent and that his name, Magra, was his way of spelling Magrath or McGrath.

In Rhode Island, we find one John Garnardi, who married one Sarah Draper in 1720 (they had six children) and one Pascal Constant Petit De Angelis, who is said to have been the son of a Neapolitan nobleman who ran away from home and went to sea. Pascal was born in the West Indies in 1763 and served during the Revolution. Later he moved to Connecticut and finally to Oneida County, N. Y., where he became a prosperous business man and a judge. Even better known is another Rhode Island pioneer, Joseph Carlo Mauran, a native of Villafranca, as related elsewhere in this volume.

We have more information about the Neapolitan innkeeper, Serafino Formicola (see the chapter on business) and Giuseppe Menghini, Mazzei's friend. Menghini was for years a servant to General Charles Lee, who left him a good-sized legacy. He married one Elizabeth Dunn. His daughter died at the age of 87 at Parkersburg, W. Va., about 1900. (See the *Lee Papers,* published by the New York Historical Society, Vols. II and IV; *Virginia Magazine of History and Biography,* July, 1903; Barry, J., *The Strange Story of Harper's Ferry,* p. 209.)

WITH OGLETHORPE AT THE FOUNDING OF GEORGIA

One of the main purposes Oglethorpe had in mind when he founded Georgia was to make of it one of the leading silk growing centers in the world. He plunged into his new venture with great enthusiasm and without regard for expense. His visions, however, were shattered after a few years spent in experimentations, including the introduction of the vine and of the olive tree (he had imported many plants from Venice to carry on his experiment). Finally he was compelled to surrender his charter.

The most proficient silk-throwers in the world in those days were the Piedmontese, many of whom had emigrated to Lyons, France. It was only logical, therefore, that Oglethorpe should have turned to Piedmont to engage the necessary men to start the industry in the new colony and to provide teachers for the apprentices he expected to recruit among the colonists. Oglethorpe, it should be recalled, was well acquainted with Italy and with the Italians, having served under Prince Eugene of Savoy. His servant, too, was an Italian named Charles Grimaldi, a man without many scruples, for during the crossing to Georgia he drank all of the several dozen bottles of Cyprus wine which Oglethorpe had ordered especially for himself. The general became so furious when he found that out, that he had ordered the rascal to be bound hand and foot, but the celebrated Rev. John Wesley, who was on board, reminded Oglethorpe that he also was liable to sin. Whereupon all was forgiven. Grimaldi settled in the new colony and became a prosperous citizen.

The first Italian to come to Georgia was one Paul Amatis. He landed with the first colonists at Charleston, South Carolina, on January 13, 1733, proceeding south, with Oglethorpe, a few days later. Paul Amatis soon called for his brother, Nicholas Amatis, then a resident of Lyons. He came over with another group of seven Italian silk experts in April, 1733. The party included one Giacomo Luigi Camuso, his wife and three children. Others came in later years, including one Joseph Ottolenghi, superintendent of silk culture in 1764. A pamphlet entitled "Directions for breeding silk-worms, extracted from a letter of Joseph Ottolenghi, Esq., later superintendent of the Public Filature in Georgia" was published at Philadelphia in 1771. In 1786, when Count Castiglioni of Milan visited Ebenezer, he was presented with some silk by one Mrs. Postell, whose name suggests its Italian origin.

THE LANDING OF OGLETHORPE IN GEORGIA
(From an old print)

Notwithstanding its initial success, however, the silk industry at Savannah was not fated to last long. Silk was last produced there in 1790. The filature was later used as city hall and public house, but was destroyed by fire in 1839.

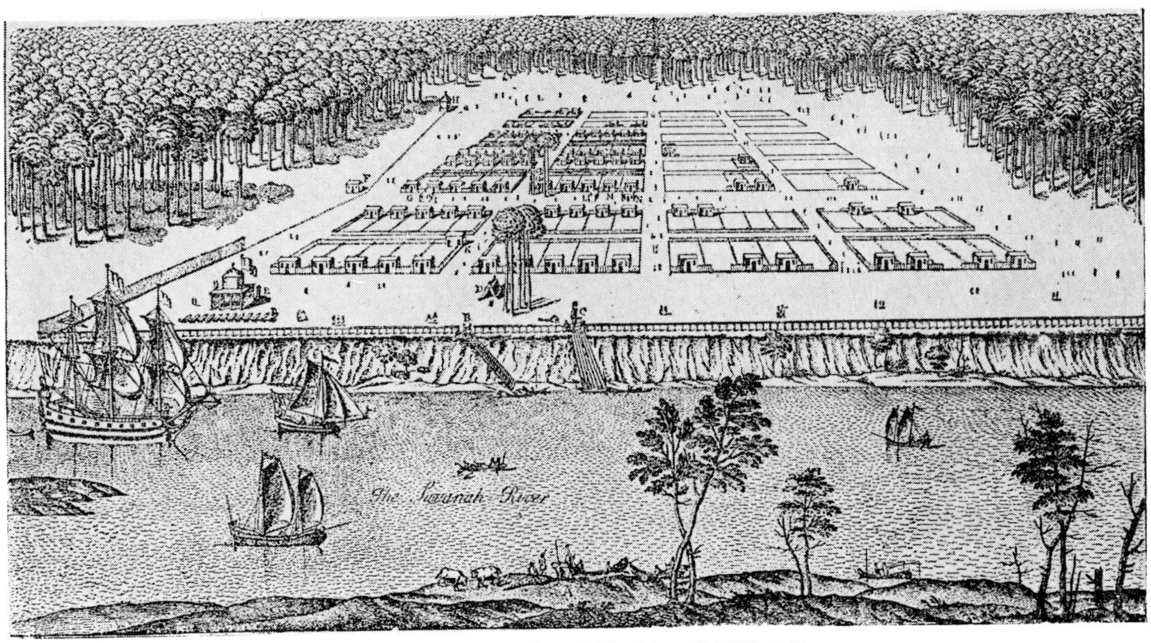

A VIEW OF SAVANNAH, GA., ABOUT 1741
(From an old print)

ONORIO RAZZOLINI ARMOURER OF MARYLAND 1732-1747

Probably the first native of Italy to occupy a public office in the Colonies—we never know when we may discover another, or half a dozen more—was Onorio Razzolini, a native of the town of Asolo, not far from Venice. It is there that Eleanor Duse is buried.

Razzolini came to America as tutor to Benedict Swingate, Lord Baltimore's illegitimate son, shortly before 1732. He was born at Asolo, about 1699, the son of Francesco Razzolini, a jurist, and Antonia de' Fabris, as we learn from *Saggio di Memorie degli Uomini Illustri di Asolo* by C. Pietro Trieste de' Pellegrini, published by the printer Zatta, at Venice, in 1780.

Razzolini was about 18 years old when he left his native town, if he died at the age of 70 in 1769, as reported in "Saggio". He returned to Italy in 1748 "much different from what he was when he left, for he brought back his wife and riches which he did not have when he went away in 1717".

Razzolini spent the longest period of his life away from home at Annapolis, Maryland. There he married Elizabeth Fleury, the only daughter of a French officer of the Roman Catholic faith, who had been president of the Parliament of Rouen. It is said that Onorio inherited his father-in-law's considerable wealth, a possible motive for his return to his native town in 1747. A year after his arrival at Asolo Razzolini built a fine villa which now belongs to the Trentinaglia family. In 1761, a year after the death of his first wife, he married again and became the father of three daughters. He died at Asolo on June 21, 1769.

Not long after his arrival at Annapolis, Razzolini became a naturalized citizen of Maryland, on July 27, 1732. Shortly after that, Charles Calvert II, Fifth Lord Baltimore, appointed him Armourer and Keeper of the Stores of Maryland, a very important position, for he was practically in charge of the defense of the Colony. It would seem also that he was a member of the Council and Keeper of the Council Chamber.

A present view of the villa Razzolini built at Asolo in 1748. Originally the villa was adorned with a majestic double stairway which led to a rotunda at the top of the building. (Courtesy, *Mayor Antonio Piscicelli of Asolo, Italy.*)

(See, Wallace, D., Onorio Razolini, Pioneer Italian, *Sons of Italy Magazine*, Boston, Nov.-Dec. 1942, Feb. 1943; *Maryland Archives*, Vols. 28, 37, and 42; *Maryland Historical Magazine*, 1921, 1926, 1927; Bernardi, Carlo, *Guida di Asolo*, Milan, 1949.)

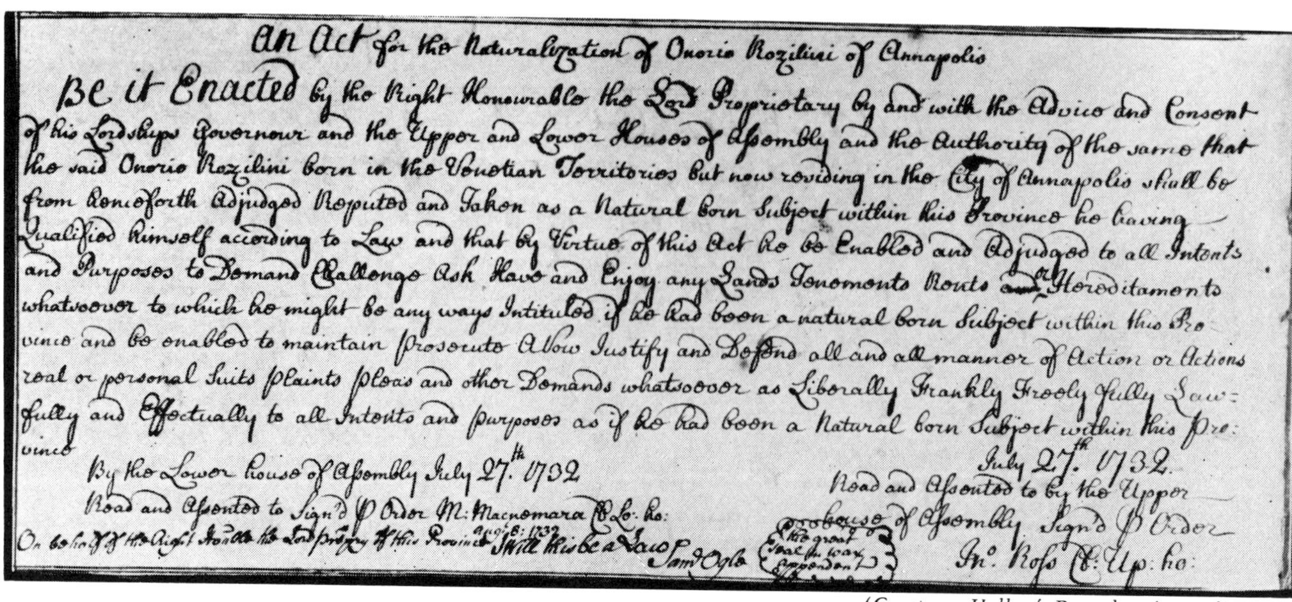

An Act for the Naturalization of Onorio Rozilini of Annapolis

Be it Enacted by the Right Honourable the Lord Proprietary by and with the Advice and Consent of his Lordships Governour and the Upper and Lower Houses of Assembly and the Authority of the same that the said Onorio Rozilini born in the Venetian Territories but now residing in the City of Annapolis shall be from henceforth Adjudged Reputed and Taken as a Natural born Subject within this Province he having Qualified himself according to Law and that by Virtue of this Act he be Enabled and Adjudged to all Intents and Purposes to Demand Challenge Ask Have and Enjoy any Lands Tenements Rents or Hereditaments whatsoever to which he might be any ways Intituled if he had been a natural born Subject within this Province and be enabled to maintain Prosecute Avow Justify and Defend all and all manner of Action or Actions real or personal Suits Plaints Pleas and other Demands whatsoever as Liberally Frankly Freely fully Lawfully and Effectually to all Intents and purposes as if he had been a Natural born Subject within this Province

By the Lower house of Assembly July 27th 1732
Read and Assented to Sign'd ℗ Order M: Macnemara Cl Lo: ho:

July 27th 1732
Read and Assented to by the Upper house of Assembly Sign'd ℗ Order
Jn° Ross Cl: Up: ho:

On behalf of the Right Honble the Lord Proprietary of this Province Aug 8: 1732 I Will this be a Law
Saml Ogle

The great Seal ... was appended

(Courtesy, *Hall of Records, Annapolis, Md.*)
FACSIMILE OF RAZZOLINI'S NATURALIZATION ACT

110 ITALIAN COLONISTS IN FLORIDA IN 1768

The second Italian mass immigration on record (the Waldenses were first in 1657—aside from the Venetian glassworkers of 1622) took place in 1768, when some 110 Italians landed in Florida with about 1,300 other immigrants from Mediterranean countries, largely Minorcans and Greeks.

They were part of a colonization project planned by Dr. Andrew Turnbull, a Scotch physician, on the east coast of Florida, between St. Augustine and Daytona Beach. He called it New Smyrna in honor of his wife's native place.

The project was a failure, for reasons which are not always clear. In our opinion, Dr. Turnbull failed where other English colonizers had succeeded, because the Italians, the Greeks and the Spaniards could not bear the truculant manners of the overseers, who, in all probability, looked down on their Mediterranean wards.

The fact is that the colonists had been hardly two months in Florida when they became convinced that they had been duped by the Scottish doctor and that instead of the promised paradise they had found only a desolate sandy shore infested with mosquitoes. The overseers, moreover, added insult to injury by treating the colonists as beasts rather than as human beings .

That much is clear from a report from St. Augustine which appeared in the *Virginia Gazette* (Purdie and Dixon) on October 27, 1768. According to it, many of the colonists "being greatly dissatisfied, formed a design of returning to their own country, to accomplish which, on the 18th of August, about 250 Greeks and some Italians rose upon and confined all the Englishmen that were there."

To effect their escape the insurgents stole all the supplies they could find and boarded a ship standing by, only to be overcome by the English, who made them prisoner. However, thirty-five of the men, including the leader, an Italian overseer named Carlo Forni, escaped in an open boat. But they were no more successful than their companions and after wandering aimlessly along the coast they, too, were seized. Whereupon three of them were sentenced to death, Forni and two Greeks. One of the latter, however, was pardoned on condition that he be the executioner of his two friends. This cruelty should suffice to give an idea of Dr. Turnbull's sense of justice.

The project, anyway, was doomed to failure. Many of the colonists died; some of them remained in Florida; hundreds of them, with their children, scattered in nearby colonies.

There is no detailed study of this episode in American colonization, with the exception of a monograph by Miss Carita Doggett, *Dr. Andrew Turnbull and The New Smyrna Colony of Florida,* which appeared in 1919. Miss Doggett's study is based on original source material but, unfortunately, she was not able to evaluate the documents at her disposal.

Remains of one of Dr. Turnbull's canals at New Smyrna, Fla. (Photo by *Van De Sande Studio, New Smyrna.*)

Without going into many details which would be out of a place in a work like the present one, the very fact that in five years the immigrants dwindled from 1,400 to 600, as Miss Doggett informs us, should give us an idea of what a miserable place New Smyra must have been in those days. (The colonists landed in 1768, and the 800 deaths occurred between 1768 and 1773—five years, according to our way of figuring, not nine, as Miss Doggett states on page 96 of her work). Even she, however, is forced to admit that the overseers were not so kind with the colonists whose "stories of the ingenious cruelties of some of their overseers are too fully and heartrendingly told to be denied" (Doggett, *op. cit.* p. 162).

To conclude, the Italians were not "a small but turbulent band" of men, as Miss Doggett labeled them, but only free men who refused to submit to slavery and risked death to obtain it. Thus, Forni was one of the first rebels who paid with his own head when his attempt to regain freedom failed; a rebel, but also one of the forerunners of the American Revolution.

(See Schiavo—*Italians in America Before the Civil War*, pp. 148-159 and 374; *Massachusetts Historical Society, Proceedings*, Vol. 3, p. 225; *Columbian Magazine*, August, 1788).

PIONEER MUSICIANS AND COMPOSERS

Although America could afford to offer few inducements to musicians before 1800, we find some Italian teachers of music in the Colonies as early as 1757, when one John Palma gave a concert in Philadelphia. Palma may have been in America long before 1757. His music, at least, was played here, for we find a "large Book of Songs" by Palma, priced at five shillings, in the inventory of the estate of Cuthbert Ogle, who died in 1755. Three compositions by Palma were included in *Hopkinson's Book,* a manuscript volume of music copied by Francis Hopkinson, the Signer of the Declaration of Independence. It is now in the Library of Congress.

Next in order of time we find Francis Alberti, a native of Faenza, Italy, who came to America not later than 1759. He may have been the same Alberti who gave a concert on April 10, 1757, which was attended by Washington, and another at Hanoverstown, near Williamsburg, Va., on May 19, 1769. According to Thomas Jefferson, "Alberti came over with a troop of players and afterwards taught at Williamsburg. Subsequently I got him to come up here (Monticello) and took lessons for several years." (Randall, H. S., *Life of Jefferson,* Vol. I, p. 131.) Alberti gave

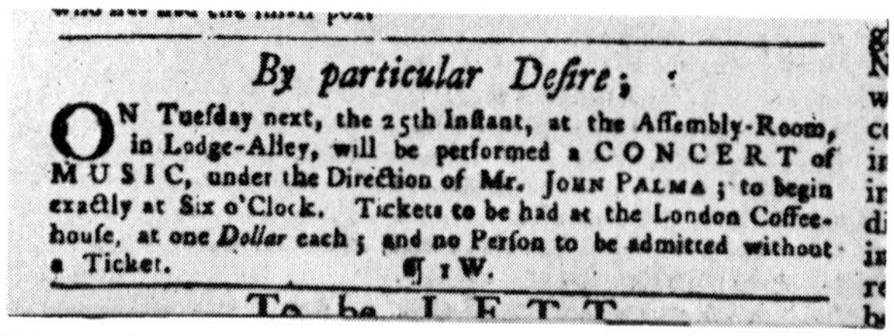

By particular Desire;

ON Tuesday next, the 25th Instant, at the Assembly-Room, in Lodge-Alley, will be performed a CONCERT of MUSIC, under the Direction of Mr. JOHN PALMA; to begin exactly at Six o'Clock. Tickets to be had at the London Coffee-house, at one *Dollar* each; and no Person to be admitted without a Ticket.

Palma advertisement in the *Pennsylvania Gazette* for January 20, 1757. (Courtesy, *N. Y. Public Library.*)

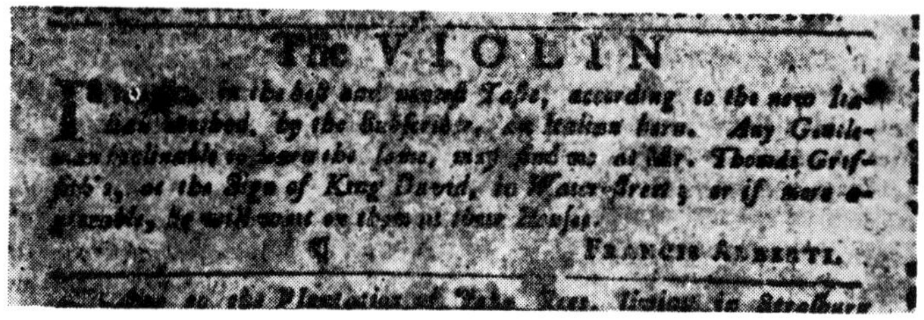

The VIOLIN

FRANCIS ALBERTI.

Alberti's advertisement in the *Pennsylvania Gazette* for November 29, 1759.

A composition by Palma copied by Hopkinson, the Signer of the Declaration, for his music book. (Courtesy, *Library of Congress.*)

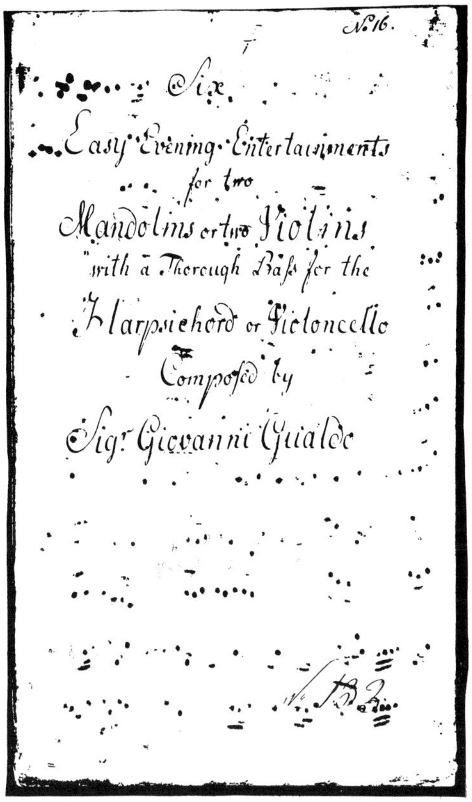

Title page of a manuscript book of compositions by Gualdo in the Library of Congress.

vocal and musical lessons, his pupils including Martha Skelton, who later became Jefferson's wife. He taught the violin, the harpsichord and other instruments. In 1774 he signed the pledge not to do business with England, known as *The Association*. After 1778 he was in Paris, where Jefferson wrote to him following Burgoyne's surrender. (Parton, *Life of Jefferson,* pp. 133 and 221.) On his 1769 concert see *Rind's Virginia Gagette,* May 11, 1769.

Giovanni Gualdo, probably the best known musician in Colonial America, arrived in Philadelphia in 1767, and lived there until he died in the insane asylum four years later. The facsimiles dealing with Gualdo's concerts which we produce in the following pages dispense us from saying more about this unfortunate man who initiated the people of Philadelphia to the appreciation of fine music.

That music conditions in the Colonies were not very promising, we may presume from the fleeting appearance of one Tioli at Providence in 1768, or by the little success which Nicholas Biferi found in New York in 1774. Biferi, together with two other Italians, Pietro Sodi, a dancing master, and Joseph Cozani, a teacher of languages, had planned the establishment of a conservatory of music in New York, where vocal and instrumental music, dancing, and both French and Italian were to be taught. The minimum of twelve pupils they depended on to start, however, did not materialize and their dreams of a conservatory vanished in thin air. They remained in America at least for some time, as we learn from the newspaper advertisements reproduced in the following pages.

Still another violinist and orchestra leader who appeared in Charleston, Philadelphia and New York between 1774 and 1783 was Gaetano Franceschini. A Trio Sonata of his for two violins, cello and continuo (harpsichord) was recorded by "New Records" of New York in 1951.

More interesting, from the historical point of view, is the appearance of "Signiora" Mazzanti, probably the first Italian woman to sing before an American audience. She appeared in New York on April 24, 1774, and rendered English and Italian songs. Whether she was the same Signora Mazzanti mentioned by Frances Burney in her diary, we do not know.

Nor should we forget a lone dancing master, one Peter Vianey (Viani), who was active in New York as early as 1768.

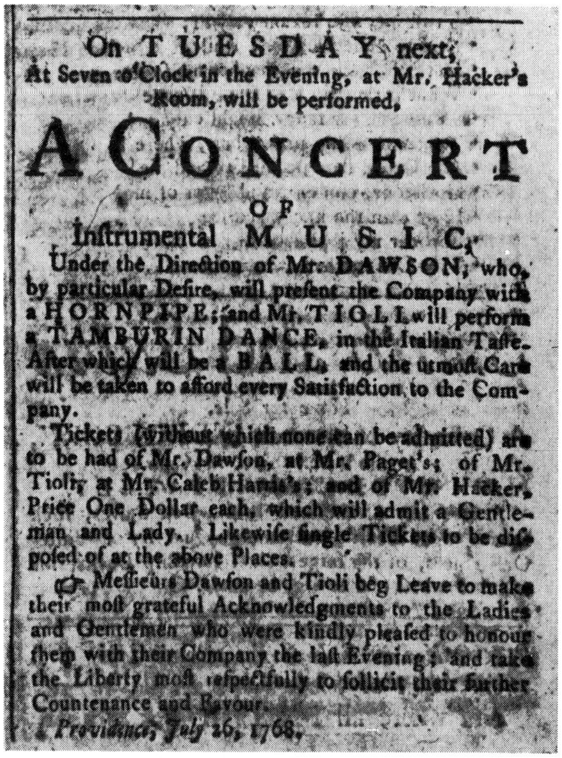
On TUESDAY next,
At Seven o'Clock in the Evening, at Mr. Hacker's Room, will be performed,

A CONCERT
OF
Instrumental MUSIC,

Under the Direction of Mr. DAWSON, who, by particular Desire, will present the Company with a HORNPIPE; and Mr. TIOLI will perform a TAMBURIN DANCE, in the Italian Taste. After which will be a BALL, and the utmost Care will be taken to afford every Satisfaction to the Company.

Tickets (without which none can be admitted) are to be had of Mr. Dawson, at Mr. Paget's; of Mr. Tioli, at Mr. Caleb Harris's; and of Mr. Hacker. Price One Dollar each, which will admit a Gentleman and Lady. Likewise single Tickets to be disposed of at the above Places.

☞ Messieurs Dawson and Tioli beg Leave to make their most grateful Acknowledgments to the Ladies and Gentlemen who were kindly pleased to honour them with their Company the last Evening; and take the Liberty most respectfully to sollicit their further Countenance and Favour.

Providence, July 26, 1768.

A concert announcement in the *Providence Gazette,* July 30, 1768. Notice Tioli's name. (Courtesy, *New York Historical Society.*)

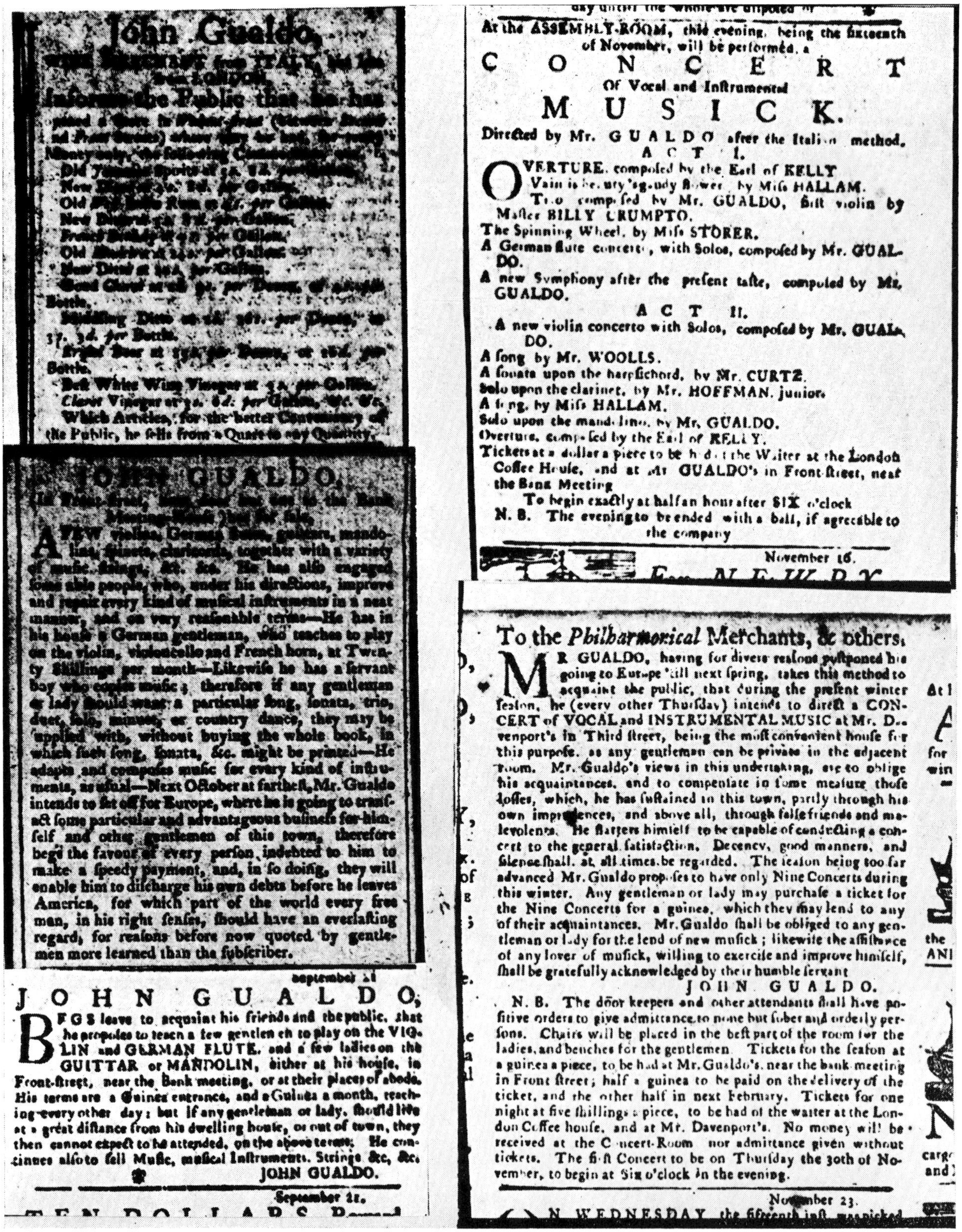

Five newspaper advertisements of some of Gualdo's concerts, which appeared in Philadelphia newspapers. (*Left, from top to bottom*) *Pennsylvania Chronicle,* Aug. 31-Sept. 7, 1767; *ibid.,* Feb. 13-20, 1769; *Pennsylvania Journal,* Sept. 21, 1769. (*Right, top to bottom*) *Pennsylvania Journal,* Nov. 16 and Nov. 30, 1769. (Courtesy, *New York Public Library.*)

Philadelphia, November 21, 1769.

To the *Philharmonical* Merchants, and others.

MR. GUALDO, having for divers Reafons poftponed his going to *Europe* till next Spring, takes this Method to acquaint the Public, that during the prefent Winter Seafon, he (every other *Thurfday*) intends to direct a CONCERT of *VOCAL* and *INSTRUMENTAL MUSIC* at Mr. *Davenport's*, in *Third-ftreet*, being the moft convenient Houfe for this Purpofe, as any Gentleman can be private in the adjacent Room. Mr. *Gualdo's* Views in this Undertaking, are to oblige his Acquaintances, and to compenfate in fome Meafure thofe Loffes, which, he has fuftained in this Town, partly through his own Imprudences, and above all, through falfe Friends and Malevolents. He flatters himfelf to be capable of conducting a Concert to the general Satisfaction. Decency, good Manners, and Silence fhall, at all Times, be regarded. The Seafon being too far advanced, Mr. *Gualdo* propofes to have only nine Concerts during this Winter Any Gentleman or Lady may purchafe a Ticket for the nine Concerts for a Guinea, which, they may lend to any of their Acquaintances. Mr. *Gualdo* fhall be obliged to any Gentleman or Lady for the Lend of new Mufic; likewife, the Affiftance of any Lover of Mufic, willing to exercife and improve himfelf, fhall be gratefully acknowledged by their humble Servant

JOHN GUALDO.

N. B. The Door Keepers and other Attendants fhall have pofitive Orders to give Admittance to none but fober and orderly Perfons. Chairs will be placed in the beft Part of the Room for the Ladies, and Benches for the Gentlemen. Tickets for the Seafon at a Guinea a Piece, to be had at Mr. *Gualdo's* near the *Bank Meeting*, in *Front-ftreet*; half a Guinea to be paid on the Delivery of the Tickets, the other half in next *February*. Tickets for one Night at five Shillings a Piece, to be had of the Waiter of the *London Coffee-Houfe*, and at Mr. *Davenport's*. No Money will be received at the Concert Room, nor Admittance given without Tickets. The firft Concert to be on *Thurfday*, the *Thirtieth* of *November*, to begin at fix o'Clock in the Evening.

Facsimile of the only known copy of a beautiful flier in red and black announcing a series of concerts by Gualdo. (Courtesy, *The Philadelphia Public Library.*)

AN ACADEMY OF MUSIC, DANCING AND LANGUAGES IN NEW YORK IN 1774

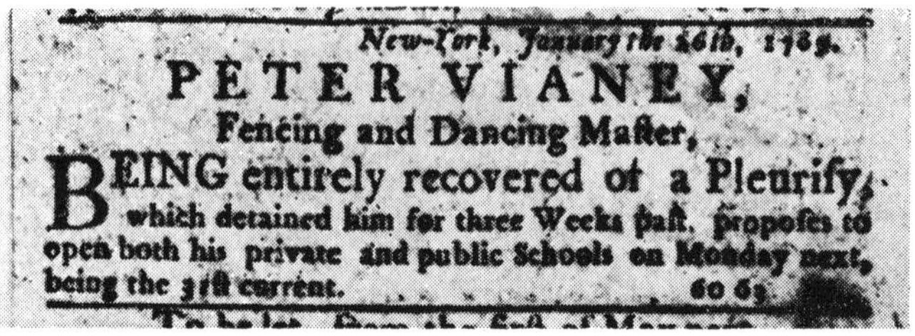

New-York, January the 26th, 1769.

PETER VIANEY,

Fencing and Dancing Master,

BEING entirely recovered of a Pleurisy, which detained him for three Weeks past, proposes to open both his private and public Schools on Monday next, being the 31st current. 60 63

One of Vianey's advertisements in the *New York Journal* for January 26, 1769. (Courtesy, *New York Public Library.*)

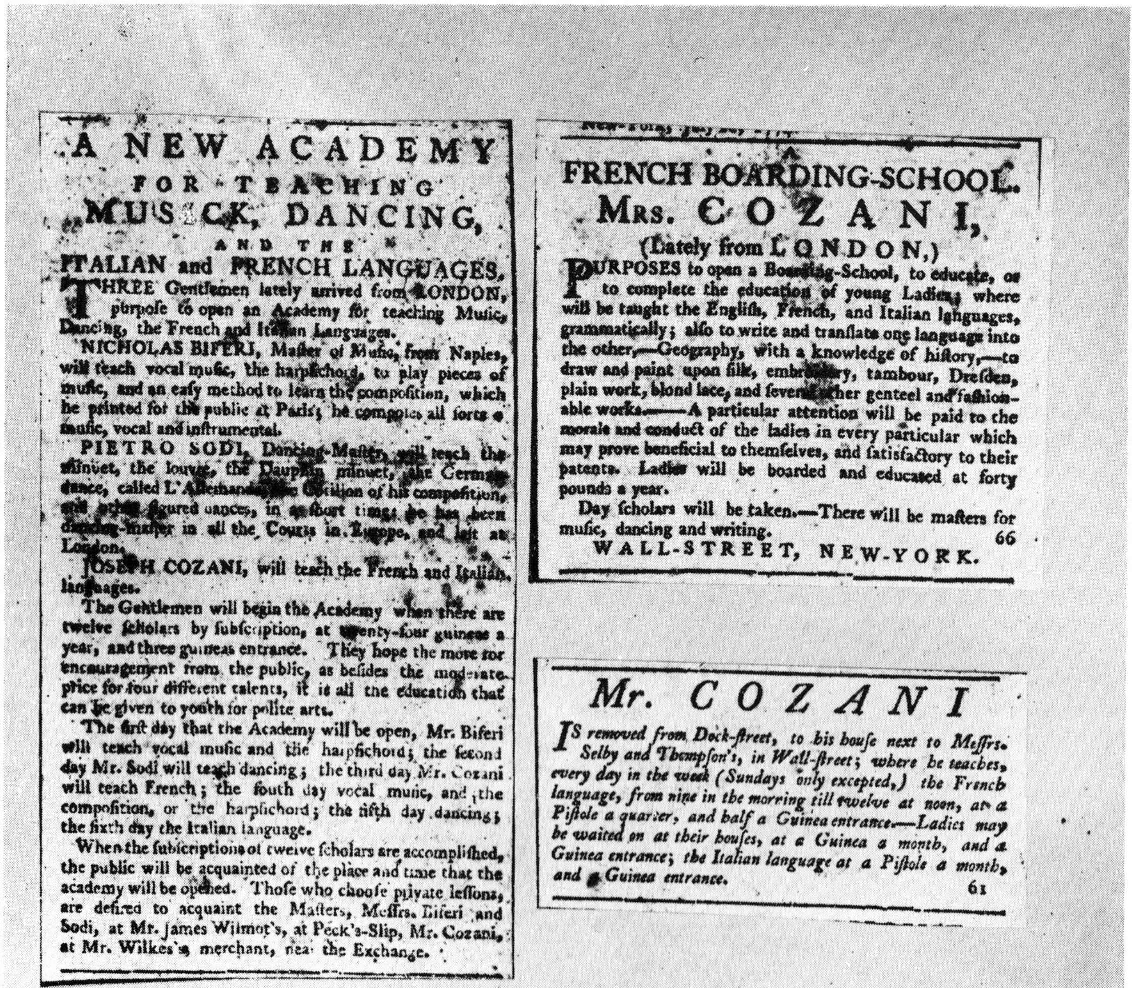

A NEW ACADEMY

FOR TEACHING

MUSICK, DANCING,

AND THE

ITALIAN and FRENCH LANGUAGES.

THREE Gentlemen lately arrived from LONDON, purpose to open an Academy for teaching Music, Dancing, the French and Italian Languages.

NICHOLAS BIFERI, Master of Music, from Naples, will teach vocal music, the harpsichord, to play pieces of music, and an easy method to learn the composition, which he printed for the public at Paris; he composes all sorts of music, vocal and instrumental.

PIETRO SODI, Dancing-Master, will teach the minuet, the louvre, the Dauphin minuet, the German dance, called L'Allemande, [illegible] Cotillon of his composition, [illegible] figured dances, in a short time; he has been dancing-master in all the Courts in Europe, and left at London.

JOSEPH COZANI, will teach the French and Italian languages.

The Gentlemen will begin the Academy when there are twelve scholars by subscription, at twenty-four guineas a year, and three guineas entrance. They hope the more for encouragement from the public, as besides the moderate price for four different talents, it is all the education that can be given to youth for polite arts.

The first day that the Academy will be open, Mr. Biferi will teach vocal music and the harpsichord; the second day Mr. Sodi will teach dancing; the third day Mr. Cozani will teach French; the fouth day vocal music, and the composition, or the harpsichord; the fifth day dancing; the sixth day the Italian language.

When the subscriptions of twelve scholars are accomplished, the public will be acquainted of the place and time that the academy will be opened. Those who choose private lessons, are desired to acquaint the Masters, Messrs. Biferi and Sodi, at Mr. James Wilmot's, at Peck's-Slip, Mr. Cozani, at Mr. Wilkes's, merchant, near the Exchange.

FRENCH BOARDING-SCHOOL.

MRS. COZANI,

(Lately from LONDON,)

PURPOSES to open a Boarding-School, to educate, or to complete the education of young Ladies; where will be taught the English, French, and Italian languages, grammatically; also to write and translate one language into the other,—Geography, with a knowledge of history,—to draw and paint upon silk, embroidery, tambour, Dresden, plain work, blond lace, and several other genteel and fashionable works.——A particular attention will be paid to the morals and conduct of the ladies in every particular which may prove beneficial to themselves, and satisfactory to their parents. Ladies will be boarded and educated at forty pounds a year.

Day scholars will be taken.—There will be masters for music, dancing and writing. 66

WALL-STREET, NEW-YORK.

Mr. COZANI

IS removed from Dock-street, to his house next to Messrs. Selby and Thompson's, in Wall-street; where he teaches, every day in the week (Sundays only excepted,) the French language, from nine in the morning till twelve at noon, at a Pistole a quarter, and half a Guinea entrance.—Ladies may be waited on at their houses, at a Guinea a month, and a Guinea entrance; the Italian language at a Pistole a month, and a Guinea entrance. 61

Facsimiles of three advertisements in *Rivington's New York Gazetteer* in 1774. (*Left*) May 5; (*Right, from top to bottom*) July 21 and June 16. (Courtesy, *New York Public Library.*)

THE SUBSCRIPTION CONCERT
Being (by Desire of many of the Subscribers) deferred 'till
THURSDAY EVENING the 24th instant,
THAT Night is allowed to be
A PUBLIC CONCERT,
FOR THE USE OF
SIGNIORA MAZZANTI,
MESSRS. ZEDWITZ & HULETT;
ON WHICH EVENING

The Gentlemen of the HARMONIC SOCIETY, have been pleased to promise their Assistance; and SIGNIORA MAZZANTI will sing several ENGLISH and ITALIAN Songs.

AFTER THE CONCERT

Proper Music will be ready to wait upon such Ladies and Gentlemen as may choose to dance.

Tickets, at a Dollar each, to be had of Mr. RIVINGTON, and of Messrs. ZEDWITZ and HULETT.

An advertisement of what is believed to have been the first concert by an Italian woman singer in America. *Rivington's New York Gazetteer,* April 14, 1774. (Courtesy, *New York Public Library.*)

At Mr. HULL's Assembly Room, will be performed a CONCERT, the 26th of this month, for the benefit of Mr. BIFERI and Mr. SODI.

THE said Concert will be divided into two acts, each act composed of four pieces. Mr. Biferi, master of music from Naples, will perform on the harpsichord a piece of music of his composition, with the orchestra; in the second act he will perform a solo, accompanied with the violin. There will follow a ball, in which Mr. Sodi will dance the louvre, and the minuet, with Miss Sodi, a young lady nine years of age; and Miss Sodi will dance a rigadoon with young Mr. Hulet. It will begin exactly at 7 o'clock.

Tickets, at One Dollar each, may be had at Mr. Gaine's, Mr. Rivington's, and at Mr. Hull's. 57

MUSIC.

MR. BIFERI, Musician of Naples, being determined to stay in this city, informs the public, that he now teaches singing after the Italian way, also the harpsichord, and the composition of music, at one Guinea for twelve lessons, and one Guinea entrance, which entrance is to be paid only by those who never had a master before. Enquire for said Mr. BIFERI, at Mr. WILMOT's, Peck's-Slip. 63

Two advertisements by Biferi and Sodi in *Rivington's New York Gazetteer* for May 19 (*above*) and July 21 (*below*) 1774. (Courtesy, *New York Public Library.*)

SIGNIOR SODI,

Late principal DANCER at the Opera in Paris and London,

ACQUAINTS the Ladies and Gentlemen of this city, that he has opened a public SCHOOL, at his Room in Chesnut-street, at the back of the Fountain Tavern, where he will teach the following Dances, viz. the Minuet, the Minuet Dauphin, Louvre, Allemande, La Bretagne, La Marie's, the Paspie, Rigadoon, New Minuet by four, New Minuet by eight, Cotillons, Cotillion step, the Hornpipe, English Country Dances, and all the Dances that are danced in the several Courts in Europe.

N. B. Signior SODI will wait on Ladies and Gentlemen at their own houses; and will likewise give private attendance, at certain hours, in his own school.—An evening school will be opened, when a sufficient number of scholars shall offer.

Signior SODI is to be spoken with at Mrs. EASTWICK's, in Walnut-street, between Front and Second-streets.

WAS brought to the house of JEREMIAH WARDER, junr. a SETTEE, by mistake. The owner, by paying the charges of this advertisement, may have it again.

GRAND CONCERT & BALL,

At the ASSEMBLY ROOM in Lodge Alley, on Friday 17th of June, 1774, for the BENEFIT of

SIGNIOR SODI,

First DANCING MASTER of the Opera in Paris and London,

IN which Mr. VIDAL, who has been a Musician of the chambers of the King of Portugal will play on divers instruments of music.

FIRST ACT.

1. A Symphony.—2. Mr. Vidal will play a Sonetta on the Guittare Italian, with the Violin.—3. A Symphony.—4. Mr. Vidal will play a Duetto on the Mandolino, accompanied with the Violin.—5. First act will finish with a March composed by Mr. Vidal.

SECOND ACT.

1. A Symphony.—2. Mr. Vidal will play a Capricio on the Guittare.—3. A Symphony.—4. Mr. Vidal will play a Solo on the Psaltery, and a Minuet imitating the Echo.—5. Second act will end with another March composed by Mr. Vidal.

After the concert, Signior Sodi will dance a louvre and a minuet with Miss Sodi; then a new Philadelphia cotillon composed by Signior Sodi. Miss Sodi will also dance a rigadoon and minuet with Mr. Hulett. A new cotillon; then the allemande by Miss Sodi and Mr. Hulett; also Signior Sodi will dance a jigg, afterwards Mr. Hulett will dance a hornpipe, and to finish with a ball for the company.

As this concert and ball is made by the desire of several Ladies and Gentlemen of this city for Signior Sodi, to show his talents as a master, he humbly requests the favour of the public to give their countenance.

Tickets to be had of Signior Sodi at Mr. Israel Jacobs's at the Bunch of Grapes in Third-street, and at the bar of the Coffee-house, at One Dollar each; to begin precisely at 7 o'clock.

Signior Sodi proposes to open a School publicly next September; in the interim will wait on any Lady or Gentleman privately at their houses or elsewhere, to teach either of the following dances, viz. Minuets, louvres, allemandoe, bretagne, rigadoon, cotillons and English country dances; care will be taken to instruct them first to walk with propriety.

Mr. Vidal acquaints the public in general, that he has bro't a parcel of fine trinkets and jewels of the newest fashion, with a variety of diamond rings, and a great quantity of instrumental strings, which are sold by him at Mr. Israel Jacobs's, at the Bunch of Grapes in Third-street.

Two of Sodi's advertisements in the *Pennsylvania Journal* for Sept. 7 (*above*) and June 15 (*below*) 1774. (Courtesy, *New York Public Library.*)

THE FIRST TEACHER OF MODERN LANGUAGES IN AN AMERICAN COLLEGE

The first teacher of the French, Spanish, German and Italian languages in an American college was Carlo Bellini, a native of Florence, who came to Virginia to join his friend, Philip Mazzei, in 1774. He was then thirty-nine years old. From then on he lived in Williamsburg.

Bellini was appointed a professor of languages at the College of William and Mary in 1778, according to a letter of his which was published in two Florentine newspapers in November of that year. A translation of that letter by Prof. A. Pace of Syracuse University can be found in the July 1947 issue of *The William and Mary Quarterly*. At any rate, Bellini was a full-fledged professor at Williamsburg in 1779. (*Virginia Gazette*, Dec. 29, 1779.)

Bellini had been hardly a year in Virginia when he joined the struggle for American independence and en listed to defend his new country. However, the danger was soon averted and the volunteers disbanded. Not before, however, Patrick Henry, who was at the head of the troops, praised him and his two Italian companions, Mazzei and the gardner, Giannini. As Bellini relates in his letter (which corresponds almost identically to Mazzei's recollection of the episode in his *Memoirs*), Henry turned to him and said: "You, Sir, render an important service to this state with your example, because barely arrived in the country, you voluntarily undertake to defend it as a soldier. You see what an effect your behavior produces on the minds of these citizens. No, you will be more useful to this very state with your ability. Go back home and be assured we shall do our best to show you our gratitude."

"I returned therefore" Bellini goes on saying in his letter, "to live quietly in the country, busying myself with studies, still-fishing, and from time to time engaging in *conversazioni* with the ladies of the province. I was then, in the situation described to you when a letter from the Governor was presented to me by a slave three quarters naked, in which I was informed that the General Assembly of the people had chosen me Secretary for Foreign Affairs and Professor at the University". From another source, a letter from James Madison to Mazzei dated July 7, 1781, we learn that "Bellini has, I understand, abided patiently in the college the dangers and inconvenience of such a situation". (Madison, *Writings*, Vol. I, p. 143.)

Bellini, however, must have made himself useful primarily as translator of official documents. Most likely he was the author of the Italian translation of the *Declaration of the Causes and Necessity of Taking Up Arms* (July 6, 1775), now among the Mazzei Papers in the Library of Congress. It is written in long hand, in large letters, on large sheets of paper, 10½ by 13½. A comparison with the Bellini letter reproduced on the next page leads us to believe that it was written by him.

As for the office to which Bellini was appointed in 1778, we are inclined to believe that he actually was Secretary for Foreign Affairs. (See Brant, I., *James Madison*, Vol. I.) The position, at any rate, was a responsible one. "From the accomplishments of Mr. Bellini", we read in a letter dated May 13, 1778, from Patrick Henry, then Governor of Virginia, to Benjamin Harrison, Speaker of the House of Dele-

WREN BUILDING CHAPEL, COLLEGE OF WILLIAM AND MARY
In that building, now restored, Bellini taught for many years. (Courtesy, *Colonial Williamsburg, Williamsburg, Va.*)

gates, "there seems no doubt of his fitness to fill the office in which Secrecy, Fidelity and Knowledge were so essentially necessary." (*Official letters of the Governors of the State of Virginia*, ed. by H. R. McIlwaine, Vol. I, p. 272.)

Bellini spent the last years of his life as a poverty stricken invalid. He died in 1803 or 1804. In 1924 a tablet in his honor, the gift of Prof. Luigi Carnovale of Chicago, was unveiled in the Library of the College where he taught for more than twenty years and which, because of him, became the first American college to offer courses in modern languages.

(On Bellini see the *William and Mary Quarterly*, for 1905, 1925, 1944, 1945 and 1947.)

ANTHONY FIVA

Bellini was not, of course, the first *private* teacher of languages in America. The teaching of Italian, for instance, was advertised in the *New York Post-Boy* on October 26, 1747, by one Augustus Vaughn. As for the first Italian teacher of languages in the Colonies, he seems to have been one Anthony Fiva, whose advertisements we have found in *Rivington's New York Gazetteer* for July 22, 1773, and May 19, 1774. (See also Chapter Ten.)

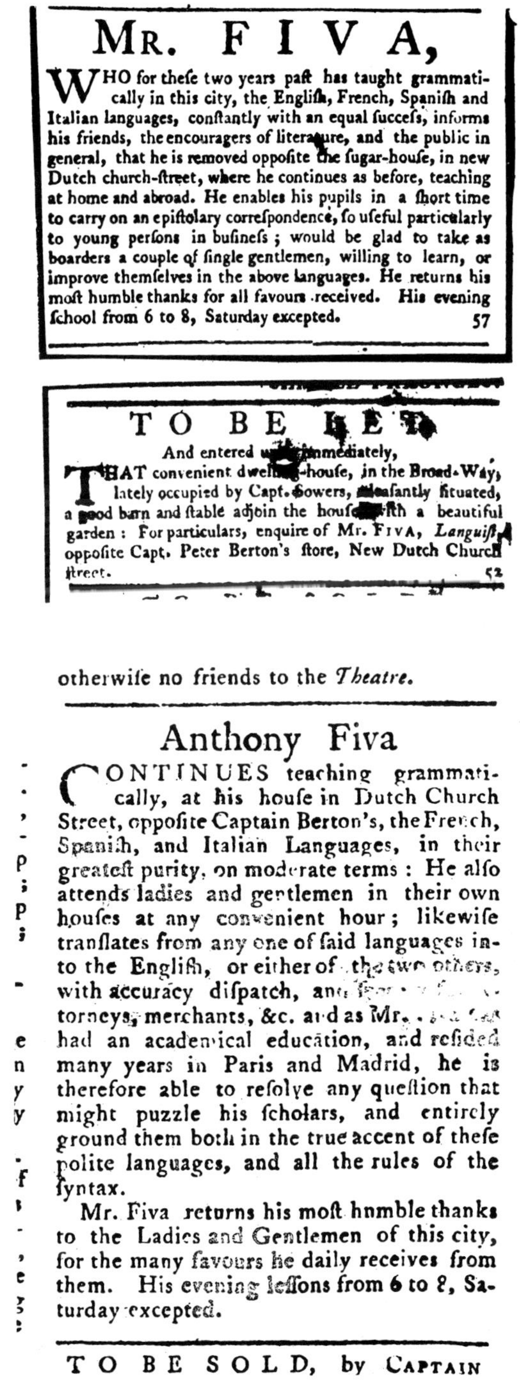

MR. FIVA,

WHO for theſe two years paſt has taught grammatically in this city, the Engliſh, French, Spaniſh and Italian languages, conſtantly with an equal ſucceſs, informs his friends, the encouragers of literature, and the public in general, that he is removed oppoſite the ſugar-houſe, in new Dutch church-ſtreet, where he continues as before, teaching at home and abroad. He enables his pupils in a ſhort time to carry on an epiſtolary correſpondence, ſo uſeful particularly to young perſons in buſineſs; would be glad to take as boarders a couple of ſingle gentlemen, willing to learn, or improve themſelves in the above languages. He returns his moſt humble thanks for all favours received. His evening ſchool from 6 to 8, Saturday excepted. 57

TO BE LET

And entered upon immediately,

THAT convenient dwelling-houſe, in the Broad-Way, lately occupied by Capt. Sowers, pleaſantly ſituated, a good barn and ſtable adjoin the houſe with a beautiful garden: For particulars, enquire of Mr. FIVA, Languiſt, oppoſite Capt. Peter Berton's ſtore, New Dutch Church ſtreet. 52

otherwiſe no friends to the *Theatre.*

Anthony Fiva

CONTINUES teaching grammatically, at his houſe in Dutch Church Street, oppoſite Captain Berton's, the French, Spaniſh, and Italian Languages, in their greateſt purity, on moderate terms: He alſo attends ladies and gentlemen in their own houſes at any convenient hour; likewiſe tranſlates from any one of ſaid languages into the Engliſh, or either of the two others, with accuracy diſpatch, and [illegible] attorneys, merchants, &c. and as Mr. [illegible] had an academical education, and reſided many years in Paris and Madrid, he is therefore able to reſolve any queſtion that might puzzle his ſcholars, and entirely ground them both in the true accent of theſe polite languages, and all the rules of the ſyntax.

Mr. Fiva returns his moſt humble thanks to the Ladies and Gentlemen of this city, for the many favours he daily receives from them. His evening leſſons from 6 to 8, Saturday excepted.

TO BE SOLD, by CAPTAIN

Three of the earliest announcements by Anthony Fiva in *Rivington's New York Gazetteer* for (*top to bottom*) July 22, 1773, and May 19 and April 14, 1774. (Courtesy, *New York Public Library.*)

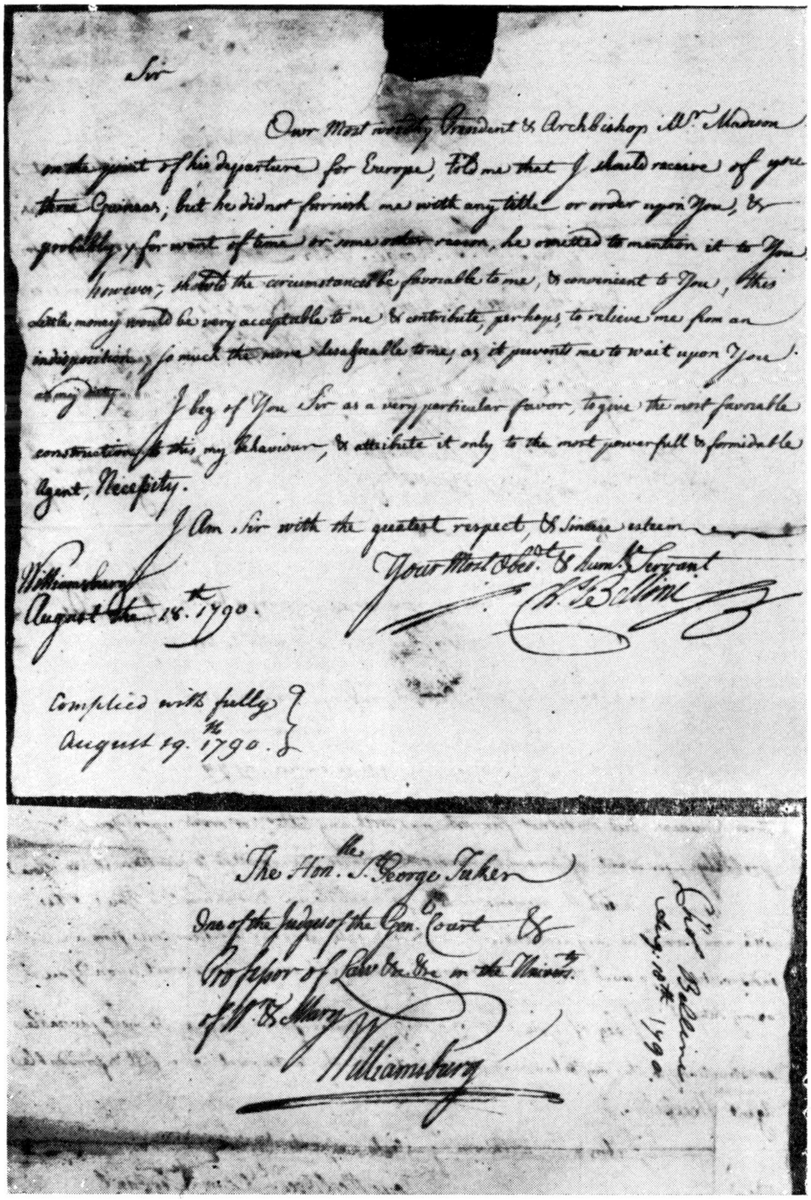

Sir

Our Most worthy President & Archbishop Mr Madison on the point of his departure for Europe, told me that I should receive of you three Guineas; but he did not furnish me with any title or order upon You; & probably, for want of time or some other reason, he omitted to mention it to You however; should the circumstance be favorable to me, & convenient to You, this little money would be very acceptable to me & contribute, perhaps, to relieve me from an indisposition, so much the more disagreeable to me, as it prevents me to wait upon You at any time.

I beg of You Sir as a very particular favor, to give the most favorable construction to this my behaviour, & attribute it only to the most powerfull & formidable Agent, Necessity.

I Am, Sir with the greatest respect, & Sincere esteem

Your Most Obet. & humb. Servant

Ch. Bellini

Williamsburg August the 18th 1790.

Complied with fully 19th August 1790.

The Hon. St. George Tucker

One of the Judges of the Gen. Court &

Professor of Law &c. &c. in the University

of W. & Mary

Williamsburg

Chs Bellini Aug. 18th 1790

Facsimile of a letter by Charles Bellini. (Courtesy, *Colonial Williamsburg, Williamsburg, Va.*)

A MAGNIFICENT SET OF FIREWORKS IN 1768

Pyrotechnics has been an Italian art for centuries past. From Italy skilled makers or displayers of fireworks were often invited to cross the Alps, as well as the English Channel, to add magnificence to royal or national celebrations.

Two of the famous Italian pyrotechnists who were called abroad in the 18th century were Carlo Vigarani and Gaetano Ruggeri. Vigarani, a member of the noted family that created in France the famous "edifices de feu", was named by the King of France in 1770 "Intendant des machines et plaisiers du Roi, inventeur et conducteur des theatres, ballets et fêtes royales." Gaetano Ruggieri was invited to England by George II, for whom he created the military school of pyrotechnics at Woolwich. He died in England in 1782 and was buried in the Cathedral of Canterbury.

When the first Italian pyrotechnists first appeared in North America we do not know. One of the very first was one Jean Gloria, mentioned by Parkman, who made the fireworks in Canada for the celebration of the marriage of Louis XIV in 1659. (Parkman, F., *The Old Regime in Canada,* 1927 ed., 203.)

The first mention of Italian firework makers in the American Colonies is about two Piedmontese brothers whose announcement appeared in the *New York Journal* for April 28, 1768. Two weeks later, on May 12, also in the same journal, they informed the public that they had served as engineers to the King of Sardinia and that they had given "very surprising Specimens of their Abilities before the Royal Family in Spain, and with great applause before his Royal Highness the Duke of Gloucester, and all the nobility at Bath." Apparently they were still, or back, in New York a year later, in June 1769. They were the first of a long line that have come over almost without interruption from year to year, up to our own days, as we shall see in later chapters.

A rare print of the most famous firework display made in London to celebrate the Peace of Aix-la-Chapelle, in 1748. It was constructed by Gaetano Ruggieri of Bologna, the founder of the Royal Laboratory at Woolwich. (From A. St. H. Brock, *Pyrotechnics,* London, 1922, 30.)

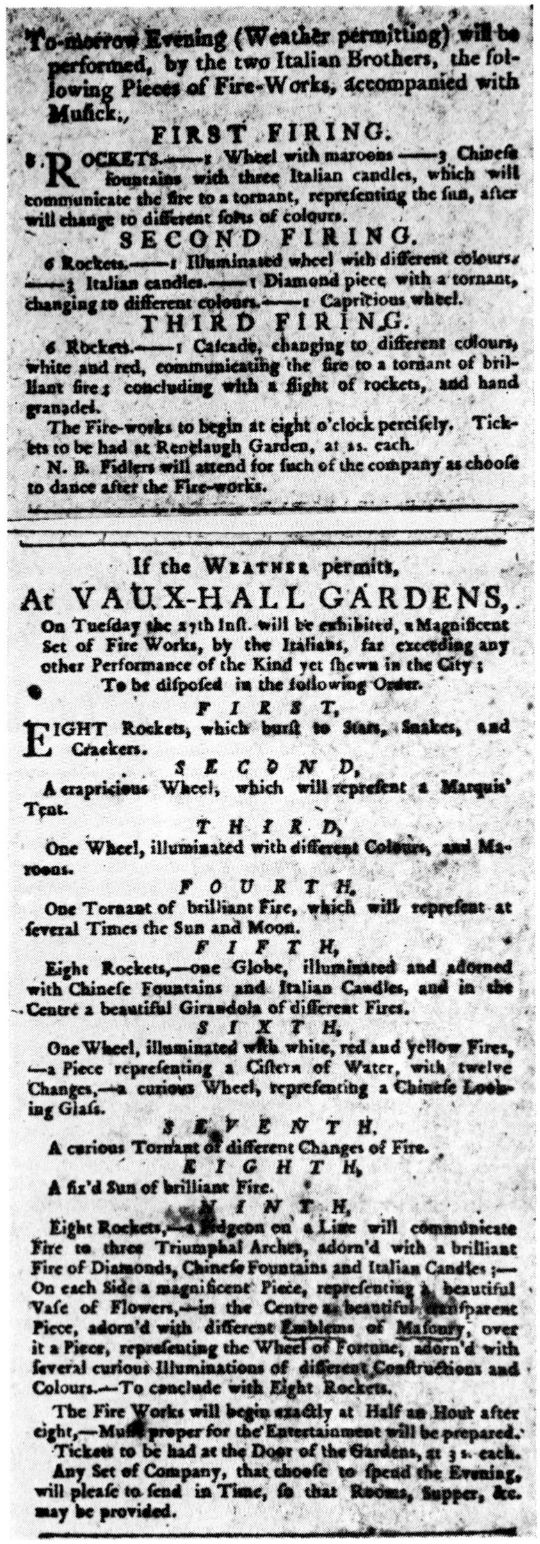

To-morrow Evening (Weather permitting) will be performed, by the two Italian Brothers, the following Pieces of Fire-Works, accompanied with Musick.,

FIRST FIRING.

8 ROCKETS.——1 Wheel with maroons ——3 Chinese fountains with three Italian candles, which will communicate the fire to a tornant, representing the sun, after will change to different sorts of colours.

SECOND FIRING.

6 Rockets.——1 Illuminated wheel with different colours. ——3 Italian candles.——1 Diamond piece with a tornant, changing to different colours.——1 Capricious wheel.

THIRD FIRING.

6 Rockets.——1 Cascade, changing to different colours, white and red, communicating the fire to a tornant of brilliant fire; concluding with a flight of rockets, and hand granades.

The Fire-works to begin at eight o'clock percisely. Tickets to be had at Renelaugh Garden, at 2s. each.

N. B. Fidlers will attend for such of the company as choose to dance after the Fire-works.

If the WEATHER permits,

At VAUX-HALL GARDENS,

On Tuesday the 27th Inst. will be exhibited, a Magnificent Set of Fire Works, by the Italians, far exceeding any other Performance of the Kind yet shewn in the City; To be disposed in the following Order.

FIRST,

EIGHT Rockets, which burst to Stars, Snakes, and Crackers.

SECOND,

A capricious Wheel, which will represent a Marquis' Tent.

THIRD,

One Wheel, illuminated with different Colours, and Maroons.

FOURTH,

One Tornant of brilliant Fire, which will represent at several Times the Sun and Moon.

FIFTH,

Eight Rockets,—one Globe, illuminated and adorned with Chinese Fountains and Italian Candles, and in the Centre a beautiful Girandola of different Fires.

SIXTH,

One Wheel, illuminated with white, red and yellow Fires, —a Piece representing a Cistern of Water, with twelve Changes,—a curious Wheel, representing a Chinese Looking Glass.

SEVENTH.

A curious Tornant of different Changes of Fire.

EIGHTH,

A fix'd Sun of brilliant Fire.

NINTH,

Eight Rockets,—a Pidgeon on a Line will communicate Fire to three Triumphal Arches, adorn'd with a brilliant Fire of Diamonds, Chinese Fountains and Italian Candles;—On each Side a magnificent Piece, representing a beautiful Vase of Flowers,—in the Centre a beautiful transparent Piece, adorn'd with different Emblems of Masonry, over it a Piece, representing the Wheel of Fortune, adorn'd with several curious Illuminations of different Constructions and Colours.—To conclude with Eight Rockets.

The Fire Works will begin exactly at Half an Hour after eight,—Musick proper for the Entertainment will be prepared.

Tickets to be had at the Door of the Gardens, at 3 s. each.

Any Set of Company, that choose to spend the Evening, will please to send in Time, so that Rooms, Supper, &c. may be provided.

Two advertisements of firework displays by two Piedmontese brothers in the *New York Journal* for April 28, 1768, and June 22, 1769. (Courtesy, *New York Public Library.*)

OLIVE OIL AND VERMICELLI

Italian products, from musical instruments and music sheets to olive oil and art wares, were imported in the Colonies, largely through England, long before the Revolution. Vermicelli (thin spaghetti) was imported as early as 1751 (*Virginia Gazette*, September 19, 1751). The English, apparently, took early to spaghetti, for in 1767 one Sam Bowen applied for permission to establish a vermicelli factory. (*Privy Council Office, Unbound Papers,* 1767.)

The early importers, however, were English or Americans. The first Italian importer to settle in New York seems to have been one Anthony Dodane, a marble cutter, who advertised the sale of chimney pieces, slabs and other marble products in the *New York Gazette and Weekly Mercury* after July 4, 1768. He also advertised in the *New York Chronicle* in September, 1769.

The first two Italian manufacturers to settle in Philadelphia and New York, so far as we know, were one Anthony Vitalli and one P. Lenzi. Vitalli advertised the manufacture of sausage in Philadelphia papers for many years after 1772.

ANTHONY VITALLI,
SAUSAGE-MAKER,
Late from ITALY,

AT his ſhop in Fourth-ſtreet, between Walnut and Spruce-ſtreets, nearly oppoſite the houſe of Edward Shippen, Eſq; and at his ſtall every market-day, oppoſite the ſign of the Indian King, ſells all ſorts of Sauſages, as they are made at Milan, Venice, Bologne and Naples, and over all Italy, fit to eat raw, broiled, fried and boiled, and others to make rich ſauces.

As he is a ſtranger in this city, he will be much obliged to the gentlemen and ladies who will pleaſe to favour him with their cuſtom, and will uſe his utmoſt endeavours to pleaſe them, having ſerved his time to this trade, in which he has obtained a ſufficient proficiency.

An advertisement in the *Pennsylvania Packet and the General Advertiser* for Dec. 9, 1772. Vitalli advertised in local newspapers over a long period of years. (Courtesy, *N. Y. Public Library.*)

Lenzi's first advertisements appeared in New York newspapers in 1774. Vitalli came directly from Italy, but Lenzi came from London, where Italian confectioners and ice cream makers have been active ever since Catherine de Medici introduced Italian pastries and ice cream into France.

P. LENZI,
CONFECTIONER,
Lately from LONDON,

TAKES this method to return his ſincere thanks to all his friends and cuſtomers for their paſt favours, and to acquaint them that he has removed from Mr. Richard Waldron near the Exchange, in Broad-Street, into Dock-Street, the 5th door from the corner of Broad-Street, juſt facing to the lamp and pump, continues to make and ſell his great variety of Engliſh, French, German, and Italian cakes, fine and rich plumb cake, preſerved pine, whole, and in ſlips, green gooſeberries, ſtrawberries, tamarinds, and other fruits preſerved, dry, or in brandy; alſo jams, paſtes, jellies, clear cakes, all ſorts of ſugar plumbs, burnt and ſugar almonds, ſhells or dragees, his fine barley ſugar, lemon, and other drops, fine ſyrup of Capillaire, and lemons, preſerved milk, candied fruits; any ſort of ice cream, or fruits; great variety of ſugar and other ornaments to ſell or to lend out, with a great many other articles, every thing warranted in perfection; as he is content with a moderate profit he will ſell at the moſt reaſonable rates, and ſpares no pains nor coſt to have every thing of the very beſt quality. He will undertake to furniſh any great entertainment whatever in as elegant a manner as any in Europe, as he has had the management of ſeveral given at balls, maſquerades, &c. in the moſt capital cities of Europe. Any perſon may be furniſhed with any article in the ſaid buſineſs without any danger or riſk, as he will warrant his ſweet meats for two or three years with good care.—He ſells a particular ſtuff for to make the hair grow long, and thicker.

N. B. Wanted an apprentice, with whom a premium will be expected. 62

One of the many advertisements inserted by the confectioner, P. Lenzi, in New York newspapers. From *Rivington's New York Gazetteer,* June 30, 1774. (Courtesy, *N. Y. Public Library.*)

WILLIAM PARSONS.
At his STORE on Cruger's Wharf,
HAS JUST IMPORTED,
Beſt Florence OIL,

Capers,	Claret,
Olives,	Green Tea,
Anchovies,	Geneva,
Malaga Wines,	Spaniſh dry Hides.

Alſo Jamaica Spirits, Sugars, Coffee, beſt Piſtol Powder, Albany Peas, a few Pieces plain Vellure, an excellent 14 Inch Cable, a quarter wore, 120 Fathom, to be ſold very reaſonable.

ROBERT BASS,
APOTHECARY in Market-ſtreet,
Has this day imported in the Mary and Elizabeth, Capt. Falconer from London,

A VERY great variety of Capital Drugs, and genuine Patent Medicines; well aſſorted for Apothecaries, Druggiſts, and Store-keepers, that purchaſe in the whole ſale way.

Alſo a quantity of French prunes, Italian Vermicelli, and a few truiſleis and morells—Rowley's Britiſh herb tobacco, and ſnuff, Keiſer's genuine famous pills, and the much celebrated arquebuſade.—Hemet's eſſence, and powder of pearl, ſo much eſteemed for the teeth and gums; Straſburgh ſnuff, fine Windſor ſhaving ſoap, &c. &c.—white flint electrical globes, large marble mortars for family uſes, fleſh bruſhes of different ſizes, elaſtic and tobacco ſyrenges, &c. &c.

A very neat collection of the fineſt colours, ſets of crayons; a variety of froſts, and bronzes; Engliſh copal varniſh, and gold lacker. Miniature frames and caſes, prepared canvas, whole, half, and three-quarter lengths, gold and ſilver leaf, gold and ſilver ſhells, tools, and pencils of moſt kinds.

Beſt Florence oil in cheſts, common oil in barrels, ſalt petre, new aniſeed, and antimony, in kegs of an hundred each; beſt refined Venetian borax, &c. &c.

All the above, with every other article of drugs, medicines, and their appurtenances, in preſent uſe and practice, will be ſold wholeſale, and retail, at the moſt reaſonable rates.

N. B. Medicines regularly and properly compounded; and all orders, preſcriptions, and family receipts, duly attended to.

Two early advertisements for Italian olive oil and vermicelli in *the Pennsylvania Journal* for September 28, 1774. (Courtesy, *N. Y. Public Library.*)

CHAPTER SEVEN

WILLIAM PACA

Signer of the Declaration of Independence

Signer of the Declaration of Independence, Chief Justice and Governor of Maryland, William Paca was born on October 21, 1740, at Wye Hall, Hartford County, Md. He died in 1796.

The first of the Paca family to come to America is said to have been Robert Paca, who arrived in 1657. In 1663 he received a grant of lands in Anne Arundel County, Md.

"A tradition in the Paca family gives its origin as Italian and of the same ancestral blood as that of Pope Leo XIII; certain it is, however, that Robert Paca, the original settler in Maryland, came by way of England, but having made no effort to locate his residence there, it was sufficient to know that he was never naturalized in the province, but was as early as 1651 granted a tract of 490 acres in Anne Arundel County for transporting nine men into the Province, according to the conditions of plantations. Other large tracts in the same county were later patented to Robert Paca. Robert Paca married the daughter of one of the commissioners appointed by Oliver Cromwell to govern Maryland. By her he had one son, Aquila, who became high sheriff." (*Baltimore Sun, July* 3, 1904.)

Mr. W. S. Paca of Chestertown, Md., a direct descendant, confirmed the family tradition regarding its Italian origins, both in a letter to the *New York Times* (July 18 1937),in a reply to a letter by the author of the present book, and in a personal interview in 1938. At that time Mr. Paca was 74 years old. On that occasion he recalled how his "aunt Pattie" used to tell him about the trunks in which the Signer of the Declaration used to bring silks from Italy. The trunks were lost in the fire that destroyed the Paca mansion in 1879, together with other precious family records.

The Paca House, now Carvel Hotel, in Annapolis, Md., immortalized by Winston Churchill, an American writer, in his novel "Richard Carvel". Built about 1763-1772 it is still one of the showplaces in the capital of Maryland. (Courtesy, *Hall of Records, Annapolis.*)

The writer, however, is of the opinion that the Paca family was related not to Pope Pecci, but to Cardinal Pacca (1756-1844) of Benevento and Naples. The Pacca family, it is interesting to recall, was allied with several noble families of Southern Italy, including the Aquila family. Is it possible that Robert called his first son Aquila in honor of his relatives across the sea? A search along these lines might prove useful. (See *Italian-American History*, Vol. I, 481-483.)

Wye Hall, William Paca's mansion on Wye Island, Queen Anne County, Maryland. (Courtesy, *Maryland Historical Society.*)

WILLIAM PACA
From the original portrait in the possession of the Maryland Historical Society. (Courtesy, *Maryland Historical Society*)

CHAPTER EIGHT

COLONEL FRANCIS VIGO

and the Conquest of the Old Northwest

COLONEL FRANCIS VIGO
A portrait in the University of Vincennes. From a photograph taken in 1929 at the request and with the assistance of the author.

No man, next to George Rogers Clark, did as much as Francis Vigo to win the old Northwest Territory. In some respects, he did even more than Clark himself.

Francis Vigo was born at Mondovi, near Turin, Italy, on December 3, 1747. At an early age, about 1774, he settled in New Orleans, later moving to St. Louis as the partner in the fur business of the Spanish Governor, De Leyba, and of Emilien Yosti, another native of Italy. Vigo's connections at that time extended as far north as Mackinac and as far east as Pittsburgh and Montreal. He was especially influential with the Frenchmen in the Illinois country (speaking French for a native of Piedmont was a common practice) and with the Indians with whom he traded. Once, asked to what he attributed his influence over them, he replied, "I never deceive an Indian."

Vigo was peacefully attending to his business when in May, 1778, Clark undertook his campaign to wrest from the British the few posts they held at Vincennes, Cahokia, Kaskaskia and, possibly, Detroit. Clark was able to raise only about 150 men and very little money or supplies. He reached Kaskaskia without much difficulty on July 4, 1778, but from then on he was beset with all sorts of troubles. Without getting into many details, Francis Vigo and other local merchants came to his rescue, Vigo alone advancing about one fourth of the total amount raised by Clark in the Illinois country. A priest, Father Gibault, also came to his assistance by enlisting the support of the French inhabitants of that post in favor of Captain Helm, the American in charge.

In December, 1778, Captain Helm, being "destitute of provisions and ammunition," wrote to Clark about it, whereupon Clark sent Vigo over to secure them from the people of Vincennes, among whom he was well known. Vigo left Kaskaskia on December 18, 1778, the day after Helm had been surprised and made prisoner by Hamilton, the British governor. Vigo, of course, did not know that the English had occupied Vincennes when he started on his trip. To make a long story short, he was captured by some Indians who plundered him of everything he possessed and took him to Hamilton. After several weeks of detention, during which Vigo kept his ears and eyes open, he was released, being a Spanish subject, on condition that he do nothing "injurious to the British interests *on his way* to St. Louis." Vigo kept his word, but no sooner had he reached St. Louis than he got in his pirogue and back he went to Kaskaskia, with the following intelligence, as stated by Clark in his letter to Patrick Henry, then Governor of Virginia, dated April 29, 1779: "that Mr. Hamilton had weakened himself, by sending his Indians against the frontiers, and block up the Ohio; that he had not more than eighty men in garrison, three pieces of cannon and some swivels mounted; and that he intended to attack this place, as soon as the winter opened, and made no doubt of clearing the western waters by fall. My situation and circumstances induced me to fall on the resolution of attacking him, before he could collect his Indians again. I was sensible the resolution was as desperate as my situation, but I saw no other probability of securing the country."

Map of the former Northwest Territory (shaded states) won for the United States by George Rogers Clark with the indispensable help of Col. Vigo. (Courtesy, *George Rogers Clark Memorial Commission of Ohio.*)

not improbable that he received instructions to help the Americans and that he kept Vigo informed of what was going on behind the scenes in Madrid, Paris and New Orleans.

In other words, Vigo's assistance, with money or with influence, was valuable, but not as valuable as the information which convinced Clark that no time was to be lost. To attempt a march through swamps and snow in February was nothing short of foolhardy, yet if Clark had remained in Kaskaskia he would have been either defeated, or compelled to leave the country.

On this point Vigo in his memorial to Congress left no doubts. "Your memorialist has not asked nor received any compensation for his services," he wrote, making it clear that he was no spy, who secured information for financial remuneration, "though he is warranted in saying, and the history of the times will prove it, that but for his own personal services, at great risk and hazard to himself, Colonel Clark would not have been enabled to have surprised Hamilton, and the garrison at Vincennes. *It was only through and by the information communicated by the undersigned that Col. Clark succeeded in surprising the post and capturing the troops under Col. Hamilton's command.*" (italics ours.)

As for the results of that victory, some historians believe that it had little to do with the winning of the Northwest Territory, a very facile conclusion that does

In a previous letter, dated two days before the famous march began, Clark wrote also to Patrick Henry: "I know the case is desperate, but Sir, we must either quit the country or attack Mr. Hamilton. No time is to be lost. Was I sure of reinforcement I would not attempt it." Vigo also informed Clark that in his opinion Hamilton was not "under much apprehension of a visit" and that if the Americans could get there undiscovered, they "might take the place." Vigo, in other words, helped Clark to make up his mind and spurred him to go. To prove his faith in the outcome, he cashed another draft for $1,452, and, it is said, fitted out at his expense a keel-boat with two cannon and forty men. He also used his influence to induce a company of Frenchmen to join the expedition. The French volunteers comprised one half of Clark's force. The rest is history.

Some writers have laid too much stress on the money that Vigo advanced to Clark and on his influence with the French inhabitants of Kaskaskia and Vincennes, whom he rallied to the American cause. All that is fine, but one must remember that Vigo was not the only man who advanced Clark some money, and certainly not the only individual who induced the French settlers to support the Americans. Father Gibault also did his share, and so did other citizens. De Leyba, too, assisted Clark.

In our opinion, neither Vigo nor Gibault had to work hard to convince any Frenchman in those days to side with the Americans. France was already at war with England and Spain was helping under cover. As for De Leyba it is

Col. Vigo's statue by John Angel in the national memorial to Clark at Vincennes, dedicated by President F. D. Roosevelt in 1936.

not take into account the most potent psychological factor that the English had lost the war and that they could not very well afford to insist in retaining what was more or less a buffer zone between Virginia and Louisiana (the territory, not the present state). Two more important factors, however, should be added.

The first, was the settlement of some 20,000 Americans following the capture of Vincennes, 20,000 resolute Americans who were determined not to fall again under British domination. The second, was the silent, or inactive, support of the Indians.

Professor James Alton James in a paper read before the Mississippi Valley Historical Association in April, 1929, stated that the disaffection among the Indians who until then had been loyal to Britain was so great that "according to British testimony the Sioux was the only nation still true to them" after the fall of Vincennes. "Three expeditions sent to intercept the Americans, retreated precipitately upon hearing the report that Clark was advancing against Detroit. A campaign against Vincennes and another against Fort Pitt were likewise abandoned."

Something here, however, does not make sense. Why would the English retreat "precipitately" if in that very summer of 1779 Clark was "forced to forego the march against Detroit . . . for want of a few men?" Propaganda, of course, or rumor, may have had something to do with it, but it is most unlikely that the English would have retreated, rumors or no rumors, had they been sure of Indian support.

Now the man who could influence the Indians to remain neutral was Vigo, the only person on the American side to enjoy a great prestige among them. "His influence is greatest among the Indians than any man I know of, and it is always exerted for the interest of his Country," wrote Major Doughty to Secretary of War Knox, who relayed the information and an account of Vigo's activities to Washington. Whereupon the President asked the Secretary to thank Vigo for "the essential services" he had rendered the Major. In 1784, Vigo, while on the way to Detroit on business, was arrested by the British and finally was released upon posting a bond of 500 pounds sterling. Vigo was accused of having helped Clark, but whether at Vincennes, or after the capture of that post, we have not found out.

Consolato Generale di S. M. il Re di Sardegna presso gli Stati Uniti d'America

N° 117.

246
1827

... li 6 Agosto 1827

Illustrissimo Signore

America, e andarlo a trovare nello Stato in cui Ella risiede.
Conservando quei suoi Parenti l'intenzione medesima e mancando tuttavia di mezzi opportuni onde intraprendere il contemplato viaggio, desiderano sapere s'Ella potrebbe provvederne, come ebbe già a farne loro l'offerta. —
A tale oggetto la prego a voler ...

Al Signor Francesco Vigo
Vincennes

Facsimile of a letter in Italian from the Sardinian Consul in Philadelphia to Vigo. From the Vigo Papers in the possession of the Vigo Chapter, D.A.R. (Courtesy, *Miss Dorothy Riker, Historical Bureau, State House, Indianapolis.*)

The two tombstones on Vigo's grave. The small one was placed at the time of his death; the larger one was erected in 1909 by the Vigo Chapter of the Daughters of the American Revolution.

Washington was so impressed with Vigo's standing with the Indians that he called him to Carlisle, Pa., in 1789, to discuss the defense of the western country. A year later, on December 20, 1790, he authorized Vigo to deliver two talks to the Chickasaws and Chocktaws and gave him a letter reading: "Mr. Vigo, the bearer, will bring you goods conformably to the treaty of Hopewell, and I shall take other measures early next year, to convince you of the further kindness of the United States. In the meantime hold fast the Chain of friendship, and do not believe any evil report against the justice and integrity of the United States," (*The Writings of George Washington,* ed. by Fitzpatrick, XXXI, 184). In other words, Vigo was chosen in order to reassure the Indians about America's good faith. The importance of that mission, at a time when the British were still trying to incite the Indians against the United States cannot be overemphasized.

Even more valuable was Vigo's assistance to General "Mad Anthony" Wayne, as it appears from a number of letters Wayne sent to Vigo in 1794 which are now in the Pennsylvania Historical Society. One of them, dated May 27, 1794, is reproduced on the next page. On July 5, 1794, Wayne instructed Vigo "to bribe or get possession of the Spanish express between Port Louis or the Mississippi and Detroit." Vigo soon got to work, as he informed Wayne on August 6. Fourteen days later Wayne defeated the Indians at the Battle of Fallen Timbers solving "for a while at least, most of the Indian difficulties." (Winsor, *Narrative and Critical History of America,* 1888, VII, 453).

Vigo rendered other services, as in 1805, when he and General Gibson were sent on a mission to the Miami, Pottawatmie, and Delaware Indians. A year later, when the University of Vincennes was organized, he became one of its first trustees. He was also instrumental in establishing the first circulating library in Vincennes. When in 1836 the State Bank of Indiana issued its first bank notes they had a "vignette likeness" of Vigo upon them.

Vigo never got the money he advanced to Clark. In 1876, or forty years after his death, the United States Supreme Court ordered the payment to Vigo's heirs of his claim which, including interest, had reached the sum of $49,898.60.

In 1800 Governor St. Clair appointed Vigo a colonel in the First Regiment of Knox County Militia, a position he held until 1810, when ill health forced him to resign. Years later a county in the State of Indiana was named in his honor. But when he died not even the undertaker could be paid the twenty dollars for the cost of the funeral. The proceeds from the sale of his property were only seventy-seven dollars and sixty-two cents.

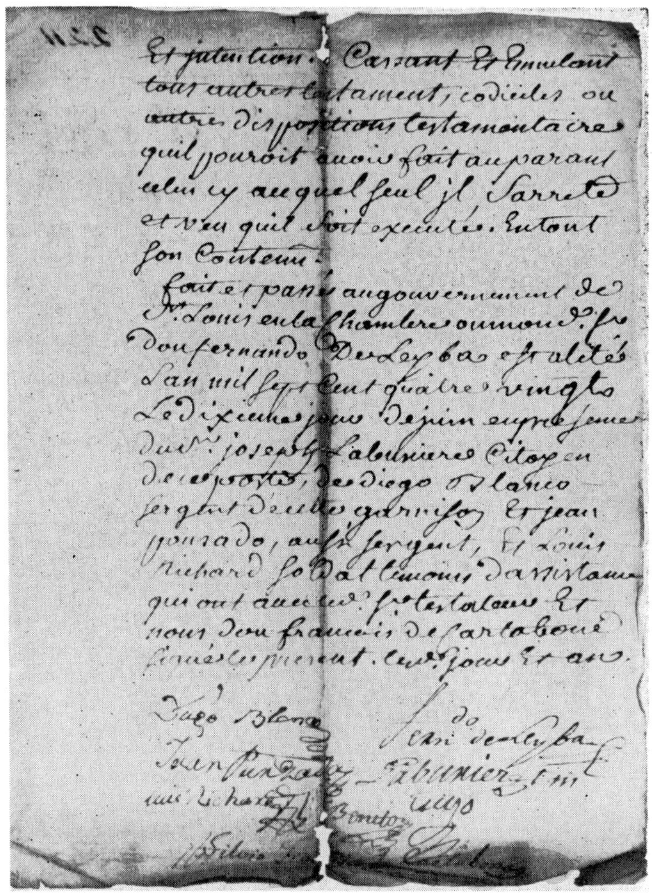
Et intention. Cassant Et annulant
tous autres testament, codiciles ou
autres dispositions testamentaires
quil pouroit avoir fait auparavant
celui cy auquel seul il sarrete
et veu quil soit executé. Entout
son Contenu.
fait et passé augouvernement de
St. Louis enla chambre ou mond. sr
don fernando De Leyba
l'an mil sept Cent quatre vingts
Le dixième jour de juin en presence
du sr. joseph Labuxiere Citoyen
de ce poste, de diego Blanco
sergent de cette garnison Et jean
Tourado, aussi sergent, Et Louis
Richard
nous don francois de Cartabone

Last page of the will of the Spanish Governor of Missouri, De Leyba, with the signature of Vigo, its executor. (Courtesy, *Pennsylvania Historical Society.*)

To recapitulate, if Vigo had not furnished Clark the vital information which prompted him to march on Vincennes in the heart of winter, Clark would have been either defeated or compelled to leave the country.

After Vincennes, if Vigo had not exerted his influence among the Indians (before the Americans warred on them and took their lands away from them) and secured their passive cooperation by not siding with the English,

1. no Americans would have been able to settle in the new country between 1779 and 1783;
2. without settlers and without Indian cooperation, Clark would have not held a vestige of possession;
3. without American possession and with the Indians on their side, the English negotiators at Paris in 1783 would have not acquiesced so easily to the boundaries demanded by the Americans.
4. Vigo's vital role in the acquisition of the old Northwest Territory is, therefore, unquestionable.

The bell in the Vigo County Court House, Vigo County, Indiana, bought with $500 bequeathed by Vigo for that purpose, in his will.

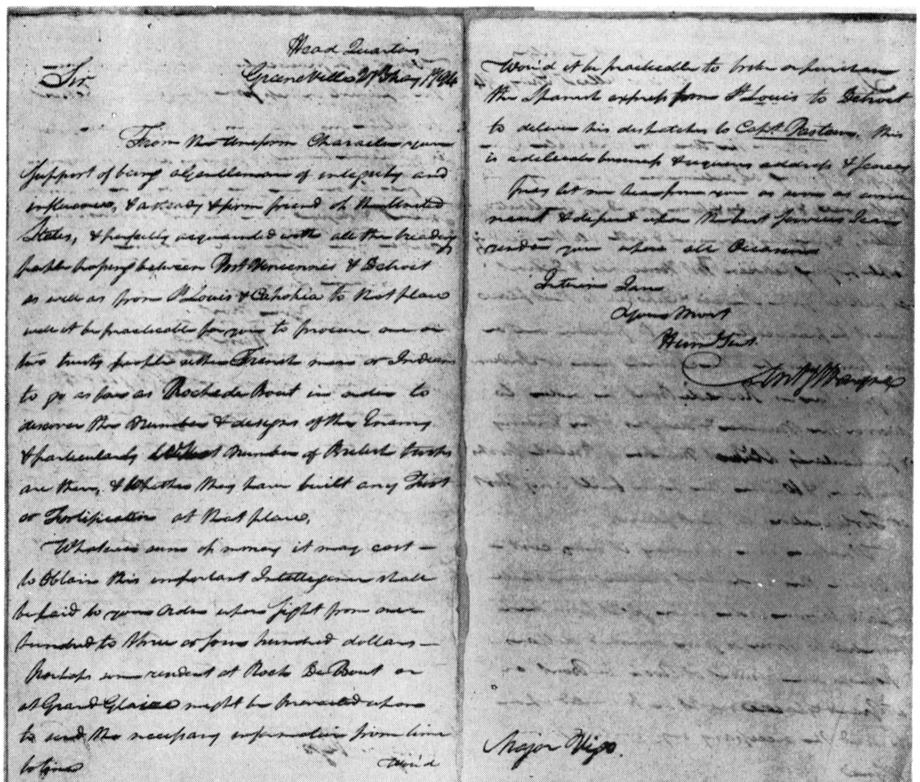

Head Quarters
Greeneville 27th May 1794

Sir

From the uniform Character & your Support of being a Gentleman of integrity and influence, & a steady & firm friend of the United States, & perfectly acquainted with all the trading paths leading between Post Vincennes & Detroit as well as from St. Louis & Cahokia to that place would it be practicable for you to procure one or two trusty people either French men or Indians to go as far as Roche de Bout in order to discover the Numbers & designs of the Enemy & particularly what Number of British troops are there, & Whether they have built any Fort or Fortification at that place,

Whatever sum of money it may cost to obtain this important Intelligence shall be paid to your Order upon sight from one hundred to three or four hundred dollars — Perhaps some resident at Roche De Bout or at Grand Glaize might be prevailed upon to send the necessary information from time to time

Wou'd it be practicable to take or purloin the Spanish express from St. Louis to Detroit to deliver his dispatches to Capt. [illegible]. This is a delicate business & requires address & secrecy

Pray let me hear from you as soon as convenient & depend upon the best services I can render you upon all Occasions

Interim I am
Your Most
Hum Servt.
Antny Wayne

Major Vigo.

Facsimile of a letter from Anthony Wayne to Vigo, in which Wayne asks for Vigo's support in his campaign against the Indians. (Courtesy, *Pennsylvania Historical Society.*)

CHAPTER NINE

PHILIP MAZZEI

One of America's Founding Fathers

Philip Mazzei was one of the fathers of the American nation and of American democracy.

The American nation, in a way, had been taking shape long before Mazzei set foot on American soil. It was not the product of any one man, or set of men; it was not due, as it has been erroneously stated, to the "genius" of any one particular ethnic group; it was not the natural by-product of the Magna Carta or other Anglo-Saxon institutions. The American nation was created primarily by the frontier, by the opportunities within reach of free men, by the spirit of independence that those opportunities made possible. The history of recent immigrants from Eastern and Southern Europe shows abundantly that a peddler from a Polish ghetto or a peasant from Sicily can attain the same degree of individuality and independence as Thomas Jefferson or James Madison—of course, relatively speaking.

The American nation was the symbol of a new way of life, of the American way of life; of a new set of standards; of lack of traditions; of economic independence, without which there can never be political freedom. Nobody showed that better than the Hessian soldiers who deserted from their army to find freedom and independence in the backwoods of Virginia.

Yet, if without the frontier there would have been only a limited economic independence, without absolute political freedom the frontier would have been meaningless.

Mazzei played a prominent role in the achievement of America's political independence. He did that (1) by hammering on the false assumption entertained at the time of his arrival in Virginia that a conflict was not inevitable and that an agreement with England was possible; (2) by trying to convince his Virginia friends, particularly Thomas Jefferson, that the English Constitution was not the model of perfection they thought it to be; (3) by writing articles in the local *Gazette* and by talking at round tables and in private homes, as well as in churches, on the political issues of the day; (4) by exerting personal pressure on influential people in Europe; (5) finally, through his book, *Recherches Historiques et Politiques*, which proved to be a most effective weapon in combating the anti-American propaganda that the British and other enemies of the United States were spreading in Europe to hamper the rising nation and particularly to discourage European emigration.

PHILIP MAZZEI
From a miniature made in Paris in 1790. (From *Philip Mazzei—Friend of Jefferson,* by Richard C. Garlick, The Johns Hopkins Press, Baltimore, 1933).

Few men in America were so well-equipped for his self-imposed task, or had so many influential friends in England and on the Continent during the crucial years of the American Revolution, as Mazzei. He put his knowledge, experience, prestige, and whatever money he had, at the service of his adopted country. No other native of Continental Europe, with the possible exception of Lafayette and Von Steuben, contributed so much to the rise of the Republic.

MAZZEI'S EARLY LIFE

Mazzei's story has been told in detail and with numerous notes and facsimiles of corroborating documents in a special monograph by the author published in 1951. Here we shall, therefore, give a brief outline of his life.

Philip Mazzei was born at Poggio a Cajano, a small town near Florence, Italy, on Dec. 25, 1730. After studying surgery until 1752, he emigrated to Smyrna, Turkey,

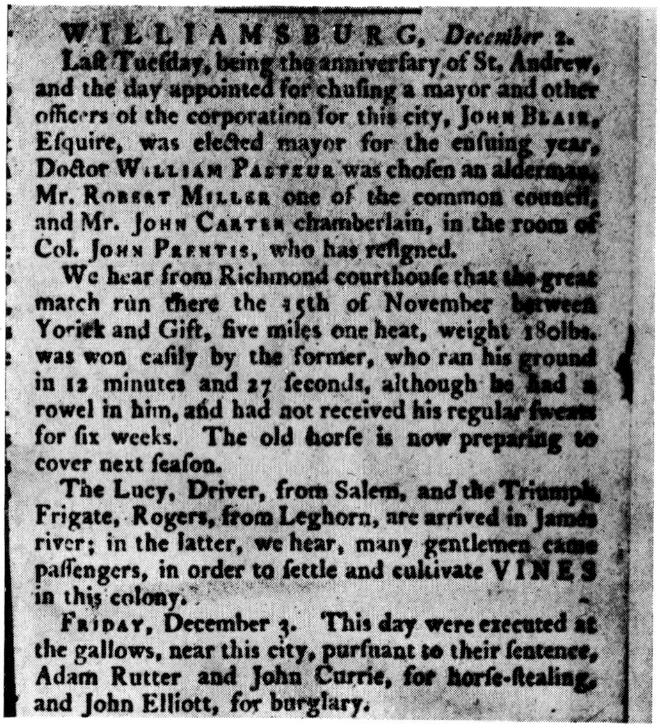

WILLIAMSBURG, *December* 2.

Laſt Tueſday, being the anniverſary of St. Andrew, and the day appointed for chuſing a mayor and other officers of the corporation for this city, JOHN BLAIR, Eſquire, was elected mayor for the enſuing year, Doctor WILLIAM PASTEUR was choſen an alderman, Mr. ROBERT MILLER one of the common council, and Mr. JOHN CARTER chamberlain, in the room of Col. JOHN PRENTIS, who has reſigned.

We hear from Richmond courthouſe that the great match run there the 15th of November between Yorick and Gift, five miles one heat, weight 180lbs. was won eaſily by the former, who ran his ground in 12 minutes and 27 ſeconds, although he had a rowel in him, and had not received his regular ſweats for ſix weeks. The old horſe is now preparing to cover next ſeaſon.

The Lucy, Driver, from Salem, and the Triumph Frigate, Rogers, from Leghorn, are arrived in James river; in the latter, we hear, many gentlemen came paſſengers, in order to ſettle and cultivate VINES in this colony.

FRIDAY, December 3. This day were executed at the gallows, near this city, purſuant to their ſentence, Adam Rutter and John Currie, for horſe-ſtealing, and John Elliott, for burglary.

The first announcement of Mazzei's arrival in America. *Virginia Gazette,* (Rind), December 2, 1773. (Courtesy, *Colonial Williamsburg, Williamsburg, Va.*)

where he spent four years. From 1756 to 1773, with the exception of two brief trips to Italy, he lived in London.

In England Mazzei earned his living as a merchant, primarily as an importer of Italian products. That, however, did not keep him from associating with diplomats, political leaders, and distinguished writers, like the famous Giuseppe Baretti. He also served as agent of the Grand Duke of Tuscany.

Having met some Americans in London, including Benjamin Franklin, he was induced to settle in Virginia and to establish an agricultural company there. Shortly after his arrival with several Tuscan gardeners at the end of 1773, a number of influential Virginians, including George Washington and Thomas Jefferson, put up the sum of 2,000 pounds sterling (about $10,000) so that he could plant grapevines and other Mediterranean plants. The venture, however, was not much of a success (he succeeded in introducing a number of vegetables which at that time were not known in America) because he soon became involved in the struggle for independence.

MAZZEI AND THE DECLARATION OF INDEPENDENCE

Mazzei was regarded so highly by his fellow-Virginians that not long after his arrival he was elected a vestryman of St. Anne's Parish in Albemarle County, and a member of the county committee, two very important positions, as explained in our monograph. When Patrick Henry with a small band of men marched against the English, Mazzei, Bellini, and one of the gardeners Mazzei had brought to Virginia, joined him, but the English withdrew and the Americans went home. In 1777 he tried again to join the Continental Army, but Patrick Henry forbade him to do so, as he could be more useful in other ways.

Mazzei remained in Virginia from November, 1773, to January, 1779, when he was sent on a special mission to Europe. During those five years he worked tirelessly to warn the Americans against the ever-growing menace from London; he kept them informed of what was going on behind the scenes in the English capital—he had friends there who sent him confidential information—he took part in the drafting of some laws and reforms, including, possibly, the first draft of the Virginia Constitution of 1776. Of particular interest is an article which he wrote in Italian and which, translated by Jefferson, is said to have appeared in the *Virginia Gazette*. That article contains words so reminiscent of those in the preamble to the Declaration of Independence that one wonders whether, or to what extent, Mazzei influenced Jefferson, or Mason, on this point. At any rate, Jefferson sent to him one of the first drafts he made of the Declaration in Philadelphia.

In 1779 Mazzei was sent to Europe as Virginia's special envoy, but because of the opposition of Franklin, who felt that the Congress and not individual states were to be represented abroad, Mazzei could not accomplish much. But he served America well just the same, through his contacts in France, Holland and Italy. While in Paris he was in close touch with John Adams and other leading Americans.

When Jefferson was sent to Europe to take Franklin's place, Mazzei paved his way and rendered his mission easier, as related in the above-mentioned monograph.

Back in America for a few months, he established a "Society of the Constitution," the main purpose of which was to "keep a watchful eye over the great fundamental rights of the people." Its members included James Madi-

MAZZEI'S ASSOCIATES IN HIS AGRICULTURAL COMPANY
(as listed in the facsimile on the opposite page)

Lord Dunmore was the governor of the Colony; Peyton Randolph was president of the first Continental Congress (1774); Robert Carter Nicholas was treasurer of the Colony; Thomas Adams, the man who induced Mazzei to settle in Virginia, was a rich merchant; George Mason was the author of the Virginia Bill of Rights; George Washington and Thomas Jefferson need no introduction; John Page of Rosewell was a member of the Virginia Convention of 1776, a member of Congress, and governor of Virginia; Benjamin Harrison was a member of the first Continental Congress, a signer of the Declaration of Independence, governor of Virginia, and father of William H. Harrison, ninth president of the United States; Thomas Mann Randolph, the husband of Martha Jefferson, was governor of Virginia, and managed Thomas Jefferson's estates during his absences; Dr. James McClurg was a delegate to the Federal Convention of 1787; Thomas Nelson Jr., a signer of the Declaration of Independence, was governor of Virginia; Allen Cooke was a member of the Virginia Convention of 1776; John Tabb was a member of the Virginia Committee of Safety; John Blair was judge of the Virginia High Court of Chancery, delegate to the Constitutional Convention of 1787, signer of the Constitution, and justice of the United States Supreme Court; Dr. Theodorick Bland, Jr. was a member of Congress; Archibald Cary was, as a recent biographer has called him, "the wheelhorse of the Revolution" because of the foundries, mills, etc. which he owned; W. Miles Cary was a member of the Virginia Convention of 1776 and is said to have been so rich that when George Washington courted his daughter he haughtily reminded him that she had a coach of her own to drive; the few others we have not identified, like John Tayloe and Charles Carter, Jr., were rich planters.

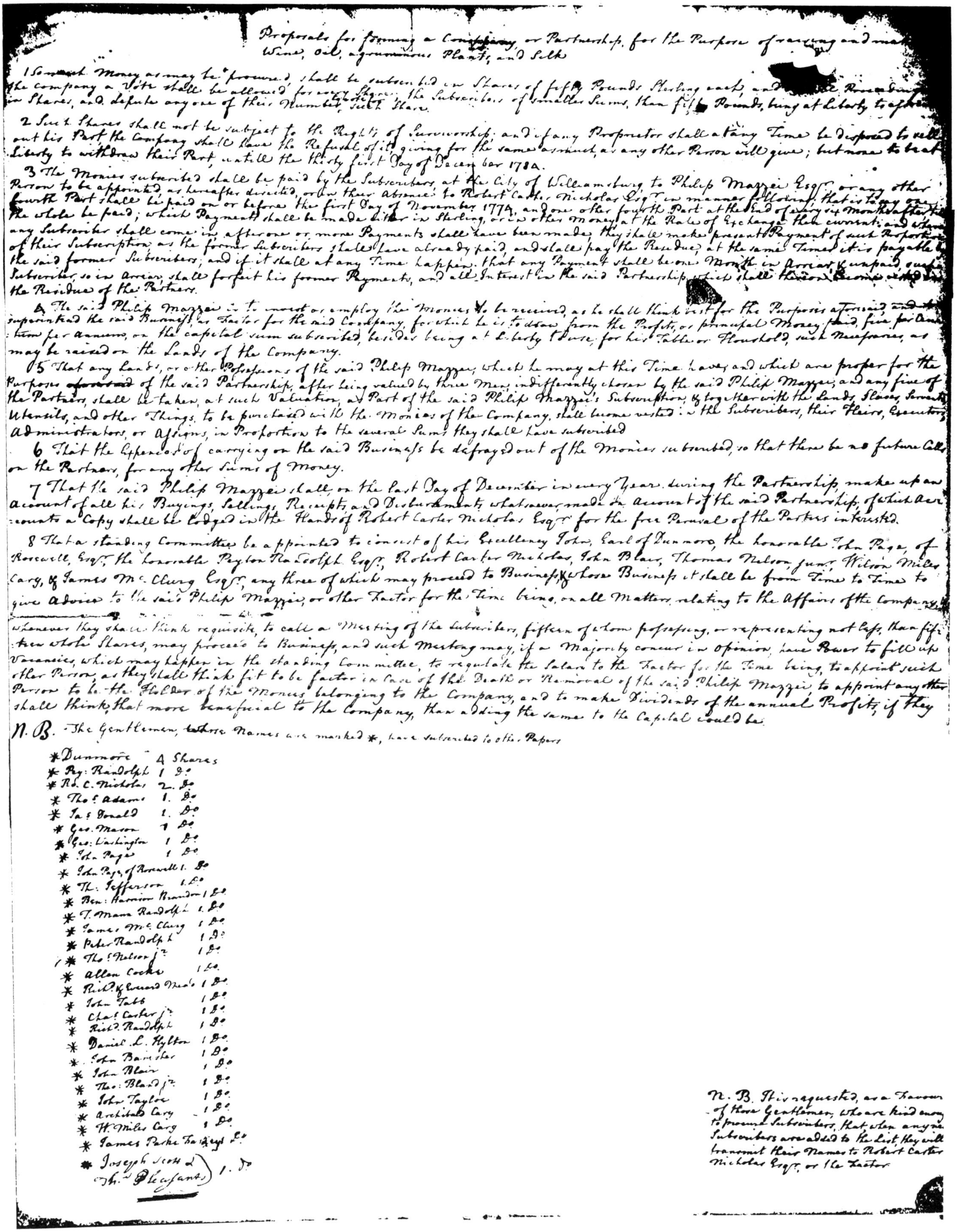

Proposals for forming a Company or Partnership, for the Purpose of raising and making Wine, Oil, agrumiuous Plants, and Silk

1 Such Money as may be procured, shall be subscribed in Shares of fifty Pounds Sterling each, and [illegible] the company a Vote shall be allowed for every Share: the Subscribers of smaller Sums, than fifty Pounds, being at Liberty to [illegible] in Shares, and depute any one of their Number, such Share.

2 Such Shares shall not be subject to the Rights of Survivorship: and if any Proprietor shall at any Time be disposed to sell out his Part, the Company shall have the Refusal of it, giving for the same as much, as any other Person will give; but none to be at Liberty to withdraw their Part, untill the thirty first Day of December 1780.

3 The Monies subscribed shall be paid by the Subscribers, at the City of Williamsburg to Philip Mazzei Esqr, or any other Person to be appointed as hereafter directed, or in their Absence to Robert Carter Nicholas Esqr in manner following, that is to say one fourth Part shall be paid on or before the first Day of November 1774, and one other fourth Part at the End of every six Months after, till the whole be paid; which Payment shall be made either in Sterling, or in other Money at the Rate of Exchange then current; and when any Subscriber shall come in after one or more Payments shall have been made, they shall make present Payment of such Proportion of their Subscription as the former Subscribers shall have already paid, and shall pay the Residue, at the same Time it is payable by the said former Subscribers; and if it shall at any Time happen, that any Payment shall be one Month in Arrear & unpaid, such Subscriber, so in Arrear, shall forfeit his former Payments, and all Interest in the said Partnership which shall thereon become vested in the Residue of the Partners.

4 The said Philip Mazzei is to invest or employ the Monies to be received, as he shall think best for the Purposes aforesaid, and to superintend the said Business as Factor for the said Company, for which he is to draw from the Profits, or principal Money paid, five per Centum per Annum, on the capital sum subscribed, besides being at Liberty to use, for his Table or Houshold, such Necessaries, as may be raised on the Lands of the Company.

5 That any Lands, or other Possessions of the said Philip Mazzei, which he may at this Time have, and which are proper for the Purposes ~~aforesaid~~ of the said Partnership, after being valued by three Men indifferently chosen by the said Philip Mazzei, and any five of the Partners, shall be taken, at such Valuation, as Part of the said Philip Mazzei's Subscription, & together with the Lands, Slaves, Servants, Utensils, and other Things, to be purchased with the Monies of the Company, shall become vested in the Subscribers, their Heirs, Executors, Administrators, or Assigns, in Proportion to the several Sums they shall have subscribed

6 That the Expences of carrying on the said Business be defrayed out of the Monies subscribed, so that there be no future Calls on the Partners, for any other Sums of Money.

7 That the said Philip Mazzei shall, on the last Day of December in every Year during the Partnership, make up an Account of all his Buyings, Sellings, Receipts, and Disbursements whatsoever, made on Account of the said Partnership, of which Accounts a Copy shall be lodged in the Hands of Robert Carter Nicholas Esqr for the free Perusal of the Parties interested.

8 That a standing Committee be appointed to consist of his Excellency John, Earl of Dunmore, the honorable John Page, of Rosewell, Esqr, the honorable Peyton Randolph Esqr, Robert Carter Nicholas, John Blair, Thomas Nelson, junr, Wilson Miles Cary, & James McClurg Esqrs, any three of which may proceed to Business, & whose Business it shall be from Time to Time to give Advice to the said Philip Mazzei, or other Factor for the Time being, on all Matters relating to the Affairs of the Company, whenever they shall think requisite, to call a Meeting of the Subscribers, fifteen of whom possessing, or representing not less than fifteen whole Shares, may proceed to Business, and such Meeting may, if a Majority concur in Opinion, have Power to fill up Vacancies, which may happen in the standing Committee, to regulate the Salary to the Factor for the Time being, to appoint such other Person, as they shall think fit to be Factor in Case of the Death or Removal of the said Philip Mazzei, to appoint any other Person to be the Holder of the Monies belonging to the Company, and to make Dividends of the annual Profits, if they shall think that more beneficial to the Company, than adding the same to the Capital would be.

N. B. The Gentlemen, whose Names are marked *, have subscribed to other Papers

*Dunmore 4 Shares
* Pey: Randolph 1 Do
* Ro. C. Nicholas 2. Do
* Thos Adams 1. Do
* Jas Donald 1. Do
* Geo: Mason 1 Do
* Geo: Washington 1 Do
* John Page 1 Do
* John Page, of Rosewell 1. Do
* Th: Jefferson 1. Do
* Ben: Harrison Brandon 1 Do
* T. Mann Randolph 1. Do
* James McClurg 1 Do
* Peter Randolph 1 Do
* Thos Nelson jr 1 Do
* Allen Cocke 1 Do
* Richd & Everard Meade 1 Do
* John Tabb 1 Do
* Chas Carter jr 1 Do
* Richd Randolph 1 Do
* Daniel L. Hylton 1 Do
* John Banister 1 Do
* John Blair 1 Do
* Theo: Bland jr 1 Do
* John Taylor 1 Do
* Archibald Cary 1 Do
* W. Miles Cary 1 Do
* James Parke Farley 1 Do
* Joseph Scott & Thos Pleasants 1. Do

N. B. It is requested, as a Favour of those Gentlemen, who are kind enough to procure Subscribers, that when any new Subscribers are added to the List, they will transmit their Names to Robert Carter Nicholas Esqr, or the Factor

Contract for the organization of Mazzei's agricultural company. (Reduced to one-fourth its original size.) Notice Washington's name, the seventh from the top. See also full list, with identifications, on the opposite page. (Courtesy, *Virginia Historical Society. Richmond. Va.*)

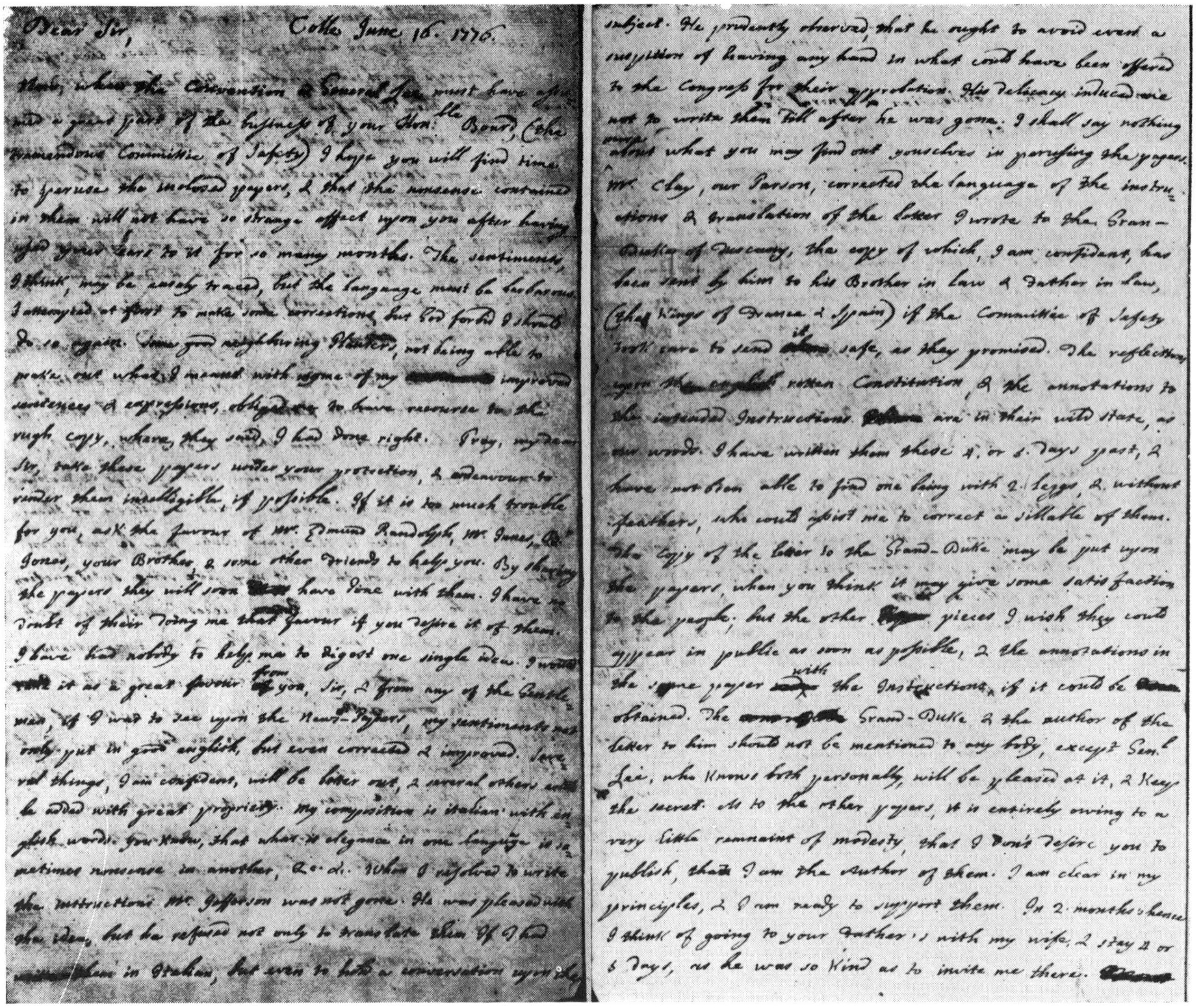

The first two pages of the letter Mazzei sent with his "instructions" to Colonel Page, during the Virginia Convention of 1776. (Courtesy, *Library of Congress*).

MAZZEI'S LETTER TO JOHN PAGE (in full)

Colle, June 16, 1776.

Dear Sir,

Now, when the Convention & General Lee must have assumed a great part of the business of your Hon.ble Board, (the tremendous Committie of Safety) I hope you will find time to peruse the inclosed papers, & that the nonsense contained in them will not have so strange effect upon you after having used your ears to it for so many months. The sentiments, I think, may be easily traced, but the language must be barbarous. I attempted at first to make some corrections, but God forbid I should do so again. some good neighbouring Planters, not being able to make out what I meant with some of my improved sentences & expressions, obliged me to have recourse to the rugh copy, where, they said, I had done right. Pray, my dear Sir, take these papers under your protection, & endeavour to render them intelligible, if possible. If it is too much trouble for you, ask the favour of Mr. Edmund Randolph, Mr. Innes, Dr. Jones, your Brother, & some other Friends to help you. By sharing the papers they will soon have done with them. I have no doubt of their doing me that favour if you desire it of them. I have had nobody to help me to digest one single idea. I would take it as a great favour from you, Sir, & from any of the Gentlemen, if I was to see upon the News-Papers, my sentiments not only put in good english, but even corrected & improved. Several things, I am confident, will be better out, & several others could be added with great propriety. My composition is italian with english words. You know, that what is elegance in one language is sometimes nonsense in another, & &. When I resolved to write the instructions Mr. Jefferson was not gone. He was pleased with the idea, but he refused not only to translate them If I had written them in Italian, but even to hold a conversation upon he subject. He prudently observed, that he ought to avoid even a suspition of having any hand in what could have been offered to the Congress for their approbation. His delicacy induced me not to write them till after he was gone. I shall say nothing more about what you may find out yourselves in perusing the papers. Mr. Clay, our Parson, corrected the language of the instructions and translation of the letter I wrote to the Gran-Duke of Tuscany, the copy of which, I am confident, has been sent by him to his Brother in law & Father in law, (the Kings of France & Spain) if the Committee of Safety took care to send it safe, as they promised. The reflections upon the english rotten Constitution, & the annotations to the intended Instructions are in their wild state, as our woods. I have written them these 4, or 5 days past, & have not been able to find one being with 2 leggs, & without feathers, who could assist me to correct a sillable of them. The copy of the letter to the Grand-Duke may be put upon the papers, when you think it may give some satisfaction to the people; but the other pieces I wish they could appear in public as soon as possible, & the annotations in the same paper with the Instructions, if it could be obtained. The Grand-Duke and the author of the letter to him should not be mentioned to any body, except Gen.l Lee, who knows both personally, will be pleased at it, & keep the secret. As to the other papers, it is entirely owing to a very little remnaint of modesty, that I don't desire you to publish, that I am the Author of them. I am clear in my principles, & I am ready to support them. In 2. months's hence I think of going to your Father's with my wife, & stay 4 or 5 days, as he was so kind as to invite me there. Your son appeared to be very glad to see me when I was there in march. 2. of my farmers thaught themselves in Paradise as soon as they saw in your father's house a specimen of the Italian buildings. They both desired to be left there. I wish you will ask your brother, after having espressed my great regard & esteem for him, if he thinks the time I have mentioned (about the 13th or 20th of August) will be agreable to your Parents for my & my wife's going there, & that he will be so good a friend to me as to let me know it with philosophical liberty, mentioning what other time I could fix, if that was not so proper. Pray, my best respects to Mrs. Page, & with the most friendly regard & esteem I have the honor to be,

Dear Sir,

your most obedient Humble Serv.t
Philip Mazzei

P.S. I will be obliged to you, Sir, if you will be so kind as to remember me to Dr. M.c Clurg, Mr. Davies, & the other Gentlemen I used to see at your house,' present my compliments to them.

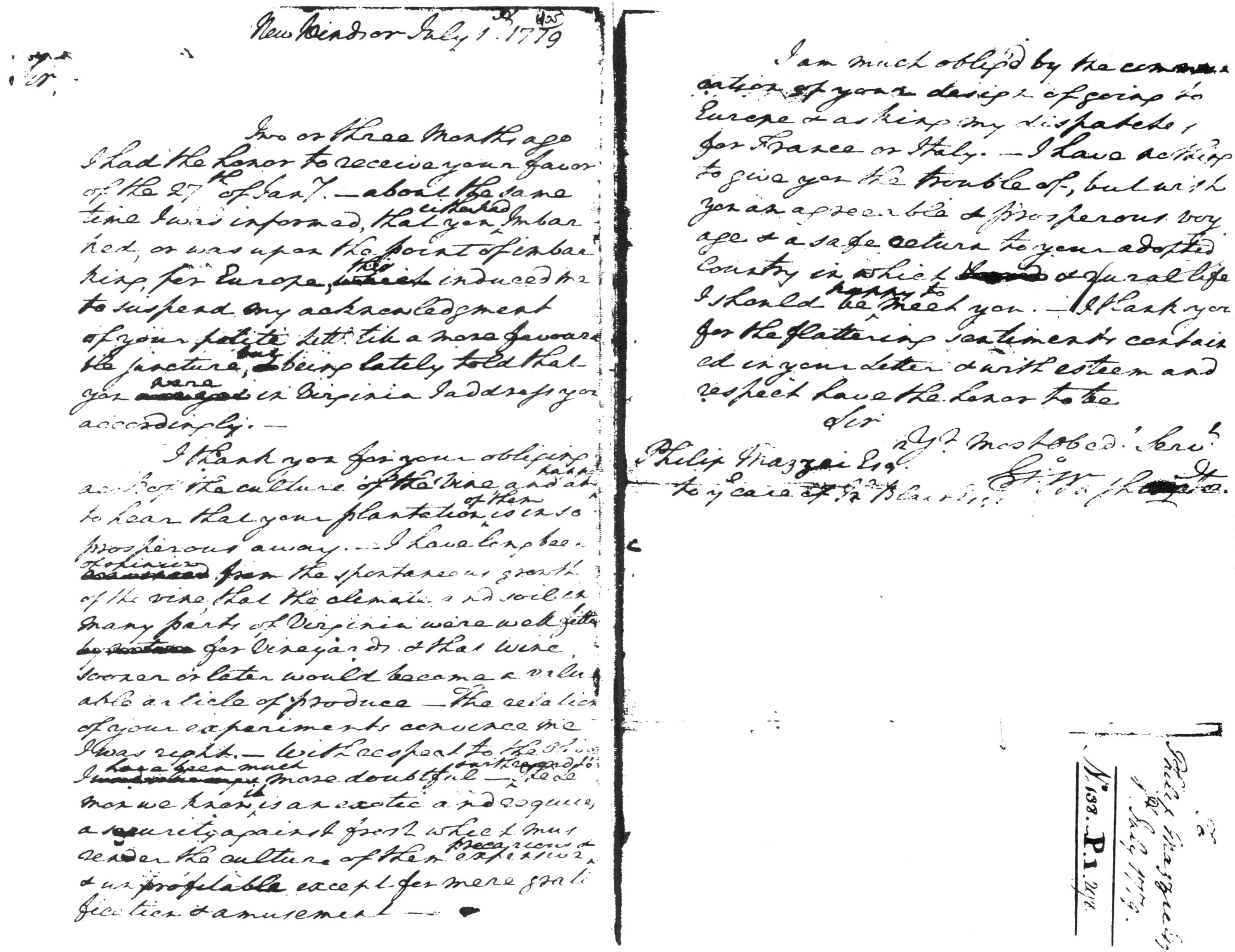
New Windsor July 1. 1779

Sir,

Two or three Months ago I had the honor to receive your favor of the 27th of Jany. — about the same time I was informed, that you either had Imbarked, or was upon the point of imbarking for Europe, this induced me to suspend my acknowledgment of your polite Lettr. till a more favourable juncture; but being lately told that you were in Virginia I address you accordingly. —

I thank you for your obliging acct. of the culture of the Vine and am happy to hear that your plantation of them is in so prosperous a way. — I have long been of opinion from the spontaneous growth of the vine, that the climate and soil in many parts of Virginia were well fitted for Vineyards & that Wine, sooner or later would become a valuable article of produce — The relation of your experiments convince me I was right. — With respect to the Olive I have been much more doubtful — the tree more we know, it is an exotic and requires a security against frost which must render the culture of them precarious & expensive, & unprofitable except for mere gratification & amusement —

I am much obliged by the communication of your design of going to Europe & asking my dispatches for France or Italy. — I have nothing to give you the trouble of, but wish you an agreeable & prosperous voyage & a safe return to your adopted Country in which a rural life I should be happy to meet you. — I thank you for the flattering sentiments contained in your Letter & with esteem and respect have the honor to be

Sir

Yr. Most obedt. Servt.

Go: Washington

Philip Mazzei Esqr.
to ye care of Mr. Blair

To Philip Mazzei Esqr. 1st July 1779.
No. 138. P.1. 290.

Letter written by George Washington to Mazzei on July 1, 1779, wishing him "a prosperous voyage & safe return." The letter is especially worthy of notice as in those days Washington was busy with war operations. (*Courtesy, Library of Congress*).

Andando VJ. in Francia senza mie lettere, parrà cosa molto strana a varj degnissimi soggetti, i quali ebbero per me una bontà grande, che io non abbia procurato Loro la sua conoscenza, dopo d'aver essi inteso da me chi è VJ. ed espresso un grandissimo desiderio di vederla in Francia. Però La prego quanto so e posso di non mancare di far visita a quelle Persone che nominerò qui sotto, dicendo Loro che i [illegible] impedito di vederla, e la mia subita inaspettata partenza non mi ha concesso altro tempo che di mandarle i nomi di quei ai quali desidero che Ella abbia la bontà di rinfrescar la memoria di me.

Al Duca de la Rochefocault La prego dire che già fatto una mediocre raccolta di Fossili, e che gli manderò la prima occasione.

A Mr. Hennin uno dei 2 bracci del Conte di Vergennes dirà l'istesso, e gli farà sentire la mia vera gratitudine [illegible] gentilezze usatemi, e la mia stima [illegible] la felice unione in Lui della filosofia e bontà alle cognizioni politiche.

A Mr. de Reynevàl l'altro braccio del Conte di Vergennes può dire che presto gli manderò la Dissertazione promessa nella mia lettera dei 29. Marzo che inclusi a Mr. de la Lucerne.

Al Conte di Vergennes vorrei che Ella trovasse l'occasione di fargli sentire che io sono in America l'istesso che ero in Francia, e che riguardo sempre Lui e il G. Washington per i 2 principali liberatori della mia nuova e cara Patria.

All'ottimo uomo e sublime Scrittore, Mr. de Marmontel partecipi l'effusione del mio cuore veramente amico, e gli domandi se ricevè la mia risposta sul preteso Legislatore Abbè de Mably, che gli mandai pochi giorni prima d'imbarcarmi. In casa sua troverà

L'Abbè Morlaix e Mr. de Florence parimente miei buoni amici, dai quali potrà farsi dar l'indirizzo del Presidente Fâcher mio grandissimo Amico [illegible] diventerà anche suo. Egli è uomo di grandissimo ingegno ottimamente coltivato e l'Abbè Mor[illegible]

2688

84

[illegible] della Francia.

Al Duca di Luxemburgo avrà la bontà di dire che ricevei la sua lettera sul punto d'imbarcarmi, che ò già cominciato a raccogliere i semi, i quali gli manderò subito che avrò trovato il resto, e che la stagione permetterà di spedir le piante.

Al Duca de la Vauguyon oltre l'espressioni di rispetto, di gratitudine, e la gentilezza usatemi tanto da lui che dalla Duchessa, vorrei che domandasse se gli pervenne la mia lettera di [illegible] sul mio figliastro, del quale [illegible] forse avrà ancora dell'amicizia per Sir J. Jay il quale vorrei che sapesse ch'io non mi sono scordato di lui. Egli è fratello di Mr. John Jay, il quale alla prima mia visita, che non mi rese [illegible] perchè mi suppose tanto oscuro quanto sapeva esserlo in bisogno di denaro, si portò meco molto freddamente. Quando poi si avvedde d'aver sbagliato, era troppo tardi per rendermi [illegible] [illegible] forza di farmi credere col mostrarsi [illegible] ufficioso ogni volta che ci incontrammo dal Marchese de la Fayette, da Mr. Adams e da Mr. [illegible] una gentile riservatezza.

Al Marchese de la Fayette bramerei che domandasse se al suo ritorno di campagna ricevè la mia lettera di Lione. Egli sa abbastanza l'amicizia e la venerazione che ho per Lui.

Al Favi che sta all'Hotel de Mirabeau rue de [illegible] giovane degnissimo, mio grande amico, e Agente del Granduca di Toscana, tra le tante altre cose dirà, che la sua partenza mi à impedito di regalare a conforma dissi a Lui esser mia intenzione, il perfetto giuoco di pedine che egli regalò a me.

Ebbi la disgrazia di non vedere il Con. di Chate[illegible]

Non posso scriver di più, la mano mi trema troppo, la posta è per partire. Mi conservi la sua stimatissima amicizia, e mi creda

All'Illmo Sig.r Tommaso Jefferson.

Suo Vero Amico, e Umilissimo Servitore
Filippo Mazzei

Ac. 4077

Contenui of Mr. Mazzei's memorand:—

[illegible]

N. B. Mazzei had twice a long conversation about Mr. Jefferson with Count de Vergennes, who expressed a great desire to see him in France.

The letter to Messrs. Van-Staphorst is to be put in the General Post-Office in France as soon as possible.

In case Mr. Jefferson would not dislike to see the observations I wrote for Count de Vergennes, on the trade between

22

America United States & the French Islands, he may apply to Marquis de la Fayette, or President Fâcher. President Fâcher has a copy of them in the original Italian Language. They were translated in French at the request of Marquis de la Fayette, who designed to give a copy of them to Marechal de Castries, Minister of Marine, from which department he expected the strongest opposition, as the Marechal does not understand Italian or English. The Marquis found them so much to his liking, that he declared them to be all axioms. The President, who was formerly Intendant in the Islands, said that Intendant will be a disagreeable imployment if my propositions are not adopted. The Duke de la Vauguyon did me the honour to say, that my conversations & writings had done great deal of good, & that he was in hope to see many of my views adopted. My answer always was that the bad, obscure, intricated system could not as yet be changed; that Turgot & Necker had plainly shown what would be the consequence for any Minister who would attempt a salutary reform, &c. In my conversations with Count de Vergennes I thought I could see that he conceived the propriety of the arguments, though it is not to be expected that he will openly agree to it, unless the times were so altered as to admit a reform. I wish it may be the case, & that Mr. Jeffer=

son, Patrick Henry, Edmund Randolph, Richard Henry Lee, James Monroe, and other prominent men of the day.

Returning to France in 1785, he decided to write a book to confute America's foes. The importance of that book has not yet been realized. In our opinion it helped not a little to destroy many falsehoods which had been scattered abroad by America's enemies; even more important may have been its influence, through its German translation, on emigration from Germany to the United States. Gorani in the third volume of his memoirs calls it "un grand ouvrage."

In 1788 Mazzei entered the service of the King of Poland as "intelligencer" (a man entrusted with securing political information) and for a time as temporary envoy. In 1792 he returned to Italy and lived at Pisa, where he died in 1816.

Upon learning of his death, Jefferson wrote to Thomas Appleton, the American consul in Leghorn: "He (Mazzei) had some peculiarities, and who of us has not? But he was of solid worth; honest, able, zealous in sound principles, moral and political, constant in friendship, and punctual in all his undertakings. He was greatly esteemed in this country." Writing on the same day to Giovanni Carmignani, a professor at the University of Pisa, he added: "His esteem, too, in this country, was very general; his early and zealous cooperation in the establishment of our independence having acquired for him here a great degree of favor."

Those words by Jefferson are Mazzei's best epitaph.

— 284 —

Frammenti di scritti pubblicati nelle gazzette al principio della rivoluzione americana da un cittadino di Virginia.

Per ottenere il nostro intento bisogna, miei cari concittadini, ragionar su i diritti naturali dell'uomo e sulle basi di un governo libero. Questa discussione ci dimostrerà chiaramente, che il britanno non è mai stato tale nel suo maggior grado di perfizione, e che il nostro non era altro che una cattiva copia di quello, con tali altri svantaggi che lo rendevano poco al di sopra dello stato di schiavitù.

Dopo esamineremo come il governo devesi formare per essere imparziale e durevole.

Questa materia è stata tanto amplamente trattata da vari scrittori di vaglia, ch'io non ambisco ad altro merito che a quello di trattarla in uno stil familiare e semplice; onde possiamo facilmente intenderci.

Gli scrittori di stile sublime mi perdoneranno; essi non àn bisogno che alcuno scriva per loro. Io scrivo per quelli, che dotati di buon senso non ànno avuto il vantaggio d'un educazione studiosa, e bramo di adattare il mio stile alla lor capacità. So bene che lo stile sublime à spesso attratto il consenso degli uomini, pur troppo disposti ad ammirare quel che non comprendono; ma è finalmente venuto il tempo di cambiar costume; il dover nostro è di procurar di comprendere per giudicar da noi stessi.

— 285 —

Tutti gli uomini sono per natura egualmente liberi e indipendenti. Quest'eguaglianza è necessaria per costituire un governo libero. Bisogna che ognuno sia uguale all'altro nel diritto naturale. La distinzione dei ranghi n'è sempre stata, come sempre ne sarà un efficace ostacolo, e la ragione è chiarissima. Quando in una nazione avete più classi d'uomini, bisogna che diate ad ognuna la sua porzione nel governo; altrimenti una classe tiranneggierebbe l'altre. Ma le porzioni non possono farsi perfettamente uguali; e quando ancor si potesse, il giro delle cose umane dimostra che non si manterrebbero in equilibrio; e per poco che una preponderi la macchina deve cadere.

Per questa ragione tutte le antiche repubbliche ebbero corta vita. Quando furono stabilite gli abitanti eran divisi per classi, e sempre in contesa, ogni classe procurando di aver maggior porzione dell'altre nel governo; cosicchè i legislatori doveron cedere ai pregiudizi dei costumi, alle opposte pretensioni dei partiti, e il meglio che poteron fare fu un misto grottesco di libertà e di tirannia.

Le loro imperfezioni costituzionali diedero origine a molti disordini, che sono stati ultimamente descritti con i più orribili colori da persone male intenzionate per indisporre il buon popolo di questo continente contro i governi repubblicani; ed alcuni uomini di buona fede ancora ànno fatto lo stesso perchè la loro inattenzione ai veri buoni principii di governo non à permesso loro di discernere, che le repubbliche.

Beginning of the first article by Mazzei to reach us. It was translated into English by Thomas Jefferson and it is said that it was published in the Virginia Gazette. From *Mazzei's Memorie*, Vol. II. (Courtesy, *New York Public Library.*)

(*On opposite page*) Facsimiles of four pages from the two memoranda in which Mazzei listed some of the influential people Jefferson would have found useful for his mission in Paris. (*From the unpublished originals in the Library of Congress.*)

CHAPTER TEN

FIGHTERS FOR AMERICAN INDEPENDENCE

If by 1776, as we have shown in the preceding chapters, there were thousands of people in the Colonies who could trace their origins to Italy, it can be safely concluded that some of them must have served during our War of Independence.

Their names, of course, are hard to identify because of the transformations they underwent through the years —especially in the case of the numerous Waldenses. Nevertheless they existed, unless the laws of nature had failed to operate.

Actually, we find officers with Italian names in the colonies, like Lupo, who was, as we have seen, a lieutenant at Jamestown as early as 1619; or like William Perone (Peyrounie), who was captain of a Virginia Regiment at Fort Duquesne, in 1755, possibly with Washington, and Captain, later Colonel, Isaac Corsa, of the Bronx, who served between 1755 and 1765.

In the numerous lists of soldiers who served during the Revolution one finds literally hundreds of names that could be taken for Italian. In New York State, to mention one instance, we find at least 49 members of the Fonda family who at one time or another served in the War. Also in New York we find one Lieutenant Bracco, who was killed in action at White Plains on October 28, 1776.

In Pennsylvania, Christopher Baldy (Baldi) of Berks County served as captain in the Continental Army and later as brigadier general. He died in Seneca County in 1809. Probably he was a member of the Baldus family, prominent in Pennsylvania. (Stapleton, A., *Memorials of the Huguenots in America,* 1901, 59.) The noted colonel, Lewis Nicola, also may have been of Italian extraction, but there is no way to deny or to affirm it, at least for the time being.

In the South, Italian names, or names that seem Italian, can be found by the score. The Taliaferros, to recall a prominent family of whose origins we are sure, were most active. One of them, Col. Richard Taliaferro, was a member of the Committee elected to enforce the *Association* in James City County of which he was a freeholder. (*Virginia Gazette,* Dec. 1, 1774.) He was killed at the Battle of Guilford Hall on March 15, 1781. Another Taliaferro, Benjamin, served as captain in the rifle corps commanded by General Morgan. Later he was president of the Georgia Senate, a member of the 6th and 7th Congress, and a judge of the Georgia Superior Court.

Monument to Major Winston at Guilford Courthouse. On one side of the stone are inscribed the names of Major J. Winston, Captain J. Franklin, and Richard Taliaferro. (Courtesy, *Guilford Courthouse National Military Park, Greensboro, N. C.*)

PASQUALE PAOLI

Italy contributed more than men to the American Revolution. Even before the conflict started, Italy was a source of inspiration to American patriots, as one can easily ascertain by the many accounts given in colonial and English newspapers and magazines of the struggle waged by Pasquale Paoli and his fellow-Corsicans for independence.

The Corsicans had been for centuries under the domination of Genoa who, to be sure, treated them more as colonial subjects than as fellow-Italians. The Corsicans tried several times to regain their freedom, as far back as 1545, but their struggle reached epic proportions in 1755 when Pasquale Paoli, assisted by Carlo Bonaparte, Napoleon's father, landed in the island from Italy and fought heroically against the Genoese. For fourteen years Paoli fought with all means at his disposal, arousing the admiration of free men all over the world, particularly in England and in America, until 1768, when Genoa sold Corsica to the French. It was then that Paoli and 400 of his fol-

The ASSOCIATION *entered into by the* AMERICAN [CONTI]NENTAL CONGRESS *in Behalf of all the Colo[nies]*

WE his Majesty's most dutiful and loyal Subjects, the Delegates of the several Colonies of New Hampshire, Massachusetts Bay, Rhode Island, Connecticut, New York, New Jersey, Pennsylvania, the Three Lower Counties of Newcastle, Kent, and Sussex, on Delaware, Maryland, Virginia, North Carolina, and South Carolina, deputed to represent them in a Continental Congress, held in the City of Philadelphia on the 5th Day of September 1774, avowing our Allegiance to his Majesty, our Affection and Regard for our Fellow Subjects in Great Britain and elsewhere, affected with the deepest Anxiety, and most alarming Apprehensions at those Grievances and Distresses with which his Majesty's American Subjects are oppressed, and having taken under our most serious Deliberation the State of the whole Continent, find that the present unhappy Situation of our Affairs is occasioned by a ruinous System of Colony Administration, adopted by the British Ministry about the Year 1763, evidently calculated for enslaving these Colonies, and, with them, the British Empire: In Prosecution of which System, various Acts of Parliament have been passed for raising a Revenue in America, for depriving the American Subjects, in many Instances, of the constitutional Trial by Jury, exposing their Lives to Danger, by directing a new and illegal Trial beyond the Seas, for Crimes alledged to have been committed in America; and, in Prosecution of the same System, several late, cruel, and oppressive Acts have been passed respecting the Town of Boston and the Massachusetts Bay, and also an Act for extending the Province of Quebeck, so as to border on the western Frontiers of these Colonies, establishing an arbitrary Government therein, and discouraging the Settlement of British Subjects in that wide-extended Country; thus, by the Influence of civil Principles, and ancient Prejudices, to dispose the Inhabitants to act with Hostility against the free Protestant Colonies, whenever a wicked Ministry shall choose so to direct them.

To obtain Redress of these Grievances, which threaten Destruction to [th]e Lives, Liberty, and Property, of his Majesty's Subjects in North Ame[ri]ca, we are of Opinion that a Non-importation, Non consumption, and [N]on-exportation Agreement, faithfully adhered to, will prove the most [sp]eedy, effectual, and peaceable Measure; and therefore we do, for our[sel]ves and the Inhabitants of the several Colonies whom we represent, firmly agree and associate, under the sacred Ties of Virtue, Honour, and Love of our Country, as follows:

First. That from and after the first Day of December next we will not import into British America, from Great Britain or Ireland, any Goods, Wares, or Merchandise whatsoever, or from any other Place, any such Goods, Wares, or Merchandise, as shall have been exported from Great Britain or Ireland; nor will we, after that Day, import any East India Tea from any Part of the World, nor any Molosses, Syrups, Paneles, Coffee, or Pimenta, from the British Plantations, or from Dominico, nor Wines from Madeira, or the Western Islands, nor foreign Indigo.

Second. That we will neither import nor purchase any Slave imported after the first Day of December next, after which Time we will wholly discontinue the Slave Trade, and will neither be concerned in it ourselves, nor will we hire our Vessels, nor sell our Commodities or Manufactures, to those who are concerned in it.

Third. As a Non-consumption Agreement, strictly adhered to, will be an effectual Security for the Observation of the Non-importation, we, as above, solemnly agree and associate, that, from this Day, we will not purchase or use any Tea imported on Account of the East India Company, or any on which a Duty hath been or shall be paid; and, from and after the first Day of March next, we will not purchase or use any East India Tea whatever: Nor will we, nor shall any Person for or under us, purchase or use any of those Goods, Wares, or Merchandise, we have agreed not to import, which we shall know, or have Cause to suspect, were imported after the first Day of December, except such as come under the Rules and Directions of the tenth Article, hereafter mentioned.

Fourth. The earnest Desire we have not to injure our Fellow Subjects in Great Britain, Ireland, or the West Indies, induces us to suspend a Non-exportation until the tenth Day of September 1775; at which Time, if the said Acts, and Parts of Acts of the British Parliament herein after mentioned, are not repealed, we will not, directly or indirectly, export any Merchandise, or Commodity whatsoever, to Great Britain, Ireland, or the West Indies, except Rice, to Europe.

Fifth. Such as are Merchants, and use the British and Irish Trade, will give Orders, as soon as possible, to their Factors, Agents, and Correspondents, in Great Britain and Ireland, not to ship any Goods to them, on any Pretence whatsoever, as they cannot be received in America; and if any Merchant residing in Great Britain or Ireland shall, directly or indirectly, ship any Goods, Wares, or Merchandise, for America, in Order to break the said Non-importation Agreement, or in any Manner contravene the same, on such unworthy Conduct being well attested, it ought to be made publick; and, on the same being so done, we will not, from thenceforth, have any commercial Connexion with such Merchant.

Sixth. That such as are O[wners] of Vessels will give positive Orders to their Captains, or Masters, n[ot to] receive on Board their Vessels any Goods prohibited by the said Non-importation Agreement, on Pain of immediate Dismission from their Service.

Seventh. We will use our utmost Endeavours to improve the Breed of Sheep, and increase their Number to the greatest Extent; and to that End we will kill them as sparingly as may be, especially those of the most profitable Kind: Nor will we export any to the West Indies, or elsewhere. And those of us who are or may become overstocked with, or can conveniently spare any Sheep, will dispose of them to our Neighbours, especially to the poorer Sort, on moderate Terms.

Eighth. That we will, in our several Stations, encourage Frugality Economy, and Industry; and promote Agriculture, Arts, and the Manufactures of this Country, especially that of Wool; and will discountenance and discourage every Species of Extravagance and Dissipation, especially all Horse-racing, and all Kinds of Gaming, Cock-fighting, Exhibitions of Shows, Plays, and other expensive Diversions and Entertainments; and on the Death of any Relation, or Friend, none of us, or any of our Families, will go into any farther Mourning Dress than a black Crape or Riband on the Arm or Hat for Gentlemen, and a black Riband and Necklace for Ladies, and we will discontinue the giving of Gloves and Scarfs at Funerals.

Ninth. That such as are Venders of Goods or Merchandise will not take Advantage of the Scarcity of Goods that may be occasioned by this Association, but will sell the same at the Rates we have been respectively accustomed to do for twelve Months last past; and if any Venders of Goods or Merchandise shall sell any such Goods on higher Terms, or shall in any Manner, or by any Device whatsoever, violate or depart from this Agreement, no Person ought, nor will any of us deal with any such Person, or his or her Factor or Agent, at any Time thereafter, for any Commodity whatever.

Tenth. In Case any Merchant, Trader, or other Persons, shall import any Goods of Merchandise after the first Day of December, and before the first Day of February next, the same ought forthwith, at the Election of the Owner, to be either reshipped or delivered up to the Committee of the County or Town wherein they shall be imported, to be stored at the Risk of the Importer, until the Non-importation Agreement shall cease, or be sold under the Direction of the Committee aforesaid: And, in the last mentioned Case, the Owne[r] [illegible] bursed (out of the Sales) the [illegible] to be applied towards relievi[ng] [illegible] the Town of Boston as are im[illegible] and a particular Account of all [illegible] inserted in the publick Papers. [illegible] imported after the said first Day [illegible] to be sent back again, without bre[illegible]

Eleventh. That a Committee [illegible] Town, by those who are qualifi[ed] [illegible] Legislature, whose Business it shall [illegible] of all Persons touching this Asso[ciation] [illegible] appear, to the Satisfaction of a Maj[ority] [illegible] Person within the Limits of their Ap[pointment] [illegible] tion, that such Majority do forthwith [illegible] published in the Gazette, to the End [illegible] British America may be publickly know[n] [illegible] the Enemies of American Liberty; and th[illegible] break off all Dealings with him, or her.

Twelfth. That the Committee of Corre[spondence] [illegible] Colonies do frequently inspect the Entries [illegible] inform each other, from Time to Time, of th[e] [illegible] every other material Circumstance that ma[y] [illegible] ciation.

Thirteenth. That all Manufactures of t[illegible] able Prices, so that no undue Advantage [illegible] Goods.

Fourteenth. And we do farther agre[e] [illegible] no Trade, Commerce, Dealings, o[r] [illegible] Colony or Province in North Ame[rica] [illegible] which shall hereafter violate, th[illegible] unworthy of the Rights of Free[men] [illegible] their Country.

And we do solemnly bind [illegible] Ties aforesaid, to adhere to th[illegible] Acts of Parliament, passed sin[ce] [illegible] continue Duties on Tea, Wine, [illegible] Coffee, Sugar, Pimenta, Indigo, foreign Pa[illegible], and Painters Colours, imported into America, and extend the Powers of the Admiralty Courts beyond their ancient Limits, deprive the American Subject of Trial by Jury, authorise the Judge's Certificate to indemnify the Prosecutor from Damages that he might otherwise be liable to from a Trial by his Peers, require oppressive Security from a Claimant of Ships or Goods seized before he shall be allowed to defend his Property, are repealed; and until that Part of the Act of the 12th of George III. Chapter 24th, entitled "An Act for the better securing his Majesty's Dockyards, Magazines, Ships, Ammunition, and Stores," by which any Persons charged with committing any of the Offences therein described in America may be tried in any Shire or County within the Realm, is repealed; and until the four Acts passed in the last Session of Parliament, viz. that for stopping the Port and blocking up the Harbour of Boston, that for altering the Charter and Government of Massachusetts Bay; and that which is entitled "An Act for the better Administration of Justice, &c." and that "[for] extending the Limits of Quebeck, &c." are repealed. And we recommend it to the Provincial Conventions, and to the Committees in the respective Colonies, to establish such farther Regulations as they may think proper, for carrying into Execution this Association.

The foregoing Association being determined upon by the Congress, was ordered to be subscribed by the several Members thereof; and thereupon, we have hereunto set our respective Names accordingly.

In CONGRESS, PHILADELPHIA, *October* 20, 1774.

Signed, PEYTON RANDOLPH, *President.*

John Sullivan, Nathaniel Folsom, } of New Hampshire.

Thomas Cushing, Samuel Adams, John Adams, Robert Treat Paine, } of Massachusetts Bay.

Stephen Hopkins, Samuel Ward, } of Rhode Island.

Eliphalet Dyer, Roger Sherman, Silas Deane, } of Connecticutt.

Isaac Low, John Alsop, John Jay, James Duane, William Floyd, Henry Weisner, S. Boerum, } of New York.

James Kinsey, William Livingston, Stephen Crane, Richard Smith, } of New Jersey.

Joseph Galloway, John Dickinson, Charles Humphreys, Thomas Mifflin, Edward Biddle, John Morton, George Ross, } of Pennsylvania.

Caesar Rodney, Thomas M'Kean, George Read, } of Newcastle, &c.

Matthew Tilghman, Thomas Johnson, William Paca, Samuel Chase, } of Maryland.

Richard Henry Lee, George Washington, Patrick Henry, Junior, Richard Bland, Benjamin Harrison, Edmund Pendleton, } of Virginia.

William Hooper, Joseph Hewes, R. Caswell, } of North Carolina.

Henry Middleton, Thomas Lynch, Christopher Gadsden, John Rutledge, Edward Rutledge, } of South Carolina.

Th: Jefferson

Val Wood

Francis Alberte

Facsimile of one of the pledges not to do business with England signed by Jefferson and Francis Alberte (Alberti). (Courtesy, *Library of Congress.*)

tions, yet they always arife naturally from her premifes." CRITICAL REVIEW.

By the special approbation of his Excellency PASCAL PAOLI, *General of the* CORSICANS,

A new and beautiful edition, *(being the third)* in one volume octavo, with a new and accurate map of CORSICA; to which is now firft added, a letter from the Right Honourable GEORGE Lord LYTTELTON to the author, and a fine engraved head of General PAOLI, done from an original portrait juft arrived from CORSICA, painted by Mr. HENRY BEMBRIDGE, and efteemed a very ftriking likenefs; an

ACCOUNT of CORSICA;

its fituation, extent, air, foil, and production: a concife view of its revolutions, from the earlieft times; its prefent ftate with refpect to government, religion, arms; commerce, learning, the genius and character of the inhabitants: with a

JOURNAL of a TOUR to that Ifland; and MEMOIRS of PASCAL PAOLI:

Alfo an original LETTER from the General of the nation, and an appendix, containing Corfican ftate papers.

By JAMES BOSWELL, Efq;

*** Mr. *Bofwell's* account of *Corfica* has been fo well received by the public, that two numerous editions of 3500 copies have been fold within the fpace of a few months; and the book is fo highly efteemed abroad, that it has been tranflated into the French and Dutch languages, and printed at *Amfterdam* and *Laufanne*.

LIKEWISE,

SHERIDAN's Britifh Education | Gray's Poems. National Debt no Griev-

Advertisement of Boswell's *Account of Corsica* in the *Pennsylvania Journal*, Sept. 21, 1769. (Courtesy, *New York Public Library.*)

lowers left the island and sought refuge at Leghorn. Eventually he moved to London, where he died in 1804.

In the American Colonies the name of Paoli became a symbol of heroism and freedom. Before the Revolution there was practically no public banquet of importance at which a toast was not offered to Paoli and his Corsicans. The town of Paoli, not far from Philadelphia, was named after him. His chief admirers, however, were the Sons of Liberty, who played such an important role in the Revolution. When the New York Battalion of Independent Foot Company was organized in 1775, it took the name of Corsicans. (*Valentine Manual*, 1849, p. 344.) More than one American called one of his sons Pascalpaoli. Even a stallion and at least one ship were called Paoli. (See Anderson, G. P., Pascal Paoli, an Inspiration to the Sons of Liberty, *Mass. Hist. Soc. Transactions*, 1927, and Kraus, M., *The Atlantic Civilization*, p. 220). How deep was American interest in Paoli's struggle for freedom may be gained from the six columns of reference to him and Corsica in the *Virginia Gazette Index*.

For *LONDON*,

The Brig *Paoli*,

James Hall, Mafter, lying at *Hancock's* Wharf, will fail in three Weeks, has good Accomodations for Paffengers.--- For Freight or Paffage apply to the Mafter on board, or to *John Hancock*, Efq; at his Store.

Bofton, Jan. 16, 1769.

ADVERTISEMENT IN THE BOSTON POST-BOY & ADVERTISER, JANUARY 16, 1769

ENGRAVED FOR THE COLONIAL SOCIETY OF MASSACHUSETTS FROM A COPY OWNED BY THE MASSACHUSETTS HISTORICAL SOCIETY

(From *Colonial Society of Massachusetts Publications*, Vol. 26.)

WITH ROCHAMBEAU AND D'ESTAING

Numerous Italians fought for American independence under the French flag. To ascertain their names is, once more, difficult because of the way they were written or copied. Philip Phinizy, for instance, came over with Rochambeau, yet his name cannot be found in the French rosters. As related in Chapter Nineteen, he was born at Parma, enlisted in the *Regiment de Gatinais* on July 22, 1777, at the age of seventeen, served during the Revolution, saw action at Yorktown, and was discharged from

The Life and education of the famous PASCAL PAOLI, *at prefent Commander in Chief of the* CORSICANS, *with a defcription of his perfon and behaviour. By* James Bofwell, *Efq; who made a voyage to Corfica, on purpofe to vifit him.*

PASCAL PAOLI, was fecond fon to the old chief Giacinto Paoli. He had been educated with great care by his father, who formed his tafte for letters, and infpired him with every worthy and noble fentiment. He was born in Corfica, where he remained long enough, to contract a love and attachment to his country, and to feel the oppreffion under which it groaned.

When the patriots were totally crufhed by the marquis de Maillebois, his father took young Paoli to Naples, where he had the advantage of attending the academy, got a commiffion as an officer in that fervice, and was much about court.

Here he lived twelve or thirteen years, cultivating the great powers with which nature had endowed him, and laying the foundation of thofe grand defigns, which he had early formed for the deliverance of his country.

His reputation became fo great among the Corficans, that he received the ftrongeft invitations to come over and take the command. He embarked in the glorious enterprife, ftimulated by generous ambition, and undifmayed by a confideration of the dangers, the cares, and the uncertainty which he was about to encounter.

There was fomething particularly affecting, in his parting from his father; the old man, hoary and gray with years, fell on his neck, and kiffed him, gave him his bleffing, and with a broken feeble voice, encouraged him in the undertaking, on which he was entering; My fon, faid he, 'I may poffibly never fee you more; but in my mind, I fhall ever be prefent with you. Your defign is a great and noble one, and I doubt not but God will blefs you in it. The little which remains to me of life, I will allot to your caufe, in offering up my prayers and fupplications to heaven for your protection and profperity.' Having again embraced him they parted.

Pafcal Paoli no fooner appeared in the ifland, than he attracted the attention of every body. His carriage and deportment prejudiced them in his favour, and his fuperiour judgment, and patriotick fpirit, difplayed with all the force of eloquence charmed their underftandings. All this, heightened with condefcenfion, affability and modefty, entirely won him their hearts. A way was open for him to the fupreme command, and he was called to it by the unanimous voice of his countrymen.

Mr. BOSWELL's Account of his Vifit to PAOLI.

WHEN I at laft came within fight of Sollacaro, where Paoli was, I could not help being under confiderable anxiety. My ideas of him had been greatly heightened by the converfations I had held with all forts of people in the ifland, they having reprefented him to me as fomething above humanity. I had the ftrongeft defire to fee fo exalted a character; but I feared that I fhould be unable to give a proper account why I had prefumed to trouble him with a vifit, and that I fhould fink to nothing before him. I almoft wifhed yet to go back without feeing him. Thefe workings of fenfibility employed my mind till I rode thro' the village and came up to the houfe where he was lodged.

I paft thro' the guards, and was met by fome of the general's people, who conducted me into an antichamber, where were feveral gentlemen in waiting. Signor Boccociampe, had notified my arrival, and I was fhewn into Paoli's room, I found him alone, and was ftruck with his appearance. He is tall, ftrong and well made; of a fair complexion, a fenfible, free, and open countenance, and a manly and noble carriage. He was then in his fortieth year. He was dreft in green and gold.

He was polite, but very referved. I had ftood in the prefence of many a prince, but I never had fuch a trial as in the prefence of Paoli. He is a phyfiognomift. In confequence of his being in continual danger from treachery and affaffination, he has formed a habit of ftudioufly obferving every new face. For ten minutes we walked backwards and forwards through the room, hardly faying a word, while he looked at me, with a ftedfaft, keen and penetrating eye, as if he fearched my very foul.

This interview was for a while very fevere upon me. I was much relieved when his referve wore off, and he began to fpeak more. I then ventured to addrefs him with this compliment to the Corficans. "Sir, I am upon my travels, and have lately vifited Rome. I am come from feeing the ruins of one brave and free people: I now fee the rife of another." He received my compliment very gracioufly.

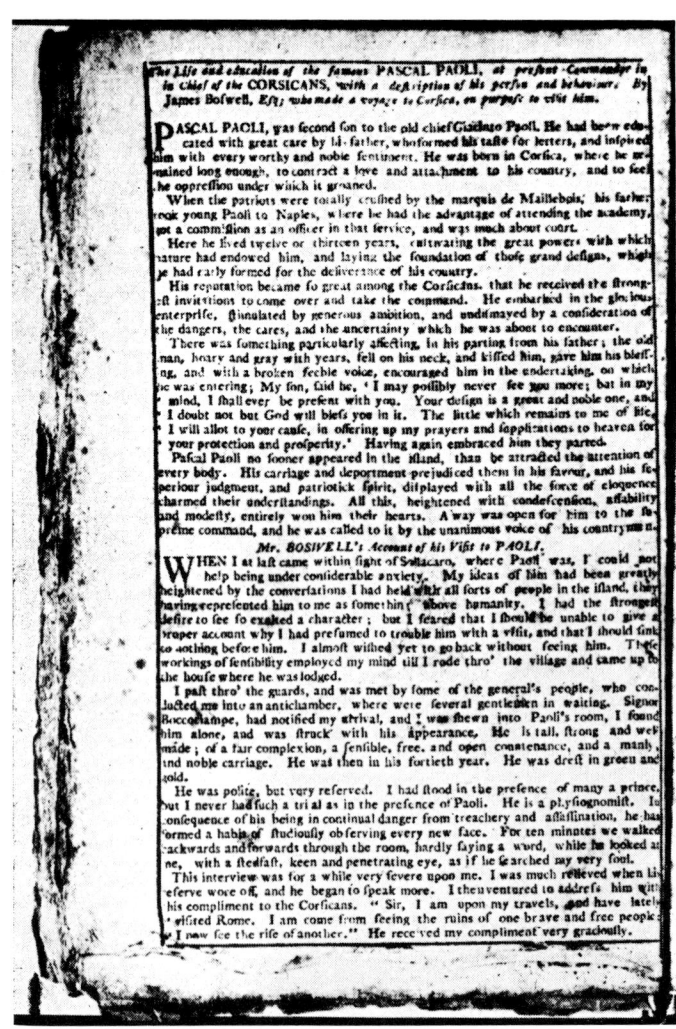

A page from James Boswell's account of his visit to Pascal Paoli. From Bickerstaff's *Boston Almanack* for 1769. (Courtesy, *New York Public Library.*)

service on January 14, 1784. Shortly after that he married Margaret Condon and settled in Georgia.

Only rarely we find the native place of the soldiers. One of them, Vincent Cussel, named Jolicoeur, was born in Italy, served in the Gatinais Regiment, and was killed in action at Savannah on October 10, 1779. (Dawson, W., *Les* 2112 *Francais Morts aux Etats-Unis de* 1777 *a* 1783, p. 41.) Another native of Italy, Biny Francois, was shipwrecked in 1782. Still another, Paly Bonnaventura, died at Yorktown in 1781. (*Ibid.*, 100.) Jean Francois of Villefranche (Villafranca), was a chaplain with the fleet of Count De Grasse. (*Am. Cath. Hist. Res. n.s.* VII, 250-257.)

Two regiments recruited mostly in Italy came over in 1779, the *Third Piemont,* with 473 men, and the *Thirtieth Du Perche,* with 1064 men. (Pascal, A., *Histoire de l'Armee,* 4 vols., Paris, 1853, II, 226.) Another regiment, the *Royal Italien,* is also said to have come over. Five members of the Scalvini family are said to have enlisted in said regiment and to have fought for our independence. One of them, Alessandro Scalvini, was introduced to George Washington, according to Amy Bernardy, an Italian writer who taught in Massachusetts not many years ago. We shall not dwell on the French officers of distant Italian extraction, like Andre' Riquetti, Viscount of Mirabeau, or the Prince of Broglie. Numerous Corsicans, at any rate, served on the ship *Le Protecteur.* (Dawson, *op. cit.*, 133.)

Whether there were any Italians who "flocked to America with Deane's commissions" (Winsor, J., *Narrative and Critical History of America,* VII, 35) deserves a close investigation, provided due attention is paid to the probable change in names. Baldeski (or Baldesqui, the paymaster of Pulaski's Legion), for instance, was not, in our opinion, a Pole, but one of the Italian Baldeschis, so well known at Perugia.

The Italians in those days were still among the leading military engineers in Europe. We would not be surprised in the least, accordingly, if some Italian, or Italian-Swiss, engineers joined Washington's cause. One of them, Rivardi, as we shall presently see, occupied a very important post in the United States Army soon after the Treaty of Paris. Another native of Italy, but not an Italian, Antonio de Cambray, covered himself with glory during the conflict. Possibly an Italian may have been the "very able engineer" mentioned by John Page in his letter of November 9, 1777, to R. H. Lee. "He understands English well and translates it into Italian, Spanish or French." (*Southern Literary Messenger,* Vol. XXVII, 1858, 258.)

He could not have been de Cambray, who sailed from Europe on November 23,1777.He was the son of a Frenchman who settled in Florence in 1745 and became a Tuscan citizen, but although the family never left Italy—where it still resides—the young Cambray cannot be considered an Italian, except as politically. About his services to America, suffice it to recall that he and another French officer, Fleury, were the only foreigners to receive two of the eight medals struck by Congress during the war. (*Franklin's Writings,* ed. by Smyth, VIII, 71.) A long and well-documented article about him, with references to unpublished material, was written by F. Massai and published in the *Atti della Societa' Colombaria,* Florence, 1937. (See also *Virginia Magazine of History,* XXIV, 169.) We mention De Cambray as typical of a class of educated Italians who in all likelihood came over during the Revolution, for the same reasons that prompted more than 200 of them to serve in the Union Army during the Civil War.

ITALIAN-BORN VOLUNTEERS

Among the first natives of Italy to bear arms against the British were Mazzei, Bellini, and the gardener, Vincenzo Rossi, who joined Patrick Henry's force as we have noted on page 138. Whether any of the other men who came with Mazzei served during the conflict, we do not know, although some of them, or their children, served in the Virginia militia. One of them, John Strobia, was a captain.

Another Italian-American volunteer was Pascal Charles Joseph De Angelis, the son of Neapolitan father and French mother. He is said to have served from 1776 (when he was thirteen years of age!) to the end of the war. He died in 1839. (*New York Evening Post,* Sept. 14, 1839.) His grandson became a justice of the Supreme Court of the State of New York.

In the *Pennsylvania Archives* (Vol. IV, 5th series, 783) we find one Peter Gully "age 20, dark complexion, born in Italy, labourer," who enlisted under Major James Moore on October 7, 1783. We have not investigated whether he had seen any previous service.

We have more information about Joseph Carlo Mauran, who was born at Villafranca, then a part of Italy (politically, Villefranche, like Nice, is a part of France) in 1748, and died in Rhode Island in 1813. During the Revolution he was master of the *Spitfire,* as early as 1776, and later of the *Washington,* apparently two armed vessels in the service of Rhode Island. (Stockbridge, J. C., *Memorials of the Mauran Family,* Providence, 1893, 132; Smith, J. J., *Civil and Military List of Rhode Island.* Providence 1900, 353, 358.)

In connection with our early men-of-war, it is interesting to recall that when the Continental Congress fitted out the first five vessels which formed the nucleus of the American Navy, three of them were named after natives of Italy, namely, Columbus, Cabot and Doria; the other two were named Alfred, after King Alfred, and Providence, after the town in which she was purchased. (Burnett, *Letters of the Continental Congress,* 1921, I, 273)—see also Neeser, R. W., *Ship Names of the United States Navy.*)

MAJOR COSIMO MEDICI OF THE NORTH CAROLINA LIGHT DRAGOONS

MAJOR COSIMO MEDICI

We do not know much about Cosimo Medici, who he was, where he came from, when he came to America, what was his occupation. We doubt very much that he was a painter by profession.

In all probability he was one of those adventurous men who joined the crew of some ship coming to the New World. We first find his name in 1767, and again in 1768, among those of persons whose letters remained unclaimed at the Norfolk Post Office. (*Virginia Gazette, Purdue and Dixon,* May 28, 1767, and Feb. 18, 1768.) In

VIEW OF CHAD'S FORD ON THE BRANDYWYNE
(From *Harper's Encyclopedia of American History.*)

1772 he was still in Virginia, where he painted the portrait of Lucy Briggs, reproduced on page 215.

Whoever he was, Medici should be honored as one of the very first men to take up arms for American independence. On April 16, 1776, Congress appointed him a lieutenant in a company of light horse to be raised in North Carolina (*Records of North Carolina,* X, 519) and was already in active service in July, 1776 (*The Lee Papers,* II, 176). Three months later, upon the resignation of Captain (later General) Jones, General Howe appointed him captain, subject to approval of the State of North Carolina.

Accordingly, on January 22, 1777, Howe wrote to Governor Caswell of that state urging Medici's appointment. "I think it but justice to him," he wrote, "to add that he has shown himself thro' the whole of his conduct here in such manner as to merit my approbation and to obtain the respect of the officers whenever he has served. I therefore hope he will have his appointment confirmed and take the liberty to solicit your interest in his behalf." Then he added: "Captain Medici having informed me, since I sealed my letter, that some malicious persons had endeavoured to asperse him in North Carolina, please give him a copy of my letter to you if he desires it." (*Records of North Carolina,* XI, 370-371.) Apparently Medici's enemies had demanded that he be court-martialed for misconduct, for Caswell replied to Howe that he could not give Medici a commission until he was cleared. Whether he was tried, or whether the charge was dropped, we do not know. We know, however, that in March, 1777, he was, as a captain, on his way to deliver a number of prisoners to the Congress in Philadelphia. (*Ibid.,* 480.) He had already taken part in the Battle of Princeton.

On September 1, Medici once more saw action, this time at the Battle of Brandywyne and later at Germantown. (*Ibid.,* 661.) Soon after the battle he rushed to North Carolina with some messages for Caswell, to whom he brought news of his son, who had been wounded at Brandywyne. He was so fatigued that he had to excuse himself for not bringing the messages in person.

During the following two years Medici was entrusted with delicate missions, including the delivery of $650,000 in loan certificates to Caswell and the purchase of horses.

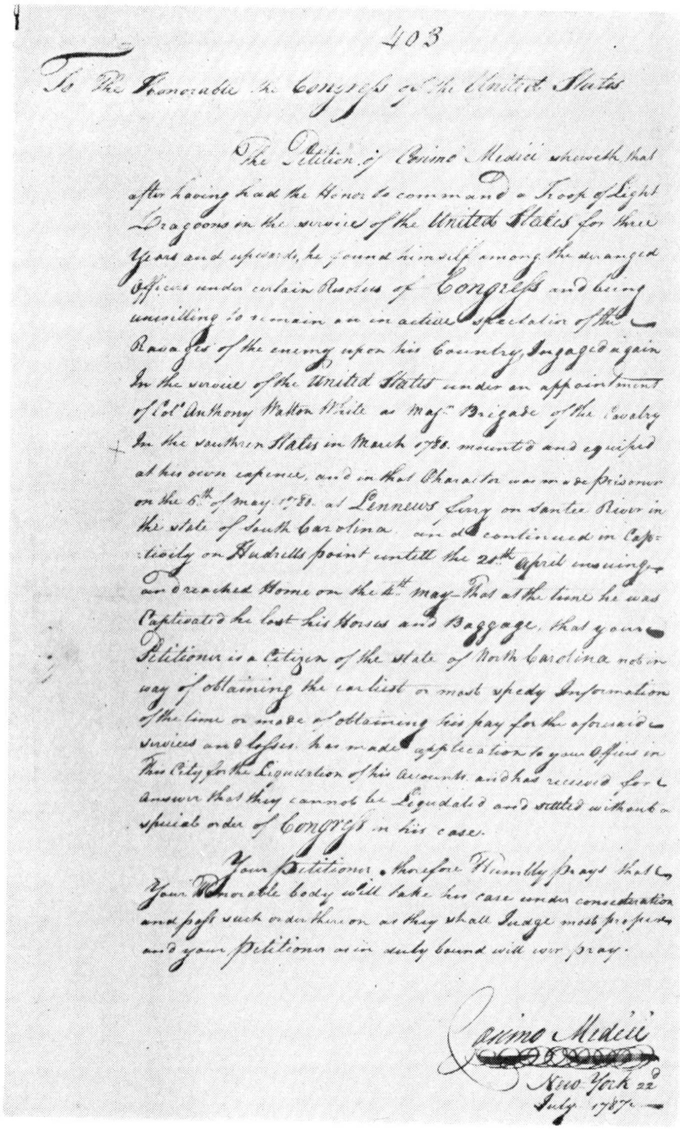

403

To The Honorable the Congress of the United States

The Petition of Cosimo Medici sheweth that after having had the Honor to command a Troop of Light Dragoons in the service of the United States for three Years and upwards, he found himself among the deranged Officers under certain Resolves of Congress and being unwilling to remain an inactive spectator of the Ravages of the enemy upon his Country, Ingaged again In the service of the United States under an appointment of Col. Anthony Walton White as Maj. Brigade of the Cavalry In the southern States in March 1780. mounted and equiped at his own expence, and in that Character was made prisoner on the 6th of may 1780. at Lennews Ferry on Santee River in the state of South Carolina. and continued in Captivity on Hadrells point untill the 20th April ensuing and reached Home on the 4th may. That at the time he was Captivated he lost his Horses and Baggage. that your Petitioner is a Citizen of the state of North Carolina not in way of obtaining the earliest or most speedy Information of the time or mode of obtaining his pay for the aforesaid services and losses. has made application to your Offices in this City for the Liquidation of his accounts. and has received for answer that they cannot be Liquidated and settled without a special order of Congress in his case.

Your Petitioner therefore Humbly prays that Your Honorable body will take his case under consideration and pass such order thereon as they shall Judge most proper and your Petitioner as in duty bound will ever pray.

Cosimo Medici
New York 22d
July 1787

Facsimile of Medici's petition to the Congress of the United States. (From the original in the Library of Congress.)

(*Op. cit.*, XIII, 58-59, 72, 297.) In 1779, however, Congress decided to disband his corps and he remained without command. Whereupon General Benjamin Lincoln recommended him to Caswell. "If your State should, as I hear they intend to, raise a Body of Horse," he wrote in June, 1779, "I beg leave to recommend him to your notice for a company, and as a person who I think will do honor to his Corps." (*Op. cit.*, XIV, 111.)

Apparently, Medici remained idle until April, 1780, when, hearing of Tarleton's raids, "unwilling to remain on in active spectation of the Ravages of the enemy upon his Country," as he wrote in his petition to the Congress of July, 1787, reproduced on page 140, he entered service once more, this time with the horses at his own expense. Two months later he was made a prisoner on the Sante River and held by the British for eleven months. According to the Committee appointed by Congress to investigate all claims, during that action Medici was in charge of four corps of cavalry, "did his duty with address and bravery," "was wounded and lost two valuable horses with his baggage." (*Journals of the Continental Congress*, 1937, XXXIV, 155. See also Vol. XXXIII.

After the war, Medici petitioned Congress for a compensation for his losses and pay, but Congress could not do anything about it, for he had failed to file his claims within the period of time allowed by Congress. He received only a few dollars for expenses incurred in 1776. The State of North Carolina, however, granted him 1872 acres of land, for 41 months of service, by warrant dated Nov. 18, 1888.

(On the American defeat on the Sante River, ascribed to the failure of the American commander to use his cavalry properly and to put out any rear guard, see: F. G. Bauer, in *Cavalry Journal*, 1938, 141; McCrady, E., *The History of South Carolina in the Revolution*, 1901, 494-495; Lee, R. E., *Memoirs of the War in the Southern Department*, 1869, 154. See also *Roster of Soldiers from North Carolina in the American Revolution*, Daughters of the American Revolution, 1932, 304.)

JOHN BELLI, DEPUTY QUARTER MASTER GENERAL, U. S. ARMY, 1792-1794.

Major John Belli, Deputy Quarter Master General of the United States Army from 1792 to 1794, and the first settler in Scioto County, Ohio, is said to have been born in Liverpool, England, in 1760. His father is said to have been French and his mother Dutch, but we are inclined to believe that his father was a native of either Italy or Italian Switzerland. The only information we have about his parents comes from an article that appeared in *The Old Northwest Genealogical Quarterly*, Vol. XII, October 1909, but it is so full of obvious errors that we can easily attribute his father's French nationality to a mistake common in such matters. Most certainly, Belli is nothing but Italian.

It is said that in 1779 he became a citizen of Holland, where on becoming of age he took Dutch citizenship. But at that time, in 1881, he is said to have gone to France, where he lived until 1883, when he came to America. Yet, among the papers left by him, there is said to have been a Dutch citizenship certificate dated 1783 and naturalization papers issued by the general court of Maryland. A search in Holland, through the courtesy of the Dutch Embassy in Washington, and in the Hall of Records at Annapolis, Maryland, has failed to produce any evidence regarding his Dutch and American citizenships.

Belli was appointed deputy quartermaster general on April 11, 1792, and served until November 8, 1794, when he resigned, after serving with Anthony Wayne in the war against the Indians. Then he purchased about 1,000 acres in Ohio, where he lived until he died in 1809, at the age of 49. One hundred years later, in 1909, his body was exhumed and reinterred, with appropriate ceremonies, in the Greenlawn cemetery in Portsmouth, Ohio.

It is interesting to recall that when Belli built his fine western home he called it Belvidere, an Italian name not uncommon in America in those days, although, according to Mencken's *The American Language*, it was first Gallicized, with two French accents, and then Americanized from the original Italian, Belvedere, into the modern form, Belvidere. However, in our opinion the name was introduced through Jefferson, in the same way that Monticello, Bentivoglio, and similar Italian names were adopted in Virginia and other places. Incidentally, Belli must have known Francis Vigo, for both of them were active under Anthony Wayne at about the same time.

MAJOR JOHN BELLI
From a painting made in Philadelphia in 1794.

(On Belli see also the *Folsom Club Publications*, No. 9, and on the Belli name in Switzerland see *Dictionnaire Historique et Biographique de la Suisse*, Vol. 2.)

MAJOR RIVARDI FORTIFIES AMERICA'S TOWNS

Major J. J. U. Rivardi was appointed by President Washington in 1794 to fortify Baltimore, Alexandria and Norfolk. He served as a major in the artillery and the engineering corps until 1802, when the corps was disbanded. Apparently then he moved to Martinique, where he died on January 4, 1808.

According to George Washington, Rivardi was a Swiss who had been in the service of Russia before coming to America. (*Washington's Writings,* XXXVI, 489.) Moreau de Saint Mery, a Frenchman who visited Norfolk in 1794, when the two met, however, tells us in his memoirs that Fort Norfolk was built "under the direction of the Italian engineer John Jacob Ulrich Rivardi." Obviously, Rivardi was an Italian Swiss; that is to say, politically he was a Swiss, racially he was an Italian.

From the voluminous correspondence about Rivardi in the National Archives, the Massachusetts Historical Society, the *Virginia Calendar of State Papers,* and the Maryland Hall of Records, (the only sources searched by us), it appears that Rivardi was most active over a period of eight years fortifying, surveying, planning, and building all over the United States, from Virginia to West Point, Niagara, Detroit, and Mackinac. Of particular interest is the survey and plan of the present city of Detroit he made in 1799. It is reproduced on this page.

From a letter he sent the Secretary of War from Philadelphia on January 16, 1801, we learn that at that time he was living there with his wife and child, but whether his family moved with him to the West Indies when he did, we cannot say.

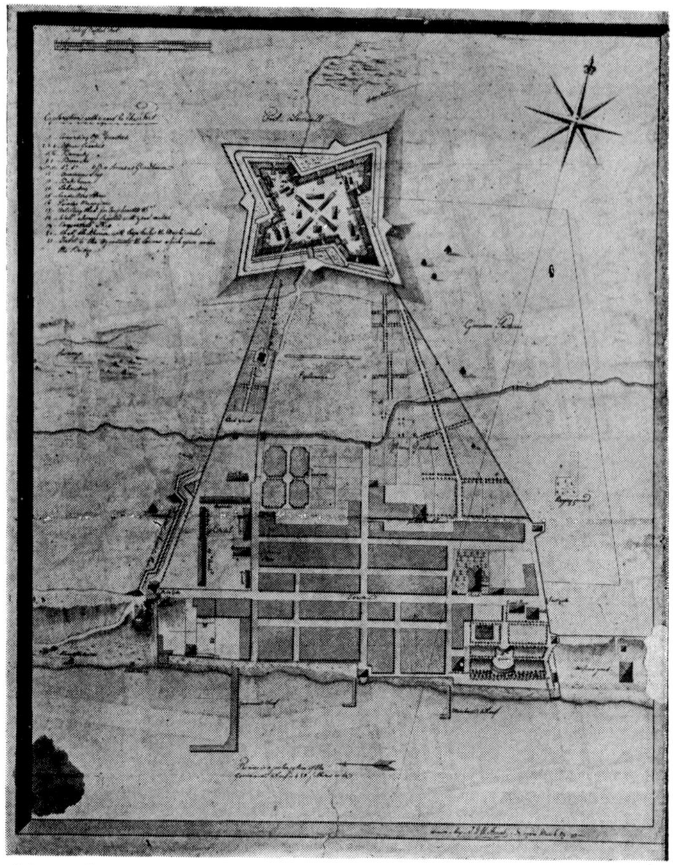

Map of Detroit, probably the earliest made of that city, drawn by Rivardi in 1799. The map, found in 1934, and now in the Clements Library at the University of Michigan, shows the old Fort Pontchartrain, and Fort Lernoult (later Fort Shelby). (Courtesy, *Detroit Trust Company.*)

AIR VIEW OF FORT NORFOLK TODAY

(Courtesy, *Corps of Engineers, U. S. Army, Norfolk, Va., district.*)

CHAPTER ELEVEN

CULTURAL RELATIONS BETWEEN ITALY AND THE AMERICAN COLONIES

At least four Italian-American professors have tried to ascertain whether Americans were interested in Italian culture during the 17th and 18th centuries, and all four of them have reached negative conclusions.

According to one of them, there was "no intellectual life to speak of" in America up to Washington's times and, after all, Italy was "the land of the dead," as Lamartine said. According to another, "throughout the 18th century very little was known in the country concerning the population and geography of Italy. The*Pennsylvania Magazine* (January 8, 1776), was the only periodical that published an article containing information on the area and population of the several kingdoms and states of the peninsula." Quoting his predecessor, he repeats that "only eight Americans visited the peninsula during the second half of the century." Rubbish.

Culture in any country, up to recent times and in certain countries even today, has been, or is, the domain of a few. Without getting into statistical comparisons, we are confident that the proportion of persons interested in culture in the Colonies, everything considered, and with due allowances for their colonial status, was not much smaller than that existing in Italy, France, or Britain at that time. In 1790, let us bear it in mind, the population of the United States was 3,900,000, as against 16 or 17 million Italians, 25,000,000 Frenchmen, and 8,892,000 residents of England and Wales alone. Virginia, to single out a state, had a population of less than 750,000 before 1800, yet she had given the nation men like Washington, Jefferson, James Madison, George Madison, Patrick Henry, George Mason, George Wythe, John Randolph, John Marshall and James Monroe. All first class statesmen, or jurists. It was not by chance that seven of the first twelve presidents of the United States came from the Old Dominion. Still limiting ourselves to Virginia, even if its intellectual life was more receptive than creative, as Prof. Wertenbaker says, "there were hundreds who were interested in literature, art, architecture, music; might themselves be amateur writers, architects, musicians." (*The Golden Age of Colonial Culture*, 109-110). Should anyone need any proof of that, he will find it in abundance in the two monumental works, *Swem's Virginia Historical Index*, and the recently published *Virginia Gazette Index*.

In the latter two volumes one will find literally hundreds of references to events that took place in Italy between 1736 and 1780. All sorts of happenings are recorded, from riots to wars, politcal news, the scarcity of bread, adulteries, murders, religious feasts, horse races, the sale of titles, taxes, absconding bankers, the Royal Academy of Painting, music, monastery life, and even the feast of San Gennaro in Naples. All parts of Italy are covered, from Palermo to Rome, Milan, Venice and Genoa, the latter city receiving more than its share of attention because of Corsica. The references to Paoli, as we have noted, take up two whole columns.

As for articles of general Italian culture, one must remember that Americans read regularly the leading London magazines of the day, and even if there had been literary and art critics in the country, they would have offered their articles for publication in England where they would have obtained a wider circulation; except, of course, for topics of immediate or primary interest to Americans. It is, therefore, in such London periodicals as *The Gentleman's Magazine* (1731-1807), that one should look for information as to the knowledge that Americans had of Italy and the Italians in colonial times.

As we have already noted, and as we point out further in the chapter on business, trade relations between Italy and American ports (not to mention those of the West

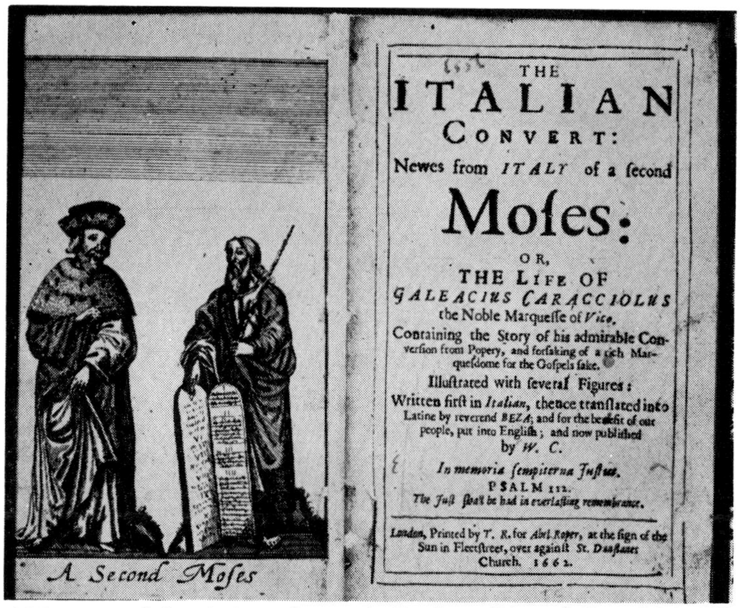

Title-page and frontispiece of an early London edition of Caracciolo's Life. (Courtesy, *New York Public Library*.)

Indies) were more frequent than it is generally believed. Now, it would have been short of human for American mariners to come home without gifts purchased in foreign ports, wine and oil, prints and statuettes, musical instruments, laces, perfumes, and even furniture. Professor and Mrs. Bridenbaugh, referring to the young men who visited Italy before the Revolution tell us that "when these graduates from the Grand Tour returned to their native shores, they furnished their homes with Italian antiquities and filled their gardens with neoclassic statuary, sought to elevate the taste of the less fortunate townsmen and in general set themselves up as connoisseurs and critics." (C. and J. Bridenbaugh, *Rebels and Gentlemen,* 1942, 122). In our opinion, much more was brought over by roving ship masters and seamen than by the young tourists. As early as 1743 Smibert had for sale in his art store "the best mezzotints, Italian, French, Dutch and English prints, in frames and glasses or without." (Quoted by Hagen, O., *The American Tradition in Art,* 1940, 59.)

More Americans than the eight recorded by the professor referred to above, visited Italy in Colonial times and shortly after; that is, besides West, Morgan, Copley, Izard, Jefferson, Carroll, Rutledge, and Shippen. The list should begin, obviously, with those who visited Italy even before they came to America. Men like John Winthrop Junior, and Robert Child, who came over in 1621 and 1640, respectively, after studying at Padua; William Penn; Benedict Calvert; Francis Daniel Pastorius ("the situation of Pennsylvania is like unto that of Naples in Italy") and not a few of our early physicians who "had doubtless touched elbows with Harvey at Padua under the tutelage of Fabricius of Aquapendente." (Blanton, W. B., *Medicine in Virginia,* 1930,80). As Dr. Blanton informs us, of the 475 English physicians listed in Munks' "Roll of the Royal College of Physicians" from 1570 to 1700, 69 were educated at Padua (*ibid.*). Others may have attended for a year or two, without graduating.

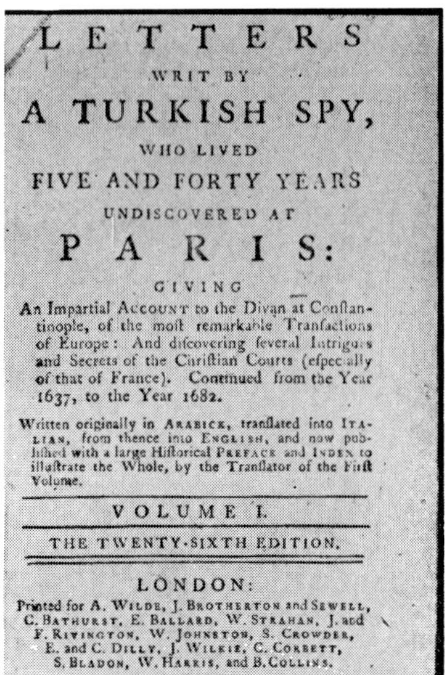
LETTERS
WRIT BY
A TURKISH SPY,
WHO LIVED
FIVE AND FORTY YEARS
UNDISCOVERED AT
PARIS:
GIVING
An Impartial ACCOUNT to the Divan at Conſtantinople, of the moſt remarkable Tranſactions of Europe: And diſcovering ſeveral Intrigues and Secrets of the Chriſtian Courts (eſpecially of that of France). Continued from the Year 1637, to the Year 1682.

Written originally in ARABICK, tranſlated into ITALIAN, from thence into ENGLISH, and now publiſhed with a large Hiſtorical PREFACE and INDEX to illuſtrate the Whole, by the Tranſlator of the Firſt Volume.

VOLUME I.

THE TWENTY-SIXTH EDITION.

LONDON:
Printed for A. WILDE, J. BROTHERTON and SEWELL, C. BATHURST, E. BALLARD, W. STRAHAN, J. and F. RIVINGTON, W. JOHNSTON, S. CROWDER, E. and C. DILLY, J. WILKIE, C. CORBETT, S. BLADON, W. HARRIS, and B. COLLINS.
MDCCLXX.

Title-page of the 26th English edition of Giovanni Marana's "A Turkish Spy." (Courtesy, *New York Public Library.*)

To that early list we may add the painters, John Smibert, who went to Italy in 1717 and came to Rhode Island in 1728, and Robert Feke, who in all probability was in Italy before 1735. (Hagen, *op. cit.* 71); possibly the two artists, John and Hamilton Stevens, who advertised in a Charleston paper in 1774, the teaching of painting "as taught in the Roman schools"; and probably also the Boston musician, W. S. Morgan, who announced in the New York *Post* for October 25, 1773, that he was a pupil of Signor Giardini, most likely in London, although a residence in Italy cannot be excluded.

It was about 1750 that it became fashionable for well-to-do American families to send their sons to Italy after they completed their studies in England. Thus the "Grand Tour," as it was known, became an indispensible part of the European education of a rich young American. (Bridenbaugh, *op. cit.*, 193-194, 210 and *passim.*) According to Dr. and Mrs. Bridenbaugh, the first American to start the custom was the young Quaker, Francis Rawle, who went over in 1748, but "the great impetus to Italian travel" occurred in 1760, when Chief Justice Allen provided his 21-year old son, John, with a letter of credit. Then he sailed for Leghorn with his cousin, Colonel Joseph Shippen, and a letter of introduction to Sir Horace Mann, the English representative at Florence mentioned by Mazzei in his memoirs. Others who visited Italy in the 1760's, besides the well-known Dr. John Morgan, were the Quaker Thomas Mifflin and the Anglicans, William Bingham and Samuel Powel. Another traveller was Henry Benbridge, who took painting lessons in Rome from Batoni and Raphael Mengs and returned to America in 1770, after he made a portrait of Paoli in Corsica at the request of James Boswell, the biographer of Dr. Johnson, as we have seen in the preceeding chapter. Breckenridge was followed to Italy by "Old Mr. Smith," a native of Long Island, who, according to Dunlap, did not succeed as a painter and became an art dealer.

Young Marylanders of "Popish persuasion," found it even more necessary to go to Europe for admission to Catholic colleges in France and Italy. (Maryland Gazette, March 21, 1754, quoted by Wertenbaker, *op. cit.*, 90). Father Carroll was only one of them. Still another man who visited Italy and returned in 1767 was Abraham Delanoy.

Not all Americans, however, looked with favor to their young men returning from Italy with new manners and affectations. As a matter of fact, the word macaroni, in the sense of fop, was first used in England about 1760. Why it was chosen by a unit of Maryland soldiers during the Revolution we do not know. Possibly their gay uniforms had something to do with it. Be that as it may, some elder Americans looked askance at Italian influences on English and American young men. "I am sorry that Luxury (Virtue's sworn Enemy) predominate too generally from the Peer to the Pedant," wrote an American from London in 1772. "Were you in England you would be astonished to see the Increase of Licentiousness since you left us; the Italian Fashions & Vices creep in upon us apace, which if not nipt in the Bud will take too deep a Root to be extirpated a few years hence." (*John Norton and Sons, Merchants of London and Virginia,* edited by Frances Norton Mason, 1937, 278). Jefferson believed that young Americans should have not been educated in Europe at all, but if any cities were to be chosen he preferred Geneva and Rome. (Jefferson to Banister, from Avignon, Sept. 19, 1785, also Feb. 9, 1785, and Nov. 25, 1785, to Elder). A visit to Italy, he wrote, also to Banister, on Sept. 7, 1786, "will certainly furnish you pleasing reflections through life." Washington, too, believed in European travel for young Americans, as he wrote to T. M. Randolph, Jr. Franklin was planning to visit Italy in 1782, but could not make it. (Franklin's *Writings,* ed. by Smyth, 1907, VIII, 315. On Jefferson and Italy see Dumbauld, E., *Thomas Jefferson, American Tourist,* 1946).

THE STUDY OF ITALIAN IN COLONIAL TIMES

In Chapter Six we have seen how the teaching of the Italian language was advertised in a New York newspaper as early as 1747. Six years later the College of Philadelphia (now University of Pennsylvania) was making inquiries "regarding the ability of a Mr. Cramer to teach the French, German and Italian languages" (Castaneda, C. E., in *Catholic Educational Review,* 1925, p. 7). In 1773 and 1774, as noted, Anthony Fiva was teaching Italian in New York City. Three years later, in December, 1777, one Daniel H. W. Mara, announced in the Virginia Gazette the opening of a school where "Arabick," Greek, Latin, French and Italian were to be taught. In 1779 Bellini was teaching his native language at the College of Williams and Mary. So much for the known teachers.

As for the colonists who could speak the language, we presume that those who had visited Italy had at least some knowledge of it. To Pastorius' ears, the Indians spoke "a language which sounds very much like the Italian" (See *Post,* Chapter XII). To some, learning it was diverting, to judge by *The Amusing Practice of the Italian Language* published by James Rivington in New York in 1782. Be that as it may, some people studied it by themselves: Franklin and Jefferson, among others. Franklin could read it, but not speak it. (B. F. to G. B. Beccaria, London, May 29, 1766).

To study and practice, books in Italian must have been on hand, but, unfortunately, very few are listed in the records which have reached us. In Virginia one Captain William Brocas, a member of the Council before 1655, left at his death "a parcel of old torn books most of them Spanish, Italian and Latin valued at 100 lbs. of tobacco" (*Virginia Historical Magazine,* 1894, 421-22). As for the books of Italian songs which were not scarce in Virginia, we do not know whether they were all music, or music and words.

ITALIAN BOOKS IN COLONIAL AMERICA

Books by Italian authors, or on Italian subjects, were not rare, even if there were not too many. Among those imported from London, we learn from the catalogues of colonial libraries which have reached us, there were, besides the Latin classics, the works of Famiano Strada, Lorenzo Valla, Polydore (an Italian resident of London), Poliziano, Boethius, Piccolomini, Baronius, Possevino, Pavone, Alciati, Castiglione, and Palladio, the latter so dear to Jefferson. The two most popular Italian books in the Colonies, however, were *A Turkish Spy* by Giovanni Marana, translated from the French, with supplementary letters probably added by Daniel De Foe, and *The Italian Convert,* or the Life of Galeazzo Caracciolo, by Nicolao Balbani. Caracciolo's life, which originally appeared in Italian at Geneva in 1587, went through several editions in French and English but none of them, according to Benedetto Croce, circulated in Italy, either in the original language or in any translation. (*La Critica,* 1933). Another Italian Protestant rather well known in the English colonies was the famous Olympia Morata. Adam Winthrop, the father of the governor, mentions her more than once in his *Commonplace-Book.* (*Mass. Hist. Soc. Proceedings,* Vol. 15, p. 241, ff.)

The subjects in which early Americans were primarily interested, outside of religion, however, were history, political philosophy, and both natural and physical sciences. Occasionally some book in German, French or Spanish was printed, but none in Italian. Those on religion were practically all by Protestant authors. One of the oldest history

252 WILLIAM AND MARY COLLEGE QUARTERLY.

	£	s	d
1 plad night gown,	0	7	6
1 new cloth Coat & Green Waistcoat	2	10	
1 old Brown Coat & 2 pair Breeches	1		
1 French grey Coat & breeches & black, silk Waistcoat	3		
An old Grey coat & Waistcoat	1		
New market coat	1	6	0
Old cloak 10s, 11 shirts 40s, 6 cravats 7s. 6d	2	17	6
5p' stockins 20s, 6 Towils 3s. 9, 4 Linnen Handkerchiefs 5s.	1	8	9
1 silk handkerchief 3s. 2 Wiggs 10 s. 2 pair shoes 10s	1	3	0
1 pr Boots 5s. 1 Hair Trunk 15s. Old Hatt 5s	1	5	0
1 Plain Gold Watch £15. 1 Spy Glass 10s. 9	15	10	9
½ lb Green Tea 4s. some Fiddle Strings 4s.	0	8	0
2 p' Temple Spectacles 5s. 2 sets shoe & knee Buckles 2s. 6 . .	0	7	6
a Fiddle & Case 21s. 6, Harpsichord and 2 Hammers &c 22£ 11. 6.	23	13	
Musick: 2 sets Pasquatis Overtures 4s each	0	8	
10 Books Handels songs	1	10	0
4 large sets Italian songs	1		
6 Sonatas by Schickard	0	4	
4 books of Symp. to Handels oratorios	0	10	
The Musical entertainment	0	5	
Lamps Songs	0	5	
Apollos Feast by Handel	0	5	
Nares Lessons 6s, Avisons Concertos 4s	0	10	
6 Concertos by Burgess & 6 by Hasse in one book	0	7	6
4 small books of Stanley	0	8	0
6 Sonatas Degeardino	0	5	0
Lamps through Bass 7s. 6, Albertis 8 Sonatas 5s	0	12	6
5 Concertos by Ramesá 4s, 2 concertos by avison 1s. 6	0	5	6
6 Concertos by Hebden in 7 parts	0	8	
1 Concerto in 7 parts by Avison	0	1	4
12 English songs by Pasquati	0	5	
1 large Book of songs Palma	0	5	
Songs in Acis and Galatea, Handel	0	5	
Alcocks Lessons 4s. Grannoms Songs 4s	0	8	
1 Vol Feltons Concertos	0	4	6
8 Concertos Avisons	0	6	0
Feltons Lessons	0	4	0
Correlli's Sonatas in Score manu	2	0	0
No. 13	0	2	6
Leveridges Songs in small	0	4	
Songs by Hasse	0	4	
Catches by Purchet & Blow	0	2	
Ballards by Grannom	0	3	6
An unbound book of Italian Songs	0	4	

A list of the effects left by a Virginian at his death in 1755, including several sets of songs and other music by Italian composers. From *William and Mary College Quarterly,* Vol. 3, 1894-1895, 251-252.

books by a native of Italy to be printed in the Colonies, was the "History of the World" by Diodorus Siculus, which appeared in Philadelphia in 1725.

INTEREST IN ITALIAN SCIENCE

More salutary and more lasting were Italian influences on science, a field in which Italy occupied a prominent place in the eyes of foreigners, to judge by the scientists among the 105 Italians who were elected to the Royal Society of London between 1700 and 1795—a most impressive figure, especially when compared to the ten Italians who were elected in the entire 19th century. (*The Record of the Royal Society of London*, 1901.)

Franklin, as we know, corresponded with quite a few Italian scientists, such as Father Beccaria, Paolo Frisi, Leopoldo Caldani and Landriani. He also corresponded with the famous political philosopher, Filangieri. Two Italians, one "Professor Famitz" of Naples, and the famous naturalist, Felice Fontana, were elected to the American Philosophical Society before 1783. Four more, Castiglioni, Andreani, Ceracchi, and Scandella, were elected between 1786 and 1798. (On Franklin and Italy see the scholarly work by Prof. Antonio Pace of Syracuse University.)

In medicine, too, Italy occupied a distinguished place in the 18th century, and Padua, with Giovanni Morgagni, was still the mecca of foreign visiting scientists. Dr. John Morgan of Philadelphia hastened to visit him when he reached Italy in 1764, but he also met other Italian scientists of the day, including a few women like the famous Laura Bassi. (See Pace, A., Notes on Dr. John Morgan . . . *Bulletin of the History of Medicine*, November, 1945). Widely read in the Colonies were the books of some Italian scientists, especially Cavallo's treatise on electricity published in 1777 at London, where Cavallo, a Neapolitan, lived for years and died in 1809.

SOCIAL SCIENTISTS

Two Italians whose works Americans read with profound interest were Gaetano Filangieri and Cesare Beccaria.

Filangieri (1752-1788), the author of the famous *La Scienza della Legislazione* (Science of Legislation) was in touch with Franklin, while the latter was in France. Filangieri had tried to settle in America soon after he got married, but Franklin advised him against doing so. "Though I am sure that a person of your knowledge, just sentiments and useful talents would be a valuable acquisition for our country, I cannot encourage you to undertake hastily such a voyage," he wrote to him from Passy on January 11, 1783. It would be interesting to investigate if Filangieri exerted any influence on the American Constitution, as it would appear from a letter sent to Bigelow by Filangieri's grandson in 1873, according to which Franklin had sent his grandfather a copy of the American Constitution, which Filangieri returned with his commentaries and Franklin sent back with commentaries on Filangieri's commentaries. (Franklin's *Works* ed. by John Bigelow, 1888, VIII, 242, note 1.) It is of further interest to recall that the Italian thinker in his famous work strongly defended the rights of the American Colonies against England. (Book II, Chap. XXII.)

Cesare Beccaria, not to be confused with Father Beccaria, the physicist, exerted a great influence on American penology with his little volume on "Crime and Punishment." Jefferson copied some twenty-six passages from it, in the original Italian. (See Chinard, G., *The Commonplace Book of T. Jefferson*, 1926.) Among the Quakers, Beccaria's opinions had "the force of axioms in the science of penal law." (See Schiavo, *The Italians in America Before the Civil War*, 1934, III.)

ART AND MUSIC

As for Italian influences on art and music in the Colonies, they were exerted primarily through London. What those influences on English life were, one may gather in part from Whitley's *Artists and Their Friends in England, 1700-1799*, or from the books by Burney and his daughter, Madame D'Arbley. (See Schiavo, *Italian-American History*, 1947, I., I.)

Then there are the crafts, but this is a field too large for investigation. We may be allowed to recall, however, that not a few of the furniture pieces that came to the Colonies from Britain's leading craftsmen, such as the Adam brothers, were the work of skilled Italian residents of London. (See, W. R. Storey, *Period Influences in Interior Decoration*, 1938.)

ITALIAN INTEREST IN AMERICA

Likewise, it is beyond the province of this brief chapter to trace Italian interest in the English-speaking Colonies and their struggle for freedom. On this point, see the article on "Some Early Italian histories of the United States" by C. R. D. Miller in *Italica* for December, 1930. On Vincenzo Martinelli see *ante*, p. 131.

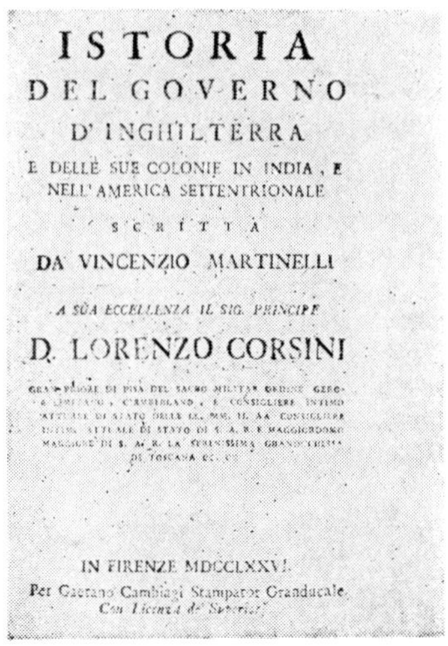
ISTORIA
DEL GOVERNO
D' INGHILTERRA
E DELLE SUE COLONIE IN INDIA, E
NELL' AMERICA SETTENTRIONALE
SCRITTA
DA VINCENZIO MARTINELLI
A SUA ECCELLENZA IL SIG. PRINCIPE
D. LORENZO CORSINI

IN FIRENZE MDCCLXXVI.
Per Gaetano Cambiagi Stampator Granducale.
Con Licenza de' Superiori.

Title-page of the first known history of the American colonies by an Italian writer.

PART II

FROM THE AMERICAN REVOLUTION TO WORLD WAR II

As stated in the foreword, the present volume deals only with the historical development of Italian immigration. No attempt, therefore, has been made to deal with its sociological aspects and implications. We cannot resist the temptation, however, from quoting two editorials which go a long way in explaining some of the problems which the Italian immigrant had to overcome.

"Antonio Agnio, a peaceable, hardworking and, so far as we know, respectable man of Italian birth, is held a prisoner at the Tombs in default of $1,500 bail—it might as well have been $15,000—to await trial at some far-off day for having shot in the leg Charles MacMahon, one of a gang of young ruffians who assaulted him as he was engaged in the lawful exercise of his vocation. Agnio, who is a bone collector, was driving through the street when he was fixed upon as a proper subject for attack by one of the street gangs which delight to rob and maltreat "Dagos". They threw stones and decayed vegetables at him, and finally jumped into his wagon and began beating him in the face. Driven to desperation, he drew a revolver and attempted to drive off his tormentors by shooting at random. One of the blackguards received a bullet in the leg, wounding him slightly. Then the ruffians of other regions, threatened to "lynch the Dago", but instead he only languishes in jail.

"Now, if this is not, on the face of it, rank injustice, we do not know what injustice is. We do not lose sight of the fact that shooting cases cannot be passed over without investigation, and that the processes of the law must often be inconvenient to innocent people. Nor should the use of firearms be encouraged among a quick-tempered people prone to violence in petty quarrels. At the same time, it is hard that the hand of the law should thus heavily be laid on the poor victim of aggression, that he should be kept from his work, that those who may be dependent on him should be left without sufficient support, while the young hoodlums are left to run at large and annoy other people. It is a notorious fact that many policemen look with good-natured toleration on the New York ruffians' attemps to "have fun with the 'Dago' and the 'Chink'." Whenever such citizens are involved in trouble with English—or rather Bowery—speaking persons, the police act on the theory that they are to blame. In three cases out of four the fact probably is that they are wantonly baited and maddened beyond what they can and far beyond what they ought to endure. They are unpopular to a certain extent because they work harder and are more thrifty than the loafers who would like to be paid twice as much for doing the same work half as well. But the abuse of them is due mainly to the mean and cowardly characteristic of the scum of all countries, the love of bullying foreigners poorer than themselves.

"The hoodlums need some severe lessons. The police should be held far more strictly to their duty of protecting Italian as well as other residents from annoyance. The Neapolitans and Sicilians may be quarrelsome among themselves, but they are usually peaceable in their relations with others. They are, indeed, so impatient as to encourage loafers to attack them. Imagine an Irishman subjected to the annoyance the Italian peddlar suffers daily. There would be some broken heads in town without fail, and the general verdict would be that the Irishman was a good fellow, who knew how to take care of himself. We should by no means counsel the Italians to meet force with force, but if every street tough who thinks it smart to stone "Dagos" could be removed to make place for a hardworking and law-abiding, if not always agreeable Italian, this city would be a more comfortable dwelling-place".

"The 'Dago' and the Loafer"—an editorial in "The New York Daily Tribune "for July 22, 1897.

"There is a self-complacency and a cool ignoring of facts in the assertions which are eminently provincial. Since the Latin race is so deficient in energy, it is rather curious that the Suez Canal, a work requiring considerable energy, should have been executed by the indolent and shiftless Latins.

"Also, it is equally strange that the same race should have tunneled Mont Cenis in half the time that an Anglo-Saxon people has occupied in the attempt to drive a smaller tunnel under the Hoosac Mountain. The accusation of want of energy and hardihood on the part of the Italians comes with a peculiarly good grace from a newspaper published in a country discovered by one Italian and named after another. Of course, since the *Commercial* has thus definitely objected to Italian immigration, it would be use to call its attention to the fact—as asserted by the police—that the Italians are the most orderly, in proportion to their numbers, of all foreigners in this city. Perhaps the *Commercial* would like to keep this country exclusively as a colony for the Emerald Isle."

An editorial in "The New York Times" for December 21, 1872, *in reply to an article in "The Commercial Advertiser", also of New York, which called the Italians deficient in "energy and hardihood".*

CHAPTER TWELVE

FROM A TRICKLE TO A FLOOD

Although a few Italians corresponded with Franklin and many more were acquainted with his scientific work and inventions, it was largely through Mazzei's efforts and the alternating fortunes of our War of Independence, that the Italians began to take an interest in the rising nation across the Atlantic. Whatever the causes, not a few Italians planned to come to America as soon as the conflict was over. Even Gaetano Filangieri, as we have seen, had planned to emigrate, but Franklin dissuaded him. Another man anxious to emigrate in 1778 was a German-Italian, one V. Bellini, a native of Gunzburg, where his father was established in business. As he wrote to Jefferson on Dec. 30, 1778, he was anxious to settle in America, "where good faith prevails". (*M.S. Library of Congress.*) We recall him as one of the many Italians, or children of Italians, who came to the United States from Germany, as Dr. Carli was to do a few years later, when he settled in Chicago at first and in Minnesota subsequently. Many Italians, indeed, must have been anxious to start a new life in the New World, to judge by the appearance in 1785 of two different Italian translations of Franklin's *Information to those who would remove to America,* one of which was printed at Cremona and the other at Padua.

EARLY ITALIAN INTEREST IN AMERICA

Italian interest in America apparently increased with the end of the Napoleonic wars. In 1816, we read in a letter to Thomas Jefferson from Thomas Appleton, the American consul at Leghorn, dated September 27, "the number of applicants to go to the United States has become incalculable; from professors of the highest services, down to the labouring peasant; and had they the means, as they have the will, Italy would be half depopulated. You will naturally infer, Sir, from thence that there is no amelioration in the political state of the country; on the contrary, it is progressing to that sort of maturity which must terminate in an universal convulsion: this is not a partial evil, but extends to the utmost limits of Italy". (*M.S. Library of Congress*—facsimile on next page.)

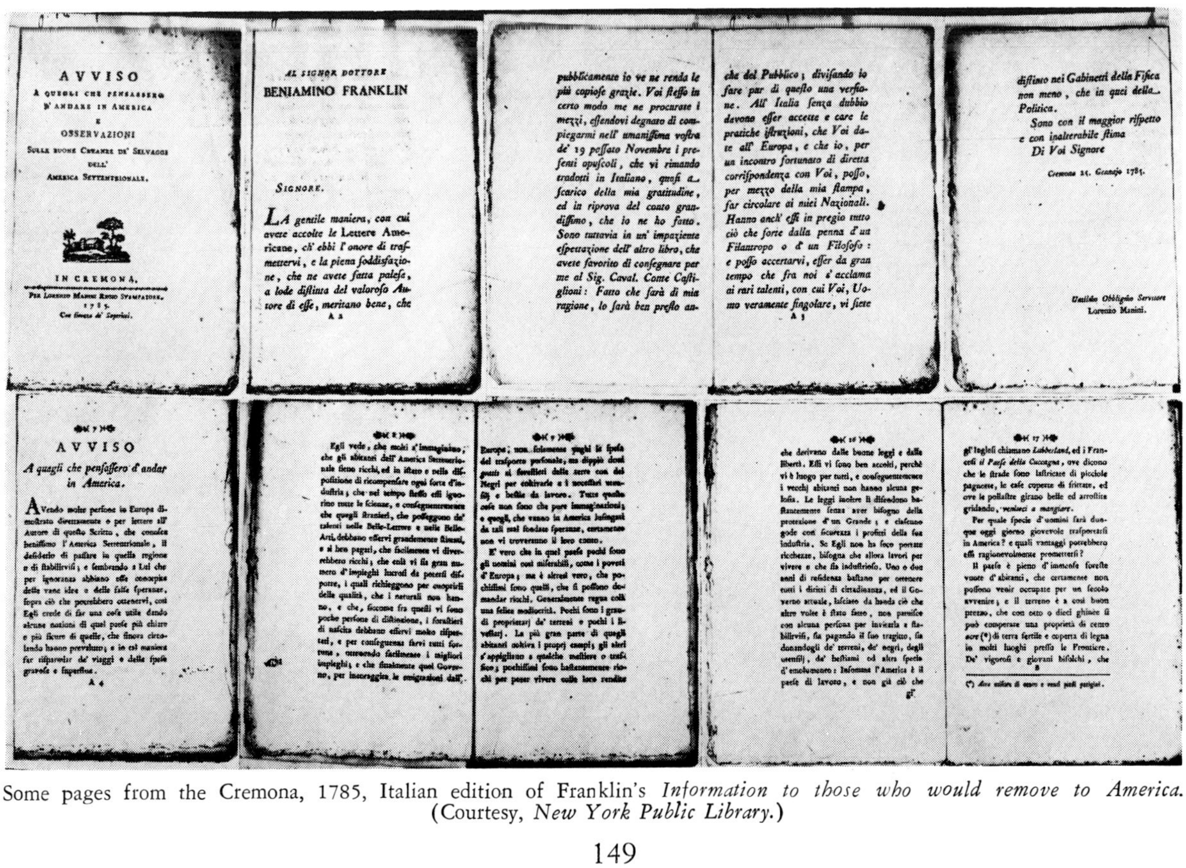

AVVISO
A QUEGLI CHE PENSASSERO D'ANDARE IN AMERICA
E
OSSERVAZIONI
SULLE BUONE CREANZE DE' SELVAGGI DELL' AMERICA SETTENTRIONALE.

IN CREMONA,
1785.
Con licenza de' Superiori.

AL SIGNOR DOTTORE
BENIAMINO FRANKLIN

SIGNORE,

LA gentile maniera, con cui avete accolte le Lettere Americane, ch' ebbi l' onore di trasmettervi, e la piena soddisfazione, che ne avete fatta palese, a lode distinta del valoroso Autore di esse, meritano bene, che
A 2

pubblicamente io ve ne renda le più copiose grazie. Voi stesso in certo modo me ne procurate i mezzi, essendovi degnato di compiegarmi nell' umanissima vostra de' 19 passato Novembre i presenti opuscoli, che vi rimando tradotti in Italiano, quasi a scarico della mia gratitudine, ed in riprova del conto grandissimo, che io ne ho fatto. Sono tuttavia in un' impaziente espettazione dell' altro libro, che avete favorito di consegnare per me al Sig. Caval. Conte Castiglioni: Fatto che sarà di mia ragione, lo sarà ben presto an-

che del Pubblico; divisando io fare pur di questo una versione. All' Italia senza dubbio devono esser accette e care le pratiche istruzioni, che Voi date all' Europa, e che io, per un incontro fortunato di diretta corrispondenza con Voi, posso, per mezzo della mia stampa, far circolare ai miei Nazionali. Hanno anch' essi in pregio tutto ciò che sorte dalla penna d' un Filantropo o d' un Filosofo: e posso accertarvi, esser da gran tempo che fra noi s' acclama ai rari talenti, con cui Voi, Uomo veramente singolare, vi siete
A 3

distinto nei Gabinetti della Fisica non meno, che in quei della Politica.
Sono con il maggior rispetto e con inalterabile stima
Di Voi Signore

Cremona 25. Gennajo 1785.

Umiliss. Obbligmo. Servitore
Lorenzo Manini.

AVVISO
A quegli che pensassero d' andar in America.

Some pages from the Cremona, 1785, Italian edition of Franklin's *Information to those who would remove to America.* (Courtesy, *New York Public Library.*)

Appleton was an easy prophet, for the revolution of 1821 was then smoldering, but he did not tell how many people left Italy for America during the following years. From Seybert's *Statistical Annals,* however, we learn that from January 1, to December 1, 1817, fifty-eight passengers arrived from Italy, of whom 7 landed at Boston, 14 at New York and 37 at Philadelphia. Whether they were all Italians, or of different nationalities, it is hard to say. Nor do we know whether any natives of Italy were included among the passengers who arrived from French ports (1,245) or from the West Indies (1,569) during the same period of time. Following the Vienna Congress of 1815 a large number of Italian officers who had served under Napoleon found themselves without jobs or a future and sought to remedy their precarious situation by emigrating to the New World. Two of them, Agostino Codazzi and Costante Ferrari, as related in a later chapter, landed at Baltimore in 1817, but they did not remain long and soon left for South America. That there were others we assume from the accounts of Italian emigrants to Latin America, or from the ever-increasing trade between Italy and the United States.

Another proof, however negative, of early Italian interest in America as an outlet for emigration we find in Father Grassi's advice to his fellow-Italians not to come over. "Those, therefore," he wrote in his *Notizie Varie* in 1818, "who might get the idea of emigrating to America would do well to take careful steps and the Italians especially should consider the proverb that he who fares well should stay at home." At any rate, according to the Rev. William Berriam, assistant minister at Trinity Church, New York, who visited Italy in 1817 and 1818, America was "the common subject of conversation at the coffee houses" in Milan. (Berriam, W., *Travels in France and Italy in* 1817 *and* 1818, New York, 1821, pp. 349 and 366.)

An American who visited Italy in 1826, one N. H. Carter, was pleasantly surprised to find "a miserably dirty tavern in the little village of Pietro", not far from Genoa, proudlly displaying a sign reading "Locanda l'Americain", an odd compound of Italian and French. At Leghorn he found that no Italian would have thought of visiting the port "without returning to the city with his hat full of American cigars". At Genoa, "by an odd coincidence, the waiter appointed to attend us has passed two or three years of life in Pearl Street, New York, making macaroni". (Carter, N. H., *Letters from Europe,* New York, 1827, Vol. II, pp. 38, 89, 43.)

EARLY ITALIAN-AMERICAN TRADE

Certainly there must have been a considerable trade between Italy and the United States by 1830 if in that year there were in Philadelphia consuls from Sardinia, Sicily and Rome. In 1831, if not before, Sicily (that is, the Kingdom of the Two Sicilies) was represented by vice-consuls at Providence, R. I., Baltimore, Md., Norfolk, Va., Charleston, S. C., and New Orleans, La., and by consuls-general at New York and Philadelphia. In the same year, Sardinia had consular representatives in Boston, New York, Philadelphia, Baltimore, Norfolk, Charleston, Mobile, and New Orleans. In 1840 the Papal States, Sardinia, the Kingdom of the Two Sicilies and Tuscany were represented by consuls in New York City. Consular agents, of course, are appointed primarily to look after a country's commercial interests; yet the very fact that the consuls of the various Italian states were all in maritime cities, leads to the assumption that not a few of the seamen who came over on trading vessels may have remained in the country. In 1851, according to the New York Italian paper, numerous Sardinian (that is, Genoese) ships were engaged in smuggling goods into the port of New York, with many members of the crews deserting ship as soon as they landed. (*Eco d'Italia,* May 10, 1851.)

The United States, on the other hand, was represented by a consular agent at Leghorn as early as 1795. In 1807, it is reported, 145 ships of American registry arrived in that Italian port, of which 85 directly from America. How-

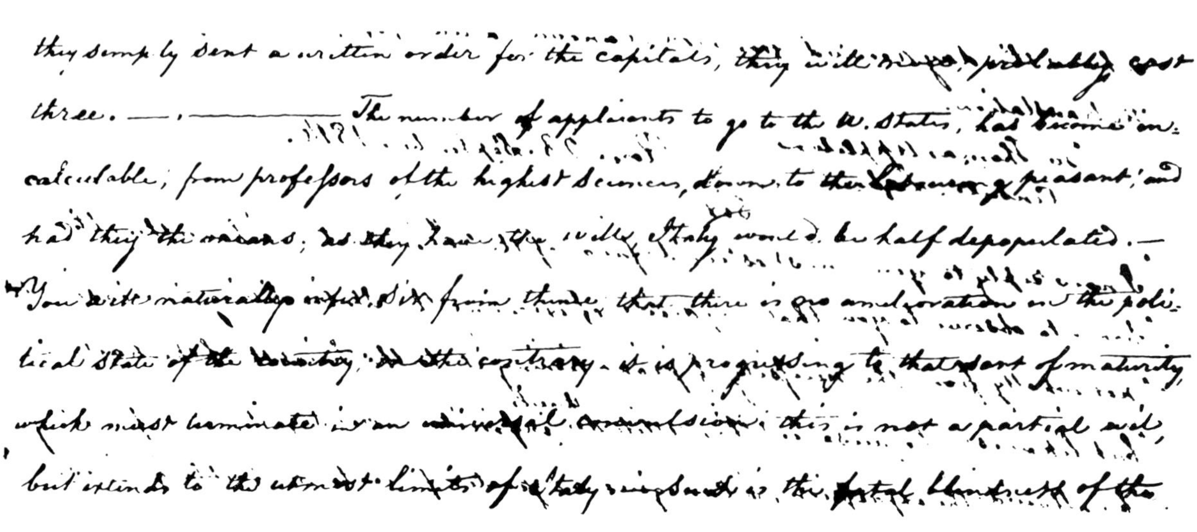
they simply sent a written order for the capitals, they will probably cost
three. — The number of applicants to go to the U. States, has become incalculable; from professors of the highest Sciences, down to the labouring peasant; and
had they the means, as they have the will, Italy would be half depopulated. —
You will naturally infer, Sir, from thence, that there is no amelioration in the political State of the country; on the contrary, it is progressing to that point of maturity
which must terminate in an universal convulsion; this is not a partial evil,
but extends to the utmost limits of Italy, in which is the fatal blindness of the

Portion of a letter which Thomas Appleton, United States Consul at Leghorn, Italy, sent to Jefferson on September 27, 1816, reading: "The number of applicants to go to the United States, has become incalculable, from professors of the highest Sciences, down to the labouring peasant; and had they the means as they have the will, Italy would be half depopulated." (*MS., Library of Congress.*)

ever, we cannot say whether by America it was meant only the United States, or, what seems more likely, the entire Western Hemisphere.

MISLEADING STATISTICS

To judge by the immigration figures of the United States Government, only 438 Italians arrived between 1820 and 1830, and 2,253 between 1831 and 1840. The figures for the latter decade, however, are somewhat strange, for they reveal only 3 immigrants in 1832, but 1,699 in 1833. Why such an extraordinary jump all of a sudden, it is hard to conjecture, even if one takes into account that a number of political exiles arrived from Italy or Austria (where the Italians had been kept in jail) during 1833.

In our opinion, the immigration figures for the period 1820-1860 are far from reliable. For instance, according to them, only 241 Italians were admitted in United States ports in the year 1848, but, according to figures in Valentine's *Manual,* during that year 321 immigrants from Italy landed in the port of New York alone. Even if the former figures were for a fiscal, rather than for a calendar year, the discrepancy can hardly be reconciled, for according to the former source 164 Italians were admitted in 1847 and 209 in 1849.

The difficulty derives primarily from the fact that before 1866 Italy was divided into so many political states that American officials often did not know whether to list a native of Venice as an Italian or as an Austrian. Actually, until 1918 the Italians from Trento and Trieste were entered in our immigration records as immigrants from Austria-Hungary, although their mother tongue was duly recorded. We may have an idea of the confusion created by Italy's political divisions from the eighth census (1860) of the population of the United States. In that report, for instance, the natives of Italy are figured at 10,518 (page XXVIII); yet from the same report we learn (on page 622) that 1,159 natives of Sardinia were not included. In more recent reports the figure has been corrected, with 11,677, instead of 10,518, natives of Italy given as residents of the United States in 1860. (From November 10, 1859, to March 17, 1861, when the Kingdom of Italy was proclaimed, Sardinia included also Lombardy, with the exception of Mantua. The other "regions", as we know, were Piedmont, Liguria, and the island of Sardinia proper.)

Before we go any further, let us note here that it is hard to tell from the 1860 census which Italian cities were included under Italy and which under other states. (Confront pages LXVI and LXXII.) Anyway, the United States census figures are way below the estimates of the Italian population made by Italian writers. In 1865, for instance, Cristoforo Negri estimated in his book *La Grandezza Italiana* that at least 50,000 Italians had landed in the United States during the preceding years and that more than 20,000 of them were in California. (*Eco d'Italia,* January 28, 1865). In 1869, according to the same newspaper, between 180,000 and 200,000 Italians were living in the United States. (See facsimile.) Even if we take into account the usual exaggeration to which Italian

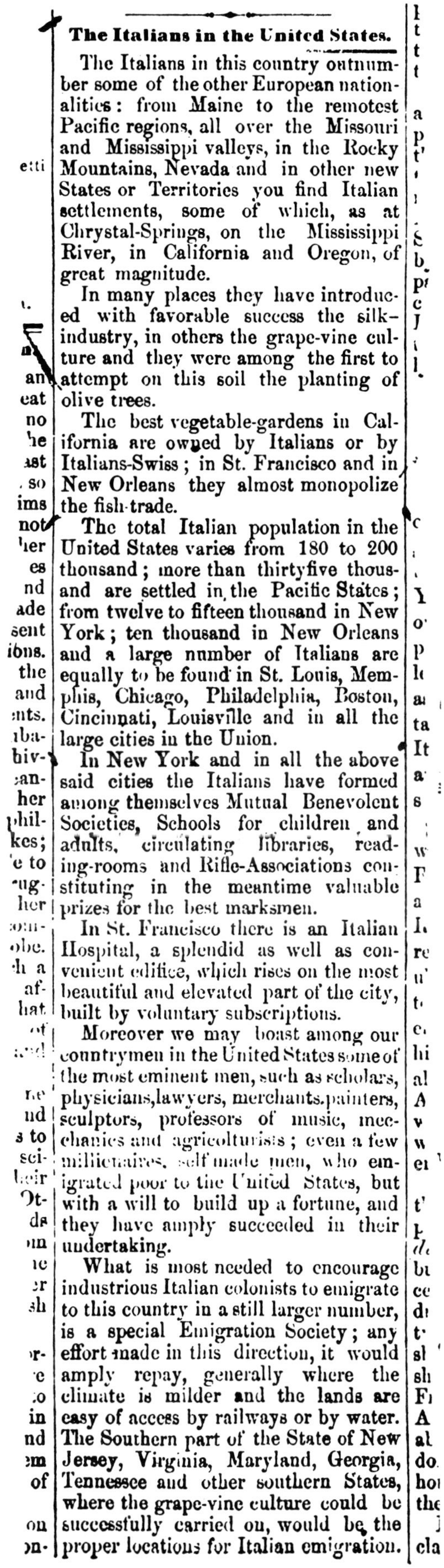

The Italians in the United States.

The Italians in this country outnumber some of the other European nationalities: from Maine to the remotest Pacific regions, all over the Missouri and Mississippi valleys, in the Rocky Mountains, Nevada and in other new States or Territories you find Italian settlements, some of which, as at Chrystal-Springs, on the Mississippi River, in California and Oregon, of great magnitude.

In many places they have introduced with favorable success the silk-industry, in others the grape-vine culture and they were among the first to attempt on this soil the planting of olive trees.

The best vegetable-gardens in California are owned by Italians or by Italians-Swiss; in St. Francisco and in New Orleans they almost monopolize the fish-trade.

The total Italian population in the United States varies from 180 to 200 thousand; more than thirtyfive thousand are settled in the Pacific States; from twelve to fifteen thousand in New York; ten thousand in New Orleans and a large number of Italians are equally to be found in St. Louis, Memphis, Chicago, Philadelphia, Boston, Cincinnati, Louisville and in all the large cities in the Union.

In New York and in all the above said cities the Italians have formed among themselves Mutual Benevolent Societies, Schools for children and adults, circulating libraries, reading-rooms and Rifle-Associations constituting in the meantime valuable prizes for the best marksmen.

In St. Francisco there is an Italian Hospital, a splendid as well as convenient edifice, which rises on the most beautiful and elevated part of the city, built by voluntary subscriptions.

Moreover we may boast among our countrymen in the United States some of the most eminent men, such as scholars, physicians, lawyers, merchants, painters, sculptors, professors of music, mechanics and agriculturists; even a few millionaires, self made men, who emigrated poor to the United States, but with a will to build up a fortune, and they have amply succeeded in their undertaking.

What is most needed to encourage industrious Italian colonists to emigrate to this country in a still larger number, is a special Emigration Society; any effort made in this direction, it would amply repay, generally where the climate is milder and the lands are easy of access by railways or by water. The Southern part of the State of New Jersey, Virginia, Maryland, Georgia, Tennessee and other southern States, where the grape-vine culture could be successfully carried on, would be the proper locations for Italian emigration.

From *L'Eco d'Italia,* New York weekly, February 19, 1869. (Courtesy, *New York Public Library.*)

newspapers in the country have always resorted for circulation and advertising purposes, we are inclined to believe that by the end of the Civil War there must have been in the country 50,000 persons who were born in Italy, or of Italian parentage, in the United States. For, it is important to bear in mind, the 1860 census did not enumerate the children of immigrants born in America, who were included among native Americans.

EXPRESS PER L'EUROPA.

THE NORTH ATLANTIC EXPRESS CO.,
DI NEW YORK.

SERVIZIO DI MESSAGGERIA DAGLI STATI UNITI ALL'ITALIA E VICEVERSA.

Officio generale N. 71 Broadway.

OFFICI ED AGENZIE IN TUTTE LE PARTI D'EUROPA.

Merci e pacchi di qualunque descrizione e valore si spediscono da e per tutte le parti d'Europa e degli Stati Uniti prezzi fissi di tariffa, abbraccianti tutto l'ammontare.

I PICCOLI PACCHI SI PAGANO ANTICIPATAMENTE.

Si spediscono e si consegnano in Italia alle seguenti rate, compreso tutte le spese, cioè:

ITALIA	Per 1 lib.	Per 2 lib.	Per 3 lib.	Per 4 lib.
Al nord di Firenze......	$1.20	$1.40	$1.60	$1.80
Al sud di Firenze......	$1.40	$1.80	$2.00	$2.60

Dietro richiesta, col mezzo postale o altrimenti, all'Ufficio Generale, di cui sopra, si spediscono gratuitamente le circolari, offerenti l'intera tariffa dei prezzi ed ogni altra informazione in proposito.

Le merci, i pacchi, ecc., spediti affrancati nell'interno degli Stati Uniti col mezzo di qualunque Compagnia di Express e diretti al NORTH ATLANTIC EXPRESS COMPANY, 71 BROADWAY, NEW YORK, verranno debitamente spediti a destinazione.

☞ Nessuna spesa qualsiasi per sonserie doganali o commissioni, imperocchè le rate della Compagnia, sopra pubblicate, coprono tutte le spese di trasporto e di consegna di qualunque genere.

W. B. FARWELL,
Agente Generale.

AGENTI IN ITALIA.
SIG. GIACOMO OCCHETTI,
Spedizioniere e Commissionario,
A TORINO, 7 Via delle Finanze,
A ROMA, 10 Piazza Rosa.

ANCONA. Carlo Perrati.—ARONA, Bellicardi e Fasana.—ASTI. Candido Carosso.—BARI. G. Tomasicchio e C.—BERGAMO, C Piantanida e figli.—BIELLA, Eusebio Bertola.—BOLOGNA. G. Gollinelli e C.—BRESCIA, Ramiro Olivari.—BRINDISI, Vincenzo Gusman.—CUNEO, Alessandro Cometti.—CREMONA, Egidio del Mare.—FERRARA, Giuseppe Mazzoni.—FIRENZE, Carlo Sestini.—FOGGIA, Achille Mongelli.—FORLI, G. M. Umilta.—GENOVA, G. Virgilio e C.—IVREA, A Longo e figli.—LUCCA. Raffaelo Ragghianti.—MILANO, Jung e C.—MODENA, Eredi di G. Poppi.—NAPOLI, Francesco Palazzi.—NOVI, G. B. Casalino.—PADOVA, Francesco Anastasi.—PARMA, Impresa Orcesi.—PAVIA, Carlo Parazzini. — PESARO, Giuseppe Girometti. — PESCARA, Cesare di F. Pepe. —PIACENZA, Impresa Orcesi.—PISA, Carlo Perroux. —RAVENNA, Clemente Triossi. — REGGIO, EMILIA, Cervo Liuzzi.—ROVIGO Domenico Turazzini.—UDINE, Francesco Parisi.—VENEZIA, T Bertina e C.—VERONA, Giuseppe Buia e C

Advertisement for parcel post service to Italy in *L'Eco d'Italia* for April 16, 1873. Only five offices are listed for cities in Southern Italy, namely: Bari, Brindisi, Foggia, Naples, and Pescara. (Courtesy, *New York Public Library.*)

THE FIRST ITALIAN COMMUNITIES IN AMERICA

Limiting ourselves only to United States census figures, in 1860 the largest "Italian" communities in North America were to be found (number of Italians in each state in parenthesis) in California (2,987), New York (1,910), Louisiana (1,279), Pennsylvania (625), Ohio (616), Missouri (603), Tennessee (379), Massachusetts (440), Virginia (263), Kentucky (234), Maryland (229), Illinois (224), Alabama (214), Mississippi (114), Wisconsin (113), and New Jersey (109). As we have already stated, those figures are not correct, but they give an idea of the distribution of the Italian population in the United States at that time. For instance, according to those figures, in 1860 there were only 49 natives of Sardinia, out of a total of 623, in the entire state of Missouri, whereas we know that most of the Italians in St. Louis at that time were natives of Liguria, then a part of Sardinia.

AFTER THE CIVIL WAR

After the Civil War the situation changed. Before 1865 only a few hundred Italians arrived in the United States every year, reaching the highest figure, with 1,414 arrivals, in 1858. After 1880 tens of thousands of Italians landed on our shores annually, with as many as 100,000 in 1900. After the turn of the century up to 1914 more than 200,000 men came from Italy year in and year out, with as many as 285,000 in 1907 and 283,000 in 1914.

Before the Civil War most immigrants came from the central northern parts of Italy; after 1880 the great majority came from the South and the island of Sicily. Before the Civil War, the Italians in the United States were scattered throughout the country, from coast to coast, wtih more Italians in California than in New York State, as we have seen; after the Civil War, most immigrants settled in the large industrial centers of the East and the Midwest. As for the alleged superiority of the immigrants who came before the Civil War, compared with those who came during the thirty years preceding World War I, it is all a question of proportion. A larger number of educated Italians (musicians, artists, educators, and other professional men) actually came after 1880 than before, but compared to the total number of arrivals for each year or decade, they represented only a fraction.

Certainly the arrival of close to 1,000,000 Italians during the last decade of the 19th century, and of more than 2,000,000 during the first decade of the 20th, was bound to create new problems and new issues with which neither the country nor the immigrants were equipped or prepared to cope. Hence the misunderstandings, the prejudices, the troubles, even the lynchings, which beset the immigrant at every step. But that was to be expected. However, as already stated, the present volume deals only with the historical development of Italian immigration, and not with its sociological implications or aspects.

FROM FLORIDA TO MARYLAND

Although the first Italians to come to the Colonies settled in the southern Atlantic states (Virginia, the Carolinas, Georgia and Florida), most of those who arrived after the Revolution chose Baltimore, Philadelphia, New York and Providence.

In Florida, as we have seen, some 110 Italians went there with Dr. Turnbull in 1768. Their children, we are inclined to believe, moved to other states, but a few remained. One of them, G. A. Pacetti, was mayor of St. Augustine, Fla., at the beginning of the Civil War. As late as 1880 only 77 natives of Italy were listed in the Federal census for that year. After 1890 the number increased, reaching 5,262 in 1930. In 1940 the figure went down to 5,138, exclusive, of course, of the children and grandchildren of the immigrants. In recent years the Italian population of that state seems to have increased, at least temporarily, because of the immigration from other parts of the country.

Among the pioneers of Italian blood in that state, we may recall Napoleon Achille Murat, the son of Joachim Murat, King of Naples, and Caroline Bonaparte, the youngest sister of Napoleon. The younger Murat came to America in 1821, six years after his father was shot at Pizzo in Calabria. He settled near Tallahassee, where he served as postmaster from 1826 to 1838. He was the author of several works in French and died in Florida in 1847. It is interesting to recall that Murat, who had been prince royal of the Two Sicilies during his father's reign, could not forget the city of his childhood, and called his Florida plantation Lipona (or Napoli, in reverse). Another son of Joachim, Napoleon Lucien, also came to America in 1825, and married a rich Baltimore girl, but he returned to France in 1849. It is not certain whether any Italians who sympathized with Murat followed him to Florida, as we are inclined to believe.

IN GEORGIA AND IN THE CAROLINAS

The highest number of natives of Italy ever recorded in any reports of the United States census for Georgia was 712, for 1930. Up to 1870 not more than 50 had been recorded. In North Carolina there were only 4 in 1850, 28 in 1890, and 445 in 1940. In South Carolina there were 59 in 1850, 344 in 1920, and 175 in 1940. Of course, those figures do not include the children of immigrants.

Yet the Italians were among the first white people to settle in those states, long before the Revolution, as we have already noted. Not only that, but the Italians have been among the leading citizens of those commonwealths, with such outstanding families as the Taliaferros, Prioleaus and Phinizys. (On Phinizy see the chapter on business.)

The identification of Italian pioneers in those three states is more difficult than in others, because of the change in names. Father O'Connell, for instance, in 1845 found an Italian at Columbus, Ga., named Strupper, and another, a Neapolitan, at Milledegville, known as Louis Valentine. From the *U. S. Catholic Miscellany* for September 8, 1824, we learn about the heroism of a native of Leghorn, one Emmanuel Carraci, who died on September 1, 1824, of yellow fever. "He is the same man who, under the name of John Roberts, while employed on board the steam-boat Columbus, so heroically hazarded his own life to save that of a fellow being, a seaman of the ship *Camillus*, as mentioned in the *Courier* of the 2nd ult. Such meritorious characters, the real 'Nobles of Nature', should not descend into the grave without a passing mark. It affords us pleas-

COSE LOCALI ITALIANE.

Lunedì sera partiva alla volta di Trenton una deputazione di Italiani onde tentare di ottenere la revisione del processo o almeno la commutazione della pena di morte pel Luigi Lusignani, condannato ad essere giustiziato a Morristown il 1° del prossimo maggio. Egli sarebbe il primo Italiano giustiziato negli Stati Uniti.

* * *

Sono giunti in questi giorni parecchi immigranti italiani, quasi tutti del territorio di Biella. Sono per la più parte minatori, scalpellini e muratori, e di apparenza molto civile. Fanno un gran contrasto colla massa degli immigranti delle provincie meridionali: tutti sanno leggere e scrivere.

COSE ITALIANE IN AMERICA

A Hazelton, contea di Lucerna, nello Stato della Pennsylvania, havvi una piccola colonia italiana composta per la più parte di Veneti e d'altri del Tirolo Italiano. Essi sono impiegati alle miniere del carbon fossile che lavorano a cottimo, e guadagnano ciascuno da 100 a 120 dollari al mese: posseggono di già un albergo di loro proprietà.

Questo è meglio che scopare le strade di Nuova York.

COSE TEATRALI.

ALLEGRETTI--ICEBERG

Refrigeratore Anti-insettico.

TEMPERATURA CONTROLLATA A PIACERE,

DAI 40 GRADI SOPRA ZERO FINO SOTTO ZERO.

I soli Refrigeratori nel Mondo che diano una equa, inodora, anti-insettica ed invariabile temperatura in ciascheduna parte delle piccole o grandi camere che vengono rinfrescate, senza produrre congelazione.

ALLEGRETTI, BADGER & CO,
131 QUARTA AVENUE, fra la 12a e 13a Strada,
NEW YORK.

Per informazioni rivolgersi ai Signori:

S. HAWK & CO, Proprietari del St. Nicholas Hotel.
DELMONICO, Quinta Avenue, ang. della 14a strada.
JERRY P. THOMAS, Caffè e Galleria, 1239 Broadway.
L. T. WARNER, M. D., 39 E. 19a strada.

SCUOLA PRIVATA ITALIANA.

I genitori che amassero far istruire i loro fanciulli nella bella lingua italiana, possono indirizzarsi alla Signora ANGELA SCOTTI, al N. 61 South Fifth Avenue.

Associazione dei Cuochi, Pasticcieri e Gelatieri Italiani e Svizzeri dei Cantoni d'Italia.

Per domande ed informazioni dirigersi all'Ufficio, aperto tutti i giorni dalle 8 alle 9 A. M., al N. 41 Settima Avenue, Restaurant Testera.

Il Segretario,
C. IGINIO MANZONI.

AVVISO.

Si richiede un bel violino, viola o violoncello italiano dell'autore "CREMONA."

Dirigersi per lettera all'Ufficio dell'Eco D'ITALIA indicando il prezzo e dettagliando lo stato dell'istrumento.

Societa' Protettrice dell'Emigrazione Italiana.

Questa Società essendosi legalmente disciolta, i contribuenti alla stessa potranno ritirare la quota del fondo rimasto in cassa devuto loro, facendone domanda al Tesoriere, Sig. M. Vanni, N. 120 Terza Avenue, fino al 30 Aprile p. v. Dopo questa data se rimarranno delle quote inesatte, il loro ammontare verrà versato al fondo del Monumento Mazzini.

P. A. PARODI, Segretario.

DA CEDERE — UN SALONE DA LIQUORI.

Some items in *L'Eco d'Italia* for April 16, 1873. (*Left to right, top to bottom*) (1) A committee of Italians going to Trenton to plead a re-trial or commutation, for the first Italian sentenced to death in the United States; (2) Arrival of Italian miners, stone-cutters and bricklayers, mostly from Biella, in Piedmont. "All of them know how to read and write, unlike those from the South"; (3) A small Italian community in Hazleton, Pa., mostly from Venetia and Italian Tyrol. "They earn from $100 to $120 a month. They own a hotel. That is better than sweeping the streets of New York"; (4) An announcement for the sale of refrigerators and (*below*) one for an Italian private school; (5) Announcement of an association of Italian and Italian-Swiss cooks, pastrymen and ice cream makers; (6) A Cremona violin wanted; (7) Dissolution of the Society for the Protection of Italian Immigrants.

ure, therefore, to add that his warm-hearted countrymen, uniting with others of their fellow-citizens, omitted nothing which could contribute to his comfort while living, and paid the last rites of respect to his remains, when no more." Also from the same newspaper, under the same date, we learn about another victim of the yellow fever, one Ann Scio, about 27 years of age, a native of South Italy. All of which leads us to believe that there must have been a small Italian community in Charleston as far back as 1824.

Another Italian who settled in Charleston in the 1840's was one Della Rocca, a political refugee from Romagna, who married a wealthy local girl. He inherited his wife's plantation with a large number of slaves whom he set free as soon as the Civil War was over. His granddaughter was a singer. (*The Confessions of a Prima Donna,* New York, Stokes, 1924.)

Two other Italian pioneers in the Carolinas were Antonio Della Torre, a partner in the store of Barelli and Della Torre in Charleston, in 1824, and Chev. Vincenzo Rivafinoli, who had failed as operatic impresario in New York in 1833-34. Both men were leading Catholic laymen. Rivafinoli, who operated some gold mines in Mecklenburg between 1827 and 1834, was responsible for the establishment of some Catholic missions in North Carolina. Nor should one forget Bishop Persico of Savannah, about whom more is said in a later chapter.

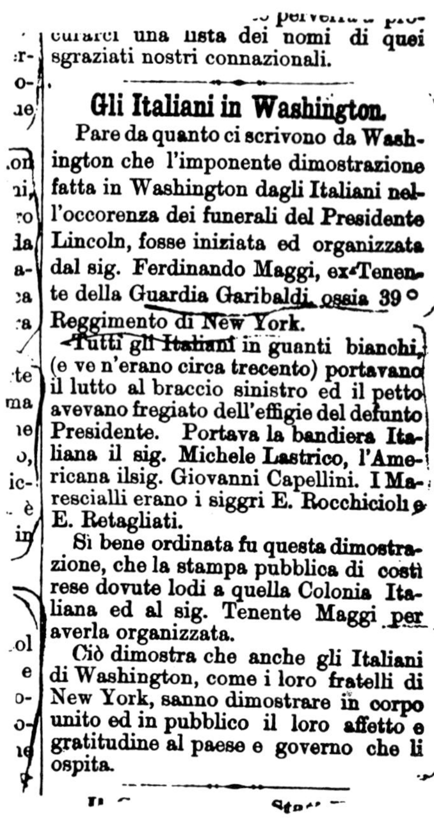
curarci una lista dei nomi di quei sgraziati nostri connazionali.

Gli Italiani in Washington.

Pare da quanto ci scrivono da Washington che l'imponente dimostrazione fatta in Washington dagli Italiani nell'occorenza dei funerali del Presidente Lincoln, fosse iniziata ed organizzata dal sig. Ferdinando Maggi, ex-Tenente della Guardia Garibaldi, ossia 39° Reggimento di New York.

Tutti gli Italiani in guanti bianchi, (e ve n'erano circa trecento) portavano il lutto al braccio sinistro ed il petto avevano fregiato dell'effigie del defunto Presidente. Portava la bandiera Italiana il sig. Michele Lastrico, l'Americana ilsig. Giovanni Capellini. I Marescialli erano i siggri E. Rocchicioli e E. Retagliati.

Sì bene ordinata fu questa dimostrazione, che la stampa pubblica di costì rese dovute lodi a quella Colonia Italiana ed al sig. Tenente Maggi per averla organizzata.

Ciò dimostra che anche gli Italiani di Washington, come i loro fratelli di New York, sanno dimostrare in corpo unito ed in pubblico il loro affetto e gratitudine al paese e governo che li ospita.

Item in *L'Eco d'Italia* for May 6, 1865, regarding the participation of about 300 Washington Italians in the Lincoln funeral procession. (Courtesy, *New York Public Library.*)

IN VIRGINIA

There never have been many Italians in Virginia at any time, even if they were among among the very first immigrants to settle there soon after the founding of Jamestown in 1607. The highest number of natives of Italy to take up residence in the Old Dominion was reached in 1910 when the census recorded 2,449 of them. In 1940 they had dwindled to 1893.

The first settlers of Italian extraction there, in all probability, were the several members of the Lupo family, followed by the Venetian glassworkers in 1622. It would seem, however, that they were preceded by a Venetian gentleman who had turned Protestant but later returned to the Catholic faith. He was in Virginia in 1613.

Mazzei, as we know, was responsible for the coming of a score or so of Tuscan gardeners and artisans. Others came at different times. Most of them became prosperous citizens, as related in the chapter on business.

IN MARYLAND

More Italians settled in Baltimore and Annapolis, possibly because of the Tolerance Act, already noted. The largest number of Italians, however, settled there after 1890, when 1,416 were recorded. The peak, with 10,892, most of them natives of Sicily and Abruzzi was reached in 1930.

IN THE NATION'S CAPITAL

The city of Washington, as we know, was laid out in 1791. The first Italians to settle there in all probability were the Sicilian musicians who organized the United States Marine Band in 1804, and the artists who were called over to decorate the nation's Capitol. During the Civil War the local Italian "colony" must have been rather well organized, if 300 of its members took part in a body in Lincoln's funeral procession. Every one of the 300 Italians wore white gloves, a black band on his left arm, and a small picture of the President on his lapel. (*Eco d'Italia,* May 6, 1865.)

In 1940, according to the United States census, there were 4,913 natives of Italy in the city. If we add those born in America of Italian parentage, including a large number of federal employees, there must be in the city probably more than 25,000 "Italians" of the first and second generations.

IN DELAWARE, PENNSYLVANIA, AND NEW JERSEY

Italian immigrants settled in what is now the State of Pennsylvania long before William Penn set foot on American soil. Most of them belonged to the group of 300 Waldenses who landed in New York in 1657 and later moved to New Castle, Del. Other Protestants, we are inclined to believe, came over after Penn got his charter. We would not be surprised in the least if even Italian Catholics came to Pennsylvania to be welcomed by Penn and Pastorius, the German immigrant leader, both of whom had been in Italy before coming to America. The melodiousness of the Italian tongue, indeed, must have left an echo in Pastorius's ears, for writing about the Indians of Pennsylvania he said that "They speak a most beautiful and grave language, which sounds very much like the Italian, although it has entirely different words". (*A Particular Geographical Description* . . . Weiss translation.) It would be interesting to ascertain whether Penn or Pastorius induced any Italian Protestants to come to America. Not a few of them, in those days, were living in Germany, Switzerland, and Holland. It would be also interesting to learn whether, or to what extent, Italian Reformists took part in the Quaker Movement and what was the nationality of Mary Lago, the mother of George Fox, the founder of the Society of Friends.

At any rate, a Jesuit priest, Father Greaton, took up residence in Philadelphia as early as 1720 and erected a chapel where St. Joseph's Church now stands. Another church, St. Mary's, was opened in 1763. It is, indeed, in the early registers of those two Catholic churches that we find the names of the pioneer Italian Catholics in the State, as we have already seen in Chapter Six. Many more will be found in the register of St. Augustine's Church, which records as its first baptism that of one Emily Frances Brasier Amabili, the daughter of Claude Amabili and Elizabeth La Fleur, who was born in Philadelphia on April 18, 1799, and baptized on October 18, 1801. In the burying grounds of St. Mary's Church we find the remains of one Louis H. Marquis of Modena, who died on September 22, 1789.

Quite a few more names can be found in the local city directory, starting from 1785, but as most of them were business or professional men, we shall deal with them in later chapters.

Probably the first son of an Italian to settle in New Jersey was William Alburtus, the son of Pietro Alberti, the Venetian mentioned in Chapter Five. He was born in Long Island in 1652 and moved to Lawrenceville, West Jersey, (now Mercer County) with his family in 1701. He served in the Hunterdon County Grand Jury in 1714 and later as constable from 1722 to 1726. In 1729 he transferred a plantation of 175 acres to one Peter Rockefeller. His name is variously recorded as Alburtus, Alburtis, and Burtis. (*Genealogical Magazine of New Jersey*, October, 1938.)

Today there are in the three states of Pennsylvania, Delaware and New Jersey probably more than 1,250,000 persons of Italian birth or parentage. In Delaware there were only 4 natives of Italy in 1860 (according to the U. S. census) and 4,136 in 1920. In 1940 there were about 3,500. In Pennsylvania the census recorded only 172 Italian immigrants for 1850 and 625 for 1860, but, in our opinion, those figures are far from correct, considering the many seamen who jumped ship at Philadelphia. In 1910

The Lincoln funeral procession on Pennsylvania Avenue, Washington, D. C.
(From *The Illustrated London News.*)

COMING OFF THE BOAT

they were close to 200,000, about the same figure of 1940. In New Jersey only 31 Italians were listed for 1850. At the end of the century, however, they had risen to 40,000. In 1930 they were close to 191,000, only to go down to 170,000 in 1940. Of course, no children of immigrants are included in said figures.

IN NEW YORK

New York City appealed at all times to Italian immigrants more than any other city in America, not excluding Philadelphia, Williamsburg, Charleston, or New Orleans. For a time, as we have seen, there were more Italians in California (largely around San Francisco), than in the entire State of New York. That was in 1860, when the American census reported 1910 natives of Italy in the Empire State, as against 2,987 in the Golden State. But that was a temporary condition created by the Gold Rush. Later many Italians moved East from California because they could not compete with Chinese labor. (*Eco d'Italia*, March 11, 1874.)

New York, more than any other city in the world, has been blessed with a cosmopolitan spirit and with an amount of freedom that one could not find even in Paris. For in Paris, one must remember, the French could turn chauvinistic at the drop of a hat; whereas in New York the most zealous patriot has always been mindful of the rights and sentiments of his "guests". There have been, of course, cases galore of intolerance and prejudice (there still are today) but compared to other leading world cities New York has been the most hospitable metropolis in the world. Certainly the first white man to visit it, Verrazzano, found its inhabitants so.

Whether the Dutch origins of the city have had anything to do with it we are not sure, although it is hard to discard such a theory. We doubt, indeed, if the English would have gone to the trouble of ransoming an Italian priest, Father Bressani, with their own money, and then sending him free back to Rome, as the Dutch did in 1644.

Be that as it may, the Italians began to flock to New York as soon as the English left it in 1783.

Beginning with 1787, just a few months after the Church of St. Peter was opened on Barclay Street, where it still stands, many are the Italian names one finds in the registers of that church, including that of Anthony Trapani, a native of Meta, near Naples, who assisted in its erection. (*Am. Cath. Hist. Researches*, Vol. VIII, p. 134). There, Philip Filicchi, Mother Seton's benefactor, was sponsor at the baptism of an Italian-American boy, Philip Ghiradini, the son of Vincent Ghiradini and Elizabeth Kearny, who was born in New York on October 10, 1787. Filicchi in 1795 was appointed as first consul-general of the United States at Leghorn, Italy. But then there are the various city directories, where one can find scores and scores of Italian names. (One, however, should be on guard; for instance, Charles Bernardi, an inn-keeper, is said to have been a Frenchman, and one John Lawrence Natali was a Negro.)

After the uprisings of 1821 a group of distinguished refugees settled in New York. From all parts of Italy, from Piedmont and Lombardy to Sicily, the victims of political tyranny continued to arrive in a steady stream until 1859, when many of them returned home. Among them a conspicuous group was that of Sicilian exiles, who began the importation of Sicilian oranges and lemons on a large scale. Then, at the outbreak of the Civil War, hundreds of veterans of the Italian wars of independence arrived to join the Union Army, as related in a later chapter.

No less distinguished was the group of Italian singers and musicians who came in, almost year in and year out, after 1826, and the Catholic priests who landed after 1848 and 1860. Their activities are described in detail elsewhere in the present volume. Finally, after the Civil War the mass immigration began, starting with 1,316 in 1866 (for the entire country), until it reached 52,000 arrivals in 1890. After that came the avalanche.

The Italian Benevolent Institute on West Houston Street, New York City, established in 1902.

CONDIZIONI DELL'ASSOCIAZIONE
PAGAMENTO ANTICIPATO.

PER UN ANNO	$6 00
SEI MESI	3 00
TRE MESI	1 50
PER LA CALIFORNIA	7 00
PEL CANADA	6 00
PER L'ISOLA DI CUBA	7 00
PEL MESSICO	10 00
PER ASPINWALL E PANAMA	7 00
PER ALTRE PARTI DELL'AMERICA CENTRALE	10 00
PER L'AMERICA MERIDIONALE	10 00
PER L'EUROPA	Fr. 35 00

L'ECO D'ITALIA.

GIORNALE SETTIMANALE.

Politica, Industria, Commercio, Scienze, Letteratura, Belle-Arti, Teatri.

ANNUNZI.

PREZZO DELLE INSERZIONI.	PER LINEA
UNA SOLA VOLTA	15 Cents
UN MESE	12 "
TRE MESI	10 "
SEI MESI	9 "
UN ANNO	8 "
INSERZIONI SPECIALI	25 "

Le Lettere NON AFFRANCATE si rifiutano.
Le associazioni datano dal 1° numero di ogni mese.

ANNO XVI. NEW YORK, 22 APRILE, 1865. NO. 16.

L' ECO D' ITALIA.
UFFICIO N° 65 NASSAU STREET.
G. F. SECCHI DE CASALI, REDATTORE E PROPRIETARIO.
NEW YORK.
22 APRILE, 1865.

Ogni comunicazione per questo giornale dev'essere diretta al Redattore e Proprietario G. F. SECCHI DE CASALI, e non ad alcuna altra persona.
I Siggri. R. MONTEFIORE e G. LEGHORA sono autorizzati ad esigere denaro dagli abbonati di New York.
—Il signor GIUSEPPE LUCCHESI è incaricato dell'Agenzia di questo giornale in New Orleans.
—L'ECO D'ITALIA è vendibile in New Orleans presso il sig. P. G. GIROUX, Strada St. Anna. No 236.
—Il sig. LUIGI JOSUE RAINUSSO è autorizzato a ricevere sottoscrizione per l'ECO D'ITALIA in Lima ed in altre parti del Perù. Egli è egualmente incaricato a stabilire altrove agenzie per questo giornale.
—Il sig. ANDREA VERZA è autorizzato a ricevere abbonamenti per questo giornale in Alessandria d'Egitto.
—Il sig. FRANCESCO QUAGLIA, residente a Guayaquil, è ora altresi autorizzato dell' Agenzia dell' ECO D'ITALIA nell'Equador ed in altre parti dell'America Meridionale.
Il sig. A. B. LONGINOTTI è autorizzato a ricevere abbonati per questo giornale in Louisville, ed in altre città del Kentucky.
Non si ricevono abboni per l' estero, compreso il Canada, che in **Oro.**

AVVISO UFFICIALE.
Consolato Generale d'Italia in Nuova Orleans.

Si dimandano notizie della esistenza e dimora dei seguenti individui:

BERARDI Dionisio, alias Eugenio GAVAZZENO—BUTTERI, Carpani Giuseppe—MAIFERO Giovanni Gaetano, di Genova—BORO Domenico—FORTI Angelo Tommaso di Bra,—BELLINI, Pietro, di Portoferrajo—MANGIAFINE Antonio, di Villafranca—BONSIGNORE Francesco, di Campo Rosso—FRASCARI Filippo, di Bologna—GHETTI Vincenzo, di Faenza—GIGLIACCIO Nicola, marinaro—PRATTINI Giuseppe, di Pallanza.

Dirigersi personalmente o per lettera al Regio Ufficio Consolare in Nuova Orleans, 23 Rampart fra Canal e Common.

Nuova Orleans, 31 marzo, 1865.
Il Regio Console Generale,
FERDINANDO DE LUCA.

Lettere degli Italiani nella Posta di N. Y.

tria, lo dimostra prepotentemente il sentimento di unità sorto come per incanto all'annuncio ferale che il suo Eletto era caduto vittima di un codardo assassino: questa calamità inaspettata ha congiunto le popolazioni del Nord in fraterno amplesso, prima a protestarsi sostenitrice del Governo la democrazia compatta sia ne'giornali sia ne'pubblici convegni. Al Sud oramai non rimane che fare adesione al Governo degli Stati Uniti, prolungare la lotta sarebbe un suicidio—il Nord unissono, non più lacerato da dissidii politici,—colosso cadrebbe come voragine sulle contrade meridionali.

Ad accertarsi di questa verità basti assistere al lutto generale in che stà avvolto tutto il paese e che prevale tuttora in tutta l'Unione, in ogni famiglia, fra il ceto ricco e povero, insomma ne pare colpita tutta la società! Dopo la morte di Washington l'istoria degli Stati Uniti non ricorda tale spettacolo di tristezza come ne fummo e ne siamo dolenti spettatori. Infatti all'annuncio della morte del Presidente Lincoln nessuno si diede più pensiero di affari, spontaneamente si chiusero i negozi, edifici pubblici e privati coperti di gramaglie, le strade deserte, cessato ogni pubblico divertimento si leggeva e si legge sul volto di tutti la più profonda mestizia!

New York, la città gaia, la metropoli commerciale del Nuovo Mondo, offre lo spettacolo di una città colpita da qualche morbo fatale, o tormentata dalla fame, o stretta d'assedio!

La banda dei congiurati, la quale si riprometteva di vendicare il Sud coll'arma dell'assassino e di far insorgere una reazione nel Nord, ha *fortunatamente* mancato al suo intento. Il Nord non esigerà dal Governo crudel...

dente Jackson, o quello in fine che nel bel seno del Senato degli Stati Uniti atterrava vigliaccamente, e a colpi di bastone quasi uccideva il degno e venerabile Senatore Sumner?

Assassinio del Presidente Lincoln.

La revoca della leva militare, il decreto della riduzione delle forze di terra e di mare, la decisione adottata nel seno del Gabinetto la sera dal 13 corrente di seguire verso i popoli del Sud una politica di conciliazione e di condono furono gli ultimi atti esecutivi del tanto compianto Abramo Lincoln.

La sera del 14 contro suo intendimento ed anche ai consigli della signora Lincoln di non intervenire allo spettacolo al Teatro Ford, il Presidente Lincoln acconsentì di andarvi onde non mancare alla parola data il dì innanzi. Il gen. Grant, il Vice-Presidente Johnson, il sig. Colfax, il sig. Stanton, Segretario della Guerra, ed altri membri del Gabinetto dovevano far parte del corteggio del Presidente, ma affari urgenti o il destino volle che non accettassero l'invito.

Alla fine del terzo atto uno sconosciuto penetra nella loggia, spara un colpo di revolver al Presidente (il proiettile colpendo il capo e fragellando il cranio) indi si slancia sulla scena e vibrando un pugnale per farsi campo fra le quinte, grida mostrando il ferro al pubblico: "*Sic semper tyrannis! Il Sud è vendicato.*"

Pervenuto a farsi adito sortì dal Teatro, e montato un cavallo sellato fuggì senza che riescisse ad alcuno di poterlo inseguire.

L'assassino era l'artista drammatico J. Wilkes Booth, nativo di Baltimore.

Contemporaneamente che ciò avvenir al Teatro Ford un altro scono...

Su tutti i Consolati in New York sventolava a mezz' asta il vessillo del rispettivo governo, ed il Console Inglese volendo dimostrare in modo più solenne il cordoglio de' sudditi britannici per tanta sciagura, convocò i suoi connazionali all'Astor House ed a questo *meeting* convennero numorosi i figli della Gran Brettagna residenti in questa città. Questo atto ed i sentimenti di simpatia espressi pubblicamente dalle autorità e popolazioni delle provincie Britanniche contribuiranno di molto a rassodare fra le due nazioni vincoli di amicizia.

Eguale dimostrazione ebbe luogo all'Albergo Delmonico per parte dei residenti francesi. Presiedeva alla riunione il Barone Gauldrée-Boileau, Console Generale di Francia, assistito dal Cav. Luigi Borg, Vice-Console Cancelliere e dal signor Paul, Console di Francia a Richmond. Il barone Gauldrée-Boileau alludendo alla morte del Presidente Lincoln commosse tutti gli astanti e le risoluzioni da lui proposte in nome dei Francesi qui residenti per essere trasmesse al Dipartimento di Stato in Washington furono accolte ed approvate da vociferosi applausi.

Anche gli Italiani propongono di manifestare questa sera al Cooper Institute il loro cordoglio per l'assassinio del Capo Magistrato degli Stati Uniti. Una simile dimostrazione, leale e concorde, sarà pegno agli Americani come i figli d'Italia, grati dell'ospitalità ricevuta, prendano parte a questa loro sciagura nazionale. La riunione sarà presieduta dal Console Generale.

Funzioni Funebri.

Non basterebbe un volume a descrivere le imponenti e com...

Programma pel trasporto
DELLE SPOGLIE MORTALI DI ABRAMO LINCOLN.

Dai giornali della capitale federale raccogliamo i seguenti particolari circa alle disposizioni stabilite pel trasporto di Abramo Lincoln da Washington fino a Springfield, nell'Illinois, ove le illustri spoglie riceveranno finale sepoltura.

Il convoglio funebre lascierà Washington alle 8 pom. venerdì 21 corrente, e arriveranno a Baltimore alle 10. Partirà da Baltimore alle 8 della sera per essere in Harrisburg alle 8½ pom., d'onde ripartirà alle 12 meridiane il dì 22 per arrivare a Filadelfia alle 6½ pom. Lascierà questa città alle 4 antim. lunedì 24, per arrivare a New York alle 10 del mattino dello stesso giorno. Lascierà New York il 25 alle 4 pom. e arriverà ad Albany alle 11 pom. Di là ripartirà alle 4 pom. il 26 e arriverà a Buffalo alle 7 antim. il 27. Indi proseguirà per la via di Cleveland, Indianopolis, e Chicago fino a Springfield, dove si calcola arriverà alle 8 antim. il 3 maggio, ove si dice, vi sia il progetto d'innalzare all'illustre vittima dell'assassinio un magnifico monumento.

La Cospirazione.

Che il Presidente Lincoln, il Vice Presidente Johnson, il generale Grant e tutti i membri del Gabinetto dovessero perire per mano di assassini, risulta evidente dalle informazioni raggiunte dalla Polizia di Washington. Appare che la cospirazione sia stata ordita mesi sono ed i cospiratori circa trenta in numero appartengono quasi tutti allo Stato del Maryland. Andato fallito in parte il cruento tentativo, i congiurati armati di tutto punto e provveduti di cavalli tentarono ...

Crediamo opportuno riprodurre in queste colonne alcuni cenni biografici del compianto defunto ex-Presidente degli Stati Uniti, e del nuovo Esecutivo sul quale sono rivolti gli sguardi di tutta la nazione:

Abramo Lincoln

nacque nella Contea di Hardin nel Kentucky il 2 febbraio 1809, conseguentemente all'epoca della sua morte aveva 57 anni. Allorchè adolescente emigrò in compagnia de' suoi genitori nella Contea di Spencer nello Stato dell' Indiana, a quel tempo, regione quasi deserta. Qui in mezzo alle selve ricevette dal proprio padre i primi erudimenti di educazione, fino a che la famiglia Lincoln passò nell'Illinois ove comperò un piccolo podere. Ne 1832 Abramo Lincoln organizzò una compagnia di volontari per la guerra contro gli Indiani della tribù Black Hawk, e ne fu nominato capitano. La sua carriera politica data dal 1834, quando venne eletto membro della Legislatura dell'Illinois.

Dedicatosi alla professione legale si trasferì a Springfield nello stesso Stato, ove si associò col sommo legista John T. Stewart. Tre volte rieletto rappresentante alla Legislatura: nel 1844 percorse gran parte dell' Illinois patrocinando colla parola ne' pubblici convegni l'elezione di Enrico Clay. Nel 1847 fu eletto rappresentante al Congresso in Washington, nel qual consesso si distinse per la sua energica opposizione alla guerra contro il Messico, tanto in voga presso il partito democratico, e nel 1858 venne sconfitto dall' Onor. Douglas pella carica di Senatore degli Stati Uniti.

Eletto il 6 novem...

The New York Italian newspaper mourns, with the rest of the country, the assassination of President Lincoln. (Courtesy, *N. Y. Public Library.*)

Funeral procession in New York City for the assassination of King Humbert I of Italy in 1900.
(From an old photograph.)

ta la Magistratura, il Clero d'ogni credo, ogni reggimento della milizia cittadina, ogni Società politica e filantropica. Una sola emigrazione, e lo diciamo con orgoglio perchè ne fummo promotori, rappresentava la propria nazionalità, e questa era la Colonia Italiana di New York, ivi accorsa in corpo di 500 circa di ogni provincia d'Italia.

Se fu un bel pensiero pel nostro egregio Console di convocarci a tale scopo pochi giorni innanzi; se le persone ivi convenute accolsero ed applaudirono l'iniziatore e coll'opera dimostrarono quanto accarezzassero l'idea di pagare un ultimo tributo all'illustre estinto, (il di cui Governo *fu il primo a riconoscere il nuovo regno d'Italia*)—l'esito riescì superiore ad ogni aspettazione, e al dire dell'*Herald* e di altri giornali di New York: "L'emigrazione Italiana offriva una bella e grandiosa apparenza, portante la Bandiera Nazionale Italiana avvolta in gramaglie, e formante un corpo unito di circa 500 persone."

Dacchè si è costituito il nuovo regno d'Italia questa fu la prima volta che gli Italiani di New York venivano convocati in pubblico convegno dal proprio Console; era la prima volta che sfilavano nelle pubbliche vie preceduti dalla loro Bandiera Nazionale, vessillo riconosciuto ed onorato da quasi tutte le nazioni, inalberato dal più prode e più magnanimo dei Re,—VITTORIO EMANUELE — piantato a piè dell'Etna e sulle sponde del Volturno dal più ardito e disinteressato Soldato che vanti l'Europa—GIUSEPPE GARIBALDI.

Convenuti martedì di buon mattino al Cooper Institute, i nostri 500 concittadini erano poco dopo organizzati militarmente e divisi in compagnie dal sig. Prati, il quale si assunse generosamente di guidarli. Giunti all'angolo di *Reade* e *Centre st.*, si fece sosta per circa tre ore onde far ala alle altre divisioni, ed alle $3\frac{3}{4}$ p. m. si incominciava in bell'ordine la marcia. I membri del Comitato signori G. F. Secchi de Casali e Carlo Ferrero, non che il Segretario della Riunione, Prof. A. Magni; ed il sig. Avv. Nash, Presidente della Società di Unione e Fratellanza Italiana, seguivano la bandiera portando armacollo una bella sciarpa di setà a tre colori, ciò che attirava lo sguardo di tutti.

Facevano parte di questa imponente dimostrazione Italiani di ogni ceto e condizione; uomini di lettere e di belle arti; industrianti ed operai tutti decentemente vestiti, o almeno secondo le loro circostanze il permettevano. Seguivano in coda alcuni ragazzi alunni della Scuola Italiana dei Cinque Punti. Tutti i membri avevano il petto fregiato della cocarda tricolore, e ci gode poter dire che non si ebbe a lamentare il benchè minimo e dispiacevole incidente. Così l'Italia era rappresentata in tale lugubre e straordinaria dimostrazione da *cinquecento* persone; e questi non erano i soli Italiani presenti alla processione, chè vi intervenne numerosa la *Loggia Massonica Garibaldi*, non che un drappello di 120 membri del 39° Reggimento, ultime reliquie della Guardia Garibaldi.

Account in *L'Eco d'Italia* for April 29, 1865, describing the participation of about 500 Italians in the Lincoln funeral procession in New York. (See below.)

The New York Italian "colony" of those days was rather unique. With the exception of the Italian community in Lisbon, Portugal, in the 16th and 17th century, where all Italians, from Piedmont to Sicily, banded together, we do not know of any community in the world in which the Italians were as united as in New York in the 1850's. They were not entirely devoid of discord, as we learn from the local newspaper of those days, but as a whole the dream of a united Italy kept them close together. At no time during the last century have the Italians been so proud and so jealous of their own good name as in those days. It seemed that each individual considered himself as the representative of the rising new Italy and duty-bound to act so as not to cast any shadow on its prestige. Evermindful of their duties as "guests" of this nation, they did all in their power to help their fellow-countrymen, to keep their beggars off the streets, to assist their needy ones. How proudly they marched in the Lincoln funeral procession, with the flag of the new Italy side by side with that of the United States, the first time in which the Italian flag, since the constitution of the Kingdom of Italy, appeared on the streets of New York! (*Eco d'Italia*, April 23-May 6, 1865—see facsimile above; *New York Herald*, April 25, 1865.)

The first association created by New York Italians was the "Società Italiana di Unione, Fratellanza e Beneficenza," organized on January 20, 1839.

APRIL 17, 1875.] HARPER'S WEEKLY. 325

THE PUBLIC HALL.

BAND PRACTICE.

THE NEW ITALIAN SCHOOL-HOUSE.

THE magnificent structure erected in Leonard Street, near Centre, for the Italian School, is the result of a movement commenced in the notorious Five Points in 1855, under the direction of Mr. A. E. CERQUA, the superintendent of the school, for the moral and mental improvement of our Italian population. For several years the movement met with only moderate success. Several times the school was closed through the opposition of the Roman Catholic priests, who worked on the superstitious fears of the Italians, and made them believe that the real object of the school was to draw them away from their religion. One Italian priest went from house to house denouncing the movement, and from the pulpit uttered fierce anathemas against those parents who permitted their children to attend the school. But notwithstanding these efforts the school gradually grew in favor with the Italians, and since 1857 the attendance has steadily increased in numbers.

Owing to the nature of the avocations followed by the pupils, the school at first held only evening sessions, from 7 to 9 o'clock; but in 1866 a day session was decided upon, and the results have shown that it was very effective in furthering the attainment of the Children's Aid Society's purpose in training the offspring of our lower classes for a life of usefulness and industry. As a compensation to parents who were thus deprived of the little earnings of the day attendants, some sixty tons of coal were for a number of years distributed by E. P. FABBRI, Esq., among the most deserving.

A question of paramount importance, however, forced itself on the consideration of the managers. Either by the exigencies of their work, or for other causes, pupils at a certain age left the institution; and it was this class which Mr. CERQUA wished not only to continue under wholesome influences, but also to utilize in the work he had undertaken. At a meeting called for the purpose he therefore proposed to the young men that they should form a society. The proposition met with great favor, and was immediately acted upon. The Italian School Young Men's Association was thus formed some four years ago. A reading-room was established, with a supply of most useful books, the gift of liberal friends. The principal newspapers are taken at the expense of the association. The young men have formed several committees for the different branches of their work, among which a visiting committee for the relief of the needy, with funds raised by their own contributions.

A number of the most industrious young men of the association, prompted by the desire of furthering their improvement, resolved to study music also. They engaged one of our best Italian professors, Maestro G. CONTERNO, and under his efficient training were soon able to form what is now known as the Italian School Band, whose proficiency in the beautiful art is really surprising, if we consider that the members of the band are occupied in shops and manufactories, and have but few hours in the evening to devote to music. Their assiduity, attention, and perseverance have elicited the admiration of all their friends, and enlisted the active interest of Messrs. E. P. and E. G. FABBRI, who liberally meet such of the attendant expenses as may be too onerous for the students themselves.

In the year 1864 a sub-committee was formed by a few of our most prominent Italian citizens, with the view of co-operating for the support of the work, which was

EXTERIOR VIEW—LEONARD STREET.

SEWING AND EMBROIDERY.

THE BOYS' WASH-ROOM.

THE NEW ITALIAN SCHOOL IN LEONARD STREET.—[J. C. CADY, ARCHITECT.]

An article in *Harper's Weekly* for April 17, 1875, about the Italian School in New York. It has been said that all the schools of Italy have not given to the Italian communities in the United States so many outstanding men as that very modest school. (Dondero, C., L'Italia agli Stati Uniti ed in California, *Italia Coloniale,* June, 1901.)

One of the floats in the evening procession which took place in Boston on Sept. 17, 1880, to celebrate the 250th anniversary of the founding of the city. It showed Europe surrounded by Germany, Britain, Italy (holding a lyre and palette, "referring to her excellence in the arts of music and painting") and France. (From the special publication printed by order of the Boston City Council.)

A rather unique organization established in 1843 was the "Italian Guard", organized by the Marquis of Sant' Angelo, a veteran of the Napoleonic wars and one of the most bizarre characters in the history of the Italians in America. More is said about him in a later chapter. The Italian Guard formed a company of the 252nd Regiment, 62nd Brigade, 31st Division, New York State National Guard. Its uniform was similar to that of the Italian soldiers who fought under General de Beauharnais, Vice-King of Italy, in Napoleon's days. Every year it used to drill at Ferrero's farm in Bloomingdale during the summer and it would give a ball in the winter. It lasted, apparently, only eight years. (*Eco d'Italia,* March 1, 1851; January 22, 1882.)

One of the first institutions the Italians created in New York was a school which they established in 1855 at Five Points, in the Chatham district, near Mulberry Street. It was supported by the local Italians, with a few Americans contributing most generously to its upkeep. Its treasurer for a time was Egisto P. Fabbri, who later became the partner of J. P. Morgan. How much the Italian community contributed to its success it is hard to say. But whatever they did was worthy of admiration, for the Italians of those days had little to spare even for themselves. One of them, however, the importer Giuseppe Fabbricotti, gave to it the sum of $1,000 in 1869. (*Eco d'Italia,* Dec. 6, 1869.)

Not all the New York Italians, however, lived in Manhattan, even in those days. Some of them lived in Staten Island, where Garibaldi resided for a time in the house of the unfortunate Antonio Meucci; others commuted, (by ferry, of course) from New Jersey; still others lived in Westchester County, at Scarsdale, White Plains, Hastings, Irvington, Tarrytown and Greensburgh (now Dobbs Ferry).

The Hastings colony formed "a picturesque and pleasant element" in the community. Antonio Bagioli, the conductor and teacher of music, built there several houses, one of which he occupied with his family, and the others he either rented or sold. Garibaldi visited there in 1850. Stephen Ferrero, the father of the Civil War General, also lived there, like the singers Salvi and Benedetti, the violinist and orchestra leader, Michele Rapetti, and the teacher of languages, Felice Foresti. (Scharf, J. T., *History of Westchester County,* Philadelphia, 1886, Vol. II.) Bagioli's daughter, Teresa, married General Sickles and was responsible for her husband's killing of her lover, Philip Barton Key, the son of Francis Scott Key, in 1859. When her husband was secretary of the American legation in London she was the lady in charge, for Buchanan, the future President of the United States, who was then our minister in the English capital, was not married.

Besides the names mentioned in Chapter Six, one finds many names which probably were Italian, in the various county histories dealing with the post-Revolutionary period. One of them was John Barbaro, of Montgomery County, near Amsterdam, who married one Sarah Van Pelten in 1791. (Pearson, J. *Contributions for the Genealogies of the Descendants of the First Settlers of the Patent and City of Schenectady from* 1662 *to* 1800, Albany, 1873, p. 7.) We have more data about a pioneer physician, Dr. John B. Marchi, who settled in Utica in 1815 and died there in 1885. (Schiro, G., *Americans by Choice,* Utica, 1940, p. 26.) (See especially Munsell's *Annals of Albany.*)

Today there are in the Empire State more than 2,000,000 people of Italian parentage or birth.

IN NEW ENGLAND

We doubt very much if there were any Italians to speak of in the New England States before 1800. Occasionally one runs across some names that are unmistakably Italian, like those of Francis Dana in Massachusetts, Diodati in Connecticut, De Angelis and Mauran (Maurana) in Rhode Island and a few others. In 1790 there were two Italian Catholics in Salem, one Peter Barrase, "an Italian", and a Mr. Frank, a "Corsican". (Lord, Sexton and Harrington, *History of the Archdiocese of Boston,* Vol. I, p. 429.) But that is about all.

Some enthusiastic people claim as Italians many pioneers who most likely were English and would have us believe that Bigelow originally was Bigello, Scott was Scotto, and so on down the line. Even Revere, which originally was Revoir, is traced to Italy, but unless more conclusive evidence is presented those claims must be relegated among myths. As for Mico, which sounds Italian but is not, that was a contraction of the French Micault.

On the other hand, if we limit our research to the post-Revolutionary period, we shall be treading on more solid ground. There are, for instance, the miniaturist Rosetti in Hartford, about 1797 and the painter Corne' in Newport

TYPICAL SCENES OF HALF A CENTURY AGO

after 1799; there are the musicians and teachers of dancing in Rhode Island, in Massachusetts and in Maine, some of whom appeared there even before the Revolution, as we have seen; there is the ship master, Dominis, in Boston, in the 1820's; as a whole, however, there is not much to brag about, however outstanding those few individuals may have been. Had there been an Italian community worthy of notice before 1840, Antonio Gallenga would have noted it in his book *Episodes of My Second Life*. Gallenga, the author of many books and the correspondent of the London *Times* for years, first came to America in 1836, returning to Europe three years later. He spent a considerable part of his American life in Boston, where he mingled in the best of circles. In Boston he met Pietro Bachi, a teacher of Italian at Harvard, and Pietro D'Alessandro, a Sicilian like Bachi, also a teacher of languages. He may have met a few other Italians, but not many, if he "used to stand still in the streets of Boston when the unfamiliar accents of our Italian dialects struck my ear, and it was as much as I could do to refrain from going up to the groups of half-tipsy, half-riotous Genoese or Neapolitan sailors from whom those voices proceded, and offering to shake hands with them for our dear country's sake". Only in New York he met "so many of the better class of my own people".

One of those sailors may have been the grandfather of Samuel E. Cassino, the publisher of *Little Folks Magazine,* for more than thirty years. In a letter to the writer in 1935, two years before his death, Mr. Cassino related that his grandfather came from Genoa, found his wife in Salem, and died there, the victim of an accident, when thirty years old. He never saw him. Since Mr. Samuel Cassino was born in Salem in 1856, we deduce that his grandfather must have come over in the 1820's. His case may have been typical of scores of others who settled here in similar circumstances.

According to the United States census, in 1850 the natives of Italy in the New England States numbered 197 in Massachusetts, 25 in Rhode Island, 20 in Maine, 16 in Connecticut and none in New Hampshire.

By 1860 Massachusetts had 440 Italian immigrants. Connecticut came next with 70. The other states trailed behind. Only after 1880 Italian immigrants began to settle in large numbers in all the New England industrial and fishing centers. Thus when the City of Boston celebrated the 250th anniversary of its settlement with an imposing parade on September 17, 1880, the Italians were ready to take part in it, with a group led by the members of the Italian Mutual Benefit and Benevolent Society of Boston, B. Brogi, commander. At the head of their group marched the Domini's Band of East Cambridge.

Today, as we know, there are hundreds of thousands of people of Italian birth or parentage in the New England states.

IN THE OHIO AND MISSISSIPPI VALLEYS

Before the Civil War few Italian immigrants moved westward from Atlantic coast ports. Rev. De Andreis and his Lazarist Fathers did in 1816. Leonetto Ciprani went all the way to California by land in the 50's. The Italian Mormon, Toronto, went to Utah in 1848. Others may have gone to Cincinnati and Chicago from Baltimore or New York. As a whole, however, the early Italian settlers in the Middle West came up from New Orleans.

Actually, to believe the census reports, in 1850 there were no Italians to speak of in the states which lie between the Alleghany and Rocky Mountains. Only one was listed for Minnesota, none, of course, for Colorado and Nebraska, which then had not been organized as territories, 10 for Wisconsin, 14 for Michigan, 6 for Indiana, 43 for Illinois. In Louisiana, however, there were 924, in Alabama 90, in Mississippi 125, in Ohio 189. In the following years the increase continued all along the Mississippi Valley, but it was not until after 1875 that the Italians began to settle in large numbers in the Middle West, practically along the railroad tracks they helped to lay down. Railroad construction, more than anything else, tells indeed the story of the Italian settlements in many Mid-Western communities which until 1875 had been more or less isolated from the rest of the country. It may suffice to recall that mileage in operation throughout the United States almost trebled in a quarter of a century, rising from 74,000 miles in 1875 to about 207,000 in 1903.

IN LOUISIANA

In 1850, according to the United States census figures, the largest Italian community in America was not in New York State, but in Louisiana, which had 924 natives of Italy, as against 833 in New York. Those figures, of course, do not include the American-born children of Italian parentage, who in Louisiana must have been in the thousands. Nor do they include the Corsicans. The fact that one finds relatively few Italian names in the city directories is of little importance, for a slight change in a vowel, and very often no change at all, made it difficult to tell whether a name was Italian, French, or Spanish. Certainly there must have been a significant number of Italians in the city if Colonel Nichols of the British Artillery, in his proclamation to the population of New Orleans on August 20, 1814, appealed to the "patriotism" of the "Spaniards, Frenchmen, Italians and Britons, whether settled or residing for a time in Louisiana". Not many years later, in 1836, when the Marquis of Sant' Angelo began the publication of his weekly newspaper *Correo Atlantico,* he had in it a section in Italian, which he would have not included had there been only a few Italian readers in the city. Three years later Sant' Angelo, the same man who in 1843 established the Italian Guard in New York City, organized "I Moschettieri di Monte Vernon" (The Mount Vernon Musketeers, so named after the "grave and cradle of Washington"). Like the New York organization, it was incorporated in the local militia and had 80 members, all Italians. (Cortese, N., *Le Avventure Italiane ed Americane di un Giacobino Molisano, Messina,* 1935, p. 97.) A pamphlet containing the names of its members is, or used to be, in the

NEW ORLEANS IN 1840
Painted by W. J. Bennett, from a sketch by A. Mondelli.
(Courtesy, *New York Public Library.*)

National Library of Naples. Four years later, in 1843, the *Societa' di Mutua Beneficenza,* the second Italian organization of its kind in the country, was organized.

More sons of Italy went to New Orleans, rather than to New York, before the Civil War, because of geographical reasons. Ever since the days of Columbus—literally, after his second voyage, as we have seen in Chapter Three—numerous businessmen from all parts of Italy, from the Alps to Sicily, settled in the West Indies to supply the Conquistadores with whatever they needed in their conquests. From Santo Domingo and Cuba as headquarters, the Italian merchants covered all the islands in the Gulf of Mexico as well as Florida, Mexico, Panama (where they had at one time a large warehouse destroyed by Morgan), and South America.

Italian emigration to the West Indies continued throughout the 17th and 18th centuries and the first half of the 19th, chiefly to Cuba, but also to Porto Rico and St. Thomas. From those islands, in the course of events, they moved to New Orleans, especially during the Spanish occupation of that city. Vigo, Cipriani, Antommarchi, Marallano, and other early inhabitants of the Crescent City, all had moved in from Cuba or nearby islands. From New Orleans to St. Louis and other communities to the North or East, was just one more step.

Thus we are not surprised to find a notable group of Italians, "chiefly mechanics, some of them refugees from the revolution of 1848", at Natchitoches before 1850. (Olmsted, F. L., *A Journey in the Seaboard Slave States,* Vol. II, pp. 282-286.) Another community not far from Natchitoches, near the present town of Homer, had been established by an Italian political refugee, Count de Leon, in 1833. A religious community, it consisted of 45 members, and it continued to thrive until about 1870, when it failed financially because of the generosity of its settlers. It is not clear, however, whether the settlers were all Italians.

During the Civil War many Italians served in the Confederate Army, but at the end of the conflict a number of them, "not being able to remain in business because of the vexing restrictions of the military authorities, disposed of their possessions at a great sacrifice and left for Mexico." (*Eco d'Italia,* Feb. 11, 1865.)

Yet the Italian communities in Louisiana continued to grow, with 1889 immigrants listed in the 1870 census. In 1880 they were 2,527 and in 1900 they had risen to 17,430.

No Italian community in the country has gone through such colorful and at times tragic circumstances as the New Orleans Italian colony, not excluding the barbarous lynchings of 11 Sicilians in 1891, which almost brought Italy and the United States on the brink of war. Eight years later five more Italians were lynched at Tallulah, La. One more Italian was lynched at Erwin, in nearby Mississippi, in 1901. In every instance the United States Government paid a large amount of money as compensation for those wanton murders.

Those shadows, fortunately, are obliterated by the achievements of the sons of Italy in the Pelican State, from the very days of Tonti to our own. An American writer, Mrs. Catherine Gibbs, has completed a whole book, *Italian New Orleans,* which reveals in all its glory the immense contribution that the people of Italy have given to the development of the city, correcting many mistaken impressions and giving back to the land of Dante many distinguished citizens who are generally labeled as French or Spanish. The achievements of some of them are described in the following pages.

IN MISSOURI

Geographical and political reasons (the Mississippi River and the Franco-Spanish domination of the valley) prompted numerous Italians to settle in Missouri, where they were among the very first inhabitants, long before it became a part of the United States and at about the time St. Louis was founded in 1764. Among the early pioneers were Francis Vigo, and a number of prominent merchants like Yosti, Bouis, Berthold, Maury, Locatell, and others. More will be found about them in the chapter on business. Here we shall recall a pioneer musician, Joseph F. Marallano (Maragliano, or Maragliani, is more likely), who came to the Untied States in 1833 and was naturalized in St. Louis in 1833 at the age of 37. In 1834, when 18 years old, he left his native Genoa for Cuba, where he lived until he moved to Missouri. (Manuscript material in *Missouri Historical Society, St. Louis.*)

Once more the U. S. census figures do not give us a faithful picture of the Italian community in St. Louis, for according to the 7th census there were only 123 Italians in the whole state of Missouri, whereas in the St. Louis city directory for 1848 we find no fewer than 37 Italians in business and in the professions, including four physicians, a lawyer, a professor, a music teacher (Domenico Ballo, later of Utah), grocers, tailors, and so on. It must be made clear, however, that not a few of those persons with Ital-

The Bartholmew Berthold home on the northwest corner of 5th and Pine Streets, St. Louis. (Courtesy, *Missouri Historical Society, St. Louis.*)

ian names were natives of Italian Switzerland and of Italian cities then subject to Austria. By 1860 the Italian population of Missouri had increased to 603 (U. S. census figures), with more than 200 Italian names listed in the local city directory for that year. A few of them had by that time moved to Kansas City. After the Civil War the immigration from Southern Italy began to move in and the population continued to grow until it reached more than 15,000 Italian-born residents in 1930. (See *Italians in Missouri,* by G. Schiavo.)

IN ALABAMA

The Italians of Alabama in pre-Civil War days lived chiefly at Mobile, a seaport. That there must have been quite a few of them, or that there was a considerable trade between that port and Genoa, we infer from the presence of a Sardinian consul at Mobile in 1831. By 1860 the trade must have increased to notable proportions, for in the local directory for 1861 we find an advertisement by a drug store reading "English, French, Spanish and Italian spoken by the attendants of this establishment," or announcements for the sale of Italian books. Ten years later, the local Italians numbered 214 (U. S. census figures), but they must have been more, as it would appear from the number of soldiers with Italian names in the Confederate Army. That explains why the son of an Italian, Constantine Lawrence Lavretta, became a member of the Alabama legislature in 1892 and mayor of Mobile in 1894, at a time when the Italians in New York could hardly get a job in the sanitation department. In more recent years the Italians moved to the Birmingham district, but at no time have they numbered more than a few thousands in the whole state.

The first Italian to settle in Alabama seems to have been one Giovanni Gradenigo, a descendant of the Venetian doges, who fell in love with a Mobile girl of German descent, married her and settled in her city. Later they moved to Louisiana where three children were born to them between 1781 and 1788.

After the Napoleonic wars a number of persons of Italian blood, including not a few natives of Corsica, settled in Alabama. One of them, Pasquale Luciani, came to America after serving nine years under Napoleon and was for some time French consul at Philadelphia. Luciani helped to establish a colony at Demopolis, Ala., in Marengo County (so reminiscent of Napoleon's famous victory in Piedmont) and died there in 1853. (Macartney, C. E. and Dorrance, G., *The Bonapartes in America,* Philadelphia, 1939, p. 221.) Another pioneer was Salvatore Bonfiglio, also a native of Corsica, who came to the United States in 1817 and married Lucinda Alden, a descendant of John Alden, in 1819. He taught modern languages at the University of Alabama and was the grandfather of Frederick Bonfils, the founder of the *Denver Post.* Two other distinguished pioneers were V. F. Corbini, who taught music at Spring Hill College in 1847, and Dr. Angelo Festorazzi of Mobile, possibly the first Italian-American to be at the head of a state medical association.

IN MISSISSIPPI

In Mississippi, as we have seen, there were at least 121 natives of Italy in 1850, but the figure went down to 114 in 1860, to rise to 147 in 1870. As a whole there have never been much more than a few thousand Italians. Most of them, however, have been substantial citizens, highly respected, and active in civic affairs. In 1869 there were about 18 Italian families at Natchez, all of them engaged in business or in farming. At that time, two men, one Gaetano Cagnone and one Ghirardelli, from Chiavari, near

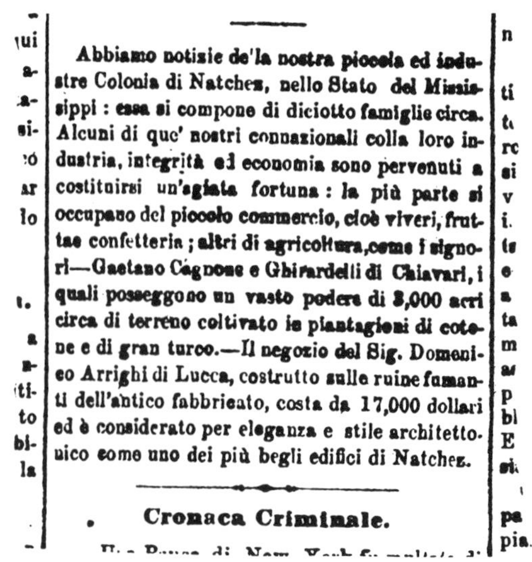

Abbiamo notizie de'la nostra piccola ed industre Colonia di Natchez, nello Stato del Missisippi: essa si compone di diciotto famiglie circa. Alcuni di que' nostri connazionali colla loro industria, integrità ed economia sono pervenuti a costituirsi un'agiata fortuna: la più parte si occupano del piccolo commercio, cioè viveri, fruttae confetteria; altri di agricoltura, come i signori—Gaetano Cagnone e Ghirardelli di Chiavari, i quali posseggono un vasto podere di 3,000 acri circa di terreno coltivato in piantagioni di cotone e di gran turco.—Il negozio del Sig. Domenico Arrighi di Lucca, costrutto sulle ruine fumanti dell'antico fabbricato, costa da 17,000 dollari ed è considerato per eleganza e stile architettonico come uno dei più begli edifici di Natchez.

Cronaca Criminale.

Item in *L'Eco d'Italia* for April 16, 1869, about the Italian community of Natchez, Miss., 18-family strong. Two of the local Italians owned 3,000 acres of land, and one owned a $17,000 building.

Genoa, Italy, owned 3,000 acres of land, where they grew cotton and corn. (See facsimile on page 164.) Two of the pioneers were active in newspaper work (in English). One of them, Paolo M. Botto, was editor and publisher of the *Natchez Democrat*, and the other, Agostino Signaigo, was editor (or member of the editorial staff, we cannot tell which) of the Grenada, Miss., *Sentinel*. More will be found about them in a following chapter. Another pioneer was one Domenico Arrighi, who married one Ellen O'Rourke, a native of Ireland. Their son, Frank J. Arrighi, who was born at Natchez in 1838, served with distinction in the Confederate Army, was wounded three times in action, and served as a public official for many years. Still another pioneer, one John Lombard, was one of the first trustees of the Catholic Board of Natchez, when it was incorporated in 1821.

IN ARKANSAS

Not many Italians settled in Arkansas before the end of the last century, even if Tonty was its founder. The people of that state, as a matter of fact, generally refer to him as the "Father of Arkansas", for it was he who first laid claim to it and established the first trading posts there. It is possible that other Italians settled in that territory in the 18th century, but their names, if any, are buried in old musty records. Only by chance we have learned of an early pioneer, one John Francis Mulletti, who in 1824 wished to donate to Bishop Rosati some 160 acres of land on the Cadron River, about thirty-five miles from Little Rock.

The best-known Italian community in that state, however, is Tontytown, established by Father Bandini in 1895, as related in the chapter on business. The highest number of Italians in the state was reached in 1910, when 1,699 immigrants from Italy were counted. In 1940 their number had gone down to 791, although there were several children of Italian parentage.

IN TENNESSEE

The Italians in Tennessee have at no time been numerous, but, like those of Mississippi, they have made up in quality what they lacked in numbers. Even today most "Italian" families in the state, chiefly at Memphis, are descendants of the pre-Civil War pioneers. That explains also why the son of an Italian became mayor of an important city like Memphis, as early (for the Italians) as 1917. He was Frank Monteverde, the son of Antonio, who settled in Memphis in 1857 and died there in 1923.

As early as 1850 there were 61 natives of Italy in the state, according to the U. S. census figures, but ten years later there were 379. In 1865 an Italian vice-consulate was opened at Memphis, with Agostino Signaigo, the poet, in charge. His brother, Captain John B. Signaigo, was nominated for alderman in the 7th district of Memphis, but we have not ascertained whether he was eventually elected.

A. Rottauzi, A. Wilhelm, *Dottori.*

Spigolature Italiane in America.

—Ci scrivono da Louisville che il ballo annuale dato nel Tempio Massonico da quella Società di Unione e Fratellanza Italiana la sera del 9 corr., riuscì oltremodo brillante: fra gli invitati eravi il sig. Paolo M. Botto, l'egregio redattore del *Democrat* di Natchez.

—Rileviamo con piacere dal *Memphis Appeal* del 6 corrente che il distinto poeta e pubblicista, signor Agostino Signaigo, redattore del *Sentinel* di Grenada, venne eletto Presidente dell'Associazione dei Giornalisti dello Stato del Mississippi.—Il sig. Signaigo tuttochè nativo d'Italia è considerato uno dei più eleganti poeti che vanti l'America.

—Un altro noto cittadino, il quale, come i signori Signaigo e Botto seppe acquistarsi fama nel giornalismo americano, è il sig. Pietro Cuneo, redattore del *Wyandot Pioneer*, foglio che pubblicasi in Upper Sandusky nello Stato dell'Ohio. Questi eletti ingegni appartengono alla Liguria e giovanetti emigrarono agli Stati Uniti.

—La sera dell'8 corr. all'Ulich Hall, in Chicago, aveva luogo il Terzo Ballo Annuale Italiano con numeroso ed attraente concorso di persone. Il *Messaggiere* di quella città dice che nel corso della cena furono fatti numerosi brindisi all'Italia, mentre l'orchestra eseguiva la marcia reale e l'inno di Garibaldi: ordine perfetto, allegria generale, festa essenzialmonte italiana.

—Il 25 gennaio u. s. moriva in San Francisco di California Francesco Ansaldo di Genova, uno de' più vecchi residenti di California: egli era molto stimato e popolare ed a' suoi funerali intervennero la Società di Beneficenza Italiana, la Compagnia Garibaldina e molti membri della Società dei Pompieri.

—Di vaiuolo cèssava di vivere in quella città Luigi Raffo in età d'anni 34: egli era nativo di Cogorno, comune di Cobrino, mandamento di Lavagna.

—Luigi Franci Leoni, nativo di Versci, Pedemonte, Svizzera, precipitato in una mina dall'altezza di circa 40 piedi, miseramente moriva la mattina del 19 gennaio.—L'*Eco della Patria* dice che il povero Franci non aveva che 29 anni!

—Lo stesso giornale annuncia la morte di Francesco Leverone di Cicagna circondario di Chiavari: egli moriva in San Francisco il 18 gennaio, in

More items about the Italians in America in *L'Eco d'Italia* for February 19, 1869. (1) A ball by the Italian Society of Louisville, Ky.; (2) Signaigo, editor of the Grenada *Sentinel*, is elected president of the Mississippi Press Association; (3) Pietro Cuneo, editor of the *Wyandot* (Ohio) *Pioneer;* (4) Third Italian Annual Ball in Chicago; (5) Death of a San Francisco pioneer; (6) Death of another San Francisco Italian; (7) Fatal accident of a Swiss-Italian miner; (8) Death of one more San Francisco pioneer. (Courtesy, *New York Public Library.*)

(*Eco d'Italia,* December 23, 1869.) During the next two decades the Italian population of Tennessee slightly increased to less than 500. Only in 1910 it reached the figure of 2,000. How rapidly the Tennessee Italians assimilated with other national groups we learn from *Eco d'Italia* which on April 2, 1873, bemoaned the Italian participation in the local St. Patrick's Day parade side by side with the Irish, who in those days and in other states, especially New York, were considered the "worst enemies of the Italians".

IN KENTUCKY

In Kentucky, too, there were quite a few Italians before the Civil War, for by 1865 there was an Italian vice-consulate at Louisville. By 1869 there was a mutual benefit society. (*Eco d'Italia,* February 28, 1865. See also facsimile on page 165.) At that time there must have been more than 300 natives of Italy in the state. According to the U. S. census, they were 144 in 1850, 235 in 1860, 325 in 1870, and 370 in 1880. At no time have they been more than 2,000.

Among the pioneers we shall recall one Colonel Mariano, who died at Lexington on June 19, 1821 and, of course, the Catholic priests who began to teach and minister there as far back as 1817.

IN OHIO

The present Italian communities in Ohio, with the exception of Cincinnati, date back, more or less, to the beginning of the present century, when there were some 11,321 natives of Italy in the entire state. In 1890 there were only 3,857. The earliest figures we have are for 1850 (189), 1860 (616) and 1870 (564). During the Civil War period most Italians resided in Cincinnati (500 out of a total of 616 in 1860), which at that time was larger than Cleveland. The fact that there was an Italian consular agent in the city as early as 1835 leads us to believe, however, that there must have been quite a few subjects of the King of Sardinia at that time, for apparently there was no direct trade with Italy that required the presence of a consular agent. Actually, the local Italian community dates back to the early years of the 19th century, as it would appear from some of the names in St. Joseph's cemetery. It is interesting to recall that as early as 1867 some 75 persons of Italian birth or extraction subscribed to a fund for the erection of a national Catholic church, but nothing came out of it. Among the noted pioneers we shall recall here only the Grasselli family.

IN INDIANA

In Indiana the Italian population rose from 6 in 1850 to 421 in 1860, to go down once more to 95 ten years later. Why such a sharp oscillation we do not know. Possibly some railroad construction would account for it. Be that as it may, the peak of Italian immigration into Indiana was reached in 1910 with 6,911 registered natives of Italy.

As for pioneers, the most famous of them all was Francis Vigo.

IN MICHIGAN

In Michigan, likewise, there were only a few Italian immigrants before the Civil War, with only 14 registered in 1850 and 87 in 1860. In 1880 there were still only about 500, but more than 3,000 had settled in the state ten years later, and twice as many in 1900. The peak was reached in 1930 with 43,087. Not a few of them were in the Lake Superior iron-ore belt.

As for the pioneers, outside of Alphone Tonti and the other Italians who followed him in the early part of the 18th century, we may recall Dr. Louis Cavalli in the 1840's, Pietro Centemeri, a musician, in the 1850's, and Pasquale Palmieri, a painter, in the 1860's. Palmieri was one of the charter members of the Detroit Italian Mutual Aid Society in 1873. More is said about them in later chapters.

IN ILLINOIS

The first Italian settler in Illinois, with the exception of De Lieto, who, as we have seen in Chapter Four, was the first permanent white settler at Chicago in 1698-1702, may have been a German-Italian, Dr. Christopher Carli, who practised in Chicago from 1837 to 1841, when he moved to Wisconsin, as related in another chapter.

The beginnings of the present mass immigration, however, date back to the construction between 1836 and 1848 of the canals that connect Lake Michigan with the Gulf of Mexico. Once more, the Italians moved in from the South, across the Mississippi, from St. Louis. That explains, in part, the labors of several Italian priests around La Salle, Peoria, and other nearby communities, between 1836 and 1850. That explains also why one of the first Italian colonies in Illinois was established at Cairo, where there must have been quite a few Italian immigrants in Civil War days, to judge by a score of names one finds among the subscribers to a monument in honor of Anita Garibaldi which was to be erected in Italy. (*Eco d'Italia,* July 8, 1865.) It was in that little town that Agostino Signaigo, later of Memphis, Tenn., and Grenada, Miss., began his newspaper career on the staff, or as editor, of the *Cairo Daily News.* (*Ibid.,* March 11 and July 8, 1865.) A few Italian Mormons lived at Nauvoo, Ill., between 1843 and 1846, as related below.

Another early group, apparently of lead workers, had settled at Galena in 1851, when an announcement for collection for their relief was published in the *Eco d'Italia* (March 29, 1851.) Father Mazzuchelli, as we know, founded the first Catholic church in the city in 1835-36, just as Father Raho and other Italian priests founded other churches and missions around La Salle and nearby communities between 1836 and 1850.

Few Italian communities in the country, if any, have increased as rapidly and as steadily as that of Chicago, which had only 100 immigrants in 1860, but increased to 552 in 1870, 1,357 in 1880, 5,591 in 1890, 16,000 in 1900, 45,000 in 1910 and 60,000 in 1920. Its first mutual benefit society was organized before 1869, for in that year the local Italians were hosts to the second annual national convention of the Federation of Italian Societies in the United States. An annual ball was also given as far back as 1867. In 1886 the first Italian-language newspaper in the middle west, *L'Italia,* was established by Oscar Durante. It is still in existence.

FROM WISCONSIN AND MINNESOTA TO IOWA AND NEBRASKA

Aside from the Italians who may have come over with Tonti or Duluth, the first natives of Italy to reach as far north as Minnesota may have been the Italian traders from St. Louis, like Vigo, whose operations extended to Mackinac. Then came the travellers, Andreani and Beltrami. Still later came Father Mazzuchelli, who labored in Wisconsin and Iowa after 1830. Dr. Carli, already mentioned, moved in from Chicago in 1841 and settled in what is now Stillwater, Minn. Another pioneer with an Italian name, one Frederick Oliva, worked as a clerk at Prairie du Chien, Wis., from 1847 to 1880. (*Guide to the Personal Papers in the MS Collection of the Minnesota Historical Society,* St. Paul, 1935.) There may have been others, besides a few missionary priests. As far back as 1869 there was a small Italian colony at Omaha, where a number of immigrants owned stores, lunch rooms, or restaurants. Most probably they had worked their way over as railroad laborers and then decided to remain. In Minnesota, at Red Wing, in 1874 there were four Genoese farmers, one confectioner who was born in Trieste, and two Piedmontese stucco workers. (See facsimiles on this page.)

RED WING, Minnesota, 2 Febbraio.

Signor Redattore,

Ciò che mi spinge a scriverle, è l'aver letto nell'*Eco d'Italia* del 28 p. p. mese un articolo sugli italiani negli Stati Uniti, dal quale rilevo come in Nuova York molti dei nostri non hanno attualmente alcuna occupazione e non pochi versano in cattive circostanze. Ebbene se ve n'hanno che siano muratori, stuccatori o scalpellini, purchè sobrii ed industriosi, io potrò essere loro utile in queste parti del Minnesota, tuttochè quelli delle due prime categorie non fossero al caso di lavorare ad uso degli Americani. Posseggo inoltre un segreto per l'arte dello stuccatore, che ben volentieri comunicherò ai miei connazionali.

Certo, la città di Nuova York non è più quella di vent'anni sono, ma la vallata del Mississippi sarà per cento e più anni avvenire la terra promessa per l'operaio intelligente ed attivo. Nel luogo da dove le scrivo siamo soltanto sette italiani; cioè, 4 del mandamento di Chiavari, i quali si applicano all'agricoltura e fanno buoni affari, uno è triestino ed ha negozio di confettureria, e gli altri 2, io e mio figlio, nativi di Gressoney nell' antica provincia d' Aosta; io faccio lo stuccatore ed il mio figlio è nel commercio. Ritiriamo i prodotti d'Italia di cui abbisogniamo dalla Casa A. CELLA E FRATELLI di New York.

Però, onde riescire fa duopo, come dissi più sopra, essere sobrii ed industriosi; i bevitori, gli infingardi ed altra simile gentaglia rimangano pur dove sono; chè questa non è la terra dei vizii o del *dolce far niente.*

C. BARELLI.

A letter from an Italian pioneer in Red Wing, Minn., inviting Italian skilled workers to settle in the Mississippi Valley, "the promised land for the intelligent and industrious worker". "There are only seven of us here, four from Liguria, one from Trieste and two from Piedmont." "Drunkards, loafers, and similar people would do well to remain where they are; this is not the land of vices or of *dolce far niente* (sweet doing nothing). From *L'Eco d'Italia,* February 11, 1874. (Courtesy, *New York Public Library.*)

RED WING, MINN.
(From Harper's *New Monthly Magazine* for 1873.)

As a whole, however, before 1870 there were only a few Italian immigrants in the states of Wisconsin, Minnesota, Kansas, Iowa, Nebraska, the Dakotas, and Montana. In Kansas and Montana, however, Italian missionaries had been at work as far back as 1836, when Brother Mazzella arrived to labor near the present city of Leavenworth. Later came Fathers Ponziglione, Urban Grassi, Ravalli, and the other Jesuit church builders.

The peak was reached in 1910 with 5,846 immigrants in Iowa, 3,517 in Kansas, 9,668 in Minnesota, 6,592 in Montana, 3,799 in Nebraska, 1,262 in North Dakota, 1,158 in South Dakota. Only Wisconsin had more Italian immigrants in 1930 (12,599) than in 1910 (9,273).

Anche a Omaha, nel Nebraska, città chiamata ad un grande avvenire per essere il centro principale della Ferrovia del Pacifico, viene di sorgere una Colonia Italiana. Ivi come a Virginia City ed a Treasure City, nel Nevada, si trovano parecchi negozi, trattorie e caffè tenuti da Italiani, alcuni fra i quali furono prevegenti a fare acquisto di terreni, che, se ora costano pochi dollari, in breve tempo potranno ottenere prezzi favolosi.

"Also in Omaha, Neb., a small Italian community is being formed. Here, as in Nevada, there are several stores and lunchrooms operated by Italians, some of whom have been provident enough to purchase land which now costs little but soon will have a high value." From *L'Eco d'Italia* for April 16, 1869. (Courtesy, *New York Public Library.*)

IN OKLAHOMA

Oklahoma was organized in 1889, when the United States government acquired most of that vast but lonely plain and opened it to settlement. Italian immigrants moved in almost at once, but apparently the new state (formed in 1907), did not offer them the opportunities they were looking for. Thus the Italian population increased from 11 in 1890 to 600 in 1900 and 2,664 in 1910, but went down after that. In 1940 there were less than 900 natives of Italy in the state, with possibly a few thousand more of Italian parentage.

IN TEXAS

The first Italians to visit Texas were, of course, the members of the unfortunate Coronado and De Soto expeditions of 1541-1542. In the following 200 years others visited and settled along the Gulf of Mexico: civilians, soldiers, and missionaries, all under the Spanish flag. The first settlers, however, moved in from Louisiana during the second half of the 16th century. One of the pioneers was Don Angel Navarro, who was born in Corsica in 1739 and made his home in the present county of Navarro, Texas (county seat, Corsicana, southeast of Dallas, so named after his son, Jose' Antonio Navarro. (See *History of Navarro County, Texas,* by W. F. Leve.) Farther west, in the present San Antonio, a pioneer Italian family was that of Cassini, which in Spanish became Cassiano. Joseph Cassini, the first settler by that name, had been a merchant in New Orleans before 1812, when he moved west. He married the widow of a former Spanish governor and became a wealthy and civic-minded American citizen.

After 1816 numerous Italians who had served as officers under Napoleon visited or settled in Texas. Some of them were at Galveston under the French General, Louis Aury, fighting for the independence of Mexico in 1818. They filled various ranks, from that of aid to the commander-in-chief, down. Others, together with French and Polish officers, joined the colony established, also in 1818,

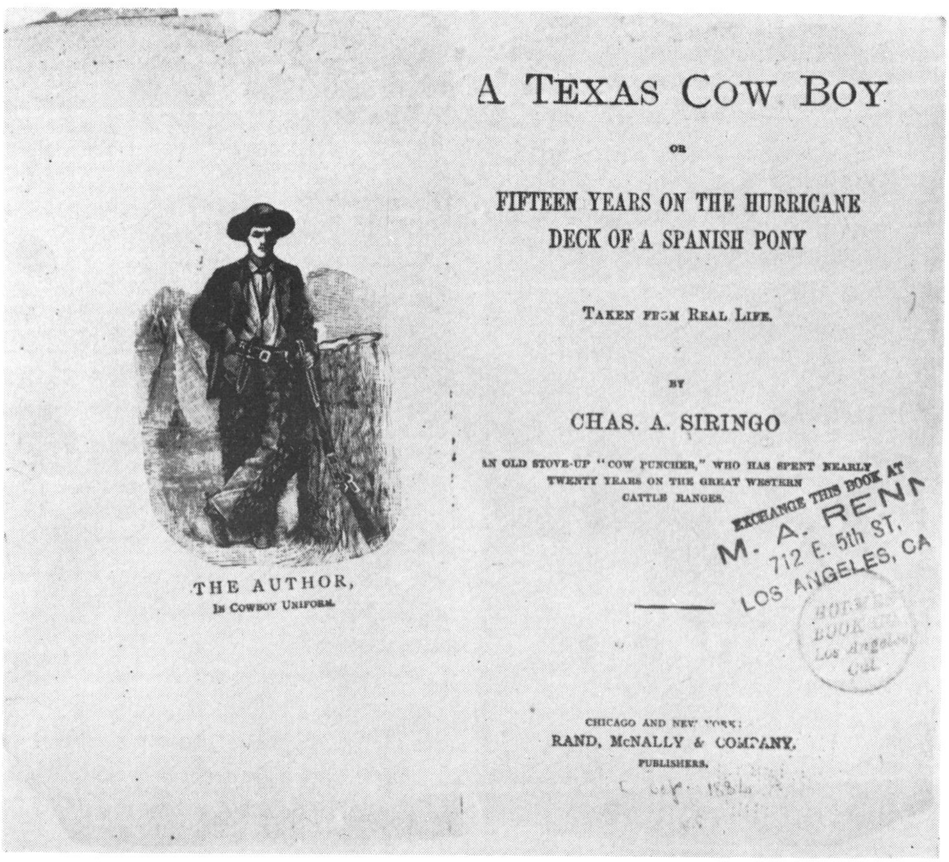

Title-page and frontispiece of the first edition of Siringo's *A Texas Cowboy,* of which more than 1,000,000 copies have been sold. (Courtesy, *New York Public Library.*)

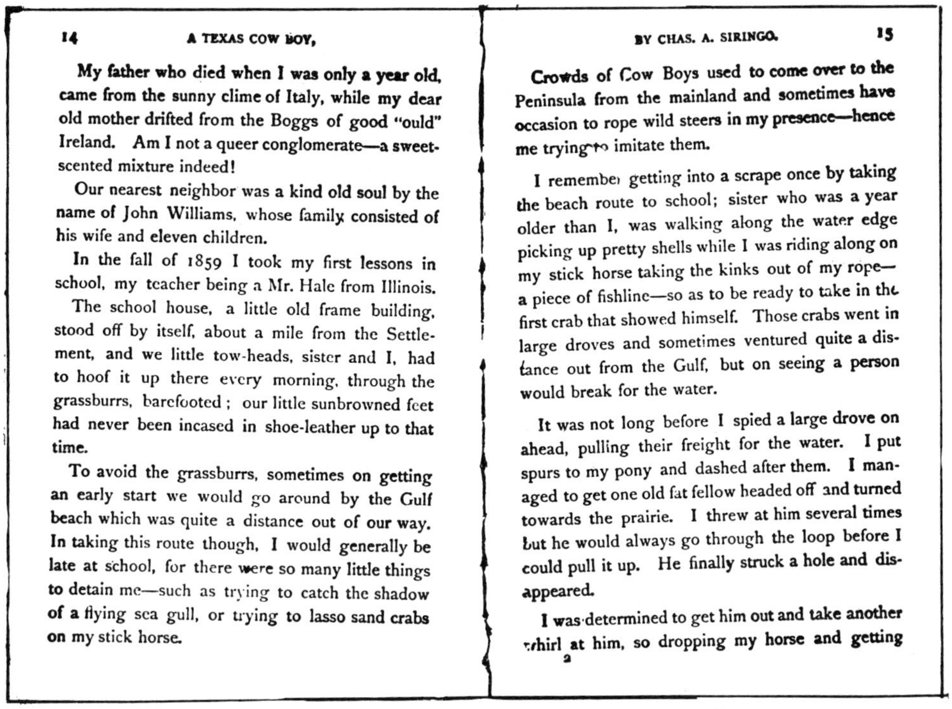

14 A TEXAS COW BOY,

My father who died when I was only a year old, came from the sunny clime of Italy, while my dear old mother drifted from the Boggs of good "ould" Ireland. Am I not a queer conglomerate—a sweet-scented mixture indeed!

Our nearest neighbor was a kind old soul by the name of John Williams, whose family consisted of his wife and eleven children.

In the fall of 1859 I took my first lessons in school, my teacher being a Mr. Hale from Illinois.

The school house, a little old frame building, stood off by itself, about a mile from the Settlement, and we little tow-heads, sister and I, had to hoof it up there every morning, through the grassburrs, barefooted; our little sunbrowned feet had never been incased in shoe-leather up to that time.

To avoid the grassburrs, sometimes on getting an early start we would go around by the Gulf beach which was quite a distance out of our way. In taking this route though, I would generally be late at school, for there were so many little things to detain me—such as trying to catch the shadow of a flying sea gull, or trying to lasso sand crabs on my stick horse.

BY CHAS. A. SIRINGO. 15

Crowds of Cow Boys used to come over to the Peninsula from the mainland and sometimes have occasion to rope wild steers in my presence—hence me trying to imitate them.

I remember getting into a scrape once by taking the beach route to school; sister who was a year older than I, was walking along the water edge picking up pretty shells while I was riding along on my stick horse taking the kinks out of my rope—a piece of fishline—so as to be ready to take in the first crab that showed himself. Those crabs went in large droves and sometimes ventured quite a distance out from the Gulf, but on seeing a person would break for the water.

It was not long before I spied a large drove on ahead, pulling their freight for the water. I put spurs to my pony and dashed after them. I managed to get one old fat fellow headed off and turned towards the prairie. I threw at him several times but he would always go through the loop before I could pull it up. He finally struck a hole and disappeared.

I was determined to get him out and take another whirl at him, so dropping my horse and getting

2

Two pages from the first edition of Siringo's *A Texas Cowboy.*

by General Lallemand, but only for a short while, for the attempt failed and they scattered throughout Central and South America, where not a few died of yellow fever. (See Codazzi's and Ferrari's memoirs, as described in the chapter on the travellers.) Not all of them, however, left, as we learn from *Olmsted's Journey Through Texas.*

Following the battle of San Jacinto not a few sons of Italy settled in the rising Republic, induced in no small measure by the written and oral propaganda of Orazio de Attellis, Marquis of Santangelo, one of the main supporters of Sam Houston. More will be found in a later chapter about this revolutionary man and his New Orleans newspaper, *Correo Atlantico.* Here we shall record only that his espousal of Texan independence was rewarded with the donation of some lands.

By 1850 there were at least 41 natives of Italy in the new state, exclusive of the natives of Corsica and probably of the natives of provinces still under Austria, like Lombardy and the Venetias. By 1860 the figure was not much higher, with only 69 reported. By 1880 they were 539. Yet at that time the Italians of Texas could boast two state legislators and a mayor. The latter, Antonio Ghio, of Texarkana, a Genoese, was one of the founders of the town, where he had moved in 1874. The legislators were L. Cardis and A. Barziza, the son of Count Barziza of Williamsburg, the friend of Jefferson. In no other state had the Italians made such a political progress. No wonder that the New York newspaper *Eco d'Italia* called Texas the "state best suited for the Italians". It still is.

The first attempt for Italian colonization on a large scale of which we know, was made about 1880 by Count J. Telfener and Chevalier L. Sala, who were planning to send over some 5,000 Italian workers. How many actually arrived we do not know, but it seems that out of one group of 1,000 some 700 were compelled to leave and found themselves stranded in other states. (*Eco d'Italia,* January 31 and February 1, 1882.) By 1890, 2,107 natives of Italy had reached Texas. In 1920 they had increased to 8,074. Since then the figure has gone down every year. As a whole, however, the Texas Italians have fared better than those of any other state in the Union, for nowhere else in the country do the Italians enjoy such a high standard of living and the respect of their fellow-citizens as in the Lone Star State; all of which does credit to the industriousness, ability and honesty of the immigrants and their children, as well as to the friendly spirit of the people of Texas.

The achievements of the Italians in that empire (it is more than twice as large as Italy) are mentioned in the following chapters. Here we shall recall a typical product of that land, cowboy detective Charles Siringo, the son of Italian father and Irish mother. Siringo, who was born in Matagorda County in 1855, was both a cowboy and a detective, but he acquired fame as the author of cowboy detective stories which became popular throughout the nation. More than one million copies of his first book, *A Texas Cowboy,* are said to have been printed and sold. He also wrote other books, all dealing with life on the range. According to the *Dictionary of American Biography,* no single writer typifies the achievements of cowboy literature, from the plane of the dime novel to one of character and distinction, as well as Charles Siringo. He died at Hollywood, Cal., in 1928.

As for the first Italian mutual aid society in Texas it seems that it was founded in 1880 by a native of the province of Parma, one Antonio Bruni of San Antonio, where he had settled in 1858. He served for a time as a member of the San Antonio City Council and died at Laredo at the age of 80 in 1925.

The Italian population of Texas reached its peak in 1920 with 8,024 immigrants. Since then, as in other states, it has gradually decreased, with 5,451 recorded for 1940.

IN NEW MEXICO

With the exception of the missionaries who arrived at Santa Fe in 1867, there were no Italians to speak of in New Mexico (one in 1850, 11 in 1860, 25 in 1870, 73 in 1880) until 1890, when 355 were recorded. The peak, with 1958, was reached in 1910. Next to the Jesuit priests, the most interesting pioneer was Sister Blandina Segale, a native of the town of Cicagna, near Genoa, Italy, who moved to Colorado in 1872 and to New Mexico shortly after. In 1881 she established the first public school at Albuquerque. Her book, *At the End of the Santa Fe Trail,* was reprinted in 1948 as the monthly selection of the Catholic Literary Foundation. Sister Blandina and her siter, Sister Justina, worked in New Mexico and Arizona until 1893.

IN ARIZONA

Arizona, as we have seen in Chapter Three, was discovered by Father Marcos de Nizas in 1539. Until 1870, however, hardly a dozen Italians had settled there. In 1910, or two years before the state was organized, there were 1,631 In recent years many Italo-Americans have moved in to enjoy the climate or to engage in farming.

One of the pioneers, Alex Rossi, settled in Tucson in 1883 and died there in 1930 at the age of 70. He had been such a legendary character, notwithstanding the fact that he was only a saloon keeper, that his death was given the most favored position in the local paper, page one, column one, and an editorial to boot.

IN COLORADO

Colorado, like California, owes its development to a gold rush, ten years after that of her sister-state, in 1859. As in California, quite a few Italians went to Colorado in search of gold as soon as the news was spread around the globe.

One of the first to reach the mining camps was Louis P. Arrighi, a native of Lucca, who arrived at Black Hawk and Central City in 1859. (*Risveglio,* Denver, July 28, 1939.) Four other settlers, the Garbarino brothers, moved in from St. Louis also in 1859, in the spring. They settled at Golden, Georgetown and Boulder. (G. Perilli, *Colorado and the Italians in Colorado,* cop. 1922.)

In 1880 there were some 335 Italians in the state, although only 6 had been registered in 1860 and 16 in 1870. In 1890 their number increased to 3,882. The rise continued until 1910, with 14,375 immigrants, but since then the number has decreased.

The Colorado Italians, like those of Louisiana, have had also their tragic days. In July, 1893, a Genoese, one Daniele Arata, was lynched at Denver. Six years later four more Italians were lynched at Walsenburg. In April, 1914, a number of Italians, including 2 women and 13 children, were burned to death in a fire. Coal mining troubles and disasters have not been rare, either.

The Italians in the state today are among the most respected citizens of their communities, with quite a few distinguished professional and businessmen. The most colorful man of Italian extraction in Colorado, however, was Frederick Bonfils, the founder and owner of the *Denver Post.* No less colorful was the first consular agent of Italy at Denver, one Angelo Cappelli, who settled in the city in 1868. His adventures from Louisiana to Colorado are vividly narrated by Adolfo Rossi in his book, *Un Italiano in America,* published in 1891. (Chapter XXXII.)

IN WYOMING

The first Italians to enter Wyoming were the immigrants headed for California and the Oregon Territory, beginning with Father Mengarini in 1841 and his Jesuit brothers in later years. Most of the laborers who went to Colorado in the 1880's also went through Wyoming. "Getting close to Cheyenne", Rossi tells us in the above-mentioned book, "we met only the usual grazing cattle and sheep". Sheep raising is one of the fields in which some Wyoming Italians are engaged on a large scale.

Who were the Italian pioneers in the state we do not know. All we know is that there were a few in the 1860's. Years ago while in Denver we were told of an Italian friend of General Grant who had a contract from the United States Army to supply it with cattle, but we have not looked into the matter. The largest number of natives of Italy in the state was reached in 1910 with 1,961 immigrants.

IN UTAH

It is not generally known that the Mormons in search for converts sent missionaries even to Italy and that a number of Italian proselytes settled at Salt Lake City in 1855, as the result of the missionary efforts of Joseph Toronto (Giuseppe Taranto) and Lorenzo Snow, one of the pillars of the Mormon Church.

Most of the Italian converts were recruited among the Waldenses of Piedmont, especially in the Angrogna and Prarostino districts in the province of Turin. Their

AN EARLY VIEW OF SALT LAKE CITY

JOSEPH TORONTO
Pioneer Mormon Leader

(Courtesy, Church of Jesus Christ of Latter Day Saints, Salt Lake City.) For an account of Toronto's early life and other pioneers in Utah by Dr. Paolo De Vecchi of New York, who interviewed them in 1880, see *L'Eco d'Italia,* Jan. 8, and April 17-18, 1881.

names, like those of most Waldenses, are rather French than Italian; hence the difficulty in telling their nationality. Several of them belonged to the Malan family of Angrogna. Others were named Bonnet, Roman, Bertoch, Barker, Francis, Ruben, Rochon, Chatelain, Rivoir, St. Germain, Lazald, Beus, Bourne, Gaudin, Pons, and Cardon. Apparently the new converts had not a clear idea of the Mormon religion, for a few of them were excommunicated for infidelity, rebellion, negligence and immorality. One of those who rose to a high position in the Mormon Church was Philip Cardon, a native of Prarostino, who came over in 1854 at the age of 53, and became Elder and High Priest. One of his eight children, Paul Cardon, who came also in 1854, was the father of 20 children and the grandfather of more than 100 boys and girls. He died in 1915 after serving honorably for many years as a prominent churchman and as the first city treasurer of Logan, Utah, the fourth largest city in the state.

Toronto, or Taranto, was born at Cagliari, in Sardinia, in 1818, was taken by his parents to Palermo, Sicily, at the age of two, and came to America as a sailor on an American vessel as a boy. In 1843, while in Boston, he joined the Mormon Church and went to Nauvoo. The Mormons were building at that time a great temple in that city, then the largest in Illinois, but as not enough money was available to finish it, Taranto, or Toronto, gave all his savings, totalling about $2,500 in gold. Brigham Young rewarded him then by putting him in charge, with one John Harris, of the cattle they drove all the way to Salt Lake City in 1848. On July 22, 1849, he was ordained a Seventy, and in October he left for Italy to make new converts. He returned to America with fourteen of his Sicilian relatives. He brought more relatives after another trip in 1875-77. He died at Salt Lake City in July 1883. One of Taranto's children, Joseph B. Toronto, was professor of mathematics and languages at the University of Utah for some 25 years and for a time acted as Italian consular representative. Joseph Toronto may have been responsible for the publication of the Italian edition of *The Book of Mormon* which appeared in 1852.

A Sicilian musician who joined the Mormons before 1850 was one Domenico Ballo whose band "was famous in the musical history of our city". He also organized a Provo Band. Ballo is said to have been a band master at West Point for a number of years before moving to Utah, but our inquiries at West Point have proved fruitless. Instead, we have found his name in the St. Louis, Mo., city directory for 1848. He was the composer of several marches and other music, and the conductor also of the Social Hall Orchestra. Neither he nor the members of his orchestra received any compensation for their work, with

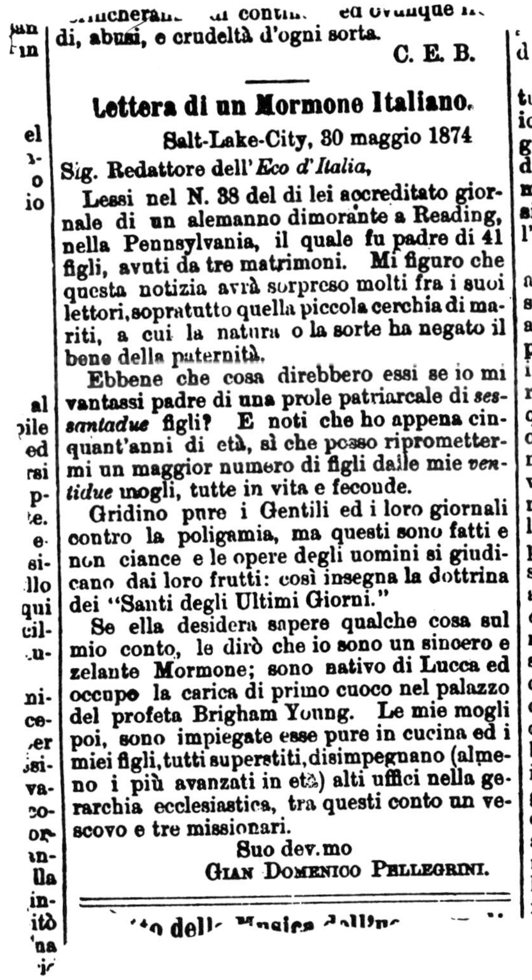

di, abusi, e crudeltà d'ogni sorta.

C. E. B.

Lettera di un Mormone Italiano.

Salt-Lake-City, 30 maggio 1874

Sig. Redattore dell'*Eco d'Italia,*

Lessi nel N. 38 del di lei accreditato giornale di un alemanno dimorante a Reading, nella Pennsylvania, il quale fu padre di 41 figli, avuti da tre matrimoni. Mi figuro che questa notizia avrà sorpreso molti fra i suoi lettori, sopratutto quella piccola cerchia di mariti, a cui la natura o la sorte ha negato il bene della paternità.

Ebbene che cosa direbbero essi se io mi vantassi padre di una prole patriarcale di *sessantadue* figli? E noti che ho appena cinquant'anni di età, sì che posso ripromettermi un maggior numero di figli dalle mie *ventidue* mogli, tutte in vita e feconde.

Gridino pure i Gentili ed i loro giornali contro la poligamia, ma questi sono fatti e non ciance e le opere degli uomini si giudicano dai loro frutti: così insegna la dottrina dei "Santi degli Ultimi Giorni."

Se ella desidera sapere qualche cosa sul mio conto, le dirò che io sono un sincero e zelante Mormone; sono nativo di Lucca ed occupo la carica di primo cuoco nel palazzo del profeta Brigham Young. Le mie mogli poi, sono impiegate esse pure in cucina ed i miei figli, tutti superstiti, disimpegnano (almeno i più avanzati in età) alti uffici nella gerarchia ecclesiastica, tra questi conto un vescovo e tre missionari.

Suo dev.mo
GIAN DOMENICO PELLEGRINI.

Letter of an Italian Mormon to the Editor of *L'Eco d'Italia* of New York (June 10, 1874). It reads in part: "What would your readers say if I were to boast an offspring of 62 children? And remember that I am only 50 years old so that I can expect a still greater number of children from my 22 wives, all of them healthy and able to procreate. . . . I am a sincere and zealous Mormon; I was born at Lucca and I occupy the position of head cook in the palace of the prophet, Brigham Young. . . . My older children hold high offices in the ecclesiastical hierarchy; one of them is a bishop and three are missionaries." (Courtesy, *N. Y. Public Library.*)

the result that often he was in financial distress, as in 1856 when, being in dire need of food, Brigham Young came to his assistance. He is said to have studied at the Milan Conservatory.

Another Italian musician at Salt Lake City in the 1850's was one Gennaro Capone, a Neapolitan band leader, who apparently left Italy for political reasons. Leonetto Cipriani, who met him in 1853, relates some interesting episodes about his life, and informs us that before moving to Utah he had been a cook at New Orleans.

The Mormon religion apparently appealed to other Italians, like one Gian Domenico Pellegrini, a native of Lucca, who in 1874 informed the editor of *Eco d'Italia* (of New York) that he was the father of 62 children and that he expected a few more from his 22 wives, all of them living and fecund. (See facsimile on preceding page.)

Yet, according to the census figures, the natives of Italy in the state are reported as one in 1850, 59 in 1860, 74 in 1870, and 138 in 1880. After 1900 came the new immigration, largely from Calabria, but also from Piedmont and other parts of Italy. (On the Italian pioneers in Utah see Daniel B. Richards, *The Scriptural Allegory in three parts,* a rare book, although of recent publication; Carter, Kate B., *Bands and Orchestras of Early Days,* a pamphlet published by the Daughters of Utah Pioneers in December, 1941; Schiavo, *Italian-American History,* Vol. I, under Ballo and Capone; bibliography in M. R. Werner's *Brigham Young,* New York, 1925; *Eco d'Italia,* January 8, April 17-19, 1881.)

ON THE PACIFIC COAST

The largest number of Italians in America at the outbreak of the Civil War was on the Pacific Coast, in and near San Francisco. Men like Gemelli-Careri and Malaspina had visited California, as we have seen, in the 17th and 18th centuries, but they did not remain. Others may have come over with the Spaniards at various times, but we have no definite proofs.

The first Italian to settle and die in California seems to have been one Juan B. Bonifacio, who arrived at Monterey in 1822 to be the stevedore of some English cargo. He was naturalized in 1829 and died about 1834 leaving a widow and three children.

During the thirty years preceding the discovery of gold several Italian seamen stopped over. One of the first Italian ships to stop at Monterey and San Francisco in 1825 was the *Flaminio Agazini.* Between 1829 and 1845 Captain John Dominis stopped on several occasions on business. He was the master of American ships, as related in a following chapter. In 1834 the Sardinian ship *Rosa* of 425 tons and 24 men, Nicola Bianchi, master, arrived at San Francisco. A year later it took a group of conspirators from San Francisco to Santa Barbara. Also in 1842, one Alberto Frescone, apparently an Italian, was established at Monterey, for his name appears on a lithograph of the city with that year's date, in the New York Public Library.

In 1836 an Italian sailor named Barnabal Costa, 36 years of age, landed at Los Angeles. In 1837 the brig *City of Genoa* arrived at Monterey from Valparaiso. Another Italian ship commanded by one Pietro Bonzi entered San Francisco Bay in 1840. Bonzi and his son, Orazio, decided to settle in California, where they were soon joined by other relatives. In 1849 one Louis Raggio opened a general store at San Luis Obispo. Raggio had come to America in 1842, when he landed at New Orleans, and had spent five years as a pilot on the Mississippi River. At San Luis he was appointed the first justice of the peace and also an associate justice in the district Court in that county.

The first considerable group of Italians arrived soon after the discovery of gold. Quite a few of them must have come over, or were headed for the west coast, if in 1851 Massimo D'Azeglio, then prime minister of Sardinia, decided to open a consulate at San Francisco, which he entrusted to Leonetto Cipriani. According to *Eco d'Italia* (April 26, 1851), at that time there were some 600 Italians in the city, with many Sardinian (Genoese) ships

SAN FRANCISCO IN 1849
(Courtesy, *Library of Congress.*)

trading in California ports. From everywhere the Italians flocked to San Francisco. Not only from Italy and other European countries, either by land or by sea (by way of Cape Horn), but also from South America, especially from Lima, Peru, where a considerable group of Italians had already been settled for years. Some Jesuit priests came down from the Oregon Country to establish the colleges of Santa Clara and later the present University of San Francisco, the former in 1851, and the latter in 1854. Some even came all the way from Australia, like the Passionist, Father Peter Magagnotto, who arrived at the end of 1849, and built the Church of St. Francis on Vallejo Street before 1853. Even an opera troupe, the Pellegrini Opera Company, found its way to San Francisco, where it opened with Bellini's *La Sonnambula* on February 12, 1851, at the Adelphi. By 1854 there were eleven opera companies in the city.

PANNING GOLD

LEONETTO CIPRIANI

Leonetto Cipriani, a controversial figure in Italian history, was born in Corsica in 1812. He had been preceded to America by his father, the owner of a large business house at New Orleans between 1801 and 1806. Leonetto first came over in 1831, but after three years in the West Indies he returned to Italy. On the way back, in 1854, he stopped in New York, where he was offered twelve acres of land north of Union Square for $20,000. He was about to purchase it when he learned that his banker had failed. He returned in 1836, and again in 1851 to open the San Francisco consulate.

Space prevents us from telling in detail the story of his life in America, which one can read in his *Avventure della Mia Vita* published at Bologna in 1934, or 46 years after his death. Briefly, Cipriani arrived in New York at the end of 1851, together with a physician, Giorgio Magnani, who was to take care of the San Francisco immigrants, and a servant. Because of the high cost of living in California he decided to send over, by way of Cape Horn, a pre-fabricated house, complete in every detail. It consisted of two stories, with 12 rooms, all furnished. It weighed 120 tons, and was made up of 1,200 separate parts, which later were assembled with 700 hooks and 26,000 screws.

Cipriani arrived in San Francisco, by way of Central America, early in 1852, but California was not what he expected it to be and he decided to spend a few years travelling through Asia. He changed his mind when he learned that a group of American financiers were planning a transcontinental railroad, but as no survey had yet been made, Cipriani decided to make one himself, and earn some extra money on the way. Accordingly, he sold his possessions for about $50,000 and on January 31, 1853, he left San Francisco for New York by way of Panama.

In New York City Cipriani purchased the instruments which he needed for the survey and started on his way back, by railroad up to Cincinnati, by boat from Cincinnati to St. Louis, and thence by covered wagon. His party consisted of 30 persons, 11 wagons, 500 cows, 600 steers, 60 horses, 40 mules and about 20,000 pounds of cargo, for a total investment of about $35,000. He reached destination safely, after an interesting detour at Salt Lake City, and even made a moderate profit on his investment. In 1855 he returned to Europe, but he came back not long after. His last trip was in 1860, when he resided in California until 1864. During this period he took an active part in the affairs of the San Francisco Italian community, and bought and sold several ranches. It seems also that he was very much interested in our own Civil War, for according to an item in the New York *Eco d'Italia* for April 26, 1862, he is said to have volunteered to kidnap General Beauregard from the midst of his own army. Lincoln, apparently, declined the offer. (On the first Italian consulate in San Francisco see Bulferetti, L., Leonetto Cipriani, console sardo in California, *Archivio Storico di Corsica,* 1939, pp. 94-102. See also Dana, J., *The man who built San Francisco,* New York, 1939, pp. 170-171; also other books dealing with Mazzini and Italian history in general, such as Oriani's *Lotta Politica.*)

GOLD SEEKERS AND STOREKEEPERS

Relatively few Italians found gold in California. Here and there we find the names of a few who amassed a little fortune, like those three immigrants who arrived from the West in New York with 120 pounds of pure gold, only to have it stolen at their hotel (*Eco d'Italia,* July 29, 1865), or the Volpone Brothers, one of whom is said to have found a treasure in gold which some Frenchmen had buried near Jamestown on a piece of land which they had purchased for a farm. Soon after the discovery of the cache he is said to have returned to Italy. That was in the 60's.

As a whole, the Italians turned almost at once into small storekeepers, largely owners of taverns, or truck gardens. Even today one finds not far from Stockton ruins of the old stores owned by the Italians during the Gold Rush, like the two Bruschi stores at Coulterville, or the Trabucco

Ruins of the main building of the Volpone brothers one mile north of Jamestown, Cal. (From *Ghost Towns and Relics of '49*, published by the Stockton, Cal., Chamber of Commerce.)

store at Mt. Bullion, all dating back to 1851. Other ruins of stores operated in the Mother Lode country, all harking back to the 50's, are those of the Trabucco store at Bear Valley, the Brunetti Dry Goods Store at Columbia, the Ghirardelli store at Hornitos, the Vignoli store at Melones, or the old homestead built by John Noce at Whiskey Slide. Finding gold nuggets along the highway was not unusual. At Butte City, three miles south of Jackson, the only ruins left of what was once a rip-roaring mining camp are the remains of the Ginocchio store, the only one in town, to which the miners flocked for their supplies. The stones for the construction of that building were brought over from China, as the miners were too busy looking for gold and could not afford to waste their time to make bricks or cut stones. The Marre family, related to the Ginocchios of Butte City, owned a wholesale liquor house in nearby Jackson. They also owned the local hotel. Jackson, now the county seat of Amador County, is only 125 miles distant from San Francisco.

THEY FOUND GOLD IN GARDENING

San Francisco, at the beginning of the Gold Rush, in 1848, had about 900 inhabitants. Within 2 years it had 25,000. Such a rapid increase in population ordinarily would create new problems everywhere, but in San Francisco it brought about chaos. As the rumors of the discoveries spread, young men and even men not so young, abandoned their occupations, their farms, their shops, their fishing boats, anything they were doing at that time, and ran to the gold-fields. Prices "skyrocketed" overnight. A boiled egg in a restaurant cost at least one dollar; shoes were selling for thirty dollars a pair, like a bottle of good whiskey. Apples could be purchased for one to five dollars a dozen. A copy of *Eco d'Italia* sold for 50 cents. The very rich people alone could afford vegetables. Only land was very cheap, as their owners abandoned it for the more promising mining camps. Some of it could be had for nothing; most of it for only a few dollars an acre.

The Italian immigrants soon realized that there was a more stable future in farming than in seeking gold and they turned over to the abandoned fields to build a little fortune. "What would this part of the country be today", we read in a correspondence from San Francisco to the New York *Eco d'Italia*, for December 9, 1865, "were it not for the thousands of Italians who cultivate the land all around? What would San Francisco be without the 300 Italian truck-gardeners or the 200 Italian fishermen?"

By 1859 the Italian community was so numerous that it could boast a weekly newspaper, a hospital, and a mutual benefit society. Three years later the Italian Club was organized. Also in that year, probably for the first time, the Italians took part as a unit in the local Fourth of July parade. There were 160 of them, all wearing black pantaloons and red shirts, with silk black scarfs around the neck in the Garibaldi fashion, and their Indian badge (coccarda) on their breasts. The community continued to grow so fast that by 1872 its mutual benefit society (Societa' Mutua di Beneficenza) could boast 1463 active members. (*Eco d'Italia*, December 28, 1872.)

IN OREGON

In the Oregon Territory (Oregon, Washington, Idaho and Western Montana) some Italian Jesuits had ventured as early as 1841, when Father Mengarini went there with Father De Smet. Others followed in 1844, and many more in the succeeding years. Until about 1880, however, there were only a few Italians in that part of the country, with the exception of the missionaries. In the present state of Oregon one finds 5 Italians in 1850, 34 in 1860, and 31 in 1870; in Washington, 11 in 1860, 24 in 1870; in Idaho only 11 in 1870. Most of them were in all probability religious workers.

A view of Portland, Oregon, in the 1850's. In the foreground, Arrigoni's "Pioneer Hotel."

The first Italian to visit the present coast of Oregon was Malaspina, followed in the 1820's by John Dominis, as related in another chapter. One of the first settlers seems to have been Captain S. N. Arrigoni, a Milanese who had gone to California in search of gold and eventually moved up north, about 1857. In Portland, where he made his home, he opened the Pioneer Hotel, "the best hostelry on the coast", with 300 accommodations. He established the first express service in the city and is said to have installed the first street lights. Later he moved to Astoria, where he operated the Occident Hotel and where he died in 1869. A city boulevard was named in his honor in recent years. (See *Vigo Review*, October, 1938, p. 12.)

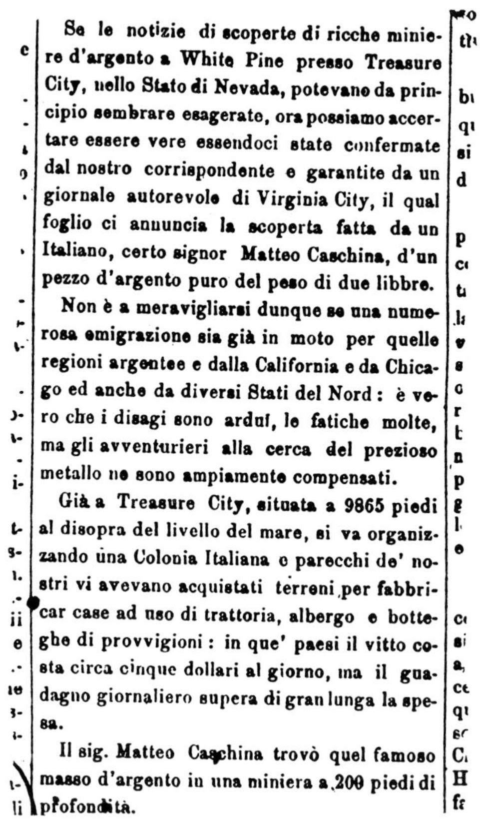

Se le notizie di scoperte di ricche miniere d'argento a White Pine presso Treasure City, nello Stato di Nevada, potevano da principio sembrare esagerate, ora possiamo accertare essere vere essendoci state confermate dal nostro corrispondente e garantite da un giornale autorevole di Virginia City, il qual foglio ci annuncia la scoperta fatta da un Italiano, certo signor Matteo Caschina, d'un pezzo d'argento puro del peso di due libbre.

Non è a meravigliarsi dunque se una numerosa emigrazione sia già in moto per quelle regioni argentee e dalla California e da Chicago ed anche da diversi Stati del Nord: è vero che i disagi sono ardui, le fatiche molte, ma gli avventurieri alla cerca del prezioso metallo ne sono ampiamente compensati.

Già a Treasure City, situata a 9865 piedi al disopra del livello del mare, si va organizzando una Colonia Italiana e parecchi de' nostri vi avevano acquistati terreni per fabbricar case ad uso di trattoria, albergo e botteghe di provvigioni: in que' paesi il vitto costa circa cinque dollari al giorno, ma il guadagno giornaliero supera di gran lunga la spesa.

Il sig. Matteo Caschina trovò quel famoso masso d'argento in una miniera a 200 piedi di profondità.

A news item in *L'Eco d'Italia* of New York (April 16, 1869) about the discovery by an Italian immigrant of a 2-pound nugget of pure silver at Virginia City. "At Treasury City (9865 feet above sea level) there are already numerous Italians, some of whom have already purchased lots to build hotels, restaurants and grocery stores . . . food costs $5.00 a day, but one earns much more." (Courtesy, *N. Y. Public Library.*)

IN NEVADA

Nevada had a few inhabitants until 1859, when silver was found in what is now Washoe County, not far from Reno. As if by magic, Virginia City sprang up and soon became the second city west of the Rocky Mountains, with a population of 35,000 in 1870 (952 in 1940). Italian adventurers flocked there, too, just as they had flocked to California in the previous years. As early as 1861, we learn from a map of the city drawn by Grafton T. Brown, one M. Crosetta operated the Virginia Saloon. (The map may be seen in the New York Public Library.) Another early establishment operated or owned by Italians, the Molinelli Hotel, can be seen still standing in that ghost town today. Other Italian business men moved or were planning to move to Treasure City, another mining center, in 1869. (*Eco d'Italia,* March 12, 1869). That some of the Italians in Nevada in those days were miners we learn from an item in the *Eco d'Italia* of New York, according to which one Matteo Caschina had found, in 1869, a nugget of pure silver weighing two pounds in a mine at a depth of 200 feet. One has, however, to pay a visit to the local cemetery to discover many Italian names, like those of the Glandoni family, one of whom, a child of six, was buried there in 1867. He may have been the brother of one John Glandoni, who was born in Virginia City in 1860 and was still living there as late as 1940. The Italian Passionist Fathers were among the first to go to Nevada, where they built the second Catholic Church in the territory. They were followed by Father Dominic Monteverde, who arrived in 1865 and remained until 1883, when he moved to Brooklyn. He organized several parishes, missions and stations.

The grave of an Italian pioneer in Virginia City, Nev. (Photo by the author.)

CHAPTER THIRTEEN

IN THE WORLD OF MUSIC

Although the natives of Italy in the United States—as distinct from those of Italian extraction—have at no time represented more than 3% of the total population of the country—until about 1870 they were hardly one tenth of one per cent—they have always played a preponderant role (way out of proportion to their number) in the musical education and in the development of the musical taste of the American people. In opera, of course, they have had no rivals—with sporadic exceptions, or until our own days—; but in teaching and even in orchestral—not to say band—music they have exerted a much greater influence than is generally recognized.

Today one has only to go through the membership lists of the various locals of the American Federation of Music in literally every state in the Union, to realize how Americans of Italian birth or extraction represent the largest ethnical group in the entire field of music, from composers and teachers to instrumentalists and singers.

The story of the Italian contribution to American music from 1757 to 1947 has been told in the 476 pages of Volume One of our *Italian-American History*. To condense it in a few pages is, obviously, impossible. We shall, therefore, limit ourselves to the highlights in each group, that is, 1) teachers; 2) opera singers and conductors; 3) band leaders; 4) conductors of symphonic orchestras; 5) composers and concert artists; 6) popular singers and orchestra leaders.

TEACHERS

As we have seen on page 112, the first Italian musicians came to the English-speaking colonies as early as 1757. Following the Treaty of Paris, they continued to arrive in a steady stream until 1800, after which hundreds of them arrived regularly every year—making up probably more than one half of the total number of professional people to land from Italy.

Two musicians who arrived before 1800 were one Trisobio, who gave concerts of vocal and instrumental music in various cities and died in Philadelphia in 1798, and Filippo Traetta, who was born in Venice in 1777 and died in Philadelphia in 1854. The son of the noted composer, Tommaso Traetta of Bitonto, Bari, he came over in 1799. Two years later, together with Graupner and Mallet he founded an "American Conservatorio" in Boston, in which he became head of the vocal department. About 1828 he founded another conservatory in Philadelphia which he headed until his death. He wrote at least three books of which we know, composed much music, from an opera to oratorios and cantatas, managed theaters in the South, where he became the friend of Madison and Monroe, and even appeared as a singer. He may have been

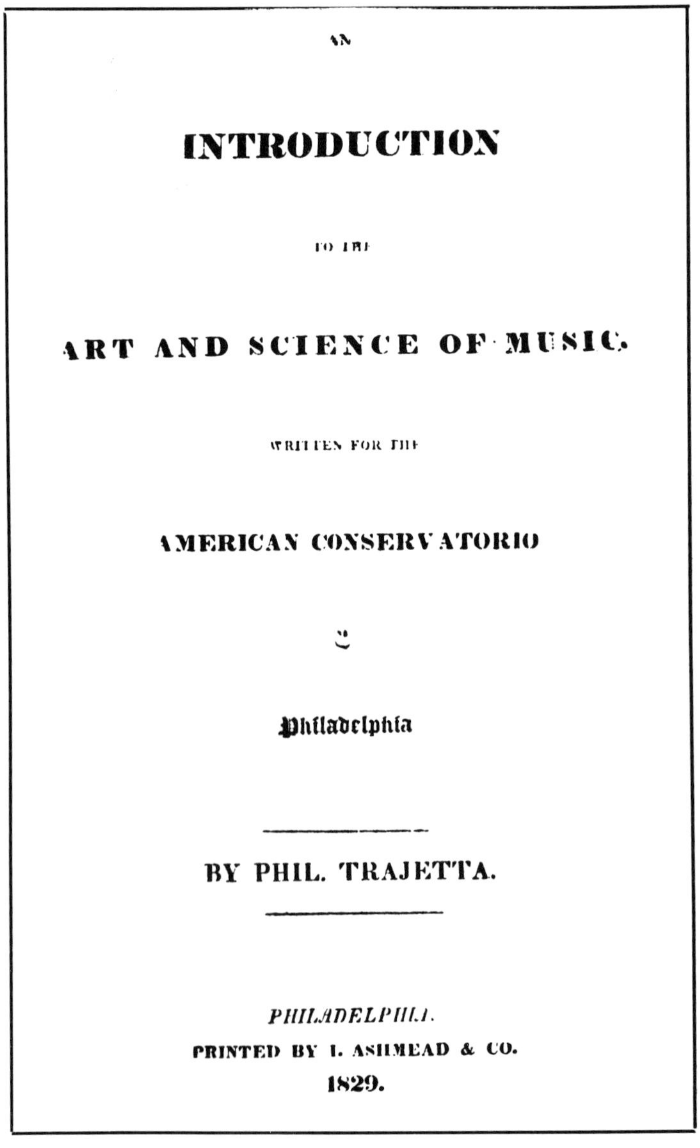
AN

INTRODUCTION

TO THE

ART AND SCIENCE OF MUSIC,

WRITTEN FOR THE

AMERICAN CONSERVATORIO

OF

Philadelphia

BY PHIL. TRAJETTA.

PHILADELPHIA.

PRINTED BY I. ASHMEAD & CO.

1829.

Title-page of one of Trajetta's books published in 1829.
(Courtesy, *Library of Congress*.)

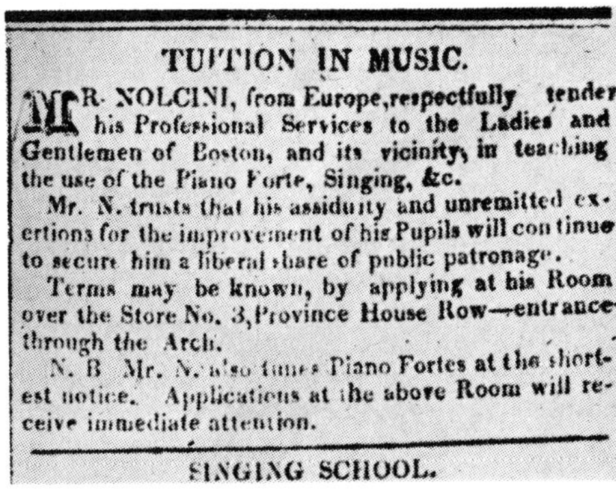
TUITION IN MUSIC.

MR. NOLCINI, from Europe, respectfully tender his Professional Services to the Ladies and Gentlemen of Boston, and its vicinity, in teaching the use of the Piano Forte, Singing, &c.

Mr. N. trusts that his assiduity and unremitted exertions for the improvement of his Pupils will continue to secure him a liberal share of public patronage.

Terms may be known, by applying at his Room over the Store No. 3, Province House Row—entrance through the Arch.

N. B. Mr. N. also tunes Piano Fortes at the shortest notice. Applications at the above Room will receive immediate attention.

SINGING SCHOOL.

One of Nolcini's advertisements in *The Euterpiad* of Boston for Nov. 10, 1821. (Courtesy, *New York Public Library.*)

manager of the Italian Theater of New Orleans mentioned in the *Moniteur* of that city between March and July, 1812. Few men played so large a role in the development of American music before 1850 as he did.

Among those who arrived between 1800 and 1825 we shall single out Masi, Nolcini and Ostinelli. Francesco Masi lived in Boston between 1807 and 1818. He taught piano, violin, cello, and practically every other instrument. In 1815 he published several waltzes and pianoforte pieces. Charles Nolcini taught in Boston and Portland between 1821 and 1829. Louis Ostinelli organized with Graupner the Philharmonic Society of Boston and was made a honorary member of the Handel and Haydn Society in which he played at one time as second violin. He is said to have been "one of the half dozen men and women to whom Boston owes its musical beginnings". His daughter, Eliza Biscaccianti, was the first Italian-American woman operatic singer.

Antonio Bagioli and Carlo Bassini were the two leading Italian musicians to settle in New York between 1825 and 1850. Bagioli came over as conductor with the Montresor Opera Company in 1832, but when that company failed he devoted himself to teaching. He wrote three books on the art of singing and composed hymns, prayers, and music. As a teacher he is said to have "attained a success probably unsurpassed by any professor in this country" in his days. His daughter Teresa married General Sickles.

Bassini came over before 1839, when he married an Italian-American girl in New York, and lived here until he died in New Jersey in 1870. He wrote several books for the cultivation of the voice and composed religious music.

IN NEW ORLEANS AND ST. LOUIS

Not all the Italian musicians settled in the North. Actually, we believe that there must have been quite a few in New Orleans, where the French language made it easier for them to earn a living. There, as early as 1791 we find one Joseph Gabriel de Baroncelli at the French Theater and a quarter of a century later Henri Corri, a member of the Corri family of musicians that settled in England and Ireland before 1800. Corri also appeared at Nashville in 1835. Signor Christiani, of the Philo-Harmonic Academy of Bologna, also left the North for New Orleans, where he had a studio on Canal Street in 1824. In St. Louis we find Maestro Joseph Marallano (Maragliano?), whose naturalization paper can be seen in the local Missouri Historical Society. Marallano left Italy in 1814, when he moved to Cuba, and thence to Missouri in 1832. On July 4, 1838, he directed the chorus for a solemn Te Deum celebrated by Bishop Rosati in the Cathedral.

AFTER 1850

After 1850, following the political upheavals in Italy, a number of distinguished Italian music teachers settled in the United States. A few of them were: Massimo Manzocchi; Achille Errani, the teacher of Minnie Hauk, Clara Louise Kellogg and Emma Abbott; the famous singer, Marietta Gazzaniga; Angelo Torriani, who taught for many years in North Carolina and New York; Antonio Barili, Adelina Patti's step-brother; Elidoro De Campi, who headed the vocal departments of several colleges of music;

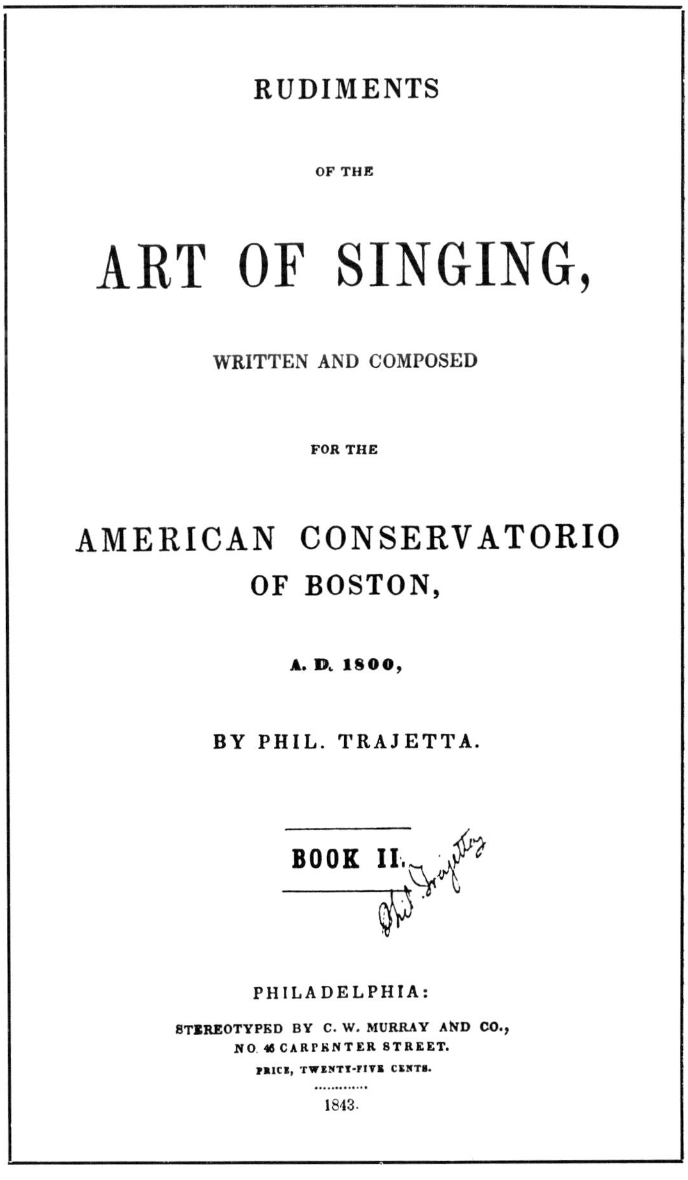
RUDIMENTS

OF THE

ART OF SINGING,

WRITTEN AND COMPOSED

FOR THE

AMERICAN CONSERVATORIO OF BOSTON,

A. D. 1800,

BY PHIL. TRAJETTA.

BOOK II.

Phil. Trajetta

PHILADELPHIA:

STEREOTYPED BY C. W. MURRAY AND CO.,
NO. 46 CARPENTER STREET.

PRICE, TWENTY-FIVE CENTS.

1843.

Title-page of another book by Trajetta. (Courtesy, *Library of Congress.*)

Eduardo Marzo, distinguished as teacher, organist and composer; P. Centemeri, who taught for years in Detroit, and later in New York; Luisa Cappiani, of Boston, one of the organizers of National Association of Music Teachers; Albino Gorno, who was associated for fifty years with the Cincinnati College of Music where he served as dean; Lino Mattioli, another noted teacher at the same college; Augusto Rotoli, who taught for 19 years at the New England Conservatory of Music; Paolo Giorza, "one of the greatest and at least the most prolific composer of ballets who ever lived"; Clito Moderati, the teacher of Emilio De Gorgoza; Pietro Minetti, a member of the faculty of the Peabody Conservatory of Music of Baltimore for about forty years; Pier Adolfo Tirindelli, head of the violin department of the Cincinnati College of Music; Romualdo Sapio, head of the vocal department of the National Conservatory of Music in New York; Giuseppe Del Puente, the famous baritone, who had a studio in Philadelphia.

SINCE 1900

Since 1900 literally hundreds of Italians have taught in American musical colleges or privately. A few names will suffice: Alfred De Voto, professor of pianoforte at the New England Conservatory of Music for more than thirty years; Giuseppe Ferrata, director of music at Newcomb College, Tulane University, for 19 years, and a noted composer; Monsignor Manzetti, one of the leading composers of church music in the United States, who taught in Cincinnati and in Baltimore; Arthuro Buzzi-Peccia, teacher of Alma Gluck and of Sophie Breslau; Aurelio Gorni, a distinguished pianist and composer, who taught at Springfield, Mass., and Philadelphia; Agide Jacchia, founder of the Boston Conservatory of Music; Ernest Consolo, the eminent pianist; Achille Alberti of Los Angeles, the teacher of Mario Chamlee; Pasquale Amato, the famous baritone, who taught at the School of Music of Louisiana State University; Vittorio Arimondi of Chicago; Sandro Benelli of New York; Domenico Brescia, professor of counterpoint and composition, and later head of the department of theory at Mills College, Oakland, Cal.; Paolo Conte, dean of the College of Fine Arts of Oklahoma Baptist University; Antonio De Grassi, musical illustrator for the University of California; Oscar Del Bianco, professor of theory at Duquesne University; Gaetano De Luca, president of the Nashville Conservatory of Music; Nicola Montani, one of the most distinguished composers of church music, author and editor of *The Catholic Choirmaster* from 1915, the year he founded it, to 1942; Angelo Testa, superintendent of the Portland Academy of Music; Pietro

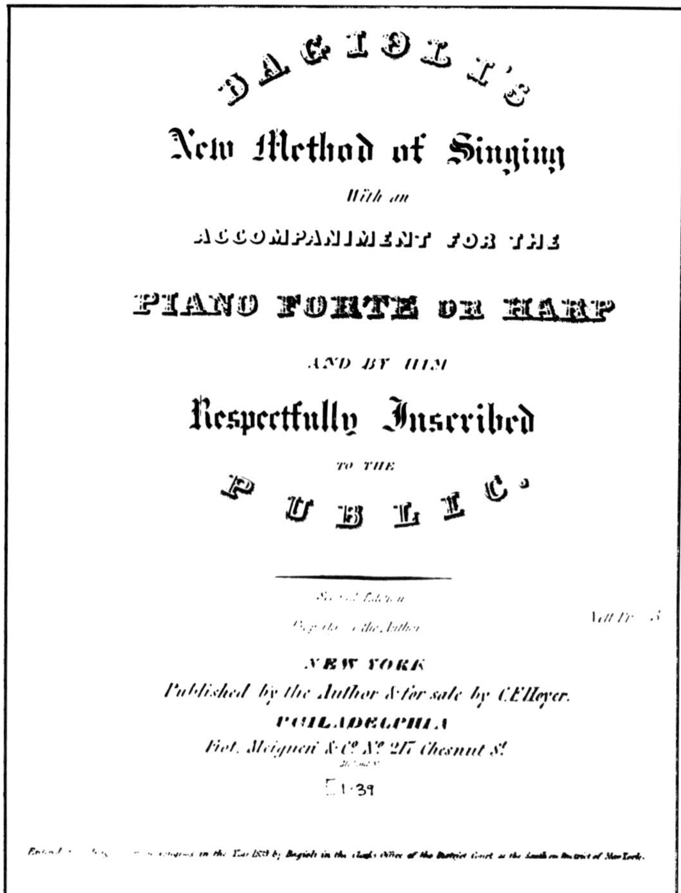

BAGIOLI'S

New Method of Singing

With an

ACCOMPANIMENT FOR THE

PIANO FORTE OR HARP

AND BY HIM

Respectfully Inscribed

TO THE

PUBLIC.

NEW YORK

Published by the Author & for sale by C.E.Hoyer.

PHILADELPHIA

Fiot, Meignen & Co. No. 217 Chesnut St.

1·39

One of Bagioli's early books published in Philadelphia in 1839. (Courtesy, *New York Public Library.*)

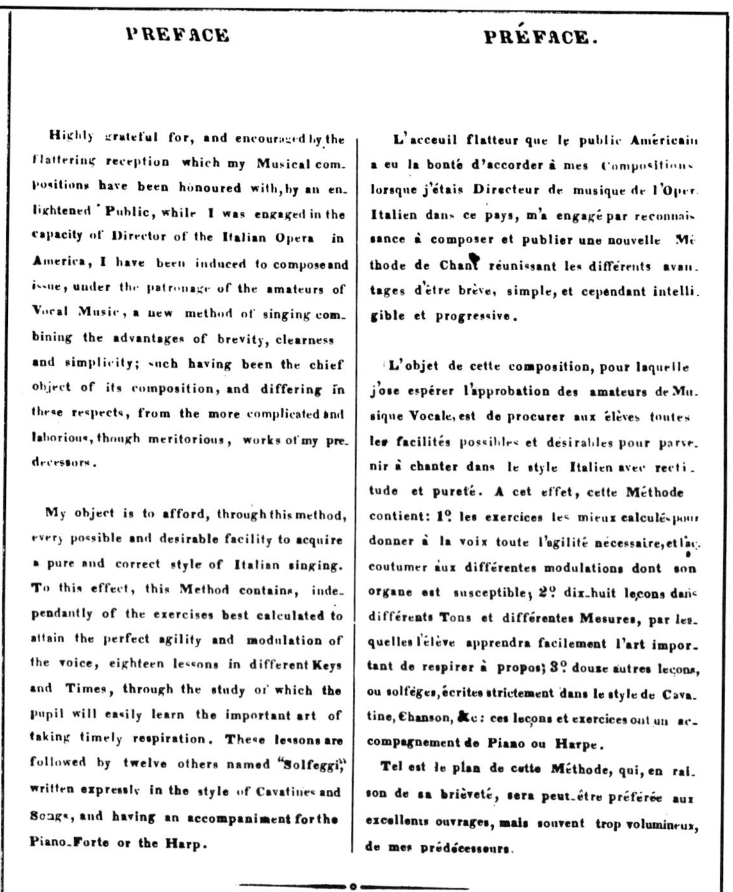

PREFACE

Highly grateful for, and encouraged by the flattering reception which my Musical compositions have been honoured with, by an enlightened Public, while I was engaged in the capacity of Director of the Italian Opera in America, I have been induced to compose and issue, under the patronage of the amateurs of Vocal Music, a new method of singing combining the advantages of brevity, clearness and simplicity; such having been the chief object of its composition, and differing in these respects, from the more complicated and laborious, though meritorious, works of my predecessors.

My object is to afford, through this method, every possible and desirable facility to acquire a pure and correct style of Italian singing. To this effect, this Method contains, independantly of the exercises best calculated to attain the perfect agility and modulation of the voice, eighteen lessons in different Keys and Times, through the study of which the pupil will easily learn the important art of taking timely respiration. These lessons are followed by twelve others named "Solfeggi," written expressly in the style of Cavatines and Songs, and having an accompaniment for the Piano-Forte or the Harp.

PRÉFACE.

L'acceuil flatteur que le public Américain a eu la bonté d'accorder à mes Compositions lorsque j'étais Directeur de musique de l'Opera Italien dans ce pays, m'a engagé par reconnaissance à composer et publier une nouvelle Méthode de Chant réunissant les différents avantages d'être brève, simple, et cependant intelligible et progressive.

L'objet de cette composition, pour laquelle j'ose espérer l'approbation des amateurs de Musique Vocale, est de procurer aux élèves toutes les facilités possibles et désirables pour parvenir à chanter dans le style Italien avec rectitude et pureté. A cet effet, cette Méthode contient: 1º les exercices les mieux calculés pour donner à la voix toute l'agilité nécessaire, et l'accoutumer aux différentes modulations dont son organe est susceptible; 2º dix-huit leçons dans différents Tons et différentes Mesures, par lesquelles l'élève apprendra facilement l'art important de respirer à propos; 3º douze autres leçons, ou solfèges, écrites strictement dans le style de Cavatine, Chanson, &c: ces leçons et exercices ont un accompagnement de Piano ou Harpe.

Tel est le plan de cette Méthode, qui, en raison de sa brièveté, sera peut-être préférée aux excellents ouvrages, mais souvent trop volumineux, de mes prédécesseurs.

Facsimile of Bagioli's preface to his "New Method of Singing." (Courtesy, *New York Public Library.*)

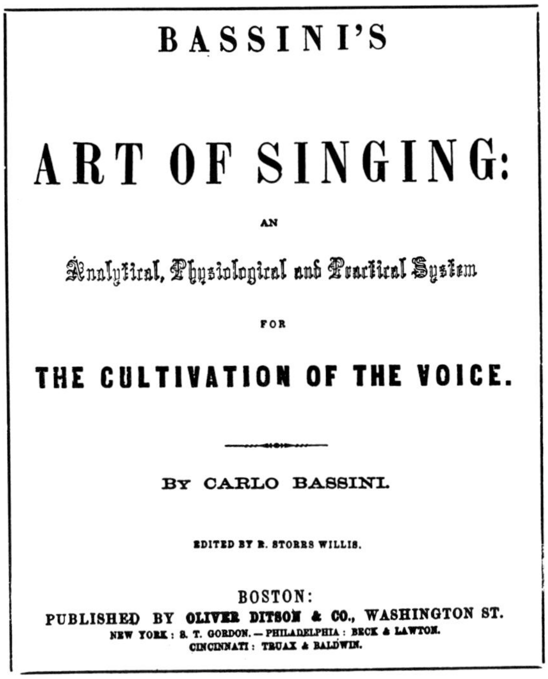
BASSINI'S

ART OF SINGING:

AN

Analytical, Physiological and Practical System

FOR

THE CULTIVATION OF THE VOICE.

BY CARLO BASSINI.

EDITED BY R. STORRS WILLIS.

BOSTON:

PUBLISHED BY OLIVER DITSON & CO., WASHINGTON ST.

NEW YORK: S. T. GORDON.—PHILADELPHIA: BECK & LAWTON.

CINCINNATI: TRUAX & BALDWIN.

Title-page of Bassini's "Art of Singing" published in 1857. (Courtesy, *N. Y. Public Library.*)

BASSINI'S NEW METHOD

FOR

SOPRANO

AND

MEZZO-SOPRANO:

BEING A

THOROUGH COURSE OF SINGING

AND

Cultivation of the Voice.

By CARLO BASSINI,

Author of "Art of Singing;" "Method for Baritone and Tenor;" "Education of the Voice;" "Seventy Melodic Exercises," &c.

BOSTON:

G. D. RUSSELL & COMPANY, 126 TREMONT ST.

Title-page of another book by Bassini published in 1869. (Courtesy, *N. Y. Public Library.*)

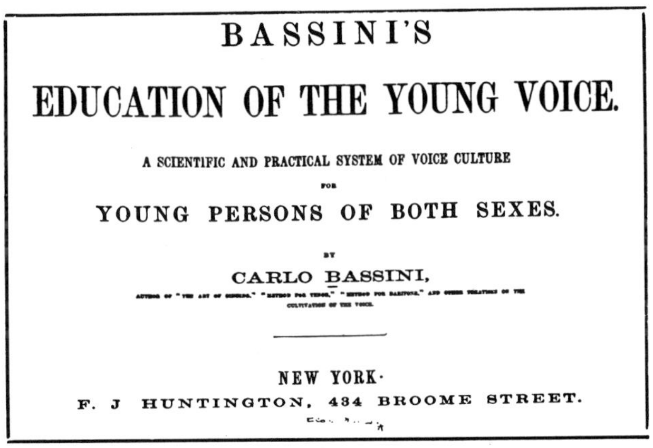
BASSINI'S

EDUCATION OF THE YOUNG VOICE.

A SCIENTIFIC AND PRACTICAL SYSTEM OF VOICE CULTURE

FOR

YOUNG PERSONS OF BOTH SEXES.

BY

CARLO BASSINI,

NEW YORK·

F. J HUNTINGTON, 434 BROOME STREET.

Title-page of Bassini's "Education of the Young Voice" published in 1865. (Courtesy, *N. Y. Public Library.*)

Yon, a renowned organist; Raoul Spoleti-Bonanno of Cleveland; Tommaso Gallozzi of Boston.

Also: Joseph Barone, founder and director of the Bryn Mawr Conservatory; Albert Bimboni of the Julliard School of Music and the Curtis Institute; Nazareno De Rubertis, professor of theoretical subjects in the University of Kansas City; Salvatore De Stefano, the well-known harpist, on the faculty of the Hartford School of Music; Vittorio Giannini, the composer, teacher of theory and composition at the Julliard School of Music; Bruno Labate, the noted oboist; Albert Martini, head of the string department at the Centenary College of Shreveport, La.; Gian Carlo Menotti, the composer, professor of composition, orchestration and dramatic forms at Curtis Institute; Rosario Scalero, head of the department of composition and theory at the same institution; Silvio Scionti, the pianist, a resident of Denton, Texas; Pasquale Tallarico, professor of piano at Peabody Conservatory of Baltimore.

PRIVATE TEACHERS

Among the private teachers of recent years we may mention Giuseppe Bambosceck; Isidore Braggiotti of California, the father of more than one distinguished musician; Maria Carreras, the famous pianist; Ferruccio Corradetti; Clemente de Macchi; Cesare Lancellotti, formerly of the Royal College of Music of London; Carolina Lazzari; Gaetano Loria, who gave lessons in speech correction to King George VI of England; Alfred Martino, teacher of Jan Peerce; Romano Romani, teacher of Rosa Ponselle; Enrico Rosati, teacher of Beniamino Gigli and Lauri Volpi; Cesare Sturani; Gilda Ruta; Agostino Carbone; Eduardo Trucco; Dino Bigalli, Ada Paggi, Mario Carboni, Vittorio Trevisan, all of Chicago; Iride Pilla and Madame Ippolito of Boston; Silvio Risegari and Giuseppe Inzerillo of Seattle; Pietro Cimini and Gennaro Maria Curci of Los Angeles; Nicholas Gualillo of Utica and Oneonta; and other too numerous to mention.

THE FIRST ITALIAN SINGERS IN AMERICA

As we have noted on page 113, the first Italian singer to appear in America seems to have been Signora Mazzanti in 1774. Then came Filippo Trisobio, who sang in Philadelphia and Baltimore between 1796 and 1798. Still later, Traetta and Comoglio sang duets together in 1809-1811, followed by Signor Chiavari and Signor Lorenzani in 1815, Signor Christiani in 1819, Anselmo Berti in 1821 (he died in New York in 1852), Signor Ramati from the Conservatory of Florence in 1825. It is, however, with the arrival of the Garcia operatic troupe in 1825 that Italian singers began to appear virtually without interruption in the United States.

ITALIAN OPERA COMES TO AMERICA

The first Italian operas produced in America, although in distorted form and in either French or English, were Pergolesi's *La Serva Padrona* and Duni's *Les Deux Chasseurs* presented in Baltimore and New York in 1790 by a French troupe from New Orleans. Four years later, Paisiello's *Orpheus et Eurydice* was given at Charleston. In 1819 Rossini's *Barber of Seville* was given in New York, but in English.

The first opera in Italian was given by the company brought to New York by Senor Garcia, a native of Seville, Spain, who opened with Rossini's *Barber* at the Park Theater on November 29, 1825. In all he gave 76 performances at the Park and Bowery theaters, remaining until September 30, 1826. His repertoire included five operas by Rossini, Mozart's *Don Giovanni,* and two operas by himself. The *Barber* alone was performed 23 times.

The cast included Carlo Angrisani, one of the leading bassos of his day, Domenico Crivelli, who became a noted

MARIA GARCIA MALIBRAN

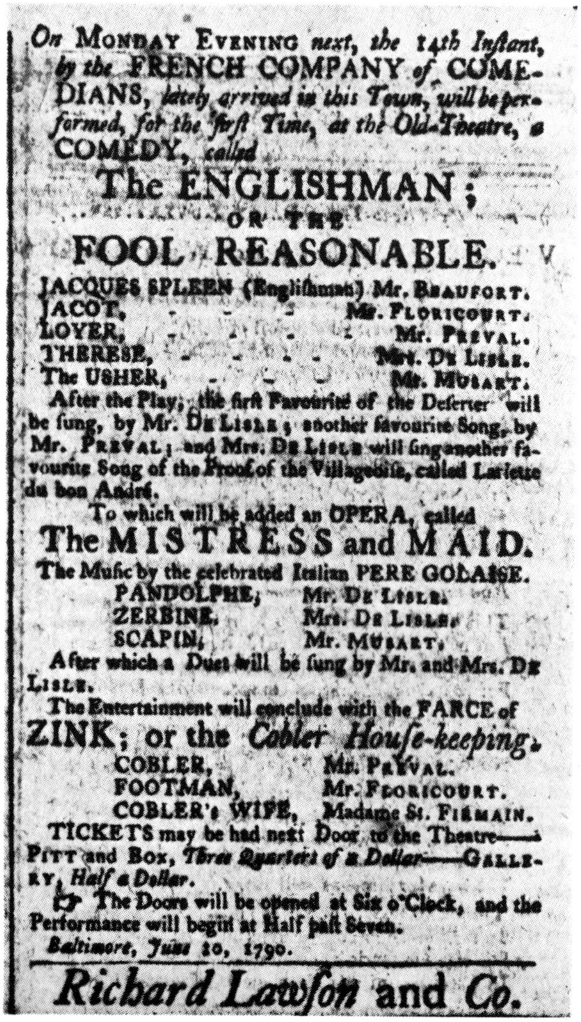

On MONDAY EVENING *next, the* 14*th Instant, by the* FRENCH COMPANY *of* COMEDIANS, *lately arrived in this Town, will be performed, for the first Time, at the Old-Theatre, a* COMEDY, *called*

The ENGLISHMAN;
OR THE
FOOL REASONABLE.

JACQUES SPLEEN (Englishman) Mr. BEAUFORT.
JACOT, - - - Mr. FLORICOURT.
LOYER, - - - - Mr. PREVAL.
THERESE, - - - - Mrs. DE LISLE.
The USHER, - - - Mr. MUSART.

After the Play, the first Favourite of the Deserter will be sung, by Mr. DE LISLE; another favourite Song, by Mr. PREVAL; and Mrs. DE LISLE will sing another favourite Song of the Proof of the Villageoise, called Lariette du bon André.

To which will be added an OPERA, called

The MISTRESS and MAID.

The Music by the celebrated Italian PERE GOLASSE.

PANDOLPHE, Mr. DE LISLE.
ZERBINE, Mrs. DE LISLE.
SCAPIN, Mr. MUSART.

After which a Duet will be sung by Mr. and Mrs. DE LISLE.

The Entertainment will conclude with the FARCE of ZINK; or the *Cobler House-keeping.*

COBLER, Mr. PREVAL.
FOOTMAN, Mr. FLORICOURT.
COBLER's WIFE, Madame St. FIRMAIN.

TICKETS may be had next Door to the Theatre—PITT and BOX, *Three Quarters of a Dollar*—GALLERY, *Half a Dollar.*

☞ The Doors will be opened at Six o'Clock, and the Performance will begin at Half past Seven.

Baltimore, June 10, 1790.

Richard Lawson and *Co.*

Announcement of the first Italian opera given in the North, Pergolesi's *La Serva Padrona.* From the June 12, 1790, issue of the *Maryland Journal.* (Courtesy, *Maryland Historical Society.*)

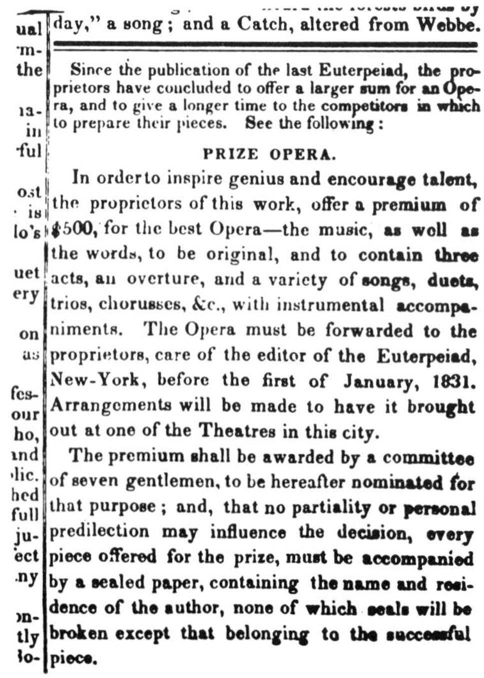

day," a song; and a Catch, altered from Webbe.

Since the publication of the last Euterpeiad, the proprietors have concluded to offer a larger sum for an Opera, and to give a longer time to the competitors in which to prepare their pieces. See the following:

PRIZE OPERA.

In order to inspire genius and encourage talent, the proprietors of this work, offer a premium of $500, for the best Opera—the music, as well as the words, to be original, and to contain three acts, an overture, and a variety of songs, duets, trios, chorusses, &c., with instrumental accompaniments. The Opera must be forwarded to the proprietors, care of the editor of the Euterpeiad, New-York, before the first of January, 1831. Arrangements will be made to have it brought out at one of the Theatres in this city.

The premium shall be awarded by a committee of seven gentlemen, to be hereafter nominated for that purpose; and, that no partiality or personal predilection may influence the decision, every piece offered for the prize, must be accompanied by a sealed paper, containing the name and residence of the author, none of which seals will be broken except that belonging to the successful piece.

Announcement of the first prize for an opera offered in the United States. From *The Euterpiad* of Boston, July 1, 1830. (Courtesy, *N. Y. Public Library.*)

THE PARK THEATER
of New York, at the time Italian opera was first given there.

THE OLD BOWERY THEATER
designed by the Italian architect, A. Sera, of Bologna.
(Courtesy, *New York Historical Society.*)

vocal teacher in London, Madame Barbieri, and Garcia's daughter, Maria, who soared to celebrity in the annals of opera as the famous Malibran. Thus, as R. G. White wrote in the *Century Magazine* in 1882, "the history of opera proper in New York begins not in the feebleness of uncertain obscurity, but in pomp and triumph."

Italian opera pleased many, but it was yet too much of a novelty to take root immediately, although it marked, as a critic wrote, "an epoch of great interest in the history of music in our country". A Boston magazine, the *Euterpiad,* even offered a $500 prize for an opera to be composed in America, but no contestants came forward.

From those days to our own, Italian opera has been produced in the United States, in both Italian and English, almost uninterruptedly, especially since the founding of the Metropolitan Opera House in New York in 1883. For almost a century and a half, scores of operatic companies have come and gone, celebrated singers have appeared year after year or for a few seasons, impresarios have been born and have died, and special theaters have been built not only in New York, but in other cities as well, from New Orleans to Chicago and from Colorado to California. As early as 1877 even the small town of Texarkana, Texas, had its opera house, built by its mayor, Antonio Ghio, a native of Genoa. Obviously, to recall the triumphs and failures of Italian opera in North America would be beyond the purpose of the present chapter. A few companies, however, deserve a special mention.

THE RICHMOND HILL THEATER

THE FIRST TROUPE FROM ITALY

The next notable operatic troupe to appear in New York, following Garcia's departure, was the company brought from Italy by Lorenzo Da Ponte under the direction of Giacomo Montresor. It opened on October 2, 1832, at the Richmond Hill Theater with Rossini's *Cenerentola* and lasted until February, 1833, when it closed at the Chestnut Street Theater in Philadelphia. It included some very fine singers, foremost among them being the mezzo-

THE OLD CHESTNUT STREET THEATER IN PHILADELPHIA

GIOV. BATT. MONTRESOR, TENOR

ADELAIDE PEDROTTI

LUCIANO FORNASARI, BASSO

MICHELE RAPETTI, VIOLINIST

soprano Adelaide Pedrotti, and the basso, Luciano Fornasari. The musical director was Antonio Bagioli, already noted; the orchestra leader was the violinist Michele Rapetti, well known in his days. The orchestra also included some of the finest players that had appeared in American cities up to that time. The chorus leader was Carlo Salvioni, the composer of the opera *La Casa da Vendere,* the first opera to have its première in New York, in 1834.

The Montresor Company did not meet with financial success, but its failure did not discourage other persons determined to establish a permanent opera house. Its prime mover, although not financially, was the indefatigable Lorenzo Da Ponte, an Italian poet of Jewish parentage who had become a Catholic, and who had acquired fame as the author of the libretto of Mozart's *Don Giovanni.* Another Italian interested in the project was Oroondates Mauran, the son of Joseph Carlo Mauran of Providence, already noted as the commander of two armed vessels during the Revolution.

LORENZO DA PONTE

Without getting into many details, in November, 1832, an association was formed to establish an opera house to be erected on the northwest corner of Leonard and Church Streets. Over $100,000 was paid in, the lots were purchased, the theater was built and a year later, on November 18, 1833, the Italian Opera House was opened with Rossini's *La Gazza Ladra.* Up to that time New York had never had a theater as magnificent as that. (See Chapter Fifteen in connection with Bragaldi and other scenic artists.) The ground of the box fronts, we learn from a contemporary writer, was white, with emblematical medallions and octagonal panels of crimson, blue and gold. The dome was painted with representations of the Muses. The sofas and pit-seats were covered with blue damask, and the floors were all carpeted." The theater, added Mr. White in 1882, was "of an exquisiteness and a splendor such as has not been since in New York." The new management was under a new impresario, Cavaliere Rivafinoli, a Milanese who later became interested in North Carolina gold mines. The leader of the chorus was the great martyr of Austrian oppression, Piero Maroncelli. The orchestra leader was Rapetti. The singers were not as good as those of the previous season.

In all the Rivafinoli company gave 80 performances, both in New York and Philadelphia, but opera was still a novelty to Americans and after another season under Porto and Sacchi, the theater was offered for sale at a public auction, but nobody would take it. It burned down on September 23, 1839.

THE ITALIAN OPERA HOUSE
on Leonard and Church Streets in New York City, built at a cost of more than $100,000 in 1932-33.

ITALIAN OPERA.

WE, the undersigned, agree to become shareholders in the ITALIAN OPERA ASSOCIATION, in the City of New-York, to the amounts affixed to our respective signatures.

The Association is divided into ninety-six shares of 1000 dollars each, payable (in case the whole shall be subscribed by the 24th instant,) one half cash on the first day of December, and the residue in notes payable on the first day of March next.

The Association is to purchase in fee simple, for 40,000 dollars, the six lots of land at the north-west corner of Church and Leonard streets, containing 100 feet on Church-street, and 151 feet on Leonard street.

Any person originally subscribing six shares, may at his election, to be signified at the time of subscribing, become a Trustee of the Association.

The property is to be holden by the Trustees in joint tenancy, with power to substitute new Trustees in the mode hereinafter specified.

The Trustees are to erect upon the land a building suitable for an Italian Opera House, with proper saloons and other accommodations, the first cost of which is not to exceed 56,000 dollars.

They are to pay all taxes and assessments to be imposed on the property, including the contemplated assessment for widening Church-street.

They are to keep the buildings in proper repair, and are at liberty to insure them against loss by fire, if in their judgment the insurance can be advantageously effected.

They are to rent the Opera House, saloons and appurtenances, for the Italian Opera or French Theatre, or both, and for such other purposes as they may deem proper and profitable.

The shares shall be transferable only on the books of the Association, which the Trustees shall keep for the purpose.

The shareholders shall be entitled to one transferable ticket for each share, entitling the bearer to free admission at every public representation in the Opera House, excepting only four benefit nights annually: and it shall be lawful for a majority of all the Trustees for the time being, in their discretion, to accept such tickets for the shareholders either in full or in part payment of the rent of the buildings;—and also to establish such regulations for the internal police and good order of the Opera House and saloons as they may deem proper.

Any person or association of persons holding six shares, and in virtue thereof entitled to six free tickets, shall be entitled to a private box—the choice of private boxes to be determined by lot after the Opera House shall be finished, preference being given to those persons originally subscribing six shares each.

Two-thirds of all the Trustees for the time being shall have power from time to time to lease the Opera House and saloons, for a pecuniary rent, to an Italian Opera Company, for periods not longer than one year each, in which case the shareholders shall be entitled to the exclusive use of their private boxes, but not to free tickets of admission, provided however that such pecuniary rent shall not be less than six per cent. per annum on the capital, and shall be paid in advance.

The Trustees once in each year shall call a meeting of the shareholders, and then exhibit a detailed statement of the affairs of the Association, and divide the surplus rents after paying the necessary expenses.

Each Trustee shall hold six shares. In case any Trustee shall have died, resigned his trust, or ceased to hold six shares, a majority of the shareholders at their annual meetings from time to time shall fill the vacancies, each share having one vote; and the remaining Trustees shall thereupon execute the conveyances necessary to substitute the new Trustees.

Before any Trustee shall resign his trust, or transfer any of his six shares, he shall by proper conveyances vest in his co-trustees his interest as trustee in the premises.

As soon as it shall be practicable the Trustees shall cause the Association to be incorporated by a law of the legislature, and shall thereupon convey the whole of the property to the corporate body to be created by that law, in which each shareholder shall receive his rateable proportion of stock.

NEW-YORK, NOVEMBER 19, 1832.

Articles of Association, made this fifteenth day of February, in the year of our Lord one thousand eight hundred and thirty-three. **Between** ROBERT RAY, GARDINER G. HOWLAND, and JOHN C. CRUGER, all of the City of New York, of the first part, and RUFUS PRIME ROBERT L. PATTERSON, OROONDATES MAURAN, SAMUEL B. RUGGLES, CHARLES HALL, I. GREEN PEARSON, MARIUS PANON, CHARLES F. MOULTON, DOMINICK LYNCH, GERARD H. COSTER, ELIHU TOWNSEND, JAMES I. JONES, EUGENE GROUSSET, JOHN N. GOSSLER, and PETER HARMONY, of the said City of the second part.

Whereas the parties to these presents have associated together for the purpose of establishing and maintaining in the said City of New York an Italian Opera House, and with this view have created a joint fund or capital, amounting to ninety-six thousand dollars divided into ninety-six shares of one thousand dollars, which have been subscribed and are now held as follows, that is to say, Robert Ray, Charles Hall, and I Green Pearson, each seven shares: Gardiner G. Howland, John C. Cruger, Rufus Prime, Robert L. Patterson, Oroondates Mauran, Samuel B. Ruggles, Marius Panon, Charles F. Moulton, Dominick Lynch, Gerard H. Coster, Elihu Townsend and James I. Jones, each six shares: and Eugene Grousset, John N. Gossler, and Peter Harmony, each one share: on each of which ninety-six shares the sum of five hundred dollars has been already paid, and the balance of five hundred dollars on each share remains to be paid by the respective holders thereof, for which they have issued their promissory notes now held by the said Oroondates Mauran, John C. Cruger and Gardiner G. Howland, Finance Committee, in trust for the benefit of the Association.

And Whereas, the said parties of the first part in virtue of a deed of conveyance to them from Russell H. Nevins, dated the twenty-first day of January, 1833, are seized as joint tenants in fee simple of all those certain six lots of land in the said City situate at the northwest corner of Church and Leonard streets; containing one hundred feet on Church street and one hundred and fifty one feet on Leonard street; and it has been mutually agreed b- ... that the said lots of land should be purch-

Facsimile of circular (*above*) and portion of the printed Articles of Association for the establishment of the Italian Opera House in New York City in 1832. (Courtesy, *New York Historical Society*.)

FERDINANDO PALMO AND HIS OPERA HOUSE

Ferdinando Palmo was one of those Neapolitans who would give anything for opera. Coming to America in 1817 at the age of 23, he spent six years in the South, until he moved to New York. At the age of 50 he had amassed a fortune of about $100,000 operating a restaurant and saloon, when he decided to establish a magnificent opera house. Within a year or so he had lost it all. "Had he remained in the macaroni and ice cream business, today he would be a millionaire," commented Secchi de Casali in his *Eco d'Italia.*

Undaunted, Palmo went back to work as a cook, until old age made it impossible for him to go on. Fortunately, however, the many people, especially among the political exiles, he had helped when he was prosperous, came to his assistance. When he died, in extreme poverty, the leading Italians in the city took him to his grave and the *New York Times*, the *New York Daily Tribune* and the *Evening Post* (the only newspapers consulted by us) devoted fine editorials to his passing.

FERDINANDO PALMO
From a portrait by Edwin White exhibited at the National Academy of Design in 1845.

Palmo's Opera House on Chambers street, between Broadway and Center street, opened on February 5, 1844, with Bellini's *I Puritani,* and continued under various managers until 1847. Of the artists who appeared there only two deserve to be remembered, Borghese and Antognini. Eufrasia Borghese is said to have been a fine soprano; Cirillo Antognini has been praised as "the greatest tenor ever heard in America". "His vocalization", wrote Mr. White in one of the *Century* articles mentioned before, "was unexceptionally pure, and his style mainly and noble. As a dramatic singer, I never heard his equal except Ronconi; as an actor, I never saw his equal except Ronconi, Rachel and Salvini."

EXTERIOR OF PALMO'S OPERA HOUSE
on Chambers Street, between Broadway and Center Street.

EUFRASIA BORGHESE

CIRILLO ANTOGNINI
"the greatest tenor ever heard in America."

INTERIOR OF PALMO'S OPERA HOUSE
(From an original drawing.)

ARDITI AND THE HAVANA OPERA COMPANY

GIUSEPPE DE BEGNIS

GIOVANNI BOTTESINI AND LUIGI ARDITI

De BEGNIS

After Palmo, other impresarios tried their hand and presented operas at Palmo's Opera House between October, 1844, and June, 1847, including Giueppe De Begnis, a remarkable buffo, and the two partners, Sanquirico and Patti. De Begnis was one of a few Italians who did not lose money (he left $50,000 at his death of cholera in New York in 1849); Salvatore Patti, a native of Catania, was a tenor, but is remembered primarily as the father of the celebrated Adelina Patti, and of her sisters, Carlotta and Amalia. Carlo Patti, his son, also had an interesting career, including a brief period of service on the staff of the Confederate General, Beauregard.

It was not, however, until the arrival of the famous Havana Opera Company, with Luigi Arditi as conductor, that opera held sway in the United States.

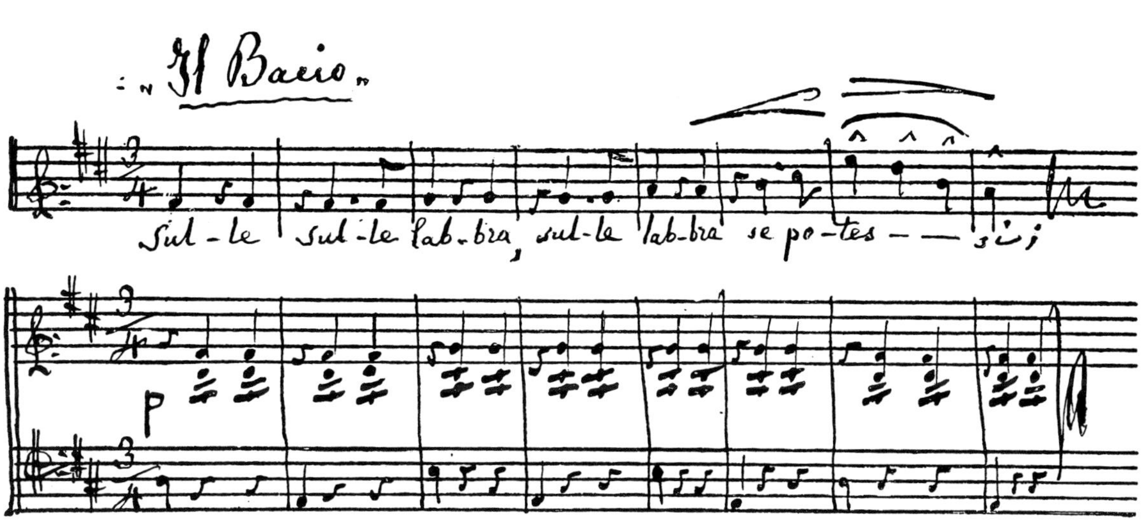

FACSIMILE OF THE OPENING BARS.

LA SPIA,

(THE SPY,)

A Grand Opera,

IN THREE ACTS,

COMPOSED BY

SIGNOR LUIGI ARDITI,

THE LIBRETTO FOUNDED ON COOPER'S GREAT ROMANCE

BY SIGNOR FILIPPO MANETTA.

New York:
PUBLISHED BY JOHN DARCIE.

Entered according to Act of Congress, in the year 1856, by JOHN DARCIE, in the Clerk's Office of the District Court, for the Southern District of New York.

Title-page of Arditi's "La Spia," the second opera based on an American subject given in the United States.

The Havana Company included at first 72, and later 83, artists, among the finest singers and musicians that had been assembled up to that time in America. Among the singers were Angiolina Bosio, one of the greatest sopranos of the 19th century, Lorenzo Salvi, a famous tenor, Ignazio Marini, a great basso, and Cesare Badiali, a noted baritone. The orchestra was under the baton of Luigi Arditi, the composer of the famous *Il Bacio* (The Kiss), and of *La Spia*, the second opera on an American subject, based on William Finimore Cooper's novel, *The Spy*, which was produced at the Academy of Music in the spring of 1856. Among the players, Giovanni Bottesini, one of the greatest contrabassists of all times. Later he became a noted conductor, especially after Giuseppe Verdi chose him to conduct the premiere of *Aida* at Cairo in 1871. "Never before had so many exquisite singers been enlisted in one enterprise", as Prof. Odell states in his monumental *Annals of the New York Stage*.

The Company appeared in New York for five successive seasons between 1847 and 1852, when its impresario, Senor Francisco Marty, discontinued his northern tours and the artists either joined other companies, returned to Europe, or settled in the United States. Arditi continued to come during a period of forty years, or until 1887.

THE ASTOR PLACE OPERA HOUSE

Opera, meantime, was getting a foothold in New York, especially among the wealthy social leaders who formed an opera association and erected what was to be the fourth "permanent" Italian opera house in the city, the Astor Place Opera House, now Cooper Union.

The new opera house opened with *Ernani* on November 22, 1847, under the management of Sanquirico and Patti. The occasion, wrote Mr. White in 1882, "was a musical event of the first importance in the musical annals of New York, and as such it was regarded by society and by musical amateurs generally. So elegant and socially impressive a spectacle as that presented by the house on the rising of the curtain had not been seen before in New York, and has not been seen since."

The artists, however, were not to be compared to those who had come from Havana, with the exception of Teresa Truffi, who, according to Mr. White, was a superb artist, although not a great singer. It was during that first season at the Astor Place Opera House that Eliza Biscaccianti, the first American-born opera singer of Italian parentage (she was the daughter of Louis Ostinelli), made her debut.

After a season under the management of Edward R. Fry, Max Maretzek, a most able Jewish impresario who had married the Italian singer and harpist, Madame Bertucca, took over and practically ruled Italian opera in New York until 1878. The Astor Place Opera House, however, did not prove a financial success, until Signor Donetti and his animal act took over the theater in 1852. That was a death blow to the good name of the house and opera moved to Castle Garden.

Among the singers who appeared at the Astor, besides the veterans of the former troupes, only Sesto Benedetti, a tenor, stood out. The husband of Teresa Truffi, he was for years the beloved of the New York public.

DEDICATION.

To WM. H. PAINE, Esq.,

Director of the Academy of Music.

DEAR SIR:—With your kind permission, I desire to dedicate to you my first Operatic Essay, and that on a truly American subject—Fennimore Cooper's Spy.—The public of America in general, and the dilletanti of New York in particular, owe you a deep debt of gratitude for your energetic exertions in endeavoring to establish Italian Opera as a fixed and permanent fact in our midst. Your time, your talent, and your purse have alike been devoted to carrying out this one great idea; and, if the patronage of the public did not at first respond to your efforts, I have reason to believe that it has now learned to appreciate them, and that your liberality, gentlemanly courtesy, and untiring desire to promote the cause of the lyric drama will meet with its well-merited reward—a more brilliant and prosperous operatic career than has been awarded to any previous director

I have the honor to remain,

Yours very obediently,

LUIGI ARDITI.

ARDITI'S DEDICATION OF HIS "SPY"

ELIZA BISCACCIANTI AS LUCIA

THE ASTOR PLACE OPERA HOUSE

SESTO BENEDETTI

TERESA TRUFFI

THE ACADEMY OF MUSIC

From 1854 until the opening of the Metropolitan Opera House in 1883, the Academy of Music was the home of opera in New York city. To be more accurate, opera was given from time to time in other theaters, such as the old Castle Garden, and the Academy continued to present operas until about 1897, but it was during the first thirty years of its existence that the Academy reigned supreme. During that period Italian opera was produced there practically without interruption, year in and year out.

The new theater, built at a cost of $350,000 on the southeast corner of Lexington avenue and Fourteenth street, opened its doors to the public on October 2, 1854, with Mario and Grisi in *Norma*. The building was torn down in 1925.

ADELINA PATTI

The greatest event in the history of the Academy of Music was the debut of Adelina Patti in *Lucia* on November 24, 1859, with Brignoli and Edgardo. She was then only sixteen years old. On that night a chapter in the history of opera was opened. "The reign of Patti", as it has been called, began.

Students of the history of opera need not be reminded of the furore that Adelina Patti created during the following forty-six years, or until 1906, when she retired from professional singing. Both in Europe and in America she had become a legend. Traveling throughout the United States in a private railroad car which is said to have cost $60,000, her earnings during three seasons from 1882 to 1885 reached the fabulous sum of $450,000. When she was scheduled to appear in a city, people used to get into line for tickets as early as five o'clock in the morning. When she appeared at the Metropolitan in 1886, with Arditi as conductor, no seat could be had for less than $10.00.

Other famous Italian singers who appeared at the Academy of Music were the celebrated tenor, Giuseppe Mario, and his wife, the equally celebrated dramatic soprano, Giulia Grisi, who appeared in 1854; Pasquale Brignoli, a noted tenor, who, as we have seen, appeared with Adelina Patti at her debut in 1859; Marietta Gazzaniga, a famous soprano already noted as a teacher; Erminia Frezzolini, a beautiful woman and a charming actress who created quite a furore, but who died in poverty having earned more money than any singer, with the exception of Adelina Patti; Giorgio Ronconi, who is said to have been one of the greatest actors that ever lived, and who taught singing in New York from 1867 to 1874; Maria Piccolomini, whose popular success "was dazzling, bewildering, incredible," surpassing even the Jenny Lind craze; Pauline Lucca and Enrico Tamberlik, who appeared together, and both of whom were famous in the annals of opera; finally, Italo Campanini, a great tenor who was chosen by Theodore Thomas for the leading role in Wagner's "Die Gotterdammerung".

The Academy of Music became the scene of even greater triumphs with the arrival of Colonel Henry Mapleson and his troupe from London. Mapleson first came in 1878 with a company of 140 persons, and returned, amid varying fortunes, until 1896, when the competition from the Metropolitan forced him to abandon the operatic field. Mapleson, as Arditi wrote of him, placed before the American world most of the principal artists of the century. The Italian singers presented by him were Adelina Patti, Sofia Scacchi, a leading mezzo-soprano who later sang at the Metropolitan, Italo Campanini, and Galassi, a baritone who became one of the idols of the New York public. Arditi was his conductor from 1879 to 1886.

THE NEW YORK ACADEMY OF MUSIC

ADELINA PATTI WITH HER FATHER

MARIA PICCOLOMINI

ANTONIO SANGIOVANNI

MARIETTA ALBONI

AGOSTINO ROVERE

THE METROPOLITAN OPERA HOUSE

Italian opera achieved its greatest triumphs in the United States with the opening of the Metropolitan Opera House in New York on October 22, 1883, reaching its peak under the management of Giulio Gatti-Casazza. Only for a short period, between 1906 and 1919, did the Metropolitan have serious competition in the Manhattan Opera Company, under Oscar Hammerstein, and in the Chicago Grand Opera Company under Cleofonte Campanini. But not for long.

Even if Gatti-Casazza had not brought together the most brilliant array of opera stars ever assembled in one company at one time, one singer alone would have been sufficient to turn all the eyes of the operatic world toward the Metropolitan. That singer was the immortal Caruso.

ENRICO CARUSO

In our century no singer has attained the summits reached by this consummate artist, for Caruso was not only a very great singer, but also a superb artist. In America, as everywhere else opera has its devotees, Caruso had become a legend even in his lifetime; it is still a legend which the greed and commercialism of some impresarios and singers of our day have unwillingly helped to grow. He died in Naples on August 2, 1921, at the age of 48.

OTHER FAMOUS SINGERS

Caruso, of course, was not the only famous singer Gatti-Casazza recruited for, or retained in, the Metropolitan between 1908, when he was lured away from the management of La Scala of Milan, to 1935, when he resigned and returned to Italy.

Limiting ourselves to the Italians, it may be sufficient to mention the Ponselle sisters, Claudia Muzio, Amelita Galli-Curci, Bruna Castagna, and Gina Cigna among the women; Amato, Gigli, Martinelli, Pinza, Nino Martini, Danise, De Luca, D'Angelo, Ruffo, Schipa, Scotti, Lauri-Volpi, among the men. The conductors included Toscanini, Serafin, Papi, Moranzoni, Bambosceck, Bellezza, Cimara, Dellera, and Sturani. Rosina Galli was mistress of the ballet and Giuseppe Bonfiglio first ballet dancer for years.

As for Gatti-Casazza's contribution to American music, the "New York World Telegram" well expressed the feelings of many critics when in an editorial on April 2, 1935, at the time of his resignation, it stated that "his twenty-seven years were a golden reign, the memory of which cannot be taken from him. He was in truth, Gatti the Great."

THE MANHATTAN AND CHICAGO OPERA COMPANIES

With the exception of Adelina Patti and Tamagno, both of whom appeared at the Metropolitan before the turn of the century, it was with the American debut of Antonio Scotti, also at the Metropolitan, in 1899, that the parade of Italian operatic stars of the first magnitude began to appear on the American stage, marching at a quickened

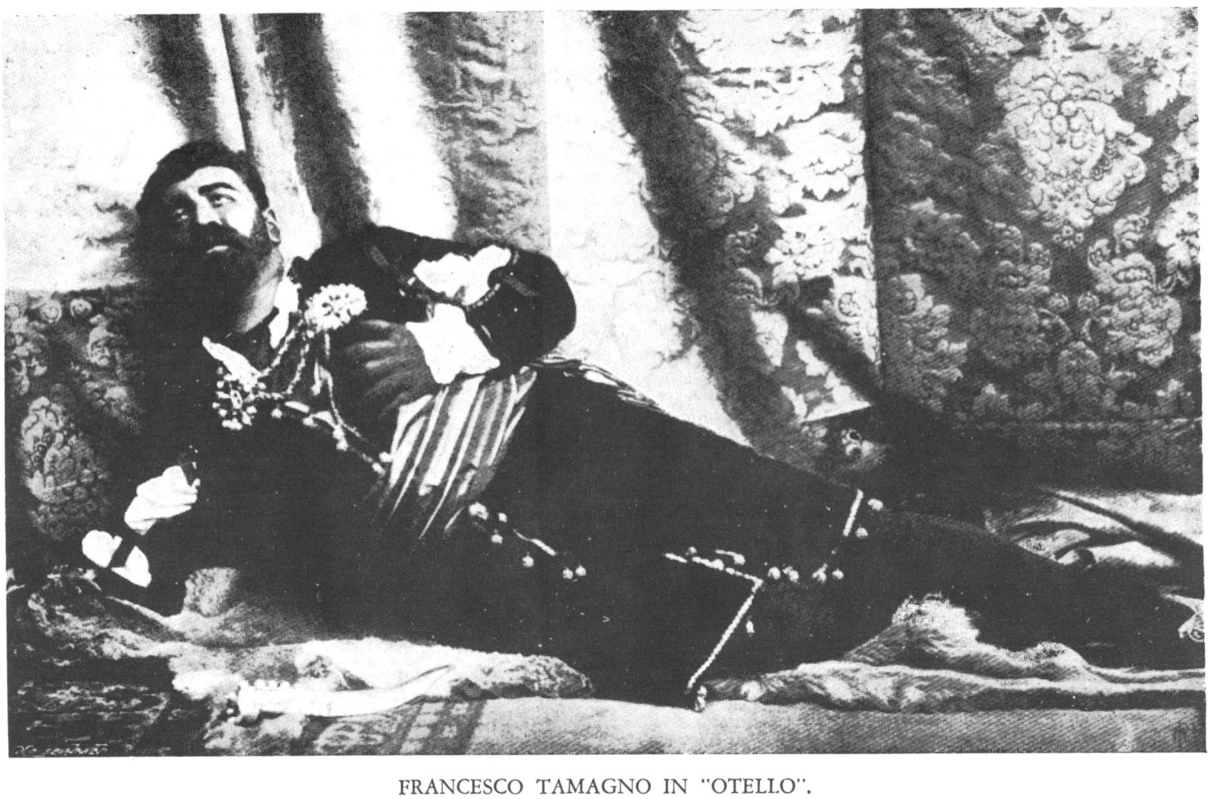

FRANCESCO TAMAGNO IN "OTELLO".

pace after 1906, when Oscar Hammerstein, a Jew who loved Italian music, organized the Manhattan Opera Company and brought to New York a galaxy of first-class singers from Italy. They included Alessandro Bonci, Luisa Tetrazzini, Giovanni Zenatello, Mario Sammarco, and Nicola Zerola. Cleofonte Campanini was his artistic director.

In the Middle West, shortly after the Manhattan Opera Company abandoned the field, Campanini continued his opposition to the Metropolitan through the Chicago Grand Opera Company (later Chicago Civic Opera Company) of which he became general manager in 1913, serving until his death in 1919.

Among the Italians he brought to Chicago, it may be sufficient to recall Luisa Tetrazzini (his sister-in-law), Zenatello, Stracciari, Amelita Galli-Curci, and Ruffo. Among the non-Italians, Mary Garden, John MacCormack, Melba, Calvé, Schumann-Heink, Nordica and Cisneros.

OTHER COMPANIES

Space prevents us from recalling, even briefly, the other operatic companies that have appeared in America during the last one hundred years. Beginning with the Pellegrini Opera Company, which offered Italian operas in San Francisco in 1851 (three years later there were eleven operatic companies in that city) to the San Francisco Opera Company, which has become one of the finest in the world under the able management of Gaetano Merola, its general director since it was organized in 1923, scores of operatic companies have sprung up and died from coast to coast.

GIULIO GATTI-CASAZZA

ENRICO CARUSO

Among the pioneer impresarios, C. A. Chizzola, Diego De Vivo, and Mario Lambardi deserve a special mention. Among those of our own days, Fortune Gallo occupies a foremost place with his San Carlo Opera Company, which he organized in 1913. He has now completed half a century of successful tours from coast to coast and even beyond, as far as Alaska and Hawaii, ever since he started in 1901. Francesco Pelosi, who died recently, organized the Philadelphia-La Scala Opera Company, which is still active; Alfredo Salmaggi has popularized opera beyond a scale ever reached by any other impresario; Filippo Ienni has also contributed his share with his Puccini Opera Company. In 1947, as recorded in Volume One of our *Italian-American History*, more than twenty-five operatic companies managed by men and women of Italian extraction were active from coast to coast.

BAND LEADERS

On September 19, 1805, fourteen Italian musicians landed from the U. S. frigate Chesapeake at the Washington Navy Yard. They had been recruited in Sicily by order of President Thomas Jefferson, who wanted to organize a popular brass band for the United States Marine Corps. The fourteen musicians were Gaetano Carusi, Domenico Guarnaccia, Francesco Pulizzi, Michele Sardo, Giuseppe Papa, Salvatore Lauria, Giacomo Sardo, Ignazio DiMauro, Pasquale Lauria, Antonio Paterno and Corrado Signorello. Also in the party were the three children of Gaetano Carusi, Samuel, 9, Ignazio, 10, and Lewis 6. Another boy, Venerando Pulizzi, 12, and some of the musicians' wives also arrived. Gaetano Carusi was the first leader of the band, now known throughout the country as the United States Marine Band.

Apparently the musicians returned to Sicily in 1816, as we learn from the autobiography of Commodore George Nicholas Hollins (*Maryland Historical Magazine,* 1939, 228 ff.), but the Carusi family came back to the United States. One of the boys, Lewis Carusi, established a dancing school in Washington, as related below. Another grandson of Gaetano, Eugene Carusi, became chancellor of the National University Law School, as related in Chapter Twenty. Gaetano Carusi wrote the music for a pantomime, *The Brazen Mask,* produced in New York in 1811. He wrote other music which can be found in the Library of Congress.

Since those early days, five more Italians have served as leaders of the United States Marine Band. They were: Venerando Pulizzi (1816-1827), Antonio Pons (1843-1844, and 1846-1848), Joseph Lucchesi (1844-1846), Francis Scala (1855-1871) and Francesco Fanciulli (1892-1897). It was under Scala that the open-air concerts at the Capitol and on the White House grounds were inaugurated. Under him the band became the finest military musical organization in the country, until John Philip Sousa led it to still greater fame. Fanciulli later organized a band which became for all intents and purposes the official band of the city of New York.

OTHER BANDS

The first Italian band to make a tour of the United States seems to have been *The Comet,* made up of Sicilians, which arrived in 1836. Some twenty years before, Francesco Masi's *Italian Band* played at dances and assemblies in Boston.

Among the pioneer band leaders born in Italy, we may recall Domenico Ballo, a Sicilian who is said to have been bandmaster at West Point and later in Missouri and Utah; one Conterno, a Piedmontese who was bandmaster of Commodore Perry's Fleet during the expedition to Japan in 1953; his son, Luciano Conterno, leader of the U. S. Navy Band at the Brooklyn Navy Yard from 1873 to 1894; Prospero Siderio, bandmaster on Admiral Dewey's flagship at the battle of Manila; Claudio Grafulla, leader of the famous New York Seventh Regiment Band; Carlo Alberto Cappa, another Piedmontese who succeeded Grafulla and became one of the most popular bandmasters of the century; and numerous other leaders of regimental bands.

In recent years the Vessella, Creatore and Rossi bands acquired fame throughout the country.

The United States Marine Band in front of the Commandant's House, Washington, D. C., about 1896. Francesco Fanciulli, leader from 1892 to 1897, shown in center foreground. (Official U. S. Marine Corps Photo.)

ORCHESTRA LEADERS

Although Italian musicians have been interested primarily in opera, they have not neglected symphonic music. Ostinelli, as we have seen, was one of the organizers with Graupner of the Boston Philharmonic Society about 1820. He was also one of the first violin concert players in the country.

It is not generally known, however, that the famous political exile, Piero Maroncelli, was one of the organizers of the Philharmonic Society of New York in 1842, which included among its pioneers C. Passaglia, librarian from 1854 to 1862, and John Godone, treasurer from 1877 until his death in 1880. Numerous Italian concert artists have appeared with the New York Philharmonic from its earliest days, including Camillo Sivori, the famous violinist who was made a honorary member in 1846, Giovanni Bottesini, the noted double-bass, and Camilla Urso, another famous violinist who appeared on numerous occasions between 1855 and 1892. We need not remind our readers that it was under Toscanini, who served as permanent conductor from 1928 to 1936, that the New York Philharmonic became known throughout the world. Nor do we need to linger on the N. B. C. Symphony Orchestra which Toscanini organized in 1937 and which he still directs. No orchestra has ever surpassed its artistic performances.

Outside New York City there is no orchestra of any importance, from Philadelphia and Boston to Cleveland, Cincinnati, Detroit, Chicago, St. Louis, Minneapolis, all the way to the Pacific coast, in which one does not find Italian conductors or outstanding soloists. Their names, too numerous to be mentioned here, will be found in chapter fifteen of volume one of our *Italian-American History*.

CLEOFONTE CAMPANINI

No less impressive is the number of symphonic orchestras organized by Italian-Americans. In 1947 not less than forty of them were active from coast to coast.

We should also mention the chamber music ensembles, from Campanari's string quartet (Boston, 1883) to the Flonzaley Quartet organized by two Frenchmen and two Italians, Ugo Ara and Adolfo Betti. Betti passed away in 1950.

Arturo Toscanini directing the N. B. C. Symphony Orchestra. (Courtesy, *National Broadcasting Company.*)

COMPOSERS

Once more, we must refer our readers to the first volume of our *Italian-American History* for the names and principal works of Italian composers in the United States.

From opera to songs, from oratorios to ballets, from marches to waltzes, literally hundreds of music compositions printed in North America have appeared under Italian names.

OPERAS

The first opera by an Italian in America was Salvioni's *La Casa Da Vendere* presented by the Rivafinoli troupe in 1834. Then came *Pocahontas* by Giuseppe Nicolao of the Palermo Conservatory, the first opera based on an American subject, produced at the Niblo Theater in 1852. (*Eco d'Italia,* January 31, 1852.) It was followed by Arditi's *La Spia* in 1856.

Other operas were composed by Luigi La Grassa, Paolo Giorza, Francesco Mancinelli, Edoardo Trucco, Domenico Brescia, Adolfo Tirindelli, and a score of others, down to Cesare Sodero, Vittorio Giannini, and Giancarlo Menotti.

One of them, *Ero e Leandro,* by Mancinelli, was produced at the Metropolitan in 1910; Floridia's *Paoletta,* the first opera ever commissioned by an American city, was produced with success in Cincinnati also in 1910; Fabrizi's *Bianca e Fernando* was given under the baton of Cleofonte Campanini in Chicago in 1914; Romani's *Fedra* had its premiere at the Royal Opera House in Rome, Italy, in 1915, and was later presented at the Covent Garden in London; Francesco Di Leone's *Alglala* was produced in Cleveland in 1924 with Edward Johnson and other noted singers; Cesare Sodero's *Ombre Russe* was given at the Malibran Theater in Florence, Italy, and over the NBC network in America in 1930; Vittorio Giannini's *Lucedia* had its world premiere in Munich, Germany, in 1934.

The best known of modern Italian-American composers is Giancarlo Menotti, whose operas *Amelia Goes to the Ball, The Medium,* and *The Telephone* have met with deserved success. *The Medium* has also been presented on the screen. His latest opera, *Amahl and the Night Visitors,* the first opera composed for television, first projected on Christmas Eve, 1951, has been called a "historic step in the development of a new idiom".

FROM SACRED MUSIC TO POPULAR SONGS

In the field of sacred music Italian-American composers have attained one of the leading places. Augusto Rotoli's *Roman Mass* is considered a masterpiece; Edoardo Marzo distinguished himself in various types of religious composition; Monsignor Leo Manzetti founded the Society of St. Gregory in America, with the assistance of Nicola Montani and Dr. John M. Petter; Montani was one of the most prolific and successful composers of church music; Melchiorre Mauro-Cottone, one of the leading organists of his day, composed many pieces for organ, voice, piano, and violin; Pietro Yon, possibly the most famous organist of our time in America, is particularly known for his *Triumph of St. Patrick* (oratorio, libretto by A. Romano), and his *Gesu Bambino,* which has become famous as organ piece as well as song.

Scores of composers of Italian birth or extraction have written popular music. One of the best known was James Monaco, who died in 1945 after writting many songs which became popular throughout the country. He also wrote the music for several motion pictures.

For that matter one has to go over the list of the members of the American Society of Composers, Authors and Publishers (ASCAP) to find the names of many Italian-American song writers.

OTHER MUSIC

There is no field of music in which Italian-American composers have not been successful, from symphonic poems to choral works, sonatas, trios and quartets for string and piano, violin concertos, organ and harp pieces, and what not. Gilda Ruta's *Concerto* was performed at the Metropolitan by Toscanini; Dante Fiorillo's symphonies have been performed by noted orchestras; Bellini's *Ninna Nanna a Liana* was played by the New York Philharmonic under Ormandy; Mennini's *Symphonic Allegro* was performed at the Metropolitan in 1945. We could go on and on.

One of Francesco Masi's waltzes published in Boston in 1815. (*Courtesy, Library of Congress.*)

PIETRO FLORIDIA

GIUSEPPE FERRATA

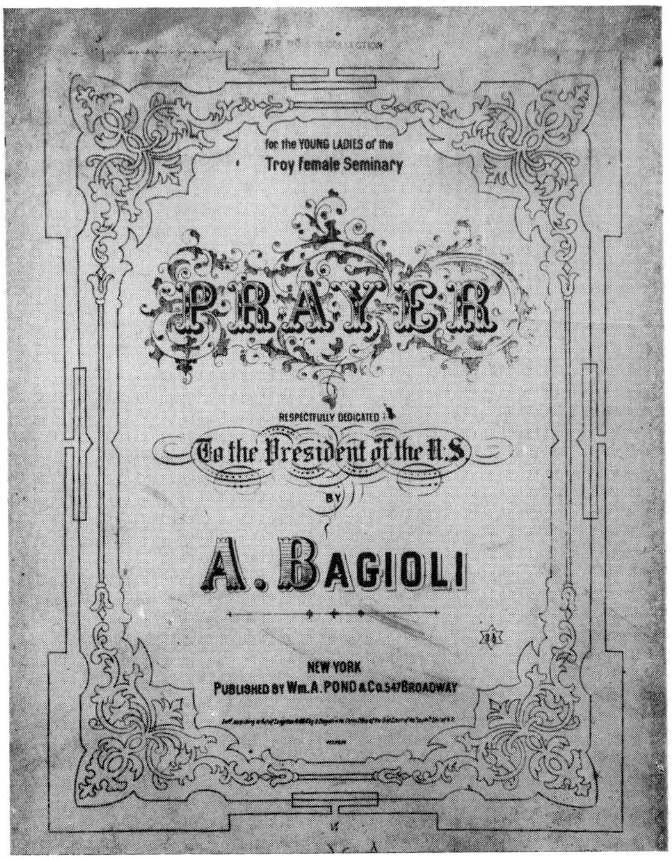

Title-page of one of Bagioli's compositions.

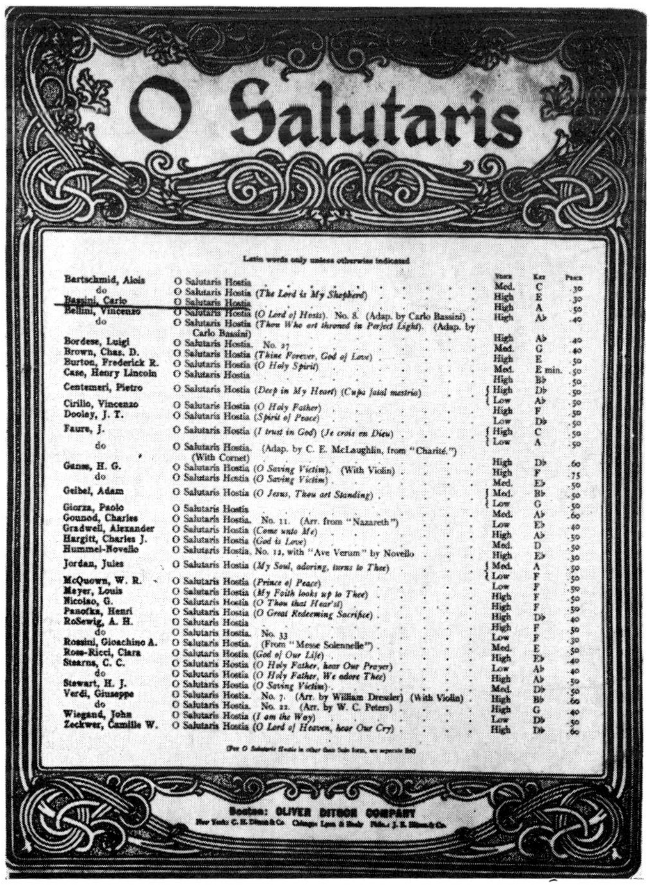

Title-page of several "O Salutaris Hostia" by various composers, including the Italian-Americans, Bassini, Centemeri, Giorza and Nicolao.

ITALIAN-AMERICAN SINGERS

A number of American stars of Italian parentage have been added of recent years to the operatic firmament: Rosa Ponselle, Carmela Ponselle, Dusolina Giannini, Elda Vettori, Santa Biondo, Nina Morgana, Carolina Lazzari, Louis D'Angelo, Norina Greco, Vivian Della Chiesa, Marguerite Piazza, Josephine Lucchese, Rose Marie Brancato, John Pane-Gasser, and others.

The chief source of operatic talent, however, still remains Italy, where the Metropolitan still has to look for superb artists like Licia Albanese and Ferruccio Tagliavini.

POPULAR SINGERS

Popular singers have become really popular only in recent years, that is, since the advent of radio broadcasting and television. Here again, Italian-American singers can be found in the front rank, with Russ Colombo and Ted Fiorito only a few years ago, and Frank Sinatra, Perry Como, Frank Parker, Alan Dale, Vic Damone, Phil Brito, Jerry Baker, Dean Martin, Frankie Laine, and others well-known to our younger generation.

As for popular orchestra leaders and artists, first places are held by Guy Lombardo, Carmen Cavallaro, "the poet of the piano", Frankie Carle, Lou Prima, and others whose racial backgrounds are hard to identify because of their professional names.

One must not believe, however, that Italian-American popular singers are of recent date. As the facsimiles on this page show they go back at least a century, and even more. Their names, however, should be sought in the annals of American vaudeville.

SIG. ABECCO'S
SENTIMENTAL
SONGSTER.

CONTAINING
ALL THE MOST POPULAR SONGS.
EUREKA MINSTREL HALL.
PUBLISHED BY D. E. APPLETON & CO.
508 Montgomery Street.
1861.

Title-page and three songs from Abecco's "Songster" published in San Francisco in 1861.

Viva l'America.

Composed by H. Millard, Esq..

Expressly for Sig. R. Abecco.

Noble Republic! happiest of lands!
Foremost of nations, Columbia stands;
Freedom's proud banner floats in the skies,
Where shouts of Liberty daily arise.
"United we stand, divided we fall,"
Union for ever—freedom to all!
Throughout the world our motto shall be—
Viva l'America, home of the free!

Chorus:

Throughout the world our motto shall be—
"Viva l'America, home of the free!

To all her heroes, justice and fame—
To all her foes, a traitor's foul name;
Our Stripes and Stars still proudly shall wave—
Emblem of Liberty, flag of the brave!
"United we stand, divided we fall,"
Granting a home and freedom to all.
Throughout the world our motto shall be—
Viva l'America, home of the free!
Throughout the world, etc.

10

WHEN THIS CRUEL WAR—CONCLUDED.

When the summer breeze is sighing mournfully along,
Or when autumn's leaves are falling sadly breathes the song,
Oft in dreams I see thee lying on the battle-plain,
Lonely, wounded, even dying, calling but in vain;
Weeping sad and lonely, hopes and fears, how vain!
—yet praying,
When this cruel war is over, praying that we meet again.

But our country called you, darling, angels cheer your way,
While our nation's sons are fighting we can only pray.
Nobly strike for God and Liberty, let all nations see
How we love our starry banner—emblem of the free.
Weeping sad and lonely, hopes and fears, how vain!
—yet praying,
When this cruel war is over, praying that we meet again.

La Neapolitaine—(Serenade.)

Sung with immense applause by Sig. R. Abecco.

Neapolitaine, I am dreaming of thee!
I'm hearing thy foot-fall so joyous and free;
Thy dark flashing eyes are entwining me yet;
Thy voice with its music I ne'er can forget.

11

LA NEAPOLITAINE—CONCLUDED.

I am far from the land of my own sunny home,
Alone in this wide world of sorrow I roam;
In the halls of the gay, or wherever it be,
Still, Neapolitaine, I am dreaming of thee!
Neapolitaine, I am dreaming of thee—
Neapolitaine, I am dreaming of thee!

Neapolitaine, art thou thinking of me?
Has absence yet banished my memory from thee?
Remember our meetings their whispers to keep,
When bright eyes are smiling all loved ones to sleep.
And yet I would not have a shade on thy brow,
As bright as thou art let it shine on me now;
For 'tis memory that brings all thy beauty to me,
Still, Neapolitaine, I am dreaming of thee!
Neapolitaine, I am dreaming of thee,
Neapolitaine, I am dreaming of thee!

"Kiss me Good Night, Mother."

As Sung by Sig. R. Abecco.

How dear to each heart is childhood's gay hours,
Their bright sunny skies and ever green bowers,
Ere the dark veil was drawn that hid from our view
Futurity's picture, so varied and true!
When the sun had gone down, being tired of play,
We watched the dim shadows of twilight so gray;

TEACHERS OF DANCING AND BALLET DANCERS

So far as we know, today there are no Italian-American dancing teachers one might call fashionable. But at the beginning of the nineteenth century, and for years until after the Civil War, dancing teachers of Italian birth or extraction were among the few patronized by Boston, New York, and Washington Society.

After Sodi, who came in 1774, as noted on page 116, the first Italian to operate a fashionable dancing school in America seems to have been Vincent Masi, who was active in Boston between 1807 and 1818, together with his brother Francesco and other relatives, all of whom played and sang at dances and assemblies. (See facsimile on page 177.)

The best known Italian dancing teacher in Boston, however, was Lorenzo Papanti (1799-1872), who came to America as a musician on the frigate Constitution, taught dancing at West Point (his pupils included Jefferson Davis and Beauregard), and for more than forty years taught dancing and deportment to Boston's upper classes. After his death his school was continued until 1900 by his son, Augustus L., who served as captain in the Massachusetts cavalry during the Civil War.

LORENZO PAPANTI
(From his portrait in the Bostonian Society.)

In New York one of the fashionable dancing academies was conducted by Stephen Ferrero, a musician who came over with the Montresor company in 1832, together with his wife, Adelaide, a singer and dancer. The academy later was managed by his son, General Edward Ferrero, who distinguished himself during the Civil War, and for a time teacher of dancing at West Point. In the same academy one Professor Planci taught modern dances in 1852. (*Eco d'Italia*, February 18, 1852.)

In Washington one fashionable school was that of Lewis Carusi at whose "assembly rooms" were given all presidential inaugural balls from John Adams to Buchanan (1825-1857). The son of Gaetano Carusi, one of the found-

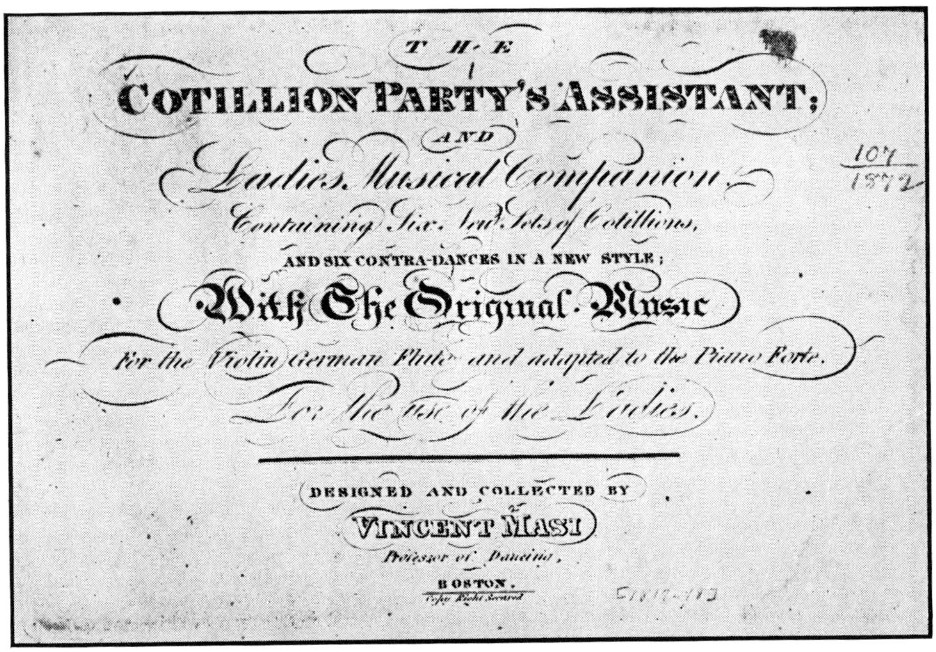

THE
COTILLION PARTY'S ASSISTANT;
AND
Ladies' Musical Companion,
Containing Six New Sets of Cotillions,
AND SIX CONTRA-DANCES IN A NEW STYLE;
With The Original Music
For the Violin, German Flute and adapted to the Piano Forte.
For the Use of the Ladies.
DESIGNED AND COLLECTED BY
VINCENT MASI
Professor of Dancing,
BOSTON.
Copy Right Secured

Title-page of a book of dance music by Vincent Masi published at Boston in 1818.
(Courtesy, *Library of Congress.*)

ers of the United States Marine Band, as we have already noted, he died in 1872.

Also in Washington in the 1860's we find Marini's school and a young dancing teacher named Buchignani, an adventurer who married Peggy Eaton, the widow of Jackson's secretary of war.

In New Orleans one Mr. Devoti conducted a deportment and dancing academy in 1842 and 1843. (*New Orleans Times Picayune,* Dec., 1842, and Jan., 1843.)

BALLET DANCERS

From the days of Baltazarini, or Beaujoyeulx, as he was called, the creator of the French ballet in the sixteenth century, to Gaetano Vestris, Maria Taglioni, Enrico Cecchetti, all the way down to our own days, the Italians have always occupied a foremost place in ballet dancing. In the nineteenth century, they were undisputed masters.

In Prof. Odell's *Annals* we find numerous names of Italian ballet dancers who appeared in America during the last century. Before 1850 there were: as early as 1803, one Signor Bologna, lately from Covent Garden, who was co-manager for a time of the Park Theater in New York; one Schinotti, who came in 1823; Angrisani, the singer, who appeared as ballet dancer at the Bowery in 1827; one Checkeni (Cecchini?) in 1827; and finally, to recall only the more famous ones, Charles and Carolina (Ronzi) Vestris, Paul Taglioni, and Giovanna Ciocca.

The Vestris came in 1828. According to Ireland, the husband had never been excelled and his wife was the peer of Fanny Ellsler.

Paul Taglioni, the brother of the celebrated Maria Taglioni, came over in 1839 and appeared in New York, Baltimore, Philadelphia, Providence and Boston, always before packed houses.

Giovanna Ciocca made her first American appearance at Philadelphia in 1852. She became popular and returned in 1857.

THE RONZANI TROUPE

The appearance of Domenico Ronzani and his company at the Broadway Theatre in New York on October 5, 1857, marks a milestone in the history of the ballet in America. The company included Domenico Ronzani, Cesare Cecchetti and his family (including the celebrated Enrico who was then five years old,) Annetta Galletti, first ballerina of La Scala of Milan, the Pratesi family, and others. In all, eighty coriphees and figurantes, and nearly a hundred males.

Ronzani was famous for his ballet *The Orphan of Geneva* which he produced all over the country, as far north at St. Paul, Minn., and then down the Mississippi to New Orleans. Financially, however, he was a failure. He returned in 1867, without more success and died in New York a year later.

Enrico Cecchetti and his little sister appeared in the ballet *Theresa.* He came back to America fifty-six years later, in 1913, when he had become the leading ballet master of the world, together with his pupil, Anna Pavlova.

Annetta Galletti also continued to appear on the American stage as late as 1875.

THE BLACK CROOK

The greatest theatrical event in the United States during the nineteenth century was the performance in 1866 of *The Black Crook,* the most extravagant spectacle America had yet seen. Its chief attraction was its ballet, with a hundred girl dancers, most of whom wore what was considered in those days to be a scanty attire. It ran for 475 consecutive perfomances from 1866 to 1868 and again for 122 more when it was revived in 1870. It is said to have netted its producers the sum of $1,100,000.

According to Miss Bonfanti, its chief ballerina, *The Black Crook* ballet had never been equalled in her lifetime. She died in New York in 1921, at the age of 70, after appearing in other productions, including *The Home of the Butterflies,* a ballet directed by one Grossi in 1871, and then for many years as premiere danseuse of the Metropolitan Opera Company.

Miss Bonfanti was assisted by Rita Sangalli, Betty Rigl and Rose Delval. The ballet, which was directed by David Costa, included the Italian dancers Adelgisa Cerebelli, Ros-

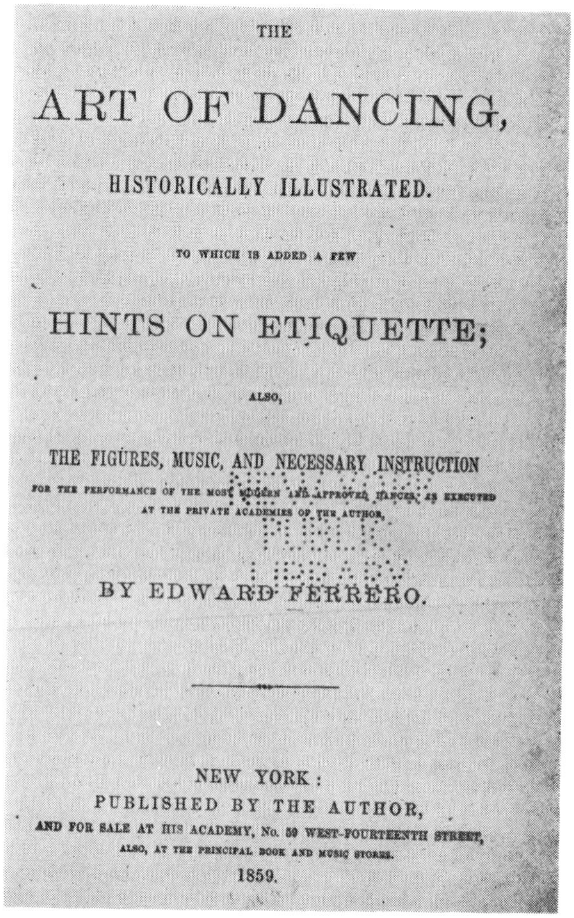
THE

ART OF DANCING,

HISTORICALLY ILLUSTRATED.

TO WHICH IS ADDED A FEW

HINTS ON ETIQUETTE;

ALSO,

THE FIGURES, MUSIC, AND NECESSARY INSTRUCTION

FOR THE PERFORMANCE OF THE MOST MODERN AND APPROVED DANCES, AS EXECUTED AT THE PRIVATE ACADEMIES OF THE AUTHOR,

BY EDWARD FERRERO.

NEW YORK:

PUBLISHED BY THE AUTHOR,

AND FOR SALE AT HIS ACADEMY, No. 59 WEST-FOURTEENTH STREET,

ALSO, AT THE PRINCIPAL BOOK AND MUSIC STORES.

1859.

Title-page of General Ferrero's book on dancing. (Courtesy, *New York Public Library.*)

CAROLINA RONZI VESTRIS
"The exquisite Vestris appeared, and all that had gone before seemed poor in comparison. With a form cast in nature's happiest mould, and a face to match; with motions graceful as a bird's in the air; with a step as free as fancy, agile as an antelope, and elastic as a bow, who was to be compared to her? . . . And whoever has heard Signorina Garcia sing, seen Kean act, and Vestris dance, has heard and seen three things well worth hearing and seeing; he has heard few superior to the former, and seen none equal to the latter."
New York Mirror and Ladies Literary Gazette, August 8, 1829.

Sheet music cover of *The Black Crook,* featuring Maria Bonfanti. (Courtesy, *New York Public Library.*)

ina Pagani, Luisa and Giovanna Mazzeri, Josephine Invernezzi, Giulia Sctti, Giuseppe Zuardi and Eugenia Zuccoli. According to Prof. Odell, *The Black Crook* revolutionized the ballet spectacle in America.

Giuseppina Morlacchi, another of the popular ballet dancers of the 70's, scored a great success in *The Bee Dance,* which is said to have been her graceful and artistic masterpiece.

The Black Crook was followed in 1868 by another spectacle of the same type, *The White Fawn,* which featured Adelgisa Cerebelli as the premiere danseuse.

During the last seventy-five years scores of ballet dancers of Italian birth or extraction have appeared on the American stage, especially in connection with opera, all the way down to Rosina Galli, Maria Gambarelli and Giuseppe Bonfiglio. Their names, too numerous to be mentioned here will be found in Odell's *Annals* or in the histories of dance in America. We shall recall only Tito Cellini's *Great Ballet* which was produced in New York in 1879.

PROFESSIONAL DANCERS

Space, likewise, prevents us from dwelling at length on the Italian-Americans who are members of outstanding professional dancing teams, like Yolanda Casazza of the Veloz and Yolanda team, Tony De Marco, Carmen D'Antonio, Fely Franquelli, and others mentioned frequently in *Variety* and *Billboard.* Some of them have appeared in motion pictures and more frequently on television.

GIUSEPPINA MORLACCHI

Another sheet music cover of *The Black Crook* featuring Maria Bonfanti in the center. (Courtesy, *New York Public Library.*)

The Enchanted Lake scene from *The White Fawn,* featuring Adelgisa Cerebelli.

CHAPTER FOURTEEN

ON STAGE, SCREEN AND RADIO

One of the features of Italian emigration of the last few centuries has been the departure of professional entertainers, from actors and ballet dancers to prestidigitators, magicians, conjurers, tight-rope walkers, bareback riders, operators of puppet shows, jugglers, equilibrists, ventriloquists, necromancers, and, in general, performers of feats of skill.

Some of them came to the United States soon after the conflict was over, either as part of other shows, or with companies of their own. Actually, as early as 1805, there was an "Italian Theater" in downtown Broadway, New York; in the 1830's, Cleveland, which was then only a village, had also an "Italian Hall", three stories high, with a theater on the top floor, but we have no information as to the origin of the name.

In Prof. Odell's *Annals of the New York Stage* one will find a more or less complete list of the various vaudeville performers who toured the country during most of the last century (all troupes of some importance visited New York)—to which one may add the names found in contemporary journals devoted to the amusement field. Here, therefore, we shall limit ourselves only to a few outstanding pioneers.

MAGICIANS AND NECROMANCERS

Next to the pyrotechnists who have been ever-present, the first Italian entertainers to perform on the American stage were the magicians, or conjurers. The most notable among them, by far, was one Signor Falconi, who appeared in American cities between 1787 and 1817 (see facsimles on next page). According to Prof. Odell, his performances are important as part of the history of prestidigitation in New York.

In 1835 one Signor Sciarra appearing at the Richmond Hill Theater in New York, promised "to swallow a sword thirty-three inches long, scabbard and all, draw the sword while the scabbard remains in his throat" and perform various feats on stilts, the slack rope, and similar stunts. His wife and children also appeared in the same act. However, he was more of an acrobat than a magician.

One Signor Francisco, a magician and equilibrist, was offered by Barnum on April 1, 1844, at his New York Museum. He later appeared in Hoboken with one Signor

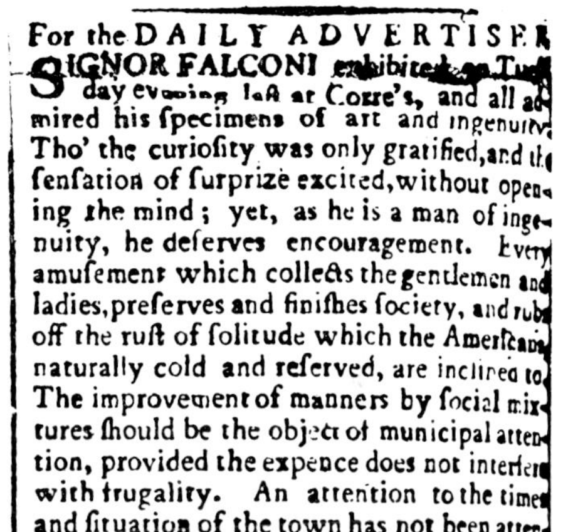

For the DAILY ADVERTISER.

SIGNOR FALCONI exhibited on Tuesday evening last at Corre's, and all admired his ſpecimens of art and ingenuity. Tho' the curioſity was only gratified, and the ſenſation of ſurprize excited, without opening the mind; yet, as he is a man of ingenuity, he deſerves encouragement. Every amuſement which collects the gentlemen and ladies, preſerves and finiſhes ſociety, and rubs off the ruſt of ſolitude which the Americans naturally cold and reſerved, are inclined to. The improvement of manners by ſocial mixtures ſhould be the object of municipal attention, provided the expence does not interfere with frugality. An attention to the times and ſituation of the town has not been attended to by this extraordinary man when he fixed his prices, which are really too high. If he would abate his price it would become the faſhionable amuſement, and would draw to Corre's room many a matrimonial couple who yawn over the frugal repaſt of ſtrawberries, and with heavy eye lids nodding like too goats ready for a *rencounter*; and alſo many lovers who conſume their hours in public endearments upon the *ſtoops*, where they often lay the foundation of conſumptive complaints, and ruin their character by endulging their lovers with pocket-hole liberties, which often inflames the curious paſſenger. The *Canaille* of Water-ſtreet, who mimick the manners of genteel people, and all the *griſettes*, ſuch as the wives of brokers and grocers, might here amuſe themſelves with innocent ſurprize, and *naive* exclamations of "*La! La! Goody ſurs; did you ever ſee the like!*" which would be a relief to the clerks and apprentices who often muſt carry their *maſters buſineſs* for their greaſy and vulgar ladyſhips, when the maſter is concerned in ſome dirty job of ſpeculation.

An editorial on the social implications of Signor Falconi's performances in the New York *Daily Advertiser* for June 30, 1787. (Courtesy, *New York Public Library.*)

THEATRE.

SIGNOR FALCONI,

Will have the Honor to give in this City his first representation of

Natural Philosophical Experiments,

THIS EVENING,

At Mr. CORRE's Assembly Room, Broadway, The doors will be opened at seven o'clock, and the performance begin precisely at eight o'clock

IT would be tedious to describe the many objects which this performance will consist of, but he can without vanity assure the Public, that they will not find themselves disappointed in their expectations. From the following list of some few of his experiments, it will give the public a small idea how far he will be deserving of engaging their attention. Having always met in Europe with general approbation, he is in hopes of having the same success in America.

1. A Sympathetic WIND-MILL, that will work or stop at the command of any of the company.

2. Some experiments of the CATOPTRIC, or appearances produced by the reflection of mirrors.

3. A number of sentiments will be handed to the company, which any person retaining in their mind, a little artificial butterfly will reply to them.

4. A small FIGURE in a Turkish dress, will answer all questions by signs, and will guess the number any lady or gentleman shall throw with two dice.

5. Likewise any lady or gentleman may throw the dice under a hat, unseen by any person, the above-mentioned Figure will tell the number.

6. To augment or diminish at pleasure the weight of gold, silver or diamonds, at the command of any of the company, the scales being at the distance of twelve feet.

7. The EXPULSION, by electricity, an entire new discovery.

8. To oblige, by sympathy, the will of three persons.

9. To tell before-hand, the combinations or arrangements of four different numbers, given by any one of the company.

There are several other experiments too tedious to enumerate, which the performer omits mentioning, not wishing to anticipate the pleasure and surprise the company may receive from them.

Every Night entirely New.

The last experiment of this first representation, and with which he will conclude, will be striking and new. The following very surprising experiment, which has been allowed by connoisseurs to be the most astonishing ever exhibited; Signor FALCONI will desire any person to write any question they may please on paper, to be signed by as many of the company as chuse. Any person is at liberty to put it into a loaded pistol, and discharge it out of the Theatre; the performer will neither see or touch the paper, and to the astonishment of the spectators, a DOVE will instantly appear with the answer in his bill.

Admittance. First Seats 8s. Second Seats 5s.

Tickets to be had of Mr. Corre, Mr. Sigismund Hugger, No. 47, Broad way, and the Printer hereof.

[illegible]

[illegible], William-street, [illegible]

SEIGNIOR FALCONI,

Will [illegible] natural and [illegible] experiments; it would be too tedious to [illegible] the many various objects that the first performance consists of.

N. B. The performer begs leave [illegible] that he is the same person who performed in this city in the year 1787, before a most respectable audience of the inhabitants, and having then met with such applause and encouragement, he has reason to believe, that, now having augmented his [illegible] to such a large extent of new experiments and novelty, he will meet still more the approbation and patronage of a generous public.

The following list of some few of his experiments, will give the public a small idea how far he will be deserving and engaging their attention.

A Small AUTOMATON,

In a Turkish Dress, will answer by signs any question put to it; it will also, among several other experiments, guess the number of dice drawn by one of the company, and what is more surprising, any one may draw two or more dice under a hat, and conceal them from any one present, and the figure will tell the number.

Some Experiments in Catoptrics,

Or, appearances produced by the Reflection of Mirrors.

Expulsion by Electricity,

An entire new discovery. To oblige by Sympathy, the will of three persons. To tell before hand, the combination or arrangement of four different numbers, given by any one of the company.

The Penetrating SPY GLASS,

The Sagacious MERMAID.

The Philosophical Piece being in the water, with a Sword in her hand, without any mechanical assistance, will perform several entertaining and instructive experiments. This ingenious discovery has been always the admiration of the learned in Europe; and the exhibitor has great reason to expect it will be equally acceptable to the spectators of this city.

The wonderful experiment of the DOVE.

If the weather permits, the performer will exhibit some Experiments in Electricity, having one of the completest machines and apparatus for that purpose. He has also one Electrical Machine chiefly intended for medical purposes, which will be for the use of such persons who are in want thereof. Also,

He has for sale, several complete Electrical Apparatus, and also mends those that are out of order

The Electrical and Perpetual Lamp,

This singular piece is actuated by the ingenious philosophical discovery of mr. Volta, fully described in Cavello's Treatise on Electricity, viz.

The Electophorus, or Perpetual Electricity, Accompanied with a surprising experiment of the Inflamable Air,

After those performances he will introduce a new kind of amusement, never seen here before, he will shew what pleasing deceptions can be invented by the power of lights, and how far the Capricks can deceive the sight, by a lively appearance of the most magnificent building in London, and other capital cities in Europe, which although the pencil of the painter could not execute, art has prevailed, and to them will be added some curious interludes.

The Result of Hunting a Boar.

With the management of a housekeeper, and the misfortune of the Well.

The Duel between the two Hunters.

With small swords.

The whole to conclude with the appearance of a SHADE, who will dance a Hornpipe in a beautiful room, as well as any dancing Master.

Seignior Falconi requests the ladies and gentlemen who may favor him with their attendance, to attend at the hour appointed, that they may not be disappointed in seeing perhaps the most pleasing performance.

Tickets Six Shillings, to be had of Mr. Gaultier, at the place of performance will begin precisely at half past seven. No money received at the door.

June 22

NEW THEATRE.

At the Assembly Room, William-street,

This Evening, July 7.

SEIGNIOR FALCONI,

Will have among several New Experiments, too numerous to be expressed herein, will be introduced a principal piece, called

A Sympathetic WINDMILL.

Which will work or stop at the command of any of the company, a curious and philosophical discovery of lighting a candle with a card, knife, or sword, without any fire.

The incomparable SWAN, and severals others too tedious to mention.

In the Chinese Shades he will again introduce Carpenter's Work-shop, with some additional improvement, to render the same more conspicuous.

The artful contrivance of Punchinello, disguised as a beggar, for stealing a Wild Boar.

The representation of that terror of Nature, a

THUNDER STORM,

At Sea. There will be seen the swelling of the sea, and the waves rolling with incredible impetuosity; the sky wonderfully covered with clouds; the natural appearance of hail, with its concomitant noise; and a ship in distress, which after a long struggle is dismasted, and goes down. The manoeuvring of the vessel in this dreadful situation will not only excite admiration to the spectators in general, but to every seafaring person present, who must acknowledge the whole calamitous scene to be exceeding natural, and the greatest piece of ingenuity of the kind ever exhibited in this part of the world. All to be accompanied with Thunder and Lightning, so near a resemblance as to astonish the company. After the storm will follow an appearance of all kinds of fish, and the result owing to the loss of the said vessel, which the exhibitor is confident will give entire satisfaction, and a perfect idea of a shipwreck, to such persons who have never seen any thing of the kind.

A DUEL between the Hunters with small swords.

Tickets Six Shillings, to be had of Mr. Gaultier, at the place of Performance, and of Mr. Charles Bernardi, no. 56, Pearl-street. Performance begins at half past seven. No money received at the door.

June 30

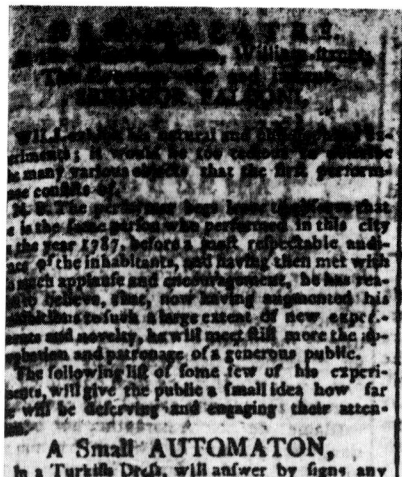

Three advertisements by Signor Falconi in the New York *Daily Advertiser* for (*from left to right*) June 25, 1787, June 22, 1795, and June 7, 1795. (Courtesy, *New York Public Library.*)

Notice in the middle advertisement the reference to Mr. Volta (the celebrated scientist) and to Cavello's (Cavallo's) Treatise on Electricity, a work published in England and well known in the United States.

Signor Falconi kept on coming to the United States as late as 1817. For his last appearance on July 1, he promised a series of optical illusions, including the Hon. James Monroe, president of the U. States, in full length, executed by one of the first painters of the city." Also the conquest of the golden fleece, and "the dance of the witches, with many improvements to render it still more conspicuous."

He may have been the same Charles Falconi whose death in New York was reported by the *Post* on July 8, 1849.

Signor Falconi in all probability was not the first Italian conjurer to perform within the present territory of the United States. As far back as 1602, we read in G. B. Harrison's "The Elizabethan Journals," Italian magicians were entertaining English audiences, as it appears from the following item under date of May 12, 1602: "There is an Italian at Court that doth wonderful strange tricks upon the cards, as telling of any card that is thought, or changing one card from another though it be held by any man never so hard under his hand. The Queen gave him 200 crowns for showing his tricks, and divers gentlemen make meetings for him where he getteth sometimes 20, sometimes 40 crowns, and yet they say he spends it strangely as he cannot keep a penny in his purse." The species, apparently, never changes.

1809

CHARLESTOWN CIRCUS.

THIS EVENING, Sept 6,

MESSRS. PEPIN and BRESCHARD, will have the honor to give their second representation—to commence with the grand Military manœuvres, with additions and alterations.

Mr. Codet and Master Diego, will, after these exercises, execute many astonishing feats of agility, &c.

Mr. Cayetano will make his second appearance, and execute many extraordinary feats of horsemanship, and several tricks with gloves, hat, hoops, &c.

Madam BRESCHARD will make her first appearance, and execute many astonishing and extraordinary attitudes, and after having leaped over several bars with her horse, will execute the great leap through two barrels with hay fire.

The Indian Horse MONARCH, recently trained by Mr. Pepin, will execute, for the first time, the scene of the Domestic Horse.

The comic scene of the MONTEANCIEL, which will be performed, for the first time, by Mr Cayetano.

Mr. BRESCHARD will distinguish himself by several extraordinary feats of horsemanship, will execute different difficult attitudes, &c. and terminate by the great leap over the four Illuminated Galleries.

The comic scene of the Brother Millers will be performed by the whole Company, in which scene the Still Vaulting will be executed.

The whole to be concluded by the infernal Horse, cured by Fire.

☞ Doors to be open at 6 o'clock, and the performance to commence at quarter past seven precisely. Box one dollar, Pit 50 cents, children half price. Tickets for sale at the Circus in Charlestown, and at Domett & Fairbanks, No. 14, Marlboro'-Street, Boston.

☞ LAST WEEK BUT ONE.

CIRCUS—in CHARLESTOWN.

THIS EVENING, Sept 21, will be presented, Grand and brilliant representations, in which Messrs PEPIN & BRESCHARD, and all the Company will distinguish themselves by a variety of new and surprising Feats of HORSEMANSHIP.

To commence by new Military Manœuvres—After the exercises of Mr. Codet and Master Diego Messrs. Pepin and Breschard, mounted on the horses Elegant and Monarch, will execute for the third time, the handsome exercise of the Minuet, and will make their horses execute every step, figure, &c according to that dance. Mr. Cayetano will perform the comic scene of the Drunken Soldier. Madam Breschard will perform many astonishing feats on one horse, and will terminate her exercises, by leaping over several bars, and through two hogsheads with her horse. The famous horse Noble, will, after having leaped over several bars, execute the extraordinary leap over two horses. Mr. Pepin, after having performed many surprising feats of address and agility, will leap over ribbands, his feet tied, and terminate with the extraordinary leap through three hogsheads.

To which will be added, for the first time this season, the Grand Pantomime of

Don Quixote de la Mancha.

Performed on foot and horseback, with combats, marches, &c. with great additions and alterations.

CHARACTERS.

Sancho, Mr. Pepin—Chief of the Robbers, Mr. Breschard—Second Chief, Mr. Cayetano—Don Quixote, Mr. Grain—Suttle Woman, Mr. La Palla—Two Travellers, Messrs. Rannon and Marret—Robbers, Travellers, &c.

The Grand Pantomime of the Battle and Death of General Malbrook, is in preparation

☞ Doors to be opened at 6 o'clock, and the performance to commence at a quarter past 7 precisely.—Box 1 dollar, Pit 50 cents—children half price. Tickets for sale at the Circus in Charlestown, and at *Domett & Fairbanks'*, No. 14, Marlboro' Street.

*** The Public are informed, that the announcing in the last bills and papers, that there would be a performance at the Circus on Saturday evening was a mistake of the person who prepares the bills for the Press. Messrs. Pepin & Breschard being well acquainted with the customs of the Metropolis, would be very sorry to do any thing in violation of them.

LAST TIME BUT ONE. [Sept?]

FOR THE BENEFIT OF MR PEPIN.

CIRCUS IN CHARLESTOWN.

THIS EVENING, Sept 28, will be given, a grand and brilliant representation of HORSEMANSHIP, in which Messrs. *Pepin & Breschard*, and all the Company, will distinguish themselves, so as to render it most agreeable.

A variety of Comic Scenes will be executed, too numerous to particularize in an advertisement.

After which will be presented, for the second time, a Grand, Pantomimic Spectacle, called,

The Battle and Death of General MALBROOK.

Performed on foot and horseback, with a variety of new Manœuvres, Attacks, and single Combats.—The taking of a Fort by assault, and honor rendered to Gen. MALBROOK after his death.

CHARACTERS

Gen. Malbrook, Mr. Pepin—French General, Mr Breschard—Mrs. Malbrook, Mrs. Breschard—Commander of the French troops, Mr. Cayetano—Commander of the English troops, Mr. Grain—First Lieutenant, Mr. Menial—Second, Mr. Codet—Page, Master Diego.

(*For description of the Pantomime, Military Manœuvres, &c. see bills.*)

Messrs. PEPIN & BRESCHARD have the honor to inform the public, that their last performance will take place Tomorrow Evening, 29th Sept. They likewise inform the inhabitants of Boston, that not having received the encouragement that they would have had, on account of the situation of their CIRCUS, they expect to return in two years, when they shall build a BRICK CIRCUS in the centre of the Metropolis, in which they hope to enlarge their company with the most agreeable performers, to give their representations in a splendid style.

☞ Doors to be opened at 6 o'clock, and the

☞ POSITIVELY THE LAST WEEK.

CIRCUS—in CHARLESTOWN.

THE Managers of the Circus, have the honor to inform the inhabitants of Boston and its vicinity, that the Circus will positively close up This Week, and that TO-MORROW EVENING, Sept 26, will be given, a grand representation of HORSEMANSHIP—which will be terminated by the celebrated Battle and death of

General Malbrook.

A Pantomime performed on foot and horseback;—with evolutions, marches, combats, single combats with the lance, sabre, &c. between an English and French general. The surrender of a fort, &c.

The Military manœuvres will be executed by sixty men, well instructed.

The etat major of the two armies, will be by all the Riders that compose the company.

Nothing has been neglected to give this representation all the order and arrangement possible.

All the Soldiers of both armies will have uniforms according to their party.

☞ This brilliant representation will be for the benefit of Mr BRESCHARD.

☞ Doors to be opened at 6 o'clock, and the performance to commence at a quarter past 7 precisely.—Box 1 dollar. Pit 50 cents—children half price. Tickets for sale at the Circus in Charlestown and at *Domett & Fairbanks'*, No. 14, Marlboro' Street.

CIRCUS—in CHARLESTOWN.

POSITIVELY THE LAST NIGHT.

ON account of a number of persons who had tickets on the night of the last performance, and could not get in, Messrs. *Pepin & Breschard* have resolved to give one more representation, TOMORROW EVENING, Oct. 3d, 1809. When will be exhibited a grand and brilliant display of HORSEMANSHIP, for the particulars of which see the bills.

To which will be added, for the second time, the Grand Pantomime of

DON QUIXOTE DE LA MANCHA,

Performed on foot and horseback, with Marches, Combats, &c.—with great additions and alterations.

CHARACTERS.

Sancho, Mr Pepin—Chief of the Robbers, Mr Breschard—Second Chief, Mr Cayetano—Don Quixote, Mr Grain—Travellers, Robbers, &c.

Tickets to be had at the Circus, and at 14, Marlboro-street. Performance to commence at a quarter past 7.

Positively the two last nights in this City.

A genteel Entertainment of Activity.

Wednesday and Friday Evenings, February the 9th and 11th, *At Corre's Hotel, Broad way*,

Mr. DONEGANI's Company

Will perform a Variety of the most curious Feats of Activity, of Tumbling, Leaping, Jumping, Dancing, and Walking on the top of a moving Ladder, &c.

Also, Balancing and Walking on the

W I R E.

The Infant HERCULES,

A boy of seven years of age, will exhibit a variety of attitudes of posture and suppleness, too numerous to detail, never exhibited in this city, and incredible to those who have never been a witness to them.

Also the BLIND FANDANGO, over Eggs, &c.

To conclude with some curious attitudes on the

R O P E.

Tickets one half dollar, children not exceeding twelve years of age one quarter dollar.—The doors will be opened at six o'clock, and the performance to begin at half after six.

Tickets to be had at the place of performance.—A few gallery Tickets, at a quarter dollar.

Mr. Donegani returns his humble thanks to the Ladies and Gentlemen, and to the Public in general.

VIVAT RE PUBLICA.

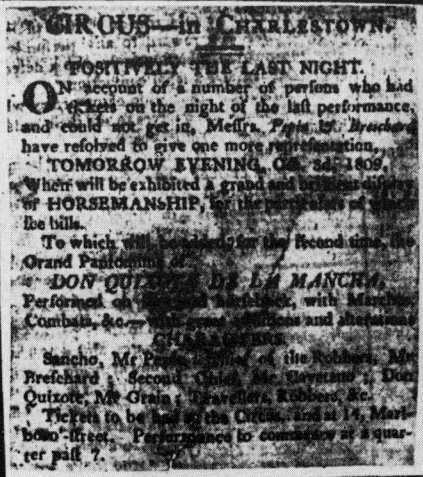

Facsimiles of some playbills announcing Gaetano's Circus in Charlestown (Boston) in 1809. (Courtesy, *Harvard Theater Collection.*) (*In right hand corner*) An announcement of a performance by Donegani's company in the New York *Daily Advertiser*, February 9, 1791. Donegani had appeared in New York as early as 1787. One Giuseppe Donegani died a very rich man at the age of 84 in 1865 at Montreal, where he had lived for half a century. (*Eco d'Italia, Sept.* 16, 1865.) He may have been the Infant HERCULES mentioned above. As for Cayetano (Gaetano Mariottini), in 1816 he was in New Orleans, where he set up his tents on Congo Square (W. A. Roberts, *Lake Pontchartrain*, 1946.) He was manager of the Olympic Circus in New Orleans when he died there on November 2, 1817. (New York *Post*, Dec. 15, 1817.)

MARIETTA ZANFRETTA, THE TIGHT ROPE DANCER
(From a print in the *Harvard Theater Collection.*)

Marietta Zanfretta, a great sensation, made her first New York appearance on Nov. 16, 1857. According to Prof. Odell, her "extraordinary performances on the tightrope are famous unto our own days. . . . Aided by Young America she made the tight rope an instrument of art." She was in New York as late as 1882. Her company included several other Italians.

Marietto and was still in New York at the Classic Museum (252 Broadway) as late as May, 1894. He may have been the conjurer Francesco Orsini, "the most wonderful and extraordinary necromancer living".

In 1847 one Signor Rossi, a "great magician", performed at Palmo's Opera House and at Alhambra Hall. He exhibited feats of skill, assisted by three other entertainers. Another magician, one Signor Miarteni, or Martino, appeared at the New Room, 332 Broadway, Manhattan, in 1848. Still another magician, Leopold Alberti, appeared in New York between 1848 and 1852, exhibiting "5 superhuman delusions" at the corner of Bleecker and Morton streets. In 1851 he was at Stoppani Hall on Chambers street, and in 1852 at Niblo Gardens, 598 Broadway. Some of those magicians may have not been Italian, for the appellative of "signor" was used freely in the profession by men of all nationalities.

ACROBATS, EQUILIBRISTS AND CLOWNS

Aside from the Italian clowns, who have been for several generations among the finest pantomimists in Europe and America (from Grimaldi to the Fratellini brothers), Italian acrobats have performed in the United States almost uninterruptedly since the Revolution. One can find most of their names in Odell's *Annals.*

Before 1800, a "Young Florentine" performed "several surprising Feats of Activity" in New York in 1791. Also in 1791 one Donegani and his "Infant HERCULES" made their appearance in New York. (See facsimile on page 205.) Two years before they had appeared in Salem, Mass.

Between 1794 and 1797 one Signor Spinacuta, a tightrope walker and music player (he was a very adaptable musician), was active in New York.

At the turn of the century, one Signor Manfredi promised New Yorkers "various feats never performed by any other person, calculated to surprize the spectator, and which have been pronounced the first of its kind ever exhibited in London, Paris, Madrid, Lisbon, Petersburgh, Constantinople, or any other of the various Capitals and Courts at which the performances have been exhibited." He was assisted by his wife and other fellow-Italians. At one of his performances he promised to "eat his supper on the Rope,

DONETTI'S ANIMAL SHOW

Donetti, like other vaudeville performers, toured the country. In the 1850's he was in New Orleans, where, according to Mrs. Catherine Gibbs, the author of a book on the Italians in New Orleans, he published a little book on monkeys. It had plates and sold for ten cents.

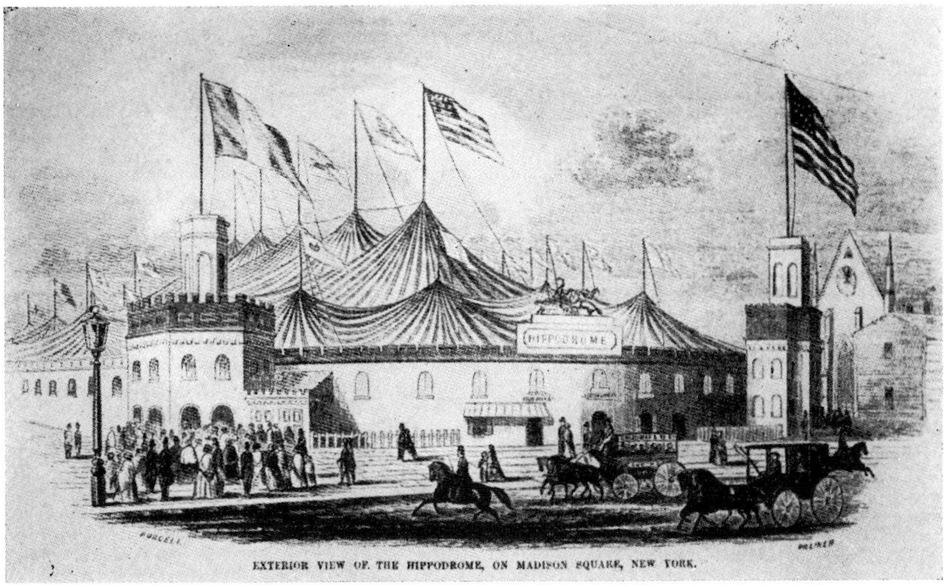

Franconi's Hippodrome on Madison Square, New York City, covered two acres of ground, with a front on Broadway 22 feet wide, extending backwards so as to occupy nearly the entire block. The company included 150 persons and 100 horses. Financially it was a success, "strangers from far and near thronging to witness the exhibition."

(From *Gleason's Pictorial. Drawing Room Companion,* June 18, 1853.) Franconi's Hippodrome, the greatest amusement place of its kind New York had ever seen, was opened on May 2, 1853, and remained opened until 1856. Franconi came from France, but the family hailed from Udine, Italy, where the first emigrant, Antonio Franconi, was born in 1737. (Hillemacher, F., *Le Cirque Franconi, Lyon,* 1875; *Lyonnet, Dictionnaire des Comediens Francais,* 2 vols.; Baron de Vaux, *Les Hommes de Cheval,* Paris, 1888.)

JIMMY DURANTE

with table, chair, bottles, glasses, and every other necessary convenience—he rises from the table quite intoxicated, and displays the most astonishing Feats of Equilibrium ever exhibited here." He called his house on Broadway. "The Italian Theater" and appeared in New York between 1803 and 1812.

The first Italian manager of a circus in the United States seems to have been one Gaetano Mariottini, who performed in Boston in 1808 and later in New Orleans, where he died in 1817. (See facsimiles on page 205.)

A juggler of some note who was in Albany in 1834 and later in New York, at first under the name of Signor Antonio and eventually as Vivalla, helped Barnum to replenish his coffers. He was balancing plates and other articles with bayonets on his nose, keeping ten plates in motion at a time, when Barnum engaged him at $12 a week, but he became so popular that the famous showman hired him out to another theater at $150 per week.

After some years in the United States, Vivalla moved to Cuba, where he was struck by paralysis and reduced to poverty, until Jenny Lind, who had gone to Havana for a concert with Barnum, was moved by his pittiful condition and gave a performance for his benefit so as to make possible his return to Italy. The poor man, however, died a few month later, (Barnum, *Struggles and Triumphs,* 1882, 322-325.)

The most famous circus brought to America in the 1850's was Franconi's Hippodrome, on Madison Square, in New York City, as illustrated on page 206. A few years later Marietta Zanfretta created a sensation with her performances on the tight rope. (See page 206.)

The story could go on to fill many pages, until we come to the circus performers of our own days, like the Christiani family, the Zacchinis, or Massimiliano Truzzi(the man who made Stalin laugh). Among those who passed away in the United States in recent years, we may recall Arnold Larchmont Novello, one of the world's greatest clown and later a noted vaudeville star, and Frederick Riccobono, who was born in Hungary of Italian parentage and died here in 1946.

PUPPET SHOWS AND ANIMAL ACTS

It is possible that Italian puppet shows were brought over in colonial times from England, where a few were given at Covent Garden before 1667, as we learn from the diary of Samuel Pepys. At any rate, the first record we have found in America is about one Dominique Vitali and Company "artists from Italy", who performed at the Roman Theatre in New York in the summer of 1819. Their puppets drank, ate, smoked and acted in other ways.

Since then we have had Vito's Fantoccini in 1829, Vivildi's figures, Rinaldi's mechanical figures, Grimaldi's Automaton Performers, Jeronelli's Marionettes, and the Italian Marionettes and Miniature Theater from Paris which appeared at the Stuyvesant Institute in 1865. Barnum also presented Italian puppet shows between 1842 and 1847.

In our own days, we have had Podrecca's marionettes which came from Italy in 1933, and, more recently, the puppet theaters conducted by Remo Bufano, Manteo, and Salici. Bufano was the victim of an air crash in 1948.

As for animal acts, besides Donetti's (see the preceding page), we may recall Bertolotti's trained fleas which drove mills, drew carriages and did other acts. Both of them were active a century ago.

VAUDEVILLE STARS

Although there have been scores of comedians and actors of Italian birth or extraction in vaudeville during the last century, only four, so far as we know, have risen to stardom: Jefferson De Angelis, Arnold Novello, Jimmy Savo and Jimmy Durante.

De Angelis, a famous comedian, was on the stage for sixty years until his retirement in 1930. He was born in San Francisco in 1859. The grandson of a Corsican immigrant, he died in 1933. We have already noted Arnold Novello. Jimmy Savo is best-known as a leading pantomimist. Jimmy Durante, of course, needs no introduction as one of the top vaudeville, radio and television stars of our generation.

FROM ELIZABETH MATHEWS TO ELEONORA DUSE

Aside from the opera stars, many of whom have been both excellent singers and superb actors, only a few actors of Italian birth or origin have appeared on the American stage. But those few have exerted an influence on the American drama which is beyond evaluation.

It would seem that some minor actors of Italian descent came over from London shortly after the Revolution, but their importance in our opinion did not warrant further research. Not so, however, with Elizabeth Mathews, even if her American appearances were not a success.

ELIZABETH MATHEWS

Mrs. Mathews, the granddaughter of the famous engraver, Francesco Bartolozzi, and the daughter of Gaetano Bartolozzi, an indolent fellow who operated a dancing academy in Paris, was born in London in 1797, where she appeared both as a singer in opera, and as an actress in English plays at Drury Lane. She came to America in 1838, but her husband, the actor Charles James Mathews, antagonized the American public and their tour ended in disaster. Her sister, Josephine (Mrs. Joshua Anderson) had a similar experience because of her husband's attitude towards the American people, who chased him out of the country.

At any rate, as students of the theater know, Elizabeth Mathews exerted a great influence on the American drama, through the innovations she brought on the English stage. (See her biographical sketch in the *Encyclopedia Britannica* or any history of the English stage. See also *The Witch of Wyck Street* by Leo Waitzkin, 1933.)

ELIZABETH MATHEWS
"As an actress she certainly stands alone. . . . Everything which she attempts seems at once stamped with the utmost finish of art." (*Knickerbocker Magazine*, New York, October, 1838.)

ADELAIDE RISTORI AS ELIZABETH QUEEN OF ENGLAND
In Giacometti's play by that title. "The role of Elizabeth was one of the most difficult for me, because in portraying that character I had to bring all my art into play." (*Memoirs and Artistic Studies of Adelaide Ristori,* New York, 1907, p. 73.)

ADELAIDE RISTORI

Few foreign actors in America, if any, have achieved the success scored by Adelaide Ristori during her three tours of 1866-1867, 1875-1876, and 1884-1885. "The advent of Ristori (in 1866) was by far the most important theatrical event that New York City had ever witnessed, and words fail to describe the furore and eclat with which the greatest living actress of the time was received. Months before, Grau (Jacob Grau, under whose management she appeared in America) had posted her portraits and spread her biography broadcast, and at the opening of the advance sale a scene, heretofore unrecordable in the annals of the box office took place. The night preceding the opening of the box office, no less than one thousand persons had remained all night in line". (Robert Grau, *Forty Years Observation of Music and the Drama,* New York, 1909, 57-

TOMMASO SALVINI AS MACBETH

"He (Edwin Booth) held in great esteem his brother-artist and friend, Tommaso Salvini, with whom he had acted, and whose farewell speech to the Senate in 'Othello' he thought unequalled in poetic beauty and musical cadence, and whose scene with Jago in the third act he considered the most powerful acting on our modern stage." (*Recollections of My Father,* by Edwin Booth Grossman, 1896, p. 16.)

THE ILLUSTRATED WEEKLY

PURE. INSTRUCTIVE. AMUSING.

Entered according to Act of Congress in the year 1874 by CHAS. CLUCAS & CO., in the office of the Librarian of Congress at Washington.

VOL. II—NO. 3. {A LARGE ENGRAVING SUPPLEMENT FREE WITH EVERY NUMBER.} NEW YORK, SATURDAY, JANUARY 15, 1876. {SUBSCRIPTION, $3.00 PER YEAR WITH CHROMO FREE.} SINGLE COPIES, 8 Cts.

THE CHARACTER OF HAMLET.

Surely, everybody must be interested in the play of Hamlet. Above all other creations in literature it embodies passages of self-analysis and suggestions of the deep mysteries of human life. It appeals to the universal consciousness.

While there is matter to engage the attention in all the characters of this greatest of dramas, yet the poet has so harmoniously subordinated these in their various positions relative to his who is the subject of the play, that, like the planets in the solar system, they, so to speak, revolve around him, the sun—the centre of influence. In reflecting upon the play, after the thoughtful reading of it, our meditations culminate in him. Regarded separately, several characters in the drama are profoundly interesting; in the contemplation of his bewilderments and woes, and the depth of his reflections, they are lost sight of, excepting only, as in the details of a portrait, they contribute to the effect of the portraiture of the young prince.

In our remarks upon Shakspeare's masterpiece, we shall, on the present occasion, restrict them exclusively to its principal character.

With respect to Hamlet's character and actions there has been a world of controversy from the time of Dr. Johnson down to the present day. The very fact of the existence of such a controversy among men of great critical ability is, of itself, sufficient proof that the subject is not free from difficulties. The phenomena of the play, so far as they are connected with Hamlet himself, must have some elements that are in real or apparent conflict with each other, in order to account for the diverse and irreconcilable judgments which have been formed concerning them. In many of the criticisms, we believe, there is a fatal flaw arising from a narrow and false philosophy of human nature itself; and in the criticism of Shakspeare pre-eminently an error of this kind will vitiate the whole. Man is a polygon of forces—the most central force of all being his will, which constitutes the very pith of his personality, and to which all other forces are more or less related. Of all the creations of Shakspeare we venture to express our conclusion that none can compare with Hamlet in the multitude of the influences under which he acted or refrained from action, and in the subtlety with which these influences operated within him; and we have every opportunity offered us of entering into the innermost recesses of his being in those numerous soliloquies in which Hamlet throws off every concealment, and reveals himself in his own language just as he feels himself to be. In these monologues Hamlet puts a window in his breast, and if we cannot read him there he must remain a mystery that will baffle the critical sphinx forever. What Hamlet was before his father's death we can learn only from incidental observations which fell from his own lips or those of others. Physically he has been traditionally misrepresented as a thin, pale man, worn down with thought and man, and that, in fact, his temperament was insuperably morbid, we have seen no proof in the play itself. The shock which was given to his whole nature by the death of his father, which he afterwards learned to be of so tragical a character, and the event which followed so close upon its heels, the marriage of his mother with the detestable fratricide, created a moral revolution within him, and shrouded his soul with a gloom to which it had been a stranger hitherto. His mother expostulated with him upon his morbid deportment in a manner which clearly shows that it was not natural to row upon a nature which, like that of Hamlet, was tender and reflective in a degree which almost wholly paralyzed his power of action. Such a calamity leaves no true, deep nature as it finds it. The fact of his mother's marriage with his uncle, two months after his father's death, was a still more intolerable grief—his mother, whom, until then, he had regarded as the most perfect type of woman on earth.

To all this must be added that Hamlet was by this proceeding cut off from succeeding to the throne; shocked, wounded, disappointed and sad- solemnly sworn that the fell deed should meet a befitting retribution, he hastens to find the king. No, he hastens to nothing. He cannot hasten. You expect that after the ghostly revelation he has just heard, and the vows he has uttered, that before another sun has set the murderer will have been discovered and sent to his account. For what hindered? His cause was dear and just. The king was accessible at any moment, and daggers were always at hand. Few young men at that day, and perhaps few still who have been disinherited, wronged, robbed of the noblest of parents by an

> As 'Well, well, we know,' or 'We could, an if we would;'
> Or, 'If we list to speak,' or 'There be, an if they might,'
> Or such ambiguous giving out, to note
> That you know ought of me: this not to do,
> So peace and mercy at your most need help you,
> Swear—"

The language we have just quoted gives the very genesis of his deliberate plot, and if more evidence were needful to complete the proof of his simulation, it is supplied by his language to his mother after the ghost has appeared to whet his blunted purpose to revenge his father's murder.

We come next to consider the motive which prompted him to simulate a disordered mind. By some critics it has been deemed to be purposeless. Such an imputation on the genius of Shakspeare we should be disposed to resent, even if the purpose lay too deep for our detection. The authority of the dramatist would carry it, with us at least, over the sagacity, or the kindness of his critics. The motive we believe to be twofold: first, for the purpose of enabling him to ascertain by facts palpable to his own senses the truth of the supernatural communication he had received from the ghost, that his uncle had been his father's murderer; and secondly, for the purpose of enabling him to break off his connection with Ophelia in such a manner as should reconcile her to the loss of a madman for a husband. Some of the critics have but insufficiently considered the profound and insatiable skepticism which was one of the chief characteristics of Hamlet's mind. While the ghost is before him, he believes in him; but when he has disappeared his faith wanes and wanes until at length, while he does not doubt that he has seen the ghost, he doubts whether it be the veritable spirit of his father. His plan, therefore, is to extort, if possible, from the very look or lips of the king himself, the confession of his crime: "I'll have grounds more relative than this."

As to Hamlet's long hesitation in putting his promise of revenge to the ghost into execution, he was a person of weak resolution, one who could not make up his mind which to choose of two courses, and consequently chose neither. He was the victim not so much of feebleness of will as of an intellectual indifference that hinders the will from working long in any one direction. He was capable of passionate energy where the occasion presented itself suddenly from without, but incapable of deliberate energy; the blade of his analysis being so subtle that it divided the finest hair of motive, leaving him desperate to choose.

Hamlet was a man—nor assuredly was he the only man—to whom the moment for action never came. He was looking for an open door of opportunity, and when it stood before him he began with new subtleties of speculation. He must fain persuade himself that he was but waiting for the tide to sail direct to his purpose; the tide rolled in free and deep, but Hamlet dare not unloose the cable. His hand was on it, but new doubts or schemes distracted him, and while he was busy with them the ebb came, and he was left dry on the shore again. This pre-

HAMLET—ERNESTO ROSSI

"His figure is not great, but well-formed; his face has not what is called plastic beauty, but it breathes sweetness and a somewhat sensuous grace. The mobility of his features is surprising, and allows of his transforming himself according to his role to the extent of not being recognized. His eyes are black, but they have not that brilliant color peculiar to the Italian. They are more liquid, and express rather tenderness than rage. When he is before the scenes, Rossi seems absolutely to lose the sentiment of his personality. He speaks, he walks, he looks, he listens, and never a word, never a step, never a look or a gesture, except according to his role. The incarnation is veritably complete. We have never seen the phenomena carried to this point. We do not think it could go beyond." (*The Illustrated Weekly,* New York, January 15, 1876, 18.)

58.) Grau made a profit of over $150,000 on her first season alone and from the sale of the librettos the management made a profit of more than $1,300 a week. As the New York *Tribune* declared on September 21, 1866, the day after her debut in *Medea*, "She is worlds in advance of any woman on the American or English stage".

Thirty-six years later, on the occasion of her 80th birthday, "even children sent me pressed flowers with best wishes, saying they had never seen me, but their mothers or grandmothers had, and had told them about me", as she related in her interview. (*The Theatre,* September 1905, 212.)

Ristori, it should be pointed out, acted in Italian, supported by an Italian-speaking cast, before an American public that could hardly understand a word she was saying. In 1885 she appeared with Edwin Booth, with an English cast, and in her performance of Schiller's *Mary Stuart* even with a German cast. During that last tour she visited sixty-two American cities.

ERMETE NOVELLI AS SHYLOCK
"In versatility and facile technic the Italian virtuoso knew more in a minute, as the saying goes, than most of our actors would in a thousand years" (Arthur Ruhl, *Second Nights,* New York, 1914, p. 47.)

TOMMASO SALVINI

Tommaso Salvini was another giant of the theater who appeared on the American stage, always in Italian, at times supported by an Italian cast, and later, with Edwin Booth, Clara Morris and an English-speaking cast. He visited the United States on five different occasions between 1873 and 1889, touring the country as far as Chicago and New Orleans. During his 1880 tour he was invited to visit the House of Representatives in Washington, causing the suspension of its activities, with the Speaker and all members of Congress rising from their chairs to applaud him. He was supreme in Shakespearean roles, particularly in *Othello.*

His son, Alexander, also appeared in America, in English, together with his wife, Maud Dixon Salvini, who died in New York in 1944. He died in 1896.

ERNESTO ROSSI AND ERMETE NOVELLI

Two more famous actors who appeared on the American stage, acting, as Ristori and Salvini did, also in Italian, were Ernesto Rossi and Ermete Novelli.

Rossi, one of the greatest interpreters of Hamlet ever born, came to America in 1881 and appeared in New York in various Shakespearean roles. He died in 1896, at the age of 68.

Novelli, one of the great actors of our century, came to America in 1907 but he did not meet with financial success because of poor management. However, he was welcomed by the members of the theatrical profession. (See *Theatre,* March and April, 1907.) Like Salvini and Rossi, he, too, was superb in Shakespearean roles.

ELEONORA DUSE

Eleonora Duse came to the United States in 1893, 1896, 1902-1903, and 1924, but she was not able to complete her last tour, for she died in Pittsburgh on April 21, 1924.

During her second tour, President and Mrs. Cleveland attended all her performances in Washington and gave a luncheon and a special performance in her honor at the White House, a privilege which they did not extend to Sarah Bernhardt, who was also appearing in America in those very days. She acted in Italian. With the exception of her third tour, when she appeared in D'Annunzio's plays, she received wide acclaim.

OTHER ACTORS

Other noted Italian actors appeared in America during the first quarter of our century, including Giovanni Grasso and Angelo Musco, both of whom acted in Sicilian. In more recent years, Mimi Aguglia, Maria Bazzi, Marta Abba and Giuseppe Sterni have appeared on both the Italian-language and English-speaking stage. All four of them are in the United States, still active, with the exception of Miss Abba, who has retired from the theater, so far as we know.

Numerous minor actors of Italian origin have performed in English-language plays for many years past. One

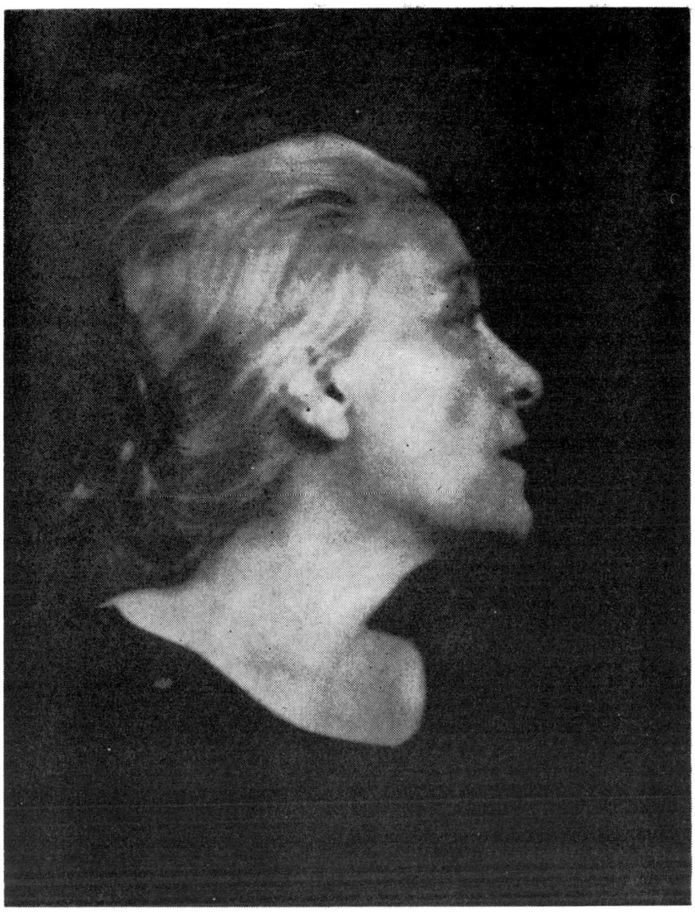

ELEONORA DUSE
"It will take one Clara Morris and one Sarah Bernhardt put together to make one Duse in the role of Marguerite Gautier in 'La Dame aux Camelias.'" (*New York Sun,* 1896.)

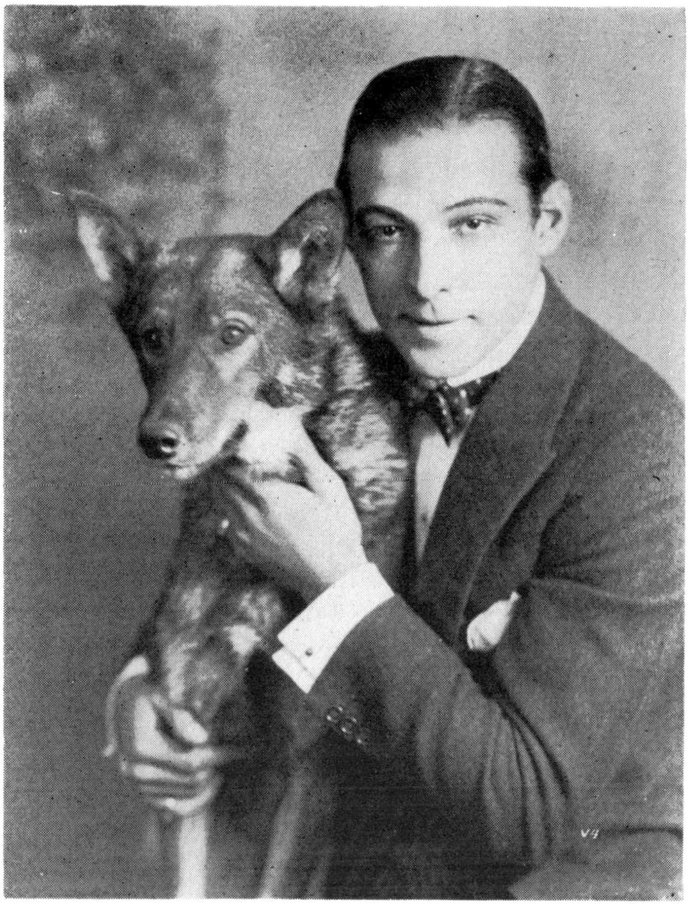

RUDOLPH VALENTINO

of the earliest, Adelina Gasparini (Adelina Ligon), was active on the New York stage in the 1870's. She died in New York in 1882. (*Eco d'Italia,* February 26, 1882.)

IN MOTION PICTURES

The greatest Italian name in American motion pictures is still Rudolph Valentino, who died in 1926. Some of his pictures are still revived from time to time.

Other motion picture actors of Italian birth or origin have been, or are, Arnold Kent (Lido Manetti), who died in 1928; Monti Banks (Mario Bianchi) who died in 1950; Bull Montana (Luigi Montagna), who died also in 1950; Elissa Landi and Henry Armetta, both of whom died a few years ago; Isa Miranda, Don Ameche, Hank Luisetti, Eduardo Cianelli, Leni Lynn(Angelina Ciofani), Lou Costello, Alida Valli, Pier Angeli, and a host of minor ones. Jackie Cooper, Alice White, Dolores Del Rio, Jean Harlow, and Evelyn Brent are said to be or to have been, partly Italian.

MOTION PICTURE DIRECTORS

Among the directors, four men stand out: Frank Capra, Frank Borzaghe, Robert Vignola and Gregory LaCava. Capra, the winner of several Academy awards, is one of the most famous directors in motion picture annals. But then there is a host of cameramen, technicians, music arrangers, scenic artists, and others whose names can be easily found in the *Motion Picture Almanac*.

FRANK CAPRA

CHAPTER FIFTEEN

IN THE WORLD OF ART

The independence of the United States prompted several Italian artists to come to America. The heroic deeds which had made it possible and the men who distinguished themselves during the struggle, obviously deserved to be immortalized on canvas and in marble. The new middle class needed artistic decorations and marble pieces for its homes and its theatres, and who could, better than the Italians, provide them? "Having understood the taste for the fine arts is rapidly increasing in these happy states they resolved to quit Italy, and to try to satisfy the respectable citizens of America, by their production." Thus two painters, Joseph Perovani and Jacint Cocchi, of the Republic of Venice, announced their recent arrival in the *Federal Gazette* of Philadelphia on September 19, 1775.

Between 1792 and 1799, aside from Medici, who came before the Revolution, at least nine painters and sculptors arrived from Italy. They were Ceracchi, Corne', Perovani, Cocchi, Rossetti, Bartoli, Iardella, Pise and Ancora. We do not include Ciceri, who was not a professional painter, nor Stagi, who was primarily an art dealer.

The portico of Trinity Church in New York City showing the Montgomery monument by J. J. Caffieri.

CAFFIERI

The first work of art by an artist of Italian blood to be erected in the United States was the monument in memory of Major General Richard Montgomery, who fell at the battle of Quebec in 1775. The first national monument erected in the country, it is in the Broadway portico of Trinity Church in New York City.

Jean Jacques Caffieri (1775-1792) was the grandson of Filippo Caffieri, a native of Rome, who was called to Paris by Mazarin. He also made a fine bust of Franklin. He never came to the United Ssates.

COSMO MEDICI

We have already met Cosmo Medici as a captain of the North Carolina Light Dragoons during the Revolution, and we have seen that he was in America at least between 1767 and 1788. Whether he was an itinerant painter before he became a soldier is hard to say, but we doubt it. By him only two portraits are known, both of which came to light on the occasion of an exhibition held at Virginia House in Richmond, not many years ago. Others may yet be found among the family heirlooms carried to the four corners of the United States by descendants of Virginia pioneers.

One of the two known Medici portraits, that of Lucy C. Briggs painted in 1772, is reproduced on the next page. To judge by our black and white photograph it looks like the work of an amateur, although if it had been painted by a native American or by some English immigrant it would occupy a prominent place among our so-called primitives, like the contortions and distortions of a Edward Hicks whose lions and "Kingdom of Peace" are imposed upon undiscerning readers as art, with "critics" and "connoisseurs" waxing sentimental about him; just as they have waxed sentimental and written volumes on the limners of a century before, whose work, as Prof. Hagen has well said, is "comparable, at best, to fifth-rate English provincial productions." (Hagen, O., *The Birth of American Tradition in Art,* N. Y., 1940, p. 15.) One does not need tio be an art critic, indeed, to agree with Mr. Saint-Gaudens that "these limners simply did not know much" (Saint-Gaudens, H., *The American Artist and His Times,* New York, 1941, p. 14) and to become aware that they simply painted as children have always painted and will always paint in any country.

Portrait of Lucy G. Briggs by Cosmo (or Cosimo) Medici. (Courtesy of *Virginia House and Mrs. John A. Coke, Jr. of Richmond, Va., owner of the painting.*)

We dwell on this point, at the very beginning of the present chapter, not to criticize anybody's taste (de gustibus non est disputandum) but because it is simply sickening to see pretentious works like the *Dictionary of American Biography* or Oliver W. Larkins *Art and Life in America* (New York, 1949) give so much space to men whose works educated Europeans would be ashamed to keep in their cellars, and completely ignore really fine paintings and sculptures by Italian-American artists.

Lest some one should try to defend their selections on the ground that those volumes deal with "American" art ists, let us reassure our readers that natives of foreign lands, even if they never became American citizens, have been included whenever the editors or compilers found it convenient. In the 20 volumes of the *Dictionary of American Biography* only two Italians are included, both foreign born; as for Mr. Larkin's work, it may be sufficient to mention that is contains not one word about Brumidi!

Getting back to Medici, to judge by the work of his contemporaries in Italy (Piazzetta, for one) he was only a third-rate painter, but it is possibile that one must see his portrait in order to discover qualities not easily discernible in black and white. According to A. W. Weddell, the "laboriously applied pigment manages to conserve a veraciousness and a feeling of character which rise superior to mere quaintness." (Weddell, *Virginia Historical Portraiture,* Richmond, 1930, p. XXX.)

Whatever the value of Medici's portraits, there is one point which we would like to stress for the benefit of future historians. Medici did not leave "a somewhat cloudy record in the Revolutionary war," as Virgil Barker states in his *American Painting,* (New York, 1950, p. 162), enlarging on an innocuous and correct statement in Weddell's book. Such kind of writing is both unfair and irresponsible. One cannot charge a soldier with cowardice or misconduct without taking the trouble of looking into the facts. Medici was a hero at Brandywine and Princeton. (For further particulars, see *ante,* Chapter Ten.)

CERACCHI

Giuseppe Ceracchi was "unquestionably an artist of the first class," as Thomas Jefferson informed the Commissioners of Washington in a letter dated April 9, 1792. He was born in Rome in 1751, but by 1775 he was in London, where he was commissioned to execute several statues for the old Somerset House and several busts, including those of Lord Shelbourne, Admiral Keppel, Sir Joshua Reynolds, now in the Royal Academy, and one of Mrs. Damer which now stands in the vestibule of the British Museum. (Whitley, W. T., *Artists and Their Friends in England,* 1928, I, 317.) From London he then went to Holland and later to Vienna, where he received a few orders from Maria Theresa and Emperor Joseph II. Back in Rome in 1785, he made the busts of Pope Pius VI, Cardinal Albani, Metastasio, and Winckelman. In 1790 he was back in Amsterdam, where he obtained a letter of introduction to Thomas Jefferson from the banking house of N. and J. Van Staphorst. Since that letter was dated October 11, 1790, it would seem that Ceracchi came to America towards the end of that year, or early in 1791, when he was in Philadelphia. On January 20, 1792, he

Trumbull's portrait of Ceracchi. (Courtesy, *Yale University Art Gallery.*)

was elected a member of the American Philosophical Society. Two months later he went to New York with two letters of introduction to Chancellor Livingston, one from Jefferson (March 6, 1792) and the other from his fellow-countryman, Count Andreani. On March 25 of the same year Jefferson gave Ceracchi another letter of introduction, this time to John Hancock.

Four months later he was back in Holland, as we learn from two letters he wrote to George and Martha Washington from Amsterdam on July 16, 1792. In 1793 he wrote to Jefferson from Munich offering him the bust he had made of him. A year later he was once more in the United States, for in March, 1794, he asked Jefferson for more letters of introduction. As his plans did not materialize, in March, 1795, he returned to Europe. There he took part in the French revolutionary movement siding with Napoleon at first, but plotting against him as soon as he became convinced that the great Corsican was not interested in the independence of Italy. Because of that plot he lost his head on the guillotine on January 30, 1802.

Ceracchi's American activities deserve a special monograph, for there is plenty of material about him in American archives, especially in the Washington and Jefferson papers in the manuscript division of the Library of Congress. He had come to America primarily to erect a national monument in honor of George Washington and the other leaders in the Revolution. The monument was to be one hundred feet high, with a Goddess of Liberty, as Ceracchi stated in his announcement, "represented descending in a car drawn by four horses, darting through a volume of clouds which conceals the summit of a rainbow.

Ceracchi's marble medallion of James Madison.

Her form is at once expressive of dignity and peace. In her right hand she brandishes a flaming dart, which by dispelling the mists of error, illuminates the universe; her left is extended in the attitude of calling upon the people of America to listen to her voice."

The main figure, of course, was to be that of George Washington, surrounded by the men who took part in the War of Independence. To that end, Ceracchi asked a number of men to sit for him, and actually made 37 models of the great men of America. Washington sat for him early in 1792, and so did Jefferson, Madison, Hamilton, John Paul Jones, John Jay, George Clinton, David Rittenhouse, and others. Later, when the plan did not materialize, Ceracchi asked the men who had posed for him, whether they wanted to purchase the busts he had made of them. Jefferson and a few others accepted the offer and paid the sculptor. Washington, however, refused to accept his bust as a gift and offered to pay for it, but Ceracchi resented the tone of Washington's reply (in Washington's own handwriting, but signed and sent in the name of his secretary, Bartholomew Dandridge) and took the bust back.

It is said that the bust was then sold to the Spanish minister in Philadelphia, Jaudenes, who sent it to Spain, as a present to Godoy, the Spanish prime minister. At any rate, it is now in the Metropolitan Museum of Art of New York. In the Gibbes Art Gallery of the Carolina Art Association of Charleston, however, there is another bust of Washington which is said to be also by Ceracchi, apparently the bust mentioned by Appleton in his letter to Jefferson from Leghorn, dated April 15, 1816. In connection with that bust, it is interesting to recall a letter dated March 1, 1793, from Amsterdam, Holland, quoted in the *New York Magazine, or Literary Repository* for May, 1793, pp. 317-318. According to it "The celebrated sculptor, Mr. Ceracchi, who returned from America last summer, arrived at Rome, and soon after his arrival commenced the sculpture of the bust of the President of the United States. The populace being informed thereof surrounded his house and threatened him with destruction. He providentially made his escape and has since arrived safely at Munich." Why the Rome populace should have tried to harm him is not clear.

It has been said also that Ceracchi in order to meet his debts had given his creditors notes for the busts "for which he had already been paid" (*William and Mary Quarterly*, January 1945, pp. 73-74). Such an impression is not well founded. Even a cursory reading of the correspondence about Ceracchi in the Jefferson and Washington papers in the Library of Congress should be sufficient to show that nobody paid the sculptor a penny and that although he made those busts at his own request, so that they could be used in the monument he was planning (Ceracchi to Clinton, Vienna, August 25, 1792, *Emmett Collection*, New York Public Library) nobody was under any obligation to pay for them. Later, when Ceracchi's dream was shattered, he asked the various men whose busts he had made whether they wanted to keep them and pay for them,

Bust of George Washington by Ceracchi. (Courtesy, *Metropolitan Museum of Art, New York City.*)

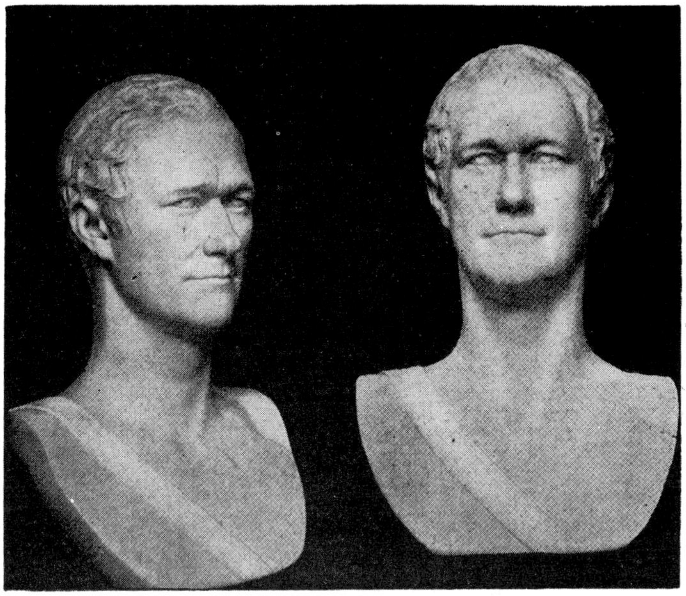

Two views of Ceracchi's marble bust of Hamilton in the New York Public Library.

Terracotta bust of George Clinton by Ceracchi. (Courtesy, *New York Historical Society.*)

Plaster bust of John Jay by Ceracchi. (Courtesy, *New York Historical Society.*)

as we have already pointed out. (See the letters by Ceracchi's widow in the Library of Congress, Dec. 31, 1802, March 10, 1805, July 5, 1805; also Appleton to Jefferson, July 5, 1805, and April 15, 1816.)

The monument, at any rate, was never erected because, as the sculptor stated in a letter to Washington dated March 28, 1795, "malicious ignorance has attacked my project" and "I am the innocent victim of intrigue" (Ceracchi to Dandridge, April 28, 1795, and to Jefferson, March 11, 1795, MS. *Library of Congress.*) His plan, however, had met with the approval of several men, including George Washington himself, who had taken four shares, for the sum of $120.00. Jefferson was in favor of it. "I have seen the model of the monument in honor of the Revolution," wrote John Jay to Egbert Benson, the first president of the New York Historical Society, on March 31, 1792. "The design appears to me to be a noble one, worthy of the attention of the United States, and honorable to the taste and talents of the artist. I think the expense proper . . . I confess to you that the effort which the measure would naturally have on the President's feelings is with me an additional inducement . . . It is only while he lives that we can have the satisfaction of offering fruits of gratitude and affection to his enjoyment; prosperity can have only the expensive pleasure of strewing flowers on his grave." (Johnston, H. P., *The Correspondence and Public Papers of John Jay,* Vol. III, pp. 417-418.)

Dejected and disgusted, after wasting a considerable amount of money and labor, in May, 1795, Ceracchi sailed for France, where seven years later he was to be executed on a public square with Arona, Le Brun and other plotters.

Ceracchi's busts, however, remain among the finest works of art ever modelled in America. Of his bust of Hamilton, for instance, it has been said that "It has been Hamilton's good fortune that his lineaments have gone down ennobled by the genius of Ceracchi and that solemn and majestic face, which would have not been particularly striking under any ordinary hand, is literally part of his fame. (Elson, H. W., *History of the United States of America,* N. Y. 1905, Vol. II, p. XI.) Engravings of Ceracchi's bust of Hamilton were made by Leney in 1815 and Durand in 1879. General Trumbull made a painting of Hamilton, but he did not succeed and he copied Ceracchi's bust. Trumbull, however, made a fine miniature portrait of Ceracchi, which is now in the Yale Collection of Art.

Even if we did not have the Hamilton busts (there are at least four of them, one in the New York Public Library, one in the Federal Museum at Wall and Nassau streets in New York, one in the New York Historical Society, and one the property of the Hon. Andrew J. Sordoni of Wilkes-Barre, Secretary of Commerce of Pennsylvania), those of Madison, Clinton, Jay and Washington should be sufficient to show that Ceracchi was an eminent sculptor. Some art connoisseurs even prefer him to Houdon.

Yet there is something else which should endear Ceracchi to Americans. While in Philadelphia in 1791 and 1792, Ceracchi, William Rush, and Charles Willson Peale tried "to form a collection of paintings and sculptures and to found a school of art." From this school, established by Peale, descended the "Columbianum" which in 1805 gave way to The Pennsylvania Academy of the Fine Arts. (Henderson, H. W., *The Pennsylvania Academy of the Fine Arts,* Boston, 1891, pp. 1-2.)

PHILIP A. PETICOLAS

There is some doubt regarding the nationality of Philip A. Peticolas, (1760-1841), one of the earliest and most prolific miniature painters in Richmond. Most authorities state that he was born in Italy, but, according to some records in the Valentine Museum in Richmond, he was born at Mezières, France. We do not know whether he was one of the so many Italians born in France of Italian parentage. The Peticolas family was prominent in educational activities in Virginia during the first half of the nineteenth century. His grandson, Arthur E. Peticolas, was a demonstrator of anatomy as early as 1849 and a professor of medicine in 1855. (Blanton, W. B., *Medicine in Virginia in the 19th Century,* 1933.) Philip is said to have painted a miniature of George Washington from life.

MICHELE FELICE CORNE'

Corne', a Neapolitan, is said to have come to America at the suggestion of the famous Salem merchant, Elias Hasket Derby, in 1799, if not before, if the date 1794 on the ship "Belisarius" now in the Essex Institute, is that of the year he painted it.

Corne' lived in Salem for several years, and then in Boston until 1822, when he moved to Newport, R. I. He painted several murals in Salem, Peabody, Mass., Providence, and Newport. In Salem he frescoed the ceiling in the cupola of the Pickman-Derby-Brookhouse Mansion. In Providence he painted numerous frescoes in the Sullivan-Dorr House, a dozen of which are reproduced in E. B. Allen's *Early American Wall Paintings* (1926, pp. 26-45.) According to Allen, "whatever his faults in drawing, Corne's colors are harmonious, and the scenes, which never repeat themselves, are delightfully decorative and effective."

Corne's painting "Columbus and the Egg" after Hogarth. (Courtesy, *Essex Institute, Salem, Mass.*)

The house which Michele Cornè built about 1822 at the corner of Cornè and Mill streets in Newport, R. I. (Courtesy, *Newport Daily News.*)

He also painted portraits and a large number of oil and watercolor paintings of ships, now scattered throughout New England, New York and Maryland, and made an illustration for Judge Joseph Story's *The Power of Solitude,* published in 1804. Corne' certainly was no Tiepolo, yet his murals are not to be despised. Some of them he painted on paper, which he later applied on the wall. The medium he used for the Sullivan-Dorr House was "some kind of water color which was applied directly to the plaster." (Allen, *op. cit.,* 35.) As for his ships and portraits, to judge by the photographs available to us, there is nothing exceptional about them. His "Columbus and the Egg" is reproduced on the opposite page.

Corne's fame in Rhode Island, ludicrously enough, seems to rest on the legend that he induced the people of New England to eat tomatoes, or "love apples," as they were known in those days. He is said to have brought some of them from North Carolina in 1819 and to have eaten them to disprove that they were poisonous. (*Rhode Island History,* July 1942, pp. 65-71 and *Rhode Island, Am. Guide Series,* Boston, 1937, p. 241.)

JOSEPH PEROVANI

Joseph Perovani and Jacint Cocchi, according to their announcement in the *Federal Gazette* already noted, arrived in Philadelphia in July, 1795, and took up residence at 87 Second Street. Who was Cocchi, and what became of him, we do not know.

Perovani, who is said to have been born in Brescia in 1765, was, therefore, about 30 years old when he came to America. He remained about five years, or until 1801, when he moved to Cuba. There he painted a "Judgement Day" "worthy of admiration" in the chapel of the Espada Cemetery, and other paintings in the Cathedral of Havana, which have been ruined by additions and corrections, with the exception of one "Ascension"' which seems to have been respected. Later he went to Mexico, where he died, the victim of cholera, in 1835. (Ramirez, S., *La Habana Artistica,* 1891.)

We do not know much about Perovani's activities in the United States. In his announcement in the *Federal Gazette* he and Cocchi offered to execute all sorts of work, from historical pieces to portraits and landscapes in oil or in fresco; and "both are able to paint any Theatre, Chambers, Department, with Plafonds in figures, and ornamented in the Italian taste; a small specimen whereof they have given in one of the saloons in the house of the Spanish minister here." All of which caused Mr. Virgil Barker to wonder "why, if the skills matched the claims, the workmen had to come so far in search of work." (Barker, *op.*

Cornè's "Bombardment of Tripoli." (Courtesy, *U. S. Naval Academy Museum, Annapolis, Md.*)

cit., 256.) The question is not too bright, especially for a man who is supposed to know something about the lives of the artists. Did not the great Leonardo Da Vinci die in France where he was compelled to emigrate to earn a living? Did not Michelangelo contemplate to cross the Alps notwithstanding the "journey is both perilous and difficult" as he wrote to his friend, Battista della Palla? (Symonds, *Life of Michelangelo,* IX, 3.) Michelangelo was then fifty-five years old, whereas Perovani was barely thirty when he crossed the ocean. Did not the famous sculptor, Lorenzo Bartolini, the protege' of Napoleon, whom he joined at Elba, plan to come to America soon after Waterloo? If he did not come, it was because Jefferson dissuaded him. "Taste for the fine arts in America," wrote Jefferson, "is not encouraging for foreign artists." Montepulciano wine, however, was appreciated, and Jefferson together with his advice sent an order for a number of bottles. (Appleton to Jefferson and vice-versa, October 25, 1815, and January 14, 1816, *MS., Library of Congress.*) As any student of emigration knows, there is more than one motive for leaving home.

At any rate, we have positive proof that Perovani was not boasting when he said that he could execute all types of painting. In 1796, we learn from Mr. Barker, he announced "an exhibition of a statue of Minerva contemplating a bust of Washington. Four months later he executed some of the scenery for the New York Amphitheatre (*Minerva,* June 8, 1796). A year later he made the decoration for the Festival Ballet Dance in honor of President John Adams at the Greenwich Theatre in New York on October 21, 1797. (Odell, *Annals of the New York Stage,* I, 473.) In Cuba, as we have seen, he painted religious paintings or murals. But then there is a portrait of George Washington—not known, to the best of our knowledge, to any of the experts on Washingtoniana—which proves that he was a distinguished painter.

That "magnificent portrait" (magnifico retrato) is said to have been presented to Godoy, but later it was purchased, with its own funds, by the Academia de San Fernando, in Madrid, where it still remains. (*Boletin de la Sociedad Espanola de Excursiones,* 1918, p. 42.) In our opinion, it was ordered by, or at the suggestion of, the Spanish minister in Philadelphia, the same Jaudenes who purchased Ceracchi's bust of Washington, to be sent also to Godoy. Jaudenes served in the United States from February 12, 1791, to April 25, 1796. We do not know, however, whether Washington ever posed for the painter. We have found nothing about him in the Washington papers, whether published or in the manuscript division of the Library of Congress. It may be possible that some reference to Perovani or to his painting exists in the official correspondence between the Spanish and United States governments.

At any rate, the painting was executed to celebrate the Treaty of San Lorenzo concluded the previous October (1795) between Thomas Pinckney and Godoy, the Prince of Peace, as it appears from the legend on the treaty. We need not describe the painting, as it is reproduced on the next page. We shall add only that at the bottom of the column the following words appear: JOSEPH PEROVANI ITALIAE IN PHILADELPHIA FECIT MDCCXCVI.

JOHN B. ROSSETTI

Perovani was preceded to America by the portrait and miniature painter, John B. Rossetti, who was active in New York between 1794 and 1795. (Grace, G. C. 1440*Early American Portrait Artists.*) In 1794 he was in Hartford (O'Donnell, J. H., *History of the Diocese of Hartford,* Boston, 1900, p. 47). Three years later he arrived in Charleston "to practice in the Line of his profession." (*Charleston City Gazette and Advertiser,* January 24, 1797.) No work of his has reached us, so far as we know.

J. BARTOLI

We do not know much more about one J. Bartoli, apparently the same "Bartello" who was employed by T. B. Freeman in Philadelphia in 1796 "to paint portraits from which engravings might be made." (Scharf and Westcott, *History of Philadelphia,* II, 1045.) In that year he made a fine portrait of the Seneca Indian Chief, Ki-on-Twog-ky, now in the New York Historical Society. Whether he was related or happened to be the same "F. Bartoli" who painted a portrait for the Royal Academy in London in 1783, it is hard to say. (Graves, *The Royal Academy of Arts,* I, 136.) Both Benezit and Mallet list him in their *Dictionnaire* and *Index,* respectively.

LEWIS PISE

In 1795 one Lewis Pise, a portrait painter, announced in the *Gazette of the United States* of Philadelphia (June 18) that he intended to remain in the city "only six or eight weeks." Apparently he remained longer than he expected. for he was still there in 1797, ready "to draw off any person's likeness." (*Federal Gazette,* April 4, 1797.) In November of that year he announced that he intended "to remain in this metropolis for a few months." (*Aurora,* Nov. 30.) Later he moved to Annapolis, where his son, Charles Constantine Pise, one of the most distinguished priests in the history of the Catholic Church in America, was born in 1801. (See next chapter.)

GIUSEPPE IARDELLA

Giuseppe Iardella, not to be confused with Francesco Iardella, the sculptor who came with Andrei in 1816 to decorate the Capitol, must have arrived before 1797, if he was brought over "to assist in decorating the mansion of Robert Morris on Chestnut Street, under the superintendence of the French architect, Major Pierre Charles l'Enfant, and had executed several pieces of work, principally in bas-relief, for that building when the failure of Morris put a stop to that work. It is believed that Iardella was the artist who executed the semi-circular pieces in relief, representing Tragedy and Comedy, which were over the windows in the wings of the old Chestnut Street Theatre. They were prepared for the Morris Mansion and were adopted

Perovani's oil portrait of George Washington. (Courtesy, *Spanish Embassy, Washington, D. C.*)

Oil painting of Ki-on-twog-ky, a Seneca chief, by F. Bartoli. (Courtesy, *New York Historical Society.*)

by Latrobe, the architect of the theatre, as appropriate ornaments for the building.

"Notwithstanding his undoubted talent as a sculptor Iardella probably became discouraged by the little profit it brought him, for he finally gave up the higher branches of art to follow the business of stone cutter. He was, until 1817, the partner of Christopher Hocker, in a marble yard on Race Street." According to Scharf and Westcott's *History of Philadelphia,* from which the above passage has been quoted, Iardella made busts for one James Traquair, a stone cutter who sold them to the public. One of William Penn was presented to the Pennsylvania Hospital in 1802. In all probability it was made by Iardella, for "much of the success of Traquair's undertaking was due to the talent of the Italian, Giuseppe Iardella, whom he employed to do his finest work." Iardella and a fellow-artist, John Dixey, made some busts of Washington, one of which is in Independence Hall. Two of his bas-reliefs are said to be still in existence, one in a tomb in South Carolina and the other in a Maryland mansion. (Article on L'Enfant in *Dictionary of American Biography.*)

PIETRO ANCORA

Pietro Ancora is, to the best of our knowledge, the last of the Italian artists to arrive before the end of the century. He lived in Philadelphia from about 1800 to the time of his death in 1844.

According to Scharf and Westcott's *History of Philadelphia* "he taught drawing and painting, but never executed any pictures for exhibition and public sale in Philadelphia. He was the first who was engaged in the importation of European paintings for exhibition and public sale in this country. This business he commenced in 1819 in partnership with Clark Bell. Mr. Ancora lived for many years, always successful, and much esteemed as a teacher." John Neagle, the painter, was one of his pupils.

Ancora is listed as "Ancora, Pietro, drawing master," in the various city directories of Philadelphia from 1805 to 1844. The 1845 directory lists only "Ancora, Jane, widow of Peter, 126 Pine." In Thieme and Becker's *Lexikon* he is said to have been a native of Naples, according to *Napoli Nobilissima,* X, 5.

PIONEER ART DEALERS

Whether or not Ancora was the first man to import European paintings for sale, he was preceded by other countrymen of his in the importation of what we might call art wares. Peter Stagi, "Italian carver of statuary to his Majesty the King of Poland," arrived from Europe in 1795. A year later he offered "a very large and elegant assortment of Statues, Busts and Chimney pieces, all of the finest marble and most exquisite workmanship." Early in February of 1797, however, he announced that he was going to embark for Europe as soon as "navigation will permit." Incidentally, he was staying at Mr. Bosio's house, corner of Lombard and Third Street. (*Federal Gazette,* Sept. 22, 1795, and March 22, 1796; *Pennsylvania Packet,* February 1, 1797.) Another early dealer, one "Provini—from Italy" offered for sale a variety of Chimney Pieces and Ornaments for buildings, together with busts of General Washington, Marquis La Fayette, Doctor Franklin, etc., made of composition equal in appearance to marble." (*Federal Gazette,* March 22, 1796.) They were preceded by John Baptist Sartori, who later settled definitely in Trenton. One of his sons became Commodore in the United States Navy. Sartori on June 3, 1794, announced in the *Federal Gazette* that "Intending in a few weeks to ship to Europe" he offered to sell "very low" the remains of his marble, consisting of Statues, Desert Tables, Guilded Tables, Busts, Vases, Pedestals, etc. And a number of elegant Pictures and Prints, some of which are framed."

THE ITALIAN ARTISTS IN THE UNITED STATES CAPITOL

The corner-stone of the United States Capitol was laid in 1793 on plans submitted by Stephen Hallet, a Frenchman, and William Thornton, an Englishman. A few months later Hallet resigned and George Hadfield was appointed in his place.

Hadfield, an Italianate if ever there was one, came to America after spending several years in Rome, where he made some drawings for the restoration of the temple in the town of Palestrina (a few miles from the Eternal City) and one of the interior of St. Peter. He was the brother of the famous Maria Louisa Cosway, the friend of Jefferson, and a resident of Italy, where she was born of English parents. Hadfield, therefore, brought to the Capitol Italian artistic traditions.

By 1805 the Capitol was just another building, with no artistic decorations of any kind, its art treasures consisting of only two paintings, if our memory does not fail us. The encyclopedic Jefferson tried to remedy the situation by asking his friend, Mazzei, to procure two sculptors for the Capitol and other buildings in the city. It was thus that the two artists, Giovanni Andrei and Giuseppe Franzoni, late in October, 1805, left Italy for the United States.

Portrait of Carlo Franzoni by Pietro Bonanni in the U. S. Capitol.

Nothing is left of the work done by the two sculptors in the nation's Capitol, except Franzoni's six columns known as the "corn-stalk columns" in the vestibule entrance to the former law library of the Supreme Court, for everything was destroyed by the fire that followed the British capture of the city in 1814. We know, however, that both Andrei and Franzoni were good artists. "I have said, that they are superior to the nature of the work they are required for, but that is not all," wrote Mazzei to Latrobe, the architect of the Capitol, on September 12, 1805. "They are able to model and make excellent statues in marble. Andrei is remarkable for exactness, Franzoni for his masterly strokes. I have heard in Florence and Rome several eminent sculptors and painters say that Franzoni will soon be a second Canova. Andrei and Franzoni are well known among men of the first class in the fine arts." (Garlick, R. C., *Philip Mazzei, Friend of Jefferson*, Baltimore, 1933, p. 151.) Franzoni, unfortunately, did not live to become a second Canova, for he died in 1815, nine years after his arrival. He was then only thirty-eight years old. Both Andrei and Franzoni were, at least on one occasion, praised by Jefferson for their elegant work (a medallion). (Jefferson to Latrobe, January 25, 1812, MS., *Library of Congress.*)

"Corn-stalk columns" by Franzoni in the U. S. Capitol.

In 1815 Andrei was sent to Italy to oversee the carving of 24 Corinthian capitals for the columns of what is now Statuary Hall. It would seem that the work was done primarily by him and one Casoni, probably related to the other Casoni who worked in the Capitol from 1853 to 1858.

Andrei returned to the United States in 1816 with two more sculptors, Carlo Franzoni, a younger brother of Giuseppe, and Francesco Iardella. Franzoni was not destined to enjoy American freedom and economic opportunities any more than his older brother, for he died in 1821, or five years after his arrival. His grandson, Charles William Franzoni, was for half a century a prominent physician and served for many years as treasurer and president of the Washington Medical Society. (*Who's Who in America*, 1920-1921.) As for Carlo Franzoni's work in the Capitol, his "Car of History" remains an eloquent proof of his artistic ability. According to Charles E. Fairman, the late curator of art of the Capitol, it is "believed to be the oldest example of the art of the statuary in any public building in the city." Of Iardella's work we have only the "tobacco capitals" in the small rotunda, for he was engaged in the general decoration of the Capitol. He died in 1831, seven years after Andrei, who passed away in Washington in 1824 at the age of 55.

Carlo Franzoni's "Car of History" over the doorway in Statuary Hall, United States Capitol. (Courtesy, *I. T. Frary.*)

BETWEEN 1815 AND 1821

With the end of the War of 1812, the fall of Napoleon, and the political upheavals in Italy which were to climax in the Revolution of 1821, many Italians sought refuge in the United States, as we have seen from Appleton's letter to Jefferson reproduced in part in facsimile on page 150.

Not less than 19 Italian painters and sculptors came to America during those six years. They were: Capellano, Bonanni, Valaperti, Causici, Cardelli, Luigi and Gennarino Persico, Mezzara, Gandolfi, Marsiglia, Giovannazzi, Meucci, Giacomo and Michele Raggi, Mondelli, Fogliardi, Pekenino and Paduany. Twenty-eight artists (including those who came after 1791) during a period in which the American people had no taste for art to speak of (Iardella was compelled to turn to stone cutting to earn a living) were bound to exert an immense influence on the aspiring American artists of those days, especially with their teaching. But then there were the scene painters, as we shall presently see.

ANTONIO CAPELLANO

Capellano, or Cappellano, had recently arrived in New York in 1814 when he was recommended to execute the sculptures for the Baltimore Battle Monument erected in 1815 to the memory of the men who had fallen during the previous year in the defence of the city. (It was during that memorable defence that Francis Scott Key wrote the Star Spangled Banner.) The monument is 52 feet high and consists of a column in the form of a bundle of Roman fasces, surmounted by a female figure, the emblematical genius of the city. It is to this monument and to the other in honor of Washington (the statue was made by Causici, as noted below) that Baltimore owes the name of "The Monumental City."

Capellano could not get to work at once, as the designer of the monument, Godefroi, was away, and was about to return to New York when he was urged to remain and received the commission for two panels which can be seen

The Battle Monument in Baltimore, Md., erected to commemorate the defence of the city in 1814. The statue is by Capellano.

today on the facade of St. Paul's Church. He received $80 for the two models. (Frary, J. T., in *Maryland Hist. Mag.* 1939, p. 64 ff.) After he finished the sculptures for the Battle Monument Capellano found full employment, both in Washington, at the Capitol, and in Baltimore. Some fifteen years later he returned to Italy, where Rembrandt Peale met him one day while promenading in the Boboli Gardens in Florence, with his wife and five children. A most industrious man, he had made enough in America to acquire a little "palazzo" in his native land. (*The Crayon,* Vol. III, 1856, January, p. 5).)

Capellano is represented in the Capitol by his "Preservation of Captain John Smith by Pocahontas" and by a bas-relief of Washington above the east entrance to the rotunda.

Capellano's "Rescue of Captain John Smith by Pocahontas", a relief panel in the stone wall of the Rotunda, U. S. Capitol.

PIETRO BONANNI

Bonanni, a fine painter, was born in Carrara in 1792, came to the United States about 1816, and died in Washington on June 15, 1821. At seventeen he received a prize from the Academy of Fine Arts of his native city for his "Death of Count Ugolino." Later he studied in Paris under David and worked in Rome.

In Washington he was commissioned to decorate the half-dome of the present Statuary Hall, which is said to be a replica of the dome of the Rome Pantheon. His work was so fine, that when the dome was taken down in 1901, it was substituted with an exact fire-proof replica of the Bonanni original. The old dome, according to Fairman, was done "with a craftsmanship so dextrous in the handling of light and shade that the caissons seemed to be in actual relief and intaglio, created an impression so realistic . . . that until one had placed his hand upon this old ceiling it was unbelieveable that the cunning of the artist could produce such a sensation of actual relief." By Bonanni we have also a self-portrait and a portrait of Carlo Franzoni, now in the office of the Architect of the Capitol, which Fairman does not hesitate to call "one of the most celebrated examples of portraiture in the Capitol Building." He is listed in the Catalogue of the Pennsylvania Academy of Fine Arts for 1819. A photograph of a "June Glow," also attributed to Brumidi, can be seen in the Frick Art Reference Library in New York. (Obituary notice in New York *Post*, June 19, 1821.)

GIUSEPPE VALAPERTI

Mystery surrounds the death of Valaperti, or Valaperta. A native of Milan, he lived in Liguria and in Spain before coming to America, for one of his sons was born in Genoa and two other children in Madrid. In 1816 he was in Vir-

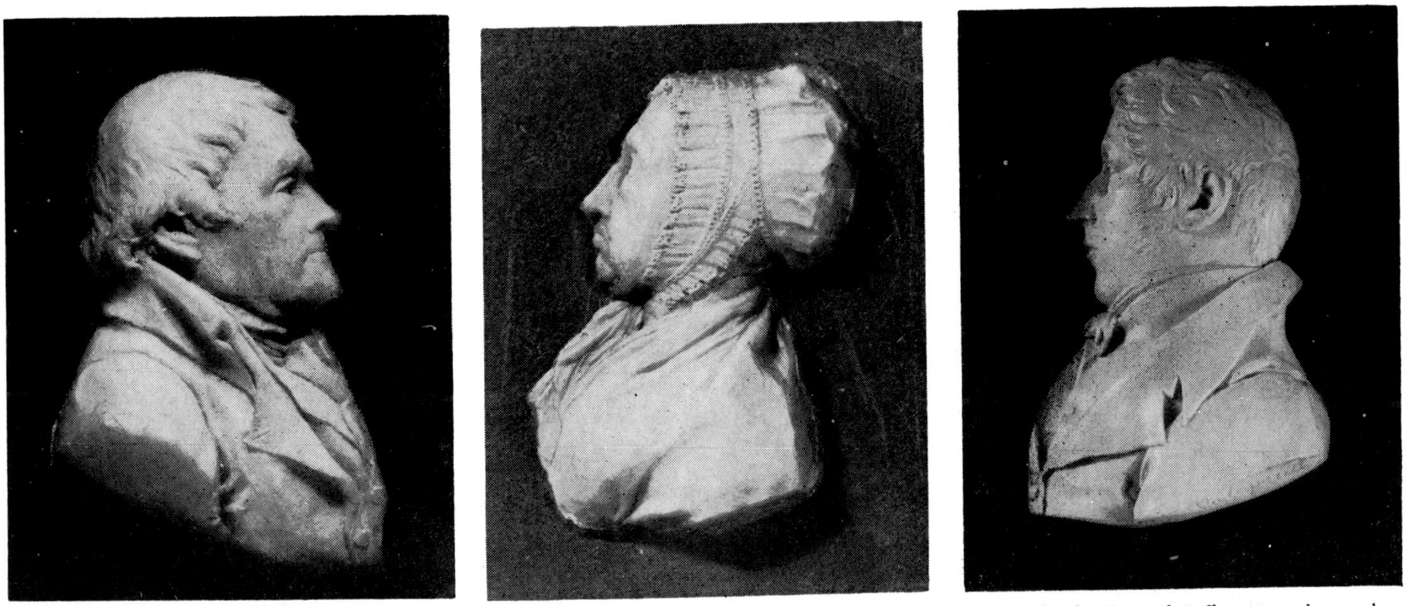

Three of Valaperti's miniature busts, each three-inches high. (*From left to right*) Red wax bas-relief on black glass of Jefferson; red wax bas-relief on clear glass, of Mrs. James Madison, President Madison's mother; ivory relief mounted on black glass of Archibald McVickar. (Courtesy, *New York Historical Society.*)

ginia, to do two of the eight red wax busts he is said to have made, one of James Madison's mother and the other of Jefferson. Five of the busts, three inches high, are in the New York Historical Society; they are those of Jefferson, James Madison, Albert Gallatin, Mrs. Madison, Sr., and James Monroe. In the same society are two fine miniature portraits in ivory of Mr. and Mrs. Archibald McVicker. (*New York Historical Society Bulletin*, April, 1927.) At that time Valaperti was employed as a "government sculptor," obviously at the Capitol. A Frenchman who met him at Monticello on that occasion refers to him as a "skillful painter and sculptor." (*Papers of the Albemarble County Hist. Soc.* Vol. IV, p. 44.) What became of him after that nobody knows, for on March 11, 1817, the *National Intelligencer* carried an advertisement announcing his disappearance.

Valaperti had been recommended by Latrobe and Thornton for the execution of a statue of Washington for the State Capitol of North Carolina. The only work of his in the Capitol is the eagle on the frieze of the south side of Statuary Hall.

"Daniel Boone and the Indians", relief panel by Causici in the stone wall of the Rotunda, U. S. Capitol.

ENRICO CAUSICI

Causici, a native of Verona, made the 16-foot statue of Washington at the top of the Washington Monument in Baltimore, the oldest monument of its kind ever erected in the United States. He received the commission to execute the statue as the winner of a national contest and worked two years on it, until it was raised to the summit on November 25, 1829. Of it, it has been said "In truth, no statue of Washington has called forth less adverse criticism."

Causici, it would seem, came over in 1816 with a plan for an equestrian statue of Washington which was to be presented to the Philadelphia Academy of Fine Arts, but while waiting for his plan to be approved he "took likenesses in alabaster, in basso or alto rilievo." For the Capitol

THE WASHINGTON MONUMENT IN BALTIMORE, MD.
(From an old print.)

Statue of Liberty by Causici in the U. S. Capitol. (Courtesy, *I. T. Frary.*)

he executed a fine Statue of Liberty and two very poor panels, "The Landing of the Pilgrims" and "Daniel Boone's Fight with the Indians." It is possible that some of the poor sculptures by Causici and other Italian artists in the Capitol were done according to the specifications of the politicians of those days and that the artists had to comply with what was wanted. In our own days, Attilio Piccirilli preferred not to mention the many pieces of statuary that came out of his shop for the decoration of Rockefeller's Riverside Church. Causici's "Liberty" and his bust of De Witt Clinton which is now in the Governor's Room at the New York City Hall, would show that he could put out some good sculpture when he wanted, or was free, to do it.

Causici is said to have died at Havana. When we do not know. We have, however, a letter of his to Robert Gilmore of Baltimore, dated New York, May 15, 1833, in which he wrote that he was about to leave for Italy, but that he planned to return to America. The letter is in the *Emmet Collection* of the New York Public Library. Another letter of his to Philip Hone, dated May 9, 1825, is in the *Dreer Collection* of the Pennsylvania Historical Society.

PIETRO CARDELLI

Cardelli is said to have been twenty-five years old when he came to New York in 1816 from his native Florence. H. W. French in his *Art and Artists in Connecticut* calls him Giorgio, but Cardelli's correspondence and his residence in New Orleans lead us to believe that his first name was Pietro.

Cardelli worked "upon capitals and ornaments" in the Capitol at least in 1818 and 1819, but even during those two years he executed busts of Jefferson, Madison, Monroe, and John Quincy Adams, and two medals mentioned in one of his letters. He seems to have travelled extensively from New England to Louisiana and to have been active over a period of more than forty years. H. W. French says that he became very popular among the first families of Hartford, Conn., and apparently of other cities, and adds that his busts were "hard, lifeless pictures, thoroughly Florentine, but said to be excellent likenesses." According to Fairman, Cardelli blamed "Bulfinch, the Architect of the Capitol, for his short-sighted attitude toward the decorative art of the Capitol during the time of the erection of the rotunda."

LUIGI AND GENNARINO PERSICO

Luigi Persico is represented in the Capitol by the "Discovery Group" on the left of the main entrance stairs (see p. 27), by the figures on the pediment and by the two statues of Peace and War, at the top of the stairs on the main entrance.

Persico's sculptures are not what one might call works of art, but then one must remember that he did exactly what he was asked to do. For instance, we know that the figures on the pediment were designed by John Quincy Adams.

Rembrandt Peale in his "Reminiscences" (*The Crayon*, January 1856, p. 5.) informs us that Persico, a Neapolitan, had been earning "a scanty subsistence in Philadelphia by miniature painting and teaching drawing" when he won a prize given by the Franklin Institute for a colossal head of Lafayette. The prize had been destined for William Rush, but Peale, who was one of the three members of the Award Committee, convinced the other two that Persico was a much better artist. "When I expatiated on the beauty of Perisco's classic creation", he tells us, "as the outburst of a genius that had been buried in obscurity, and almost in despair, they agreed with me in voting it the palm of excellence. The language of our decision aroused the torpid ambition of the young sculptor, who proceeded to Washington, to be employed in the costly decoration of the Capitol."

Actually, Persico did not obtain the Capitol commission as easy as that, for several members of the Senate Committee were opposed to him and wanted to appoint a native

East pediment by L. Persico over the Rotunda entrance to the U. S. Capitol. (Courtesy, *I. T. Frary.*)

artist, but Buchanan, a friend of Persico, whom he had known since they lived in the same town of Lancaster, Pa., espoused his cause and he got the "contract." Persico was also supported on that particular occasion by the Artists' Fund Society of Philadelphia, which sent the Senate a memorial, signed by John Neagle, urging his appointment on the ground that "both as an artist and as a man, he is entitled to distinguished consideration." (*Papers of Lancaster Hist. Soc.* Vol. 16, No. 3.) In 1837 Persico went to Italy to execute the work, which was erected in 1844.

Luigi Persico lived in Lancaster as a portrait painter in 1819. A year later he moved to Philadelphia, where he made at least three fine busts, one of Nathaniel Chapman, another of Nicholas Biddle (made in 1837) and another of one Dr. Togno, apparently a fellow-countryman. (Two of the busts are reproduced in an article on Persico by Edward Biddle in the Philadelphia *Evening Bulletin* for Feb. 8, 1913.) It would seem also that he worked in the Capitol long before he was given the commission for the "Discovery Group," as John Quincy Adams in his *Diary*, under date of June 30, 1828, mentions meeting Persico on the Capitol grounds. In all probability Persico designed the "Liberty" which appears on the U. S. coins of 1826 and later years.

Luigi Persico's brother, Gennarino Persico, was also active in Philadelphia and in Virginia. In 1822 he had a studio as drawing master and miniature painter in Philadelphia. Twenty years later, in September, 1842, he opened "The Southern Boarding and Day School" in Richmond. He still had a studio there in 1856. By him we have three crayon portraits which are now in Lynchburg, Va., and a portrait which was exhibited at Virginia House. He was the teacher of Jacob Schoener, a minor painter.

FRANCESCO MEZZARA

Among the portrait painters who exhibited at the Pennsylvania Academy of Fine Arts in 1823, we find one N. Mezzara, most likely the same man mentioned by Da Ponte as one of the teachers of Italian in New York in the 1820's. Probably he was the same Francis Mezzara who in 1817 was fined the sum of $100 for appending the ears of a jackass to the portrait of a gentleman who refused to accept the portrait he had painted of him. He may have been related to the Pietro Mezzara who made a colossal statue of Lincoln in San Francisco in 1869. Mezzara's case reminds that of another Italian, one Joseph Chiappi, who in 1814 was likewise fined in New York for ridiculing a fellow-countryman of his, Lorenzo Astolfi of Philadelphia, in his wax museum. (*Ladies Weekly Museum*, Sept. 20, 1817.) Odell (*Annals*, II.) mentions a singer by that name in New York in 1821.

MAURO GANDOLFI

Gandolfi was one of the finest artists, of any nationality, ever to visit and live in the United States. The son of a painter, he was born at Bologna in 1764, but at 15 he enlisted in a regiment that was going to France. For a time he lived in Paris, where he made beautiful watercolor por-

Three crayon portraits by Gennarino Persico. (*Top*) Augustine W. Cross of Lynchburg, Va. (*Bottom*) Unknown portraits owned by the Marshall Lodge of the Masons, Lynchburg, Va. (Courtesy, *The Valentine Museum*, Richmond.)

MAURO GANDOLFI
Self-portrait in the Pinacoteca of Bologna, Italy. (Courtesy *Frick Art Reference Library*, New York.)

traits, and later in London and Rome. In 1817 he was in the United States, but did not remain long. He painted also oils and was excellent as an engraver. As a man, says Dunlap, "his conduct was that of a detestable profligate," "as an artist, he deservedly ranks high." He died at Bologna in 1834. According to Dunlap, he induced the painter, William Main, to follow him to Italy, but once there he left him to himself. Gandolfi wrote a book, *Viaggio Agli Stati Uniti d'America,* published in 1819, of which only one copy is known to be in existence. (Revelli, P., *Terre d'America e Archivi d'Italia,* 1926, p. 115.)

GERLANDO MARSIGLIA

Marsiglia was one of the founders and one of the first fifteen Academicians of the National Academy of the Arts of Design in 1826, serving until the time of his death in 1854. In New York, where he settled in 1817, "his merits as an artist . . . rendered him eminently successful." (*Catalogue—Dunlap Exhibition, Stuyvesant Institute,* 1838.) According to Dunlap, "he has painted many portraits and other compositions of merit. He finishes with care and colors with great clearness and brilliancy—not always with harmony. His productions of the complicated kind are remarkable for great beauties and obvious faults. He . . . is esteemed for his amiable manners and correct deportment." His portrait of Von Steuben (a copy, after Pine) is in the New York City Hall.

Miniature on ivory of Pierre Toussaint by Antonio Meucci. (Courtesy, *New York Historical Society.*)

ANTONIO MEUCCI

Antonio Meucci, "a miniaturist from Rome," not to be confused with the inventor by the same name, was a resident of Charleston, S. C., where he lived at 157 King Street, according to the 1822 city directory. Between 1823 and 1826 he was active in New York, and after 1827 in New Orleans. Some of his miniature paintings are in the New York Historical Society, others in the Delgado Museum in New Orleans. Two, which he painted at Saratoga Springs in 1824, belong to private families, and two more are in the Gibbes Art Gallery of Charleston. He also painted the scenes for the Orleans Theatre in 1827. Photographs of ten of his miniatures can be seen in the Frick Art Reference Library.

GIACOMO AND MICHELE RAGGI

Jefferson must have been well satisfied with the work done by the Italian sculptors in the Capitol, for when he founded the University of Virginia in 1819, once more his eyes turned towards Italy. That is how Giacomo and Michele Raggi, two Tuscan brothers, were engaged in November, 1818, to carve the columns for the Rotunda (now Library) and others buildings of the new institution.

Giacomo apparently returned to Italy to oversee or do the actual carving, returning to America in February, 1824. The marble was shipped during the following year. For some seventy years the Raggi columns added beauty to Jefferson's pet project, until a fire destroyed them in 1895. A few of the least damaged capitals, we understand, are now scattered in the university museum gardens.

As for Giacomo Raggi, we come across him once more in New York in 1829, when he presented a petition to the City Common Council for permission to erect a fountain in Bowling Green at his own expense "but depending upon the inhabitants of the vicinity for remuneration." But fourteen years had to elapse before the fountain "was made to play for the first time." (Stokes, *Iconography,* Sept. 21 and Nov. 30, 1829, June 30, 1843.)

OTHER LITTLE-KNOWN ARTISTS

Other men about whom we have scant information were: One "Signore Gorme," who exhibited paintings at 234 Broadway, New York City, in 1810. They took up some 400 square feet of space. Whether he was an artist, or just a dealer, we do not know.

Ottaviano Giovannazzi, the sculptor of a bust of Thomas A. Emmett, New York State Attorney General in 1812, now in the New York City Hall.

Lewis Paduany (Padovani?), a miniturist, listed in the New York City directory for 1819 and noted by Da Ponte as a teacher of Italian.

Michele Pekenino, a Piedmontese architect and engraver. In 1822 he made an engraving of Decatur, from an original portrait by Stuart. He is mentioned by Dunlap and listed in Thieme and Becker.

Dunlap mentions also an engraver named Casali who was active in New York at about the same time as Pekenino. He may have been a relative of the other Casali who was active in London half a century before, unless Dunlap attributed to a contemporary resident of New York some engraving made by the London artist.

From Dunlap we learn the names of one T. Simmone, who engraved a few plates in New York about 1814, and of one Francesco Scacki (Scacchi), who produced "a large and poorly executed etching of the Battle of New Orleans."

SCENE PAINTERS

In two fields Italian artists in America were pioneers and undisputed masters throughout the first half of the nineteenth century: scene painting and mural painting.

Not being sure of the nationality of one Ignatius Shnydore who abandoned scene painting for other more remunerative forms of painting, including "rooms painted in the Italian mode," in 1788, we shall begin with Charles Ciceri, a Milanese.

Dunlap gives a long account of Ciceri's American activities in his *History of the American Theatre*. A jack-of-all trades, Ciceri was theatre machinist, business man, musician, and, above all, scene painter. He came to New York from Philadelphia in 1793 to paint the scenes for *Tammany*. For several years after that he painted scenes in New York, including those for the new Park Theatre, which opened in 1798. Ciceri was also in charge of machinery and of the stage. Later he began to trade in merchandise between New York and Paris, until he acquired a little fortune which enabled him to return "in competence to his native country, from whence he sent his friendly remembrances to one who had not provided so well of old age as he had done." Since Dunlap died in 1839 at the age of 73, Ciceri's "remembrances" must have been sent in the 1820's. Ciceri's name appears several times in Odell's *Annals*, Vol. I.

In 1826 we find two Italians at work, painting scenes. One of them, one Aperasso (A. Perazzo?) painted the scenes for Parson's Theatre in Albany. "A genius in his way" and "an excellent artist," he was tall and absent-minded, falling so frequently from his scaffolds that he never recovered fully from his falls. (Munsell, J., *History of Albany*, Vol. II, p. 51.) The other was Signor Sera, not Serra, as spelled in Odell's *Annals*.

Sera occupies a prominent place in the history of theatrical architecture in the United States, for he built the best theater in the country up to that time, the second Bowery Theater, in 1828. Two years before he had decorated the Park Theater.

The *New York Mirror and Ladies' Literary Gazette* for August 23, 1828, devoted a long article to the description of the new Bowery Theatre, together with a full plate illustration at the right hand corner of which the name of "Sera, Arch." plainly appears. "The scenery, too, as far as we have seen it, is of the most beautiful kind." "To Mr. Sera, the architect, who designed the whole, and to whose tasteful pencil all the rich decorations of the interior are to be ascribed, too much praise cannot be accorded."

In 1827, as we have seen, Antonio Meucci painted the scenes for the Orleans Theater in New Orleans. (*Louisiana Quarterly*, January, 1945.)

In 1833, when the Italian Opera House was opened in New York, it revealed to astonished Americans who had never traveled abroad, a luxury beyond imagination. "The whole interior," we learn from Ireland's *Records of the New York Stage*, "was pronounced magnificent and, with the scenery and the curtains which were beautiful beyond all precedent, was the conjoint production of the distinguished Italian artists, Bragaldi, Albe (Albi) and Guidicini. The ground of the box fronts was white, with emblematical medallions, and octagonal panels of crimson, blue and gold. The dome was painted with representations of the Muses. R. G. White in his article on "Opera in New York" in the March, 1882, issue of *Century Magazine* tells us that the theater "was decorated by some of the most skillful Italian artists of the day, who were brought from Europe for this purpose."

Mario Bragaldi, according to Dunlap, was one of the finest scene painters and decorative artists of the age. He painted scenes for other theaters, including those of the Astor Place Opera House in 1847, together with Allegri, Monachesi and Guidicini, to whom we may add other scene painters of the period, like Capelli, Collinca, and Millini, or Molini. Their names occur frequently in the second, third, fourth, fifth and sixth volumes (up to 1850) of Odell's *Annals*. Monachesi, as we shall presently see, was also a fine portrait painter as well as muralist.

In the South, the leading scene painter was Antonio Mondelli. From an announcement that appeared in a Nashville paper in September, 1830, it would seem that he had been at work in New Orleans since 1818. "The celebrated Mondelli," it stated, "is engaged and will labor incessantly to produce the powerful effects of his pencil, which have been the admiration of New Orleans for twelve years." Mondelli, who studied at Milan, created "scenic effects that were described as elaborate and amazing. Real waterfalls, moving boats, storms, forest settings, and clever use of lights are all described in the newspaper accounts." (Hunt. D. C., The Nashville Theatre, 1830-1840, in *Birmingham Southern College Bulletin*, May, 1935, p. 25.) Mondelli was also the chief scenic artist for the St. Charles Theater of New Orleans, which opened in 1835. (*Louisiana Hist. Quart.*, 1945.)

Mondelli added to his income by giving private lessons in painting and drawing. In Nashville he charged $18 for the drawing course, $24 for the painting course and $28 for all branches in general.

Another Italian artist who settled in New Orleans as early as 1820 was one Fogliardi, who designed the scenery for the St. Philip Theater. He also opened the first art academy in New Orleans. Costantino Beltrami, the discoverer of the sources of the Mississippi, described his decorations as "superb" and "marvellous," (Beltrami, *A Pilgrimage in Europe and America*, II, 526-530).

After 1850, numerous Italian artists found work painting scenes for theaters not only in New York, but throughout the country. The names we have mentioned so far, however, should be sufficient to show to what extent Italian painters blazed the trail and set the example.

MURAL PAINTERS

Mural painting, whether in homes, churches, or public institutions, was introduced into America by Italian artists. It is not of recent date, as stated in *The History of American Painting* by Isham and Cortissoz (1936 ed. p. 580), which asserts that "John La Farge practically invented the subject with us in 1876." Architect G. E. Hamlin simply dismisses the work of the Italian artists in the U. S. Capitol by dubbing them "second-raters." (Article on Mural Painting in *Encyclopedia Americana.*) More recently, Homer Saint-Gaudens agrees with his friend, Mr. Cortissoz (The *American artist and his times*, 1941, p. 152), even if he recalls Cornè, who, as we have seen, painted many murals in New England homes some three quarters of a century before La Farge. Cornè, however, did not paint all his murals on wall paper strips, as Mr. St. Gaudens states on page 151 of his book. Most of them, as we have seen, were on plaster. Even before Cornè, Perovani, as we have also noted, painted a ceiling in one of the rooms of the Spanish minister in Philadelphia in 1795. Bonanni, as we have pointed out, painted frescoes in the United States Capitol as far back as 1817, and Italian scene painters frescoed quite a few theaters between 1826 and 1850. When the Tivoli Theater was built in New York in 1840, it had "a grand saloon, painted by Signor Capelli, the ceiling being the most finished, artistically in New York." (Odell, *Annals*, IV, 435.) Aperasso, as we have seen, used to fall frequently from his scaffolds, way back in 1828.

As for La Farge's church murals, he was also preceded by the Italians. As far back as 1832 Nicola Monachesi painted frescoes in the old Cathedral of St. John the Evangelist and in the churches of St. Mary, St. Joseph, St. Augustine and St. Philip, all in Philadelphia (*Am. Cath. Hist. Soc. Records*, II, 122, and Thieme and Becker, *Allgemeines Lexikon der Bildenden Kunstler*), "which brought him prominent notice. These, painted upon wet plaster, are said to have been the first real frescoes executed in the country" (Champlin and Perkins, *Cyclopaedia of Painters and Paintings*, 1887). He painted frescoes in other churches, in homes, and in the Philadelphia Merchants Exchange in 1833-34.

Among other early fresco painters we find G. Uberti, who decorated the Church of St. Augustine, also in Philadelphia, in 1836 (*Ibid.* I, 171); Ferdinando Rossini, who decorated the French Church on Canal Street, in New York, in 1851 (*Eco d'Italia*, July 5, 1851); Gaetano Alessandrini, who decorated the Passionist Monastery and the Church of the Blessed Paul of the Cross in Pittsburgh in 1858 (Ward, *The Passionists*, 114 and 158); the painter Pellegrini, who "contributed not a little to make the Church of the Sacred Heart (of New York) the most elegant temple in the United States (*Eco d'Italia*, June 11, 1864); F. Augero, who was also a decorator of churches (*Eco d'Italia*, April 23, 1865 and *New York Herald*, April 13, 1865).

Dominick Canova of New Orleans, a nephew of the famous Antonio Canova, painted the beautiful murals in the St. Louis Hotel, those of the Baptist Theological Seminary, and others in public buildings in Louisiana before the Civil War; Ciceri, another "French painter," probably a Milanese who came to America by way of France, decorated the French Opera House in New Orleans in 1859; Primo Boretti, who died in New York in October, 1865, was considered "a celebrated fresco painter," (*N. Y. Daily Tribune*, Oct. 18, 1865); G. G. Garibaldi was an "architectural decorator and artist in fresco, in New York, in 1869 (*Eco d'Italia*, Dec. 2, 1869); Giovanni Rossi was called to St. Louis, also in the same year, to paint frescoes in various public buildings (*Ibid.*, March 5, 1869); Filippo Donnarumma painted frescoes in the home of F. W. Tucker, 49th Street and Fifth Avenue, New York, in the Brougham Theater and in churches (*Ibid.* Aug. 27, Sept. 10, 1869 and Dec. 28, 1872).

The list could go on, especially in the 80's and the 90's.

COSTANTINO BRUMIDI

The greatest fresco painter to come to America from Italy was Costantino Brumidi.

A native of Rome, Brumidi worked for three years in the Vatican until 1852, when, at the age of forty-seven,

COSTANTINO BRUMIDI
Self-portrait in the U. S. Capitol.

he came to America. In New York, where he settled at first, he engaged in portrait painting and in church murals and decoration. After a visit to Mexico City he made his home in Washington, where he lived from 1852 to the day of his death on February 19, 1880.

One of Brumili's first murals was the panel on Statuary Hall showing Cornwallis asking for a truce, still "the best example of fresco painting in the United States" after almost a century. His laurels, however, rest on his famous "Apotheosis of Washington" in the canopy of the rotunda of the Capitol and on his frescoes in the President's room, where he painted the portraits of Columbus and Vespucius shown on pages 45 and 49. Like other Italian artists, Brumidi was the object of attacks by men who wanted to have the work done by native artists. A fine book about his work by Mrs. M. C. Murdock appeared in 1950.

VINCENTI, CASONI, BUTTI, GAGLIARDI AND COSTAGGINI

Literally scores of Italian sculptors and carvers have worked in the decoration of the Capitol since the days of Brumidi. Among them we may single out Francis Vincenti, Guido Butti, Tommaso Gagliardi, Vincent Casoni and Filippo Costaggini.

Vincenti, who worked in the Capitol from 1853 to 1858, is the author of the two busts of Indians in the gallery floor of the Senate wing. One of them is reproduced on this page.

Casoni worked as a decorative sculptor from 1855 to 1858. Later he established himself in business in New York, where he did marble and architectural work for numerous buildings, including the old Tribune Building. He died in New York in 1875. (Obituary in *N. Y. Tribune,* April 10, 1875.)

Butti, according to Fairman, was "the most versatile of all, being an excellent designer and modeler, as well as a sculptor of distinction." A colossal plaster model of Washington by him was exhibited at the National Academy in 1853.

Bust of Thomas Crawford by Tommaso Gagliardi in the U. S. Capitol.

Bust of Chippewa Chief by Vincenti in the U. S. Capitol.

Gagliardi, to whom we owe the bust of Thomas Crawford in the Senate wing of the Capitol, is said to have been the most famous carver of them all. He was associated with Larkin G. Mead in the construction of the Lincoln Monument at Springfield, Ill. Later he went to Japan, where he founded the School of Sculpture of the Tokyo Royal Academy.

Costaggini continued Brumidi's work on the frieze of the rotunda, completing almost two thirds of it. He also painted the portrait of Senator Morrill of Vermont in the Senate gallery. Later he worked as a free lance artist, primarily as a church decorator in Baltimore, Philadelphia and New York. He died in Baltimore in 1904. (*Art Annual,* 1905.)

OTHER PRE-CIVIL WAR ARTISTS

In the various city directories, from the East and South to the Mississippi Valley, as well as in the catalogues of the National Academy of Design, of the Pennsylvania Academy, and similar institutions, one finds literally scores

Brumidi's "Apotheosis of Washington" in the ceiling of the Rotunda, U. S. Capitol.

Upper portion of the Rotunda in the U. S. Capitol showing the fresco frieze by Brumidi and Costaggini. (Courtesy, *I. T. Frary.*)

of Italian artists at work between 1830 and 1865. Names like F. M. Terrigi, portrait and historical painter, 1824-25; Charles Canda, teacher of drawing and painting (*N. Y. Ev. Post,* Sept. 19-26, 1832); G. Chizzola (National Academy of Design, 1837 exhibit); Spiridione Gambardella, who made a portrait of Felice Foresti, and who exhibited at the National Academy between 1838 and 1868; C. Capelli, already noted as a scene painter, who exhibited at the National Academy in 1843; one Mrs. Balmanno, who exhibited at the National Academy also in 1843; Thomas C. Ambrosi, a painter, listed in the Philadelphia city directory for 1846; one Parmacelli, who painted a portrait of Mayor Clinton, now in New York City Hall, mentioned in Valentine's *Manual* for 1848, p. 329; one Brunetti, who exhibited a Panorama of Jerusalem in New York in 1848 (Odell, *Annals,* V, 402); Giuseppe Gerosa, who exhibited at the National Academy between 1849 and 1863; Francis Pedretti, a fresco painter, who lived in Cincinnati from 1854 to the time of his death in that city in 1891 (Greve, C. T. *Centennial History of Cincinnati,* Vol. II); Anthony Piatti, sculptor, who exhibited at the National Academy between 1850 and 1857; Nestore Corradi, friend and companion of Garibaldi while the famous General lived in New York, where Corradi died in 1891 (photograph of his portrait of Garibaldi in Frick Art Reference Library); Francis Augero, portrait painter, who exhibited at the National Academy between 1854 and 1870 (photographs of two of his portraits in Frick Library and notice in *Eco d'Italia,* April 12, 1851); Raffaello Genovese, historical and portrait painter of Palermo (*Eco d'Italia,* Nov. 5, 1851); Philip Guelpa and Jean B. Guelpa, fresco and portrait painters, respectively (*Boston Almanac,* 1856 and 1858); Pasquale Palmieri, a fresco painter, who settled in Detroit in 1858 and died, apparently in Buffalo, in 1916 (*Carroccio,* April, 1932, p. 151 and *Atlantica,* March 1931, p. 139); La Mano, scene painter at Barnum's in 1859 (Odell, *Annals,* VII, 154); Louis Del Noce, painter, who exhibited at the National Academy in 1862 and 1863; G. C. Citaroto, a Sicilian sculptor who was in Chicago in 1865 and later executed a memorial to General Sherman's daughter in Cincinnati (*Eco d'Italia,* Feb. 11, March 18, April 13, 1865); Fabrino Julio, who was born at St. Helena of Italian father and Scotch mother, and settled in New Orleans in 1861, where he painted his "Last Meeting of Lee and Jackson"; Tito Conti, an ornamental sculptor (d. 1910), who opened a studio in Boston in Civil War days; and finally one Pietro Mezzara of San Francisco, whom Gottschalk calls "eminent sculptor" in his *Notes of a pianist* (1881, 395). Mezzara did a colossal statue of Lincoln which was placed in front of the Lincoln House in San Francisco. (*Eco d'Italia,* Sept. 9, and Dec. 9, 1865; Dana, J., *The man who built San Francisco,* 1939, 207.) Another statue of his was erected in Union Square, also in San Francisco (*Eco d'Italia,* Oct. 8, 1869). Whether he was related to the other Mezzara mentioned in the preceding pages, or to the sculptor Joseph Mezzara, a native of New York who was active in Paris from 1852 to 1875, we have not been able to ascertain.

NICOLA AND FILIPPO MONACHESI

Nicola Monachesi, as we have seen, painted murals in Philadelphia churches, homes and public buildings, as far back as 1832. He painted many portraits, including one of Lorenzo Da Ponte, and probably also for his patrons, Girard, Madam Rush and Joseph Bonaparte. He also painted a large picture "The Murder of Jane McCrea" which was exhibited at the Pennsylvania Academy of the Fine Arts in 1832. A native of Tolentino, in the province of Macerata, Italy, where he was born in 1795, he died in Philadelphia in 1851. He had studied painting at the Academy of S. Luca in Rome, under Landi.

Another painter by the same name, Filippo Monachesi, probably a brother, also was a resident of Philadelphia as early as 1831. Both Nicola and Filippo had their studio at 98 Locust Street and later at 156 Pine Street. Filippo seems to have been primarily a mural painter.

NICOLINO CALYO

Calyo is best remembered for his paintings of New York City after the Great Fire (of 1835), and for his views in gouache and pastel. His paintings are scattered in various museums from New York to Baltimore, including some at the New York Historical Society and the Museum of the City of New York. In 1856 he, his son and another painter did the drapery and the act drop for Laura Keene's new theatre in New York City. (Odell, *Annals, VI,* 540.)

His picture of the "Philadelphia Waterworks" "was popular on Staffordshire china. He also painted in Charleston and Richmond." (*Two Hundred and Fifty Years of Painting in Maryland*, pp. 48-50 and 109-110.)

Calyo lived a most adventurous life. He was born at Naples (or in the Kingdom of Naples, probably Calabria) in 1796, the son of a colonel. In 1821 he took part in the revolutionary movement that spread all over Italy and was compelled to leave his native land. For several years after that he lived in Malta and in Spain, coming to America in the 1830's. While here, Napoleon III was frequently his guest. In 1842 (most likely in 1840), he went back to Spain, where he was appointed painter to Queen Mother Christine, herself a Neapolitan princess, executing for her a portrait which was at one time, and probably still is, in the royal palace in Madrid. Calyo remained only a short while in Spain and returned to New York where he lived most of his remaining years. He died in New York in 1884. (*New York Daily Tribune*, December 14, 1884.)

His son, Annibale Calyo, followed on his father's footsteps and became scene painter at the Academy of Music after his brother-in-law, Giuseppe Allegri, relinquished the place when he returned to Italy. Annibale Calyo died in New York in June, 1883. (*Eco d'Italia*, June 2, 1883.)

Terpsichore, one of the nine muses painted by Fagnani. (Courtesy, *Metropolitan Museum of Art, New York City.*)

FRANCESCO ANELLI

Anelli, a painter, must have been quite active, for in the Frick Art Reference Library alone we find twelve or thirteen photographs of portraits painted by him. In this page we reproduce that of Edwin Smith in the New York Historical Society. In June, 1848, he exhibited at the Middle Reformed Protestant Dutch Church of Brooklyn, a 500-foot long canvas entitled "The End of the World." (Odell, *Annals*, V, 411.) He exhibited at the National Academy of Design from 1836 and was still in New York in 1878.

Anelli's portrait of Edwin Smith. (Courtesy, *New York Historical Society.*)

LATILLA AND FAGNANI

In 1849 two outstanding artists, Eugenio Latilla and Giuseppe Fagnani, settled in New York.

Latilla, an honorary member of the National Academy of Design from 1847 to 1860, was the son of Italian father and English mother. He came to America preceded by an excellent reputation which he acquired during the years he lived in London and on the Continent. Tuckerman, who knew him, says that "as a portrait painter he had skill and taste: painted portraits of 50 of the most eminent American clergymen," and "proved of signal benefit to the School of Design." Also according to Tuckerman, "two houses in New York bear witness to his superior taste and execution in encausting painting." Later he devoted himself to rural architecture and lived the last years of his life at Chautauqua, where he died in 1860. (Tuckerman, H. T., *Book of the Artists*, 1867, 418-420; lso, Francis, J. W., *Old New York*, 1880, Vol. IV, 301.)

Fagnani was born in Naples in 1819 and died in New York on May 22, 1873. He came to America in 1849 with his friend, the English Ambassador, Henry Bulwer. His portrait of Henry Clay, the first portrait of a Speaker owned by the United States Government, is in the United States Capitol. He acquired fame in America with his Nine Muses, for which nine American society women posed. They are now in the Metropolitan Museum of Art. Photographs of other portraits by him are in the Frick Library. According to Mr. Barker, "he caused a corruption in public taste." (*op. cit.*, 400.) His self-portrait, however, is in the "Galleria degli Uffizi" in Florence. (See *The art life of a 19th century portrait painter, Joseph Fagnani*, by Emma Fagnani, 1930, and *Eco d'Italia,* Aug. 20, 1869.) His son, Charles Prospero, taught for years at the Union Theological Seminary in New York as related in Chapter Twenty.

FROM THE CIVIL WAR TO OUR OWN DAYS

PALMA DI CESNOLA

The greatest Italian name in American art after the Civil War is that of Luigi Palma Di Cesnola. How he served with distinction as a Colonel and as a Brigadier General in the Civil War, winning the Congressional Medal of Honor, is told in Chapter Twenty-two. Here we shall dwell, however briefly, on his work as director of the Metropolitan Museum of Art from 1879 to the time of his death in 1904.

The Metropolitan Museum, it is well to remember, was established in 1870, in a private house on Fourteenth Street, until a permanent building was erected on its present site in 1879. It was then that Di Cesnola was appointed as its first director. In that same year, Princeton University bestowed upon him the honorary degree of Doctor of Laws.

One cannot recount in a few lines all the difficulties the new director had to overcome almost to the very end of his life. For one thing, the American people did not have much use for art, and to many of them the museum was a waste of money. (It was not many years ago that Calvin Coolidge said to Homer Saint-Gaudens, "What is the use of art," (*op. cit. p.* 15), just as another New Englander wrote in 1719, that "The plowman that raiseth grain is more serviceable to mankind than the painter who draws only to please the eye" (Hagen, *op. cit.*, p. 2).

Then, Cesnola was a foreigner, and to some people a swindler, who had sold a lot of ruins to the Metropolitan Museum for $60,000, referring by that to his famous collection of Cypriote antiquities, worth at least $200,000 and for a part of which he had been offered $50,000 by the British Museum. But Cesnola was an American and envisioned New York as one of the centers of art and culture in the world.

THE METROPOLITAN MUSEUM OF ART
as it looked in 1888, nine years after Di Cesnola became its director.
(Courtesy, *Metropolitan Museum of Art, New York City.*)

So vicious were the attacks against Cesnola that once he could not refrain himself any more and replied in such violent terms to one of his critics that he was sued for libel. The trial lasted three months, but Cesnola won the case. When he died his pallbearers were some of New York's leading figures, including J. Pierpont Morgan and Carl Schurz. The *Scientific American* summed it up in a few words, when in its editorial of December 3, 1904, it wrote that "The Metropolitan Museum of Art, as we know it today, may be regarded as a monument to his energy, enterprise and rare executive ability." Only three months before his death the *Arena* had stated in its issue of September 1904 that "New York, therefore, had its solid rise in the founding of the noble institution, and in the determined character and genius of General L. P. di Cesnola almost from the beginning. Not until the Cyprus collections arrived was there any strong artistic impulse in the greatest city in America. They formed the nucleus around which one of the greatest art institutions of the civilized world has been formed."

FORGOTTEN ARTISTS

Scores upon scores of Italian artists arrived in America in the half century following the Civil War. Among them a distinguished place is occupied by the architectural sculptors and mural painters, the carvers and the decorators, from whose scalpels and brushes came many of the statues, architectural ornaments and frescoes which adorn our squares, our public buildings and the finest churches in our cities. Their names are now forgotten, except in some rare article or official report. To cite only one instance, most of the better-known statues by Daniel Chester French, Saint-Gaudens, McMonnies, Bartlett, and other famous American sculptors, were enlarged from the sculptors models and carved into marble by the six Piccirilli brothers and their father, Giuseppe. Also from their studio came the marble decorations and statues that adorn the Customs House, the Stock Exchange, the old County Court House, all in New York, down to Riverside Church and Rockefeller Center in recent years. But then there are those statues whose artists are entirely forgotten, like the sculptor of the victory statue on top of the monument in Capitol Park at Harrisburg, which, according to the *Encyclopaedia Britannica*, was executed in Rome, in 1868.

To trace their names is beyond the purpose of the present article. We shall, therefore, follow the Roman proverb "ab uno disce omnes" and recall only a few of the more prominent ones.

LUIGI GREGORI

In the first chapter of the present work we have already seen three of the paintings about Columbus' life which Luigi Gregori did for Notre Dame University.

When Father Edward Sorin, founder of that famous institution, went to Rome to look for an artist to decorate the University Chapel, Pope Pius the Seventh recommended Mr. Gregori. From information kindly furnished to the writer in 1933 by Paul R. Byrne, the University Librarian, we learn that Gregori came here on a three year contract to paint the fourteen Stations of the Cross. It took him two years to complete this set but in the meantime he was also engaged in decorating the ceiling of the chapel as work progressed. One of his murals, "Columbus's Return and Reception at Court" was used by the United States Government as the design on the ten cent stamp issued at the time of the Columbian Exposition. He also painted many portraits and did altar pieces for the Catholic Cathedrals of Baltimore and Dubuque. A native of Bologna, Gregori returned to Italy in 1891 and died there in 1896 in his seventy-seventh year. We recommend his work to those students of art who may still be under the impression that it was La Farge to paint the first murals in American churches. His self-portrait, reproduced on this page, is in the "Galleria degli Uffizi" in Florence. A photograph of his portrait of General Sheridan is in the Frick Library. (See *Ill. Cath. Hist. Rev.* April, 1922, and *Cath. Hist. Researches*, April, 1887, 94.)

LUIGI GREGORI
Self-portrait in Galleria dagli Uffizi, Florence.
(Courtesy, *Notre Dame University.*)

Rebisso's statue of Grant in Lincoln Park, Chicago. (Courtesy, *Department of Parks, City of Chicago.*)

LOUIS T. REBISSO

Rebisso (1837-1899) came to America in 1857, but his better-known monuments were executed in the 1880's and '90's. A native of Genoa, he lived for a while in Boston, and then, for the rest of his life at Cincinnati, where he taught sculpture at the McMicken School of Art and Design.

Rebisso executed several equestrian monuments, including those of Grant in Lincoln Park in Chicago, General McPherson in Washington, and General Harrison in Cincinnati. According to Loredo Taft, Rebisso's chief contribution to American sculpture was as a teacher, particularly of men like Niehaus, Barnhorn and Borglum, for his statues were "uniformly commonplace, not good enough to be considered seriously from an artistic standpoint, nor bad enough to be picturesque." (Taft, L., *History of American Sculpture,* 1925 ed., 523.) Another expert who had the opportunity to examine the Grant statue closely proclaimed it the work of a genius. His statue of McPherson "bears a near inspection much better than some others in the city." (*Am. Archit. and Bldg. News,* October 24, p. 55, and 31, p. 69, 1891.) For the Grant statue fifteen sculptors, including E. C. Potter and C. E. Dallin, competed, but Rebisso was awarded the commission. Joseph Sibbel was also one of his pupils. (Biographical sketch in *Encyclopedia Americana.*)

ADOLFO APOLLONI AND TOMMASO JUGLARIS

Apolloni (1855-1923), the famous sculptor who became mayor of Rome and senator of the Kingdom of Italy, lived in Boston and in Providence between 1879 and 1883. For a while he taught at the New England Conservatory. He married a native of Providence, but after his wife's death in 1883 he returned to Italy. Two of his works were shown at the World's Columbian Exposition in 1893. His "Poet" is in the Boston Museum.

Juglaris, a native of Piedmont, was a painter. He came over at about the same time as Apolloni, and also settled in Boston, where he was artistic director for a chromolithographical firm. He, too, later moved to Providence where he taught "figure, ornament, composition and design" at the Rhode Island School of Design as late as 1891. (*The Craftsman,* 1905, 43-54.)

LOUIS AMATEIS

Amateis (1855-1913), a sculptor, was born in Piedmont and came over in 1883. He executed numerous busts from life (Andrew Carnegie, President Arthur, James G. Blaine) and several monuments, including that to the heroes of the war of 1836 in Galveston, Texas. From 1892 to 1899 he was head of the department of fine arts, founded by him, at the Columbian (now George Washington) University. He executed a pair of bronze doors for the United States Capitol, which have never been hung and are now on exhibition at the west entrance of the New National Museum Building in Washington. Of his four sons, two are architects, and one is a well-known sculptor.

Trentanove's statue of Marquette in the United States Capitol

GAETANO TRENTANOVE

Trentanove, a native of Florence (1858-1937), executed many statues, although he is best known for that of Marquette in the United States Capitol. He also did the statues of Daniel Webster and Albert Pike in Washington, the Kosciusko equestrian statue in Milwaukee, two war memorials at Oshkosh, and Appleton, Wis., the monument to the Confederate soldiers at Springfield, Mo., and other works.

GIUSEPPE COSENZA

Cosenza (1846-1922), a painter, was born in Calabria and came to the United States in 1886. He painted portraits, marine views, and miniatures, now scattered in Italy, Paris, London and New York. In 1892 he served as vice-president of the International Jury for Fine Arts at the Chicago World's Fair. Of his four children, one became an engineer, the other a pianist, and the third, Mario E., dean of Brooklyn College. (See, Comanducci, A.M., *Dizionario illustrato dei pittori e incisori Italiani moderni,* 2nd ed., 1945; Della Rocca, *L'arte moderna in Italia,* 1883, 217-221 ill.)

VITTORIO CIANI

Also in the 80's came to America Vittorio Ciani of Florence, the sculptor of the bust of George Clinton in the United States Capitol. He did also "The Landing of the Pilgrims" in New England and New York. He died at Perth Amboy, N. J., in 1908.

C. S. PIETRO

An exceptional, although little known, sculptor who died in New York in 1918 at the age of thirty-one was C. S. Pietro, a native of Palermo. His bust and statue of his friend, John Burroughs, and his head of a child (one of the Vanderbilts) are real gems. He is represented at the museums of Boston, Toledo, Cleveland, Hartford and St. Louis. (See *Art and Archeology,* Sept.-Oct. 1918, 313 and 341.)

ALBERT OPERTI

Operti (1852-1927), a native of Turin, lived a full life. A cadet in the British Naval Marine as a young man, he came to the United States in the 1870's, and became a caricaturist and scenic artist. Later he made two voyages to the Arctic regions with Admiral Peary, serving at the same time as special correspondent for the "New York Herald." He made the first casts ever made of North

Greenland Eskimos for the Museum of Natural History of New York, and numerous paintings and magazine illustrations showing life in the Polar regions. Two paintings of his "The Rescue" and "Farthest North" were executed for the U. S. Army and Navy departments. He also illustrated several books. In 1893 he was selected by the U. S. Government as its representative artist at the World's Columbian Exposition in Chicago. (See *Natural History*, Vol. 27, 628-631; *Who's Who in America; Who's Who in New York.*)

VINCENZO ALFANO

A native of Naples, Alfano (1854-1929) came to America in 1896. He executed many of the sculptures for the Pennsylvania Capitol at Harrisburg, the Court House at St. Louis, Mo., the pediments of several buildings and churches, including the Church of St. John the Baptist in New York. Referring to Alfano's little work "Tout danse devant le Grand Perturbateur," Loredo Taft said that "no sculptor of American birth has yet attained to the 'chic' and dainty charm of that fantastic relief." (*op. cit.* 468.) On his work, besides Thieme and Becker, see *Brush and Pencil, July*, 1905, and *Who's Who in America.*

FLORIANO IACCACI

August Florian Iaccaci, as he was better known, was born in France and educated in part in Italy. His mother was a native of Italy, and his father was of Italian extraction. He came to America as a boy, and rose to a distinguished position as one of the editors of "McClure Magazine" at its foundation, and for several years as art editor of "Scribner's Magazine." As a decorative artist, he is best known for his murals in the Minnesota Capitol and in the old Potter Palmer residence in Chicago. He was also the author of several books. On the occasion of his death in France on July 22, 1930, the "New York Times" devoted a long editorial to his work as an artist and a public- spirited citizen.

JOHN RAPETTI

Rapetti, a distinguished sculptor, was born in Como in 1862 and died in New York in 1936. As a young man he went to Paris, where he worked as one of Bartholdi's assistants in the casting of the Statue of Liberty. (His name is engraved in the crown of the statue as one of its creators.) He came to America in 1889 to work on the art exhibits at the Chicago Exposition, but shortly after that he settled in New York. His works include the statues of Hamilton and Jefferson on the campus of Columbia University; the statue of General Grant in Grant Park, Brooklyn; the statues of Greely at Chappaqua, N. Y., and of Admiral Farragut in Washington Square, New York; a magnificent "Pieta"; much of the ornamental relief work at the St. Alban's Cathedral in Washington; a bust of a girl which won first prize at the Paris World's Fair in 1900; the statue of Nathan Hale at St. Paul, Minn.; the marble bust of Chief Justice Fuller, U. S. Supreme Court, Washington; a statue of "Peace" at the Hague, Holland; busts of Hamilton, Franklin, and other famous Americans. His portrait of an old woman, "Nearing Home," is now in the Corcoran Art Gallery in Washington. (*New York Times*, June 23, 1936.)

ATTILIO PICCIRILLI

No Italian artist in the United States in recent years has been more loved and more respected by Americans of all racial backgrounds than Attilio Piccirilli (1868-1945). A native of Massa Carrara, he studied sculpture at the Accademia of San Luca in Rome, coming to the United States with his father and brothers in 1888. From 1898, when he made the MacDonough monument in New Orleans, to the very time of his death, Attilio Piccirilli gave America and the world of art numerous memorials and statues, beginning with the monument to the heroes of the Maine (he defeated forty-nine rivals in a national contest), to the Firemen's Memorial on Riverside Drive, both in New York, the Marconi Monument in Washington, the bust of Jefferson on the rotunda of the State Capitol at Richmond, Va., the statue of James Monroe at Ash Lawn, Va., and the war memorial for the City of Albany. He also did numerous medals, medallions, doors, friezes, and other sculptural pieces. His "Frageline" is in the Metropolitan Museum. In 1932 the Thomas Jefferson Memorial Foundation awarded him the gold citizenship medal. (See, Lombardo J., *Piccirilli*, 1944.)

Maine Monument at the entrance to Central Park, New York City, by Attilio Piccirilli. (Courtesy, *New York City Park Department.*)

ARTISTS WHO HAVE DIED IN RECENT YEARS

Among the artists who have died in recent years, we may recall Ernesto Bagni Piatta, designer of the Navy and Marine Memorial to be erected in Washington; James Novelli, sculptor of numerous groups for parks and places in New York; Michele Falanga, painter, one of the founders of the Leonardo Da Vinci Art School; Attilio Pusterla, painter of the murals in the Ottawa Parliament building and the New York County Court House; Edmund Pizzella, noted for his pastels of American women; Raffaello Menconi, whose sculptures adorn the U. S. Customs House in New York and other buildings in other cities, including one at Yale University; Vincenzo Miserendino, sculptor of many statues; Ettore Caser, muralist and associate member of the National Academy of Design; Gottardo Piazzoni, painter of the murals in the San Francisco Public Library; Joseph Stella, possibly America's leading abstractionist painter; André Durando, the painter of the murals in the Boston Opera House; Ercole Cartotto, who painted the portraits of President Coolidge, Chief Justice Stone, and other prominent men; Beniamino Bufano, the sculptor who designed the buffalo on the nickel, and executed a huge statue of Saint Francis in San Francisco; Salvatore Scarpitta, a noted sculptor, active for years in California; Stephen Pichetto, art restorer for the Metropolitan Museum and consultant to the National Gallery in Washington.

"Heroic Sacrifice", main figure in front of Cenotaph to the memory of the heroes of the Alamo at San Antonio, Texas, by Pompeo Coppini.

TODAY'S ARTISTS

It would be impossible in a chapter as this one even to list the more than 300 names of artists of Italian birth or extraction who are at present active from the Atlantic to the Pacific. In sculpture alone, close to twenty per cent of the artists represented at the 1940 exhibit of the National Sculpture Society had Italian names, or, to be more exact, 24 out of a total 122 exhibiting members. There were also four invited artists.

Among the sculptors, it may be sufficient to mention Paolo Abbate, Edmund Amateis, Olympio Brindesi, E. Cadorin, Vincent Carano, Gaetano Cecere, Enrico Cerracchio, Pompeo Coppini, Gemma D'Auria (Mrs. Percy Houston), Anthony De Francisci, Giuseppe Donato, Alfeo Faggi, Archimede Giacomantonio, Arthur Ivone, Salvatore Lascari, Leo Lentelli, Thomas Lo Medico, Oronzio Maldarelli, Pietro Montana, Joseph Nicolosi, Joseph Pollia, Onorio Ruotolo, Antonio Salemme, Victor Salvatore, Concetta Scaravaglione, Cesare Stea and Ettore de Zoro.

Among the painters, three men would head the list: Jon Corbino, a Sicilian, called the Rubens of New England; Luigi Lucioni, a Milanese, famous for his etchings; Arturo Noci, a Roman, noted for his portraits. Others who occupy prominent places in painting are Vincent Canade, Ercole Cartotto, Dane Chanese, Carlo Ciampaglia, Gustavo Cimiotti, Alfred Crimi, Joseph De Martini, Frank Di Gioia, Rosario Gerbino, Louis Guglielmi, Aldo Lazzarini, Peppino Mangravite, Felix Martini, Vincenzo Maragliotti, Athos Menaboni, Umberto Romano, Francesco Spicuzza and Nicola Ziroli. Some painters are also good sculptors, and vice-versa.

The illustrations of books and magazine articles are both numerous and distinguished. Men like La Gatta, Calapai, Cimino, De Feo, Patri, and a score of others. Anthony and Joseph Mungo, brothers, occupy a unique place for their illuminations and miniatures. More numerous are the directors and staff members of art departments of magazines and newspapers.

Church decorators, both mural painters and sculptors, are not numerous—about a dozen or so—but what they lack in number they make up in artistic skill. Men like Raggi and Zucchi in New Jersey, Cangelosi in Chicago, Tommasi (a sculptor), La Russa and D'Ambrosio in New York, and others in the South and on the West Coast, such as Rev. Sciocchetti in San Francisco.

Not a few Italian-American artists are engaged in teaching in art schools or in the art departments of our leading universities. The painter, Sante Graziani, is dean of the Whitney School of Art of New Haven; Albert D'Andrea, the only American to be elected to the Royal Society of Arts in England in 1947, is chairman of the art department of the College of the City of New York.

Giovanni Castano of Boston, Giuliano Acampora of New York, Pasquale Farina of Philadelphia, are among the experts on whom American galleries and museums often call upon to restore works of art or to express their opinion regarding doubtful paintings.

ARCHITECTS

The first architect of Italian extraction, although of way back, seems to have been Colonel Taliaferro, who designed the house in Williamsburg he later gave to his son-in-law, George Wythe, the Signer of the Declaration of Independence. But the first professional architect of Italian birth in all probability was one Sera of Bologna who built, as we have seen, the new Bowery Theatre in New York in 1828.

Italian priests designed a number of churches from Philadelphia to Iowa, all the way to New Orleans and San Francisco. Father Tornatore was one of the two men who designed the Cathedral of S.S. Peter and Paul in Philadelphia. Father Mazzuchelli, it is said, designed the Iowa State Capitol. Father Cambiaso, who designed the old Jesuit Church on Baronne Street in New Orleans, is said to have been the first man in the world to use reinforced concrete for foundations.

Many Italians have served as professional architects since the Civil War. Antonio di Nardo of Cleveland, who died in 1948, taught architecture at Western Reserve University and at the Carnegie Institute of Technology. Richard H. Granelli was recently awarded the Paris Prize of the Beaux-Arts Architects. Olindo Grossi is chairman of the department of architecture at Pratt Institute, Italo Ferrari, who died in 1951, was professor of architecture at Cooper Union for twenty years. He designed ships and helped design the Criminal Courts Building, the Frick Museum, the Hayden Planetarium, the J. P. Morgan Bank, and numerous other office buildings. Others have designed apartment houses, and whole housing projects. Among them, Rosario Candela of New York and John Guarino of Boston, stand out. But there are others, as one can easily find out from the member list of the American Institute of Architects. Landscape architects, like the late Ferruccio Vitale, have also distinguished themselves.

CRAFTSMEN

In the many books dealing with handicrafts in America one finds scores of names of craftsmen of Italian birth or extraction. They are especially skillful in jewelry designing, bookbinding, cameos, leather tooling, wood carving, wrought iron work, and similar crafts in which Italians have excelled for centuries.

In mosaics and terrazzo work they lead. When in 1941 the National Gallery of Art was built in Washington, most of the marble work was entrusted to an Italian firm of Louisville, Ky., which installed all the interior marble, all the marble mosaics, the Louis XIV fountains, the travertine stone and similar works. All the mosaic in the Memorial Church of Stanford University were made in Italy, sent to Stanford in sections, and put in place by Italian workers who were sent over for that exclusive purpose. Actually, all over the country, from the Atlantic to the Pacific, there are not many public buildings in which the terrazzo and mosaic work was not executed by plans.

Italian names of craftsmen are found also in Colonial time, but it would be idle to speculate about their nationality. We believe, however, that following the special emigration of Italian skilled workers to the West Indies in 1751, a few Italian craftsmen may have come over, either on some of the many American ships that traded with those islands, or by the way of New Orleans and the West Indies, as related in Chapter Twenty-One.

Jon Corbino's oil painting "Flood". (Courtesy, *Montclair, N. J., Art Museum.*)

ITALIAN ART AT THE GREAT EXHIBITION.

of the back porch, a sound as of exhortation greeted their ears, through the open window of the kitchen, and they turned and beheld seated around the cooking-stove (for the thermometer had gone down among the eighties) a dusky company of three. The new driver was smoking his pipe and looking somewhat somnolescent; but Peggy, leaning back in her chair with an expression of superlative content, was listening to a burly Boanerges, who was sawing the air with his right arm and rehearsing his next Sunday's sermon.

In the front part of the house, sounds of music were to be heard issuing from the sitting-room.

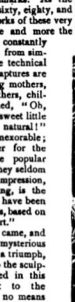

"VANARELLA." BY F BARZAGHI.

Florence and her visitor were singing *Adeste Fideles* at the melodeon.

"Let us go back to the dining-room and get our tea," said Ellen, "and leave the sitting-room to those imbeciles. This establishment is fairly swarming with lovers."

"It is said that one wedding makes many," returned Dr. Woodson, "and perhaps it was having so much sentiment around us that put us in the way of being sentimental."

"Yes," returned Ellen; "in regard to love, we may say, as Mrs. Rollins did once, when asked if chicken-pox were contagious, 'I don't know whether it is contagious or not, but it is powerful catchin'.'"

ITALY AT THE EXHIBITION.

BY BRONSON HOWARD.

Nothing in Memorial Hall or the Art Annex, at the Centennial Exhibition, attracted so much attention among the great throngs of visitors as the Italian sculptures. Certain critics of New York and elsewhere in this country began to decry these works early in the season, and some went so far as to speak of the sculptors as "stone-cutters." Within a few weeks after the tenth of May it became evident to every observer on the grounds, that the hearts of the American people had been reached by these "stone-cutters," with their inartistic (?) chisels. Even with a daily attendance of from ten to twenty thousand only, there were crowds of people in the art galleries, and in no part so many as in the Italian department. Men and women stood in groups before each of the figures representing familiar incidents in domestic life, or quaint conceits of the imagination, commenting upon them, and exchanging enthusiastic remarks. As the number of visitors increased to sixty, eighty, and then a hundred thousand, the works of these very bad Italian artists became more and more the chief centres of attraction. One constantly heard expressions of satisfaction from simple-minded people, to whom the technical merits which throw critics into raptures are of no interest whatever. Young mothers, young girls, grandmothers, fathers, children, even bachelors, exclaimed, "Oh, the little darling!" "What a sweet little rogue!" "How perfectly natural!" The critics, however, were still inexorable; they allowed nothing whatever for the effect of these works on the popular heart; they seldom do this; they seldom admit that any deep, popular impression, be it of book, statue, or painting, is the slightest evidence that they may have been incorrect in their own impressions, based on what they term the "canons of art."

The announcement of awards came, and the people, ignorant of these mysterious canons, had what may be called a triumph, Of thirty-five medals awarded to the sculptors of all countries represented in this branch of art, sixteen went to the Italian "stone-cutters." I by no means believe that the inexperienced eye can detect the merits of many good works of art; and many tawdry works, like veiled faces, figures with nets thrown over them, elaborate bits of fancy-work, etc., often receive undeserved praise from a crowd of visitors. But works which actually touch the hearts of thousands of people, as many of these Italian figures have done during the past six months, must have decided merit. If a critic does not discover it, it is his business to study them conscientiously until he does. A single incident which came under my notice, reminded me that one old lady might give a better criticism than the most learned of art pedants, without the utterance of a single word. A motherly woman, apparently a farmer's wife, and one who had nursed half a dozen babies or more, perhaps, stood before the figure of a chubby boy. As I was watching her, she extended her hand, as if unconsciously, and patted the urchin gently on the calf of his leg, with a tender maternal expression, which convinced me that the artist in Italy knew more of babies than I did; he had brought himself into full sympathy with this American mother, four thousand miles away from his studio

The artist of The Weekly has portrayed this week a number of the sweet domestic figures contributed to the Italian department, with some of those showing merely a pretty conceit developed in forms of airy grace and beauty. Of the former class are "You're Jealous," by Zannoni—a little girl holding a kitten in her arms, while a small dog at her feet looks up indignantly. Here we have a conflict of races, which we have all studied in our own early lives, and we each recognize a familiar incident of childhood days. "Vanarella" is the pretty name of another piece, by Barzaghi. Every woman remembers when she first tried on her mother's skirt, and longed to be "old" as earnestly as she now, perhaps, longs to look young; nor can any bearded man who remembers his first boots, fail to sympathize with the opposite sex in the emotions which this figure arouses. Of the fanciful designs none, perhaps, was so dainty in idea as Donato Barzaghi's "Love's Blind." The lithe, graceful figure of the young girl has that exquisite chastity which nothing but full drapery or perfect nudity can give to a work of art. Cupid hovers above her shoulders, and, in covering her eyes, illustrates a truth, expressed in the title, which no philosophical observer of society denies. "Love's Mirror," by P. Caputti Cantalamessa, of Rome, is a still lighter subject—pure fancy indeed—the observer being left to make what he can out of a Cupid, a mirror, and a beautiful girl. Each reader's imagination must supply the story; if each should send a solution to the editor of The Illustrated Weekly, I dare say he would have a very interesting budget of ideas.

The largest picture of the page gives a glimpse of the main corridor of the Annex which was lined on each side by Italian sculptures and paintings. The first figure and the third are two more of those charming child studies so numerous in this department. "The First Friend," by the sculptor of "Love's Blind," Barzaghi, shows a little girl and her pet with that mysterious friendship between early youth and dumb animals which we, in after life, can remember but not appreciate nor understand. "A Wounded Friend," by Prof. Antonio Tantardini, of Milan, illustrates this same friendship, saddened by sympathy with the suffering of a pet—a girl sits upon a stool, holding the little animal in her arms and looking up with a face full of tenderness and affection. Childhood offers many gentle lessons for maturity to study. "The Discarded," by Andrea Malfatti, of Milan, is a domestic study, but of an entirely different character. A young girl, or rather a young woman, for a fully developed affection has made her such, is just experiencing that first agony which comes when the discovery is made, too late, that "Love is blind." She crushes a letter in her hand, and an expression of deep pain is given in her attitude as well as in her face. The drapery of this figure was one of many remarkable studies presented us by the Italian artists. They have a wonderful skill in the manipulation of marble, giving it the appearance of whatever substance they desire to illustrate. The satin drapery of this statue was as realistic as if it were the result of the painter's, rather than the sculptor's art. The quaint figure of a lad, having the air of an accomplished courtier, with a manuscript and a pen, represents the Italian dramatist of the last century, Carlo Goldoni, in his youth. The expression of attitude and face, showing a comic humor and a maturity beyond his years, seems strangely inappropriate to the size of the urchin, yet it is historically correct. The boy wrote a little comic drama at the age of eight years, and assumed the *rôles* of female characters, on the public stage of Perugia, at thirteen.

A number of Italian paintings hang on the wall beyond the sculptures above mentioned. The two studies of female heads are by Lodovico Accarisi, of Florence, the one on this side being a portrait of a Moorish woman, with the sumptuous drapery peculiar to her race and sex. The larger painting in the centre, by Prof. Ferdinando Cicconi, of Ancona, represents an historical scene of the most profound importance in the shaping of human events, despite the religious calm which pervades the picture. Christopher Columbus is just entering the monastery of La Rahida, near Palos, on the shore of Andalusia, welcomed by the noble Juan Perez de Marchena, to whose active interest in his plans the success of the great discoverer was undoubtedly due. Wearied and disgusted by his futile efforts to interest the Court of Portugal, Columbus departed for that of Spain, obliged to work his way by sea and land, according to the exigencies of his poverty. If he had not stopped at the gate of this monastery near Palos, the discovery of America would have been indefinitely postponed, and it is probable that the name of Columbus would not have been associated with it.

Columbus begged bread at the convent for his little son. The superior, Juan Perez, became deeply interested in him, retained him as a guest nearly two years, and secured him that introduction to the Court of Spain which resulted finally in the equipment of the little fleet which crossed the Atlantic. Juan Perez was one of those who persuaded Queen Isabella to recall Columbus, after he had left her presence, discomfited and unsuccessful, and to promise him her royal assistance. It was from the harbor of Saltez, near Palos, that the explorers sailed. It would be impossible, perhaps, for an artist to choose another scene in the history of the world as quiet, gentle, and peaceful as this—merely three monks welcoming a weary traveler—yet so significant of mighty changes involving the happiness of the human race and the progress of civilization.

"LOVE'S BLIND." BY F. BARZAGHI.

"Who was the meekest man, my son?" said the superintendent of a boy's Bible class in this state. "Moses, sir." "Very well, my boy, and who was the meekest woman?" "Please, sir, there never was no meekest woman."

THE SPANIARD'S VICTIM.

BY A MINER.

Two men were prospecting far up among the Nevada mountains.

"We are too high, and I know it. Who would be fool enough to look for gold or silver here? I have no mind to go further chasing a midge. Where do you make us out to be, Senor Brent?" said one.

Brent threw himself down among the sparse sage brush, and began studying a chart which he took from his pocket.

"Not far out of our way. That must be Prime Peak yonder. Our course lies south by west from here across the gorge."

"It might as well be across perdition!" said the other, grumblingly.

But Brent checked his complaint, with a stern look.

"You knew that we had difficulties to face in the start. If we are to be comrades, we must share the hardships as well as the rewards—if any come. That we are such was not of my seeking, Sanmara."

The brow of the Spaniard lowered for a moment, then cleared.

"You are right, Senor Brent. I esteem myself fortunate in having gained your confidence. Come, let me see if I cannot redeem myself by finding a short way out of our trouble. The map, if you please."

It was given. An hour was spent while the two men ate a lunch, rested, and explored the edge of the gorge in the hope of finding a place for descent. The sheer rocky wall, broken here and there by a sharp cleft or rugged point, seemed inaccessible to man. But this pair of adventurers had come prepared for such emergencies.

Brent, who had information of a supposed rich deposit, had been long contemplating the trip, and hesitated only for lack of a partner he could trust. Sanmara was not the man he would have chosen. But accident had revealed to the Spaniard some knowledge of his purpose, and he had at least bravery to recommend him. They had shaken hands over a solemn compact, and set forth secretly, loaded with tools and provisions, on their search. Among other things, they had a coil of light, strong rope. Selecting the best spot for their purpose, they made one end fast, and flung the other down the precipice.

"We will lose our rope, provided we are able to scale the other side."

"We will not have another such occasion for it, if the chart is correct. We must follow the water course until we can ascend. I am the lighter weight. I will go down and explore the bottom, and you can lower the things when I make sure all is right."

Suiting the action to the word, Brent drew off his boots, and seized the rope, and began to descend hand under hand.

Far down the darkness of that deep, narrow gorge was impenetrable. At the first jutting irregularity, a hundred feet below the verge, Brent planted his feet firmly, and steadying himself by the rope, peered down. There was a glint of water and a faint reverberating echo, and a depth of twilight which would have made a weaker brain reel. He drew closer to the wall, and plunged his arm into a crevice, while he turned his face upward for a glimpse of the blue heavens to dispel the other gloomy picture. But the sight he saw was one to strike a thrill of terror to even his brave soul. Sanmara was peering down at him with what might have been the face of a satyr.

He held a naked blade flashing in the sunshine, and, while Brent watched him, cut the rope through with a single blow.

"Farewell, senor," his mocking voice rang echoing down the space, "farewell, and a pleasant sojourn in the Lost Gulch. It was true instinct told you you could not trust me, senor, though, if you had been wise, you would have hidden your suspicions. I will start the diggings with a comrade more to my taste, if the prospect holds good; let that console you."

Brent's rifle was strapped to his back. After the first instant of stupefied horror and surprise, he snatched it hastily loose, with the stern passion which treason will excite in the true Western man. But before he could take aim, that mocking face was withdrawn from above, and he was alone! Half way down the Lost Gulch, on a rounding knob, with a perilous foothold scarcely three square feet in extent.

He had always considered that abyss the merest myth. It was not down on any map he had ever seen, and the improbable stories regarding it had been told, with slight variations, of other mysterious recesses and haunted mines and bottomless

"YOU'RE JEALOUS." BY A. ZANNONI.

depths, which closer knowledge of the subjects had quite exploded. His situation was not quite desperate while he retained his hold of the rope, as he did.

It was but a few minutes' work to draw up the ends. With the coil at his feet, he began looking for some projecting roughness to which he might fasten it. Nothing of the kind met his sight. The crevice in the rock presented some trifles of crumbling fragments, the deposits of wind and storm. Besides these there was only the slippery bulge on which he stood.

He proceeded to tie one end of the rope about his waist, and, with the coil upon his arm, stepped to the edge, following the zigzag crevice with his eye as far as it could possibly reach. Satisfied, he began to follow it in reality, clinging to the crack with his hands, and seeking any roughness in the wall for his feet. It was a desperate move, which strained every muscle to its utmost tension. But he made his way slowly, stopping to rest whenever the aperture would admit his arms, taking every step with cool deliberation, where to have missed one would have precipitated him to sure destruction. At the best, it was a tedious, an awful task. His hands and feet, torn and bleeding, marked the course he went. Strong and inured to hardships, he was growing dizzy and faint, and gasping for breath, while great drops started out from his forehead and rolled down his face, when the object that he sought was found.

He slipped the loop he had already prepared on the end of the rope over an upright section, and made a turn about his body under the arms, thus supporting his weight while he rested again before commencing the actual descent. This was accomplished tediously and with effort, but in entire safety. It was scarcely more than mid-afternoon on the open mountain. But long before Brent reached solid footing below, the blackness of Tartarus reigned there. He flung himself down on the damp, slimy bottom, in a state of complete prostration, from which he lapsed imperceptibly into sleep.

It was still dark for hours after he awoke. But with the first faint light that struggled there he started to explore the unknown chasm. It was a wild, sepulchral sort of cañon, a mile in length, and nowhere more than fifty yards in width. The only vegetation was a coarse, reed-like grass, that grew in clumps near the water's edge. The stream flowed with a swift rush, which was not betrayed by its smooth, black surface, but only showed when some object was caught and borne onward by its force. It entered the top of the cañon by a fall, and left it in a manner which Brent could only conjecture. The stream widened into a miniature lake, flowing smoothly against the rocky barrier, under which he was convinced it had some subterranean outlet. Stars shone in the glimpse of blue at the top at mid-day. The air was chilly and vault-like, the water ice-cold from the mountain springs. In all the round of the desolate place there was not a break nor the semblance of a path by which the prisoner might hope to effect his escape.

He had some provisions in his pockets—dried buffalo meat chiefly. He had his rifle, ammunition, and knife with him. He had also a box of matches. There was an abundance of fuel, fortunately, drifted upon the banks. He made his provisions last a week, and in all that time the only living thing he saw was an eagle which flew slowly over the gorge. He fired at it without effect, and kept watch afterwards constantly with his gun at his side, but no repetition of the opportunity came.

To describe the life he led, day after day, or to attempt to delineate the stages of hope, despondency, and final despair through which he passed, is beyond the power of words. One day something shot into the air, and fell with a dull thud almost at his feet. It proved to be an ordinary rabbit, which had either run unheeding or been driven over the precipice, and with it the pangs of hunger were for the time appeased. At another time when he was in the vicinity of the fall, a fish leaped upward, and, describing a curve, fell back into the stream. When, in no manner discouraged by its first failure, it repeated the operation, Brent sent a bullet into its head, and dashing into the water, secured a fine specimen of a fresh-water salmon. But it was the only fish he ever saw in the Lost Gulch.

SOME ITALIAN GEMS IN THE ART ANNEX

A page from "The Illustrated Weekly" of New York for Dec. 2, 1876, devoted to the Italian works of art exhibited at the Philadelphia Centennial Exhibition in 1876. (Courtesy, *New York Public Library.*)

CHAPTER SIXTEEN

MISSIONARIES AND RELIGIOUS EDUCATORS

All statements in the present chapter are fully documented in Volume Two of "Italian-American History." The reader is referred to it for additional details.

Italian missionaries played a most important role in the establishment of the Roman Catholic Church in the the United States. They did not come over to minister to immigrants; they came over 1) to convert the Indians and 2) to seek an asylum.

It so happened, therefore, that before 1880 there were more Italian priests in the United States than during the next quarter of a century, when millions of immigrants landed on our shores from Italy. It so happened also that probably half of the Italian priests who arrived before 1870, were engaged in educational activities, from the District of Columbia to the Pacific Coast, as professors of theology and languages—and even science—as well as presidents or founders of colleges and universities; the others were laying the foundations of the Catholic Church west of the Mississippi. A notable few, nevertheless, were organizing parishes in the East.

The first group arrived between 1818 and 1830 and consisted primarily of Lazarist Fathers, or members of the Congregation of the Mission, who labored between Missouri and Louisiana in the West and Philadelphia and Baltimore in the East. To them one lone Dominican must be added, Father Mazzuchelli.

The second group arrived between 1840 and 1870 and was made up largely of Jesuits, with a relatively few Franciscan, Passionist, Servite, and Capuchin Fathers. During this period only a handful of Italian secular priests labored in the United States; but, what they lacked in numbers, they made up in quality.

PIONEER LAYMEN

Even before any Italian priest began his labors in America, natives of Italy helped to establish some of the first parishes and erect some of the first churches in the United States.

In New York, Antonio and Filippo Filicchi became the benefactors of Mother Seton and helped her to establish her Order of the Sisters of Charity. Anthony Trapani, a native of Meta, near Naples, was one of the first trustees of St. Peter's Church on Barclay Street. Charles Del Vecchio, a Milanese, was active in the recently established parish of the Old St. Patrick's Cathedral on Mott Street, and was elected vice-president of the New York Catholic Benevolent Society, the first Catholic organization of its kind in the country, in 1816. (Incidentally, old St. Patrick's Cathedral was built by an Italian mason named Morte.)

In New Jersey, Giovanni Battista Sartori built the first Catholic Church in the state, that of St. John the Baptist, at Trenton, in 1814. In Philadelphia, several Italians were active in local parish affairs at the beginning of the last century. In Louisiana, in Virginia, in Alabama, in South Carolina, in Mississippi, in Arkansas, in Georgia, in Indiana, in Illinois, and later in California and Colorado, Italian Catholics did their share to the best of their abilities.

OLD ST. PETER'S CHURCH
on Barclay Street, New York City, as it looked in 1785. At least one Italian, Anthony Trapani, assisted in its erection and served as trustee.

THE FIRST CATHOLIC CHURCH IN NEW JERSEY
An early photograph of the Church of St. John the Baptist, Trenton, N. J., erected in 1814 by John Sartori.

THE FIRST PRIESTS

The first Italian priest to labor in the United States, so far as we know, was Father Nicholas Zucchi of the Society of the Faith of Jesus, who came to Maryland in 1803. He died at Taneytown, Md., in 1845, after serving as prefect at Georgetown College.

In 1810, one Rev. B. Torelli and one Rev. Bonavita were stationed in Philadelphia and New York, respectively, and Rev. Giovanni Grassi began his labors at Georgetown.

THE FIRST PRESIDENT OF GEORGETOWN UNIVERSITY

Father Giovanni Grassi, S.J., a native of Bergamo, became president of Georgetown College in 1812, two years after his arrival, and out of a small school he created the first Catholic University in the United States. Under him Georgetown acquired such a prestige (even Protestants sent their sons to study there) that soon there were more applicants than accomodations.

Father Grassi had been proposed as Bishop of Detroit, but he was anxious to return to his native land, where he became provincial and assistant for Italy to the General of the Society of Jesus.

THE ITALIAN LAZARISTS IN MISSOURI AND IN THE EAST

The first important group of Italian Lazarists, or members of the Congregation of the Mission, landed in Baltimore on July 26, 1816. They were headed by Father Felix De Andreis, a native of Piedmont, and included Father Giuseppe Rosati, several priests and a few brothers. From Baltimore, they proceeded, most of the way on foot, to Pittsburgh and from there on a flatboat (a regular boat was a luxury) to Kentucky, where they spent a year teaching theology and other subjects.

In 1817, they resumed their voyage until they reached Missouri, settling at St. Louis. At nearby Perryville, a year later, Father Rosati built the Seminary of St. Mary, the first Catholic institution of its kind west of the Mississippi. From Missouri they scattered throughout the South, all the way to New Orleans, laboring among the Indians and the French-speaking settlers. Most of them became pastors and builders of churches, convents and other institutions.

One of them, Father Philip Borgna, became rector of the Cathedral of St. Louis, vicar general of the diocese, and later director and professor of theology at Mt. St. Mary's College, Emmittsburg, Md. For a time he taught at Fordham in New York. Another priest, Father Francis Cellini, was pastor of several parishes, built more than one church and served as vicar general of St. Louis. He is said to have been very skillful as a physician, and to have vaccinated probably all the children of his parishes. Still another Vincentian, Father Louis Moni, served as rector of the Cathedral of New Orleans from 1829 until he died at Mobile, Ala., in 1842. In all more than forty Italian-born priests served in Missouri and Louisiana between 1820 and 1850.

BISHOP ROSATI

The outstanding Italian priest in Missouri, to our own days, was Bishop Joseph Rosati (1789-1843). A native of Sora, near Naples, he was twenty-seven years old when he came to the United States, but he possessed such organizing qualities that two years later, upon the death of Father De Andreis, he succeeded him as superior. Seven years later, with the creation of the diocese of St. Louis, he was elevated to the rank of bishop, remaining in charge for thirteen years until he was sent on a diplomatic mission in 1840.

Bishop Rosati's accomplishments are told by the 34 churches, 9 of stone, 10 of brick, 25 of wood, attended by 68 priests in 1838. He also built colleges, academies, convents, an orphan asylum, a hospital, and, above all, the old Cathedral of St. Louis which he began in 1830 and finished in 1834. Of historical interest is also Father De Smet's mission to the Indians of the Northwest, which he authorized shortly before he left his see.

A flatboat on the Ohio River at the beginning of last century.

BLESSED FELIX DE ANDREIS
First Superior of the Congregation of the Mission in the United States. An artist's conception. (Courtesy, *Congregation of the Mission,* Perryville, Mo.)

JOSEPH ROSATI
FIRST BISHOP OF ST. LOUIS

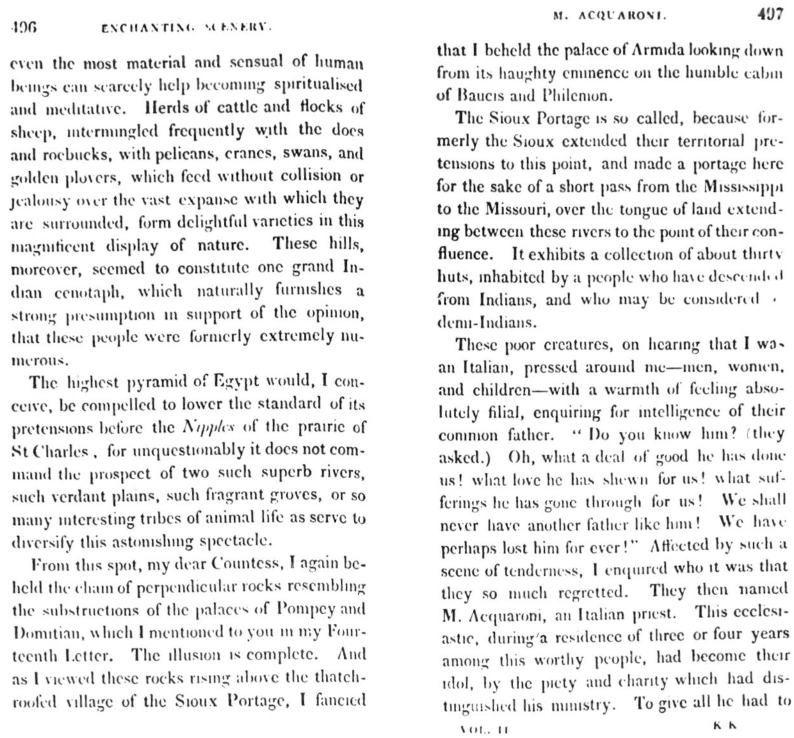

496 ENCHANTING SCENERY.

even the most material and sensual of human beings can scarcely help becoming spiritualised and meditative. Herds of cattle and flocks of sheep, intermingled frequently with the does and roebucks, with pelicans, cranes, swans, and golden plovers, which feed without collision or jealousy over the vast expanse with which they are surrounded, form delightful varieties in this magnificent display of nature. These hills, moreover, seemed to constitute one grand Indian cenotaph, which naturally furnishes a strong presumption in support of the opinion, that these people were formerly extremely numerous.

The highest pyramid of Egypt would, I conceive, be compelled to lower the standard of its pretensions before the *Nipples* of the prairie of St Charles, for unquestionably it does not command the prospect of two such superb rivers, such verdant plains, such fragrant groves, or so many interesting tribes of animal life as serve to diversify this astonishing spectacle.

From this spot, my dear Countess, I again beheld the chain of perpendicular rocks resembling the substructions of the palaces of Pompey and Domitian, which I mentioned to you in my Fourteenth Letter. The illusion is complete. And as I viewed these rocks rising above the thatch-roofed village of the Sioux Portage, I fancied

M. ACQUARONI. 497

that I beheld the palace of Armida looking down from its haughty eminence on the humble cabin of Baucis and Philemon.

The Sioux Portage is so called, because formerly the Sioux extended their territorial pretensions to this point, and made a portage here for the sake of a short pass from the Mississippi to the Missouri, over the tongue of land extending between these rivers to the point of their confluence. It exhibits a collection of about thirty huts, inhabited by a people who have descend-d from Indians, and who may be considered - demi-Indians.

These poor creatures, on hearing that I wa- an Italian, pressed around me—men, women, and children—with a warmth of feeling absolutely filial, enquiring for intelligence of their common father. "Do you know him? (they asked.) Oh, what a deal of good he has done us! what love he has shewn for us! what sufferings he has gone through for us! We shall never have another father like him! We have perhaps lost him for ever!" Affected by such a scene of tenderness, I enquired who it was that they so much regretted. They then named M. Acquaroni, an Italian priest. This ecclesiastic, during a residence of three or four years among this worthy people, had become their idol, by the piety and charity which had distinguished his ministry. To give all he had to

VOL. II KK

A page from Beltrami's *A Pilgrimage in Europe and America* praising Father Acquaroni's work among the Indians of Arkansas.

THE LAZARISTS IN THE EAST

The first Lazarists in the East went there in 1841 at the invitation of Bishop Kenrick of Philadelphia to take charge of the Seminary of St. Charles Borromeo. The small group was headed by Father Maller, a Spaniard, and included two Genoese priests, Fathers John B. Tornatore and Anthony Penco. Both of them remained in Philadelphia until 1852. Father Tornatore is said to have drawn, together with Father Maller, the plans for the Cathedral of Philadelphia; Father Penco served as a member of the board of trustees of the Seminary of St. Charles Borromeo, and for a time was president of St. Joseph's Seminary at Fordham, N. Y., and of St. Vincent's College at Cape Girardeau, Mo.

THE FIRST CATHOLIC CHURCH IN THE BRONX

In New York, the outstanding Lazarist was the Piedmontese Father Felix Villanis, who became director of St. Joseph's Seminary at Fordham and taught at St. John's College soon after his arrival in 1840. Later he served as pastor in various parishes and built several churches, including that of St. Raymond, the first Catholic church in the Bronx.

In Maryland, Father James F. Burlando, who served as director of the Sisters of Charity from 1853 to 1873, is said to have done "more than anyone else to develop the growth of the Emmittsburg school during his long administration." Also in Maryland, Father Giustiniani was active from 1854 to the time of his death in 1866, after thirty-one years of service in America. He is remembered as the builder of the beautiful Church of the Immaculate Conception in Baltimore which was dedicated in 1857, and probably more as a "worker of miracles." It is said that more than one person given up as hopeless recovered after a visit from Father Giustiniani.

Of course, scores of Italian Lazarist Fathers served as pastors and teachers in various colleges and seminaries, from Missouri and Louisiana to New York State, Pennsylvania and Maryland. Their names, as indicated at the beginning of the present chapter, will be found in Volume Two of our *Italian-American History*.

THE OLD CATHEDRAL OF ST. LOUIS, MO.
Erected in 1831-34 by Bishop Rosati.

ST. MARY OF THE BARRENS
The first seminary built by Father Rosati in 1818 at the Barrens, now Perryville, Mo. It was the first Catholic seminary west of the Mississippi. It is now used as the motherhouse of the Western Province of the Lazarists in the United States. (Courtesy, *Congregation of the Mission,* Perryville, Mo.)

THE PHILADELPHIA CATHEDRAL
which is said to have been designed by Fathers Tornatore and Maller.

ST. VINCENT'S COLLEGE, CAPE GIRARDEAU, Mo.
Opened in 1844 with Rev. H. Figari, C.M., as its first president, and Rev. C. M. Barbieri, C.M., as vice-president. (Courtesy, *Congregation of the Mission, Perryville, Mo.*)

SEMINARY OF ST. CHARLES BORROMEO
at 18th and Race Streets, Philadelphia, 1839-1871.

REV. FRANCIS BURLANDO

REV. JOSEPH GIUSTINIANI

FATHER MAZZUCHELLI AND OTHER PIONEERS IN THE MIDDLE WEST

FATHER SAMUEL MAZZUCHELLI

FATHER MAZZUCHELLI

Founder of the Order of the Dominican Sisters of the Holy Rosary, or of Sinsinawa, builder of twenty churches, from Wisconsin and Illinois to Iowa, architect, philologist, educator, Father Mazzuchelli holds one of the foremost places in the annals of the Catholic Church in the United States. "At his entrance into his labors," wrote Archbishop Ireland, "Mazzuchelli was the solitary priest, from the waters of Lake Huron and Michigan to those of the Mississippi River across the widespread prairies and forests of Wisconsin and Iowa. . . . Others followed in his footsteps; he had been the pathfinder in the wilderness."

Father Mazzuchelli was born in Milan in 1806 and came to the United States at the age of 21 in 1827. Three years later he was ordained a priest in Ohio. During the following thirty-four years, until he died in 1864, he was always on the go, on horseback, most of the time alone, from Mackinac, where he began his labors in 1830, to Galena, and from Sault Ste. Marie to Iowa City. At one time he declined an appointment as bishop—like several other Italians, mostly Jesuits, to whom a similar honor was offered—for he preferred to be among the humble people of his parishes. When the First Territorial Legislature of Wisconsin was organized in 1836, he received the honor of opening its first session with a prayer. In 1833 he published at Green Bay an almanac in the Chippewa language which is considered as the first book printed in Wisconsin. To his Irish parishioners, who loved him, he was "Father Kelly."

Father Skolla's sketch drawn in 1845 of St. Anne's Church, Mackinack Island, where Father Mazzuchelli began to labor in 1830.

OTHER PIONEERS IN THE MIDDLE WEST.

At about the same time that Bishop Rosati and Father Mazzuchelli were laboring in Missouri and in Wisconsin, Father John B. Raho was laboring in Illinois, where he organized, and in several instances built, nineteen parishes of which we know, beginning with the one at La Salle in 1838 and ending with one at St. Augustine in 1844, scattered over one third of the state of Illinois. It was in the present diocese of Peoria, in the village of Kickapoo, that Father Raho in 1839 laid the cornerstone of the first permanent Catholic Church in Illinois. He also built the first Catholic Church in La Salle.

Other Italian priests who labored in Illinois in the 1840's were Father Parodi, Father Rinaldi, Father Montuori, and several other Italian Lazarists. Father Raho later became the first vicar general of Los Angeles.

In Kentucky and Tennessee Fathers Savelli, Orengo and D'Arco were active after 1842. Father Pozzo, a Dominican, taught theology at Somerset, Ohio, from 1841 to 1844. Father D'Arco was chancellor at Nashville in the 1850's. Father Olivetti labored in Ohio between 1839 and 1845.

PEORIA, ILL., IN 1831.

JESUIT PIONEERS—FROM OREGON TO MARYLAND

In the cemetery of Mount St. Michael, outside the city of Spokane, Wash., there is a corner in which many of the Jesuit Fathers and Brothers of the Rocky Mountain Missions are buried. It is as impressive a graveyard as any in the country—a kind of Westminster Abbey or Santa Croce, but on a much smaller scale, obviously. No less impressive is the other small patch of land in the cemetery of Santa Clara, Cal., in which are buried other pioneer members of the Society of Jesus. From Father Mengarini to Father Cataldo they seem to be all there.

The tombstones in those two small cemeteries tell the story of the Italian pioneer Jesuits who labored from Montana to the Pacific Coast, all the way from Alaska to San Jose', Cal. The first was Father Mengarini, who went to the Oregon Territory with Father De Smet in 1841. A distinguished philologist, he wrote several Indian grammars and dictionaries and is said to have discovered one of the sources of the Missouri River.

Among the other pioneers in the West we may single out:

Father Michael Accolti, a native of the province of Lecce, who came over in 1840, was chosen superior of the Oregon Mission in 1850, taught ethics and other subjects in California, and served as a priest until he died in 1878. A great executive, he had been proposed as a bishop, but he declined the honor, just as Father Mengarini had done before him.

Father Anthony Ravalli, a native of Ferrara, spent forty years in Montana, where he built the first Catholic Church in the state and where he labored not only as a priest but also as a physician. To him the Flatland Indians of Montana owe a great debt.

Father Urban Grassi, a native of the province of Voghera, built the first Catholic church for white people in Montana and labored throughout the Northwest from 1861 to the time of his death in 1890.

Father Joseph Giorda, one of the most conspicuous figures in the history of Catholicity in Montana, Idaho and Washington, was born in Piedmont. He began to work among the Coeur d'Alene Indians in 1861, and spent the rest of his life in Montana and Idaho until he died in 1882. He served two terms as superior general of his province, but is especially remembered for his dictionary of the Kalispel language.

Father Camillus Imoda, a native of Turin, arrived in Montana in 1859 and spent the rest of his life there until 1886, when he died. After 1883 he served as vicar-general of the diocese of Helena, Montana.

Father Lawrence B. Palladino, a Genoese, served as president of Gonzaga College from 1894 to 1897, and as vicar general of the diocese of Helena for some years. His book, *Indian and White in the Northwest,* is indispensable as a source for the study of the history of the Catholic Church in Montana and nearby states.

IN CALIFORNIA

The Jesuit Fathers in California devoted themselves primarily to teaching.

The pioneer was Father John Nobili, a Roman who landed in Oregon in 1844, but after five years moved to San Francisco together with Father Accolti in order to establish a college there. Two years later, with only $150 to start with, he laid the foundations of the present University of Santa Clara. He died of lockjaw in 1854 at the age of forty-three.

Among the successors of Father Nobili at Santa Clara we may recall: Father Felix Cicaterri, a native of Velletri, who came to America in 1848 after serving as rector of the Jesuit college in Vienna; Father Masnata, a Genoese, who served as president of both Santa Clara and Saint Ignatius College; Father Aloysius Brunengo, of Turin, who is

(*Above*) A section of the cemetery of Santa Clara, Cal., in which the Jesuit pioneers are buried. (*Left*) A similar section in St. Michael's Cemetery, Spokane, Wash. (Photos by the author.)

The first Roman Catholic Church in Montana, built by Father Ravalli.

best remembered as professor of the now flourishing "Institute of Law of St. Ignatius Institute"; finally, Father John Pinasco, the last of the Italian pioneers to serve as president of Santa Clara. At present (1951) Father C. J. Gianera is in charge.

THE UNIVERSITY OF SAN FRANCISCO

The college of St. Ignatius, now University of San Francisco, was started by Father Anthony Maraschi, a Piedmontese, in 1855. A learned man, he came to America in 1848 and for a while taught philosophy at Holy Cross and Loyola College, Baltimore. He died in San Francisco in 1897.

Other noted Jesuits at St. Ignatius College were: Father Congiato, a Sardinian, who served as president of both Santa Clara and St. Ignatius Colleges, and as superior of the California and Rocky Mountain Missions, with which was connected for more than forty years; Father Aloysius Varsi, also a Sardinian, who came to America in 1861 and spent thirty-six years of continuous work in California, during which he built the college and new church at their present locations; Father Bayma, an intellectual giant, who served as fourth president of St. Ignatius, but is remembered chiefly for his book on molecular mechanics, a work which is said to have been a century before its time; Father Neri, a distinguished Piedmontese scientist, whose experiments were "forerunners of modern electrical applications"; Father Anthony Cichi, a native of Sardinia, also another of the pioneer scientists on the West Coast; Father Dominic Giacobbi, a native of Corsica, one of the founders of the Jesuit magazine *America* in 1909; and finally Father Giuseppe Chianale, a Piedmontese, who spent fifty-years in the Northwest as a missionary and professor of philosophy until he died in 1941. He was the last of the pioneers whom the writer was privileged to meet at Spokane in 1936.

Of course, scores of other Italian Jesuit Fathers labored in the Northwest during the second half of the last century. Their names and some of their activities will be found in Volume Two of *Italian-American History*, as we have already indicated.

THE JESUIT FATHERS IN THE EAST AND IN COLORADO

Not all the Jesuits who came from Italy between 1848 and 1871 went to the West Coast or to the Rocky Mountains. Some of them remained in the East, while others settled in Colorado and New Mexico.

WOODSTOCK COLLEGE

The greatest institution established and developed by the Italian Jesuits in the East is the College of the Sacred Heart at Woodstock College, the first scholasticate established by the Jesuit Fathers in the United States, and still their leading institution of its kind in North America.

The man who conceived and erected Woodstock College was Father Angelo M. Paresce, provincial of the Maryland province of the Society of Jesus from 1861 to 1869 and rector of the college from 1869 to 1875. A native of Naples, he came to America in 1845 and died in Maryland in 1879.

FATHER MAZZELLA

Father, later Cardinal, Camillus Mazzella, one of the outstanding men in the history of both the Society of Jesus and the Catholic Church, was born in the province of Benevento, in southern Italy, and came to America in 1867. He taught theology at Georgetown and Woodstock until 1878, when Pope Leo XIII called him to teach at the Gregorian University in Rome. In 1897 he was made a cardinal. Four of his important works on theology were written while he lived at Woodstock.

OTHER NOTED JESUITS

Other noted Jesuits who taught at Woodstock were: Father Sestini, a Florentine, who is remembered as a scientist and as the founder of the *Messenger of the Sacred Heart* in 1866; Father Emilio De Augustinis, a Neapolitan lawyer who joined the Society of Jesus at the age of twenty-six and rose to a position of prominence among its theologians; Father Sabetti, the author of a *Compendium Theologiae Moralis* of which thirty-four editions had been published up to 1939; Father Charles Piccirillo, a former editor for twenty-three years of *Civilta' Cattolica*, and the man to whom Woodstock owes its museum of natural history.

Elsewhere, Father Anthony Ciampi served as president of Holy Cross College for three terms between 1851 and 1873, and Father Nicholas Russo was president of Boston College from 1887 to 1888. Father Ciampi also served as president of Loyola College in Baltimore in 1863.

FATHER CATALDO—FOUNDER OF GONZAGA UNIVERSITY

The greatest Jesuit missionary in the entire Northwest was Father Joseph Cataldo, a native of the town of Terrasini, in the province of Palermo, who landed in Boston in 1862.

One of the great builders of the Northwest, regardless of creed or nationality, he has been called the Father of the City of Spokane, a title which in all probability he deserves. Begining in 1865 among the Indians of Idaho, he served as missionary in the Northwest and in Alaska, as superior of all Jesuit missions for seventeen years, as founder of churches, convents, academies, and other Catholic institutions from Wyoming to Washington. His crowning achievement, however, was the founding of Gonzaga University in 1881. When he became superior, there were in the entire Northwest 43 Jesuit Fathers and Brothers; when he left sixteen years later, they numbered more than 150.

On March 13, 1928, a month before he died, the Spokane Chamber of Commerce gave a luncheon in his honor at which all the civic institutions in the city were represented. The next day he was honored by Gonzaga University. On March 15, a great civic reception was held also in Spokane, at which the highest state and city dignitaries intervened. The Italian consul at Seattle, one Signor Alfani, sent his regrets. Father Cataldo was then 91 years old.

FATHER JOSEPH CATALDO

A memorial to Father Cataldo erected in 1936 in front of the mission built by him in 1866, the first among the Spokane Indians. (Photo by the author.)

Father Cataldo's grave in St. Michael's Cemetery, Spokane, Wash. (Photo by the author.)

IN COLORADO AND NEW MEXICO

In 1867 a number of Jesuits of the Neapolitan province, headed by Father Donato Gasparri, a native of the province of Foggia, arrived to labor in Colorado, New Mexico and Texas. In all probability, more than one hundred Jesuits, both Fathers and Brothers, of the Province of Naples, labored in those three states until our own days. The last of the pioneers was Father Salvatore Giglio, who died at Pueblo in 1943.

In all, the Jesuits of the Neapolitan province remained in the United States as an independent group for fifty-two years, or until 1919. During this period of time they erected 14 parochial and 50 mission churches, organized 17 parishes and about 100 missions and stations, and built a number of convents, schools, hospitals and other institutions, including Regis College at Denver.

FATHER PONZIGLIONE

We cannot conclude these summary notes about the Italian Jesuits in the United States without mentioning Father Paul M. Ponziglione, a missionary who spent forty years among the Indians of the Middle West from Kansas to Wyoming. Suffice it to say that he established 61 missions and took a prominent part in the establishment of 82 more. We do not know exactly how many churches he built; in Kansas alone he built at least seven, besides several schools for boys and girls. The son of a count, he was born in Piedmont and came to America in 1848, laboring among Indians and whites until 1891, when he retired to Chicago, where he died in 1900. While in Chicago he founded the Guardian Angel's School, out of which was born the Church of the Holy Guardian Angel.

THE ITALIAN PASSIONISTS

The Order of the Congregation of the Passion was introduced in the United States by Father Anthony Calandri and remained under the administration of Italian-born provincials for almost half a century, with one exception. During this time the Passionist Fathers established their monasteries at Pittsburgh, Dunkirk, West Hoboken, Marysville, Cal., Baltimore, Cincinnati, Louisville, St. Louis, and St. Paul, Kansas. Those are facts that Italian-Americans should do well to remember, for it seems that our American Passionist Fathers are trying to make people forget the labor of their Italian pioneers.

The founder, Father Anthony Calandri, arrived in Pittsburgh on December 8, 1952, together with two more priests and a brother. One of the priests, Father Parezyki, was a Pole. On April 7, 1853, the cornerstone of their first monastery, on Pittsburgh's South side, was laid. The Province of the Blessed Paul of the Cross was created in 1863, with Father John Dominic Tarlattini as first provincial. He was followed by Fathers Calandri, Tarlattini, once more, Stefanini, Carunchio, Murmane, and Baudinelli. All of them, with the exception of Father Murmane, were natives of Italy.

Another Passionist, Father Peter Magagnotto, landed in California even before the arrival of Father Calandri. Coming from Australia, from 1849 to 1853 he lived in San Francisco, where he built the first church of Saint Francis on Vallejo Street. He also served as the first vicar general of the archdiocese. Later he and other Italian Passionists labored in Nevada and Utah, where they established a number of parishes and missions. Also in Nevada, a Genoese priest, Father Dominic Monteverde, who was ordained in San Francisco in 1864, organized one parish and eight missions. Later he moved to Brooklyn. (See *Ital-Am. Hist.* Vol. II, 840.)

FATHER PAMPHILUS OF MAGLIANO

THE FRANCISCAN FATHERS

The first Italian Franciscan Father to settle in the United States seems to have been The Rev. Francis Caro, a Sicilian, who became the first pastor of the Church of St. Joseph, Roswill, Staten Island, in 1855.

In that year several Franciscan Fathers, headed by the Rev. Pamphilus of Magliano, a town in the Abruzzi, arrived from Italy and settled in the diocese of Buffalo. In less than twelve years the tireless pathfinder created six monasteries, five parishes, twenty-two mission churches, a college, a seminary, and an academy for young women, besides two new communities of sisters. All the parishes were in New York State, with the exception of one at Houston, Texas, and another at Towanda, Pa. The college founded by Father Pamphilus was St. Bonaventure's College at Allegany, N. Y., one of the best-known small colleges in the country today.

In Connecticut, another distinguished Franciscan, Father Leo Rizzo of Saracena, a native of Calabria, was active from 1865 to the day of his death in 1897. During the Civil War he served as a chaplain with the Ninth Connecticut Volunteers.

ST. BONAVENTURE'S COLLEGE, ALLEGANY, N. Y.
Founded by Father Pamphilus of Magliano.

FATHER PAMPHILUS OF MAGLIANO

A tablet in the vestibule of the Catholic Cathedral of New Orleans which credits Pauline Jaricot as the foundress of the Society of the Propagation of the Faith, whereas it has been established that the Society was founded by Father Angelo Inglesi. (Photo by the author.)

THE FRIARS MINOR CONVENTUALS

The Italian Conventuals in the United States have not been numerous at any time; nevertheless they made up in labors what they lacked in numbers. They included: Father Joseph Lesen, an Italian despite his German name, who served as provincial from 1880 to 1889; Father Francis Gatti, superior of the Conventual missions in Texas, college rector and teacher; Father Caesar Cucchiarini, who was active in the Mohawk Valley in New York State between 1865 and 1890; Father Peter M. Giachetti, who built more than twelve churches in New Jersey between 1865 and 1892; and Fathers Salvatelli and Marzetti, who pioneered in St. Louis Mo., and Alton, Ill.

THE SERVITES

A small, but important, group of Italian Servites, or Servants of Mary, arrived at Green Bay Wis., in 1870. From there they spread to Chicago,where they were the first to minister to Italian immigrants. Their leader was Father John Morini of Florence, a learned theologian who had introduced the Servite Order in England.

PIONEER SECULAR PRIESTS

One of the first Italian secular priests in the United States was Father Angelo Inglesi, the real founder of the Society of the Propagation of the Faith, notwithstanding the tablet in the vestibule of the Cathedral of St. Louis in New Orleans, according to which the Society was founded by Madame Jaricot.

IGNAZIO CARDINAL PERSICO
Bishop of Savannah, Ga., from 1870 to 1872.

Other pioneers included:

Bishop Ignazio Persico of Savannah, Ga., a Capuchin, who served from 1870 to 1872, when he returned to Italy.

Father Constantine Pise, to whom goes the double honor of having written the first Catholic novel in America and of having been the first and only Catholic chaplain the Congress of the United States ever had. He was born in Annapolis in 1801, the son of the painter Pise already noted by us, and was the author of various novels as well as of a five-volume history of the Catholic Church.

Father Michael Olivetti who was active in Ohio and, after 1847, in the Lake Champlain district.

Father Izzi and Father Neno, the first two Italian Augustinians to come to the United States. Father Izzo became pastor at Mechanicville, N. Y., in 1867.

Father Venuta, a former member of the Sicilian Parliament, who came over in 1848. He built two churches in New Jersey, where he died in 1876.

Monsignor De Concilio, a Neapolitan, pastor of St. Michael's Church in Jersey City from 1860 to the time of his death in 1890.

Father Joseph M. Finotti, literary editor of the Boston *Pilot* for many years and the author of several books.

Father Frigueglietti, one of several Italian pastors in New England, who built four churches at, or near, Quincy, Mass.

Father Eugene Vetromile, a native of Gallipoli, in the province of Lecce, who came to America in 1840 and spent more than twenty-five years among the Indians and French-Canadians of Maine. He wrote several books, some of which are reproduced in facsimile in the present chapter.

Fathers Joseph Rolando and Joseph Nardiello, pastors in New Jersey after 1870 and 1878, respectively.

Father Gaetano Mariani, pastor of the Church of St. Mary Magdalene de Pazzi, in Philadelphia, the first Italian parish in the United States, organized in 1852.

Father Gaetano Sorrentini, pastor at Monterey, Cal., in 1857, and at the Italian Church in Philadelphia in 1866, succeeding Father Mariani.

Last, but not least, Father Eugene Bononcini, a native of Modena, who labored in Kansas after 1866 and died at Toluca, Ill., in 1907.

NO RUM, NO FIRE-WATER
Illustration from Father Vetromile's book "The Prayer Song" in one of the Indian languages of Maine.

THE PORTAGE
An illustration from Rev. Vetromile's "History of the Abnakis" in Indian dialect and English, showing how the Indians and the missionaries carried their canoes when crossing over land.

REV. EUGENE BONONCINI
Pioneer priest in Kansas

REV. EUGENE VETROMILE
Pioneer priest among the Indians of Maine.

INDIAN GOOD BOOK,
MADE BY
Eugene Vetromile, S. J.,
INDIAN PATRIARCH,

FOR THE
BENEFIT OF THE
PENOBSCOT, PASSAMAQUODDY, ST. JOHN'S,
MICMAC,
AND OTHER TRIBES OF
THE ABNAKI INDIANS.
THIS YEAR ONE THOUSAND EIGHT HUNDRED AND FIFTY-SIX.
OLD-TOWN INDIAN VILLAGE,
AND BANGOR.

NEW YORK:
EDWARD DUNIGAN & BROTHER,
151 FULTON STREET.
1856.

OF VETROMILE'S
NOBLE BIBLE.
Such as happened Great-Truths.
MADE BY
EUGENE VETROMILE,
INDIAN PATRIARCH,
Corresponding member of the Maine Historical Society, &c.,
FOR THE BENEFIT OF
THE PENOBSCOT, MICMAC,
AND OTHER TRIBES OF THE
Abnaki Indians.
OLD TOWN, INDIAN VILLAGE, AND BANGOR. 1858.

NEW YORK–VILLAGE:
RENNIE, SHEA & LINDSAY.
1860.

Entered according to Act of Congress, in the year 1856, by EDWARD DUNIGAN & BROTHER, in the Clerk's Office of the District Court for the Southern District of New York.

ALNAMBAY ULI
AWIKHIGAN,
KISI TUNESSA
Eugin Vetromile, S. J.,
ALNAMBAY PATLIAS,
ULIHALAKONA
PENAUBSKET, SYBAYK, ULASTOOK,
MICMAC,
TEBA MINAKTAKIK ETALAUNSISIK
WANBANAKKI ALNAMBAK.
YO PEMIKATOOK NEKUTAMQUÀKE NSANSOOK KESSAKTEKOY TEBA NONINSKA
TEBA NEKUTANS.
PENAUBSKET ALNAMBAY
UDENEK,
TEBA KANDOSKIK.
NEW YORK:
EDWARD DUNIGAN & BROTHER,
151 FULTON STREET,
1856.

AHIAMIHEWINTUHANGAN;

THE PRAYER SONG,

ARRANGED BY
REV. EUGENE VETROMILE, S. J.

NEW YORK:
PUBLISHED BY EDWARD DUNIGAN & BROTHER,
(JAMES B. KIRKER,)
NO. 371 BROADWAY
1858.

THE LORD'S PRAYER IN MICMAC HIEROGLYPHICS.

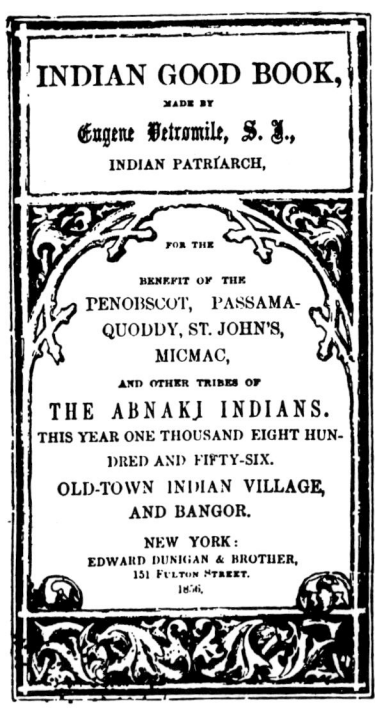

Title-pages of five of Rev. Vetromile's books and (*bottom right*) a page from "The Abnakis and Their History." (Courtesy, *The New York Public Library.*)

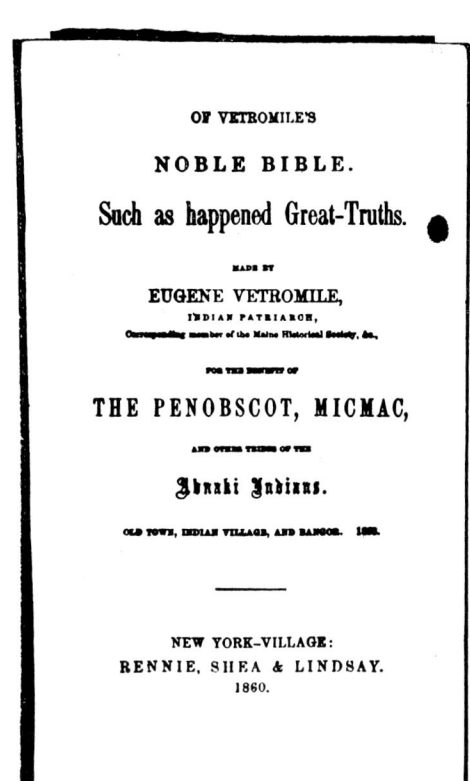

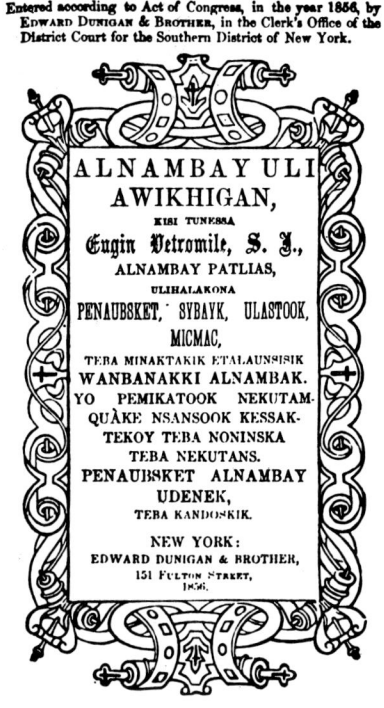

ST. FRANCES XAVIER CABRINI

RELIGIOUS ORDERS

Although the Franciscans and the Servites ministered to Italian immigrants from Civil War days, it was with the arrival of the Scalabrinian Fathers in 1888 that Italian priests came to the United States with the sole purpose of taking care of their fellow-immigrants. In 1897 the first Salesians landed in San Francisco, and a year later in New York, also to take care of the local Italians.

Today the more important Italian religious orders in the country include the Stigmatine Fathers, the Pallottine Fathers, the Sylvestrine Benedectines, the Capuchins, the Augustinians, the Oblates of St. Joseph, and a few less numerous ones.

RELIGIOUS ORDERS OF WOMEN

The first, or at least, the most distinguished Italian nun in the United States, previous to the arrival of Mother Cabrini, was Sister Tommasini of Parma, who came over in 1848 to spend sixty-five years in the service of the Society of the Sacred Heart in North America. She served as mistress general of Manhattanville, superior vicar of Canada, and local superior in Cuba, Louisiana, and Mexico. She had been preceded to the United States by Mother Marie Therese Trincano, who came in 1847 and helped to found quite a few of the schools or academies which the Society established in North America. She died in 1868.

In the 1870's the Segale Sisters and the Bentivoglio Sisters began to labor in the Middle West. All of them were born in Italy. Sister Justina and Blandina Segale were active in Ohio, Colorado, New Mexico and Arizona until the second decade of our century. One of them, Sister Blandina, wrote a book, *At the End of the Santa Fe Trail,* which was the monthly book selection of the Catholic Literary Foundation not many years ago.

The Bentivoglio Sisters arrived in 1875, but they had to overcome many difficulties before they were able to introduce the Order of the Poor Clares in the United States.

Over and above all of them stands, of course, Saint Frances Cabrini, the foundress of the Order of the Missionary Sisters of the Sacred Heart and the first American citizen to be elevated to sainthood. In 1950 her Order conducted 14 colleges, 98 schools, 28 orphanages, 8 hospitals, 4 dispensaries, 3 training schools for nurses, 4 ambulance services, 6 day nurseries, 2 rest homes and 2 preventoriums. The members of the community, close to 3,700, are scattered from the Atlantic to the Pacific.

Since the turn of the century other Italian orders of sisterhoods have settled in the United States, such as the Missionary Zelatrices of the Sacred Heart, the Salesian Sisters, the Venerini Sisters, the Religious Teachers Filippini, etc.

THE BENTIVOGLIO SISTERS
(*Left*) Mother M. Costanza and (*Right*) Mother M. Maddalena, Foundress and Abbess of the Order of St. Clare in the United States.

CHAPTER SEVENTEEN

EARLY TRAVELLERS

From time immemorial, travel in foreign countries has always been one of the main aspirations of the educated Italian; not travel with a Baedeker or in search of night clubs and taverns; but travel as the source of new impressions; of learning; of new vistas for the mind; travel primarily as an opportunity for research and discovery. The Italians have always travelled for the same reasons that prompted Lanfranc and Anselm, both Archbishops of Canterbury, to roam through France in the 11th century; or Marco Polo and Giovanni da Pian del Carpine through Asia in the 13th; or Aeneas Sylvius and Ciriaco of Ancona in search of manuscripts and inscriptions in the 15th. Benzoni, as we have seen, was the first man to come to the New World in search of Indian lore and antiquities.

American independence aroused the interest of the Italians, as we have noted at the beginning of Chapter Twelve. Certainly a small nation that could successfully defy the might of powerful England was an object of admiration; but America was a new world in every meaning of the word, a world full of surprises not only for the student of political science, but especially for the naturalist, the geographer, the astronomer, the ethnologist.

We are not amazed, therefore, if at all times serious Italians have come to our continent to roam, and see, and note down. From what they wrote one certainly could compile a most interesting anthology about America of yesterday, something which, unfortunately, we cannot do even summarily in the present chapter.

IL VIAGGIO AEREO
DELL' ILLUSTRE CAVALIER MILANESE
DON PAOLO ANDREANI
nell' Anno 1783
ESPOSTO
DAL CANONICO CARLO CASTELLI
IN UNA LETTERA
DIRETTA
AL SIG. FAUJAS DE SAINT FOND,
Celebre Istorico delle esperienze ariostatiche.

MILANO

PER LI FRATELLI PIROLA
Impressori dell' Eccellentissima Città
dicontro al Teatro grande alla Scala.
Con Permissione.

Title-page of Canon Castelli's account of Andreani's first air ascension in Italy in 1783. (Courtesy, *Library of Congress.*)

Here we shall refer briefly to a few travelers who arrived before 1825 and to list a few who came between 1825 and 1850. As for those who paid us a visit during the second half of the century, the reader is referred to Dr. Andrew J. Torrielli's book, *Italian Opinion on America.* One more observation is necessary at the outset: not all early Italian travellers in the United States came over to visit our country; many of them simply took advantage of their stopover at some Atlantic port, on their way to Central America, to take a glance at our country.

COUNT CASTIGLIONI

Count Luigi Castiglioni, a native of Milan (1757-1832), was probably the first Italian traveler of distinction to visit the United States. He came over in 1785 and remained until 1787, traveling, meantime, in every one of of the Thirteen States. In 1785 he was the guest of George Washington at Mount Vernon; a year later he visited Ezra Stiles, president of Yale College, at New Haven, as we learn from Stiles' diary (August 27, 1786, *Manuscript,* Yale University); also in the same year, while in Philadelphia, he was made a member of the American Philosophical Society. Back in Milan, in 1790 he published his *Viaggio Negli Stati Uniti,* in which he related his American experiences and described many plants he noted during his travels. His book was translated into German.

COUNT ANDREANI

Count Paolo Andreani (1764-1823), a native of Milan like Castiglioni, is best known as one of the pioneers of aeronautics, and as one of the first men to ascend in a balloon in February, 1783. He made the first ascensions in Italy and the fourth and fifth in the world. He was elected member of several scientific societies, including the Royal Irish Academy of Dublin, and the American Philosophical Society.

In 1784 Andreani made a scientific expedition in Scotland and Ireland; in 1790 he was in London (*Thraliana,* 2 vols. Oxford, 1942, 765). A year later he was exploring the Lake Superior region, noting his observations in a journal which has been quoted by the Duke de la Rochefoucault Liancourt in his *Travels Trough the United States of North America,* (4 vols., London, 1799, I, 575-591). "The abilities and character of Count Andreani," the writer informs us, "inspire great confidence in the exactness of the information which he has collected."

Andreani is also mentioned in *A Tour To The Lakes* by Th. L. McKenney, published at Baltimore in 1827. Quot-ing one Mr. Johnson, an early resident of Minnesota, McKenney tells us: "In the year 1791, Mr. Johnson remembers to have been on Le Point. and to have seen a scientific Frenchman, or Italian, with his instruments adjusted, taking observations; and endeavouring to ascertain the longitude. He told him he had visited the highest mountains and among these, Mt. Blanc; and his ulterior object had relation to the question regarding the formation of the earth at the poles. His name was Count Andrian. Does anybody know any thing of the result of the Count's investigation? Few people would suppose that this extreme point, so far beyond the bounds of civilized life, and so far in the interior, had ever been the theater of such scientific investigations." (*A Tour of the Lakes,* 263.) It seems also probable that Andreani circumnavigated Lake Superior, "one of the first white persons of whom there is record to accomplish that feat." (Smith, G. H., Count Andreani: A forgotten traveler, *Minnesota History,* March, 1938; see also North American Review, Vol. 24, 344.)

Andreani, as we have seen in Chapter Fifteen, wrote a letter to Chancellor Livingston of New York University in 1792, recommending the sculptor Ceracchi. He was also in close touch with other outstanding Americans, including Dr. William Thornton of Philadelphia, in whose company he toured Europe (Jackson, J., *Early Philadelphia Architects and Engineers,* Philadelphia, 1923). He came to America with a letter of introduction from John Paradise to George Washington, to whom he brought a copy of Alfieri's *Ode to America,* but apparently he later made, or was said to have made, some remarks about the United States which prompted Washington to refer to him in indifferent terms. At any rate, Andreani was in good terms with Thomas Jefferson and James Madison, as we learn from a letter he wrote to Madison from New Orleans in March, 1808. In that letter, which is in French, Andreani offered to write for the benefit of President Jefferson an interesting account of the political situation in Louisiana, where he had lived for many years, and where he had no political or commercial ties. Thus, he wrote, he would have been able to judge with impartiality. The letter is in the Manuscript Division of the New York Public Library.

(On Andreani see Mancini, L., *Grande Enciclopedia Aeronautica,* Milan, 1936, and Caproni, Guasti, Tiurina e Bertarelli, *L'aeronautica italiana nell'immagine,* 1487-1875, Milan, 1938.)

Andreani brings to our mind another early Italian resident of Philadelphia who was also interested in aeronautics. He was Joseph Ravara (or Ravera, a well-known Piedmontese name), consul general of Genoa in Philadelphia, who was very much interested in the ascensions that Blanchard made in 1793 and 1794. Ravara was planning to ride in Blanchard's balloon and raised some money to finance its undertaking, but the ascension did not take place. (See Scharf & Westcott, *History of Philadelphia,* I, 471, and the papers of Thomas Jefferson in the Library

The Lake Superior region, as drawn by Joseph Scott for his "United States Gazetteer" published in Philadelphia in 1795, the earliest of such books published. (From Winsor's *Narrative and Critical History of America.*)

of Congress, under May, 1793.) Another Italian who was interested in areonautics while in the United States was the political exile, Quirico Filopanti, as related in Chapter Twenty.

DR. GIOVAN BATTISTA SCANDELLA

The facsimile of Scandella's obituary reproduced on the next page dispenses us from repeating the information about his life contained therein.

Dr. Scandella came to America with letters of introduction to some of our outstanding citizens. Washington, whom he visited in 1796, referred to him in a letter as "Dr. Scandella, who gave me the pleasure of his company in June last, and whom I found a very sensible, and well informed man." (*Writings,* Vol. 35, 506.) Latrobe, the architect of the Capitol, decribed him in his *Journal* as a "Venetian gentleman of the most amiable, fascinating manner, and of the best information upon almost every scientific subject, who speaks English perfectly and who has now travelled through all the country between the St. Lawrence and the St. James River." On April 20, 1798, Scandella was elected a member of the American Philosophical Society. (Reference to Scandella will be found in Dunlap's *Diary,;* Thacher, J., *American Medical Biography,* II, 91; Oberholtzer, E. P., *Literary History of Philadelphia,* 1906, 159, *The Autobiography of Benjamin Rush,* Princeton, 1948; Stokes, *Iconography of Manhattan Island;* Hardie, J., *An account of the Malignant Fever,* 1799.)

EUSEBIO VALLI

Eusebio Valli (1762-1816), an eminent pathologist (Castiglioni, A., *History of Medicine*), is probably the first hero in the medical annals of the New World. The forerunner of Pasteur, he laid the foundations of modern vaccinotherapy. (Arcieri, G., Agostino Bassi, N. Y., 1938.)

After some years in the Orient, where he experimented on the plague, and a few more as a military physician in Dalmatia and in Spain, he came to North America to study the yellow fever, hoping to develop some type of preventive vaccination. It was in the course of those experiments that he died, the voluntary victim of the yellow fever, at Havana, Cuba.

Valli arrived in the United States in April, 1816, with a letter of introduction from Carlo Botta, the famous historian, to Thomas Jefferson. A few days later Jefferson invited him to his house. "As it would be mortifying to me," he wrote, "to lose by any occasional absence the pleasure of receiving you here, I take the liberty of mentioning that three or four times a year I visit a distant possession and sometimes make considerable stays there, but as these visits are fixed to no particular times, a previous notice of that which will best suit yourself will enable me to accomodate my movements to yours."

On June 3, Valli sent Jefferson a 19-page letter in which he explained in detail his theories about the yellow fever, ending with the announcement that he was leaving for Havana, where he was planning to inject himself with the sweat of the dying and the bile of the dead, and to risk his life in the interest of science. A few months later he was dead.

146 MEDICAL REPOSITORY.

tivity as its leader. Mr. J. however, found afterwards, that if the ears of a blinded bat were filled with pomatum, it was no longer able to fly steadily and with exactness."

[For the above information we are chiefly indebted to the (London) Monthly Magazine for May, June, July and August last.]

MEDICAL OBITUARY.

Died, Sept. 16, 1798, I. B. Scandella, M. D. aged 28. The fate of this gentleman was, in a remarkable degree, to be lamented. He was a native of the Venetian State. His family were opulent and high in rank. He had received the best medical education, but had consecrated his faculties to the general improvement of science, and the benefit of mankind.

Having resided for some time at London in the capacity of Secretary to the Venetian Embassy, he conceived the design of visiting America. His country's service no longer demanding his attention, he proposed to gratify a liberal curiosity in surveying the principles and structure of a rising empire.

He first arrived at Quebec, and thence took various journeys through the southern and western districts. His personal merits secured him the esteem of the persons among us, most eminent for their knowledge and talents. His candour and blameless deportment made him be regarded with peculiar tenderness by all who knew him. His chief attention was directed to agricultural improvements and projects, justly conceiving that mankind would derive most benefit from the perfection of this art.

Having spent two years in this country, and accomplished the purposes which brought him hither, he embarked for Europe in June, 1798. The vessel proving unfit for the voyage, he returned to Philadelphia, the port from which he had set out. Shortly after he came to New-York, and engaged a passage in a packet which was speedily to sail from this harbour. The detention of his baggage, which was daily expected from Philadelphia, occasioned him the loss of this opportunity. An epidemical disease had meanwhile made its appearance in both cities. Notwithstanding its greater progress and malignity in the latter city, his concern in the welfare of a helpless family, whom his departure had deprived of their only useful friend, induced him to return thither. After enduring the continual loss of rest, and exposing himself to the influence of an infected atmosphere for ten days, he set out on his return to New-York. He had scarcely arrived before symptoms of disease appeared, which, on the sixth day terminated in death.

Scandella's obituary in the *Medical Repository,* Vol. 2, No. 2, 1798. (Courtesy, *New York Public Library.*)

(Below). Last paragraph of Dr. Valli's letter to Jefferson, dated June 3, 1816. It reads in part: "Being convinced of the contagious character of the yellow fever I propose to contract the disease with the sweat of the dying and the bile of the dead . . . if it should be written in the Book of Destiny that I fall a victim in the great experiment my death will not be without glory." (Courtesy, *Library of Congress.*)

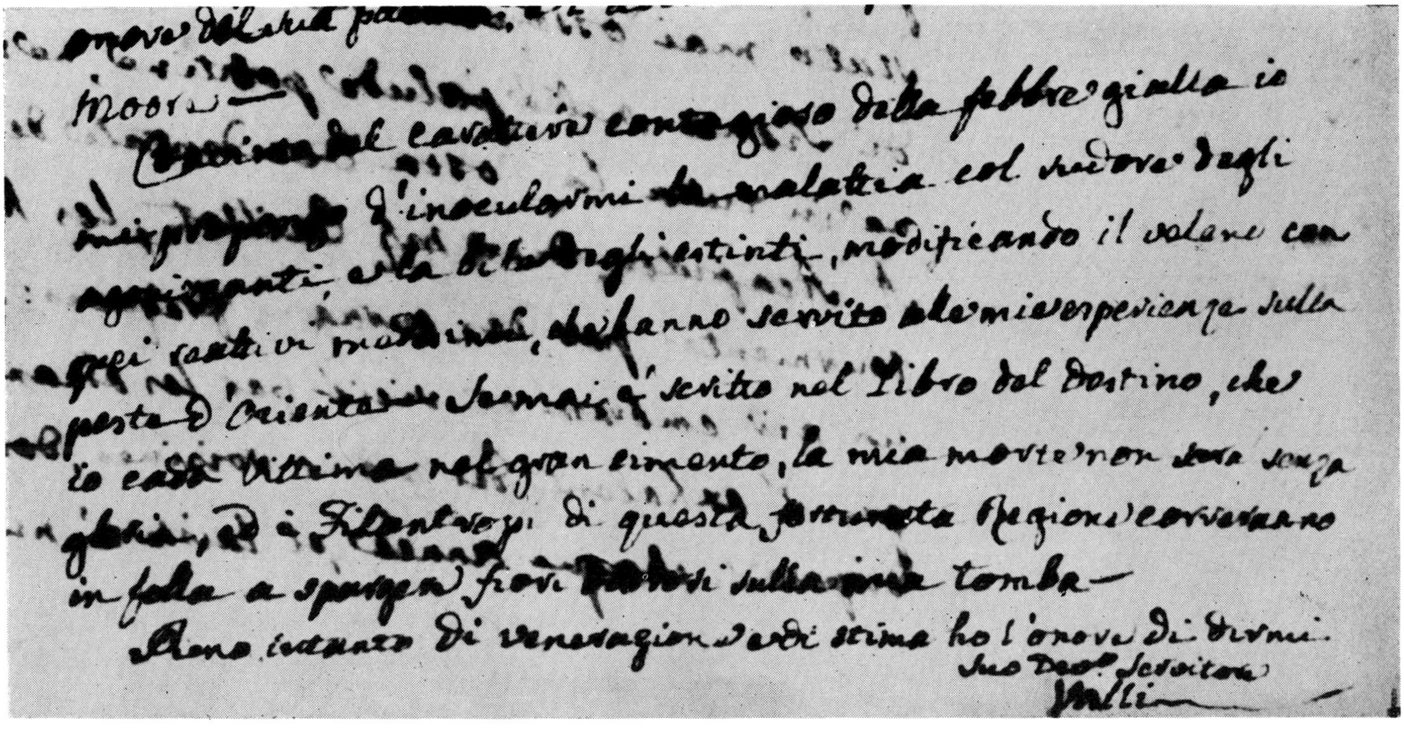

BELTRAMI DISCOVERS THE SOURCES OF THE MISSISSIPPI RIVER

Giacomo Costantino Beltrami, the discoverer of the sources of the Mississippi River, has been called "perhaps the most picturesque and unique figure in the series of many explorers of the area of Minnesota." He explored the Lake Ithasca region nine years before Henry Schoolcraft, to whom the honor of the discovery has been generally credited.

Beltrami was born at Bergamo, Italy, in 1779, and had served as a judge, when the fall of Napoleon, whose follower he was, compelled him to leave his home. In 1821 he decided to visit Europe, and later America, where he landed in November, 1822.

While here he made up his mind to find the sources of the Mississippi River, moved only by the desire of achieving glory. In August, 1823, he plunged into the wilderness of Minnesota, at first with two Indians and a white guide, and then by himself.

Alone, without knowledge of the country, with scanty provisions, Beltrami carried on, paddling a birch canoe; but, as he was inexperienced at paddling, the canoe upset, drenching his provisions. He then decided to proceed in "Chinese style," or by towing his canoe behind. He had gone alone for four days when he fortunately met a party of Indians, one of whom he persuaded to take him to Red Lake, where they arrived on August 19. By canoe he then proceeded to what is now known as Mud Lake, and finally, on the 28th, he reached a small lake which he called Lake Julia, in honor of the Countess Medici-Spada, and which he proclaimed to be the real source of the Mississippi River.

Covered with animal skins sewed with animal senews, with the bark of a tree as a hat, hungry and tired, Beltrami resumed his march towards civilization, until he reached New Orleans. There, in 1824, he published his first book, *La Decouverte,* in which he described, in the form of letters, his adventures and his observations. Four years later he published in London a more lengthy account in two volumes, under the title of *A Pilgrimage.*

Beltrami's book was not well received in some circles which he had criticized, yet, as we have fully demonstrated in *The Italians in America Before the Civil War,* there is no doubt that he was the discoverer of the sources of the Father of the Waters.

Back in Europe, Beltrami was made honorary member of many academies and learned societies. In 1834 he represented the Historical Institute of France at the Scientific Congress of Stuttgart. Lafayette honored him with his friendship. Chateaubriand acknowledged in his *Voyage en Amerique* that some of his descriptions of the United States were based on Beltrami's books. James Fenimore Cooper is also said to have used those volumes with profit. To remember his feat in the United States one will find on the map Beltrami County and Beltrami Village, both in Minnesota.

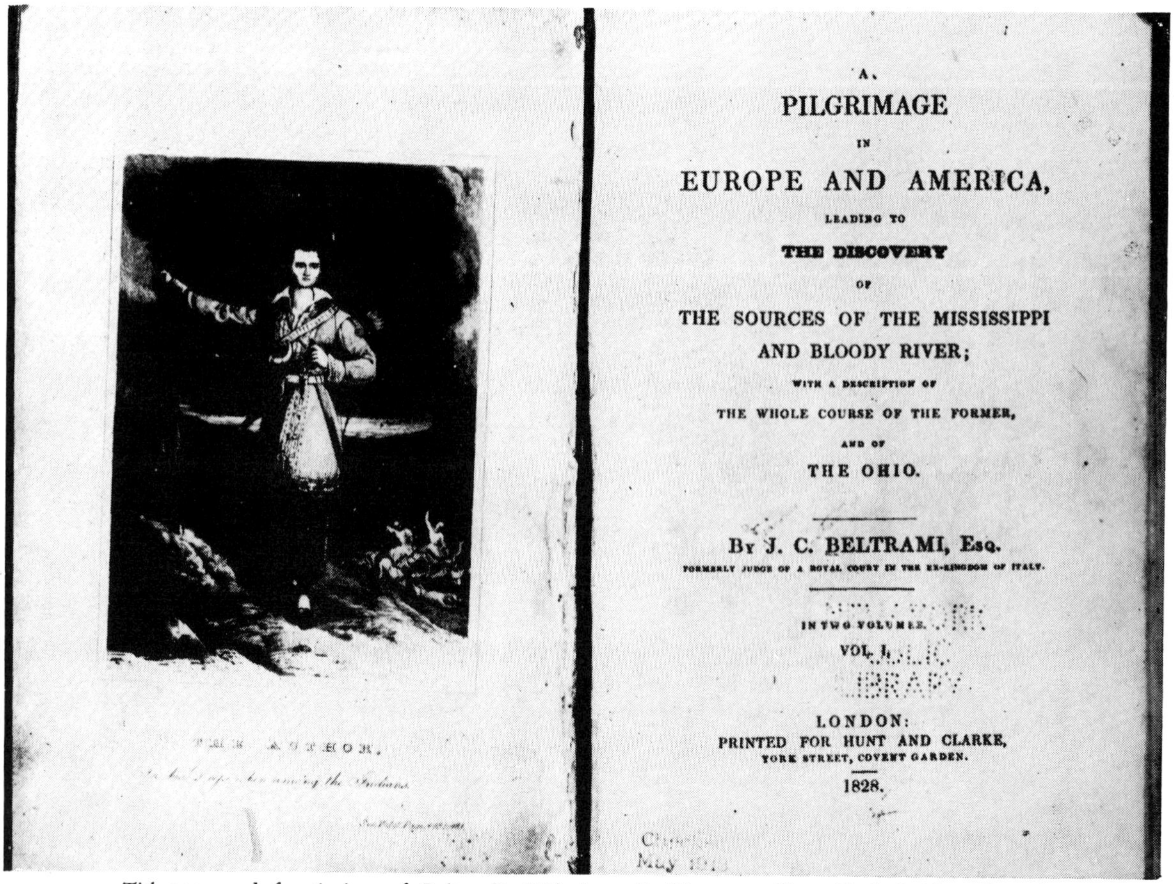

Title-page and frontispiece of Beltrami's "Pilgrimage." (Courtesy, *New York Public Library.*)

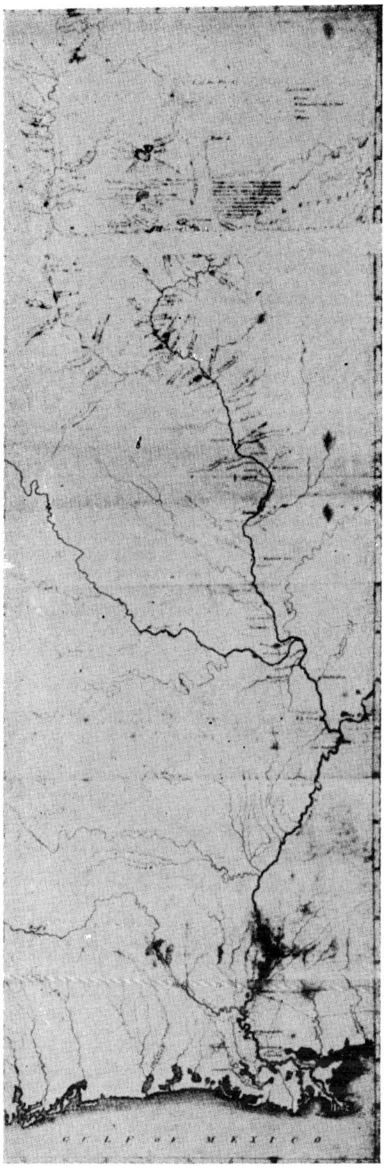

Map of the Mississippi River prepared by Beltrami. The upper part is the first complete map of the head of the River.

GIACOMO COSTANTINO BELTRAMI
A portrait by Enrico Scuri presented to the Minnesota Historical Society in 1865 by the City of Bergamo, Beltrami's native place.

BELTRAMI SURPRISED BY THE INDIANS
(From W. Glazier's *The Headwaters of the Mississippi,* New York, 1893.)

I shall limit myself to remark, that some of the beautiful situations, which one meets in the valley of the river of St. Peter, afford interesting scenery for descriptions; that some new traits of the savages, some curious anecdotes, and the history of the swan, the musk-rat, the buffalo, the wolves, merit all the attention of the reader. The wars, the horrors, and policy of the colony of Pembonel, and of the *North West* and *Hudson Bay* companies, offer a new proof that civilized man is more barbarous than the savage.—The dogs, also, act a part there, which add something to the natural history.

The eighth letter is the Achilles and the Hercules of my work; it is the shield upon which I repose myself.

I tremble every time, when I think upon the terrible situation in which my savage guides left me; and I feel with pride, that I have been more than human in not trembling then. And the sources of the *Bloody River* to the north going to throw themselves into the *Frozen Ocean!*... and the sources of the Mississippi to the south!... and the waters flowing on one side towards the Pacific, and on the other, towards the Atlantic!.. and the phenomenon of that lake, which is only surmounted by the Heavens!...Those enchanting situations! That silence! That sombre solitude!—My poor savage repast! My bark porringer!—What an assemblage of wonders, of thoughts, and of feelings, surrounding the eyes, and the soul! . . .—What an exalted idea of the Almighty, of the Great Architect of the Universe! . . .—Ah! Yes! It is with the

most devout enthusiasm, I exclaimed, ***how happy is one to believe!*** It is here that my hypocritical calumniators ought to be confounded. . . . But, where religion is only a calculation, all good profession of faith is useless; in order to please them, one must believe as they wish, and blindly serve their ambitious projects, and their culpable policy. And these bitter and delightful remembrances! . . .—*Infandum regina jubes renovare dolorem.*—Let us only stop here a moment to allow some souls of sensibility to consecrate again their tears of regret and veneration to the most pure virtue, to the rarest friendship.—Such tears are equally honourable to the beings who weep, and to those who are the subjects of them.

In the 9th, 10th, and 11th letters, I have conducted the reader to the western sources of the Mississippi; I have marked, *with exactitude*, the places, where Messrs. Pike and Schoolcraft have arrived before me; I have shown him the entire course of this great river, all the lakes and rivers which flow into it; I detain him at the most interesting spots, to inspire his admiration; and, with incontestible evidence, I prove that the Mississippi is the first river in the world, and I hope that the Americans will find some new proofs of my esteem in the new reflections that I offer them there.

The picture of the dreadful Bacchanals at Leech Lake is of a horror entirely new, and I believe, that the terrible dangers, from which I have escaped, only through the miraculous interposition of that *Providence*, which has never abandoned me in this perilous

6

not always explain ourselves with *veni, vidi, vici*, and much less can it be expected here, where I have to contend with powerful enemies, Envy, Malice and Ingratitude.

First, let me say a word, with some reflections, upon what has been said, and done, for, and against my book, in order, that the public may the more properly appreciate this unusual attempt.

At New-Orleans, I was deemed worthy of Paradise, in England, I was assigned to the Infernal Regions, and the Holy Alliance have condemned me to Purgatory.—No matter:

> Integer vitæ scelerisque purus
> Non eget Mauris jaculis neque arcu:

Happily till now I have escaped the darkness of *limbo!*

I have been told, that the Bishop of Louisiana has accused me at the court of Rome, as an arch-heretic, and has inscribed my name on his *Index*, whilst some prelates, and other respectable clergymen of devout and orthodox Mexico, have proclaimed me as a defender of the faith.

At Philadelphia, the editor of the National Gazette, *the friend of Major Long*, (and whom all the world knows very well,) has prostituted truth, evidence, and the good sense of the public, to the necessity, which he cannot resist, of being malicious, and rude. See his paper of the 11th or 12th August, 1824.—Mark, I have committed no other fault towards him, but that of treating him with much politeness; which I have done also towards many others who have conspired with him, and sought, by secret and base devices, to prejudice the public of Philadelphia against my poor book.

The first article which appeared in this city, in the Commercial Advertiser of July 25th, compared me almost to Columbus, &c. &c. Exaggerated praise is no criterion; and it is always suspicious in the eyes of the judicious; but the writer speaks truly of the perfidious conduct, which for a year and a half, kept concealed 400 copies of my book at Philadelphia, whither I had sent them from New-Orleans, to be distributed among the different cities of the East, and which had I not returned from Mexico, and made some enquiries respecting them, would never again have seen the light. A second article in the Evening Post of the 11th of August, gives me at first, praise without bounds; but concludes by accusing me of a disposition to satire, which does not constitute a just criticism; and a third article, a generous Mæcenas, under the signature of "Army," grants me a certificate, as if the self-evident truth of my book required testimony.

The National Advocate, whilst honouring me with his approbation, which I duly appreciate, seems to cast some doubt on my discovery, for in saying "this is the first important work on the topography of that section of our country, *written in the French language*," the reader is naturally led to conclude, that there had been others written in English; the praise is therefore *equivocal*.

Another journalist has amused himself with throwing oblique glances, with a quantity of "*not without*," upon the offering which a worthy son of unhappy Italy thought his duty to make to his country, and to friendship. The editor has all the means of announcing his opinion without marring articles confided to his paper, and which he was not asked to comment upon;

Four pages from Beltrami's Pilgrimage in which he describes his discovery of the sources of the Mississippi River and tells of the praise and criticism with which the announcement of his discovery was received.

OTHER EARLY TRAVELLERS

OTHER EARLY TRAVELLERS

Two early travelers who stopped in the United States long enough to take part in some local figthing, were Agostino Codazzi and Costante Ferrari. Both of them acquired distinction in South America, especially Codazzi, who became chief of staff and colonel in the engineering corps of Venezuela, governor of a province, explorer, map maker, and scientist. His memoirs contain some enthusiastic pages about the United States.

Codazzi and Ferrari landed at Baltimore in August, 1817, but they did not remain long. After a brief stop in New York, where they met other Italian officers, they headed for Texas, where they joined the "army" of the French corsair, Louis Aury. After another trip to Florida, in which they took part in some skirmishes, they proceeded to Venezuela.

Two other Italians who arrived before 1820 were Casimiro De Lieto, the friend of Palmerston and Gladstone, and Giuseppe Rondizzoni, who became a general in Chile. Both of them stopped over to visit Joseph Bonaparte at Bordentown, N. J. (*Rassegna Storica del Risorgimento,* March, 1938, and *Almanacco del Tamburino,* Rome, 1934.)

In the 1830's we find Antonio Gallenga (see next chapter); Antonio Montresor, a physician, who came to join his father, the impresario noted in Chapter Thirteen (*Atti e Memorie dell'Accademia di Storia dell'Arte Sanitaria,* Nov.-Dec., 1936); and Count Francesco Arese (the hand some Italian Count, as he was known in New York Society —*Eco d'Italia,* August 13, 1859), who came to be with his friend, Louis Napoleon Bonaparte, just exiled by Louis Philippe. His notes, *A Trip To The Prairies And In The Interior Of North America*, were published in New York in 1934.

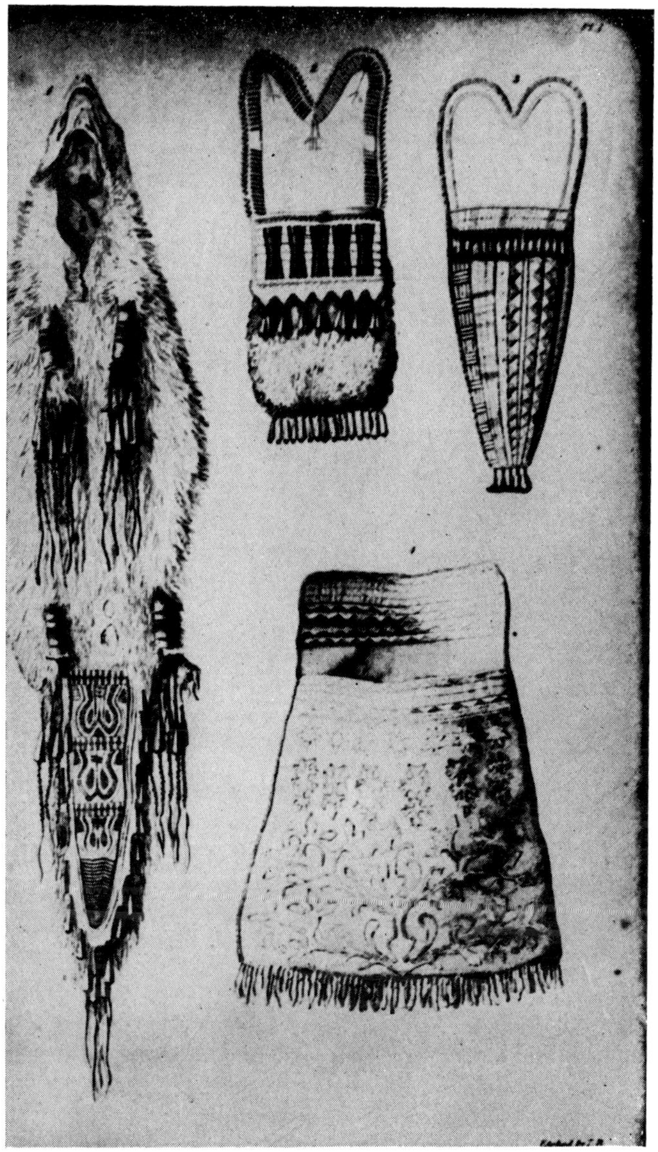

Some of the Indian articles Beltrami brought back with him to Europe from his exploration voyage in Minnesota. 1. A medicine sack, made of the coat of an animal; 2. a pouch (Sioux); 3. a knife sheath (Cypowais); 4. a woman's apron-pouch. (From Beltrami's *Pilgrimage.*)

AGOSTINO CODAZZI

In the 1840's Gaetano Osculati (1808-1894), a noted globe-trotter, and Carlo Ghega (1800-1860), a famous engineer, visited us. Ghega wrote (in German) a book on American railroads, and another on the Bank of the United States.

After 1850 we find Count de Cassato and Count de Malaperta (Gottschalk, *Notes of a Musician,* 90); Camillo Ferri-Pisani, who wrote *Lettres Sur Les Etats-Unis,* Paris, 1862; Giulio Adamoli, a noted engineer and traveler (*Nuova Antologia, Living Age,* 1922); Count Luigi Pennazzi (*Rassegna Italiana,* 1930); Giovanni Capellini, 1833-1922, a geologist who left us a book of scientific observations; Adriano Lemmi, the head of the Italian Masonry, who accompanied Kossuth in 1851; and many others whom space prevents us from listing.

CHAPTER EIGHTEEN

EDUCATORS AND WRITERS

Intermingled with the musicians, artists and missionaries who came over before the mass immigration from Italy began in the 1880's, were a few physicians, lawyers, one lone dentist, some engineers, and quite a few teachers of languages.

TEACHERS OF ITALIAN

Most of the Italian teachers of languages in the United States during the 19th century were "improvised" teachers, that is, men who found in the teaching of their native language, and occasionally French and Spanish, the only honest way of eking out a living. Most of them were political refugees, and a few out-and-out adventurers; in a good many cases men without a trade, technical knowledge, or business ability, possessing only a university degree in jurisprudence or "belles lettres".

As related below, the first Italian teacher of languages we have found in the United States soon after the Revolution was James Puglia. A few years later came Lorenzo Da Ponte, who arrived, as we have seen, in 1805. In 1820, as he tells us in his *Storia della Lingua e della Letteratura Italiana in New York* (1827), there were only three teachers of Italian in New York, one of whom was Rapallo. A few years later we find ten. They were besides Da Ponte, and Rapallo: Aloisi, Padovani, Mezzara, Casati, Ferrari, Strozzi, Sega and de Attellis.

Antonio Rapallo was the only friend Da Ponte had among those teachers. "After teaching languages for many years (he has excellent knowledge of many of them) he studied law and succeeded. He honors me with his friendship and is one of the few teachers of Italian who did not become my enemy." (Da Ponte, *op. cit.*, 3.) His son, Charles Antonio, became Judge of the Court of Appeals of the State of New York in 1870.

The others, with the exception of Sega and De Attellis, do not seem to have attained any distinction. Giacomo Sega, whose name we have found listed in the Philadelphia city directory as "teacher" at 283 Walnut Street, between 1830 and 1833, wrote at least three books. Padovani and Mezzara we have already met as artists. Whether they were artists who turned to teaching as a side line, or vice-versa, we cannot say.

Orazio de Attellis, Marquis of Sant'Angelo, was one of the most peculiar characters ever to come to America, as related below. Here we shall recall only that he opened four private schools, three in New York and one in New Orleans, between 1824 and 1836.

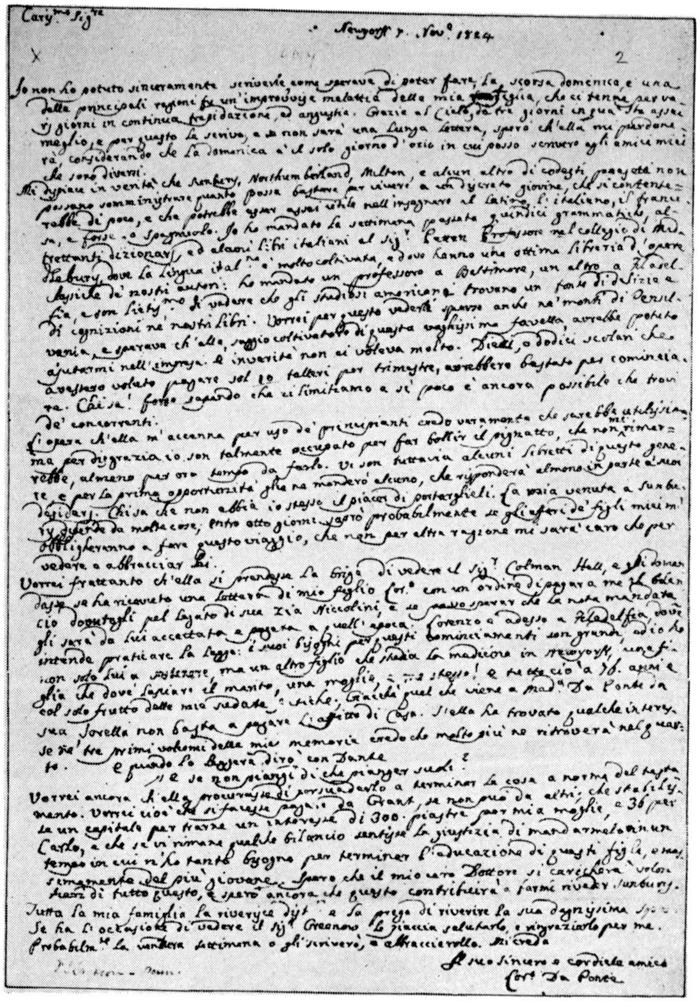

A letter written by Da Ponte in 1824 in which he tells of the progress of the study of the Italian language in the United States. (Manuscript, Emmett Collection, *New York Public Library.*)

Among the other teachers of Italian in the United States in the 1820's we may recall Donato Gherardi, a Tuscan who taught for years at Cambridge, Boston, and Northampton. In 1825 he married Jane Bancroft, the sister of George Bancroft, well known as Secretary of the Navy and founder of the United States Naval Academy. (Howe, M. A. De Wolfe, *The Life and Letters of George Bancroft*, 1908, I, 13.; Nye, R. B., *George Bancroft*, 1944, 73.) Later he, his wife and their first two children moved to Louisiana, where their son, Bancroft Gherardi, 1832-

1903, was born. More will be found about Admiral Bancroft Gherardi and his son, Rear Admiral W. R. Gherardi, in the last chapter of the present work. It is interesting to recall that when Gherardi joined the famous Round Hill School at Northhampton, Italian was to be learned "as a recreation." (Long, O. W., *Literary Pioneers,* 94; see also, Bassett, J. S., The Round Hill School, *American Antiquarian Society,* April, 1917, and Elliott, M. H., *Uncle Sam Ward and His Circle,* 1938, 22.)

Charles Nolcini, the musician, taught Italian at Portland, Me., and Boston. (*Italian-American History,* I, 383-384.)

Lorenzo L. Da Ponte, the son of Lorenzo, began by practising law, but later he taught Italian at Maryland University and New York University, as well as privately. He was a prolific writer. After his death in 1840, his wife, who was the niece of President Monroe's wife, moved to New Orleans, with her children. (Da Ponte, *Memoirs,* note by A. Livingston, p. 430.)

Pietro Bachi, a Sicilian, came to America, apparently as the result of a love affair. He taught Italian, Spanish and Portuguese at Harvard from 1826 to 1846, and wrote several grammars and anthologies. He died in Boston in 1853. Gallenga speaks highly of him in his *Episodes of My Second Life,* 1885, 37-42; see also, *Appleton's Cyclopaedia of American Biography,* I, 128; the general catalogues of the Library of Congress and the New York Public Library, and Marraro, H. R., Pioneer Italian Teachers of Italian in the United States, *Modern Language Journal,* Nov. 1944. Other material about Bachi can be found in the Corporation records and official correspondence of Harvard College.)

Antonio Gallenga, who arrived in Boston in 1836 and for a while gave Italian lessons in Boston, tells us about another Sicilian, Pietro D'Alessandro, a political exile who had been in his own country "a romantic, tragic and elegiac poet", who too, became in America a "marchand de participes".

Moving south in 1838, Gallenga found Borsieri and Signor Interdonato in Philadelphia, and Foresti, Castiglia (De Castillia), Maroncelli, and other political exiles in New York, all trying to earn a living by teaching Italian.

Pietro Borsieri, a Milanese (1786-1852), was one of the heroes of the Risorgimento and came to America in 1836 after spending twelve years in the dungeons of Spielberg. He taught at Philadelphia and at Princeton for about two years until 1838, when he returned to Italy. He translated H. M. Brackenridge's *History of the War between the United States and England in the years* 1812-1815, which appeared in Milan in 1821. (See *Enciclopedia Italiana.*)

Gallenga does not say anything about Signor Interdonato, except that he was "a Roman, the handsomest youth that ever came out of Italy, a learned youth, highly accomplished, all our ladies and young ladies running mad after him". (*loc. cit.* 186.)

Piero Maroncelli was one of the most famous Italian exiles to come to America, and is well known to readers of Pellico's *My Prisons.* He lived in New York from 1833 to the time of his death in 1846 at the age of 47. While with us he taught Italian and music and was one the organizers of the Philharmonic Society of New York. (*Italian-American History* I, 363-369.)

ELEUTERIO FELICE FORESTI
Professor of Italian at New York University and U. S. Consul at Genoa, Italy. (From a portrait by Michael De Santis, apparently after Monachesi's portrait, presented to Columbia University in 1929 by Mr. and Mrs. Ludwig G. Foresti.)

Gaetano De Castillia (1795-1870) remained in America about three years, for he returned to Italy in 1839, on the same boat that carried Gallenga, the Sedgwicks, who were going to England, and three American painters—Verbryck, Gray, and Huntington—who were going to Rome. (Gallenga, *op. cit.,* 236.) For a while he had two classes of Italian, one private and the other at Agthorp College, but he expected to have two more. (De Castillia to Theo. Dwight, New Haven, Feb. 10, 1837, MS. *Pennsylvania Historical Society.*) Later he became a senator of the Kingdom of Italy.

Eleuterio Felice Foresti, "a man whose strength of character bore up most heroically against the cruel hardships of fifteen years' imprisonment" (Gallenga, *op. cit.,* 187), also came over in 1836. He taught at New York University from 1842 to 1856, and had just begun to serve as American consul in Genoa, Italy, when he died three months after he took his office in 1858. He wrote a grammar and a reader for beginners. He was very active in New York. (*Eco d'Italia,* March 18-19 and 25-26, 1883.)

At Yale, Luigi Roberti and Giuseppe Artoni taught Italian, and the latter, for a time, French, between 1842 and 1847.

In Philadelphia and in New York, G. F. Secchi de

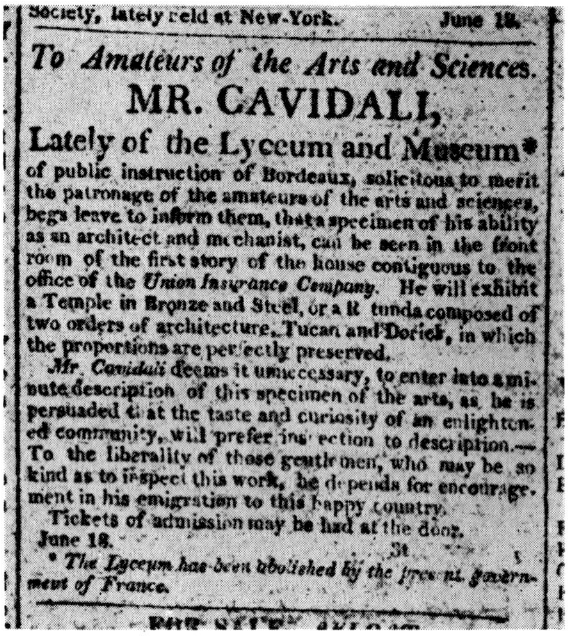

Society, lately held at New-York. June 18.

To Amateurs of the Arts and Sciences.

MR. CAVIDALI,

Lately of the Lyceum and Museum*

of public instruction of Bordeaux, solicitous to merit the patronage of the amateurs of the arts and sciences, begs leave to inform them, that a specimen of his ability as an architect and mechanist, can be seen in the front room of the first story of the house contiguous to the office of the *Union Insurance Company*. He will exhibit a Temple in Bronze and Steel, or a Rotunda composed of two orders of architecture, Tucan and Dorick, in which the proportions are perfectly preserved.

Mr. Cavidali deems it unnecessary, to enter into a minute description of this specimen of the arts, as he is persuaded that the taste and curiosity of an enlightened community, will prefer inspection to description.— To the liberality of those gentlemen, who may be so kind as to inspect this work, he depends for encouragement in his emigration to this happy country.

Tickets of admission may be had at the door.

June 18. 3t

* *The Lyceum has been abolished by the present government of France.*

One of Cavidali's advertisements in the *Norfolk Gazette*, June 18, 1816.

Casali, the founder and editor of *Eco d'Italia*, taught Italian, French and other subjects between 1845 and 1846, at a time in a private school where he worked 17 hours a day for $300 a week. (*Eco*, June 28-29, 1883.)

OTHER PIONEERS

In Northern New York State, we find one S. Pinistri, teacher of drawing and Italian "for some time past in some of the most respected families" in Albany, N. Y., about 1820. (Marraro, *op. cit.*)

In the *Boston Almanac* for 1844 we find Gaetano Lanza and Levina Buonocore listed as teachers, the former of Italian and French, and the latter without further indication. Lanza was the father of Gaetano Lanza, the Massachusetts Institute of Technology professor emeritus, as related in the next chapter. The family moved to Charlottesville, Va., in 1858, where the elder Lanza taught foreign languages at the University of Virginia from 1858 to 1861. His son also taught there in the School of Mathematics from 1869 to 1871.

In the same *Boston Almanac* for 1844 we find an item about one Adelbert B. Ptolemius, an Italian, who "attempted to shoot John Scott, Mayor of Philadelphia. He asked for private conversation, and after being shown into an anteroom, desired to be provided with a place for teaching languages. As Mr. Scott turned to go out, the fellow fired a pistol at him. The ball passed through the coat and vest, and slightly lacerated the flesh. As usual, the villain was called insane and perhaps truly."

Also in Philadelphia in the 50's we find one Vincenzo D'Amarelli, who is said to have taught Italian language and literature at the University of Pennsylvania. A native of Rossano, in Calabria, he seems to have been related to another teacher of languages, Dominic Anthony Vincent, who is said to have been born in Paris of Italian parents.

IN THE SOUTH

In the South, four teachers with Italian names were active between 1816 and 1829. One, Mr. Cavidali, advertised in the *Norfolk Gazette* for June 18, 1816, the exhibition of "a Temple in Bronze and Steel, or a Rotunda composed of two orders of architecture, Tuscan and Dorick, in which the proportions are perfectly preserved", as "a specimen of his ability as an architect and mechanist", but later he turned to teaching Italian and French.

In Richmond, at about the same time, Ferdinand Isovazzi and Carlo Deharo (De Caro, or De Carlo?) taught French, Spanish and Italian, and "Senior" Pudiani conducted a school of fine arts. Most probably he also taught languages. (Meagher, M., *Education in Richmond*, 1939.)

Salvatore Bonfiglio, or Sauveur Bonfils (1795-1849), as noted on page 201, taught languages at the University of Alabama between 1832 and 1836 and at Transylvania University in later years. A native of Tempio, Corsica, he was educated in Rome, Italy, and came to the United States in 1817, where two years later he married Lucinda Alden, a descendant of John Alden. He was the grandfather of Frederick Bonfils ,the founder of the *Denver Post*.

AFTER 1850

After 1850 the number of Italian teachers in American Institutions of learning and especially in private schools increased considerably. We have already noted the religious educators. Two of them, Monti and Botta, arrived before the Civil War, like one G. B. Fontana, who published an Italian grammar in New York in 1864.

Luigi Monti, we learn from a letter he sent to President Buchanan, "was born in Palermo, Sicily, in 1830. My father was a commander in the navy. I was graduated at the Jesuit College in 1846, went to sea for my health in an American ship, and crossed twice the Atlantic; I entered the University of Palermo in 1847, took an active part in the Revolution of 1848-'49 with my fellow-students and was obliged to emigrate. I came to America in 1850 and established myself in Boston as a teacher of my native language. I was appointed instructor in Italian at Harvard University in 1854. In 1855 I published a grammar of the Italian language and a reader, which are now textbooks at the University."

In 1861 Monti was appointed American consul at Palermo, serving there for twelve years, after which he returned to the United States to teach and lecture. He will be remembered as the Sicilian in Longfellow's *Tales of Wayside Inn*, and the author of a book, *Adventures of a Consul Abroad*. (See *Italian-American History*, I, 489-490; *Eco d'Italia*, Feb. 23, 1881.)

Vincenzo Botta (1818-1894) was the son of the author of the History of the War of Independence of the United States, which went through at least seven editions. A member of the Italian Parliament, he came to America in 1853 to study American conditions, but once here he married an Irish young lady, Anne C. Lynch, and remained for the rest of his life. For forty years, or from 1854 to 1894,

ADVENTURES

OF

A CONSUL ABROAD.

BY

SAMUEL SAMPLETON, ESQ.,

LATE UNITED-STATES CONSUL AT VERDECUERNO.

BOSTON:
LEE AND SHEPARD, PUBLISHERS.
NEW YORK:
CHARLES T. DILLINGHAM.
1878.

Title-page of Luigi Monti's book about his life as U. S. Consul at Palermo.

Botta was nominally professor of Italian at New York University, but as he related only a few months before he died to Prof. Carlo Speranza, his position was just an honorary one, for he never delivered a single lecture. Another honorary position which he enjoyed for thirty-one years was that of vice-president of the Union League Club of New York. His home, which Emerson called "the house of expanding doors," was for many years the meeting place of many of the noted literary and social figures of America.

SINCE THE CIVIL WAR

After the Civil War not a few of the Italians who served as officers in the Union Army remained to teach. More numerous were those who arrived with the immigration tide, educated men without any particular skill, who found temporary occupations as teachers of languages not only in private schools but especially in music colleges from New York to California. A few were lucky enough to join the faculties of our best known universities. Meanwhile the new generations of native Americans of Italian parentage were gradually spreading into educational fields other than language instruction.

EDWARD CHIERA

As representative teachers of subjects other than languages, we shall recall four men who passed away in recent years: Edward Chiera, Henry Suzzallo, Charles Prospero Fagnani, and Carmon Ross.

Edward Chiera, professor of Assyrology at the University of Chicago and one of America's leading Orientalists, was born in Rome in 1885 and came to America in 1910. He taught at the University of Pennsylvania from 1913 to 1927 and at the University of Chicago from 1927 until the time of his death in 1933. He will be remembered for his success in deciphering in 1924 a Babylonian tablet giv- the story of Adam and Eve similar to that found in the Genesis, but at least 1,000 years older, and for his excavations in the Tigris Valley near Bagdad in 1928 and 1929, during which he brought to light many important findings, including the famous Sumerian tablets. A rather long account of his activities appeared in the *New York Herald-Tribune* for June 22, 1933, at the time of his death. (See also, *Dictionary of American Biography.*)

HENRY SUZZALLO

One of the nation's most distinguished educators who passed away also in 1933 was Henry Suzzallo. President of the University of Washington from 1915 to 1926 and president of the Carnegie Foundation for the Advancement of Teaching during the last three years of his life, Professor Suzzallo played a most prominent role in American education for many years. He was born in San Jose, Cal., in 1875, the son of Italian immigrants. The fact that his parents had come from Dalmatia, has led some people not acquainted with the history of that part of Europe to believe that he was of Jugoslav extraction. That he was of Italian extraction, however, he himself confirmed to this writer who asked him about it on the occasion of a lecture Dr. Suzzallo delivered at New York University in 1929. An editorial about his contribution to American education appeared in the *New York Times* on September 26, 1933.

FAGNANI AND ROSS

Charles Prospero Fagnani (1854-1940) was born in New York, the son of the painter, Giuseppe Fagnani. Professor emeritus of Old Testament, Literature and Exegesis at Union Theological Seminary from 1915 to 1926, he was the author of several books and a honorary member of the Union League Club of New York.

Dr. Carmon Ross, who died in 1946, was born in the province of Salerno, Italy, and brought to America by his parents when he was a child. Here his name was changed from Carmine Cortazzo into Carmon Ross. He served as president of Edinboro (Pa.) State Teachers College from 1924 to 1940, and for several years as executive director of the Public Education and Child Labor Association of Pennsylvania. (See *Italian-American Who's Who,* and *Atlantica Magazine,* May 1934, 196.)

OTHER EDUCATORS

Today literally hundreds of men and women of Italian birth or extraction are active in American education in practically every state in the Union. Professors of, or instructors in, languages, sociology, economics, political science, comparative philology, psychology, philosophy, theology, they are all doing their share in making America a center of learning. One name may suffice: that of Angelo Patri, one of the great pioneers in modern education, who came from his native Italy as a boy in the 1880's.

We only regret that we cannot afford to dwell on the contributions to American learning made by some of the men who passed away in recent years, men like Dr. Alberto Bonaschi, Professors Lipari, Marinoni, De Salvio, Cadicamo, Marchisio, Zema, and last, but not least, Alfonso Arbib Costa, an Italian of the Jewish faith, who for about half a century honored the New York Italian community.

PIONEER WRITERS AND NEWSPAPERMEN

For various reasons, it is not easy for a man or woman to write a work of literary merit in a foreign language. There are exceptions, of course, such as Rafael Sabatini in our own days, but the exceptions are so rare that they simply confirm the rule. Even for native-born Americans of foreign parentage it is not very easy to acquire a place in American literature, although the exceptions here are not so rare. For one thing, young authors need encouragebent, something very few Italian-American writers have received. The policies of some of our newspapers, besides, make it rather difficult for beginners to become known.

Nevertheless, there are and have been Italian-American writers who acquired a little distinction in the 19th century and others who deserve to be better known. Cora Fabbri, for instance: a young poetess who died at San Remo, Italy, in 1892 at the age of twenty.

CORA FABBRI

We do not know much about Cora Fabbri with the exception of the little information contained in her obituary in the *New York Times* (January 14, 1892) and in the fine article Enrico Nencioni (1837-1896), a leading poet and critic, devoted to her in the famous magazine *La Nuova Antologia* of Rome (February 16, 1892).

Cora Fabbri was born in New York, the daughter of Ernest G. Fabbri, a member of the firm of Fabbri and Chauncey, who died in 1883, and the niece of Egisto Fabbri, the partner of J. P. Morgan. She began writing verse at an early age, some of her poems appearing in American periodicals. Not long after her father's death the family moved to Italy, where Cora Fabbri wrote her poems.

Not all of Cora Fabbri's verses are perfect, but they are so full of "essentially poetical and lyrical images and expressions" that they may be considered "worthy of any eminent poet", as Nencioni said. One, however, does not need to accept the verdict of the Italian critic. Her book of *Lyrics*, published in New York in 1892, will prove a revelation to any one who takes the trouble of perusing it in the New York Public Library.

Cora Fabbri, of course, was not the first Italian American poet or writer. Father Pise, as we have seen, acquired distinction as a poet and author of religious works. Father Finotti, the editor of the Boston *Pilot* for many years, wrote several lives of saints and novels. His brother, G. M. Finotti, who died in South Dakota in 1889, also devoted himself to literary pursuits. (*Italian-American History,* II, 372.)

AGOSTINO SIGNAIGO

Agostino Signaigo, a native of Italy, is said to have been outstanding "in the Americas" as a "poet, linguist, political writer, and as a student of all branches of learning" (*Eco d'Italia,* Aug. 12, 1865), but we have not been able to find any of his verses or other writings to express a personal opinion. In 1865 he was editor of the Cairo, Ill., *Daily News,* but later he joined the Grenada, Miss., *Sentinel.* In 1869 he was elected president of the Mississippi Press Association.

The first native of Italy to be on the staff of a metropolitan daily newspaper as editorial writer was in all probability George Bendelari (1851-1927), a native of Naples, who came to the United States at the age of four, with his father, Enrico, the friend of Meucci. He was educated at Harvard and at Leipzig, Germany, received an honorary degree of Master of Arts from Yale in 1888, taught languages and history at Harvard, Yale and Columbia from 1878 to 1894, and then joined the New York *Sun* as editorial writer. (*New York Times,* Aug. 13, 1927; *Who's Who in America,* 1924-'25.)

ITALIAN AUTHORS IN AMERICA

It is not generally realized that among the men and women who have come to America from Italy during the last half century, there have been quite a few who have written Italian verse and prose of some distinction, even if only two or three of them will ever be mentioned in future histories of Italian literature. Poets, playrights, novelists, essayists, translators in prose and verse, they would have made a name for themselves in the United States had it not been for the language barriers. Here we shall not deal with them as, in a sense, they are not a part of the American scene. They deserve a special monograph.

CONTEMPORARY ITALIAN-AMERICAN WRITERS

As for writing in English, Italian-Americans have made a good beginning, with a number of poets whose verses have appeared in the several anthologies published annually in the United States; with biographers like Frances Winwar (Francesca Vinciguerra); with novelists like Jerre Mangione, Oscar De Liso, John Fante, Pietro di Donato, Michael De Capite, Nicholas Cosentino, or Guido D'Agostino. We might also include Bernard De Voto and Hamilton Basso, whose grandparents came from Italy about a century ago. Nor should we forget Sacco and Vanzetti, the two humble workers whom prejudice and hysteria "railroaded" to the electric chair. Their immensely moving and impressive letters, however, are already a part of American literature and are included in the anthologies. (Se Joughin, G. L., and Morgan, E. M., *The Legacy of Sacco and Vanzetti,* 1948.)

WRITERS ON VARIOUS SUBJECTS

Generally speaking, it would not be hard to compile a list of 500, or even 1,000, books authored by Italian-Americans during the last forty years, from politics to history, economics, sociology, mathematics, medicine, advertising, and even dogs, or golf. Before the Civil War several of the political exiles like Maroncelli, Foresti, Filopanti, Secchi de Casali, contributed articles on current Italian politics to leading newspapers and magazines, from Virginia to New England. Secchi de Casali, the editor of *Eco d'Italia,* contributed to the *Saturday Evening Post,* the *Whig Democratic Review,* the *New York Tribune, New York Herald,* and other periodicals. (*Eco,* Feb. 4-5, 1883.)

The first best-seller written by an Italian-American still remains *A Texas Cowboy* by Charles Siringo, of which more than 1,000,000 copies are said to have been printed, as we have already noted on page 169. (See facsimiles.)

JAMES PHILIP PUGLIA

An early Italian-American writer to take an interest in American politics was James Philip Puglia, one of the most active political pamphleteers the Federalists had on their side. He wrote numerous articles, several pamphlets, three plays based on current political events, and at least two books.

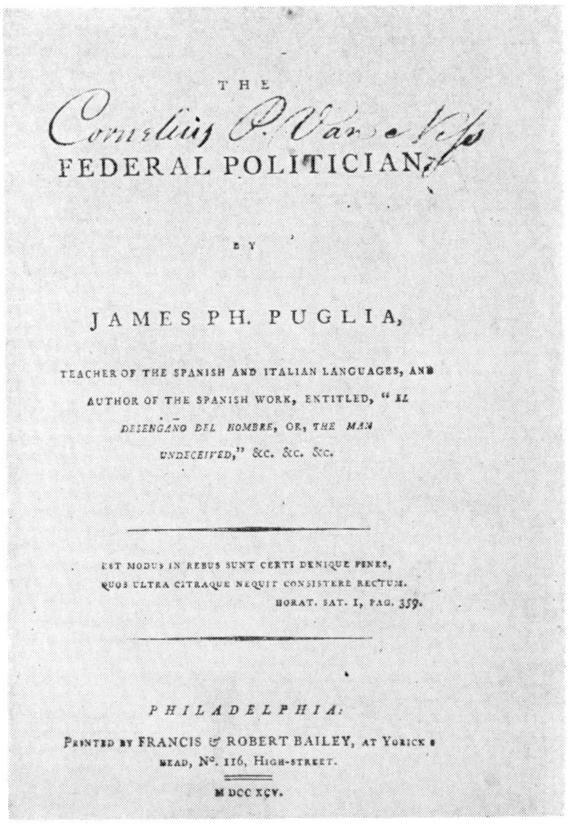
THE

FEDERAL POLITICIAN,

BY

JAMES PH. PUGLIA,

TEACHER OF THE SPANISH AND ITALIAN LANGUAGES, AND AUTHOR OF THE SPANISH WORK, ENTITLED, "EL DESENGAÑO DEL HOMBRE, OR, THE MAN UNDECEIVED," &c. &c. &c.

EST MODUS IN REBUS SUNT CERTI DENIQUE FINES, QUOS ULTRA CITRAQUE NEQUIT CONSISTERE RECTUM.
HORAT. SAT. I, PAG. 359.

PHILADELPHIA:

PRINTED BY FRANCIS & ROBERT BAILEY, AT YORICK'S HEAD, No. 116, HIGH-STREET.

M DCC XCV.

Title-page of one of the early books by James Puglia, published at Philadelphia in 1795. Notice his title as "teacher of the Spanish and Italian languages." (Courtesy, *New York Public Library.*)

We do not know exactly where Puglia was born, but we are inclined to believe that he was a native of Italy, although his family had emigrated to Italian Switzerland some two hundred years before his birth. His father, John Dominick, was born at Blenio, in the Canton Ticino. From 1775 to 1782 young Puglia studied at Savona, a city near Genoa, after which, apparently, he travelled, as his father wished him to do, until he reached America. At any rate, he was here as early as 1792, for we find him listed as "Spanish interpreter" in Hardie's *Philadelphia Directory and Register* for 1793. In 1794 he was a private in the local militia. (*Pennsylvania Archives,* Series 6, Vol. 5, 509.)

It was in that year, 1794, that Puglia's first book printed in the United States, *El Desengaño del Hombre,* in Spanish, appeared in Philadelphia. A year later he published a *Federal Politician,* a book of 284 pages, and *The Blue Shop, or Impartial Humorous Observations on the Life and Adventures of Peter Porcupine.* Porcupine was the pseudonym of William Cobbett, as students of that period know. Puglia often attacked him, under the name of Quick Silver. (See Clark, M. E., *Peter Porcupine in America,* 1939, 69.)

We need not dwell here on all that Puglia wrote during the next quarter of a century, or until his last book known to us, *El Derecho del Hombre,* a translation of Paine's *Rights of Man,* appeared in Philadelphia in 1822. It is in that book, a copy of which we consulted at the Huntington Library in San Marino, Cal., that one will find a list of Puglia's published and manuscript writings and a reference to his Italian nationality.

Puglia is said to have served as health officer for the city of Philadelphia and to have lived for a number of years in Harrisburg, where he was "worshipful Master" of Perseverance Lodge No. 21 of the Masons. (*Notes and Queries,* Harrisburg, 1894, Series I, Vol. I, 51.) From a letter he wrote to Jefferson, to whom he dedicated his comedy, *The Embargo,* we learn that William Warren, the manager of the Chestnut Street Theater refused to produce it because he was opposed to Puglia's political ideas. (Puglia to Jefferson, June 21, 1808, and Jefferson to Puglia, June 24, 1808. *MS. Library of Congress.*) That he never became a rich man we learn from his *Short Extract* (also in the Huntington Library), or summary of his *El Desengano del Hombre,* which he wished to publish in an English translation, provided he could get enough subscriptions. "The low circumstances of De Puglia (who must get his living like the birds of the forest) are great impediments to his sparing time for study." Whether Puglia's *Embargo* was ever produced on the stage we do not know. (See Hornblow's *History of the Theatre in America,* 1919, I, 212, and Quinn's *History of the American Drama,* 2nd ed. 1943, 136.)

ORAZIO de ATTELLIS

Orazio de Attellis, marquis of Sant'Angelo, was born at Sant'Angelo Limosano, in the province of Campobasso, Italy, on October 22, 1774, and died at Civitavecchia on January 10, 1850.

He came to America in 1824 after spending thirty-four years in Europe plotting and fighting. In 1812 he was with Napoleon during the famous retreat from Moscow. Previously he had seen action in Italy and in Spain. He had been arrested, sentenced to death, pardoned, exiled. Out of the army, he had been a law clerk, a newspaperman, a teacher of languages in France, a public official. At fifty he had packed more adventure and more dangers in his life than two or three men his age.

A month after his arrival in New York, de Attellis paid a visit to Joseph Bonaparte at Bordentown, met Lorenzo Da Ponte, and three months later opened a school in New York, as we have seen. As restless as ever, the following year he decided to move to Mexico, took part in Mexican politics for a year, and then decided to return to the United States. From 1827 to 1832 he lived in New York teaching and writing until he went back to Mexico City to establish a college at the suggestion of Santa Anna. (*El Correo Atlantico*, May 30, 1836.) On the way over he stopped for a while at New Orleans, where he contributed a series of articles to the local *L'Abeille,* all in favor of the Mexican general.Harmony between the two, however, did not last long and soon they separated. De Attellis thereupon published a newspaper, *El Correo Atlantico,* but not for long, for Santa Anna expelled him from Mexico. Resuming publications in New Orleans, he carried on an intense propaganda for the independence of Texas, in Spanish, English, and even in Italian and French.

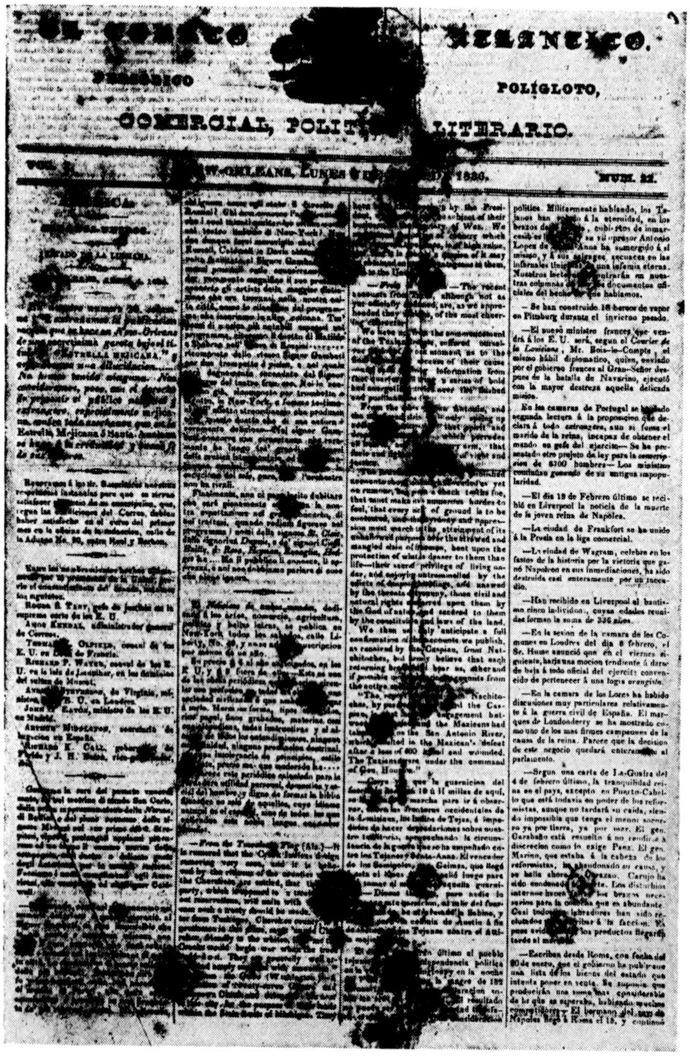
POLIGLOTO,

LITERARIO.

Front page of one of the early issues of the *Correo Atlantico* published by De Attellis in New Orleans in 1836. Notice the various articles in Italian, English and Spanish. Other items were in French. (Courtesy, *Library of Congress.*)

So well and so strongly did Attellis defend the right of Texas to independence that in 1839 he "was rewarded with a grant of a large tract of land and with the honor of having a set of *El Correo* kept permanently in the Texas state archives." (See Cortese, N., *Le Avventure Italiane ed Americane di un Giacobino Molisano,* Messina, 1935, 95.) He also received a large sum in payment of his claims against the Mexican Government. How much land he actually received we have not tried to ascertain, but that *El Correo Atlantico* is kept on file in the Texas State Library in the State Capitol at Austin, has been confirmed to us by the Texas State Archivist.

From 1836 to 1848 de Attellis lived in New Orleans, Philadelphia and New York, taking active part in local Italian affairs, organizing two military units, as we have noted on page 200, lecturing and writing. He was most active on the Texas Question, possibly because of his claims.

During this period de Attellis published at least fifteen pamphlets, thirteen of which are listed by Cortese and two which are in the Yale University Library. One of them (1834) is in defense of the Italians who had been attacked by the *Philadelphia Ledger.* (In America, sir, you have only seen, with but a few exceptions, Italian orange and fig sellers, or a few Italian artists or professors, seeking in privte and tranquil pursuits, an honest livelihood.) Thereupon he challenged to duel "sword in hand" the editor and another "half a dozen insolent scribblers of your stamp."

In seven letters which appeared in the Washington *Index* in 1842 and later in pamphlet form, he severely critized President Tyler and his Secretary of State, Daniel Webster. In 1844 he came out for Henry Clay, "the greatest and best American," against Polk, "an ambitious and evil demagogue". He even found time to get in more trouble, for, having attacked Senator McRoberts of Illinois, he was sued for libel and made to pay.

His American citizenship, however, saved him from ending his life in prison when he returned to Italy in 1848, at the age of seventy-four, as bellicose as ever. He died there two years later.

As for his political pamphleteering, it would seem that they played a role not only in the independence of Texas but especially in the settlement of American claims against Mexico. (See also *Eco d'Italia,* January 22, 1882, and April 1, 1883.)

PIONEER EDITORS AND PUBLISHERS

In the various county histories of the United States or in Mott's *History of American Magazines* one will find names of editors or publishers which seem Italian, such L. B. Alberti, contributor to the Baltimore *Portico;* John Bisco, founder of *The Broadway Journal;* John Dominey, one of the principal movers and stockholders of *The Republican,* a newspaper published first in 1811 in the Lake Champlain Valley; or even the well-known John Fenno. But it is hard to prove whether or not they were of Italian extraction or birth.

THE FIRST ITALIAN-AMERICAN NEWSPAPERS

Coming to more solid ground, the first native of Italy to publish a newspaper in the United States seems to have been Orazio de Attellis with his *Correo Atlantico,* as we have seen. Thirteen years later, in 1849, Secchi de Casali became editor of the *Europeo-Americano* (The European-American), a weekly in Italian and English which included among its contributors several well-known writers of the day. It lasted only nine weeks, for after the fall of the Roman Republic the Italian Cause seemed lost and its supporters lost enthusiasm. Not so Casali. With $78 in subscriptions, only half of which had been paid in, he started all over again and put out, also in 1849, *L'Eco d'Italia,* a weekly which was to last until 1894, for a time even as a daily.

Many, of course, were the sacrifices undergone by the young editor, who on occasions had to pawn some of his family heirlooms, including his gold watch and his wife's earrings, which his ever-precarious finances never allowed him to reclaim.

No sooner had *L'Eco* come out than an ex-priest tried his hand at journalism and published another weekly in Italian, *L'Esule* (The Exile). It died shortly after it was born. In 1851 Felice Foresti started a weekly of his own, *Il Proscritto* (The Expatriate), which lasted about two years. Also short-lived was the *European Mercury,* in English, which Luigi Tinelli founded early in 1852.

Two more Italian papers tried their wings in the 50's. The first was *La Gazzetta Italiana* of Philadelphia, published by one A. Balbo, a Piedmontese who in 1853 had been manager of La Gazette Francaise. Balbo, however, went a little too far in his attacks against an ex-priest, one Baldassare, a contemptible individual, according to Casali. Supported by a group of anti-Catholics, Baldassare sued for libel and succeeeded in having Balbo sentenced to one year in jail. After which he moved to New York, where he opened a drug store. The second weekly, *L'Eco della Patria,* was founded by Federico Biesta in San Francisco on March 19, 1859.

Also in 1859 James R. Del Vecchio founded what we might call the first American newspaper published by an Italian-American in the United States, the *Brooklyn Standard,* a weekly for the first two years and a daily for about six months in 1861, when it suspended publication apparently because of Del Vecchio's enlistment in the Union

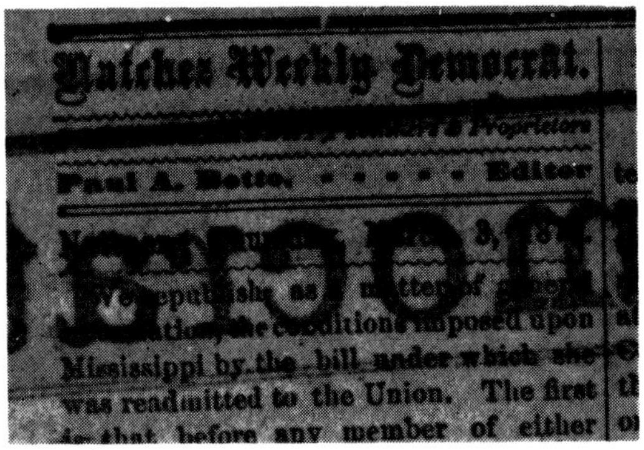

Masthead of the *Natchez Weekly Democrat* showing the name of Paul A. Botto as editor. (Courtesy, *Mississippi State Library.*)

Army, in which he served as a quarter master, with the rank of captain. His fellow-citizens in 1862 presented him and General Spinola, both of the Empire Brigade, with the gift of a sword, sash and pistols. Del Vecchio was discharged in 1866 with the rank of Lieutenant Colonel, U. S. Volunteers, by brevet, "for gallant action or meritorious conduct during the war." He then resumed the publication of his newspaper, which continued under its own name until 1877, when it was merged with the *Brooklyn Union* to form the *Standard-Union.* A set of its first 52 issues is in the Queens Public Library. (See also Stiles, *History of the City of Brooklyn,* 3 vols. 1870, II, 449 and III, 940.)

In the 1860's, an *Almanacco Italiano,* the first Italian almanac printed in the United States, was put on sale in January, 1862. Also in the 60's, Paolo M. Botto was editor and co-publisher of the *Natchez Democrat,* a weekly, and Pietro Cuneo was part-owner of the Medina, Ohio, *Gazette,* and then publisher and editor of the *Wyandot Pioneer* of Upper Sandusky, Ohio, the name of which he later changed into *Wyandot County Republican.* (*Italian-American History,* I, 493. See facsimiles, *ante,* 165.)

At Woodstock, Md., Father Sestini founded in 1866 the *Sacred Heart Messenger,* probably the Catholic magazine with the largest circulation in the world. He served as editor from 1866 to 1881.

On the West Coast, Biesta was making progress, for

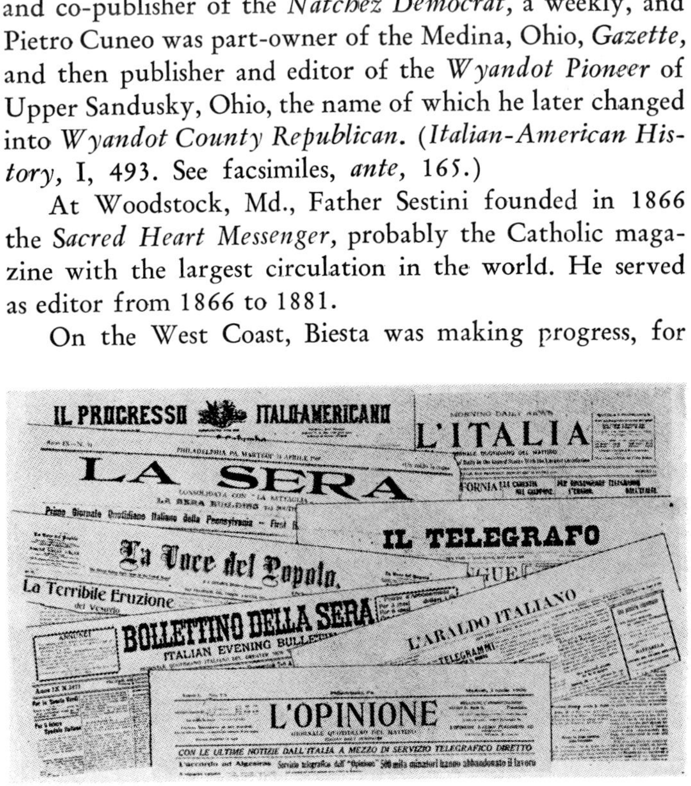

Some of the Italian-language daily newspapers published in the United States at the beginning of the century.

ETTORE PATRIZI

in 1869 he began the publication of the *Illustrated San Francisco News,* in English. Six years later, in 1875, the first Italian religious weekly in the United States, *Osservatore Cattolico,* made its appearance.

Biesta, meanwhile, was meeting opposition in San Francisco. A Piedmontese loyal to the House of Savoy and to monarchy, he never missed an opportunity to criticize the local political exiles, men of Republican principles, who naturally resented Biesta's monarchical attitude. Supported by the local Italian-Swiss residents, they decided to start a newspaper of their own, and put out *La Voce del Popolo,* which in the 90's became a daily.

In the East, Casali remained in undisputed control of the field until about 1871, when the first Italian-language daily newspaper appeared in New York. Published and edited by Cesare Orsini and Giuseppe Norton, two fine journalists, it was named *L'Unione dei Popoli* (United Peoples). It lasted about six or seven months.

Nine years later, in 1880, an ambitious young Tuscan, Carlo Barsotti, started a new daily, *Il Progresso Italo-Americano,* which soon took the lead, even after *L'Eco d'Italia* also appeared as a daily, starting with its issue of March 14, 1881. In 1888 another daily, *Cristoforo Colombo,* began its publication in New York, but after seven years of hard life it was purchased by Mr. Barsotti.

Ever since those days, *Il Progresso* has been the leading Italian-language newspaper in the United States, under the leadership of its founder until he died in 1927, and under the management of Generoso Pope from 1928 until 1949, when he also passed away. Since then it has been published by his two sons. For twenty years it was edited by Italo Falbo, an outstanding journalist who relinquished the editorship of a daily newspaper in Rome, Italy, to come to New York. He died in 1946 at the age of seventy.

Getting back to the 80's, another Italian daily founded in 1886 was *L'Italia* of San Francisco, still in existence. It, too, has served the Italian people well, especially under the editorship of Ettore Patrizi, one of the finest gentlemen this writer had the privilege of counting among his friends. From 1893 to the time of his death in 1945, Ettore Patrizi was the exponent on the West Coast of the best that the Italian immigrant could offer to both Italy and America.

HUNDREDS OF WEEKLY NEWSPAPERS

During the last seventy-five years literally hundreds of Italian weekly newspapers have been published in the United States. Among those still in existence, we shall recall, in chronological order, *L'Italia* of Chicago, founded in 1886 by Oscar Durante, translator of De Amicis' "Cuore", Rome correspondent, for a time, of the *Chicago Tribune,* and the first man to carry U. S. registered mail across the Island of Porto Rico in two covered wagons in 1898; *Il Corriere del Connecticut,* established in New Haven in 1893; *La Follia* of New York, the most popular weekly in the Italian language in the United States, founded in 1893

Some of the weekly newspapers in the Italian language published in the United States at the turn of the century. Five of them are still in existence.

by Marziale Sisca and by his brother, Alessandro (Cordiferro), a poet whose death a few years ago is still mourned by an army of friends; *La Gazzetta del Massachusetts*, a weekly founded in 1896 by James Donnarumma, whose unflagging devotion to Italy and America and whose unswerving principles can hardly be matched; *Il Pensiero* of St. Louis, founded in 1904 by Luigi Carnovale, as pure an idealist as ever lived anywhere, and edited since 1917 by Dr. Cesare Avigni, a scholar of the old school; *L'Opinione* of Philadelphia, a daily, founded in 1905 by C. A. A. Baldi, now managed, for many years past, by Remo Zuecca, one of the ablest newspaper managers in the country; *Il Risveglio* of Denver, founded by Frank P. Mancini, still its publisher and editor, in 1907, when he was only 16 years old; *L'Italo-Americano of Los Angeles,* the only Italian newspaper in Southern California, founded in 1908, and now edited by Cleto Baroni, another man who has devoted the best years of his life to the advancement of his people; *La Tribuna* of Detroit, founded in 1909 by Vincenzo Giuliano, to whose idealism and sacrifices the Italians of Michigan owe more than a debt of gratitude for his immense contribution to their prestige and welfare; *The Texas Tribune* of Dallas, formerly all in Italian, and now in English with a column in Italian, founded by Charles Papa, a self-made man, under whose leadership it became one of the most successful Italian weeklies in the country. Among those which recently suspended publication, worthy of mention is also the *Unione* of Pueblo, Colorado, founded by H. Chiariglione in 1897, and published for many years by Vincenzo Massari. Last but not least, we cannot omit *The Italian News* of Boston, the only Italian weekly in the English language in the United States, founded in 1921 and still published and edited by Principio Albert Santosuosso, a veteran of the *Boston Post* and the *Boston Journal,* whose devotion to the Italian people has a few peers among the children of Italian immigrants. A place by itself is occupied by *The Rubicon, American Critical Review,* which has been published monthly since 1941 by Luigi Criscuolo of New York.

MAGAZINE PUBLISHERS

One could write a history of the intellectual development of the Italian immigrant in the United States simply by a study of the scores of monthly publications that have appeared in Italian-American communities during the last fifty years. Most of them have been of a general cultural type, but a few have specialized in musical activities, social studies, art, medicine, business, and even baking, shoe repairing and barbering. We shall recall *Il Carroccio*, a bilingual magazine edited by its founder, Agostino De Biasi, from 1915 to 1937; *Columbus,* also started in 1915, and still published by its founder, Vincenzo Campora, an unrepentant idealist, who sacrificed his entire life to create another cultural link between Italy and the United States; and finally, *The Rivista d'Italia e d'America,* founded in Rome, Italy, in 1923, and then continued in New York under the name of *Atlantica* from 1928 to the time of his death in 1942, by Dr. Filippo Cassola. The writer may be allowed here to pay a special tribute to Dr. Cassola, whom he came to know rather intimately during the years he was connected with him as managing editor of his magazine, as well as a friend. If there ever was a man who ran after a chimera, that man was Dr. Cassola. Completely devoid of personal ambition, with no desire whatever except that of promoting the intellectual development of the Italians in America and to reveal to their children the glorious heritage of Italy, Dr. Cassola spent more than $75,000 without ever anticipating a financial return.

The most popular magazine in the Italian language in the United States today is *Divagando,* published by Divagando Corporation, Charles L'Episcopo, President.

CONTEMPORARY EDITORS AND PUBLISHERS

One has only to go through the recent annual editions of *Editor and Publisher* to find an impressive array of Italian names, as editors and even publishers of daily newspapers. But, for that matter, a glance at some of our popular magazines is enough to reveal many Italian names on editorial staffs.

CHAPTER NINETEEN

ANTONIO MEUCCI

INVENTOR OF THE TELEPHONE

The electric telephone was invented by Antonio Meucci many years before Alexander Graham Bell applied for his famous patent on February 14, 1876.

Of course, this is not the first time that Meucci has been proclaimed the inventor of the telephone—we are fully aware of that; but, with all due repect to all previous students of the subject, not one of them has ever produced the right kind of evidence that would satisfy the most skeptical scientist.

Yet, during the last sixty-five years anyone who had known how to go about it could have found in the archives of the Supreme Court of the United States and elsewhere in Washington all the evidence needed, just as we found it in December, 1951.

The most important piece of evidence on Meucci discovered by us is the official court record of the case of the American Bell Telephone Company versus the Globe Telephone Company, Antonio Meucci and others, which was tried before Judge Wallace of the United State Circuit Court for the Southern District of New York from 1885 to July 19, 1887, when Judge Wallace rendered his decision.

ANTONIO MEUCCI

According to Judge Wallace, Meucci was an impostor, knew that he had invented nothing worth while, had only foolish notions about electricity, and most certainly could not have invented a telephone resembling Bell's.

But, as they say, there are two sides to every story. In the following pages we shall, therefore, present the other side, using, of course, the very evidence which, in our opinion, Judge Wallace failed to use with judicial equanimity and impartiality. Lack of space, unfortunately, prevents us from reproducing in facsimile all the pertaining evidence from the 1,000-page printed Record—something which we intend to do as exhaustively as possible in a separate volume. The evidence given in the present chapter, nevertheless, should be enough for any unbiased scientist or lawyer to draw his or her own conclusions.

MEUCCI'S SCIENTIFIC LEARNING

Meucci was not a science professor; but, to judge by the many inventions he patented, and by those which he did not patent, he knew more about the various branches of science than many college professors of his day. His inventions and experiments cover various fields, from paraffine candles and wood pulp paper to electric therapy and submarine telephony. At one time he was interested in the electrification of railroads and in a canal steamer; at another in the mummification of human bodies; still at another in a piano with glass keys.

Ever since he was a boy in his native Florence, where he was born in 1808, he had been interested in mechanics. In 1835, he moved to Havana, Cuba, where he worked for years as theater machinist. It was there, while treating some patients with electric therapy that he conceived the idea that speech could be transmitted electrically. That was in 1849.

Coming to the United States in 1851 with a capital of $20,000, he bought a home at Staten Island and established a candle factory in which Giuseppe Garibaldi, who lived in Meucci's house during his American residence, worked for a time. Then he had a brewery. Still later he became interested in other business ventures. But Meucci was too trustworthy, and a very poor business man at that, to succeed in business.

During all this time he had never abandoned the idea of the telephone. Actually he constructed several instru-

Patents Granted to and Applications and Caveats Filed by Antonio Meucci.

22,739. January 25, 1859. Appl. Nov. 15, 1858. Candle Mold. Ass'd to Domenico B. Lorini, Nov. 29, 1858. Recorded Feb'y 24, 1859, Z4, p. 29. E. S. Renwick, att'y. W. E. Rider, witness.

Caveat. April 9, 1859. Galvanic Battery.

Caveat. June 6, 1860. Candle Apparatus. E. S. Renwick, att'y.

Application. June 6, 1860. Dry Galvanic Battery. Rejected. E. S. Renwick, att'y.

30,180. Sept. 25, 1860. Appl. Apparatus for moulding candles. Ass'd to N. Y. Parafine Candle Co., May 28, 1860, U5, p. 66; W. E. Rider, witness to ass't. E. S. Renwick, att'y. [Possibly the ass't relates to caveat of June 6, 1860.]

36,192. Aug. 12, 1862. Appl. May 7, 1862. Lamp burner. W. E. Rider, witness. Ass'd to Antonio Jané, May 13, 1862, N6, p. 390. E. S. Renwick, att'y.

36,419. Sept. 9, 1862. Appl. June 16, 1862. Imp't in treating mineral oils for paint. Ass'd to Antonio Jané, June 12, 1862, O6, p. 207. Munn, att'y.

38,714. May 26, 1863. Appl. April 3, 1863. Preparing hydrocarbons for paint. Ass'd to Mrs. Esterre Meucci (wife of A. M.), March 13, 1863, R6, p. 413. Munn & Co., att'ys.

44,735. October 18, 1864. Appl. Sept. 12, 1864. Removing gum, &c., from vegetable material for paper pulp. Ass'd to Wm. E. Rider, Nov. 26, 1864, S7, p. 17. E. S. Renwick, att'y.

46,607. Feb. 28, 1865. Appl. Jan'y 17, 1865. Making wicks out of vegetable fibre. Ass'd to W. E. Rider, Jan'y 19, 1865, S7, p. 344. E. S. Renwick, att'y.

47,068. March 28, 1865. Appl. Feby 21, 1865. Imp't on 44,735. Ass'd to W. E. Rider, Feby 11, 1865, R7, p. 389. E. S. Renwick, att'y.

2 MEUCCI'S PATENTS,

British 758 of 1865. Same as 44,735 and 47,068.

Italian. Nov. 3, 1869. Ditto.

53,165. March 13, 1866. Appl. Aug. 3, 1865. Treating vegetable fibre for paper pulp. Ass'd to David Whiting, Mch. 15, 1866, A9, p. 307; W. E. Rider and Jas. C. McAndrew, witnesses. E. S. Renwick, att'y.

Caveat. Dec. 28, 1871. Sound Telegraph. T. D. Stetson, att'y. Witnesses, Shirley McAndrew and Fred. Harper.

122,478. Jan'y 21, 1872. Appl. Nov. 20, 1871. Effervescent drinks. Shirley McAndrew, witness. Ass'd to Alex. McAndrew, Dec. 17, 1871, C15, p. 103. Ass'd to Mrs. Esterre Meucci (wife of A. Meucci) March 4, 1872, V14, p. 434; B. Bertolino, witness. T. D. Stetson, att'y. Final fee paid Dec. 20, 1871.

Caveat. Dec. 9, 1872. *Caveat* for Sound Telegraph renewed. Stetson, att'y.

Caveat. July 7, 1873. Screw steamer for canals. T. D. Stetson, att'y.

142,071. Aug. 26, 1873. Appl. July 9, 1873. Angiolo P. Agresta and Antonio Meucci, inventors. Sauce for food. T. D. Stetson, att'y.

1,503. Oct. 21, 1873. Appl. July 9, 1873. Trade mark for same. Stetson, att'y.

Caveat. Dec. 15, 1873. *Caveat* for Sound Telegraph renewed. Stetson, att'y.

Caveat. April 23, 1874. Refining, &c., mineral oil. T. D. Stetson, att'y.

Caveat. July 2, 1874. *Caveat* for canal steamer renewed. Stetson, att'y.

168,273. Sept. 28, 1875. Appl. July 23, 1875. Lactometer. Ass'd to Giuseppe Tagliabue, July 17, 1875, O19, p. 431. Van Santvoord and Hauff, attorneys.

183,062. Oct. 10, 1876. Appl. Dec. 1, 1875. Hygrometer. L. D. Cunningham, witness. Ass'd to Esterre Meucci, his wife, Nov. 29, 1875, R19, p. 477; witness Luigi Tartarini. Esterre Meucci appoints Antonio Meuicí, "my husband," her atty. about this,

CAVEATS AND APPLICATIONS. 3

Nov. 30, 1875, U19, p. 292; Leonard D. Cunningham, witness. T. D. Stetson, att'y.

Application. Mch. 6, 1878. Ornamental candles for Christmas trees. Ass'd to Mrs. Esterre Meucci Feby 28, 1878, O22, p. 284. Rejected. Munn & Co., att'ys.

Application. Aug. 1, 1878. Preventing noise on Elevated R. R. Rejected. Hughes & Morris, att'ys.

Application. July 2, 1880. Wire for electrical purposes.

Application. July 8, 1880. Marine Telegraph, serial No. 13,140.

Application. January 6, 1881. Postage and revenue stamps, and process for making same. Ass'd to Scott Lord, Jr., Dec. 30, 1880, D26, p. 382. Rejected. Brown & Brown, att'ys.

279,492. June 12, 1883. Appl. March 8, 1883. Plastic paste. A. Meucci & Torello Dendi. T. D. Stetson, and Munn & Co., att'ys.

Deed. Sept. 22, 1880. A. Meucci to W. W. Goodwin, James Work, Robt. R. Dearden & Alfred P. Willoughby. Recites that A. Meucci did, about 1871, make certain inventions for sound telegraphs and telephones, and did thereafter, July, 1871, file a caveat on said inventions, and did subsequently file his applications for improvements upon the same, and renewed the caveat. Grants the same. Refers to application prepared contemporaneously with deed. Agrees to deliver to them all affid., models and evidences in the hands of his attorneys, M. Lemmi & C. Bertolino. Recorded Oct. 3, 1883, P30, p. 63.

Deed. A. Meucci to Goodwin *et al.*, recorded Dec. 7, 1883, Q30, p. 130. Witnessed by Charles Bertolino and G. B. Edwards. Assigns appl. for Marine Telegraph filed July 8, 1880, serial No. 13,140.

Deed. Same to same. Dec. 4, 1883, recorded Dec. 7, 1883, Q30, p. 130. Assigns appl. about to be made for method of and apparatus for transmitting sound telegraphically.

4

Summary by Dates of Filing.

1858. Nov. 15. Candle mold, 22,739.....Renwick.
1859. June 6. Caveat for candle app..... "
" Appl. for dry battery. Rej .... "
Sept. 25. Apparatus for molding candles, 30,180........ "
1862. May 7. Lamp burner, 36,192.....Renwick.
June 16. Treating oils, 36,419..... Munn.
1863. April 3. do. do. 38,714..... "
1864. Sept. 12. Wood pulp, 44,735.....Renwick.
1865. Jan'y 17. Wicks of fibre, 46,607..... "
Feb'y 21. Veg. fibre, 47,068....... "
Aug. 3. " " 53,165....... "
English 758 of 1865.
Ital. Nov. 3, 1869.
1871. Nov. 20. Effervescent drinks, 122,478,.................Stetson.
Dec. 28. Sound telegraph. *Caveat*. "
1872. Dec. ditto renewed. "
1873. July 7. *Caveat* for canal steamer. "
" 9. Sauce, 142,071.......... "
Oct. 21. " trade mark, 1,503. "
Dec. 15. Sound tel. caveat renewed "
1874. April 23. Refining oil. *Caveat*... "
July 2. Canal steamer. *Caveat renewed* .... "
1875. July 23. Lactometer, 168,274.....Van Santvoord.
Dec. 1. Hygrometer, 183,062.....Stetson.
1878. Mch. 6. Ornamental candles. Rej. "
Aug. 1. Prev. noise on el. R. R. Rej.....................Hughes & Morris.
1880. July 2. Appl. for wire for el. purposes.................
July 8. " marine telegraph
1881. Jan'y 6. Postage stamps. Rej....Brown & Brown.
1883. Mch. 8. Plastic paste.............Stetson, Munn.
Dec. Sound telegraph........

A partial list of Meucci's inventions, as recorded in the United States Patent Office. (Courtesy, *National Archives and Records Service,* Washington, D. C.)

ments through which he and his friends spoke for years. In 1860, when a friend of his, Enrico Bendelari, left for Italy, he asked him to find some well-to-do Italians to help him finance his invention. But Bendelari did nothing about it. The idea of being able to talk through a wire over a distance of miles seemed too preposterous in those days, as we shall presently see.

To make a long story short, Meucci, notwithstanding the lack of support, continued his investigations, making several instruments, "trying and trying again," just as his famous countryman, Galileo, had taught. During this time his financial conditions were getting from bad to worse. He had lost all his money, so much so that he had to resort to public charity or to the assistance of the New York Italians. To top it all, while going home one day on the ferryboat, its boiler exploded, killing more than 100 people. Meucci was seriously injured and was compelled to remain in bed for six months. With no money in sight, one day his wife sold his telephone instruments to a junk dealer for $6.00.

In 1871 Meucci finally decided to patent his telephone invention, but his lawyer, Mr. Stetson, wanted $250 to prepare the necessary documents. Meucci had no money. All he could get together from three friends who took an intestest in his invention was $20, just enough to pay for a caveat. In 1872 and 1873 he renewed the caveat—the sum of $10 needed on each occasion having been advanced by a friend.

THE STRANGE CASE OF MR. GRANT

Not long after he received his caveat, Meucci tried to get some capitalist interested in his telephone invention. Once, accompanied by a friend, Angelo Bertolino, he approached Mr. Edward B. Grant, who was then vice-president of the American District Telegraph Company of New York, and begged him to let him use his wires to test his telephone. Grant took the detailed description that Meucci had brought with him and turned it over to his assistant, Mr. George F. Durant, who had a desk next to his, and who was then superintendent of the New York division of the American District Telegraph Company. At the time he testified in the Meucci (or Globe) case in 1886 he was vice-president and general manager of the Bell Telephone Company of Missouri.

After that first interview, Meucci and his friend, according to Mr. Durant's deposition, "called repeatedly, at intervals, perhaps of two weeks or a month. And I had told Mr. Grant that I didn't see anything in the papers at all; that I thought the man was a crank, although when they came I treated them very politely, and told them I had been pressed for time and had not given the matter any attention. After they called several times, Mr. Grant suggested that I had better hand the papers to him, which I did, and was very glad to get rid of them."

During the course of his testimony, Mr. Durant, of course, denied that Meucci wanted to test his telephone, but made the damaging admission (of paramount importance, as we shall presently see) that Meucci in his transmission of "some signals or sensations" had used a wire and that "on that wire they had a galvanic battery of several cells."

After calling fruitlessly on Mr. Grant for a couple of years (Mr. Durant admitted to only "four or five months perhaps") Meucci asked Mr. Grant to return his papers to him (according to Mr. Durant they were ten or a dozen pages), only to be told by Mr. Grant that he did not have them any more and that he did not know what had become of them.

Meucci's visit to Mr. Grant reminds us of the visit another Italian, Antonio Pacinotti, paid to the Froment machine shop in Paris, and of the long talk he had with the shop mechanic, Zenobe Theophile Gramme, about his recently-invented ring-winding dynamo. Gramme, like Grant, also told Pacinotti that he would look into the matter, until not long after that interview, in 1870, it was announced that Gramme had invented a ring-winding dynamo like Pacinotti's. Only the description of his invention in the scientific magazine "*Nuovo Cimento*" of Florence in 1865 saved Pacinotti from being robbed of the honor, although Gramme got the millions. All that Pacinotti received was the Volta prize of 50,000 francs bestowed on him by the Government of France.

Getting back to our story, when Meucci learned about Bell's telephone he protested, but what could an old and poor foreigner who could hardly speak English do against a company that was backed by millions of dollars?

Even Garibaldi, at his friend's request, tried to get the Italian Government to support Meucci's claims, but as history proves, Italian bureaucrats and politicians have never lifted a finger to help Italian inventors. The case of Marconi is typical.

For a time some wealthy Americans and Englishmen took an interest in Meucci's invention; men like Robert Garrett, president of the Baltimore and Ohio Railroad, and other millionaires, including William H. Vanderbilt of New York and James McHenry of London. (*Philadelphia Times*, Aug. 26, 1884.)

Later Meucci assigned his telephone invention to the Globe Telephone Company, one of several firms that had been formed to dispute Bell's title to originality. In September, 1885, the Globe Company issued a circular announcing that it had secured title to Meucci's invention and invited the public to purchase the instruments which it was planning to make without infringing on the Bell patent. Two months later the Bell Company brought suit against the Globe Company, Meucci, and others for infringement of its patents. The case was concluded on July 19, 1887, when Judge Wallace rendered his decision, as already indicated.

The defendants immediately appealed the case to the Supreme Court of the United States in order "to hear the said cause anew." On November 18, 1887, Judge Lacombe, also of the United States Circuit Court for the Southern District of New York, allowed the appeal and ordered the American Bell Telephone Company to appear on the second Monday of October, 1888. The case came up for a hearing

118 CAVEAT.

PETITION.

The petition of Antonio Meucci of Clifton in the County of Richmond and State of New York, respectfully represents:

That he has made certain improvements in Sound Telegraphs, and that he is now engaged in making experiments for the purpose of perfecting the same preparatory to applying for Letters Patent therefor. He therefore prays that the subjoined description of his invention may be filed as a Caveat in the Confidential Archives of the Patent Office.

119 ANTONIO MEUCCI.

OATH.

STATE OF NEW YORK, }
County of Richmond, } ss.:

ANTONIO MEUCCI, the above-named petitioner, being duly sworn, deposes and says that he verily believes himself to be the original and first inventor of the improvement in Sound Telegraphs, described and claimed in the foregoing specification; that he does not know, and does not believe, that the same was ever before known and used; and that I am a citizen of the United States.

120 ANTONIO MEUCCI.

Subscribed and sworn to before me, }
this 23d day of December, 1871, }

JOSEPH DOYLE,
Justice of the Peace.

The following is a description of the invention sufficiently in detail for the purposes of this Caveat:

I employ the well-known conducting effect of continuous metallic conductors as a medium for sound, and in-

crease the effect by electrically insulating both the conductor and the parties who are communicating. It forms 121
a speaking Telegraph without the necessity for any hollow tube. I claim that a portion or the whole of the effect may also be realized by a corresponding arrangement with a metallic tube.

I believe that some metals will serve better than others, but propose to try all kinds of metals.

* * The system on which I propose to operate and calculated, consists* in isolating two persons* separted at considerable distances from each other by placing them upon glass insulators employing glass, for example, at the feet of the chair or bench on which each sits and 122
putting them in communication by means of a telegraphic wire. I believe it preferable to have the wire of larger area than that ordinarily employed in the electric telegraph but will experiment on this. Each of these persons holds to his mouth an instrument analogous to a speaking trumpet in which the word may be easily pronounced and the sound concentrated upon the wire. Another instrument is also applied to the ears in order to receive the voice of the opposite party. 123

All these, to wit, the mouth utensil and the ear instruments communicate to the wire at a short distance from the persons. The ear utensils being of a convex form like a clock glass enclose the whole exterior part of the ear and make it easy and comfortable for the operator The object is to bring distinctly to the hearing the words of the person at the opposite end of the telegraph.

[Marginal notes:] Isolating or not. It may be founded necessary for the person communicating the message to be isolated, but* the person receiving to be in electrical connection with the ground

Both the utensils for mouth & ears *must* be metallic conductors of electricity

NOTE.—Marginal notes on this Exhibit K are in *red ink*, beginning with the *stars* and the word *isolating*, and ending with the word *electricity*. (See certificate to the caveat.)

124 To call attention, the party at the other end of the line may be warned by an electric telegraph signal or a series of them. The apparatus for this purpose and the skill in operating it need be much less than for the ordinary telegraphing.

When my sound telegraph is in operation the parties should remain alone in their respective rooms and every practicable precaution should be taken to have the surroundings perfectly quiet. The closed mouth utensil or trumpet and the enclosing the persons also in a room alone both tend to prevent undue publicity to the communication I think it will be easy by these means to prevent the communication being understood by any but the proper persons

125 It may be found practicable to work with the person sending the message insulated and with the person receiving it in free electrical communication with the ground. Or these conditions may possibly be reversed and still operate with some success.

Both the conductors or utensils for mouth and ears should be,—in fact I may say—must be—metallic and be so conditioned as to be good conductors of electricity.

I claim as my invention & desire to have considered as such for all the purposes of this Caveat

The new invention herein set forth in all its details, combinations and sub-combinations.

And more specifically I claim—

126 FIRST—A continuous sound conductor electrically insulated.

SECOND—The same adapted for telegraphing by sound or for conversation between distant parties electrically insulated

THIRD—The employment of a sound conductor which is also an electrical conductor as a means of communication by sound between distant points.

FOURTH—The same in combination with provisions for electrically insulating the sending and receiving parties.

FIFTH—The mouth piece or speaking utensil in combination with an electrically insulating conductor. 127

SIXTH—The ear utensils or receiving vessels adapted to apply upon the ears in combination with an electrically insulating sound conductor.

SEVENTH—The entire system comprising the electrical and sound conductor insulated and furnished with a mouth piece and ear pieces at each end adapted to serve as specified.

In testimony whereof I have hereunto set my name in presence of two subscribing witnesses.

ANTONIO MEUCCI 128

Witnesses:
SHIRLEY McANDREW.
FREDK. HARPER.

[K3319]

Facsimile of Meucci's caveat with the changes made on the margin by Thomas D. Stetson, the attorney who prepared it and filed it.

before the Supreme Court in Washington during the term of October, 1891, but since the appellants had failed to present the transcript of the record, in pursuance of the 10th rule of the Court, Chief Justice Fuller on March 10, 1892, dismissed the case and ordered the appellants to pay the sum of $4,138.11. To put it another way, the Globe Telephone Company abandoned the case.

Why? Simply because by the time the case came up for a hearing, Meucci had been dead more than two years, and since the Globe Company had asked not for a review of the case but for a new trial, the interrogation and cross-examination of Meucci was no longer possible; Bell's patents, moreover, were about to expire; finally the Bell Company had grown to such formidable power that it had become hopeless to grapple with it. Money had won.

Thus, to all intents and purposes, Meucci's claim to priority in the invention of the telephone had been decided from the legal point of view and Meucci had lost.

But, over and above all individual judges and any or all national courts, there is the court of the public opinion of the world. It is to that court that we submit now *all* the evidence in the case, namely, the evidence contained in the official court record of the case of the American Bell Tlephone Company versus the Globe Telephone Company, Meucci, and others.

We shall do that by quoting first in italics Judge Wallace's decision, point by point, followed by our proofs. For a full documentation, however, the reader must wait for our forthcoming volume on Meucci or consult the printed record and the other documents in the archives of the Supreme Court in Washington and in the National Archives of the United States. The full text of Judge Wallace's decision can be found in 31 *Federal Reporter*, 729.

JUDGE WALLACE'S DECISION AND THE EVIDENCE IN THE CASE.

1) *"That he (Meucci) did not believe he had accomplished anything of practical commercial utility is a reasonable inference from the fact that he did not communicate his invention to those who would have been likely to appreciate it, and assist him in perfecting and introducing it to the public."*

That is not true. On the other hand, the Record proves abundantly,

a) That as early as 1860 Meucci asked his friend, Enrico Bendelari, who was then about to go to Italy, to get some people in Italy interested in his invention. The proof of that can be found in *Eco d'Italia* of New York, October 13, 1865, still available in the New York Public Library. Judge Wallace himself admits it in his decision (not quoted above).

b) On January 19, 1872, three weeks after he had secured his caveat and four years before Bell filed his application, Meucci wrote a letter to his attorney, Thomas D. Stetson, who had prepared his caveat, informing him that two of his three partners had withdrawn from the partnership they had formed for the development of his telephone and added (the spelling is as in the original letter): "I now ask you if you, perhaps with your influence and acquantance about the city if you would try to find some gentleman acquantance in Telegraphic bueseness and having some means to join in and replace the other two, in this way it would facilitate me very much in my experiments for having some interesting parties connected that aare allready acquantens in Telegraphic buseness";

c) There is, above all, the evidence about Meucci's many calls at the office of Mr. Grant as we have already noted. How Judge Wallace could afford to state that Meucci did not try to communicate his invention to those who could "assist him in perfecting and introducing it to the public," when he had Durant's sworn deposition glaring in his face, it is most difficult to understand. Durant, we wish to stress it once more, was a witness for the Bell Company and one of its top officials.

2) *"Between 1859 and the time of his application for a caveat he filed many applications for patents for other inventions. During the years 1859, 1860, and 1861 he was in close business and social relations with William E. Ryder, who was interested in his inventions, paid the expenses of his experiments, and, in connection with others whom he introduced to Meucci, invested a considerable amount of money in Meucci's inventions, and their use in business enterprises. He was a constant visitor at Meucci's house, lived near him, and seems to have been his closest personal friend and business adviser.*

"Their intimate relations continued until 1867, when Ryder became satisfied that Meucci's inventions were not sufficiently practical or profitable to devote more time and money to them, and their intimacy ceased, although as late as 1871 he interested himself for Meucci to dispose of some of his inventions. During all these years, according to the testimony of Mr. Ryder, he never heard from Meucci, or anybody else, of Meucci's telephone.

"In 1864 and 1865 David H. Craig was a partner with Meucci and Ryder in the paper manufacture.

"He had been intimately associated with others in telegraph inventions and patents, and his interest in such matters must have been known by Meucci. He never heard from Meucci or otherwise, that Meucci had invented or was experimenting with the telephone.

Judge Wallace attaches much importance to the testimony of William E. Ryder (as the name is spelled in the Record), a man who, in our opinion, should have been prosecuted for perjury, for it is simply too absurd to believe, as Judge Wallace believes, that during his many years of close association with Meucci, whose house he visited constantly, "he never heard from Meucci or anyone else, of Meucci's telephone." Judge Wallace himself states in his decision that "There is no reason to doubt that for many years prior to 1865, and from that year until he applied for a caveat, he had been experimenting with telephonic and electric apparatus with a view of transmitting speech, and during this time had convinced himself that he had made interesting discoveries, which might eventually become useful ones. To this extent he is corroborated by the testimony of a number of witnesses. But the proofs fail to show that he had reached any practical result beyond that of conveying speech mechanically by means of a wire telephone."

The fact is that Ryder took advantage of Meucci's good faith, converting to his own use most of the sum of $5,000 which he received on account of one of Meucci's inventions and which he should have divided with Meucci, "besides a certain amount that my wife (Meucci's wife) had given him for safe keeping." Rider, of course, tried to justify his actions in this matter, but his explanations are far from satisfactory, as shown in the Record. Rider certainly was interested in Meucci's inventions and got several people with money interested in them. The fact that he did nothing about Meucci's telephone may be explained by the skepticism which people in those days had about talking through a wire.

SKEPTICISM ABOUT THE TELEPHONE

According to Mr. Watson, Bell's collaborator, the Scotch inventor had a hard time trying to convince his own financial backers—Hubbard and Sanders—who "were insisting that the wisest thing for Bell to do was to perfect the harmonic telegraph; then he would have money and leisure to build air castles like the telephone." (Watson, Thos. A., *The Birth and Babyhood of the Telephone,* 13.) Bell himself made a similar statement during his cross-examination by the counsel for the Government, during the case of the United States Government versus the American Bell Telephone Company, in 1892. According to him, his financial backers, Hubbard and Sanders, "considered the multiple telegraph as being more valuable than the speaking telephone."

Even after Bell had obtained his patent and succeeded in transmitting speech through the wire, people were skeptical. His exhibit at the Philadelphia Centennial Exhibition had been ignored until the Emperor of Brazil, whom Bell had met in connection with his work of teaching the deaf, was induced to try Bell's telephone. The rest is history.

One more thing may show how little faith even people who were supposed to know had in the telephone. In the fall of 1876, after the Philadelphia success, Mr. Hubbard offered to sell Bell's telephone invention to the Western Union Company for $100,000, but the offer was declined. As Mr. Watson informs us, "Two years later the Western Union would gladly have bought those patents for $25,000,000." (Watson, *op. cit.*, 24.)

942.
909

38 PROOFS FOR GLOBE TELEPHONE COMPANY.

112 find that I entered anything about this case during that month or the succeeding.

THOMAS DREW STETSON.

Sworn and subscribed before me, this 9th day of January, 1886,

JOHN A. SHIELDS,
U. S. Commissioner

Defendants' Exhibit No. 149.

113 [Record, p. 37.]

I, THOMAS D. STETSON, of the City, County and State of New York, hereby make oath that I am well acquainted with Mr. Antonio Meucci, of the Town of Clifton, Staten Island, in the State of New York, since the year 1871, when I acted as his patent attorney, through the assistance of Mr. A. Bertolino who acted as Mr. Meucci's translator and interpreter of Italian into the English language, to caveat in the United States Patent Office Mr. Meucci's invention of what is now known as the telephone; and that from his verbal explanation and the description contained in the caveat I verily believe him to be the first and original inventor thereof.

114 And I further state that, from knowledge gained through an intimate acquaintance with the affairs of Mr. Meucci since 1871, to the best of my knowledge and belief Mr. Meucci has been too poor to pay the money necessary to complete his patent application and to introduce his invention, and has been physically unable to earn the necessary means.

And that I, as Mr. Meucci's attorney, sent to the Patent Office the several fees for his caveat and its renewal, and the receipts therefore were received by me for the years 1871, '2, '3 and until the 28th of December, 1874.

And I further state that this affidavit is entirely volun-

943
910

DEPOSITION OF THOMAS D STETSON 39

tary and made in justice to Mr Meucci without receipt of any payment or promise of compensation, and that I have no business interest with him. 115

THOMAS D STETSON

Sworn before me, this 14th day of July, 1880,

ANGELO BERTOLINO,
[L. S.] Notary Public,
N Y Cy

Complainants' Exhibit K.

[Record, p. 37.]

[2—175.] 116

DEPARTMENT OF THE INTERIOR.

UNITED STATES PATENT OFFICE.

To all Persons to whom these Presents shall come, Greeting:

THIS IS TO CERTIFY, That the annexed is a true photo lithographic fac-simile of the petition, oath and specification (except marginal notes in red ink, which have been added by hand, as the pencil marks were two faint to photograph). In the matter of the Caveat of Antonio Meucci.

Filed December 28th, 1871, for Improvement in Sound 117
Telegraphs.

[SEAL.] IN TESTIMONY WHEREOF I, M V Montgomery, Commissioner of Patents, have caused the seal of the Patent Office to be affixed this 12th day of January, in the year of our Lord one thousand eight hundred and eighty-six, and of the Independence of the United States the one hundred and tenth

M. V MONTGOMERY
Commissioner

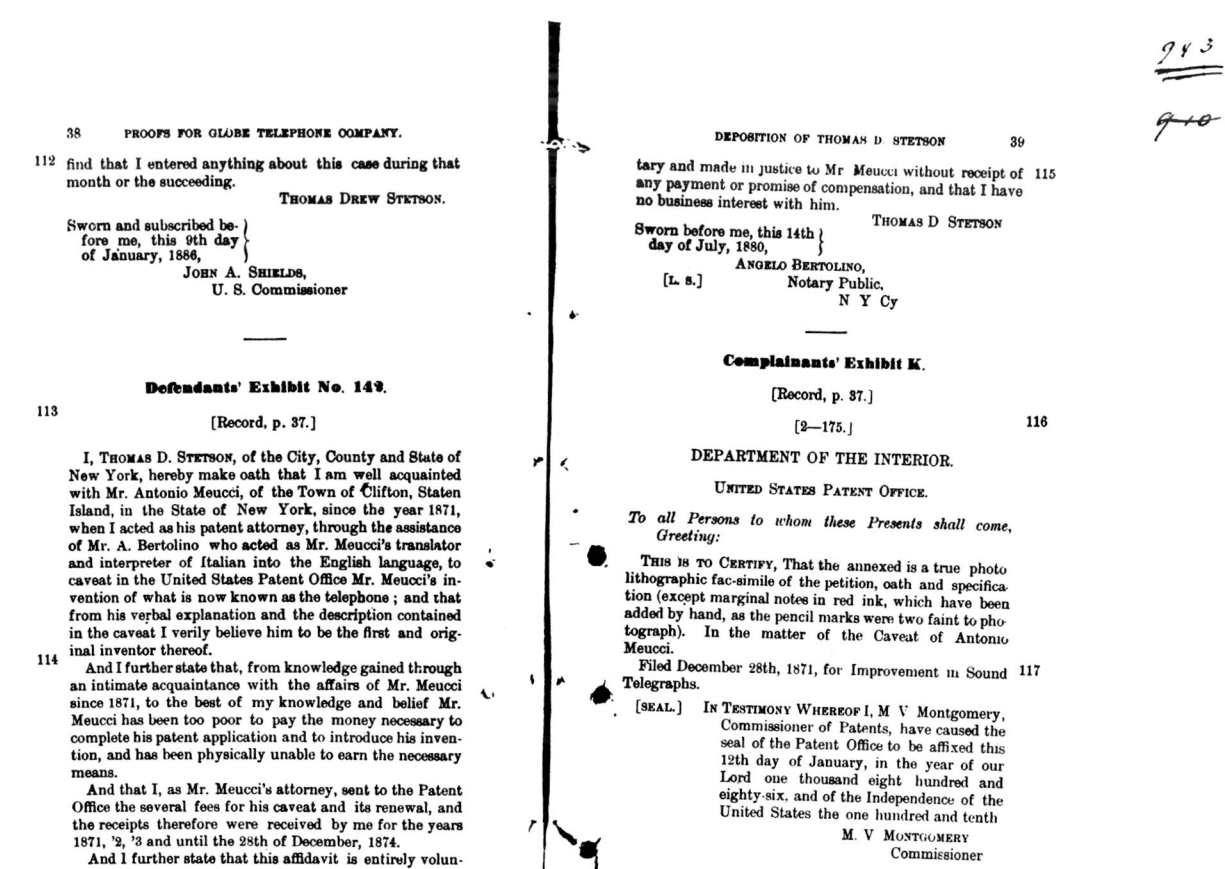

Affidavit by Thomas D. Stetson which Judge Wallace completely disregarded notwithstanding its paramount importance. (From the Record in the U. S. Supreme Court, Washington, D. C.)

528 EVIDENCE FOR COMPLAINANTS.

tion. No. 1 is a pasteboard box; No. 2, mouthpiece; No. 3, bobbin full of insulated copper wire, the extremity of which passes through the bottom of the box to connect with the wire from the battery; No. 4, bar of tempered steel; No. 5, conductors going from the bobbin to the battery; No. 6, metallic diaphragm; No. 7, bottom of the box. Please state if an instrument made according to that pattern will transmit articulate speech when properly adjusted by a screw placed in the bottom of the box, as indicated in the drawing?

Fig 14

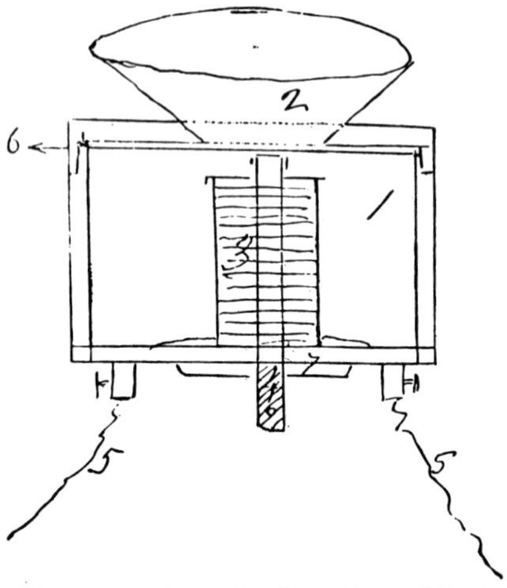

DEPOSITION OF CHARLES R. CROSS. 529

Ans. If the diaphragm at 6 were made of iron or steel, it doubtless would transmit speech. I do not observe, however, that Mr. Meucci makes any reference to the use of diaphragms of either of those materials.

[*The cross-examination of Mr. Cross not being completed this day (May* 1, 1886), *complainants' time for taking testimony is hereby extended to Saturday, May* 8, 1886.

The further cross-examination of Mr. Cross is adjourned to Monday, May 3, 1886, *at* 2.15 P.M.]

BOSTON, May 3, 1886.

Met pursuant to adjournment, all the parties being present as stated before.

CHARLES R. CROSS, *further cross-examined.*

By Mr. HUMPHREYS. *Cross-Int.* 255. I believe you have testified, have you not, that Figs. 5, 7, 8, 11, 13 and 14 of Mr. Meucci's testimony, by using them with an iron diaphragm, will transmit speech?

Ans. I do not recollect that I have testified at all to that effect.

Cross-Int. 256. Have you not just testified that instruments made after the pattern of Fig. 14, using an iron diaphragm and a steel magnet with a coil, will transmit speech?

Ans. It is true that Fig. 14, when thus made, will transmit speech, and my remembrance is that I have testified to this effect regarding it.

Cross-Int. 257. Have you not also testified with reference to Fig. 13 to the same effect?

Ans. As far as I remember, I have done so; undoubtedly, Fig. 13 does, if the diaphragm is constructed of iron.

Cross-Int. 258. Will not Fig. 11 also do the same?

Ans. I should think that Fig. 11 would transmit speech, if the diaphragm at 6 were made of iron.

Cross-Int. 259. The same of Fig. 8?

Ans. I think I have already said that even if the diaphragm at 4 were made of iron, I thought it very doubtful whether speech could practically be transmitted with Fig. 8.

Two pages from the deposition of Prof. Cross of the Massachusetts Institute of Technology, who testified for the Bell Telephone Company. Notice his flat denials and then his admissions. (From the Record in the Supreme Court, Washington, D. C.)

As late as February 16, 1877, the *Chicago Tribune* in its defense of Gray's claim to the invention of the telephone stated that "Talking by telegraph and other sport of that description Mr. Gray has not paid much attention to as yet, because there is no present indication in it of anything more than sport; but the principles involved in it were discussed by him and have all been used by him in a practical manner."

That was eight months after Bell had demonstrated his telephone at the Philadelphia Centennial.

A year later, in 1878, Appleton's *Annual Cyclopaedia* stated: "The telephone has been regarded as a toy, or a curiosity to play with; but while it is undoubtedly extremely interesting as a novelty, it is very much more than this. . . . The telegraph was much longer regarded as an impracticable invention. . . ."

Gray himself wrote to Bell in March 1877: "I do not however claim even the credit of inventing it, as I do not believe a mere description of an idea that has never been *reduced* to *practice*—in the *strict sense* of that phrase—should be dignified with the name of invention."

Mr. W. C. Langdon, who until a few years ago was historical librarian of the American Telephone and Telegraph Company, seized this admission by Gray to prove that Gray had not preceded Bell in the invention of the telephone and added that Gray "was not deceived, as Meucci was, by any one. He was competent to reach the truth of the matter from his own knowledge of electricity." (Langdon, Myths of Telephone History, *Bell Telephone Quarterly*, April, 1933.)

Mr. Langdon, however, ignored the fact that Meucci's telephone had been in use for many years before Bell applied for his patent—a little thing which makes a whale of a difference.

Getting back to Rider's deposition, one must bear in mind that at the time Rider testified in court against Meucci, Mr. Dickerson, the attorney for the Bell Company, was also counsel for the Goodyear Company and that Mr. Rider's father was half owner of the Goodyear patent.

As for Craig's testimony which Judge Wallace finds so important, it is irrelevant to the case for the same reasons shown above. In court, for instance, Mr. Craig, who is supposed to have had such a deep interest in telegraph inventions, was forced to admit that he had never heard of the telephone invention of the German, Philip Reis, until after he had left the Associated Press in 1866, although Reis's invention dated back to 1860. Bell was well acquainted with it. Craig had no direct dealing with Meucci. Rider communicated with Meucci in French.

MR. STETSON'S LETTERS AND DEPOSITION

"*Before consulting Mr. Stetson, Meucci prepared a description of his invention, intending to make an application for a patent. After consulting Mr. Stetson, he concluded to make application for a caveat only. With the aid of an interpreter, and the manuscript containing the description, Mr. Stetson prepared the formal application. After it had been prepared by Mr. Stetson, it was sent by him to Meucci, and returned by the latter with amendments to be inserted in it. It is sufficient to say that the application does not describe any of the elements of an electric speaking telephone. . . .*

387 388

564 EVIDENCE FOR COMPLAINANTS.

Cross-Int. 410. The next paragraph reads: "Uniting the two extremities of the cord of copper to the ground it becomes well conductive, taking the electricity of the earth." Would that aid in any manner to render a telephonic apparatus effective?

Ans. This paragraph is exceedingly vague, and it is difficult to understand the idea which was in the mind of the person writing it. It is, of course, a well-known fact that the earth will serve instead of a return wire for telephonic or telegraphic apparatus.

Cross-Int. 411. In the second paragraph on page 2, I ask you if there is not a statement of a magneto telephone, *multum in parvo*, in a few words, describing a magneto telephone, provided you use a metallic diaphragm, or one of iron or steel?

[*Complainants object to the question because the second paragraph is only part of a long description, all of which should be read.*]

Ans. I do not find any such description.

Cross-Int. 412. It is a fact, nevertheless, is it not, that a strongly magnetized iron, protected or surrounded with a bobbin, placed in close proximity to an iron diaphragm, will transmit speech without the aid of a battery?

Ans. There is no doubt that in a magneto transmitter there is a strongly magnetized bar of steel or iron surrounded by a bobbin, and having a proper iron diaphragm in close proximity to it. This will transmit speech without the aid of a battery.

Cross-Int. 413. I ask you if you take the description of diaphragm given by Mr. Meucci in his description of Fig. 5, where he says, animal membrane with a hole in the centre, as shown by No. 6, over which a steel tongue was placed; then in Fig. 7, animal diaphragm with a hole in the centre with a metallic tongue of iron under it serving as a valve; then, Fig. 8, membrane of metal; Fig. 10, membrane at the bottom of the tube, sometimes of iron; Fig. 11, membrane, sometimes mineral; Fig. 13, metallic membrane; Fig. 14, metallic diaphragm; and qualify them all with Mr. Meucci's statement as to how a diaphragm should be made in his memorandum book, Aug. 17, 1870, "Fabric of cotton, flax, silk, saturate with starch very thick, and the starch dissolved in a solution of nitrate of silver and then paraffine has given a good diaphragm, only to use this quality of membrane it is necessary to put in the centre a

DEPOSITION OF CHARLES R. CROSS. 565

small disk of iron or platinum metallic iron, in order that it can have action on the centre of the bobbin and communicate the electricity in its vibration with the sound of the word." Now I ask you if Mr. Meucci's description of a diaphragm, as given in his deposition herein read to you and explained from his memorandum book, is not a better, more sensible, more scientific description of a diaphragm necessary for telephonic purposes than that given by Prof. Bell in his first patent, No. 174,465, when he says, "I include in the category of bodies capable of inductive action, brass, copper and other metals, as well as iron and steel"?

[*Question objected to because it is not a correct statement, either of Mr. Meucci's testimony or of the Exhibit* 109, *alleged to be his memorandum book; and particularly objected to because there is no mention of a steel tongue in his description of Fig.* 5. *The reference to Fig.* 10 *is objected to specifically as a misquotation, the statement in the deposition being, "membrane at the bottom of the tube, sometimes of animal substance, sometimes of iron, sometimes of copper, and sometimes of different materials." The reference to Fig.* 11 *is objected to, the statement being, "membrane, sometimes mineral, sometimes of other substances that I have elsewhere indicated." The passage from the alleged note book is also objected to because the same page contains descriptions of other diaphragms of manila paper, etc., without any reference to any metal disk connected with them.*]

Ans. Neither in the statements of Mr. Meucci, to which I suppose you refer, nor in any statements of his in his deposition, affidavit, memorandum book, or anywhere else that I have seen, is there the slightest description, hint or intimation of any kind as to the nature of the diaphragm which was necessary for use in an electrical speaking telephone. On the contrary, his language is such as to show most conclusively, to my mind, that he did not have the slightest suspicion of the necessity of having the diaphragm made of a substance which should be capable of inductive action. The statement made by Mr. Bell, which you quote, read in connection with the remainder of the patent, is perfectly clear, scientific and proper.

Cross-Int. 414. Brass and copper are wholly unsuitable, are they

Two more pages from the deposition of Prof. Cross revealing his habit of denying without regard to the available evidence. (From the Record in the U. S. Supreme Court, Washington, D.C.)

"*A letter written by* Mr. Stetson *of the date of January* 13, 1872, *is in evidence, and is important as confirmatory of the conclusion that beyond this the invention was only inchoate. This letter was written to Meucci when the latter was in communication with Mr. Stetson in reference to obtaining a patent for the invention. In this letter Mr. Stetson, in substance, advised Meucci that his invention was not in a condition to patent; telling him that it was 'an idea giving promise of usefulness' and the proper subject of a caveat, but requiring many experiments to prove the reality of the invention.*"

Judge Wallace here twisted the facts to suit his thesis in order to prove, through Stetson's letter, that Meucci's invention was not in a condition to patent and that it was advisable to apply for a caveat rather than a patent.

According to Meucci, whose veracity nobody has the least reason to doubt, having decided to protect his invention, he "went to Angelo Bertolino, and asked him to make a translation of what I had written of my invention, in order to submit it to Mr. Stetson, to apply for a patent. We went together to Mr. Stetson, who allowed me only one hour to speak, at the end asking me two hundred and fifty dollars to obtain the patent, and twenty dollars for the caveat. In view of the scarcity of money, I preferred the caveat, not having the two hundred and fifty dollars for the patent." Since Meucci was on relief, his friends gave him the twenty dollars for the caveat. Some other friend advanced the sum of ten dollars which he needed to renew the caveat in 1872 and 1873. Finally, "I had no more means to pay, and I couldn't find anybody willing to give me anything, because they did not believe in my invention. I was so poor that the Poor Commissioner of Staten Island furnished me with coal and groceries in order not to let me starve. I asked other persons for the money, but they told me that it was not convenient to spend more money to renew the caveat; that it was better that the money was used for my maintenance or something else necessary." In those days some Italians used to give Meucci one dollar a month each to provide for his support.

Stetson testified that "I am quite sure that I did not fully understand the invention; what I did understand I put into such shape as I thought was proper for a caveat"; that he did not remember, one way or the other, whether any drawing was furnished by Meucci; that he did not remember whether he was solicited to secure a patent (there is a letter to that effect); that he could not well remember details of something that had taken place more than fourteen years before.

Later, with the help of his notebook, Stetson said that all he was able to devote to Meucci's invention was one half hour for his conversation with the inventor, one hour to dictate the caveat, and another half hour to add an amendment. The defendants then produced a letter from Meucci to Stetson which was delivered on January 12, 1872, saying in part: "Could you at an early date give me an estimate of the cost of preparing all necessary documents for the application to the U. S. for a letter Patent to Cover all the separate points claimed in the caveat specifications?"

To that letter Stetson replied with the letter mentioned by Judge Wallace to the effect that Meucci's "telegraphing will have to be experimented with considerably before it will be ready for a patent. . . . It is in just the right condition for caveat—just an idea which gives promise of usefulness, but not yet ready to be put fully into condition for use. I advise making a good many experiments, to prove the reality of the thing." Whereupon Meucci asked Stetson, as already mentioned under No. 1, to find some persons with means to take the place of the two Italians who had withdrawn from the contract. On January 19, 1872, Stetson replied that he was too busy and that he could not take any interest in his invention.

Stetson's letter of January 19 should be enough to lead one to the conclusion that he did not realize the importance of Meucci's invention, just as the Western Union officials and Elisha Gray himself did not realize the value of Bell's patent even after Bell had demonstrated his instrument at Philadelphia. Now it is absurd to assume that Stetson knew more about electricity than Gray.

Meucci was poor, had no wealthy friends, and lawyers usually are "too much occupied," as Stetson was, when there are no fees in sight. After Bell obtained his patent and the telephone was a success, Stetson changed his mind about the value of Meucci's caveat and advised him to test his telephone at the Western Union shop. That was in April, 1877. At that time he felt that "the thing was valuable," although Meucci had made no improvements on it since 1871. All of which goes to show that Meucci besides protesting tried to prove the validity and priority of his invention as soon as he heard of Bell's patent.

At any rate, the telephone was too big a thing for a poor man like Meucci. On March 25, 1875, he wrote to Stetson: "I shall continue on small affairs, as I believe as you do that they are the best."

On September 28, 1885, Stetson wrote a letter which he never mailed, to William Goodwin of the Globe Telephone Company. In it he expressed doubt as to the drawings which Meucci said he handed to him, or to any reference to a battery in Meucci's talks with him. But he added: "I am now statisfied from Mr. Meucci's statements that he had actually invented all those things earlier than December, 1871. But, like many inventors, he did not take the trouble, or did not consider it policy to give those details in his caveat." It is possible that Meucci may have done just that, since a caveat does not offer as much protection as a patent. In connection with his invention of a spiral cord, on October 14, 1875, Meucci begged Stetson to "secure me something to guard and protect myself as I much fear, the capitalist with whom I am associated, can and will take advantage of me."

On September 28, 1885, Stetson wrote another letter to Mr. Goodwin, in substitution of the one mentioned above. In this one, which he mailed, he wrote that having tried to remember what happened at the time Meucci asked him to prepare his caveat, he still could not "recollect any of the circumstances," and added: "It was not my custom at that time, and has never been since, to bestow as much care on the preparation of a caveat as on an application for a patent. . . . The caveat itself is proof positive that Mr. Meucci had at that time the idea of communicating spoken words by the aid of electricity . . . It is sometimes held that a caveat is also proof that the idea is imperfect, incomplete, but this should be qualified; it is simply proof that some point about the matter is thus incomplete; it may have been some unimportant point which he held to be in that condition. The main idea of communicating spoken words by a telegraphic wire, and that electricity was to aid in it, and that communication was to be promoted by the insulation of the wire, is very plainly set forth in the caveat."

In the above-mentioned *Myths of Telephone History*, Mr. Langdon would have us believe that in 1885 Meucci became the dupe of Dr. Beckwith of the Globe Telephone Company and that "out of Beckwith's exploitation of him arose the myth of Antonio Meucci as the inventor of the telephone." Mr. Langdon, unfortunately, did not learn all the facts in the case, for he does not seem to have known about Stetson's advice to use the Western Union shop in 1877, or about an affidavit dated July 14, 1880, by Stetson. Judge Wallace also ignored that affidavit, whereas he attached so much importance to the other letter Stetson wrote on January 13, 1872. The affidavit, however, is so important that we reproduce it here.

MEUCCI'S CAVEAT

4) Judge Wallace admits that Meucci transmitted speech through a wire, and then adds:

"But the proofs fail to show that he had reached any practical result beyond that of conveying speech mechanically by means of a wire telephone. He doubtless employed a metallic conductor as a medium for conveying sound, and supposed that by electrifying the apparatus or the operator he could obtain a better result.

"The caveat itself is sufficient to indicate that he had reached no practical result. There is no reason to doubt that his application contained the best description of his invention which he was then able to give. . . . It is sufficient to say that the application does not describe any of the elements of an electric speaking telephone. Its opening statement refutes the possibility that Meucci understood the principle of that invention. Meucci states that he employs:

"The well-known conducting effect of continuous metallic conductors as a medium for sound, and increases the effect by electrically insulating both the conductor and the parties who are communicating."

"As originally expressed by Mr. Stetson, it contained this statement:

"The system on which I propose to operate consists in isolating two persons, separated at considerable distances from each other, by placing them upon glass insulators, employing glass, for example, at the feet of the chair or bench on which each sits, and putting them in communication by means of a telegraphic wire.'

"As amended pursuant to Meucci's instructions, this statement was qualified as follows:-

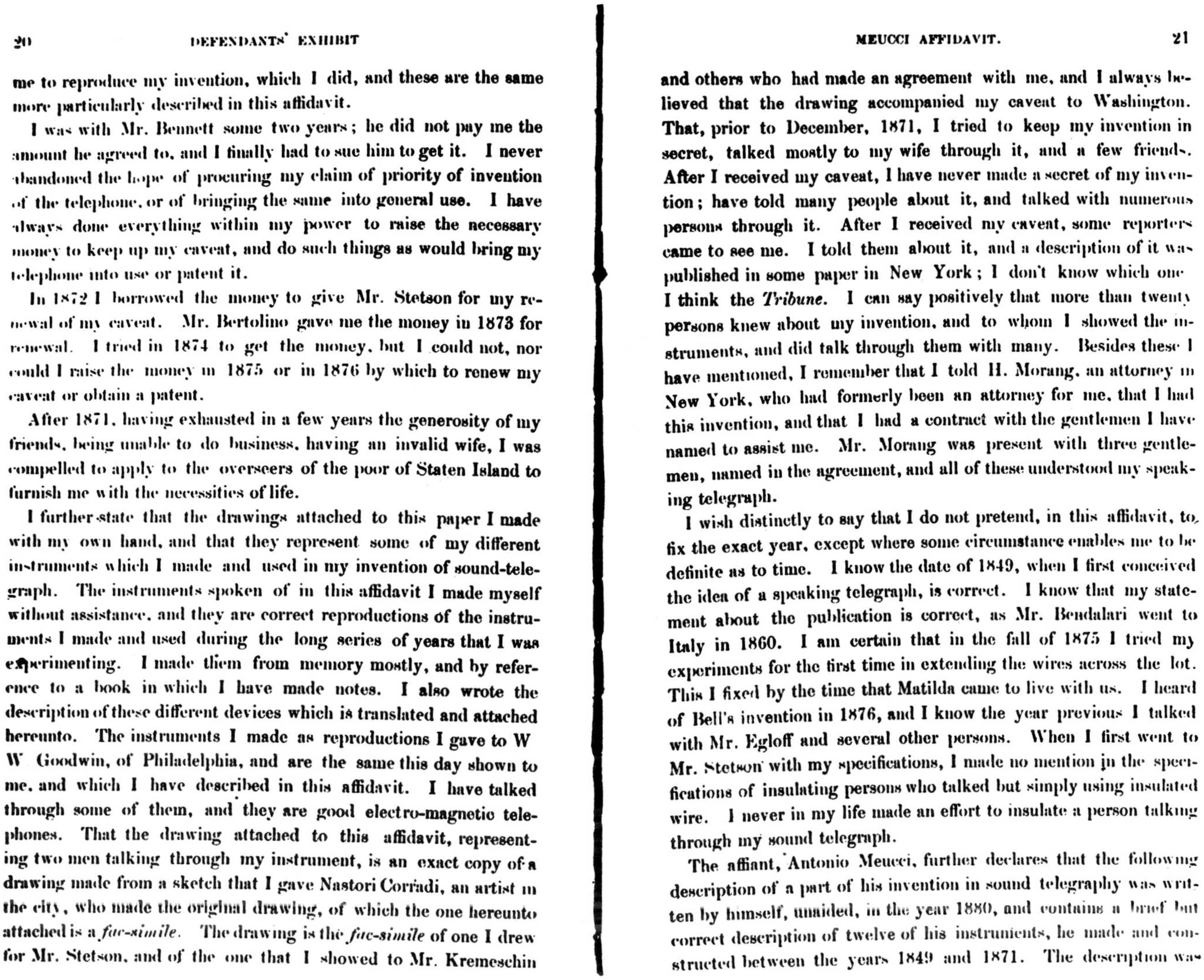

20 DEFENDANTS' EXHIBIT

me to reproduce my invention, which I did, and these are the same more particularly described in this affidavit.

I was with Mr. Bennett some two years; he did not pay me the amount he agreed to, and I finally had to sue him to get it. I never abandoned the hope of procuring my claim of priority of invention of the telephone, or of bringing the same into general use. I have always done everything within my power to raise the necessary money to keep up my caveat, and do such things as would bring my telephone into use or patent it.

In 1872 I borrowed the money to give Mr. Stetson for my renewal of my caveat. Mr. Bertolino gave me the money in 1873 for renewal. I tried in 1874 to get the money, but I could not, nor could I raise the money in 1875 or in 1876 by which to renew my caveat or obtain a patent.

After 1871, having exhausted in a few years the generosity of my friends, being unable to do business, having an invalid wife, I was compelled to apply to the overseers of the poor of Staten Island to furnish me with the necessities of life.

I further state that the drawings attached to this paper I made with my own hand, and that they represent some of my different instruments which I made and used in my invention of sound-telegraph. The instruments spoken of in this affidavit I made myself without assistance, and they are correct reproductions of the instruments I made and used during the long series of years that I was experimenting. I made them from memory mostly, and by reference to a book in which I have made notes. I also wrote the description of these different devices which is translated and attached hereunto. The instruments I made as reproductions I gave to W W Goodwin, of Philadelphia, and are the same this day shown to me, and which I have described in this affidavit. I have talked through some of them, and they are good electro-magnetic telephones. That the drawing attached to this affidavit, representing two men talking through my instrument, is an exact copy of a drawing made from a sketch that I gave Nastori Corradi, an artist in the city, who made the original drawing, of which the one hereunto attached is a *fac-simile*. The drawing is the *fac-simile* of one I drew for Mr. Stetson, and of the one that I showed to Mr. Kremeschin

MEUCCI AFFIDAVIT. 21

and others who had made an agreement with me, and I always believed that the drawing accompanied my caveat to Washington. That, prior to December, 1871, I tried to keep my invention in secret, talked mostly to my wife through it, and a few friends. After I received my caveat, I have never made a secret of my invention; have told many people about it, and talked with numerous persons through it. After I received my caveat, some reporters came to see me. I told them about it, and a description of it was published in some paper in New York; I don't know which one I think the *Tribune*. I can say positively that more than twenty persons knew about my invention, and to whom I showed the instruments, and did talk through them with many. Besides these I have mentioned, I remember that I told H. Morang, an attorney in New York, who had formerly been an attorney for me, that I had this invention, and that I had a contract with the gentlemen I have named to assist me. Mr. Morang was present with three gentlemen, named in the agreement, and all of these understood my speaking telegraph.

I wish distinctly to say that I do not pretend, in this affidavit, to fix the exact year, except where some circumstance enables me to be definite as to time. I know the date of 1849, when I first conceived the idea of a speaking telegraph, is correct. I know that my statement about the publication is correct, as Mr. Bendalari went to Italy in 1860. I am certain that in the fall of 1875 I tried my experiments for the first time in extending the wires across the lot. This I fixed by the time that Matilda came to live with us. I heard of Bell's invention in 1876, and I know the year previous I talked with Mr. Egloff and several other persons. When I first went to Mr. Stetson with my specifications, I made no mention in the specifications of insulating persons who talked but simply using insulated wire. I never in my life made an effort to insulate a person talking through my sound telegraph.

The affiant, Antonio Meucci, further declares that the following description of a part of his invention in sound telegraphy was written by himself, unaided, in the year 1880, and contains a brief but correct description of twelve of his instruments, he made and constructed between the years 1849 and 1871. The description was

Two pages from Meucci's sworn affidavit. Notice his reference to the drawing made by the painter Corradi and his denial of any mention in his specifications of insulating anybody. (Courtesy, *National Archives and Records Service,* Washington, D.C.)

"'It may be found practicable to work with the person sending the message insulated, and with the person receiving it in free electrical communication with the ground. Or these conditions may possibly be reversed, and still operate with some success.'

"It is idle to contend that an inventor having such conceptions could at that time have been the inventor of the Bell Telephone.

"The application does, however, describe a mechanical telephone, consisting of a mouthpiece and earpiece connected by a wire.

"Without adverting to other evidence tending to indicate that Meucci was merely an experimentalist who had not produced anything new in the art of transmitting speech by electricity, it suffices to say that his pretensions are overthrown by his own description of the invention at a time when he deemed it in a condition to patent, and by the evidence of Mr. Stetson."

Judge Wallace seems to have relied on the conclusions reached by Prof. R. Cross of the Massachusetts Institute of Technology, Bell's good friend and the technical expert of the Bell Telephone Company. In an affidavit sworn by Prof. Cross on April 22, 1886, which was introduced before the Circuit Court of the United States for the Eastern District of Louisiana, Prof. Cross said in part:

"That caveat (Meucci's) plainly and well decribes what is known as a lover's telegraph or string telephone, transmitting sound mechanically in the well-known manner . . . the caveator appears . . . to have got hold of the foolish notion that by means of 'electrifying' the apparatus of the operators or both he could enhance that effect. Nowhere in the caveat is there any statement of the employment of magnets or electro-magnets, or coils of wire, or diaphragms, or any of those instrumentalities which go to make up an electric speaking telephone."

Mr. Langdon, in the above-mentioned article on *Myths of Telephone History,* also stresses that in his caveat:

"Meucci stated that his 'system consisted in isolating two persons by placing them on glass insulators, employing glass for example at the feet of the chair or bench on which each sits.' Probably he thought this would keep electricity in, prevent it from escaping. Nowadays of course everyone knows that the glass insulation would prevent there being any electric current at all. But Meucci's apparatus would work equally well with the insulation and

without. Certainly; because it worked by physical and not by electrical impulse."

The evidence in the Record leads us to disagree with Judge Wallace and to believe that Meucci's application *did not* contain "the best description of his invention which he was then able to give."

a) As we have seen, Mr. Stetson testified that he had been able to devote to the preparation of Meucci's caveat only two hours, including half an hour for his interview with Meucci. Bell, on the other hand, "had to devote considerable time to drafting the specifications and claims which ultimately resulted in his basic U. S. Patent No. 174,465, granted March 7, 1876, covering the telephone." (Quoted by F. L. Rhodes in his *Beginnings of Telephony,* New York, 1929, 26.)

b) Meucci's original description was much longer than the one prepared by Stetson for the application. According to Meucci's lawyer, the description he gave to Mr. Grant covered "ten or twenty pages of manuscript," but according to Mr. Durant, the vice-president of the Bell Telephone Company of Missouri, they were ten or a dozen pages . . . not very closely written; it was written in a pretty bold hand." (Mr. Durant must have had a wonderful memory to have been able to remember such a detail so well after fourteen years.) Mr. Durant reminds us of the fact that the caveat does not mention any battery, whereas Mr. Durant stated unequivocally that Meucci's description of his invention included a battery of several cells. No further comment on this very important point is necessary.

c) The fact that on January 12, 1872, or *fifteen days after the caveat was granted,* Meucci asked Mr. Stetson for an "estimate of the cost of preparing all necessary documents for the application to the U. S. for a letter Patent to Cover all the separate points claimed in the caveat specifications" shows clearly, as Mr. Stetson stated, that, "like many inventors, he (Meucci) did not take the trouble, or did not consider it policy to give those details in his caveat." If the caveat had been complete, there would have been no necessity to prepare any "necessary documents."

d) The caveat was prepared by Mr. Stetson who added or cut out what he considered necessary to add or to eliminate in the caveat. In his deposition Mr. Stetson testified that "it is never practicable to be absolutely certain that one understands another fully; in this case, I am quite sure that I did not fully understand the invention; what I did understand I put into such shape as I thought was proper for a caveat." As we have already seen, in his letter of September 28, 1885, to Mr. Goodwin, Mr. Stetson stated: "It was not my custom at that time, and has never been since, to bestow much care on the preparation of a caveat as on an application for a patent" and then added: "It would have been in accordance with my practice to have added some ideas of my own; I judge that the direction that much care should be taken to provide a quiet room for the listener had such origin; it seems to me quite probable that the direction that the wire should be larger than ordinary telegraph wire was also my addition."

e) One of the chief charges made against Bell by other contenders for the invention, as sworn in court, was that Bell's application of February 14, 1876, was not for a telephone, but for "certain impracticable devices to be used in harmonic multiple telegraphy" and that "the apparatus decribed in his application was worthless (*New York Times,* editorial, September 20, 1885). That charge, of course, was untenable, for Bell in his application clearly described the principle of the transmission of the human voice by electricity, just as Meucci did in his caveat.

To quote the dissenting opinion of Justice Bradley of the Supreme Court of the United States in the so-called Telephone Appeals on March 19, 1888, "Yet the proof amounts to demonstration, from the testimony of Mr. Bell himself and his assistant, Watson, that he never transmitted an intelligible word through an electrical instrument, nor produced any such instrument that would transmit an intelligible word, until after his patent had been issued." (126 U. S., 576.)

But, as Mr. Chief Justice White declared in the majority opinion in the same case, "the law does not require that a discoverer or inventor in order to get a patent for a process, must have succeeded in bringing his art to the highest degree of perfection. It is enough if he describes his method with sufficient clearness and precision to enable those skilled in the matter what the process is, and if he points out some practical way of putting it into operation. This Bell did. (U. S. 126,536.) Judge Wallace also subscribed to that legal principle, and refers to it in his decision on the Meucci case.

f) Meucci swore that he gave Mr. Stetson a drawing of two men talking to each other through a wire which had been made by the artist, Nestore Corradi, in 1857, but when a search for it was made in the Patent Office in Washington it could not be found. (*New York World,* October 2, 1885, page 5.) Corradi also swore that he had made the drawing, a copy of which Meucci had kept for himself. Mr. Stetson, however, did not remember anything about a drawing being attached to the caveat, one way or the other, just as he had not remembered anything about the battery. Bell's mention in his deposition of the fact that Gray's caveat of 1876 had drawings, on the other hand, leads us to assume that drawings were required of caveats as well as patents.

Meucci's drawing is important because it tells more than the caveat itself, and Judge Wallace, who took plenty of irrelevant testimony in consideration, such as Craig's deposition, or Prof. Cross's inconsistent conclusions, should have taken it into account.

g) At the time Judge Wallace rendered his decision (July 18, 1887) Meucci's caveat had expired by more than twelve years and, therefore, even if it had described an electrical telephone in every detail, it would have not affected the legality of Bell's patent, unless it could have been proved that Bell had stolen Meucci's invention.

In other words, Meucci's caveat was only a small part of the evidence, no matter how valuable because of its documentary character; but it was not all the evidence which Judge Wallace should have taken into consideration, as we shall presently see.

190

191

206 EVIDENCE FOR COMPLAINANTS.

two weeks or a month. And I had told Mr. Grant that I didn't see anything in the papers at all; that I thought the man was a crank, although when they came I treated them very politely, and told them I had been pressed for time and had not given the matter any attention. After they called several times, Mr. Grant suggested that I had better hand the papers to him, which I did, and was very glad to get rid of them.

Int. 15. Do you know where the papers are now?

Ans. I do not.

Int. 16. Did these two men ever explain to you anything about any experiment they had made, or what did they tell you on that subject?

Ans. At the time the papers were handed to me, this gentleman who spoke English described to me the contents of the papers, which related to some experiment they had had, and the gentleman who was with him listened very attentively to the explanation; and it seems to me that it was in relating this story that they referred to some apparatus which was stuck in the mouth. I remember distinctly when the gentleman described about the device being placed in the mouth, and the other man having it in the mouth, that some sensations were produced; and this gentleman who was with him seemed to confirm what he said by gestures, by pointing to his mouth particularly. Apparently, he understood everything that was said, although he didn't say a word himself.

Int. 17. Did they tell you where they had made any of these experiments? Did they mention the place?

Ans. I think it was in Cuba. My recollection is that this man was a dentist and an experiment was made with his assistant. It is so long ago that I have forgotton that part of it. That is my best recollection about it.

Int. 18. Did they bring you any instruments at any time?

Ans. No, sir; no instruments were brought.

Int. 19. Did they bring you any drawings at any time, or make any there?

Ans. No, sir; the papers contained no drawings of any kind; it was all manuscript.

DEPOSITION OF GEORGE F. DURANT. 207

Int. 20. Did they tell you that they had got, or had had an actual practically successful speaking telephone, or anything of that kind?

Ans. No, sir, they did not; they told me that these experiments had been made, and that certain sensations were produced, but they never mentioned a speaking telephone to us.

Int. 21. When you examined the papers and heard their description, did you find in their papers or their description anything which led you to believe that an electrical speaking telephone for the transmission of speech by electricity could be made out of them, or anything of that kind?

Ans. No, sir; my impression was that the man was a crank; the electrical part of the papers was nonsense to me; I could't make anything out of it.

Int. 22. You have been, then, an electrician for eight or ten years, I understand you?

Ans. Yes, sir.

Int. 23. Was an electrical speaking telephone a thing which your company would have liked to have had at that time?

Ans. Oh yes, sir; any improvement in our apparatus would be taken very readily by our people.

Int. 24. Tell me generally the nature of your business, in order that the Court may understand whether a speaking telephone would be adapted for your business and uses.

Ans. Yes, sir; we could apply it very readily; our business at that time was the introduction of the messenger box into the houses and offices of our customers, from which a series of signals could be sent to the central office, or district office, as we call it, and the number of signals which could be sent were very limited.

Int. 25. What were the signals for?

Ans. For messengers, policemen, fire apparatus and carriage. As we got along in the business we found a great many demands for special calls that couldn't be met by our boxes, and a great many different apparatuses were experimented with to increase the number of calls to the box and make the service more flexible; but it was very limited even then, and anything of that kind, a speaking telephone particularly, would have been taken very readily.

Two pages from the deposition of George F. Durant, Vice-President and General Manager of the Bell Telephone Company of Missouri. Notice on page 206 his reference to Meucci as a ctank and on page 207 his denial that a speaking telephone was ever mentioned, notwithstanding the fact the Meucci's caveat was already on file with the U. S. Patent Office. (From the Record in the U. S. Supreme Court, Washington, D. C.)

ACOUSTIC VERSUS ELECTRIC TELEPHONE

Judge Wallace, Prof. Cross and Mr. Langdon insist that Meucci invented a string telephone, sometimes called acoustic or mechanical telephone. According to Bell, "in the lover's telephone or telegraph the two membranes are mechanically connected together by means of a stretched string. The function of one membrane is to pull the other, through the intermediary of the string." (Bell's deposition, p. 213.) Just before he made that statement Bell had declared: "I am not conscious of having ever seen a lover's telegraph or telephone with metal diaphragms." Since the words "acoustic" or "mechanical" may confuse the reader, let us explain that an acoustic telephone is nothing more nor less than one of those telephones children the world over have been making for centuries past by attaching a wire or string to a membrane in a little box of cardboard used as transmitter or receiver.

To contend that Meucci and an outstanding patent attorney with Stetson's experience could not tell a string telephone from an electric telephone is simply too preposterous.

As Stetson declared, "the caveat itself is proof positive that Mr. Meucci had at that time the idea of communicating spoken words by the aid of electricity." Others who have studied the caveat have reached the same conclusion. Only a few years ago, an English scientist, Mr. William Aitken, stated in his book *Who Invented the Telephone,* (London and Glasgow, 1939): "the caveat, however, clearly proves that they (Meucci's) instruments were electrical. Meucci was unfortunate in his poverty and business relationships, but the mere fact that he submitted his invention to an official of a telegraph company is fairly conclusive that he had produced an apparatus that would transmit speech electrically, in the way claimed in his caveat."

Judge Wallace and Mr. Langdon, in support of their conclusion that Meucci knew nothing about electricity have stressed the paragraph in the caveat in which Meucci states that his "system consists of isolating two persons by placing them on glass insulators."

Meucci's affidavit is clear on this point. He swore: "When I first went to Mr. Stetson with my specifications, I made no mention in the specifications of insulating persons who talked by simply using insulated wire. I never in my life made an effort to insulate a person through my sound telegraph." That the paragraph about insulation may have been included by Mr. Stetson without Meucci's knowledge (we have noted how it was his practice to add ideas of his own) we infer from the fact that after he sent Meucci the first draft of the application, he inserted the paragraph about insulating only one person. Apropos of the word insulating, we wonder if Meucci knew the difference (in English, of course) between insulating and insulated. We have alredy seen how in his letter to Stetson dated January

19, 1872, he wrote "interesting parties" when obviously he meant "interested parties."

Anyway, the insulation of the persons has only a secondary importance. The words "practicable" and "these conditions may possibly be reversed" which Meucci uses in his caveat show that he intended to experiment further on that point.

What counts in the telephone is not the insulation or absence of insulation, but the use of electricity and the right construction of the instrument for the electrical transmission of speech. That Meucci used electricity is clear from the caveat; that his instruments (he made more than one) were practical electrical telephones we learn most conclusively from the other evidence Judge Wallace completely ignored, although Prof. Cross carefully studied it.

MEUCCI'S FUNDAMENTAL INVENTION

Meucci's claim as inventor of the telephone rests not so much on his caveat of 1871 as on the various telephones he had made previous to that year and which he had used for communication in his home. All of them, as we know, had been sold by his wife for $6.00 as junk while he was in bed recovering from the injuries sustained in the ferryboat explosion. Fortunately for him, starting with 1860 he had been noting down in a memorandum-book "the ideas that came to me concerning the telephone, and other memoranda. " Thus, when he was asked to produce the instruments that he had invented and constructed, he had no difficulty in making new models.

Of course, Meucci's memorandum-book, a printed copy of which can be found in the New York Public Library, came for a very close scrutiny by the counsels for the Bell Company, but no matter how hard they tried to find something that would question its authenticity, they were bound to admit that it was genuine. Mr. Storrow, the able counsel for the Bell Company, actually proved that Meucci's copy-book used to belong to the firm of Rider and Clark, which had gone out of existence in 1867, but then Mr. Rider had to admit that he had advised Meucci to note down his ideas as they came to him. Meucci did that at first in a pocket notebook, beginning with 1860, but later copied the first notes in the larger book. At any rate, the fact that Meucci got the book before Rider severed his connection with him in 1867 proves that Meucci could not have "invented" the memorandum-book to support his claims after Bell came out with his patent.

One entry alone, under the date of August 17, 1870, may be sufficient to show that at least five years before Bell, Meucci had a clear conception of the real problem involved. His note reads: "Fabric of cotton, flax, silk, saturated with starch very thick, and the starch dissolved in a solution of nitrate of silver and then paraffine has given a good diaphragm, only to use this quality of membrane it is necessary to put in the centre a small disk of iron or platinum metallic iron, in order that it can have on the centre of the bobbin and communicate the electricity in its vibration with the sound of the word." Any scientist will be satisfied by that description of the value of the diaphragm in Meucci's invention, that his telephone was electric and that he did not intend to use electricity, as Prof. Cross stated, only "to increase an effect already attained by the well-known sound-conducting effect of a wire."

Prof. Cross, however, was so ready to deny everything that might be construed as favorable to Meucci that he denied that too. In another instance he was pinned down by Meucci's counsel to say whether some of the instruments made by Meucci could transmit speech electrically if equipped with an iron diaphragm. He quickly denied that, but then, when pressed he had to admit that some of Meucci's telephones were electrical telephones. (See facsimiles.)

Finally, not being able to deny the evidence, he concluded in the affidavit mentioned above: "I have read Mr. Meucci's deposition. I am unable to find in it an adequate description of the operation of those instruments, or any evidence that even at the time of giving the deposition he had such knowledge of the essentials of all the different parts indicated and their operation upon each other, and the operation of the instruments as a whole, must have preceded the construction of the first of those having cores, coils and operating diaphragms by a man who had invented them out of his own knowledge and had not simply copied them from information obtained from' others."

In other words, Meucci was a dishonest man who had stolen his ideas from Bell.

Of course, we know that Meucci was a most honest man, as we shall presently demonstrate. But granting for a fleeting second that he had opened one of Bell's instruments and examined it carefully, he would have copied only one type of transmitter or receiver. Instead, he produced twelve different instruments in court, including a double-pole telephone. Evidently, Prof. Cross was not well acquainted with the elements of logic.

But even if that were not sufficient, Meucci must have been some kind of a wizard, for a man close to 78 years of age, if he could reply without a moment's hesitation and with full competence to the questions fired at him by his cross-examiners, as well as counsel, and draw with such accuracy, right on the spot, the various instruments he had made, without being tripped once. His deposition and the obvious sincerity of his answers leave no doubt as to the originality of his invention, as well as to his knowledge of scientific subjects in general and electricity in particular.

SCIENTIST VERSUS INVENTOR

Mr. Langdon, in the above-mentioned article of his informs us that "Meucci thought he was using electricity. But with all respect be it said, he was mistaken—nor is it surprising that he should be. He was not a trained scientist; his various inventions were not the result of systematic scientific research, as were the inventions of Edison, Elisha Gray or of Bell."

Had Mr. Langdon been acquainted with all the experiments with electrical instruments that Meucci had made over a period of years, he would have not treated him as a boy who could not tell a string telephone from a scientific instrument. That argument may be permissible in a court room, even by a man with an ax to grind like Prof. Cross, but certainly not by a historian.

To quote Sir Oliver Lodge, "the articulating telephone is an instrument of absurd simplicity. It was invented by one who was no professed electrician, who was not really learned in physical science, but was interested primarily in introducing precision and clear intelligibility into human speech." (*Journal of the British Institution of Electrical Engineers,* Vol. 64, 1098-1114.)

Thomas A. Watson in his pamphlet on *The Birth and Babyhood of the Telephone* quotes his electrical mentor, Moses G. Farmer, "perhaps the leading practical electrician of that day," to the effect that "if Bell had known anything about electricity he would never have invented the telephone."

Writing to his parents from Washington in February, 1875, Bell himself declared that "I felt that I had not the electrical knowledge necessary to overcome the difficulties." In his deposition of 1892, while under cross-examination by the counsel for the Government, Bell clearly stated that he had never pursued any course of study concerning electricity at any of the schools attended by him and could not remember any book on electricity he had ever studied until more recent years. His own friend, Prof. Cross, stated that when Bell attended his (Prof. Cross's) Lowell lectures in 1873-1874, "he gave more attention, so far as time was concerned, to acoustic apparatus than to electrical apparatus."

Edison, a trained scientist, spent over $100,000 and months of experimentation before he could find the right kind of fibre for his incandescent lamp; yet, a poor Piedmontese with no laboratory to speak of, and an amateur compared with Edison, Alessandro Cruto, produced a platinum filament after tinkering for only a few weeks. His small lamp factory remained in operation for more than thirty years, until World War I, when it closed down for financial reasons.

Arturo Malignani, to recall another inventor, could not be compared with Edison, either, by any means; yet he, without money, succeeded in doing what Edison was not able to do with his great laboratories and an army of research assistants. Malignani invented a method for getting the vacuum in incandescent lamps that "revolutionized the art of lamp exhaustion." His patent was assigned in 1895 to the General Electric Company, which has been using his method ever since. (Howell and Schroeder, *History of the Incandescent Lamp; Vigo Review,* April, 1938.)

MEUCCI'S INTEGRITY

Judge Wallace concludes his decision with the implication or insinuation that Meucci was a confidence man. He says:

"The evidence leaves the impression that his speaking telegraph would never have been offered to the public as an invention if he had not been led by his necessities to trade on the credulity of his friends; that he intended to induce three persons of small means and little business experience, who became his associates under the agreement of December 12, 1871, to invest in an invention which he would not offer to men like Ryder and Craig; and that this was done in the hope of obtaining such loans and assistance from them as he would temporarily require."

A thorough study of the record has convinced us that with the exception of slight errors due to the lapse of so many years, Mr. Storrow, the Bell counsel, was not able to find Meucci guilty of a single misrepresentation. He even checked the passenger lists of the ships that left for Europe in 1860, to verify whether Bendelari had actually gone to Italy as Meucci had sworn. Meucci's memorandum-book was the object of a thorough investigation, with the result that its authenticity was proved. The files of *L'Eco d'Italia* were searched, Mr. Storrow combing the country for missing issues, some of which he found in New Orleans. Mr. Storrow and his colleague, Mr. Dickerson, cross-examined Meucci as thoroughly as they knew how, obtaining in every instance replies that were both prompt and to the point.

Meucci, let us proclaim it to the world, was a very honest man; too honest for his own good. Had he not been honest he would have not ended on relief. Even Mr. Rider, who testified against him, promptly admitted in court that Meucci was "the last man in the world that would take anything that didn't belong to him, if he knew it."

Over and above all legal considerations, the respect that he enjoyed over a period of forty years in such gossipy, cynical, and hypercritical community as the New York Italian colony, should be enough to prove his perfect integrity. Garibaldi, as we know, had the greatest respect for him, tried to secure the interest of the Italian Government in his invention as late as 1881 (he died in 1882), and up to the last letter he sent him addressed him as "dear boss," in remembrance of the days he had spent at Staten Island making candles in Meucci's factory.

During the last few years of his life the Italian Government, probably the most ungrateful and neglectful government in the world, so far as its citizens are concerned, granted him a small pension; the Italian Freemasonry, of which Meucci was a member, also helped him with a small monthly allowance.

When he died, the Italian Government (Crispi, the immortal Crispi, was prime minister at that time) ordered that Meucci's funeral be held at its expense, the only instance, so far as we know, in the history of the Italians in America in which a similar honor has been bestowed on anybody. All of New York's newspapers devoted long obituaries to his passing.

As stated in the *New York Herald* for October 19, 1889, Meucci "died in the full belief of the priority of his claim as inventor of the telephone, which, during the intervals of his sickness, he declared must be recognized sooner or later."

DID SOMEONE STEAL MEUCCI'S INVENTION?

In the circular distributed by the Globe Telephone Company in 1885 a comparison was made between the telephone invented by Meucci and the other bearing Bell's name, leading to the conclusion that "it is one of the most remarkable instances on record that inventions of so important a character and so entirely similar could have been made by two persons who never had met or held communication with each other. . . . As we have before suggested, the coincidence is one of the most remarkable on record. It is not reasonable to at least infer, that by some means the ideas of Antonio Meucci may have been *Telephoned* to others and *their* ideas been moulded into form that he set out, and he thereby been deprived of the rights justly due him?"

The charge is a serious one, however possible; but there is no way to prove it. All one can offer is circumstantial evidence.

1) As we have seen, soon after he obtained his caveat, Meucci handed the description of his invention to Mr. Grant at the American District Telegraph Company. According to Meucci, he never got his papers back.

2) The American District Telegraph Company of New York was closely connected with the Western Union, a company which, if we are to believe the *New York Times* (editorial, January 14, 1881, page 4), was not very scrupulous in those days.

3) In 1875 Mr. Orton, the president of the Western Union, was on friendly terms with Bell and his future father-in-law, Mr. Hubbard, both of whom he met in Washington in March of that year, as we learn from Bell's deposition.

4) The Western Union later became interested in telephony through its subsidiaries, the Gold and Stock Telegraph Company and the American Speaking Telephone Company, which controlled various telephone patents, including those of Dolbear and Gray.

5) The Western Union in 1879 reached an agreement with the Bell Telephone Company, as a result of which it retired from the telephone business, turning to the Bell Company all the 56,000 telephones it had installed in 55 cities. In return the Bell Company agreed to pay to the Western Union for a term of 17 years 20 per cent of all rentals and royalties for licenses and leases of telephone patents and equipment in the United States, amounting to $1,164,563.

6) On the same day that Bell applied for his patent, on February 14, 1876, an American inventor, Elisha Gray, applied for a caveat for a telephone invention of his own two hours after Bell had left the same Patent Office. Incredible as it may seem, three weeks after he filed his application Bell received his patent.

7) Gray later charged that "Mr. Bell's attorneys had an underground railroad in operation between their office and Examiner Wilbur's room in the Patent Office, by which they were enabled to have unlawful and guilty knowledge of Gray's papers as soon as they were filed in the Patent Office." The Supreme Court, however, rejected the charge as the evidence presented by Gray was not *sufficient* "to brand Bell and his attorneys and the officers of the Patent Office with that infamy which the charges made against them imply." (126 U. S.)

8) Bell testified in court that while he was experimenting with his apparatus, he was afraid that Gray spied on him and removed it from Williams' shop to private rooms on Exeter Place, in Boston. In 1877, however, Gray, who seems to have been more candid than Bell, in a telegram to Bell said: "There is no evidence that either knew that the other was working in this direction."

9) As already stated, the drawings which Meucci said he gave to Stetson in order to be attached to his application for a caveat had disappeared when a search for them was made in the Patent Office before 1885.

10) In 1875 Bell's Washington attorneys, Pollock and Bailey, made a search in the U. S. Patent Office in connection with Bell's application for his multiple telegraph patent. Bell testified that in February, or March, 1875, he met Mr. Wilbur, the Patent Officer Examiner. Most certainly Bell's attorneys must have found then Meucci's caveat which had expired only two months before, in December, 1874. Less than three months later, on June 2, 1875, Bell is said to have made his famous discovery.

11) The U. S. Government in 1885 brought suit against the Bell Telephone Company for fraud. The case, however, never came to trial, partly because of the death of the counsel in charge for the Government, but also because the Bell patents had expired by lapse of time. Political and financial pressure, one presumes, may have had something to do with the Government's abandonment of the case. In all, the Bell Company was involved in some 600 lawsuits, most of which were settled out of court.

12) On February 1, 1887, the *New York Times* printed a story which had appeared the day before in the *Chicago Evening Journal*, according to which, one Mr. E. B. Welch, president of the Mexican Telephone Company of Boston, had made an offer to Meucci, in 1883, for the assignment of his invention rights for a sum of more than $180,000. But nothing came out of it. A day later, that is, on February 2, 1887, the *New York Times* published a brief account from Boston of an interview with Mr. Welch, in which he denied that he had been at any time an official of the Bell Telephone Company, but admitted that he had opened negotiations with Meucci in 1883, but at his own personal instance. According to the sworn affidavit of Meucci's attorney, Mr. Lemmi, Welch had told him in 1883 that years before he (Welch) had asked Mr. Grant what had become of Meucci's papers but was told that he had given them back.

Welch's denial of his connection with the Bell Company for a while fooled us, for we had taken it at face value. Fortunately, in the 25th street branch of the New York Public Library we found the Boston Directory for 1883 in which E. B. Welch and the Mexican National Bell Telephone Company are listed both at exactly the same office address, 95 Milk Street, Room 67. The American Bell

Telephone Company is listed at the same street address, 95 Milk, but in Room 62.

That Mr. Welch was well acquainted with other officers of the Bell Company appears from Mr. Durant's admission that he knew him. Durant, as we have seen, was the gentleman in the American District Telegraph Company to whom Mr. Grant turned Meucci's papers.

What really happened nobody knows. Certainly nobody can prove whether Bell or Gray learned of Meucci's invention through a routine search in the Washington Patent Office, and supplemented it with more ample and more direct information through Mr. Grant's office. Certainly nobody has been able to explain why and how Bell and Gray happened to file their applications for a similar invention ("the description is substantially the same as yours"—Gray to Bell, Chicago, Feb. 21, 1877) on the same day, with a difference of only "an hour or two" between them.

Probably Elisha Gray was right when he wrote on a scrap of paper which was found among his effects after his death: "The history of the telephone will never be fully written: it is partly hidden away in 20 or 30 thousand pages of testimony and partly lying on the hearts and consciences of a few whose lips are sealed—some in death, and others by a golden clasp whose grip is ever tighter." (Quoted by Langdon in the article cited.)

52 COMPLAINANTS' EXHIBIT

possession of the proper parties to demonstrate the truthfulness of the foregoing statements.

By way of illustrating the similarity of the claims, we call attention to two cuts of models of Antonio Meucci's invention, one certified to as of 1857, and the other of 1867, and also a cut of the Bell telephone It will be seen that a diaphragm and a magnet are properly placed in a case with wires running from the same for attachment to the transmitting wires Upon reference to the Bell telephone, while differing somewhat in shape and proportions, it will be found that the essentials of the Meucci device are the same.

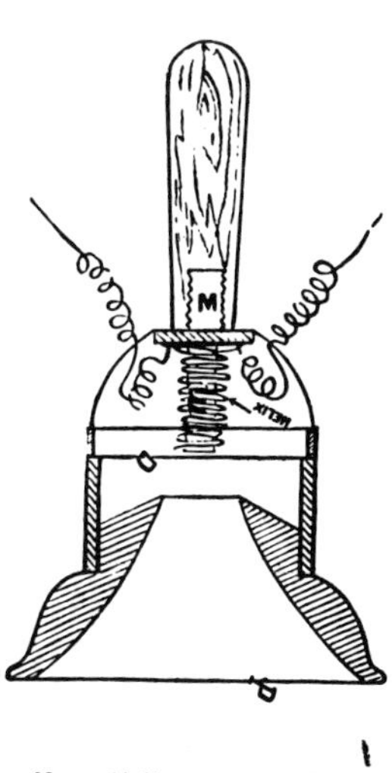

Meucci's Telephone. — 1857

M — Magnet

D — Diaphragm

P — Mouth or Ear Piece.

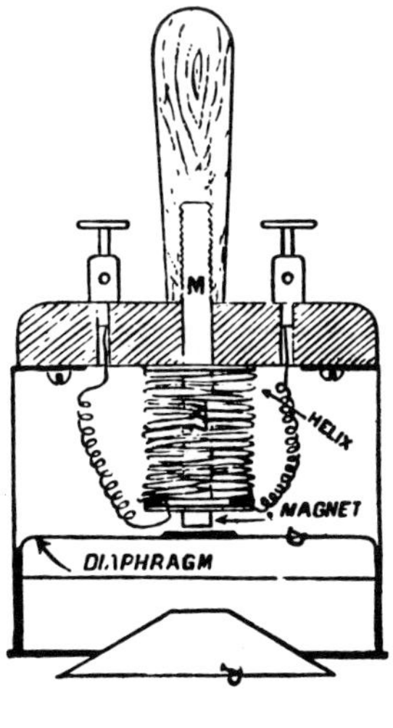

Meucci's Telephone. — 1867.

M — Magnet.

D — Diaphragm.

P — Mouth or Ear Piece.

CIRCULAR GLOBE TELEPHONE CO 53

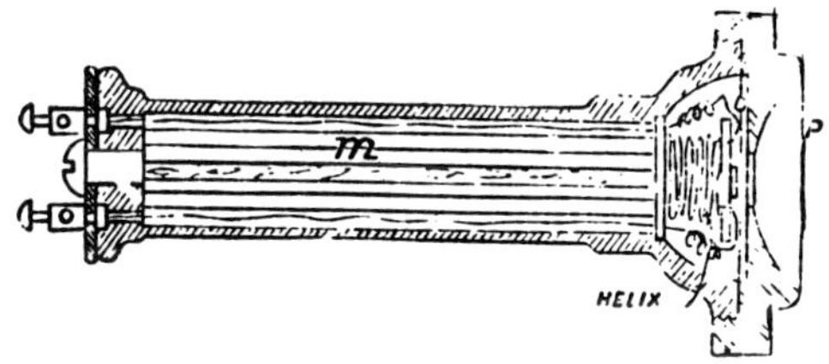

Bell Telephone.

M — Magnet.

D — Diaphragm.

P — Mouthpiece.

Let any one read the claims of Antonio Meucci of 1871, compare the description of the instrument where he speaks of its shape and application to the mouth and ear, and his description generally, as to how it is to be used, with those of the Bell claims (remembering that Meucci's description was written five years prior to the application of Bell), and with it consider Meucci's inability to speak the language of the country, his destitute condition, his persistent and earnest efforts, with all these difficulties before him, in his endeavor to bring his invention before the world; and having done so, it is respectfully submitted that it is one of the most remarkable instances on record that inventions of so important a character and so entirely similar could have been made by two persons who never had met or held communication with each other.

Other parties have laid claim to priority of invention of the telephone, and have presented evidence in substantiation of their claims, but they have failed in the one important particular: they did not, as was done by Meucci, file their claims in the Patent Office years before those of Bell; and in none of the claims they presented did they set them forth in the clear and distinct language to be found in the caveat of Antonio Meucci.

As we have before suggested, the coincidence is one of the most remarkable on record. Is it not reasonable to at least infer, that by some means the ideas of Antonio Meucci may have been *Telephoned* to others and *their* ideas been moulded into form that he set out, and he thereby been deprived of the rights justly due him?

Two pages from the circular issued by the Globe Telephone Company. (From the Record in the U. S. Supreme Court, Washington D. C.)

CHAPTER TWENTY

PROFESSIONAL MEN AND PUBLIC OFFICIALS

America, generally speaking, never was the land of opportunity for the Italian professional man. Language difficulty was, of course, the chief barrier; but then there were mental habits, cultural traditions, environmental backgrounds which an educated man could not very well discard. Marriage into an American family, especially of the upper class, made things much easier, but how many could do that?

Even after 1880, when the mass immigration began, the only professional men born in Italy who could look forward to a future in America were the physicians who settled and practised almost exclusively in Italian-speaking communities. In recent years Italian scientists, primarily physicists and chemists, have found responsible positions in American universities, but their work has been almost exclusively in laboratories, where ability to speak English well is not a prerequisite. The other exceptions, as we have seen, are the artists and the musicians who speak an international language. There are, of course, the children of the immigrants; but that is another story, as related below.

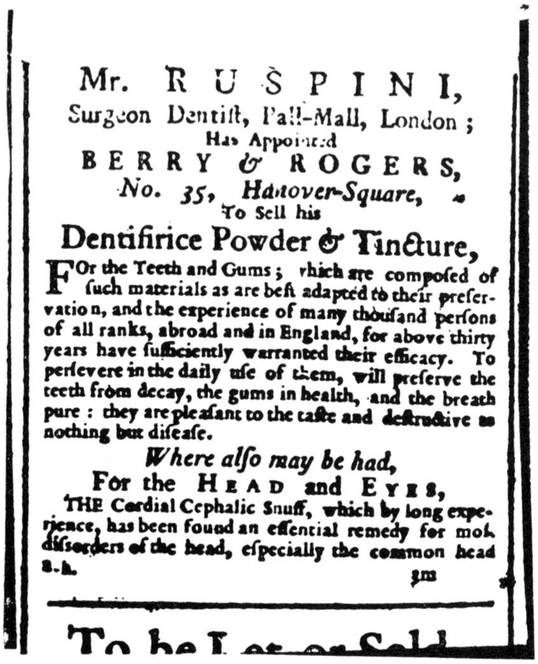
Mr. RUSPINI,
Surgeon Dentiſt, Pall-Mall, London;
Has Appointed
BERRY & ROGERS,
No. 35, Hanover-Square,
To Sell his
Dentifirice Powder & Tincture,
FOr the Teeth and Gums; which are compoſed of ſuch materials as are beſt adapted to their preſervation, and the experience of many thouſand perſons of all ranks, abroad and in England, for above thirty years have ſufficiently warranted their efficacy. To perſevere in the daily uſe of them, will preſerve the teeth from decay, the gums in health, and the breath pure: they are pleaſant to the taſte and deſtructive to nothing but diſeaſe.
Where alſo may be had,
For the HEAD and EYES,
THE Cordial Cephalic Snuff, which by long experience, has been found an eſſential remedy for moſt diſorders of the head, eſpecially the common head a-h.

One of the advertisements inserted by Dr. Ruspini in New York newspapers. (From the *New York Daily Advertiser,* May 27, 1786.)

DR. BERTOLDI

Aside from those who came on temporary visits, or were going through the United States on their way to Central and South America, like Scandella in 1798 and Valli in 1816 (Mazzei did not come to practice medicine or surgery), the first Italian physician to arrive after the Revolution was in all probability Dr. Francis Bertody, or Bertoldi, who married Ursula Plimpton of Wrentham, Mass., on January 16, 1785. He is said to have graduated from the University of Padua and to have served for a time as personal physician to the French Dauphin. On June 19, 1788, he became an American citizen, the act of naturalization stating that he was from the Kingdom of "Persia," a word which some people meant to have been "Prussia," but which could have been just as easily Austria, which in those days ruled over parts of Italy. Having not examined the original documents we refrain from any speculation. At any rate, a son of his was still living in Boston in 1859. (*Mass. Hist. Soc. Proc.* IV, 362; *Vital Records of Wrentham, Mass., to the year* 1850, Boston, 1910.)

A DENTIST OF 1786

On May 26, 1786, a dentist named Ruspini landed in New York, but we do not know whether he settled in America or returned to London, where his father, Chevalier Bartholomew Ruspini, practised dentistry and was well known as the author of a *Treatise On The Teeth* which ran into at least eight editions. (*New York Directory* for 1786, pp. 141 and 187.)

In the New York directory for 1791 we find one Dr. George Alberti with offices at 59 Mulberry Street, possibly the same Dr. George F. Alberti who was connected with the Bank of the United States in Philadelphia, where he died on June 12, 1837, at the age of 72. We have no information as to his origins.

We know more about Dr. De Angelis, a "practitioner of medicine in the Hospitals of Naples and a member of the faculty of New York," who came over in 1798 and died in New York on April 26, 1841, at the age of 83. He left three sons, Gideon, Joseph, and Lorenzo, and a daughter who married one Frederick W. Hadley. In 1825 he advertised the sale of his "celebrated bilious pills" and "other useful medicines" in the *New York Daily Advertiser* for July 1.

Dr. Giuseppe Gherardi, the brother of Prof. Donato Gherardi and the uncle of the future American admiral by that name, was in New York in 1823, as we learn from Da Ponte, but apparently he did not remain long.

DOCTORS MAURAN AND DA PONTE

The first sons of Italian immigrants to graduate as physicians from an American college were in all probability Dr. Joseph Mauran and Dr. Charles Grahl Da Ponte.

Dr. Mauran was born in Providence, the youngest of the ten children of Joseph Carlo Mauran, a native of Italy, and Olive Bicknell Mauran. He graduated from Brown College in 1816 and from the New York College of Physicians and Surgeons in 1819. He died on June 8, 1873, after serving for two terms as president of the Rhode Island Medical Society and as a trustee of the New York College of Physicians and Surgeons. He was one of the founders of Rhode Island Hospital and a prominent man in the development of the Providence Bureau of Health. (*National Cyclopaedia of American Biography*, X, 275; Stockbridge, J. C., *Memorials of the Mauran Family*, 1893, p.116.)

Dr. Da Ponte, the son of the poet Lorenzo, practised medicine in New York in 1828. In 1831 he was in New Orleans, and later at Easton, Pa. (Da Ponte's *Memoirs*, Abbot tr., 430, note 1.)

DR. JOSEPH CARLI
The son of an Italian merchant in Frankfort-on-the-Main, Germany, he was one of the founders of the city of Stillwater, Minn., a member of its first city council, chairman of its first board of health, county physician and business man. (Courtesy, *Minnesota State Med. Assoc.*, Minneapolis.)

OTHER PIONEERS

Other pioneers were: one Dr. Braretta, who owned a tavern in Baltimore in 1839, but whether he was an Italian or of Italian descent we cannot say (Kimel, S. *The Mad Booths of Maryland*, New York, 1940, 58); Dr. Francesco Antommarchi, Napoleon's physician at St. Helena, who was a resident of New Orleans in 1834, when he presented to the city one of the five original bronze casts of Napoleon's death mask and a bust of the Emperor long preserved in City Hall (*Cuba Contemporanea*, Vols. 3 and 4; Cipriani, *Avventure*, I, 79); Dr. A. Natili, who is said to have been a professor of medicine at the University of Pisa and lived in New Orleans, where we find him in 1850, and later in New York, where he died in 1864 (*Eco d'Italia*, Feb. 6, 1864, Aug. 13, 1881, April 22, 1883); Doctors Albuzzi, Bartolotti, Biamonti, Bianchi and Valletti, whose names we find in the New Orleans city directories between 1838 and 1843; Doctors Bassa, Lumachi, Petri and Vitali, listed in the 1848 St. Louis city directory; Dr. Magnani, who landed in San Francisco with Leonetto Cipriani in 1851; Dr. Louis Cavalli, who conducted a private museum of natural sciences in Detroit as early as 1846, and whom we find listed as an importer of French wines and liquors in the local directory for 1852; Dr. Christopher Carli, already noted on pages 166 and 167, a native of Germany of Italian parentage, who practised in Chicago from 1837 and 1841 and in Wisconsin and Minnesota from 1841 to the time of his death in 1887 (*Minnesota Medicine*, July-Sept. 1938, pp. 502-571, 655).

In 1815 "Dr." John Marchisi, a Piedmontese, settled in Utica, where he was one of the first men to operate a pharmacy, but he had no medical degree. He died in Utica in 1885 at the age of 95. It is interesting to note that in the Utica directory for 1817 he is listed as John M'Kisse. (Schiro, G., *Americans by Choice*, Utica, 1940, 26-83.)

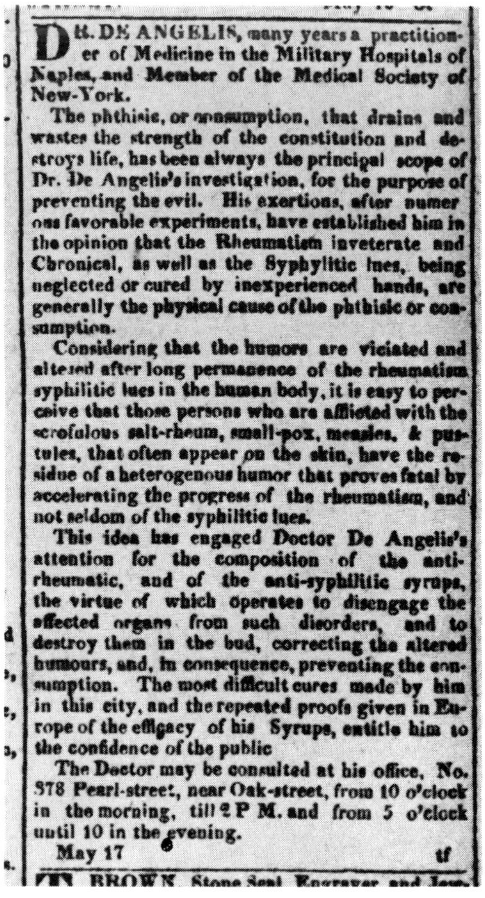

DR. DE ANGELIS, many years a practitioner of Medicine in the Military Hospitals of Naples, and Member of the Medical Society of New-York.

The phthisic, or consumption, that drains and wastes the strength of the constitution and destroys life, has been always the principal scope of Dr. De Angelis's investigation, for the purpose of preventing the evil. His exertions, after numerous favorable experiments, have established him in the opinion that the Rheumatism inveterate and Chronical, as well as the Syphylitic lues, being neglected or cured by inexperienced hands, are generally the physical cause of the phthisic or consumption.

Considering that the humors are viciated and altered after long permanence of the rheumatism syphilitic lues in the human body, it is easy to perceive that those persons who are afflicted with the scrofulous salt-rheum, small-pox, measles, & pustules, that often appear on the skin, have the residue of a heterogenous humor that proves fatal by accelerating the progress of the rheumatism, and not seldom of the syphilitic lues.

This idea has engaged Doctor De Angelis's attention for the composition of the anti-rheumatic, and of the anti-syphilitic syrups, the virtue of which operates to disengage the affected organs from such disorders, and to destroy them in the bud, correcting the altered humours, and, in consequence, preventing the consumption. The most difficult cures made by him in this city, and the repeated proofs given in Europe of the efficacy of his Syrups, entitle him to the confidence of the public

The Doctor may be consulted at his office, No. 378 Pearl-street, near Oak-street, from 10 o'clock in the morning, till 2 P M. and from 5 o'clock until 10 in the evening.

May 17 tf

An announcement by Dr. De Angelis in the New York *Evening Post* for May 18, 1816. (Courtesy, *New York Historical Society*.)

AFTER 1850

The political upheavals of 1848-1860 caused a large number of professional men to leave Italy. Some of them, as we have seen, came to the United States.

At any rate, in *Wilson's Business Directory* for the

city of New York we find as early as 1857 at least half a dozen Italian-American physicians practising in Manhattan, including Dr. Salvatore Caro, Dr. G. Ceccarini, Dr. C. Fio, Dr. Miliano (Milano), Dr. Nicholas Sposato, and others.

Dr. Caro, a native of Canicatti, Sicily, came to America in 1853, and settled in Elizabeth, N. J., where he operated a drug store. Later he moved to New York, and spent the rest of his life there until he died in 1881. (*Eco d'Italia*, May 1, 1881.)

Dr. Giovanni Ceccarini, the first chairman of the Sanitary Committee of the Department of Health of the City of New York in 1870, and a noted surgeon, came over in the 50's. (*Italian-American History* Vol. I, 511-512.)

After 1860 we find quite a number of physicians and druggists with Italian names listed in the various city directories, but none of them, so far as we know, achieved specials distinction, with the exception of Dr. Formento and Dr. Verdi. Occasionally we find a dentist.

DR. FELIX FORMENTO.

DR. FORMENTO

Dr. Felix Formento was born in New Orleans in 1837, but in 1851 he went with his parents to their native Piedmont, where he studied at the University of Turin. After he received his medical degree at the age of 20, he went to Paris for post graduate work, returning to Italy in 1859 to serve as a surgeon in the Piedmontese Army during the

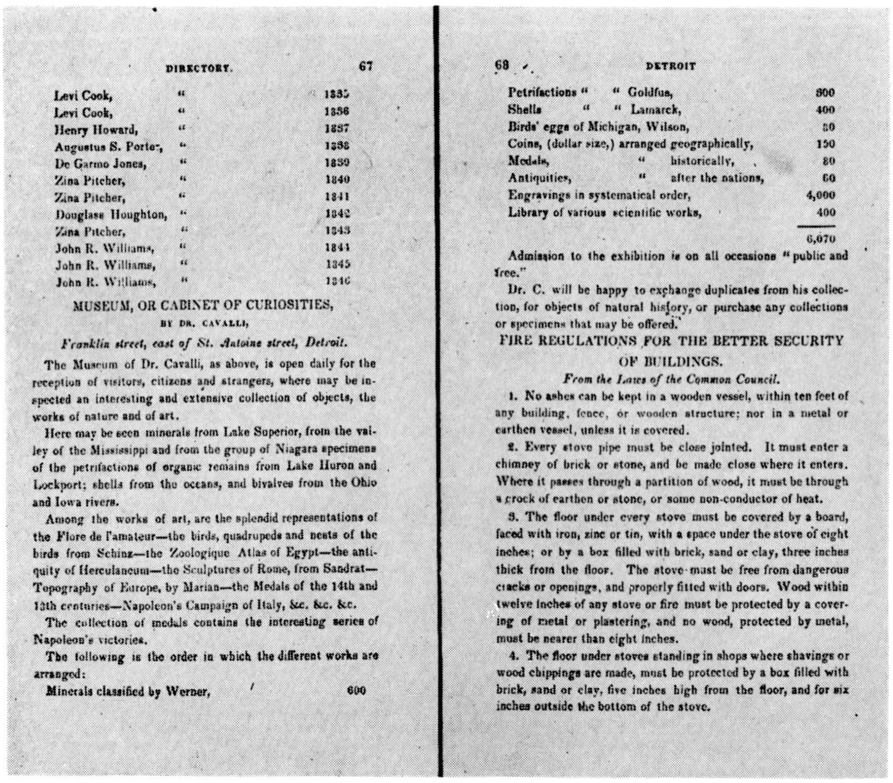

DIRECTORY. 67

Levi Cook,	"	1835
Levi Cook,	"	1836
Henry Howard,	"	1837
Augustus S. Porter,	"	1838
De Garmo Jones,	"	1839
Zina Pitcher,	"	1840
Zina Pitcher,	"	1841
Douglass Houghton,	"	1842
Zina Pitcher,	"	1843
John R. Williams,	"	1844
John R. Williams,	"	1845
John R. Williams,	"	1846

MUSEUM, OR CABINET OF CURIOSITIES,

BY DR. CAVALLI,

Franklin street, east of St. Antoine street, Detroit.

The Museum of Dr. Cavalli, as above, is open daily for the reception of visitors, citizens and strangers, where may be inspected an interesting and extensive collection of objects, the works of nature and of art.

Here may be seen minerals from Lake Superior, from the valley of the Mississippi and from the group of Niagara specimens of the petrifactions of organic remains from Lake Huron and Lockport; shells from the oceans, and bivalves from the Ohio and Iowa rivers.

Among the works of art, are the splendid representations of the Flore de l'amateur—the birds, quadrupeds and nests of the birds from Schinz—the Zoologique Atlas of Egypt—the antiquity of Herculaneum—the Sculptures of Rome, from Sandrat—Topography of Europe, by Marian—the Medals of the 14th and 13th centuries—Napoleon's Campaign of Italy, &c. &c. &c.

The collection of medals contains the interesting series of Napoleon's victories.

The following is the order in which the different works are arranged:

Minerals classified by Werner,	600

68 DETROIT

Petrifactions " " Goldfus,	800
Shells " " Lamarck,	400
Birds' eggs of Michigan, Wilson,	80
Coins, (dollar size,) arranged geographically,	150
Medals, " historically,	80
Antiquities, " after the nations,	60
Engravings in systematical order,	4,000
Library of various scientific works,	400
	6,070

Admission to the exhibition is on all occasions "public and free."

Dr. C. will be happy to exchange duplicates from his collection, for objects of natural history, or purchase any collections or specimens that may be offered.

FIRE REGULATIONS FOR THE BETTER SECURITY OF BUILDINGS.

From the Laws of the Common Council.

1. No ashes can be kept in a wooden vessel, within ten feet of any building, fence, or wooden structure; nor in a metal or earthen vessel, unless it is covered.

2. Every stove pipe must be close jointed. It must enter a chimney of brick or stone, and be made close where it enters. Where it passes through a partition of wood, it must be through a crock of earthen or stone, or some non-conductor of heat.

3. The floor under every stove must be covered by a board, faced with iron, zinc or tin, with a space under the stove of eight inches; or by a box filled with brick, sand or clay, three inches thick from the floor. The stove must be free from dangerous cracks or openings, and properly fitted with doors. Wood within twelve inches of any stove or fire must be protected by a covering of metal or plastering, and no wood, protected by metal, must be nearer than eight inches.

4. The floor under stoves standing in shops where shavings or wood chippings are made, must be protected by a box filled with brick, sand or clay, five inches high from the floor, and for six inches outside the bottom of the stove.

Two pages from the Directory of the City of Detroit for 1846 with a description of Dr. Cavalli's Museum. (Courtesy, *Detroit Public Library.*)

War against Austria. In 1860 he returned to New Orleans where he lived until he died in 1907 at the age of 70.

Dr. Formento was considered one of the most prominent surgeons in the South, which he served as chief surgeon of the Louisiana Hospital at Richmond during the Civil War and as a member of the Louisiana State Board of Health.

DR. VERDI

Dr. Tullio Suzzara Verdi is remembered as the personal physician of Secretary of State Seward and as the man whose name one of the plotters of the Lincoln assassination used in order to gain admittance to Seward's home. He was born at Mantua in 1829, served for a while in the Sardinian Army, and then decided to emigrate to the United States. Arriving here with only five dollars, he taught Italian for a while at Brown University in Providence. Later he studied at Hahnemann College in Philadelphia, from which he received his degree of doctor of medicine in 1856. Thus it would seem that he was the first native of Italy to graduate from an American medical school. A year later he moved to Washington. His marriage to a Pittsburgh society woman in 1860 admitted him to the best circles in the nation's capital, where he became personal physician to society and political leaders.

In 1871 he was appointed a member of the first and only Board of Health of the District of Columbia, serving as secretary and chairman of its Sanitary Committee. In 1873 he visited Europe as Sanitary Commissioner. One of the organizers of the Homoeopathic Hospital in Washington, he was also one of the charter members of the Homoeopathic Medical Society of the District of Columbia. He died in Milan, where he had gone hoping to restore his health, on November 26, 1902.

Dr. Verdi wrote a number of books, some of which can be found in the New York Public Library and in the Library of Congress. His brother Ciro served as assistant surgeon with the Union Army during the Civil War.

SINCE THE CIVIL WAR

The Italian physicians who have practised in the United States since the Civil War are too numerous to be mentioned. We shall recall only a few.

Dr. Peter Charles Remondino came to America from his native Turin at the age of eight in 1854, was educated in Illinois and Minnesota, and graduated from Jefferson Medical College in 1865. During the Civil War, while he was still a student, he served with the Union Army; later he was a surgeon with the French Army during the Franco-Prussian War; in 1873 he settled in San Diego, where he died on December 10, 1926.

Dr. Remondino was editor of the *Natural Popular Review*, a Chicago journal of preventive medicine, after 1892; a lecturer on the history of medicine at the University of Southern California; president of the San Diego Board of Health; author of several books on medicine and other scientific subjects.

Dr. Paolo De Vecchi, another Piedmontese who, like Dr. Remondino, served during the Franco-Prussian War, but as a member of the Piedmontese Ambulance, came to the United States to study American orthopedical methods, just as he had done in England and other countries. Once here, however, he decided to remain, married an American woman, and spent twenty-five years in San Francisco. In 1905 he moved to New York, where he remained until he died in 1931. The author of several books on surgery and other subjects, he had been considered for years as the dean of Italian physicians in the United States.

DR. TULLIO SUZZARA VERDI

Dr. Augustus Ravogli, one of Cincinnati's most distinguished physicians and surgeons, was born in Rome in 1851; studied medicine in Rome, Vienna, Prague and Berlin; served as a surgeon with the rank of major in the Italian Army and came to America in 1880. A professor of dermatology at the University of Cincinnati for years, he was the author of two books and a contributor to several medical journals. He died in 1934.

Dr. Antonio Lagorio was born in Chicago in 1857 and received the degree of doctor of medicine from Rush Medical College in 1879. Later he studied at Rome and Genoa, the city of birth of his parents. Loyola University (Chicago) conferred on him the degree of Doctor of Laws.

Dr. Lagorio was the most prominent Italian in Chicago up to the time of his death on November 24, 1944. The director of the Chicago Pasteur Institute which he founded in 1890, he served for years as member and president of the Chicago Public Library Board, and as trustee of the House of Correction.

Dr. Angelo Festorazzi of Mobile, Ala., the grandson of an Italian immigrant and a graduate of Spring Hill

College in 1884, was probably the only man of Italian extraction to serve as president of the Medical Association of Alabama.

Dr. F. H. Masi of Norfolk, Va., probably the descendant of one of the men who came over with Mazzei in 1773, served as the first treasurer of the Virginia Pharmaceutical Association when it was organized in 1882.

Dr. Annina Carmela Rondinella, who died in Wellesley, Mass., at the age of eight-four in 1949, graduated from the Women's Medical College in Philadelphia in 1899, probably the first woman of Italian extraction to receive a medical degree in the United States. After serving as assistant dean of the Women's Medical College, she set up the medical department of the Connecticut College for Women in 1915, later moving to Wellesley. At the time of her death she was consulting ophthalmologist emeritus at Wellesley College.

Dr. Paul Mazzuri, who died at the age of 82 in his native New Orleans in 1947, was closely associated with Walter Reed in the fight against yellow fever, as related in Chapter Twenty-Two.

Dr. Charles J. Imperatori, who was born in New York City of Italian parentage in 1878, was for years professor of laryngology at Columbia University and of otolaryngology at New York University. During World War I he served as lieutenant-colonel with the U. S. Army Medical Corps. The co-author of a well-known book on the diseases of nose and throat, he served as president of the American Laryngological Association and of the American Bronchoscopic Association and as governor of the American College of Surgeons. He died in 1950.

Dr. Italo Frederick Volini, to recall another distinguished physician who died also in 1950, was the head of the School of Medicine of Loyola University in Chicago from 1929 to the time of his death.

Coming to our own days, one could easily compile a very long list of physicians and surgeons born in Italy, or in the United States of Italian parentage, who occupy prominent places in various branches of medicine. Space, unfortunately, prevents us from even mentioning their names, many of which, however, can be found in the *Italian-American who's who.*

In the United States there are today possibly more than five thousand physicians and dentists, besides some 3,000 pharmacists, of Italian birth or extraction. Many of them have served as presidents of state, county, and local professional organizations. Not a few are full professors in America's leading medical schools. Many more served as majors, colonels, and one or two, if we are not mistaken, as generals in the U. S. Army or with corresponding ranks in the U. S. Navy during World War II. More than 300 of them are Fellows of the American College of Surgeons. Quite a number of them have written books on medical subjects or are regular contributors to leading American and foreign scientific publications. There is possibly no noted hospital in the United States in which one does not find some Italian-American physician or surgeon in a responsible position, often at the head of a department.

In various parts of the country Italian-American physicians, dentists, and pharmacists have organized professional organizations of their own, and even a college medical fraternity. In the past they have published medical journals in both English and Italian, but today there is only one left, the magazine *Alcmeone* published by Dr. Giovanni Arcieri of New York, an authority on the history of medicine, on which he lectures at the University of Rome.

ENGINEERS AND SCIENTISTS

To judge by the material and notes collected by us during the last twenty-five years or so, no Italian engineers and scientists to speak of came to the United States before World War I. But somehow we feel that our lack of material in this field must be due largely to the little interest we have had in scientific pursuits and consequently our little acquaintance with technical publications. We feel confident, therefore, that a proper search along those lines is bound to reward the investigator. Special attention should be paid to the 300-odd volumes of the *Gazette* published by the United State Patent Office. But then there are the various city directories and the advertisement pages of local newspapers. For instance, in the Detroit city directory for 1855 we find one Angelo Paldi listed as architect and draftsman for the Commissioner of Water Works (his wife is listed as midwife) and a few years later we find one Enrico Ressell, an engineer from Trieste, who had patented in Washington an invention of his for some kind of propeller, or rudder. (*Eco d'Italia,* July 22, 1865.)

LUIGI D'AURIA

Luigi D'Auria was a lecturer on applied mechanics at the University of Naples and an engineer on the general staff of the Italian Army when he came over in 1876 with his young wife—a Russian princess—to visit the Centennial Exhibition at Philadelphia. Instead of returning to Italy, however, he decided to make his home in the city of Brotherly Love, where he lived until he passed away on August 4, 1916. Upon the death of his first wife he married the daughter of Brigadier General Henry M. Robert, formerly Chief of Engineers, U. S. Army. Their daughter, Gemma D'Auria (Mrs. Percy H. Houston of Los Angeles), is a fine sculptress and poetess.

Luigi D'Auria invented a pumping engine which is still in use throughout the United State and Canada (Greene, A. M., *Pumping Machinery,* 2nd ed., 1919, p. 104), but should be remembered for his contributions to the study of tides and stellar dynamics which appeared in

LUIGI D'AURIA
Mechanical Engineer and Inventor

GAETANO LANZA, JR.
Professor Emeritus, Massachusetts Institute of Technology.

the *Journal of the Franklin Institute* (1890) and in the bulletin of the Astronomical Society of France (1913). He was active in American engineering circles for years, serving on various committees, including the section on gas engines and prime motors at the International Electrical Exhibition held in Philadelphia in 1884, of which he was secretary.

GAETANO LANZA

Gaetano Lanza, as we have seen on page 266, was the son of the Sicilian language teacher by the same name. He was born in Boston in 1848, studied at the University of Virginia, where he taught for two years until 1871, when he joined the Massachusetts Institute of Technology.

Prof. Lanza was connected with that famous institution for forty-one years, twenty-nine of which he spent as head of the department of mechanical engineering, the largest in the Institute. In 1912 he was made professor emeritus, retired to Philadelphia and joined the Baldwin Locomotive Works as consulting engineer.

Prof. Lanza's contribution to American science and engineering may be judged by the books and the more than one hundred articles and pamphlets which he wrote. His treatise on applied mechanics went through nine editions.

Upon his death in Philadelphia in 1928 his body was returned to the Univeristy of Virginia, where it was interred in the University cemetery. To his alma mater he bequeathed $10,000 and his entire scientific library.

(On Prof. Lanza see *Who's Who in America*, 1928-29; *Technology Review*, May, 1928; *Transactions of the Am. Soc. of Mech. Eng.*; *Journal of Franklin Institute*; *Engineering Index*.)

GIUSEPPE FACCIOLI

Giuseppe Faccioli, who died in Pittsfield, Mass., in 1934 at the age of 57, was considered the friendly rival of Charles Steinmetz because of his internationally-known experiments on artificial lightning. A native of Rome, he came to America in 1904 and was connected with the General Electrical Company from 1907 to 1930, when he retired as chief engineer. In 1932 he received the Lamme Gold Medal of the American Institute of Electrical Engineers. A cripple like Steinmetz, he also did his work in a wheel chair. (See *Dictionary of American Biography* and *National Cyclopaedia*, Vol. 24.)

OTHER NOTED ENGINEERS

Guido Pantaleoni was born at Macerata in 1858 and came to America in 1883. A resident of St. Louis, he was connected for years as an engineer with the Westinghouse Electric Manufacturing Company, which sent him on important missions to China, Japan, India, South America and other parts of the world.

Philip Torchio, chief electrical engineer and vice-president of the Consolidated Edison Company of New York, was born in Vercana (Como), Italy, in 1868 and came to America in 1893, after graduating from the University of Pavia and the Royal Polytechnic of Milan. The holder of numerous patents on improvement in cables, storage batteries and electrical control, he served at one time as president of the New York Electrical Society. He was also president of the Bank of Naples Trust Company of New York from 1930 to 1941, and mayor from 1928 to 1931 of Bronxville, N. Y., where he died on January 14, 1942.

Gerardo Immediato was born in Italy in 1876 and died in New York in 1939. Until the time of his retirement in

1936 he was professor of mechanical engineering at Brooklyn Polytechnic Institute. Previously he had served as designing engineer in charge of subway construction for the City of New York.

William Bruno, a native of Italy who died in Brooklyn in 1943, was a pioneer in the development of the teletype and short wave radio. At the time of his death he was consultant to the U. S. Government in connection with his work on radar.

Gian Giacomo Ponti is said to have served as assistant to Steinmetz at the General Electric Company. Later he returned to Italy, where he became professor at the Royal Polytechnic Institute in Turin and president of the local power company.

Ugo D'Annunzio, the son of the celebrated poet, was an expert in aeronautics. He died in New York in 1945 at the age of 56.

Mario Lorini, who died in Yonkers at the age of 88 in 1943, took part in the construction of the Croton Dam.

Bancroft Gherardi, the grandson of the language teacher noted on page 264, was chief engineer and vice-president of the American Telephone and Telegraph Company.

Albert Andriano, who was born in Missouri in 1865, invented a number of telephone and electrical devices.

Fred Zonino, who died at Waterbury, Conn., in 1946 at the age of 59, was at the time of his death chief industrial engineer of the footwear division of the United States Rubber Company.

LIVING ENGINEERS

A summary examination of *Who's Who in Engineering, American Men of Science,* and similar yearbooks, will reveal a number of Italian-Americans who hold important positions in the field of engineering.

Joshua D'Esposito, born and educated in Italy, came to the United States in 1898 at the age of 20, joined the Pennsylvania Railroad as a draftsman in 1904, and rose to the position of assistant to the chief engineer in 1913. During World War I he was assistant manager of the Emergency Fleet Corporation, United States Shipping Board, Washington, D. C. Between 1919 and 1925 he was in charge of the construction of Union Station of Chicago and was responsible for a great deal of the designing of that building. He is now one of the outstanding consulting engineers in the country.

Guglielmo Marconi at the receiving set at St. John's, Newfoundland, December 12, 1901.

Giuseppe Mario Bellanca, one of the pioneers of aviation, was born at Sciacca, Italy, in 1886, and came to the United States in 1911. He designed and built the first cabin monoplane in the United States, the transatlantic monoplane "Columbia," and the first transpacific monoplane, "Miss Veedol." He also designed and built the planes on which Boardman and Polando flew to Turkey in 1931 and Pangborn and Herndon flew from Japan to the United States.

Dr. Cesare Barbieri of New York, noted inventor and mechancial engineer. (See *post,* pp. 342-343.)

Peter L. Bellaschi, a native of Piedmont, was ten years old when he came to America in 1913. Since 1928 he has been connected with the Westinghouse Company at Sharon, Pa., where he invented the Lightining Stroke Current Generator and the full Lightining Stroke Generator. Under his direction the first lightning stroke current and the full lightning stroke were developed in the Westinghouse laboratory.

Guglielmo Camilli was born at Castelmadama, near Rome, in 1898, was educated in Turin, and came to America in 1924. Since 1926 he has been in charge of the development of high-voltage instrument transformers at the General Electric Laboratory in Pittsfield, Mass. In 1938 he directed the construction of 50 instrument transformers used at Boulder Dam. He has more than 40 patents to his name.

Alfred F. Gambitta, a native of the province of Messina, was also educated in Turin. One of the leading high voltage transmission engineers in the country, he has been in charge of the construction of some of the outstanding electrical underground transmission lines in the United States.

Eugene Mirabelli is assistant professor of structural design at the Massachusettes Institute of Technology.

Panfilo Trombetta of Milwaukee, an electrical engineer, new heads a company of his own, manufacturing solonoids, solonoid brakes and industrial controls.

Alfred A. Ghirardi of Darien, Conn., is the author of a number of textbooks on radio, and editor of, and contributor to, magazines on radio and television.

We do not have much information regarding:

Frank E. La Cauza, a native of Sicily, professor of electrical engineering at the Postgraduate School of the U. S. Naval Academy, Annapolis; Domenico Pietro, a native of Piedmont, dean of engineering, Georgia School of Technology, Atlanta; Louis Fopeano, curator of civil engineering, Museum of Science and Industry, Chicago; Louis M. Rossi, vice-president of the Bakelite Corporation; Alfred Ferretti, professor of mechanical engineering at

Northeastern University; Ralph Montonna, professor of chemical engineering at the University of Minnesota; Victor Ronci, vacuum tube engineer, with the Bell Telephone Company, holder of numerous patents; other professors on the faculties of our colleges and universities.

It should not be necessary to stress the contribution of Marconi to American civilization, even if he was not a resident of the United States, except on brief visits.

SCIENTISTS

In other fields of science, outside of electrical and mechanical engineering, one finds a number of Italian-American scientists, but their names are harder to bring to light as in many cases they are connected with governmental and industrial laboratories where the scientist works almost anonymously.

QUIRICO FILOPANTI

The first Italian scientist to seek and find asylum in America was probably the political exile Quirico Filopanti (Giuseppe Barili, or Barilli, 1812-1894). Patriot, scientist, political leader, he came to America after the Fall of the Roman Republic of 1849, which he served as secretary of the triumvirate with Mazzini. We do not know exactly how long he lived here; by 1866, however, he was back in Italy fighting side by side with Garibaldi. A professor of mechanics at the University of Bologna, he is also remembered as the author of several books on history and religion.

Of interest to us is his plan for air navigation with an airship of his own for the construction of which he expected to raise the necessary funds in the United States. The Washington *Daily Globe*, however, did not deem Filpanti's plan practical, but, retorted New York's *Eco* d'Italia, "Columbus and Fulton also had to struggle against the prejudices of their century." Apparently the plan was abandoned. (*Eco d'Italia*, Feb. 8 and March 22, 1851.)

ENRICO FERMI

Of course, the leading Italian scientist in the United States, in every branch of science, is Enrico Fermi, a native of Rome, winner of the Nobel Prize for physics in 1938. A member of the General Advisory Committee of Scientists for the Atomic Energy Commission, he directed the building of the first self-sustaining nuclear chain reactor and was the outstanding figure in the making of the atom bomb. In 1946 he was one of the five top scientists on whom the Government bestowed the Medal of Merit, the highest award that the Government can make to civilians. In 1948 he was named honorary chancellor of Union College, Schenectady, for 1947-48. Prof. Fermi was born in Rome in 1901 and came to the United States in 1939.

More Italian and Italian-American scientists have been, or are, associated with the Manhattan District Project or with the Atomic Energy Commission than it is generally realized. Only from time to time their names become known in connection with some announcement of public interest.

In 1948, for instance, Alfonso Tammaro was named manager of the Chicago operations office of the Atomic Energy Commission, to coordinate the activities of twenty-nine Mid-Western industrial and academic institutions. Joseph T. Gemmi, a Newark architect, was one of the men who designed the buildings and equipment for the production of atomic bomb parts at Decatur, Illinois. Armando Spadetti, formerly at Johns Hopkins University, also worked at Oak Ridge, Tenn. Dr. Albert Ghiorso has been active in the peace-time development of atomic energy. Theirs are only four of the names that have come to our attention.

A number of Italian-American scientists are connected with the Bureau of Standards in Washington. One of them, Frederick D. Rossini, a native of Monongahela, Pa., is chief of the section on thermochemistry and constitution of petroleum, as well as editor of the *Journal of the Washington Academy of Science.*

At Bethesda, Md., near Washington, William V. Consolazio, a former Harvard biochemist, and one of the designers of the National Naval Medical Research Institute, is chief chemist of the institute. Under his direction the Navy perfected the process for making sea water drinkable. Another process for desalting sea water was developed by a New York firm which included among its research chemists and engineers an Italian-American, Vincent J. Calise.

In Cincinnati, George Sperti, who was born in Kentucky in 1900, is research professor and director of research at the Institutum Divi Thomae of the Athenaeum of Ohio. One of the six American scientists honored by Pope Pius XI in 1936 with membership in the Pontifical Academy of Sciences, he has several inventions to his name, including the well-known Sperti Sun Lamp.

Salvatore Pagliuca, a Neapolitan, was for years chief meteorologist of the Harvard Blue Hill Observatory and of the Yankee Network Weather service. He died in 1944, the victim of an automobile accident while serving as a major in the U. S. Army.

E. O. Fenzi, who was born in Florence in 1843 and died in North Africa in 1924, came to America in 1893, and spent the next sixteen years at Santa Barbara, Cal. According to Dr. Popenoe of the U. S. Department of Agriculture, he introduced more plants in California than any other man. "California gardens will be more beautiful for all time, and California orchards will contain a greater number of delicious fruits because of his sojourn at Santa Barbara." (*Journal of Heredity*, 1922.) In 1922 the American Genetic Association awarded him the third Frank W. Meyer Medal which was presented to him by the American minister in Rome. (*Vigo Review*, April, 1938.)

The few names mentioned by us at random show that both natives of Italy and Americans of Italian extraction have not neglected the field of science. But we have not even scratched the surface. A more methodical study of the subject, and especially of college and university catalogs, is bound to reward the researcher with an abundant crop of names and facts.

INVENTORS

The same thing may be said of the thousands of patents issued by the U. S. Patent Office to men with Italian names, from industrial processes to mechanical devices for war and peace. We could mention a number of them which we have in our files, but the field is so vast that we prefer not to dwell on it at all. We shall recall only an Italian inventor, an old Piedmontese sergeant named Lamberti, the owner of a hat store on Dock Street in Philadelphia about 1846, who is said to have invented a sewing machine. (*Eco d'Italia,* January 7-8, 1883.)

Bronze tablet in honor of Guglielmo Marconi by Pietro Montana, offered by the Italian Professional Women of America to Fordham University in 1938.

ATTORNEYS AT LAW, JUDGES AND PUBLIC OFFICIALS

MEMBERS OF THE BENCH AND BAR

Inability to speak the English language well and to pronounce it without an accent has kept many a talented native of Italy from practicing law in the courts of the United States. There have been, of course, a few Italian-born lawyers, beginning with Antonio Rapallo, already mentioned by us, who became an attorney in New York in the 1820's.

Before the Civil War at least three natives of Italy were members of the New York Bar: Luigi Tinelli, who became U. S. Consul in Portugal, as related below; G. Gajani, a former member of the Roman Bar (*Eco d'Italia,* March 26, 1859); and Augusto Fransioli. After 1880 we find a number of lawyers with Italian names listed in city directories from New York to San Francisco, but in all probability they were natives of the United States.

Even among the American-born children of Italian parentage there were not many attorneys at law before World War I. Today, as we know, there are more than 1,000 Italian-American lawyers in New Yory City alone. Not a few of them, like Charles J. Margiotti of Pittsburgh, have acquired a national reputation. Scores of them have been admitted to practice before the Supreme Court of the United States.

Among those who achieved prominence in the past, we may recall Eugene Carusi, the son of Nathaniel Carusi, a native of Sicily, who came with his father, Gaetano Carusi, to organize the U. S. Marine Band in 1805. Eugene Carusi was admitted to the bar in 1857 and continued to practice in Washington for more than half a century. In 1869 he was one of the organizers of the National University Law School, which he served as chancellor from 1906 until his death in 1924. He was succeeded by his son, Charles Francis Carusi, who served until he died in 1931. Charles Carusi was for four years president of the District of Columbia Board of Education.

JUDGES

If we want to go back to colonial days we can easily find a number of judges of superior courts of Italian descent, like Paca or Benjamin Taliaferro (1750-1821).

Before 1850, Pascal Charles De Angelis, who died in Oneida County, N. Y., in 1839, often presided over the deliberations of the Oneida County Court of General Sessions; in Missouri, Francis Yosti of St. Charles, the son of the Piedmontese immigrant, Emilian Yosti, served as county judge, and Eugene Napoleon Bonfils, the son of the Corsican teacher of languages, Salvatore Bonfiglio, served as probate judge, both in the 1850's. In California, Louis Raggio became a justice of the peace in San Luis in the 1840's and later served of justice of the County District Court. Since then, of course, there have been numerous judges of Italian extraction.

The three outstanding Italian-American judges of the past were Rapallo in New York, Longino in Mississippi and Angellotti in California.

Charles Antonio Rapallo (1823-1887), the son of Antonio, was justice of the Court of Appeals of the State of New York from 1870 to 1887, the highest judiciary position ever attained by an Italian-American in the Empire State.

Andrew Houston Longino (1854-1942), was the son of an immigrant whose name was shortened from Longinotti. He served as member of the Mississippi State Senate from 1870 to 1884, and then as U. S. District Attorney from 1888 to 1890, presiding judge of Mississippi from 1894 to 1899, and then governor of Mississippi from 1900 to 1904.

Frank M. Angellotti, the son of Giuseppe Angellotti, served as district attorney of Marin County, Cal., from 1885 to 1891, as judge of the Superior Court from 1891 to 1903, associate justice of the Supreme Court of California from 1903 to 1915, and as chief justice from 1951 to 1921, when he retired.

In our own days only two Italian-Americans are justices of the highest court in their states, Justice Capotosto in Providence, since 1935, and Justice Musmanno of Pennsylvania, since January, 1952. In 1947, C. Thomas Schettino was appointed lay judge of the Court of Errors and Appeals of New Jersey.

Since 1923, when the late Salvatore Cotillo became the first native of Italy to become a judge of the Supreme Court of New York, more than a score of Italian-American attorneys have been elected or appointed justices of superior courts (Supreme Court in New York, Court of Common Pleas in Pennsylvania, Superior Court in Massachusetts). Italian-American judges of lower courts, from general sessions or district courts, to municipal or magistrates courts, are more than one hundred. The names of those who served before 1947 will be found in Volume One of our *Italian-American History*.

FEDERAL OFFICIALS

Charles Joseph Bonaparte, a descendant of Napoleon, served as U. S. Secretary of the Navy and later as Attorney General of the United States under Theodore Roosevelt, but he cannot be considered an Italian-American, in the same sense that sons of Italian immigrants are.

EUGENE CARUSI
One of the founders of the National University of Law, Washington, D.C., 1866.

In the latter category, the first to rise to a prominent federal office was Anthony Caminetti (1854-1923) of California who served as Commissioner General of Immigration from 1913 to 1921. A similar office was held in 1947 by Ugo Carusi, a native of Italy, who served for about fifteen years as executive assistant to the attorney general of the United States and then as Commissioner General of Immigration and Naturalization.

In recent years the highest federal office filled by the son of an Italian immigrant has been that of director of the Office of Price Stabilization held by Michael V. Di Salle, former mayor of Toledo, from 1950 to 1952. Literally hundreds of Italian-Americans hold responsible positions in the Federal Government.

JOHN PHINIZY
Mayor of Augusta, Ga., 1837.

IN THE DIPLOMATIC AND CONSULAR SERVICE

To the best of our knowledge, only one American of Italian extraction has held ambassadorial rank in the diplomatic service of the United States, although there have been quite a few Italian-Americans who have served as attaches at embassies and legations. He is John J. Muccio of Providence, R. I., American Ambassador in Korea. A century ago Teresa Bagioli, the daughter of the noted conductor of the Italian Opera House in New York, served as mistress of the American legation in London where her husband, the future General Sickles, was serving as attache under James Buchanan, our bachelor minister.

In the consular service, however, there have been scores of men born in Italy, or of Italian parentage in the United States. That was especially so immediately after the Revolution when a number of Italians served as American consuls in Italy, Morocco, the West Indies, Constantinople, Portugal, and other countries. Men like Joseph and Girolamo Chiappe, Joseph Ceronio, Francis Dainese, Filippo Filicchi, and others. Foresti, already noted, was appointed consul at Genoa in 1858, but he died three months after he arrived there. Luigi Monti, also noted on page 266, served at Palermo, in Sicily, from 1861 to 1873. Gen. Luigi di Cesnola served as consul at Cyprus before he became director of the Metropolitan Museum of Art, and his brother acted as vice-consul at Pathos, also in Greece. Luigi Tinelli, the political exile and lawyer already noted by us, was United States Consul at Oporto, Portugal, from 1841 to 1852.

STATE OFFICIALS

Besides Governors Longino of Mississippi and Paca of Maryland, only one Italian-American has served as head of a state government. He is U. S. Senator John O. Pastore, who became Governor of Rhode Island in 1945. He is also the first Italian-American to serve as a United States Senator.

Charles Poletti served as lieutenant-governor of New York State from 1939 to 1942, and Louis W. Cappelli held the same office in Rhode Island from 1941 to 1944.

In the past only a few Italian-Americans have held office in state cabinets. The first was Adolphe V. Coco, who served as attorney-general of Louisiana from 1916 to 1924. In Pennsylvania, Charles J. Margiotti served as attorney-general under three governors between 1935 and 1951. In Connecticut Francis A. Pallotti served as secretary of state from 1923 to 1929 and as attorney general from 1938 to 1941. Also in Connecticut, C. John Satti and Charles J. Prestia have served as secretaries of state and F. M. Anastasio and Joseph A. Adorno, as state treasurers. At present (1952), besides Mr. Adorno, five Italian-Americans are members of state cabinets: Andrew J. Sordoni, Secretary of Commerce of Pennsylvania; Edward Corsi, Commissioner of Labor of New York State; John J. Del Monte, Commissioner of the Massachusetts Department of Labor and Industries; Frank Annunzio, director of the Illinois Department of Labor; Joseph F. Di Domenico, Commissioner of the Maryland Department of Labor and Industry. In Alaska Leo Sarella is Commissioner of the Department of Mines.

LEGISLATORS

As noted, there is only one Italian-American member of the United States Senate, John O. Pastore. Congressmen have been more numerous, ever since Francis B. Spinola was elected in 1886, followed, four years later, by Anthony Caminetti. Their names, likewise, will be found in Volume One of *Italian-American History*. Today (1952) there are one each from Connecticut, Massachusetts and Michigan and two each from New Jersey and New York.

The members of state senates and assemblies, of course, reach into the hundreds, beginning with General Spinola in 1853, or with one of the grandsons of Count Barziza of Venice, who was a member of the Texas Assembly in 1874.

MAYORS

The first son of an Italian immigrant to become mayor of an American city was in all probability John Phinizy, the son of Ferdinand Phinizy of Parma, who became mayor of Augusta, Ga., in 1837.

Other pioneer mayors were: G. A. Pacetti of St. Augustine, Fla., at the beginning of the Civil War; Antonio Ghio, a native of Genoa, who served as mayor of Texarkana, Texas, from 1880 to 1886; Constantine L. Lavretta of Mobile, Ala., who served from 1892 to 1898; Frank L. Monteverde, who was mayor of Memphis, Tenn., from 1918 to 1921.

During the last twenty years scores of Italian-Americans have been mayors of large American cities, like La Guardia in New York, Rossi in San Francisco, Maestri in New Orleans, Celentano in New Haven, Di Salle in Toledo, D'Alessandro in Baltimore, Spagnola in Youngstown, Villani in Newark, De Guglielmo in Cambridge, Mass., Olgiati in Chattanooga, Fontana in Aliquippa, Pa., Levanti in Fitchburg, Mass., De Sapio in Hoboken, Vaccarella in Mt. Vernon, N. Y., Ruffu in Atlantic City, Martini and De Muro in Passaic, N. J., De Vita in Paterson, N. J., Casassa in Revere, Mass., Paonessa in New Britain, Conn., Parente in Monessen, Pa., Imburgio in Melrose Park, Ill., and scores of others in smaller communities. Of course, we need not say much about Mayor Impellitteri of New York, a native of Sicily, who won a smashing victory against Tammany Hall at the polls in 1950.

COUNTY AND CITY OFFICIALS

To list all the descendants of Italian immigrants who have held county and city offices during the last 250 years one should go back to William Alburtus, the grandson of the Venetian Cesare Alberti, who served as constable in Hunterdon County, N. J., from 1722 to 1726. The list of course would cover literally thousands of names. We shall recall, therefore, only two pioneers, Charles Del Vecchio, who became one of New York's first three fire commissioners in 1839, and Dr. Giovanni Ceccarini, who was one of the first four health commissioners and chairman of the Sanitary Committee, also in New York City, in 1870.

CHAPTER TWENTY-ONE

IN BUSINESS, FINANCE, AND AGRICULTURE

Most of the preceding chapters had already been written and set into type, when we found an item in the *Virginia Gazette* for November 21, 1751, which confirms our early suppositions regarding Italian immigration to Louisiana before 1800. The item, dated Madrid, July 23, reads: "The necessity of stocking our Possessions in the West-Indies with a great Addition of European Colonists, especially Handicraftsmen and Labourers, having been laid before his Majesty . . . ; these Representations having been approved by the Council, it has been resolved to make the most encouraging Offers of Privileges, Immunity and pecuniary Assistance, to any Italian families who will enter themselves to settle in the King's American Dominions, and there follow the same Trades and Occupations by which they maintained themselves at home."

How many Italian families accepted the offer we are not able to say without further research in Spanish and Central American archives; nevertheless, we are inclined to believe that at least a number of families must have emigrated to the New World from those parts of Italy which at that time were under Spanish rule, namely, Naples and Sicily, which were under Charles III, and parts of northern Italy, wihch were under his brother, Don Philip. The two rulers, one must remember, were the sons of Philip V and of Elizabeth Farnese of Parma. Charles III, especially, was closely identified with Italian affairs and enjoyed for years, even after he became King of Spain in 1759, the advice of his celebrated minister, Bernardo Tanucci. One should also bear in mind that in 1763 all Louisiana, which then extended from the Gulf of Mexico to the Rocky Mountains, was ceded to Spain, who ruled over until 1801.

MISSOURI PIONEERS

Before 1800, old Louisiana, and particularly what is now Missouri, offered a larger field of activity to Italian immigrants, in part because most of the settlers in those days spoke French, but also because St. Louis was then, and has been ever since, the largest raw fur center in the United States. That explains why one finds more prominent Italians in St. Louis and New Orleans before 1800 than in any other part of the country, with rare exceptions. The inducements to Italian settlers offered by Spain, moreover, confirm our theory of 1929, when our book *The Italians in Missouri* was published, to the effect that many of the settlers whose names seem French or Spanish, actually were Italians: men like Sanguinet, Morelle, Tardiveau, Lamy, Puricelly, and so on.

BARTHOLOMEW BERTHOLD
From a medallion in the possession of the Missouri Historical Society, St. Louis.

Some of the early settlers in St. Louis who became prosperous merchants were Emilien Yosti, Antoine Bouis, Bartholomew Berthold, Evariste Maury, Charles Sanguinet and Gregoire Sarpy. Besides, of course, Colonel Francis Vigo.

Yosti was born in Novara about 1740 and died in St. Louis in 1818. He was one of the earliest real estate operators in the city, a member of the first grand jury in 1804, and the owner of a tavern, or inn, in which was held the first court of justice as soon as St. Louis became a part of the United States. He was a partner of Francis Vigo (a fellow-Piedmontese) and was prominent in the organization of the civil government in Missouri. His son Francis, who was born in St. Louis in 1798, lived an eventful life. In 1830 he started for Santa Fe, New Mexico, where he arrived after 90 days, and where he operated a store for two years. On his way back he was attacked by the Indians and for 17 days he trudged through swamps or over hills and rocks without food until at the confluence of the Red Fork and Arkansas River he was helped by some friendly Indians. In 1834 he settled in St. Charles, Mo., where he served as a judge of the County Court for four years and became president of the First National Bank of St. Charles. He was a Catholic and a Democrat. In Missouri and other parts of the country one finds today several prominent men named Yost, but whether they are descendants of the immigrant Piedmontese we cannot say. In 1915 one of them, Casper S. Yost, was editor of the well-known newspaper *Globe-Democrat* of St. Louis.

Bouis was born in Genoa in 1752, emigrated to New Orleans in 1780 and settled in St. Louis in 1782. He was the father of ten children, one of whom, André V. Bouis, became a school teacher, and another, Pascal V. Bouis, graduated from West Point as a second lieutenant in the artillery in 1806 and was killed in a duel about 1811. Thus he seems to have been the first Italian-American to graduate from the United States Military Academy. AntoineBouis was also the grandfather of Alexander Lesueur, who became secretary of state of Missouri and was for many years editor of the Lexington (Mo.) *Intelligencer.* The elder Bouis must have been active in the fur business, according to a *Map of the Trans-Mississippi Territory,* 1807-1843, in which we find Fort Defiance, or Fort Bouis, on the White River, just south of the present city of Bismarck, N. D.

Bartholomew Berthold, a partner in the American Fur Company, one of the largest firms of its kind in the history of that industry, was born at Trento, Italy, in 1780, the son of Alessandro Bertoldi and Maddalena Beltrami. In 1809 he settled in St. Louis, where in 1811 he married Pelagie Chouteau, a member of the famous family that founded the city half a century before. Shortly after his marriage he formed a partnership with Auguste Chouteau, which lasted until Berthold's death on April 20, 1831. He had four sons and two daughters. Fort Berthold in the Upper Missouri region was named after him. He, Chouteau and others are said to have been connected with John Jacob Astor as partners, according to an item in *St. Louis Republican* for May 26, 1875, but we have found no reference to it in any of the biographical accounts of Astor or in Chittenden's *The American Fur Trade of the Far West.*

Gregoire B. Sarpy is said to have been born in France, the son of Charles Sarpy and Suzanne Trenty, both of whom, we are inclined to believe, were natives of Italy. Together with Charles Sanguinet he was a partner with Manuel Lisa in the Missouri Fur Company. He is said to have been the first man to attempt the navigation of the Missouri River with a keelboat. A fort was named after him on the Yellowstone.

John B. Zenoni was another Italian who was associated with Lisa in the Missouri Fur Company when it was reorganized in 1820. He was one of the early shareholders of the Bank of Missouri when it was established in 1816.

Charles Sanguinet also was a shareholder in the same bank, but for only two shares, like Zenoni, as compared to five shares each ($100 a share) subscribed by Yosti and Maury and thirty shares ($3,000) subscribed by Berthold and Chouteau (*Missouri Gazette,* Sept. 14, 1816). He is said to have come to St. Louis in 1775 and to have been the son of Joseph Sanguinette, a surgeon major in the French service in Canada.

Evariste Maury arrived in St. Louis from Nashville, Tenn., in April, 1816, when he opened a coffee-house in the Old Sanguinet Mansion on Second Street. A few months later, as we have seen, he became a shareholder in the Bank of Missouri; in 1817 he was operating a hotel of his own, "The Planters Hotel;" in 1819 he announced that he was going to "his native country in the state of Venice, Italy" (see facsimile) and shortly after that he advertised the publication of the St. Louis *Enquirer* together with another man from Tennessee, Isaac N. McHenry. He must have been a man of means, to judge by

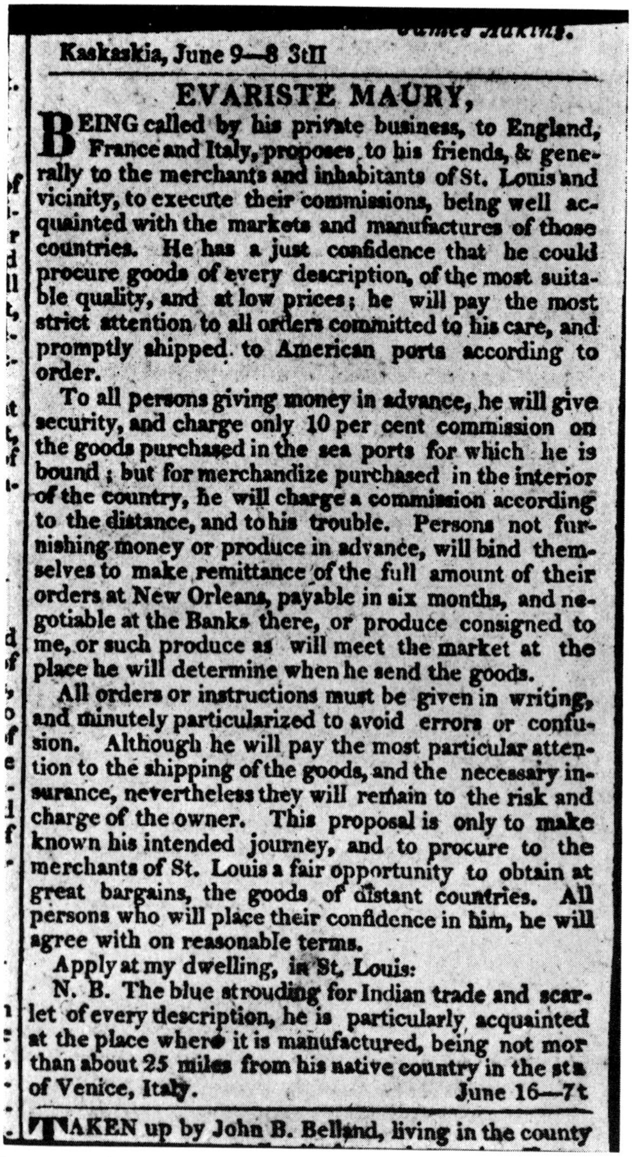

Kaskaskia, June 9—8 3tII

EVARISTE MAURY,

BEING called by his private business, to England, France and Italy, proposes to his friends, & generally to the merchants and inhabitants of St. Louis and vicinity, to execute their commissions, being well acquainted with the markets and manufactures of those countries. He has a just confidence that he could procure goods of every description, of the most suitable quality, and at low prices; he will pay the most strict attention to all orders committed to his care, and promptly shipped to American ports according to order.

To all persons giving money in advance, he will give security, and charge only 10 per cent commission on the goods purchased in the sea ports for which he is bound; but for merchandize purchased in the interior of the country, he will charge a commission according to the distance, and to his trouble. Persons not furnishing money or produce in advance, will bind themselves to make remittance of the full amount of their orders at New Orleans, payable in six months, and negotiable at the Banks there, or produce consigned to me, or such produce as will meet the market at the place he will determine when he send the goods.

All orders or instructions must be given in writing, and minutely particularized to avoid errors or confusion. Although he will pay the most particular attention to the shipping of the goods, and the necessary insurance, nevertheless they will remain to the risk and charge of the owner. This proposal is only to make known his intended journey, and to procure to the merchants of St. Louis a fair opportunity to obtain at great bargains, the goods of distant countries. All persons who will place their confidence in him, he will agree with on reasonable terms.

Apply at my dwelling, in St. Louis:

N. B. The blue strouding for Indian trade and scarlet of every description, he is particularly acquainted at the place where it is manufactured, being not mor than about 25 miles from his native country in the sta of Venice, Italy. June 16—7t

TAKEN up by John B. Belland, living in the county

Maury's advertisement in the Missouri Gazette for June 9, 1819. (Courtesy, *Missouri Historical Society of St. Louis.*)

the large amounts of money involved in some of his transactions, as it appears from documentary material about him in the Missouri Historical Society of St. Louis.

Maury's case is another proof of the difficulty the historian finds at every step when trying to identify names which seem to be Italian. In the *Dictionary of American Biography,* for instance, one finds more than one noted man named Maury, all from Tennessee, but none of them seems to be of Italian origin. In the case of Evariste Maury, however, we have his own statement regarding his place of birth.

FROM LOUISIANA TO MICHIGAN

A larger number of Italians must have engaged in business in Louisiana, even if they did not have the same opportunities they could find in fur trading west of St. Louis. Unfortunately, not much printed material is available, nor have we been able to conduct a personal search in state and city archives, both in Louisiana proper and in the West Indies.

Nevertheless, from the meagre data at our disposal, it appears evident that quite a few Italians were living in New Orleans as early as 1805, as it appears from the names listed in the city directory for that year. Other information we gain from memoirs and travel accounts, like Cipriani's *Memorie della Mia Vita,* from which we learn that his father had a wholesale house in the city between 1801 and 1806, or from the journal of James L. Cathcart, who tells us of a native of Trieste who lived in Bayou Plaquemine in 1819 and was granted a franchise for maintaining a ferry service across the bayou. His name was Giovanni Questi. Some time later, as we have noted on page 172, Louis Raggio spent five years as a pilot on the Mississippi River before he moved to California in 1847.

The 1838 directory lists a number of Italians in business in New Orleans, including J. H. Vigo, the nephew of the famous Colonel, who operated a grog shop. Others owned grocery stores, dry goods stores, coffee houses, tailor shops, and similar small businesses. One M. S. Cucullu was president of the Merchants' Insurance Company (capital $300,000) and director of the Levee Steam Cotton Press Company, in which we find, also as a director, H. Gally, vice-consul of Sicily. J. A. Barelli was director of the Gas Bank and Eagle Insurance Company. L. D. Coco was cashier of the Avoyelles branch of the Union Bank of Louisiana. G. Rossi earned his living as an apothecary (druggist). Mondelli, the painter, operated a wholesale and retail store in which he sold paints, oils, glass, and various other products. Vito Viti was listed as an importer of fancy goods. He was in all probability the same Vito Viti who later moved to Philadelphia, where he died on June 5, 1874, less than a month after he had secured the approval of a state law against vagrant children. (*Eco d'Italia,* May 16, 1874, and Philadelphia papers, June 6, 1874.) In the same directory we find J. D'Ambrogio as First Lieutenant of the Orleans Carabineers, F. Generelly as First Lieutenant of the Orleans Dragoons and A. Mondelli, the painter, as captain of the Orleans Lancers. In the 1845 directory Mondelli is listed as head of the Grand Lodge of the I.O.F. of Louisiana. By the time of the Civil War, the retail fruit, vegetable, fish and oyster trade was "almost exclusively in the hands of the Italians, two thirds of whom are engaged in this business." (*Eco d'Italia,* March 5, 1869.) By that time a number of well-to-do Italian merchants had sold out their businesses "at a great sacrifice" and left for Mexico because of the many restrictions imposed by the military authorities. (*Eco d'Italia,* Feb. 11, 1865.)

Moving up North, we find a number of Italian small businessmen listed in the St. Louis city directory for 1848: grocers, barkeepers, confectioners, one tinner, one paper hanger, one importer of cigars, one shoemaker, two owners of fruit stores, one drayman, one soda manufacturer, and one peddler. There were also several physicians, as already noted in the preceding chapter, and one attorney, Philip Mauro.

Even in Detroit we find a sawyer as early as 1837, a carpenter in 1845, and the ever-present maker of plaster of Paris figures in 1850. In Cleveland the earliest businessman with an Italian, or apparently-Italian, name found by us is one Joseph De Core, boot and shoemaker, who announced the opening of his shop in the *Cleaveland Register* for August 14, 1819.

THE GRASSELLI CHEMICAL COMPANY

Before the advent of the railroad, Cincinnati was more accessible than Cleveland, Detroit, or Chicago, because it could be reached by water through the Mississippi and the Ohio Rivers. As we have seen on page 166, there was an Italian consul in Cincinnati as early as 1835, obviously because either there was a sizeable Italian community or because, as it seems more likely, there was considerable trade with Italy. At any rate, it was in Cincinnati that Eugene Ramiro Grasselli established a small chemical manufacturing plant in 1839.

The son of Giovanni Angelo Grasselli, a chemist from the small town of Torno, on the Lake of Como, Italy, who had emigrated to Strasbourg, Alsace-Lorraine, Eugene arrived in 1836, settling in Cincinnati three years later. Under the management of his son, Caesar A. Grasselli, who was born in Cincinnati in 1850, the family business expanded considerably until it was moved to Cleveland, where it became one of the largest industrial firms in the country.

One of the captains of industry who made Cleveland a manufacturing center, Caesar A. Grasselli was president of two savings banks and a director of several large corporations. In 1910 King Victor Emmanuel of Italy conferred upon him the Cross of Chevalier of the Crown of Italy. The town of Grasselli, Indiana, was named after the founder of the family in the United States.

IN THE EAST

It is not possible to say how many business men of Italian birth or extraction were active in the East before or shortly after 1800. The local city directories ordinarily would be the best source of information, but not in the case of foreign names. A change in a letter of the alphabet, the addition of a vowel or a consonant, would transform a name to the point that its origin is completely lost. Who could, for instance, guess from the listing of Anthony Trepan in the 1789 New York directory that the correct name was Trapani? Ravera, who later became consul of Genoa in Philadelphia, is listed as Revira, a name which would seem more Portuguese than Italian.

Nevertheless, between 1787 and 1793 we find a number of Italian names in the directories published in New York in those years. Names like those of John Grandine, "cordwainer" (shoemaker); Anthony Leto, hair-dresser; Roderick La Testa, baker; John Roma, sail maker; John Annelly, gunsmith; Evangelist Chighizala, mariner; Petro Castelli, Italian stay-maker; Mrs. Ferrari (Farrari, Ferrara) operator of a boarding house. The names which could be either Spanish, Italian, or Portuguese are more numerous.

Limiting ourselves to men who, we know, were born in Italy, we might begin with the Milanese scene-painter, Charles Ciceri, about whom Dunlap has left us a rather long account in his *History of the American Theater*. Ciceri's life was typical of that of many other Italians of hi day who sought adventure abroad. After roaming through France and Belgium and serving three months in the French cavalry, he enlisted in a regiment destined for St. Domingo, where he spent several years until he returned to Europe. Later he decided to carry some merchandise to St. Domingo, but his ship was wrecked near the Bahamas, he lost everything and finally was carried to Providence, R. I., eventually finding his way to Philadelphia and New York. According to Dunlap, after some years as a scene painter, Ciceri began to import French merchandise and apparently was successful, for later he returned to Europe with a competence.

In New York, with the exception of Oroondates Mauran (1791-1846) who, as we have seen, was one of the owners of the Italian Opera House building and of the Staten Island Ferry, in partnership with Commodore Cornelius Vanderbilt (he was also one of the oldest members of the Union Club), we do not know of any Italian who became prominent in business or finance until we come to Fabbri and Morosini, as related below.

One could, of course, mention scores of men who operated small businesses (how small we do not know). Men like Anthony Trapani (1757-1840), a native of the province of Naples, who began the importation of Italian oranges and lemons; Philip Cioffi, a musician who became a distiller (1828); Dominic Mazzinghi, another musician who sold pianos (1803); Theobold Monzani, who manufactured flutes and other instruments between 1835 and 1865; Salvator Rosa, who was awarded a prize for his display of musical instruments at the Mechanics' Fair in 1857; Gaspar Godone, piano maker (1830); a number of men and women engaged in the making of theatrical costumes; a lithographer named Risso (1833); several operators of wax museums; several shopkeepers (grocers and fruit dealers); quite a few confectioners; a number of importers of alabaster and marble ornaments and statues; and then hairdressers, shoemakers, and what not—but not many.

MAKERS OF THERMOMETERS AND BAROMETERS

One line of business in which the Italians became leaders was the manufacture of thermometers and barometers, beginning with Joseph Donegany, who announced his arrival from Philadelphia in the *Daily Advertiser* of New York on October 15, 1787. Another pioneer in the same business was Giuseppe Tagliabue, the man to whom Meucci assigned one of his patents in 1875 and who is said to have offered Meucci one dollar for a pair of binoculars worth two hundred dollars. He came over about 1831 from Como and was succeeded by his son, Charles J. Tagliabue, who was born in New York in 1852. The firm is still in existence in Brooklyn, but, so far as we know, no Italians are connected with it in an executive capacity. Another man from Como, also a friend of Meucci, Gaetano Negretti, was manufacturing barometers in New York in the 1850's.

Making thermometers and barometers, like plaster of Paris figurines, seems to have been a specialty with the Italians in those days. As early as 1822-24, two of them were active in this line of industry in New Orleans. One of them was Pier Antonio Maspero "of Italy" who died in that city at the age of 50 in September, 1822 (*Louisiana Courier*, Sept. 17, 1822) and was listed as a maker of barometers in *Paxton's City Directory* for that year; the other was one Peter Bello, who had a full-page advertisement in the city directory for 1823-24 and died in New Orleans at the age of 43 in 1824. (*Louisiana Courier*, September 16, 1824.) More, we suppose, could be found in other cities during the same period.

Charles Del Vecchio, the same man who became one of New York's first fire commissioners in 1839, was listed, together with John and Joseph Del Vecchio, as manufacturers of looking glasses in 1833. He also did all the gold emblems, mouldings and ornaments for the Italian Opera House on Leonard Street, his mirrors especially having been of a superior quality. (See Ormsbee, T. H., *The Story of American Furniture*, N. Y., 1938, 40-44.) Also in the same line of business was Joseph Bonfanti, whose gift and jewelry store in downtown Broadway was one of the largest in the city at the time of his accidental death in 1838. Nearby, one Stoppani operated an establishment which was patronized for its bath tubs, which in those days were something of a rarity in private homes.

In the food business, a Genoese was manufacturing macaroni on Pearl Street in the 1820's (Carter, N. H., *Letters from Europe*, N. Y. 1827, II, 43). In 1865 A. Zerega had a macaroni establishment in Brooklyn. The importation of Italian food products as a regular business, however, began with the arrival of the Italian exiles in the 1830's and 1840's. One of them, the famous General Joseph Avezzana (1797-1879), a native of Chieri, near Genoa, came to New York in 1834 after fighting with the Spanish

GENERAL AVEZZANA
(From *Gems for the Fireside,* 1854)

and Mexican armies. Here he worked as a commission merchant until 1848, when he returned to Italy to serve as minister of war in the ill-fated Roman Republic. Back in the United States in 1849, thanks to his American passport, he remained until 1861. His daughter, the widow of General Saint-Seigne, died in New York in 1925.

Still another political exile who became a prosperous businessman in New York was Giuseppe Albinola, a martyr of the Spielberg, who died in New York in 1883. (*New York Times* and *Evening Post,* editorial note, both of June 6, 1883.)

The first importer of Italian food products on a large scale seems to have been Michele Pastacaldi, a native of Leghorn, who died in New York in 1862 at the age of 47. (*Eco d'Italia,* Nov. 29, 1862.) Also noted in those days was Ottaviano Fabbricotti, who died in 1869, also in New York. (*Eco d'Italia,* Sept. 10 and Dec. 6, 1869.)

By 1885 Italian trade with the United States had developed to the point that an Italian chamber of commerce became a necessity in San Francisco, where one was organized in that year. On January 12, 1888, another Italian chamber of commerce was established in New York, with a membership that included several large firms, like that of Antonio Zucca, who came from his native Trieste in 1867 and was doing a business of more than a million dollars a year by the end of the century. He served as president of the Italian Chamber of Commerce in New York from 1899 to 1908.

IN THE SILK BUSINESS

Ever since the days of Oglethorpe, a number of Italians have tried to introduce silk culture in America, but sooner or later their experiments have failed. About 1837, Luigi Tinelli (1799-1873), already noted as United States Consul at Oporto, tried the breeding of silk worms, at first at Weehawken, then at Albany and Poughkeepsie, but he was no more successful than the others. A few years later, in 1869, an Italian-Swiss, Vincenzo Tagliasecchi, established a small plant at St. Charles, Mo., but we doubt if he met with success. (*Eco d'Italia,* July 16, 1869.) Tinelli, however, developed a prosperous import-export business. Later, as related in the next chapter, he served as a colonel in the Union Army. (See Castelli, G., *Luigi Tinelli,* Milan, 1949; *Eco d'Italia,* May 31, 1873; Sept. 9, 1865.)

In more recent years a number of silk mills were established in New Jersey and in Pennsylvania by Italian capitalists, or by immigrants who made their small fortunes in the United States. Among the pioneers we shall recall Joseph Ratti and Celestino Piva. Ratti, an uncle of the late Pope Pius XI, founded the Bloomsburg Silk Mill at Bloomsburg, Pa., in 1888 and several other mills in nearby towns. In 1905 he donated a hospital which at first was named Joseph Ratti Hospital, but in 1912 the name was changed into Bloomsburg Hospital, to dispel the impression that it was a private institution. At least that was the reason advanced for the change. He died in 1906 at the age of 61 in his native Rogeno, near Como, Italy. Celestino Piva, who died in 1936, was one of the leading businessmen of New York at the beginning of the century. He owned or controlled four large silk mills at Allentown, Pa., West Hoboken, Hackensack, N. J., and Norwich, Conn., with 2,000 looms and 2,500 employees, of whom about 1,000 were Italians. His importation of raw silk alone amounted to more than $8,000,000 a year. He is best remembered, however, as the publisher of a daily in the Italian language and as the principal supporter of the first Italian Home and Dispensary on West Houston Street in 1904.

The Jersey Shore, Pa., silk mill, one of several plants owned and operated by Giuseppe Ratti in 1900.

IN THE RESTAURANT BUSINESS

Today we all know that a considerable number of the finest restaurants in the United States are owned and operated by natives of Italy. A century or so ago, one could find, at least in New York, a few first-class Italian restaurants like Palmo's, La Maison Dorée, owned by a Piedmontese named Francesco Martinez, or the Moretti Cafe. The most famous of them all, of course, was Delmonico's, operated by two brothers and four nephews who were born in Italian Switzerland. Their first restaurant was opened at Beaver and William Street in 1835, followed by others along Broadway and Fifth Avenue. Like other Swiss citizens of Italian blood, both in New York and California, the Delmonico brothers took an interest in the affairs of the Italian community. (*Eco d'Italia,* Dec. 21, 1865.)

EARLY FINANCIERS

As we have said, the only natives of Italy to gain positions of prominence in business or finance during the 19th century in New York were the Fabbri brothers and Giovanni Morosini. To them we might add Louis Herman Augustus Zerega di Zerega, who was born at St. Thomas, in the West Indies, in 1833 and died in New York about 1910. A member of the firm of Cromwell and Zerega, later L. H. Zerega and Co., he was one of the founders of the New York Cotton Exchange. His daughter Paula, who died in England in 1946, married the son of the fourth Duke of New Castle.

The older of the two Fabbri brothers, Egisto, came to New York from his native Florence in the late 40's, followed by his brother Ernesto a few years later. In 1852 they were in business at 167 Broadway, as we learn from a plan they had submitted to President Fillmore for a 40-foot statuary group "Columbus Unveiling the New to the Old World" which was to be erected in Washington. (MS., *Buffalo Historical Society.*) A quarter of a century later, in 1876, he became a member of the banking firm of Drexel, Morgan and Company, which he represented on the board of directors of the Pennsylvania Railroad. He was also a director of numerous other companies, including the Edison Electric and Light Company, of which he was treasurer. He retired in 1885, "to Pierpont's great regret, because he was very fond of him". (Satterlee, H. L., *J. Pierpont Morgan,* N. Y., 1939, 156, 197, 208, 234.) He was also treasurer of the first Metropolitan Opera House Company.

His brother Ernesto entered the fur house of John Randall and Company as a clerk, but soon became a partner and married Randall's daughter. In 1865 he became a member of the firm of Fabbri and Chauncey, commission merchants, of which Egisto was the senior partner. He was a director of several large corporations, including the Edison Company, the U. S. Rolling Stock Company, the Orient Mutual Insurance Company, and the Central and South American Telephone Company. He died in New York in 1883. (*Evening Post,* July 3, 1883.) His daughter, Cora Fabbri, died in Florence in 1892, as we have noted. Another son of his, Ernesto G. Fabbri, who married the granddaughter of William H. Vanderbilt, died in California in 1943, at the age of 69. Both Egisto and Ernesto G. Fabbri, Sr., took an active interest in the affairs of the Italian community, unlike many prominent Italian-Americans of today.

Giovanni Morosini was another poor boy who became one of the chief stockholders of the Erie Railroad Company, a millionaire banker, and the partner of J. Gould. He died in 1918. Of his children, Giulia, famed for her beauty and expert horsemanship, married a policeman whom she later divorced. She died in 1932 leaving more than one million dollars in cash and a most valuable collection of European and Oriental art, including many rare coins and a notable group of early European arms and armor which she bequeathed to the Metropolitan Museum of Art, together with the famous Morosini Mansion at Riverdale. Her sister Victoria died, also in New York, in 1933, after many years of seclusion. Having incurred her father's wrath for eloping with her coachman (in 1884), she was compelled to go to work as a chorus girl, her husband becoming a car conductor. Two years later they parted. In 1906 she was found in the convent of the Sisters of St. Joseph at Rutland, Vt., under the name of Marie Baldwin. Morosini's last son, Giovanni P., died in New York at the age of 75 in 1935. Another son, Attilio, had died in 1924. All were buried at their mausoleum in Woodlawn Cemetery. (See *New York Times Index* under the above dates.)

IN PHILADELPHIA

In Philadelphia one could begin with that musician-cafe owner, Vincent M. Pelosi, who had a restaurant in Philadelphia before he moved across the river to Camden in 1788. (See facsimile.) Or one could mention some of the names listed in the various issues of the local city directory between 1799 and 1802. Da Ponte in his *Memoirs* mentions at least two Italian businessmen in the City of Brotherly Love, the confectioner Astolfi and Joseph Mussi, the friend of Bishop Carroll, as well as of Count Castiglioni, who remembered him in his *Travels in the United*

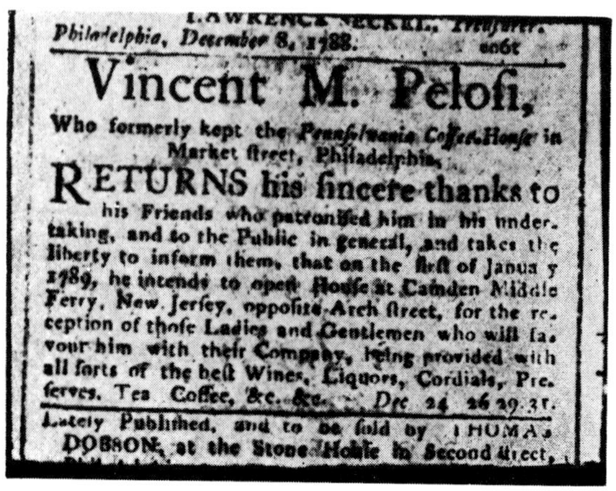

Philadelphia, December 8, 1788.

Vincent M. Peloſi,

Who formerly kept the *Pennſylvania Coffee-Houſe* in Market ſtreet, Philadelphia,

RETURNS his ſincere thanks to his Friends who patroniſed him in his undertaking, and to the Public in general, and takes the liberty to inform them, that on the firſt of January 1789, he intends to open Houſe at Camden Middle Ferry, New Jerſey, oppoſite Arch ſtreet, for the reception of thoſe Ladies and Gentlemen who will favour him with their Company, being provided with all ſorts of the beſt Wines, Liquors, Cordials, Preſerves, Tea Coffee, &c. &c. Dec 24 26 29 31.

Lately Publiſhed, and to be ſold by THOMAS DOBSON, at the Stone Houſe in Second ſtreet,

Pelosi's advertisement in the *Pennsylvania Packet* for Dec. 31, 1788.

States. We shall, however, limit ourselves to only one man, Paolo Busti, veritably one of the most outstanding executives in America during the first half of the nineteenth century.

PAOLO BUSTI
Founder of Buffalo, N. Y.

PAOLO BUSTI

Paolo Busti, founder of the city of Buffalo, and a native of Milan, Italy, came to America from Amsterdam about 1798, as the general agent of the Holland Land Company, which at that time owned some 3,000,000 acres of land in the northern part of New York State and Pennsylvania. Why he should be considered the rightful founder of Buffalo has already been told in our book *The Italians in America Before the Civil War*. Here we shall add only a brief passage from a biographical sketch of Busti which we have found in manuscript form in the archives of the Historical Society of Pennsylvania. It was written in 1886 by one Loren Blodget, who learned many of the facts about Busti from a relative who was a neighbor of Busti and knew him personally. It reads:

"The first General Agent of the purchasers of land made by citizens of Amsterdam, Holland, in Western New York and Western Pennsylvania was Theophilus Cazenove, who acted as such from 1793 to 1798; but he did little toward the settlement of the lands, and he was succeeded in 1799 by Paul Busti, who established his general office in Philadelphia beginning at once an active system of survey and settlement of all these lands. He directed all the work of Joseph Ellicott, the chief surveyor who had gone to Canandaigua, New York, in 1798, and who subsequently laid out in proper form all the lands of the Holland Land Company's purchase in New York State. Agent Busti also had the direction of the survey and settlement of the purchases in Western Pennsylvania made by the same Amsterdam merchants, and sent H. J. Heinekoper as the first resident agent to Cassewago, now Meadville, in 1804. From this time forward, and during the entire period of the settlement of the seven or eight large counties occupied by the Holland Land Company as proprietors, the firm and enlightened policy of Agent Busti is to be credited with all the important results. These liberal acts of management and settlement of the millions of acres embraced in these purchases, and forming now the richest portions of Western New York and Western or Northwestern Pennsylvania, constitute the enduring memorial of Paul Busti, who, during all this period was a resident and prominent citizen of Philadelphia."

Busti, wrote the *American Daily Advertiser* of Philadelphia on August 17, 1824, at the time of his death, "possessed a refinement of manners—a comprehensive knowledge of things, and an intelligent spirit, which contributed to the delight of the learned and the pleasure of social intercourse. He spoke several of the European languages well, which enabled him to maintain a correspondence with foreigners of the first distinction . . .In the infancy of these settlements he extended every patronage and encouragement to promote their success. To his judicious management, prudence and circumspection, and to the liberal policy, uniformly enforced, are these regions, so lately a wilderness, mainly indebted for their rapid progress in population and improvement—rapid, perhaps, beyond a parallel and now assuming the first rank in physical strength and respectability."

Busti, we might add, was also one of the first prominent real estate operators in the Philadelphia area.

IN THE SOUTH

In the South, outside of New Orleans, and besides the silk men who came over with Oglethorpe in 1732 or the descendants of the Florida settlers of 1768, the first Italians in business found by us shortly after the Revolution are Formicola, Strobia, one Bonisola, and some of the men of came with Mazzei in 1773.

Serafino Formicola, a Neapolitan, is said to have come over with Governor Dunmore. Shortly after the hostilities he owned a hotel, the Charlton House, in Williamsburg, which is said to have been the fashionable meeting place of those days. (Hawthorne, H., *Williamsburg, Old and New*.) About 1780, when he was 37 years old, he moved to Richmond, where he owned the famous Eagle Tavern, on two different locations. It was patronized by Washington and other leaders. At that inn Aaron Burr was arraigned before Chief Justice Marshall in 1807. (*Diary of George Washington*, April 26, 1786; Dumbauld, E., *Thomas Jefferson, American Tourist;* 1946, 42-46.)

Formicola married one Matilda Newman in 1774. They had one daughter, Evelyn Formicola, who is said to have been one of the leading belles of Williamsburg. She married Stewart Bankhead, one of whose descendants is said to be now a leading motion picture actress. Evelyn's daughter, at any rate, married Col. Henry Garnett of Westmoreland in 1817 and her son, Thomas Bankhead, the grandson of

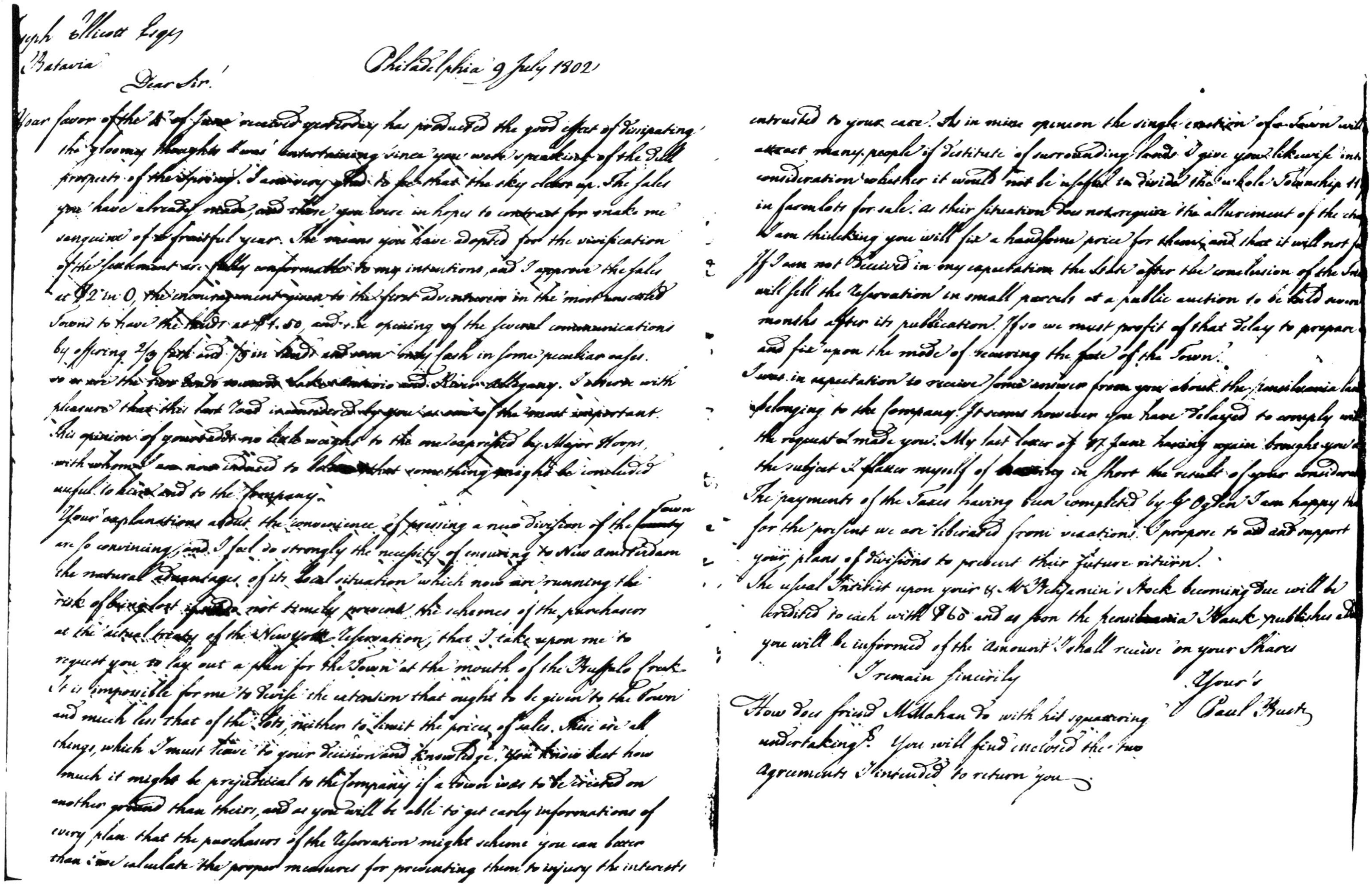

Joseph Ellicott Esqr
Batavia

Philadelphia 9 July 1802

Dear Sir

Your favor of the 8th of June received yesterday has produced the good effect of dissipating the gloomy thoughts I was entertaining since you wrote speaking of the [illegible] prospects of the Spring. I am very glad to feel that the sky clears up. The sales you have already made, and those you were in hopes to contract for make me sanguine of a fruitful year. The means you have adopted for the [illegible] of the settlement are fully conformable to my intentions, and I approve the sales at $2 in 10, the encouragement given to the first adventurers in the most unsettled Towns to have the land at $1.50 and the opening of the several communications by offering 2/3 cash and 1/3 in land and even only cash in some peculiar cases. [illegible] Lake Ontario and River Allegany. I observe with pleasure that this last road is considered by you as one of the most important. This opinion of yours adds no little weight to the one apprised by Major Hoops, with whom I am now induced to believe that something might be concluded useful to him and to the Company.

Your explanations about the convenience of pressing a new division of the Town are so convincing, and I feel so strongly the necessity of ensuring to New Amsterdam the natural advantages of its local situation which now are running the risk of being lost if we do not timely prevent the schemes of the purchasers at the actual treaty of the New York Reservation, that I take upon me to request you to lay out a plan for the Town at the mouth of the Buffalo Creek. It is impossible for me to devise the extension that ought to be given to the Town and much less that of the Lots, neither to limit the prices of sales. These are all things, which I must leave to your decision and knowledge. You know best how much it might be prejudicial to the Company if a town was to be erected on another ground than theirs, and as you will be able to get early informations of every plan that the purchasers of the Reservation might scheme you can better than me calculate the proper measures for preventing them to injure the interests entrusted to your care. As in mine opinion the single erection of a Town will attract many people if destitute of surrounding lands I give you likewise into consideration whether it would not be useful to divide the whole Township 11 in farm lots for sale. As their situation does not require the allurement of the [illegible] I am thinking you will fix a handsome price for them, and that it will not [illegible] If I am not deceived in my expectation the State after the conclusion of the [illegible] will sell the Reservation in small parcels at a public auction to be held [illegible] months after its publication. If so we must profit of that delay to prepare and fix upon the mode of securing the fate of the Town.

I was in expectation to receive some answer from you about the Pennsilvania land belonging to the Company. It seems however you have delayed to comply with the request I made you. My last letter of 17 June having again brought you [illegible] the subject I flatter myself of [illegible] in short the result of your [illegible]

The payments of the Taxes having been completed by G. Ogden I am happy that for the present we are liberated from vexations. I propose to aid and support your plans of divisions to prevent their future return.

The usual Interest upon your & Mr Benjamin's stock becoming due will be credited to each with $60 and as soon the Pennsilvania Bank publishes [illegible] you will be informed of the amount I shall receive on your Shares

I remain sincerely

Yours
Paul Busti

How does friend McMahan do with his squattering undertakings? You will find inclosed the two Agreements I intended to return you

Photostat copy of the letter Paul Busti sent to Joseph Ellicott, his surveyor, on July 9, 1802, authorizing him to lay out a plan for the city of Buffalo. On July 26 Busti cancelled his instructions, but on December 14 he confirmed them once more "having received from Holland the long wished for almost unlimited authority of acting according to the best of my knowledge." Notice, beginning with the 15th line on the left, the words: "Your explanation about the pressing of a new division of the town are so convincing and I feel so strongly the necessity of insuring to New Amsterdam the natural advantages of its local situation which now are running the risk of being lost if we do not timely prevent the schemes of the purchasers at the actual treaty of the New York reservation, that *I take upon me to request you to lay out a plan for the town at the Buffalo Creek* (italics ours). (Courtesy, *Buffalo Historical Society.*)

the Italian immigrant, was killed at the Battle of Chancellorville. Be that as it may, Formicola became a man of consequence, just as the Marquis of Chastellux had foreseen when she stopped at his Richmond inn in 1781. In 1786 he subscribed the sum of $500 towards the erection of Quesnay's Academy of Science and Fine Arts. (Meagher, M., *History of Education in Richmond*, 1939, 22; Mordecai, S., *Richmond in By-Gone Days*, 1860, 206; Crozier's *Virginia County Records*, Vol. 9, 118; Little's *History of Richmond*, 73; *Virginia Magazine of History and Biography*, Vol. 10, 101, Vol. 27, 339, Vol. 30, 245; *William and Mary Quarterly*, II, 114; *Virginia Gazette* (Purdie), January 19, 1776; Chastellux, *Travels in North America*, 1828 ed., 276; *Virginia Independent Chronicle*, June 20, 1787; Schoepf, *Travels in the Confederation*, 1911, 64.)

Giovanni Strobia seems to have been one of the gardeners who came with Mazzei in 1773. From a letter that Jefferson wrote to Bellini on April 26, 1799, we learn that he "has got rich as a grocer in Richmond . . . is in flourishing circumstances". His name appears frequently in the *Virginia Calendar of State Papers* (Vols. 4, 6, 8 and 9), between 1785 and 1802, when he resigned as a captain of the militia. He died in 1809. (*Richmond Enquirer*, March 17, 1809.) His son, John H. Strobia (1785-1856), married Ann Marie Lambert, the eldest daughter of Col. (later General) D. Lambert, mayor of Richmond. When he died he was "buried with honors by the Richmond Light Infantry Blues of which he was active and later honorary member". He was one of the city's leading citizens (*Richmond Despatch*, Oct. 16, 1856) and is said to have been one of the patrons of local artists, including Robert M. Scully. (Dunlap, *Rise and Progress of the Arts*, III, 194.) Another of Giovanni's sons, Francis Strobia, was born in 1787 and died in 1815.

Jefferson, in his letter to Bellini mentioned above, tells also of Anthony Giannini, who "has raised a large family, married several of them, & after thriving for a while has become embarassed . . . Francis, his brother in law & Anthony Molina have done terribly well." Anthony Giannini in 1784 bought land on Buck Island Creek. "In 1792 he petitioned for liberty to build a mill on that stream. One of the same name, no doubt a son, became a Baptist minister in 1807." (Woods, E., *Albemarle County in Virginia*, 1901, 360.) Woods also mentions one Francis Modena, a carriage maker by trade, who died in 1826.

Antonio Sylvester Bilisoly (Bonisola, or Buonisola—literally translated, "good island") was born at Ajaccio, like Napoleon, in 1750, came to America with De Grasse in 1777 and served at Yorktown. After a brief residence in Haiti, where he married Adelaide Accinelli, the daughter of an exiled Acadian who owned a coffee and sugar plantation, he settled in Norfolk in 1799, later moving to Portsmouth, Va., where he died on October 6, 1845. His son, Joseph A., a native of Norfolk, was engaged in shipbuilding for about four years, but later became a merchant. Three of Joseph's sons became physicians. (*Eminent and Representative Men of Virginia and the District of Columbia*, 1893, 397-399.)

FERDINAND PHINIZY

Ferdinand Phinizy (Finizzi), a native of Parma, Italy, also come with the French, with whom he served during the Revolution. After the war he settled in Georgia, where he became a prominent merchant. During the War with the Indians (1792-1794) he equipped a company of soldiers and received the rank of captain at first, and major later. He died in 1818 at the age of 57, leaving an estate of $120,000 and five children (three sons and two daughters). Their descendants have been bankers, prominent lawyers, planters, publishers of newspapers, trustees of educational institutions, directors of railroad and insurance companies, and civic leaders. One of Ferdinand's sons, John Phinizy, graduated from the University of Georgia in 1811, served as mayor of Augusta, Ga., and was a prominent banker and merchant, as we have seen in the preceding chapter. (See also F. P. Calhoun, *The Phinizy Family in America*.)

GIUSEPPE VANNINI AND LUIGI CHITTI

Another pioneer settler in the South was Giuseppe Vannini of Florence, who worked as a surveyor in Virginia as early as 1806 and as a captain "in a company of heroes" during the War of 1812. The good friend of President Monroe, he is said to have submitted to him a plan for the accumulation of capital (apparently a lottery) which is said to have been accepted (Monroe to Vannini, December

FERDINAND PHINIZY

29, 1815) and put into operation in several states. In 1831 he returned to Italy and lived in Naples until 1839, when he came back hoping to salvage whatever he could from the failure of the Bank of the United States where he had his savings. He died in Brooklyn on October 17, 1853. (*Eco d'Italia,* Oct. 22, 1853, June 3-4, 1883; *New York Times,* Oct. 19, 1853, Evening Post, Oct. 18, 1853.)

Vannini reminds us of another financier, Luigi Chitti (1784-1853), a native of Castelnuovo in the province of Reggio Calabria, who died in New York less than two months before, on September 2, 1853.

Chitti was probably the most distinguished Italian economist to come to the United States as a political exile. After the fall of the Republic of Naples, of which he was secretary of finance in 1821, he escaped abroad and for a while taught political economy and finance at the universities of Madrid and Brussels, serving also as president of the Bank of Ghent, Belgium. While in Europe he wrote a number of books on political economy and finance, which can be found in the Library of Congress and in the British Museum. He was especially well known in Great Britain, where he shared the friendship of Cobden and Robert Peel. Cavour also numbered him among his friends. Here he contributed to American publications, including the *Merchant's Magazine* in which at least one of his articles appeared in December, 1851. When he died, a poor man, the Italian Society of New York donated a lot for his grave in the Bay Cemetery, near Greenville. The leading Italian refugees in the city at that time took part in his funeral, with Foresti delivering the funeral oration. But thirty years later no tombstone nor any other marker indicated his place of burial. (*Enciclopedia Italiana Treccani; Eco d'Italia,* Dec. 13, 1851, January 10, 1852; Feb. 18, 1883.)

OTHER PIONEERS

A search of the various city directories throughout the East, as well as on the Pacific Coast, will reveal an impressive number of Italians in business before 1880, that is, before immigration from Italy acquired impressive proportions. Most of them were operators of one-man shops, such as barbers, shoemakers, grocers, fruit dealers. Occasionally one finds an Italian in an unusual occupation for his race in those days, like one William Pardua who was a coach builder in Bridgeport in 1855, or one John Cairoli who was listed as a manufacturer of teeth in the Bridgeport city directory for 1869. In the same publication, for the same year, one Attilio Zaiotti is listed as chemist and one Wentzel Malletta as stone cutter. In California, as early as 1856 we find the firm of F. Argenti, Cavallier and Co., Paris, bankers, with offices on Montgomery Street, one door north of Jackson (*Evening Bulletin,* April 1, 1856). Argenti may have been the same F. Felice Argenti who came over as a political exile in 1836.

The trunk which Phinizy bought at Naples before coming to America with Rochambeau's forces.

Worthy of notice in the East is Giovanni Battista Sartori, who began the manufacture of calico and later of macaroni in the early years of the last century. Joseph Bonaparte, King of Spain, is said to have been godfather to one of his fourteen children, one of whom, as related in the next chapter, became commodore in the United States Navy, and another an assistant surgeon, also in the Navy. (Stock, L., American Consuls to the Papal States, *Cath. Hist. Soc. Rec.* New Series, IX, No. 3; *A History of Trenton,* 2 Vols., Princeton, 1929, I, 447, II, 660.)

A RAILROAD BUILDER IN TEXAS

The first Italian merchant in Texas was in all probability Angelo Navarro, a native of Corsica, who was one of the founders of the city of San Antonio in 1777. His son, Jose' Antonio Navarro, already mentioned by us, was one of first land commissioners to serve in 1834-35 and a member of the convention that declared the independence of Texas from Mexico. (*The Writings of Sam Houston* ed. by A. W. William and E. C. Barker, Vol. VII, 396, note 1.) Still another pioneer merchant was one Cassiano, or Cassini, who moved to Texas from New Orleans in 1812. Half a century later another Italian mentioned by Martin Maris in his *Souvenirs D'Amerique* (Brussels, 1863) operated a hotel in a small Texas town. Adolfo Rossi mentions an Italian who owned a clothing store in New Mexico in the 1870's. However, one must come to 1879 to find a prominent Italian business man in the Southwest, like Count Giuseppe Telfener, a poor man who rose to riches in his native Italy.

We do not know much about Giuseppe Telfener, a native of Foggia, who was made a count by King Victor Emmanuel II in 1877. By that time he was a millionaire, and the owner of Villa Potenziani and other palaces in Rome. In 1879 he married the sister of the millionaire John William Mackay (1831-1902), the Irish immigrant who also rose from poverty to riches.

Not long after his marriage Telfener planned to send some 5,000 Italians to Texas, but of the 1,000 who got there, about 700 had been compelled to return to the East, or found themselves stranded, by January, 1882. Telfener had purchased several hundred thousand acres of land at 75 cents an acre in El Paso County and had built 92 miles of a projected New York, Texas and Mexican Railway, from Rosenberg Junction to Victoria, but was unable to continue and abandoned everything in 1884, when he returned to Rome. Three years later his creditors obtained a judgement for $384,900 for non-fulfilment of land purchase, and the railway became a part of the Southern Pacific System. (*New York Tribune*, April 1, 1879; *Eco d'Italia*, January 31, 1882; *New York Times*, March 10, 1887; Spreti, *Enciclopedia Storico-Nobiliare Italiana*, VI, 567.)

IN BANKING

Since the days of the Fabbri brothers and Morosini a number of natives of Italy have risen to prominence in banking and finance. Among the pioneers we will recall only Salvatore Cantoni, a native of Venice, who arrived in 1860 and became a member of the New York Stock Exchange in 1879; Joseph Francolini, a native of Corleto Perticara, who came over in 1886, and ten years later founded the Italian Savings Bank of which he became president; Armando Pedrini of Bologna, one of the founders of the Bank of Italy, and later vice-president of Transamerica Corporation; Francesco Belgrano, who died in 1928 in San Francisco, where he was outstanding in financial circles.

Among the sons of Italian immigrants, the foremost name, of course, is that of Amedeo Peter Giannini, the giant of the West, and the founder of the Bank of Italy of California which now, under the name of Bank of America, has become the largest banking institution in the world. (See Dana, J., *A. P. Giannini;* Joseph M., Big Bull of the West, *Saturday Evening Post,* Sept. 13 & ff., 1947.)

Among the sons of Italian immigrants who became outstanding bankers one might recall John King Beretta, the son of a Milanese, who was born at Fort Smith, Ark., in 1861, founded the Bank of Laredo, Texas, in 1892, and became president of the National Bank of Commerce of San Antonio, Texas; Victor H. Rossetti, also the son of a poor immigrant, who became president of the Merchants Bank of Los Angeles, and was a director of numerous important corporations, until he died in 1946; James A. Bacigalupi, one of the early executives in the Bank of Italy; literally scores of bank officials from presidents and controllers down. One has only to go through the latest edition of the Bankers Directory to find an imposing list of banking executives of Italian extraction.

SINCE THE CIVIL WAR

Between the Revolution and the Civil War most of the Italian immigrants were artists, musicians, professional men of various types, political exiles, priests, soldiers. Here and there we find a man engaged in business pursuits, like Garibaldi, who for a short time worked for Antonio Meucci making candles, or the itinerant vendor of statuettes. Yet as early as 1851 there must have been a number of Italian laborers in New York City and vicinity, if *L'Eco d'Italia* on July 5th of that year published an advertisement calling for 500 workers needed in railroad construction in New York State and 200 in Staten Island. "Italians are preferred"—so the advertisement said.

After the Civil War mass immigration from Italy began, largely from the small towns and farm districts of the Peninsula. Unlike their predecessors, most of the new immigrants were unskilled workers, men without education and with a high degree of illiteracy, whose sole aim was to make a few thousand dollars as soon as possible and then get back to their native village. Of course, as we know now, it did not work out that way and sooner than they expected they decided to spend the rest of their lives in their adopted country. At any rate, because of various circumstances, such as language barriers, the self-imposed necessity of pinching the penny, employment possibilities, and other factors, the immigrant settled among the "paesani" (men from the same "paese" or town—by illation, from the same country) and formed the first little Italies in the United States. To cater to their needs a new class of tradesmen and artisans arose or found the possibility of plying at one's occupation: grocers, barbers, shoemakers, tailors, importers of food products, macaroni manufacturers, sausage makers, steamship ticket agents, labor contractors, foreign exchange dealers, publishers of weekly newspapers and magazines, and even teachers of music and languages.

Most of the immigrants, however, found employment as laborers in the construction or maintenance of our railroad system, in industry, and occasionally in commerce. Little by little they branched out, they learned the secrets of some industrial activity, especially in the manufacture of men's and women's clothes, or such items as concrete blocks. The fruit peddler became first the owner of a fruit store and later a commission merchant; the little grocer became an importer; the clothing worker became a subcontractor; the bricklayer or the mason became a road builder or general building contractor; the shoemaker developed into a shoe manufacturer; the man with some education became a real estate or insurance agent. With rare exceptions, everybody started on the proverbial "shoestring".

In recent years the progress of industrialization has acquired a quickened pace, with the sons of the immigrants pushing into such fields as foundries, manufacture of machines, electric appliances, steel products, making of radio and television sets (among the largest in the country), and what not.

The office of the Bank of Italy which A. P. Giannini opened in San Francisco soon after the disastrous earthquake of 1906. Out of the Bank of Italy was born the Bank of America, now (1952) the largest banking organization in the world.

IN AGRICULTURE AND IN MARITIME TRADE

Relatively few Italians, compared to the millions who have entered the United States during the last century, have engaged in agricultural pursuits. For one thing, the immigrants who arrived before World War I came over to make a little fortune and then go back to Italy; secondly, they could make more money working in a factory or as a railroad laborers than as a farm hands; finally, their inability to speak English forced them to live near people who could speak their language and who could come to their rescue in case of need. Climate or urge for sociability had nothing to do with it. Truck gardening, besides, has always appealed to the Italian, who finds a genuine joy in growing vegetables or fruits.

Notwithstanding the relatively small number of Italians in agriculture, their contribution to American living has been out of proportion to the value of their crops in dollars and cents. For the Italians, starting with Mazzei (and probably even before him), have introduced a variety of products which have changed American diet and contributed in no small measure to the health of the American people.

FATHER PIETRO BANDINI
(1853-1917)
Founder of Tontitown, Ark.

The first notable group of Italians to engage in agriculture in the United States settled around San Francisco, where about 300 of them were said to supply most of the vegetables consumed in that city as early as 1865. (*Eco d'Italia*, Dec. 9, 1865.) By 1920 they had increased to 30,000 for the whole state, or one third of the total number of farmers in California; we do not know, however, whether the children of Italian parentage were included. At present it is not uncommon to find Italians owning from 1,500 to 2,000 acres of land each, with some of them specializing in only one crop, such as lima beans, or artichokes, spinach, tomatoes, egg plants, cauliflowers, and so on. Although of late they have lost ground as owners of wineries, they still are among the largest growers of grapes in the country.

Other noteworthy Italian agricultural communities can be found near Bryan, Texas, Independence, La., Vineland and Hammonton, N. J., Fredonia and Canastota, N. Y., Valdese, and St. Helena, N. C., Daphne, Ala., Tontitown, Ark., Paw Paw, Mich., Rosati (formerly, Knobview) and Marshfield, Mo., Natchez, Shelby and nearby places in Mississippi, the entire Delta region of Louisiana, from Shreveport and Baton Rouge to the Gulf of Mexico. Near every large city in the country, besides, one is likely to find a number of small farms of 10 to 40 acres each owned by natives of Italy or by their sons. In the Mississippi Delta the Italians are said to have cleared and reclaimed 2,000,000 acres of land. In New York State alone in 1920 they owned 1,782 farms covering 103,142 acres for a total value of $14,380,236.

The Italians grow almost exclusively vegetables or fruits, which they send to the nearest market. There are, however, a few large cotton and sugar plantations in Louisiana and Texas, alfalfa farms in Southern California, and mushroom establishments near Philadelphia. Grapes, however, take the first place both in tonnage and dollar value.

(*Left*) An Italian family at Daphne, Ala., and (*right*) a view of Tontitown, Ark., at the beginning of the century.

An Italian farmer in his vineyard near Humboldt, Tenn., about 1900.

Among the leading Italian agriculturists of the past, it may be sufficient to mention Secondo Guasti, Andrea Sbarboro, L. Schiappa Pietra, Marco J. Fontana, P. C. Rossi, and finally the most outstanding of them all, Joseph Di Giorgio, who owned or controlled more than 40,000 acres of fruit land from California to Florida, at the time of his death in 1951.

As Prof. Lansen has said in his book *The Immigrant in American History*, the Italians "by patient experimentation introduced into commercial orchards fruits that the native had long attempted vainly to grow . . . American diet is healthier and more varied because of Italian gardeners and Italian cooks."

Farm scene at Vineland, N. J. a few years after its establisment.

BENI STABILI

—:o:—

DA VENDERSI

A

VINELAND.

TUTTI QUELLI CHE DESIDERANO PODERI.— Da vendersi a VINELAND agli agricoltori, giardinieri e coloni braccianti Italiani e Ticinesi un bel terreno coltivabile, suolo vergine, a $25 per acre, pagabili in sei anni.

Il terreno è eccellente, grasso e produttivo, molto vicino, mediante le strade ferrate, ai grandi mercati di New York e Filadelfia, dove da 20 a 40 acri costituiscono un buon podere se in parte rigoglioso di frutti.

Da questa località la più grande e variata quantità di frutti è spedita al mercato, in confronto di qualunque altra postura di eguale area negli Stati Uniti. Essa sorge nel mezzo di fiorente borgata con belle strade, magazzini, scuole e manifatture.

Le donne appartenenti alle famiglie coloniche ed altri affini potranno ottenere un buon lavoro nelle fabbriche di paglia, di scarpe, e nelle manifatture di bottoni, di pannilani ed in altri rami d'industria.

Già molti agricoltori Inglesi, Svizzeri, Italiani e Scozzesi vi hanno preso stanza e vivono prosperamente. Togliete le vostre famiglie dall'ozio, causa di tanti vizi.

Un bel numero di giardinieri dei dintorni di Nuova York vi si sono stabiliti.

VINELAND per l'agricoltura e commercio è uno dei punti più adatti nel circondario. L'agricoltura vi è più vantaggiosa che all'Ovest a causa della vicinanza dei mercati.

CONDIZIONI.

Per venti acri o più si deve pagare 1/6 in contanti, il rimanente si pagherà semestralmente cogli interessi legali nello spazio di sei anni.

Per dieci acri ¼ in contanti, e con pagamenti semestrali si salderà il debito coi dovuti interessi nello spazio di 5 anni.

Per cinque acri metà in contanti.

Per acquisto di terreni rivolgersi al Signor G. F. SECCHI DE CASALI, Redattore dell'ECO D'ITALIA, 51 Liberty Street.

Si danno e si spediscono gratuitamente le informazioni più ragguagliate.

Advertisement in *L'Eco d'Italia* of New York on January 3, 1874, offering farm land at Vineland, N. J. at $25 an acre, payable one half at the time of the purchase and the balance within five years, plus interest.

ALESSANDRO MASTROVALERIO
(1855-1944)
Founder of the agricultural settlement of Daphne, Ala., in 1888, and editor from 1898 to 1928 of the weekly newspaper *La Tribuna Transatlantica* of Chicago. (*Vigo Review*, May, 1938.)

Another subject which we recommend for a detailed investigation is the history of the Italians in the maritime trade and fishing industry of the United States. From colonial days to our own, not many Americans have been anxious to go out to sea, except as skippers or masters, with foreigners, to no small extent from Mediterranean countries, making up the crews. Aside from that, it is fair to assume that a country with such a long coastline as Italy must have contributed a good share to our merchant marine. The Venetian Alberti who settled in New Amsterdam in 1635 came as a seaman. So did Pascal De Angelis, the Neapolitan who died in Newport, R. I., in 1770, and others whose names we have recorded in the preceding pages.

JOHN DOMINIS

The first native of Italy to serve as master of American vessels may have been Giovanni Dominis of Trieste, who is best remembered as the father of John Dominis, the prince consort of Queen Liliuokalani of Hawaii, and as the man who brought the first cargo of salmon from the Columbia River. Out of that first shipment was born the profitable salmon trade betwen the West Coast and New England. Incidentally, Dominis was the first man, according to Bancroft, to plant peach trees in Oregon. He was active between 1823 and 1840.

OTHER SEA CAPTAINS

S. Pizzati, a Sicilian captain who was born in Palermo in 1839 and died in New Orleans on Dec. 30, 1915, is said to have been the first captain to take a steamship to Honduras for the purpose of bringing back bananas to the United States. Be that as it may, the banana trade with Honduras rose to vast proportions with the three Vaccaro brothers, all natives of Sicily, whose firm, the Standard Fruit and Steamship Company, was capitalized at $50,000,000 in 1926, with a fleet of many ships. Felix Vaccaro, the last of the three brothers, died in 1943.

Other Italians who owned ships before the Civil War were Egisto Fabbri, already noted by us, in New York; Marquis Niccolo Reggio, who settled in Boston in 1832 and died in New York in 1867; Zerega di Zerega of New York, also noted by us as one of the founders of the New York Cotton Exchange. Secchi de Casali, the editor of the New York Italian weekly, was one of the stockholders of the North American and Italian Steamship Company organized in 1865. (*Eco d'Italia*, May 6, 1865.) On the Pacific Coast, Nicholas Larco owned several vessels which brought coolies from China and also traded with South America.

ITALIAN FISHERMEN

A rather large number of Italians have engaged in fishing ever since Civil War days. How many at any given period we cannot say. We know, however, that as early as 1869 there was an association of Italian fishermen in San Francisco. (*Eco d'Italia*, March 19, 1869, and April 6, 1881.) In our own days, hundreds, if not thousands, of natives of Italy are engaged in fishing, from New England to Florida, and from the Gulf of Mexico to the California Coast, all the way up to Alaska. That their number has not been insignificant we learn from the fact that at the beginning of World War II some 700 Sicilian fishermen in Boston alone were forbidden from fishing in New England waters. In California, it is said, the fresh fish industry is in the hands of the Italians to the extent of 80 per cent. Also owned by Italians are several fish canneries on the Pacific Coast.

THE BARK SMYRNIOTE (1861)
owned by Marquis Nicholas Reggio of Boston, which plied between the United States and Mediterranean ports.

CHAPTER TWENTY-TWO

IN THE UNITED STATES ARMY AND NAVY

To unearth the names of the natives of Italy or of the Americans of Italian origin who served in the armed forces of the United States from the War of Tripoli to World War II, one would have to search a mountain of muster rolls, registers, regimental books and what not. Even then the search would be largely a waste of time, for many registers are missing and in those which are still in existence it is often practically impossible to identify one's national origins, so garbled up and so hard to read are many of the names. All one can do, therefore, is to assume that out of the millions of citizens of Italian extraction born in America ever since the Revolution, some of them must have served in the Army and Navy of the United States.

On the other hand, we have positive data about the birthplaces of a relatively small number of soldiers and sailors born in Italy or of Italian parentage in the United States. It is, accordingly, to them that we shall restrict our investigation.

IN THE WAR OF TRIPOLI

All students of American history will recall how in 1801 the United States, although young and weak, compared to the great powers of those days, chose to defy the Barbary pirates, preferring war rather than to pay tolls to those early racketeers who demanded a sum of money for each ship that entered the Mediterranean.

It is also well known how in the early stages of that war the frigate *Philadelphia* ran aground at the entrance of the port of Tripoli and was seized by the enemy, who floated it again, manned it and kept it ready for battle—thus humbling the pride of the very young American Navy. But only for a brief period of time, for no sooner had the ship been seized by the pirates than Commodore Edward Preble, the commander of the American squadron, conceived a bold plan to "enter the harbor at night, board the *Philadelphia* and burn her."

The plan was carried out most brilliantly and Stephen Decatur, who was in charge of the expedition, acquired national fame and one of the highest places among our naval heroes.

It is very little known, however, that the man who, in a sense, was responsible for the success of the raid was Salvatore Catalano, a young Sicilian seaman who volunteered to pilot Decatur's ketch, the *Intrepid,* into Tripoli and through his intimate acquaintance with the harbor, the people and their language, was able to bring the *Intrepid* close to the *Philadelphia* without arousing the suspicions of the pirates. The fact that the expedition had to wait nine days outside the port for the propitious time to enter, explains the difficulty of the operation.

THE BURNING OF THE PHILADELPHIA IN TRIPOLI HARBOR IN 1804
An exploit made possible "in the greatest degree" by Salvatore Catalano.

Decatur himself was the first to pay tribute to Catalano, when in his report to Commodore Preble, written at sea, while returning from the raid, he stated: "It would be injustice in me, were I to pass over the important services rendered by Mr. Salvadore, the pilot, on whose good conduct the success of the enterprise in the greatest degree depended."

Catalano served as a pilot on other American War vessels, including the two frigates, *Constitution* and *Congress.*

In 1806 he came over on the *Congress* by order of the Secretary of the Navy and served at the Washington Navy Yard until the time of his death on January 4, 1846. He was born in Palermo about 1771.

ITALY HELPS THE UNITED STATES

Catalano was not the only Italian who rendered valuable services to the United States during the War of Tripoli. Aside from the fact that the King of the Two Sicilies (Naples and Sicily) allowed the U. S. Navy to use the port of Syracuse as its base during the conflict, six Italian gunboats and two Italian bomb vessels took part in Commodore Preble's attack on Tripoli, all manned by Italian gunners and seamen. They were "of very essential service to the squadron under my command in the several attacks which we made on the City and shipping of our common enemy—the Tripolines", Commodore Preble wrote on December 15, 1804, to the Neapolitan minister of war, adding: "I with great pleasure acknowledge the gallant conduct of the Neapolitan Gunners and others of His Majesty's subjects attached to them" (the gunboats). Preble considered the assistance rendered by the Italians so valuable that he asked for more vessels, but Italy refused as they were needed for the protection of the country.

Commodore Barron, who succeeded Preble, renewed the request, making it clear that "the operations of our squadrons will, I fear, be comparatively weak and ineffectual for want of those succours from which we derived such essential advantage during the last campaign. . . . I consider them, indeed, as indispensable to ensure our success."

(Moran, C., Commodore Preble's Sicilian Auxiliaries, *U. S. Naval Institute Proceedings,* January, 1939, 80-82; see also *Naval Documents related to the U. S. Wars with the Barbary Powers,* 6 vols.)

IN THE WAR OF 1812

Because of the difficulties already mentioned, we have not examined the various available registers of the men who served in the War of 1812, in the various campaigns against the Indians, and in the War with Mexico.

We know, however, that during the War of 1812 Carlo Mauran, a son of Joseph Mauran of Providence, served as first lieutenant in 1813; Vannini, the economist, as we have seen, served as a captain, apparently with a Virginia military unit; Joseph Lametti, a native of Modena, served as a lieutenant and later as a captain in the 9th Regiment of the New York State Artillery. He died in New York on May 8, 1848, at the age of 44, and was buried in the cemetery of St. Patrick's Old Cathedral on Mott and Prince Streets. There, on February 22, 1930, the Society of the War of 1812 placed a marker at his tomb.

FOR THE INDEPENDENCE OF TEXAS AND IN THE WAR WITH MEXICO

Somehow, we are inclined to believe that a number of natives of Italy took part in the struggle for the independence of Texas. Some of them were residents of Louisiana, like one Prospero Bernardi, who served under Sam Houston, was honorably discharged in 1837, and received a grant of 1280 acres of land. Others were residents of Mexico, including not a few officers who had fought for the independence of that country.

Among the latter, General Avezzana, the famous minister of war of the Republic of Rome and a merchant in New York for many years, as we have seen, joined the Mexicans in their fight for freedom. Santa Anna made him a colonel and governor of two provinces, but later the two became enemies, and after a brief struggle Avezzana repaired to New York. De Attellis, the editor of *Correo Atlantico,* also was a friend of Santa Anna for a time, until he, too, opposed his designs and found shelter in New Orleans. We have not the least doubt that de Attellis helped Sam Houston's cause (the independence of Texas) in no small degree. Among the Italians who remained loyal to Santa Anna was General Vicente Filisola, who took command of the Mexican troops after Santa Anna was captured by the Texans at the Battle of San Jacinto. At that time Filisola possessed a colonization grant for 600 families on the Trinity River in East Texas, but he lost it when the Mexicans were defeated. (*The Writings of Sam Houston,* ed. by A. W. Williams and E. C. Barker, I,301, note 2.)

One of the most prominent pioneers in Texas, as we have already noted, was Jose' Antonio Navarro, the son of a Corsican immigrant, who served as land commissioner in 1834-35, was a member of the convention of 1836 that declared the independence of Texas and was a signer of both the Declaration of Texan Independence as well as of the first Constitution of Texas. He was the only native of the state who sat in the convention that accepted annexation. (*Ibid.,* VII, 396, note 1.)

Among the men of Italian extraction who served during the Mexican War, we have some information about the future Commodore Louis C. Sartori, who served as a lieutenant on the bomb schooner *Stromboli* and was present at the capture of Tabasco; the future Admiral Bancroft Gherardi, who served as a midshipman in 1846, at the age of 14; Louis Gally of New Orleans, who served as major, (as we have seen, he was consul of Sicily in that city); William Trovillo, who served with the Louisiana Battalion of Volunteer Artillery (later he served as a captain in the Union Army); Lieutenant-Colonel Herny Forno, who served with Walton's Regiment of Louisiana; N. C. Barrabino, a surgeon in the Navy; Lieutenant-Colonel Charles Fiesca of the Louisiana Volunteers; Lieutenant-Colonel Christian C. Nave of the Indiana Volunteers; First Lieutenant John Phinizy, Jr., of the Georgia Volunteers; and others whose names are doubtful.

IN THE CIVIL WAR

During the Civil War thousands of foreigners served in the Union Army; relatively few offered their services in defense of the Confederate cause. Most of them were veterans of the wars for the independence of Germany, Hungary, Poland, Italy, and other countries, who were induced by Union agents in Europe to join their forces.

Certainly the cause for which the North was fighting had an immense appeal for the veterans of the Risorgimento, many of whom hastened to join the Union Army. Most of them were commissioned officers; not a few, however, were non-commissioned officers and privates, as it appears from the names which have reached us. (See facsimiles on pages 319 and 322.) At any rate, the Italians must have been among the first to fight for the Union if as early as November, 1861, a number of them had already enlisted in the *Enfants Perdus* regiment. Two months later, we learn from *L'Eco d'Italia,* some of those who had been encouraged by the American Legation in Turin to come over, had already met with disappointment and returned to Europe; others found themselves stranded in New York; still others, veterans of the battles of Montebello, San Martino and Volturno, were compelled to accept lower ranks than those they had held in the Italian army because they could not speak English. Carlo Lombardi of Brescia, for instance, had to enroll as a private although he had served as a captain with Garibaldi. A month later, however, he was commissioned a second lieutenant in the 39th U. S. Colored Infantry, with which he served until he was killed in an explosion at Fort Fisher, N. C., in January, 1865. (*Eco,* April 13, 1865.) A few were planning to emigrate to Mexico. (*Eco,* Jan. 25 and Feb. 15, 1862.)

GARIBALDI IS OFFERED A COMMAND IN THE UNION ARMY

At the beginning of the Civil War, at a time "when our new regiments need experienced officers", Garibaldi was offered the command of a division on the direct authority of President Lincoln, but Garibaldi could not accept, at first because the situation in Italy was such that his services might have been needed at home, later because he was not in good health. However, as he wrote on September 10, 1861, "if war should by evil chance continue in your country, I will overcome all obstacles which hold me back, and will hasten to come to the defence of that people which is so dear to me." A year later Garibaldi's coming to the United States was still a topic of conversation, but *L'Eco d'Italia* was decidedly against it. "If Garibaldi should come to America", it stated in an editorial, "just imagine what would happen in the United States, where the Hughes (Cardinal Hughes) and the Corcorans are the heroes of the party." (*Eco,* Oct. 18 and 25, 1862.) That Garibaldi and all Italian liberals were for the Union appears clearly from the letter which he addressed to Lincoln shortly after the Proclamation of Emancipation. (See facsimiles below; on the offer of a command to Garibaldi see N. Nelson Gay in *Century Magazine.* Nov. 1907, p. 63, and *Mass. Hist. Soc. Proc.* III series, I, 320. See also H. N.

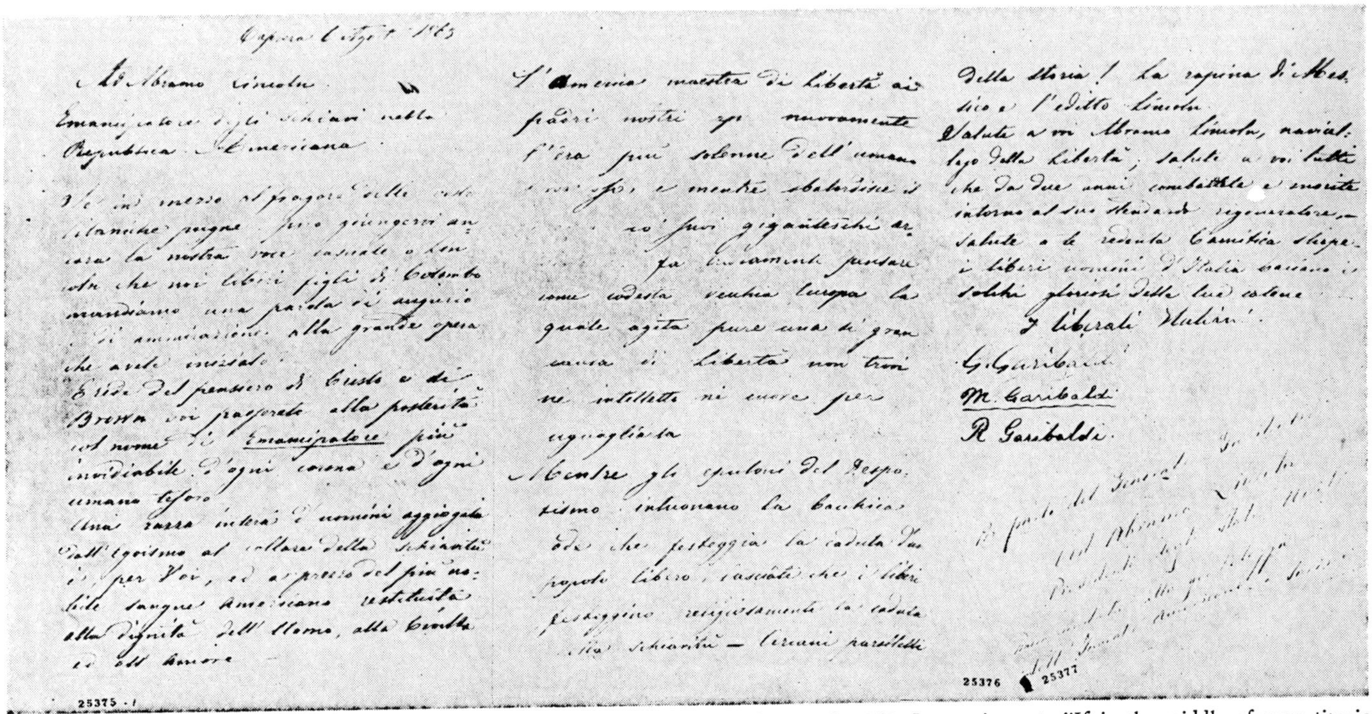

Copy of a letter sent by Garibaldi and other Italian liberals to Lincoln on August 6, 1863. It says in part: "If in the middle of your titanic struggle our voice may still reach you, Oh Lincoln, allow us, free sons of Columbus to send you a word of good wishes and admiration for the great work begun by you. The heir of Christ and Brown, you will go down in history under the name of Emancipator, a title to be envied more than a crown or any human treasure. A whole race of men enslaved by selfishness, is by you, at the cost of the most noble American blood, given back to the dignity of Man, to Civilization and to Love. America, the teacher of freedom to our fathers, opens once more the most solemn era of human progress. . . . Greetings to you, Abraham Lincoln, Pilot of Liberty! Greetings to you all who during the last two years have been fighting and dying around its regenerating standard—greetings to you, redeemed Hamitic race, the free men of Italy kiss the glorious marks of your chains." (Courtesy, *Library of Congress.*)

ARRUOLAMENTO.

HEAD--QUARTERS

GARIBALDI GUARD,

89° Reggimento N. Y. S. Volontario.

Questo bel Reggimento partito uno dei primi pel teatro della guerra, e che ha cosi valorosamente combattuto il di 8 giugno alla battaglia di Cross-Key, chiede 100 uomini a compimento del suo effettivo.

I Francesi, Svizzeri, Belgi, Italiani, e Spagnuoli che verranno a schierarsi sotto la bandiera di questo reggimento vi saranno accolti con una viva simpatia dai loro compatrioti, che vi entrarono al momento della sua formazione.

Le condizioni le più vantaggiose saranno fatte agli arruolati

L'ufficio d'arruolamento è sito N. 53 e 55 Franklin Street, ed aperto dalle 9 di mattina alle 4 di sera.

Il Capitano reclutante
V. CHANDONÈ.

SPINOLA EMPIRE BRIGADE.

SIEGEL SHARP SHOOTERS.

T. H. BRONLIK COLONNELLO COMANDANTE.

Si desiderano 40 individui per formare una compagnia nel detto Reggimento.

La paga di ciascun arruolato sarà dai dollari 13 ai 23 per mese.

Questa correrà, a datare dal giorno dell'arruolamemto e sarà inoltre immediatamente vestito, alloggiato e nutrito.

100 dollari sono garantiti come premio Le reclute volontarie riceveranno subito il quarto di questa somma, più un altro regalo di dollari 50 per parte dello Stato di New York.

Un mese di paga sarà dato in anticipazione, ciò che in totale un uomo riceverà, il giorno che sarà incorporato definitivamente, la somma di dollari 88.

I posti di Bass' ufficiale sono ancora vacanti ; ma non saranno ammessi a questi gradi che persone competenti e che s'impegnino ad occuparsi della formazione della compagnia.

L'ufficiale di reclutamento è reperibile al N. 84 Grand Street.

Capitano P. SALVOTTI, italiano e vero amico de' suoi connazionali.

Luogotenente D. FONTAINE già ufficiale al servizio di diversi eserciti d'Europa.

(*Above*) Two advertisements for volunteers in *L'Eco d'Italia* for July 26, 1862. (*Right*) Two more advertisements in the same newspaper in November, 1862, for the sale of pills and ointments to men in the Army and Navy of the United States. (Courtesy, *New York Public Library.*)

Gay, Garibaldi's American contacts, *Am. Hist. Rev.*, Oct., 1932.)

THE GARIBALDI GUARD

Although Garibaldi did not come over, his name became the battle cry of the Garibaldi Guard, a regiment of volunteers officially known as the 39th New York Infantry. It consisted at first of 830 men, of whom about 50 were Italians. (*Eco,* March 1, 1862.) The others were Germans, Hungarians, French, Swiss, Spaniards and Portuguese. The Italians included Col. Repetti, Major (later Lt. Col.) Tinelli, Captains Osnaghi, Venuti, and Salviatti, and at least six first lieutenants and six second lieutenants. It was probably the most picturesque organization in the entire Union Army and served with distinction in numerour battles, from the First Bull Run to Appomattox. Its casualties were heavy.

OFFICERS OF ITALIAN BIRTH OR EXTRACTION IN THE UNION ARMY

As the following list shows, the "Italians" were scattered throughout the Union Army. They included:

GENERALS

Major General Edward Ferrero, the hero of numerous actions, from the Battle of Roanoke Island to Second Bull Run, Chantilly, Antietam, Jackson, and other engagements.

AMICI E PARENTI

DEI

BRAVI SOLDATI E MARINAI.

PILLOLE ED UNGUENTO

DI

HOLLOWAY.

Tutti coloro che hanno Amici e Congiunti nell'armata e nella Marina, dovrebbero aver cura che fossero abbondantemente provvisti di queste Pillole ed Unguento, e se mai i bravi Soldati e Marinai avessero trascurato di procacciarsene, nessun regalo sarebbe loro tanto utile quanto questi farmachi. Sono stati esperimentati essere l'amico costante del Soldato nell'ora del bisogno.

TOSSI ED INFREDDATURE AFFLIGGONO LE TRUPPE.

Saranno immediatamente alleviate ed effettivamente curate facendo uso di queste meravigliose medicine, ed osservando alla lettera le Direzioni che sono affisse ad ogni Vasettoo Scatola

MAL DI TESTA, PERDITA DELL'APPETITO, INCIDENTI AI SOLDATI.

Queste sensazioni che tanto ci affiggono, derivano generalmente da dispiacieri o noje, respiro represso, cibi o bevande malsane, che sconvolgono l'azione naturale del fegato e dello stomaco. Bisogna che recate sollievo a questi organi, se desiderate ristabilirvi in salute Le Pillole, prese secondo la ricetta stampata, produrranno immediatamente un'azione salubre sia nel fegato che nello stomaco e come conseguenza naturale curati del mal di testa stabilito l'appetito.

DEBOLEZZA PRODOTTA DA SOVERCHIA FATICA.

Sparirà per mezzo di queste inestimabili Pillole, ed il Soldato ne acquisterà maggior vigore. Non lasciate gli Intestini senza la dovuta azione. Sembrerà strano che le Pillole d' Holloway sieno raccomandate per la Disenterie e Flusso, molti supponendo che aumenterebbero il rilascio. Questo è un grande errore, dacchè queste Pillole assesteranno ogni disordine nel fegato e nello stomaco, ed in tal modo rimuovono dal sistema tutti gl umori acri. Questa medicina tonica darà vigore a tutto il sistema organico per disordinato che fosse, mentre salute e forza seguono in ogni caso. Nessun'altra cosa arresterà si efficacemente il rilascio degli Intestini come questa celebre medicina.

VOLONTARJ ALL'ERTA! INDISCREZIONI DELLA GIOVENTU'.

Piaghe ed Ulceri ed Enfiature, possono con certezza essere curate radicalmente se si prendono le Pillole notte e giorno, e se si fa abbondante uso dell'Unguento come è prescritto nelle ordinazioni. Se si usano diversamente, cureranno in un luogo per ricomparire i mali in un'altro. Mentre questo Unguento sradicherà gli umori dal sistema e ristabilirà l'Infermo in uno stato salutevole e vigoroso. Richiede soltanto un poco di perseveranza in casi ostinati per produrre una cura perfetta.

PER FERITE CAGIONATE O DALLA BAJONETTA, SCIABOLA O PALLA, PIAGHE O CONTUSIONI.

[illegible] cui vanno sogetti i Soldati e i Marinai, non vi sono medicine tanto sicure e convenevoli come le Pillole e l' Unguento di Holloway. Il povero soldato ferito e quasi agonizzante può avere le sue ferite medicate all'istante, se volesse provvedersi di questo Unguento senza pari, che si dovrebbe far penetrare nella ferita e sciolto tutto all' intorno, poscia avvolto in un pezzo di lino, e compresso da un fazzoletto. Prendendo notte e giorno 6 o 8 Pillole, per rinfrescare il sistema e prevenire l'infiammazione.

Ogni Zaino di Soldato e Cassa del Marinaio dovrebbero essere provveduti di questi infallibili rimedj.

AVVISO!—Nessuna è genuina salvo che le parole "HOLLOWAY, NEW YORK AND LONDON," sia discernibili come a Marca-d'acqua in ogni foglio del libro delle prescrizioni all'intorno d'ogni vaso o scatola ; lo stesso può vedersi sui fogli attraverso il lume di una candela. Si darà un generoso compenso a chiunque renderà informazion che possano tendere alla detenzione di ogni persona o parti contrafacenti le medicine o vendendo le medesime, sapendo che sono spurie.

— Vendibili all'Ufficio del Prof. Holloway, No. 80 Maiden Lane, New York, e da tutti i principali Farmacisti e Venditori di Medicine, in tutto il mondo civilizzato, in scatole a 25 cents, 62 cents, e un dollaro.

☞ Si risparmia considerevolmente comperando i vasi o scatole più grandi.

N. B.—Direzioni per guida degli 'infermi d' ogni malattia sono affisse ad ogni scatola.

Yorktown, 1° Luglio 1862.

Signor Redattore dell'*Eco d'Italia*,

Lo interesse, che mostrate nel propugnare nel vostro settimanale giornale il dritto, e la giustizia di chiunque si rivolge alla persona vostra rende arditi i sottoscritti Italiani al servizio federale nel Battaglione des *Enfants Perdus* a voler appoggiare colla stampa le loro preghiere che inviano al Presidente del Comitato Militare, perchè sia loro data la paga che li compete, come ogni altra truppa in campo.

Il battaglione non ha percetto alcun soldo dal 26 Novembre 1861, epoca della sua organizzazione, e parecchi de' postulanti già contano l'ottavo mese di servizio.

Sicuri di conseguir dalla vostra bontà il chiesto favore, come quelli che più vi sono a cuore quali vostri concittadini, vi fanno riverenza e si soscrivono

Pietro Fona;—Giuseppe Peraani;—Pietro Camparo;—Giuseppe Giacomelli;—Domenico Ferrari;—Camillo Brega;—Giustini Camillo;—Giuseppe Zannelli;—Carlo Casanna;—Turchi Francesco, Sergente-Maggiore;—Carlo de Rizzi.

A letter in *L'Eco d'Italia* for July 11, 1862, in which some Italian soldiers of the *Enfants Perdus* battalion complain that they had not received their pay since it was organized on November 26, 1861. It was signed by ten privates and one sergeant. At least one of the officers of that regiment. First Lieutenant Tancredi Bonino, was an Italian. (Couresy, *New York Public Library.*)

Burnside's bridge at Antietam carried at the point of the bayonet by General Ferrero's second brigade, on Sept. 17, 1862. (From Harper's *History of the Great Rebellion.*)

The Garibaldi Guard being reviewed by President Lincoln and General Scott on July 4, 1861. Note the Italian flag with the words "Dio e Popolo" (God and the People) which had flown over the Roman embattlements during the ill-fated Roman Republic. (From *The Illustrated London News.*)

Ferrero was born in Madrid, where his parents happened to be during an operatic tour, in circumstances similar to those of Adelina Patti's birth. But the fact that he was born in Madrid does not make him a Spaniard, just as General George Meade, who was also born in Spain, was not a Spaniard but an American. The famous painter, John Singer Sargent, was born in Florence, Italy,but he is rightly considered as an American. "The laws of Spain, while regarding the child of an alien as an alien, give him the right, on attaining his majority, of electing to be a citizen of the country of which he resides" (Hall, W. E., *A Treatise On International Law*, 8th ed., 1924, 277.) Ferrero was only about one year old when his parents brought him to America.

Brigadier General Francis Spinola, a native of Long Island, was a politician. He was appointed a brigadier general by Lincoln "for meritorious conduct in recruiting and organizing a brigade of four regiments and accompanying them to the field." He was wounded twice at the battle of Wapping Heights, during which he led his brigade in a bayonet charge.

Colonel Luigi Palma di Cesnola, a Piedmontese, received the brevet rank of brigadier general from Lincoln just before the end of the war, and was awarded the Congressional Medal of Honor. Later, as we have seen, he became the director of the Metropolitan Museum of Art of New York.

Colonel Enrico Fardella also was made a brigadier general by brevet towards the end of the war for distinguished services at Plymouth, N. C. The member of a distinguished Sicilian family, he was in business in New York for many years as an importer. (*Eco d'Italia*, January 8, 1869.)

COLONELS AND LIEUTENANT COLONELS

Bachia, Richard A., Lieutenant Colonel, 87th New York Infantry. Colonel for gallant and meritorious services, 1866.

Del Vecchio, James R., Assistant Quartermaster with rank of Captain. Lieutenant Colonel by brevet.

Gandolfo, John B., Lieutenant Colonel, 178th New York Infantry.

Maggi, Albert C., Colonel, 3rd Massachusetts Infantry.

Navone, Luigi, Colonel, unit unknown.

Piepho, Carlo, Colonel, 108th Ohio Infantry.

Repetti, Alexander, Lieutenant Colonel, 39th New York Infantry. (See, Caddeo, R., *Le Edizioni di Capolago*, Milan, 1934, 368.)

Sceva, Benjamin, Lieutenant Colonel, 10th New York Cavalry. Colonel by brevet for gallant and meritorious services. After the War he practiced law in New York City.

Tinelli, Louis W., Lieutenant Colonel, 90th New York Infantry. Colonel by brevet. See *ante*, p. 299.

MAJORS

Crapo, Angelo, by brevet, U. S. Volunteers.

Corsa, William H., by brevet, New York Volunteers.

Cremony, John C., California Cavalry.

Danesi, John, F. L. W., served as Captain, 25th New York Cavalry. Commissioned Major, declined.

Paldi, Angelo, First Michigan Cavalry. See *ante*, p. 294.

Venuti, Edward, 52nd New York Infantry. Formerly with 39th New York Infantry. Killed in action at Gettysburg, July 2, 1863.

CAPTAINS

Alberti, Alexander, Fifth Michigan Infantry.

Barto, Alfonso, 52nd Illinois Infantry.

Belotti, George B., 62nd New York Infantry.

Biscaccianti, Alessandro, Assistant Quartermaster.

Capelli, James F., 16th Massachusetts Infantry.

Castello, Edward, 7th Missouri Infantry.

Cipriani, Alfred, 53rd New York Infantry.

De Vecchi, Achille, Massachusetts Light Artillery.

Fariola, O. L. F. E., 77th U. S. Colored Troops.

La Fata, Charles G., 62nd New York Infantry.

Leoni, Georgi, First Mississippi Cavalry.

Osnaghi, Cesare, 39th New York Infantry (Garibaldi Guard).

Pelosi, Louis, 26th Wisconsin Infantry.

Pizzalo, Charles, 26th Wisconsin Infantry. Killed at Chancellorsville.

Rolli, John G., 12th Ohio Infantry.

Salviatti, Ercole, 39th New York Infantry.

Serviere, Alphons, 46th New York Infantry.

Venturi, Severi, 59th New York Infantry. Wounded in two battles.

Shericardi, Rudolph, 39th New York Infantry.

Stephani, Charles, 5th Missouri Infantry.

Trovillo, Wm. H., 87th Pennsylvania Infantry.

Valentini, Count Edward Valentino, aide-de-camp.

FIRST LIEUTENANTS

Allegretti, Ignazio, 29th New York Infantry.

Bixio, Oliviero, 24th New York Cavalry.

Bonino, Tancredi, 194th New York Infantry.

Bonta, James W., 3rd New York Artillery.

Cassinone, Frederick, 3rd New York Artillery.

Castello, John, 28th U. S. Colored Troops.

Castello, Thomas, 170th New York Infantry.

Colani, Giovanni Mario, 39th New York Infantry.

Conterno, Ottavio, 12th New York Cavalry.

Corrello, Alfred A., 7th West Virginia Infantry.

Dal Molin, Antonio, 39th New York Infantry.

Ferrari, Hannibal, 120th U. S. Colored Troops.

Fontana, Andrew, 39th New York Infantry.

Garbanati, Frederick, 2nd New York Cavalry.

Gianini, Charles A., 55th New York Infantry.

Ginochio, Noel B., 25th New York Cavalry.

Lucia, J. H., 17th Vermont Infantry.

Maggi, Ferdinando, 39th New York Infantry. Wounded in action.

Marochetti, Alberto, 103rd U. S. Colored Troops.

Marriccini, Octave, Enfants Perdus.

Modica, Joseph A., 11th New Hampshire Infantry.

BRIGADIER GENERAL FRANCIS B. SPINOLA

BRIGADIER GENERAL LUIGI PALMA DI GESNOLA
Winner of the Congressional Medal of Honor

COLONEL LUIGI TINELLI

REAR ADMIRAL BANCROFT GHERARDI
(Courtesy, *Naval Records and History, U. S. Navy Department.*)

L'ECO D'ITALIA.

GIORNALE SETTIMANALE.

Politica, Industria, Commercio, Scienze, Letteratura, Belle-Arti, Teatri.

NEW YORK, 3 LUGLIO, 1862.

CARTEGGIO DELL' ECO D'ITALIA.

La Guardia Garibaldi alla battaglia presso Shenandoah. – Valle del Shenandoah, 29 giugno 1862.

Alla testa dell'armata, formanti l'avanguardia, erano due deboli reggimenti d'Irlandesi, sotto il comando del bravo colonnello francese Clousery.

Alle 11 antimeridiane dell'otto giugno, li esploratori di questa piccola Brigata, giunsero in faccia dell'inimico che trovavasi in posizione fortissima su di una linea in colli boschivi, avanti e lungo i quali si estendeva una vallata piana ed aperta affatto e larga di circa 800 passi. Appena veduta il nemico la nostra avanguardia scendere nella valle, incominciò il fuoco. Si fu allora che il colonnello Albert, capo dello Stato Maggiore di Fremont, richiese il primo battaglione del reggimento Garibaldi Gardes che a regolare distanza seguiva l'avanguardia, ed ordinò al sig. capitano Odoardo Venuti che lo comandava, stante l'assenza del colonnello e tenente colonnello del reggimento, di discendere fino al limitare del bosco che occupavano e che faceva fronte alla posizione del nemico e di dividersi la sudetta vallata.

Giunto il detto capitano abbasso e sulla estremità del bosco, sciolse quattro compagnie e le distese in bersaglieri ed appoggiando circa 2000 passi a destra, si assicurò, mediante una rapida conversione a sinistra che fece fare alla compagnia di testa, nulla avendo a temere pella sua destra dall'ala sinistra del nemico, circondo in tale guisa un colle boschivo, sporgente per almeno 400 passi nella detta vallata, che era occupato per quanto parve da una forza rimarchevole stante l'incessante pioggia di palle che di colà cadevano sulla catena. Veduta quindi il detto Capitano l'importanza del momento, fece suonare lungo tutta la catena la conversione a sinistra a passo di corsa, facendo quindi passare colla massima velocità una compagnia all'ala destra per rinforzarla; fece cessare il fuoco e proibì di sradicare le siepi per non perder tempo, ma di abbatterle, e di disporsi all'assalto dopo di aver ordinato di porre la baionetta in canna. A 300 passi circa veduta la sua ala destra ben sostenuta dalla aggiuntavi compagnia e la sua sinistra dal resto del reggimento fece suonare la carica, e al grido di Viva Garibaldi, viva l'Unione, [illegible] la catena unanime e colla risolutezza di provetti veterani, si mise in marcia a passo di corsa [illegible] bosco.

A [illegible] circa dalla posizione del nemico [illegible]rò il fianco sinistro che rimase vicino [illegible] mentre appunto che voltatosi animava le [illegible] compagnie ad accelerare per quanto [illegible]ero il passo onde unirsi agli altri [illegible] nemico, ma siccome il colpo fu di nessun [illegible] effetto non si crede ferito e continuò la sua [illegible]ando colla voce e coll'esempio i suoi bravi [illegible] che come leoni slanciavansi all'assalto, in ispecie la [illegible] compagnia, (c.) compagnia Italiana, che innanzi a tutte le altre correvá intrepida e non curante la grandine di palle che li fulminava.

Poco dopo sentendosi il bravo capitano Venuti venir meno pose la mano ove credea esser ferito, e la ritirò bagnata di sangue, ciò che lo convinse di aver riportata una grave ferita, ma continuò non pertanto la sua marcia infondendo sempre coraggio e risolutezza ai suoi soldati e pregando il Dio delle battaglie di sostenerlo in quel momento, sul dubbio che vedendolo i suoi commilitoni cadere non venisse lor meno l'ardore, e soltanto non potendo più sorreggersi si appoggiò ad una siepe col trombetta a lato che continuamente suonava l'assalto ed ebbe tanta forza di rimanervi sino a che vide entrare nel bosco tutta quanta la truppa e quindi si abbandonò sul terreno.

Mi si assicura che se il battaglione avesse un solo istante titubato, avrebbe dato campo al nemico dieci volte superiore di riaversi dallo sgomento di un attacco sì ardito e [illegible], e veduto il piccolo numero di assalitori li avrebbe egli pure respinti alla baionetta e sarebbero stati tutti irreparabilmente perduti, e ciò anche dacchè il battaglione di riserva, che dovea sostenerli, non avendo seguito il passo di corsa era rimasto a troppa distanza per giungere in tempo a prestar loro assistenza.

Il capitano assistito dal trombetta Goetz Eugenio, francese, giovinetto dai 17 ai 18 anni potè trascinarsi all' ambulanza ove il Dottor Wolf chirurgo in capo del reggimento lo medicò, dopo avergli estratta la palla, assicurandolo di pronta guarigione per non essere stata offesa veruna parte vitale.

La condotta, in questo fatto d'armi, del reggimento Garibaldi Gardes, si distinse oltremisura avendo per tre volte assalito e prese le posizioni al nemico e più non si potea aspettare da gente che avea eseguito un si brillante attacco.

Gl'Italiani di detto reggimento che viemaggiormente si distinsero per coraggio e risolutezza e che furono i primi ad attaccare e respingere il nemico, furono il Capitano Odoardo Venuti, i sergenti Feralasco, Maggi, Roux e Castelvecchio. i quali alla testa della compagnia animavano colla voce e coll'esempio i soldati; i caporali Griffo, Rizzi, Nalucer ed i soldati Angiò, Bottero, Pantaloni, Johnson, Rivera, Rocca, Pis, Valdees Zenz, erano sempre i primi a slanciarsi colla baionetta al petto od alle reni del nemico, facendo strada ai loro compagni che molto bene li emulavano.

I feriti poi italiani furono Olivari, Piccioni, Samaniego e Godini, i tre ultimi leggermente.

Il contegno in questa battaglia sanguinosa, di di tutta la divisione Blenker in generale, fu ammirabile e da provetti e bravi soldati, e si distinsero specialmente, dopo il Garibaldi Gardes per coraggio e risolutezza, i Cacciatori Blenker N° 8 Volontari di New York de'quali la meta resto sacrificata per una inesplicabile cattiva direzione, come pure la batteria del capitano Schirmer che molto massacro fece dei nemici per l'abilissima e intrepida condotta del detto capitano.

Il Generale Blenker dimostro il massimo sangue freddo fra la piu fitta moschetteria e mitraglia e diresse la sua divisione con intelligenza e bravura.

Il colonnello Clousery non smentı la fama della sua bellicosa nazione, egli si diportò valorosamente, come pure il colonnello Gilsa il quale riporto una ferita in una coscia.

Si assicura che per questo brillante fatto d'armi doveva l'armata di Jackson restare totalmente disfatta al punto dal non poter salvar se stesso, e ciò pel valoroso ardore delle truppe federali, sostenute da una eccellente e ben guidata artiglieria e pei brillanti attacchi da esse sopportati contro un nemico di forze assai superiori ed avente le migliori posizioni, che quantunque forti e coperte non sarebbero bastate a raffrenare l'ardore di quel pugno d'uomini, sino a che non fossero state conquistate, e posto inoltre il nemico ad una completa impossibilita di comunicazione co'suoi diversi corpi, e colla perdita inoltre di tutta la sua artiglieria situata alla sua sinistra, dopo che si fosse respinta la sua destra fuori del bosco sulla pianura, che si estendeva dal piede del versante opposto, fino quasi alle rive del Shenandaoh e quivi l'artiglieria e moschetteria l'avrebbe a bell'agio distrutta, facendo dalla cavalleria inseguire altresi i fuggiaschi che avessero cercato di salvarsi dalla parte del fiume.

Tale pare fosse il piano del Generale Blenker, il quale non ebbe l'esito felice di cui punto non dubitava, stante l'ordine pervenutogli del Generale Fremont, per tre volte consecutive, di una immediata ritirata che dovè eseguire a malinucore, sebbene avesse fatto conoscere al medesimo, che il nemico era inseguito e ributtato da ogni parte per cui non dubitava della certa e completa vittoria; ritirata misteriosa che fu eseguita col dispetto e la rabbia delle truppe.

Impegnati nel combattimento furono i due deboli reggimenti del colonnello Clousery, poca cavalleria *Mounted Rifles*, l'artiglieria del bravo capitano Schirmer e la divisione Germanica.

In complesso la battaglia non fu nè perduta nè vinta, avendo le parti belligeranti pernottato nelle già possedute posizioni, e Jackson levò allo albeggiare il campo passando con tutta comodità il Shenandoah e distruggendo quindi il ponte.

La perdita per quanto risulta fu assai maggiore dalla parte dei confederati, e si contano da quella dei federali morti, il luogotenente Lessein francese e 15 soldati, il sottotenente Riege tedesco e 50 soldati.

An account of the Battle of Cross Keys, near Shenandoah, Pa., in *L'Eco d'Italia*. It tells how Capt. Odoardo Venuti, who was in command of the Garibaldi Guard in the absence of its colonel, was wounded in the action. The Italians who distinguished themselves on that day were, besides Capt. Venuti, sergeants Feralasco, Maggi, Roux and Castelvecchio; corporals Griffo, Rizzo, and Nalucer; privates Angiò, Bottero, Pantaloni, Johnson, Rivera, Rocca, Pis, Valdees, Zens. The Italians who were wounded in that battle, besides Venuti, were Olivari, Piccioni, Samaniego and Godini. Evidently, not all the Italians were commissioned officers. A week later, on July 11, the same newspaper published a correction to the effect that the Garibaldi Guard suffered the heaviest losses in that battle. (Courtesy, *New York Public Library*.)

Monument to the Garibaldi Guard (39th New York Infantry) on Cemetery Ridge at Gettysburg. The Guard included some 50 Italians, of whom about 17 or 18 were officers. At least 8 Italians from New York State alone died at Gettysburg on July 1-3, 1863. The name of one of them, Major Venuti of the 52nd New York Infantry, appears on the New York State Monument in the cemetery. The others were: Private Paolo Boni and Sgt. Geoge Bonin of the Garibaldi Guard; Private Peter Capallo, Corp. Charles Cavello, Private John Carmine, Private Christiana, Private Torango. There were others whose names are hard to classify.

Ornesi, Francesco, 39th New York Infantry.

Palmieri, Casselli A., 84th U. S. Colored Troops.

Papanti, Augustus L., 2nd Massachusetts Cavalry. (Son of the Boston dancing teacher, Lorenzo Papanti.)

Patrullo, Andrew, 27th New York Infantry.

Polizzi, Domingo, 101st New York Infantry. Came over with Fardella.

Sanno, James M., 7th New York Infantry.

Sansoni, Anthony J., 8th California Infantry.

Scala, Raphael, 3rd New York Cavalry.

Secondo, Rolando, 1st Louisiana Infantry.

Serini, Philip, 2nd New York Artillery.

Sivori, Constant, 55th New York Infantry. Wounded at Fredericksburg, Second Bull Run, and Antietam. A native of Genoa, he died in 1864, either in action or of wounds received in battle. (*Eco,* January 23, 1864.)

SECOND LIEUTENANTS

Addi, Thomas J., 39th New York Infantry.

Bertholdi, Charles, 4th New York Cavalry.

Bogialli, Giovanni, 39th New York Infantry.

Cala, Christopher, 4th New York Cavalry.

Crasto, Roch, 101st New York Infantry.

De Rudio, Carlo C., 2nd U. S. Colored Troops. See below.

Ernesti, Frederick, 29th New York Infantry.

Georgi, Joseph, 103rd New York Infantry.

Lacca, Horace, 22nd New York Infantry.

La Roza, George, 133rd New York Infantry.

Lombardi, Charles V., 39th U. S. Colored Troops. Killed by an explosion at Fort Fisher. Had lived several years in New Orleans.

Marchisi, Henry, 117th New York. (Son of Dr. Marchisi of Utica, N. Y.)

Modica, Frank P., 16th New Hampshire Infantry.

Nesi, Giovanni, 39th New York Infantry. Died of wounds received in action.

Raffo, Anthony, 17th West Virginia Infantry.

Ronzone, Silvio, 39th New York Infantry.

Samsa, Giovanni, 39th New York Infantry.

Sortore, Samuel, 5th New York Cavalry. Commissioned but did not serve as first lieutenant. Killed in action in 1864.

Tinelli, Frank B., 13th New York Artillery. Brother of Col. Tinelli.

Veride, Ciro P., 101st New York Infantry. Brother of Dr. Tullio Suzzara Verdi.

Zenetti, Arnold, 132nd New York Infantry. Killed in action at Bachellor's Creek, N. C.

SURGEONS

Margiarotti, Regola, Assistant Surgeon, 2nd New York Cavalry.

Piero, Francis L., Assistant Surgeon, 3rd Arkansas Cavalry.

Pierucci, Celso, Surgeon, 83rd U. S. Colored Troops.

Nortoni, Edward W., Assistant Surgeon, 4th Massachusetts Infantry.

CHAPLAINS

Rev. Leo Rizzo of Saracena, 9th Connecticut Infantry.

Rev. James Titta, 11th Pennsylvania Cavalry.

Rev. Prezza, Samuel, a Franciscan, like the two above, unit unknown.

Rev. Bixio, a Jesuit, at Libby Prison, Richmond.

MEDALS OF HONOR

As we have seen, General De Cesnola was awarded the Congressional Medal of Honor for gallantry in action. Two more men with Italian names were also awarded the highest decoration the United States Army can offer for bravery. One of them, Joseph H. De Castro, of Boston, a corporal with the 19th Massachusetts Infantry, was honored for his capture of the flag of the 19th Virginia Regiment. We are not positive, however, as to his nationality. In Italy, there are many people named Castro, but the name could just as easily be Spanish or Portuguese.

Another man who was awarded the Medal of Honor was Orlando E. Caruana, a native of Malta. He may have been related to one Carmelo Caruana, also of Malta, who "may be considered a distinguished part of our colony because of the interest which he has always displayed in anything which may be of advantage to the Italian name and to our cause." (*Eco d'Italia,* Nov. 11, 1865.)

IN THE NAVY

In the naval records of the Civil War one finds a number of officers with Italian names, like Joseph J .Tinelli (the brother of the Colonel), who was acting master; Alfred L. B. Zerega, of New York, also known to us, who served in the same capacity; Eugene Biondi, of Paterson, N. J., also acting master; Charles W. Sartori, a brother of the commodore, acting assistant surgeon; George A. Falconi, pilot of the U. S. S. Hartford; Lorenzo Frank Papanti, the son of the Boston dancing teacher, acting master's mate; James Como, acting engineer; Domingo Castano, third assistant engineer; Thomas Pentony, acting third assistant engineer; John S. Pera, acting second assistant engineer; and so on and on. More numerous are the names of the seamen. Of special interest to us is the record of Frank Bonistalli, one of the pioneer Italian merchants in Pittsburgh, who came over in 1861 and served until the close of the hostilities. In 1889 he was a prominent member of the Grand Army of the Republic and an importer of Italian products. He was the partner of Ernest Bisi, probably the first manufacturer of macaroni in the Pittsburgh district.

ADMIRAL GHERARDI AND COMMODORE SARTORI

So far as we know, only two sons of Italian immigrants have reached the highest ranks in the United States Navy.

The first was Louis G. Sartori, the son of Giovanni Battista Sartori of Trenton, the man who built the first Catholic church in New Jersey, Papal Consul, and businessman. He was born in New Jersey about 1812, was appointed to the Navy in 1829 and commissioned a lieutenant in 1841. As we have noted, he was present at the capture of Tabasco during the Mexican War. At the outbreak of the Civil War he was commissioned as commander and took part in several actions. In 1866 he was made a captain serving in command of the navy yard at Mare Island, Cal., until he was retired in 1874, a year after he was commissioned as commodore. In 1898 a bill was introduced in the House of Representatives for his promotion to rear admiral. He died a few months later, on January 11, 1899. (*New York Times,* Jan. 14, 1899; *Appleton's Cyclopædia of American History.*)

Rear Admiral Bancroft Gherardi is said to have been "one of the conspicuous figures in the development of the modern navy of the Nation". The son of the language teacher already noted, he was born in Jackson, La., in 1832, was commissioned a lieutenant in 1855, and a lieutenant-commander in 1862. During the Civil War he distinguished himself at the Battle of Mobile Bay under Farragut. He was made a rear admiral in 1877, was commandant of the New York Naval Yard after 1887, and served until 1894, when he was placed on the the retired list. He died in 1903. (*New York Times,* Dec. 11, 1903.) His son, Walter R. Gherardi, also became rear admiral and was for a time commandant of the Boston Navy Yard. He died in San Francisco on July 25, 1939.

WHO INVENTED THE MONITOR?

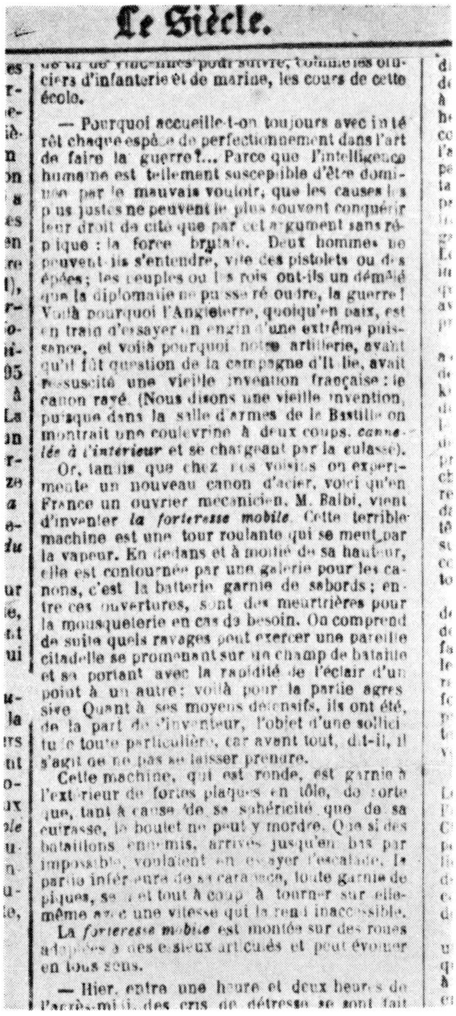

Le Siècle.

ciers d'infanterie et de marine, les cours de cette école.

— Pourquoi accueille-t-on toujours avec intérêt chaque espèce de perfectionnement dans l'art de faire la guerre?... Parce que l'intelligence humaine est tellement susceptible d'être dominée par le mauvais vouloir, que les causes les plus justes ne peuvent le plus souvent conquérir leur droit de cité que par cet argument sans réplique : la force brutale. Deux hommes ne peuvent-ils s'entendre, vite des pistolets ou des épées; les peuples ou les rois ont-ils un démêlé que la diplomatie ne puisse résoudre, la guerre! Voilà pourquoi l'Angleterre, quoiqu'en paix, est en train d'essayer un engin d'une extrême puissance, et voilà pourquoi notre artillerie, avant qu'il fût question de la campagne d'Italie, avait ressuscité une vieille invention française : le canon rayé. (Nous disons une vieille invention, puisque dans la salle d'armes de la Bastille on montrait une coulevrine à deux coups, *cannelée à l'intérieur* et se chargeant par la culasse).

Or, tandis que chez nos voisins on expérimente un nouveau canon d'acier, voici qu'en France un ouvrier mécanicien, M. Balbi, vient d'inventer *la forteresse mobile*. Cette terrible machine est une tour roulante qui se meut par la vapeur. En dedans et à moitié de sa hauteur, elle est contournée par une galerie pour les canons, c'est la batterie garnie de sabords; entre ces ouvertures, sont des meurtrières pour la mousqueterie en cas de besoin. On comprend de suite quels ravages peut exercer une pareille citadelle se promenant sur un champ de bataille et se portant avec la rapidité de l'éclair d'un point à un autre : voilà pour la partie agressive. Quant à ses moyens défensifs, ils ont été, de la part de l'inventeur, l'objet d'une sollicitude toute particulière, car avant tout, dit-il, il s'agit de ne pas se laisser prendre.

Cette machine, qui est ronde, est garnie à l'extérieur de fortes plaques en tôle, de sorte que, tant à cause de sa sphéricité que de sa cuirasse, le boulet ne peut y mordre. Que si des bataillons ennemis, arrivés jusqu'en bas par impossible, voulaient en essayer l'escalade, la partie inférieure de sa carapace, toute garnie de piques, se met tout à coup à tourner sur elle-même avec une vitesse qui la rend inaccessible.

La *forteresse mobile* est montée sur des roues adaptées à des essieux articulés et peut évoluer en tous sens.

— Hier, entre une heure et deux heures de l'après-midi, des cris de détresse se sont fait

Facsimile of an item in *Le Siecle* of Paris for October 21, 1860, in which the Italian engineer Giacomo Balbi describes a "mobile fortress" similar to the turret which Ericsson built on the Monitor. Balbi's turret, however, was for use on land. (Courtesy, *Bibliotheque Nationale,* Paris, and Dr. Vinay, of Turin, Italy.)

All American school boys have heard, more or less, of the *U. S. Monitor,* the famous ironclad designed by John Ericsson, and of the battle which it had with the *Merrimac* off Hampton Roads on March 9, 1862.

Ericsson, a distinguished inventor and engineer, has generally been given credit for his revolutionary innovation, although it seems established that an American, Theo. Ruggles Timby, had patented a revolving gun turret some ten years before the Swedish-born inventor built the *Monitor.* During our research, however, we have found an item which we report for all that it may be worth. It bears the title (translated from the Italian) "The true inventor of the turret applied to the Monitor" and it appeared in the New York newspaper *L'Eco d'Italia* of November 15, 1862, reprinted from the magazine *Italia Militare,* obviously a publication of the Italian armed forces.

According to that article the turret which Ericsson erected on the *Monitor* was invented by one Giacomo Balbi, an Italian engineer who had been a resident of France during the previous eight years. In 1854, according to Balbi, he proposed his "mobile fortress" to Marshal Vaillant and three years later he presented his plan to Napoleon III, who received him on May 8, 1857. At any rate, a description of Balbi's invention appeared in the *Siecle* of Paris for October 21, 1860. (See facsimile on this page).

Whether or not Ericsson was acquainted with Balbi's invention it is hard to say. It is interesting, however, to note that in an article that he wrote for *The Century Magazine* (Vol. XXXI, p. 280-299) Ericsson mentions that he, too, presented a description of an iron-clad steam-battery to Napoleon III in 1854, the same year that Balbi presented his drawing to Marshal Vaillant (page 298).

IN THE CONFEDERATE ARMY AND NAVY

According to *L'Eco d'Italia* for May 3, 1862, there were at that time some 10,000 Italians in New Orleans alone. In our opinion, those figures are not highly exaggerated, if we include the children of Italian parentage and the natives of Corsica, as well as of other parts of Italy, such as Venice, Trento, and Trieste, which at that time were not a part of the Italian Kingdom. How else can one explain the fact the the European Brigade of New Orleans alone included some 500 Italians, who were serving as a unit known as the Italian Guards, under Major Della Valle? (Lonn, E., *Foreigners in the Confederacy*, 1940, p. 114.) As Dr. Lonn has stated, "the writer examined few muster rolls without Irish, Italian and Spanish names".

In other Southern states one also finds numerous Italian names. In Georgia, the Phinizy family contributed one colonel, two captains, one of whom died at Manassas (see photograph on this page), one sergeant and one financial agent. In Alabama, Sylvester Festorazzi served as a captain in the infantry; in Virginia, Alfred Pico was captain of an Italian company; in Mississippi, Frank J. Arrighi served as a captain in the infantry and was wounded at Antietam, Chancellorsville and Spottsylvania.

Among the leaders, we have some information about General Paul Sanguinetti, who was still living in 1939, when he was adjutant of the Confederate veterans, and Dr. Fromento, who, as we have noted, was in charge of the Louisian hospital in Richmond. We do not know whether

Captain Jacob Phinizy who gave his life for the Confederacy at Manassas in 1862. Five other members of the same family served with the South, one as a colonel, two as captains and one as a sergeant.

General E. H. Lombard, who was frequently mentioned for bravery in the field, was of Italian origin. (*New York Times*, May 6, 1903.) General Beauregard is said to have been a descendant, on his mother's side, of the famous Este family of Italy. In connection with him, it is interesting to recall that Leonetto Cipriani (see *ante*, p. 173) had planned to capture him, but his offer was declined. (*Eco*, April 26, 1862.)

IN THE INDIAN CAMPAIGNS AND IN THE SPANISH-AMERICAN WAR

Following the Civil War, the Italians continued to contribute their share to the armed forces of the United States, both as regular members of the Army and as volunteers.

In the campaigns against the Indians two men especially distinguished themselves: John Martini, a trumpeter, and Lieutenant Charles C. De Rudio. Martini served from 1874 to 1904, when he retired as a sergeant and spent the rest of his days in Brooklyn, where he died in 1922, at the age of 71. He was with Custer at the battle of the Little Horn and blew the officers' call on that fateful day. Shortly after that General Custer ordered him to bring a message to Col. Benteen asking for reinforcement; a providential order for Martini, who thus escaped the general massacre. (*Italian-American History*, I, p. 369.)

De Rudio lived a most adventurous life. A native of Belluno, Italy, he fought for the Roman Republic in 1849, when he was only 17 years old; nine years later he took part with Felice Orsini in the attempted assassination of Napoleon III; sentenced to spend the rest of his life at Devils Island, he escaped from French Guinea to the United States; during the Civil War he served, as we have seen, as a lieutenant; he re-enlisted after the War and served in the cavalry as a lieutenant until 1882, when he was made a captain. He retired in 1896 at the age of 64.

De Rudio had a narrow escape at the battle of the Little Big Horn, when his horse was killed under him and for 42 hours he remained surrounded by savages, until he fought his way to freedom and was able to rejoin the few survivors of his regiment. According to *Eco d'Italia* (May 24, 1881), he distinguished himself in so many actions, that "had he been an American or an Irishman he would be a general, or at least a colonel, today." (See *New York Times*, March 22, 1881, for a violent editorial against him for his part in the Orsini plot, and *Frontier and Midland Magazine*, Jan., 1934; also *N. Y. Tribune*, July 6, 1876, for the Battle of the Little Horn.)

We have no information about one George Ferrari, a native of New York, who was awarded the Congressional Medal of Honor for bravery in action at Red Creek, Arizona, in 1869.

Hundreds of Italian-Americans fought during the Spanish-American War. We shall mention only one of them, Colonel Luigi Lomia, a native of Canicatti', a town in Sicily, who came to America at the age of 14 in 1857, graduated from West Point in 1867, saw service as a lieutenant in Cuba, and rose to the rank of colonel. Lomia taught languages at West Point from 1868 to 1870, was a professor of military science at the University of Ohio and at the University of Wisconsin from 1876 to 1891 and served as military attache' in Rome in 1898. He died at New Rochelle, N. Y., in May, 1918.

IN WORLD WARS I AND II

There are no official figures regarding the national origins of the Americans who served during the First World War. According to Mr. George Creel, who was in charge of propaganda during the conflict, "The Italians in the United States are about four per cent of the whole population but the list of casualties shows a full ten per cent of Italian names. More than 300,000 Italians figure on the Army list and in defense of the inner lines as well as on the firing-lines they proved their devotion to their adopted country. There was no shipyard, ammunition factory, airplane factory, steel mill, mine, lumber camp, or docks in which the Italians did not play a large part, in actual and efficient work. In some places, such as mines and docks, the Italians reached fully thirty per cent of the total number of employees working at all times with full and affectionate loyalty toward the Government of the United States. For instance, when a strike was threatened in one of the big industrial centers, it was an Italian who jumped on a box and cried:" If you leave work now, you will be as though you were sneaking back out of a trench, abandoning your comrades at a time of a fight, when they need you most. And the strike was averted."

According to Major General C. H. Bridges of The Adjutant General's Office, "it may be stated that of a total of 3,138,261 applicants for adjusted compensation for service in the Army during the World War, 350,712 are shown to have been born in foreign countries. Of the latter number 89,662 are shown to have been born in Italy". Apart from the fact that the figures quoted by General Bridges refer only to the Army and do not include the Navy, Marine Corps, or Merchant Marine, they are by themselves illuminating.

Taking the United States population as a whole, there were in 1920 some 105,710,000 souls in the country, of whom 13,710,000 were born abroad. Of the latter, 1,615,000 were natives of Italy. Thus less than 3 per cent of the total population of the United States served in World War I. Of the Italians in the country, on the other hand, more than five and one half per rent served in the Army. In other words, whereas the natives of Italy represented about one and one half per cent of the total population, they contributed almost three per cent of the total number of men serving in the Army, or about twice as much as their population expectation. These figures, moreever, do not take into account those men who were born in the United States of Italian parentage, or the very important fact that as Italy joined the Allies almost two years before the United States, a very large number of Italians had returned to serve in the Italian Army and thus were prevented from joining the armed forces of the United States. In 1915 alone 90,258 Italians returned to Italy.

Regarding the number of Italian-Americans who served in the United States Navy and in the Merchant Marine there are no figures, but their number must have been rather impressive. As a matter of record, the first American seaman to give his life for the United States in World War I was the Italian-American John Isidore Eopolucci.

First enlisted Marine to receive the Congressional Medal of Honor in World War II. (Official Photograph, *U. S. Marine Corps.*)

The role played by the Italians in the First World War is best attested by the 83 distinguished Service Crosses awarded to natives of Italy, besides another score to soldiers born in America of Italian parentage, exclusive of those men who had Americanized their names. For instance, how could one tell the national origins of Lieutenant Bryan T. Burt and Corporal William Green, both of whom were born in Italy?

To them one must add the names of Private Valente, who was awarded the Congressional Medal of Honor; Col. Conrad H. Lanza, who was awarded the Distinguished Service Medal for his work as chief of the artillery of the First Army, A.E.F.; Major William Verdi (a noted professor of surgery at Yale University) who was also awarded the Distinguished Service Medal for his services as surgical consultant and specialist in surgery at the front.

Worthy of note was also Major Onorio Moretti, a native of the province of Caserta, who died in San Diego, Cal., in 1939. Major Moretti enlisted in the army in 1898, spent four years in Cuba and served as assistant professor of military science and tactics at Yale University from 1916 to 1917. After he retired from the army, he became a

Methodist minister and organized several small churches in Colorado and New Mexico. He is remembered for his "Moretti's Bible", a textbook on military science of which more than 40,000 copies were sold. (*San Diego Union*, October 24, 1939.)

IN WORLD WAR TWO

There are no figures on which one can figure exactly to what extent, or in what proportion, Americans of Italian birth or extraction contributed to our victory in World War II. A summary study, however, leads us to the belief that they contributed more than their share in dead and wounded.

Let us take, for instance, the "Honor List of the Dead and Missing for the State of New York" published by the War Department in June, 1946. According to it, the casualties for the five New York City boroughs totalled 16,107; of them, at least 3,147, as checked by us, had Italian names. In other words, close to 20 per cent of the casualties for the City of New York were Americans of Italian descent. Using the same percentage basis, New York should have had in the 1940's close to 1,560,000, men, women and children of Italian origin, or 20 per cent of New York's population (7,835,000). It is more than doubtful that there are that many Italian-Americans in the city even today, in 1952. Therefore, it is safe to assume that the New York "Italians" contributed more than their share in soldiers killed in action or while in the service.

Let us take other sample figures. According to the lists published by the U. S. Navy Department (including, of course, those for the Marine Corps) in 1946, the states of New Jersey, New York, Connecticut, Rhode Island and Massachusetts had 11,720 men killed in action. Of them, as checked by us, some 1,451, or more than 12 per cent of the total, had Italian names. Here and there, of course, we may have included some non-Italian casualty; on the other hand, most surely we must have missed quite a few men with Anglicized names.

Another way of measuring the contribution of a particular ethnic group is to count the number of decorations awarded to each unit. Or one could single out the exploits of individual soldiers, like Don Salvatore Gentile, America's leading ace, credited with 30 Nazi planes, and Major A. Martini of San Francisco, who shot down 22 German planes in 15 minutes of furious combat over Paris. Obviously, such an investigation would be beyond our inquiry. On the other hand, it might be sufficient to list the Italian-Americans who were awarded the Congressional Medal of Honor and the Navy Cross. The two lists follow:

MEDALS OF HONOR (Army)

1. 1st Lt. W. C. Bianchi of Minnesota. Third man to receive the Medal of Honor in World War II.
2. Major Ralph Cheli of Bethlehem, Pa. Missing in action.
3. Pfc. Frank J. Petrarca of Cleveland, Ohio. Killed in action.
4. Staff Sgt. Arthur De Franzo of Saugus, Mass. Killed in action.
5. Pfc. Gino J. Meli of Peckville, Pa.
6. Tech. Sgt. Peter J. Dalessandro of Watervliet, N. Y.
7. Pfc. Mike Colalillo of Duluth, Minn.
8. Sgt. Vito R. Bertoldi of Decatur, Ill.
9. 2nd Lt. Robert M. Viale of Ukiah, Cal. Killed in action.
10. Pfc. Joseph Cicchetti of Waynesburg, Ohio. Killed in action.

MEDALS OF HONOR (Marine Corps)

11. Gunnery Sgt. John Basilone of Raritan, N. J.
1. Corp. Anthony Peter Damato of Shenandoah, Pa.

NAVY CROSSES

1. Ensign R. Mazza of Pepaluma, Cal. (Also awarded a Gold Star in lieu of Second Navy Cross.)
2. Lt. Herman Joseph Rossi, Jr., of Wallace, Idaho. (Also awarded a Gold Star in lieu of Second Navy Cross.)
3. Lt. Henry V. Bonzagni, Jr., of Melrose, Mass.
4. Lt. Patsy Capano of Fall River, Mass.
5. Ensign Salvatore John Cavallaro of New York City.
6. Lt. (jg.) Alfred Michele De Cesare of Pueblo, Colo.
7. Lt. Donald Domenic Di Marzo of Long Beach, Cal.
8. Machinist's Mate First Class Ernest J. Gentile of Leominster, Mass.
9. Lt. Com. Orazio Simonelli of Portland, Oregon.
10. Lt. Emil Bernard Stella of Hurley Wis.

Both lists do not include, so far as we know, more recent awards.

HIGH-RANKING OFFICERS

The lists examined by us reveal an incredibly large number of Italian-Americans who served as colonels and lieutenant colonels in the army, or as commanders in the navy. To the best of our knowledge, however, only four men of Italian ancestry held the rank of brigadier generals: Daniel Noce of Denver, Colorado; Robert V. Ignico of Boston Mass.; Ralph Palladino of Winchester, Mass., and Joseph T. Michela of Duluth, Minn., who also served as United States Military Attache in Russia.

Of the four, General Noce played a prominent role during the war as chief of the amphibious operations of the United States Army in the European Theater. The leading American expert on offensive landing operations, he was awarded the Distinguished Service Medal "for meritorious service in planning and organizing the Engineer Amphilian Command", namely, the landing of the United States Armed Forces on the shores of Africa, Italy and, later, of France.